Eugene E. Carpenter A...

Holman
Treasury of
KeyBible
Words

200 Greek and 200 Hebrew
Words Defined and Explained

HOLMAN
REFERENCE

NASHVILLE, TENNESSEE

Holman Treasury of Key Bible Words
Published in 2000 by B&H Publishing Group,
Nashville, Tennessee

ISBN 978-0-8054-9352-8

Some of the articles written by Philip Comfort were adapted from previously published works, now no longer in print. These works, whose copyright is held by the author, Philip Comfort, are as follows: *I Am the Way, Opening the Gospel of John* (with W. Hawley), *The Origin of the Bible, The Complete Guide to Bible Versions, The Quest for the Original Text of the New Testament, Early Manuscripts and Modern Translations of the New Testament*.

Scripture marked ASV are taken from the American Standard Version © 1901.

Scripture marked KJV are taken from the King James Version.

Scripture marked HCSB are taken from the Holman Christian Standard Bible. © 2000 by Broadman & Holman Publishers. All rights reserved.

Scripture marked NLT are taken from the *Holy Bible,* New Living Translation ©1996 by Tyndale Charitable Trust. All rights reserved.

Scripture marked NKJV are taken from *The Holy Bible*, New King James Version ©1982 by Thomas Nelson, Inc.

Scripture marked NRSV are taken from the New Revised Standard Version Bible ©1989. The Division of Christian Education of the National Council of Churches of Christ in the United States of America.

Scripture marked RSV are taken from the Revised Standard Version of the Bible © Copyright 1952 and © 1946, by the Division of Christian Education of the National Council Churches of Christ in the United States of America.

Scripture marked TLB or "LIVING" are taken from the *The Living Bible,* ©1971 owned by assignment by KNT Charitable Trust. All rights reserved.

Scripture marked "Amplified" are taken from the The Amplified® New Testament, Copyright © The Lockman Foundation 1954, 1958, 1987.

Text copyright (c) 2000 by The Livingstone Corporation.
Design and Composition by Design Corps.

Library of Congress Cataloging-in-Publication Data

Carpenter, Eugene E., 1953-
        Treasury of key Bible words / by Eugene E. Carpenter and Philip W. Comfort.
                p. cm.
        Includes index.
        ISBN 0-8054-9352-2
Bible-Dictionaries. I. Comfort, Philip Wesley. II Title.

BS440.C342000
220.3-dc21   00-044440

220.3
Bible-Dictonaries

Printed in the United States of America
9 10 11 12 13   18 17 16 15 14

New Testament

Introduction

The Holman Treasury of Key Bible Words

Your Invitation to Dig Deeper

Agape. Charis. Shama'

These Greek and Hebrew words communicate much more than "love," "grace," and "to hear," respectively. A one-word, or one-sentence, definition of a biblical word like the Hebrew word *shama'* simply won't do. Certainly, *shama'* may mean "hear." But, its real significance lies in the fact that the word is part of the great Israelite call to worship, the Shema: "Hear, Oh, Israel, the LORD our God is one . . . " (see Deut. 6:4-5). "Hear" is the constant cry of the Old Testament prophets (see, for example, Isaiah 48:1; Ezekiel 18:25). And, it's clear from the contexts where this word is used that it means much more than "hear." It embraces the ideas of understanding and obeying. A simple definition won't suffice for a word that has such depth.

This book is an invitation for you to dig deeper into the biblical languages. Dr. Eugene Carpenter, professor of Hebrew at Bethel College, has identified 200 Hebrew words that deliver key insights into the meaning of Scripture. And, Dr. Philip Comfort, professor of New Testament at Trinity Episcopal Seminary, has identified 200 key Greek words that the New Testament writers used in significant ways. In *The Holman Treasury of Key Bible Words*, you will find only those Greek and Hebrew words that will open new horizons of meaning beyond their straight-forward English translation. You won't have to wade through an entire Greek or Hebrew dictionary to find those penetrating insights from the ancient languages that you need for your lesson or personal study of Scripture.

Discover what Paul meant by "grace" or "mercy." Dig deeper into the meaning of the word "covenant" in the Old Testament. Dr. Carpenter and Dr. Comfort have collected key insights, culled from years of intensive study of the biblical languages.

Our prayer is that these 400 word studies will enrich your study of God's Word.

The Publisher

How to Use The Holman Treasury of Key Bible Words

In the first half of this book, you will find 200 key Hebrew words in alphabetical order according to their most common English translation. For instance, if you want to learn about the meaning of the Old Testament word for "covenant," you would look under "C."

In the second half of this book, you find 200 key Greek words in alphabetical order according to their most common English translation. For instance, if you want to learn about the meaning of the New Testament word for "grace," you would look under "G."

Each word study includes:
- The English translation of the key Hebrew or Greek word
- The transliteration of the Hebrew or Greek word
- A pronunciation spelling of the Hebrew or Greek word
- The associated *Strong's Concordance* numbers, if you want to look up the word in another lexicon
- A succinct definition, along with an overview of how the word is used throughout Scripture
- A list of key Bible passages where the word can be found

You can use *The Holman Treasury of Key Bible Words* as a handy reference book for your study. Or, you can read through all 400 word studies, using the studies as starting points for your own study of each biblical concept—whether it is "covenant" or "love." Either way, you will want to include *The Holman Treasury of Key Bible Words* in your library of Bible reference tools.

Transliteration Chart

Hebrew				Greek			
א	'	ל	l	α	a	ξ	x
ב	b	מ	m	β	b	ο	o
ג	g	נ	n	γ	g	π	p
ד	d	ס	s	δ	d	ρ	r
ה	h	ע	<	ε	e	σ	s
ו	w	פ	p	ζ	z	τ	t
ז	z	צ	ts	η	ē	υ	u
ח	ch	ק	q	θ	th	φ	ph
ט	t	ר	r	ι	i	χ	ch
י	y	שׂ	s	κ	k	ψ	ps
כ	k	שׁ	sh	λ	l	ω	ō
		ת	t	μ	m	·	h
				ν	n	ῥ	hr

Old Testament Words

Abomination

See also: *Abomination of Desolation, p. 220*
Hebrew expression: *shiqquts*
Pronunciation: *shihk QOOTS*
Strong's Number: *8251*

Abomination describes detestable and vile acts, objects, or images. The Hebrew word *shiqquts* for abomination describes this and more. In the Hebrew Bible, the word does not describe something vile in the eyes of Israelites or other people—but primarily of something vile and abominable in the eyes of God. This word was used to describe the idolatrous practices of the pagans, as well as the horrible things God's rebellious people would do. The original root of *shiqquts* was *shqts*, which carries the idea of "blemish" or "impurity." The Hebrew language formed a verb from this root that meant "to make detestable" or "detest" (Lev. 11:43; Deut. 7:26). From this same root, *shiqquts*, "abomination," was coined with all of the negative connotations mentioned above.

In Daniel, the Hebrew word *shiqquts* referred prophetically to the statue of Zeus, a Greek god set up by Antiochus Epiphanes on an altar (Dan. 9:27; 11:31; 12:11). *Shiqquts* also pointed further ahead to the "abomination of desolation" spoken of by Jesus (Matt. 24:15) and the book of Revelation (Rev. 13). Comparing or replacing the holy God of Israel, free from moral or ethical blemish, with an immoral, corrupt concept of a god is indeed an "abomination" and a "vile thing" in the Lord's eyes. The Sidonian goddess Ashtoreth, the Ammonite god Milcolm, and the Moabite god Chemosh were all described by *shiqquts*—abominations. Ezekiel condemns the "vile images" of the Israelites for making, tolerating and worshiping these "abominations" (Ezek. 5:11; 7:20), "detestable things" (KJV), and "idols" (NLT). The Temple of the Lord was full of these idolatrous, unclean images and pictures in Ezekiel's day (Ezek. 8). Israel is described as "lusting" after their *shiqqutsim* (Ezek. 20:30). Hosea puts the matter most daringly. He observed that the problem of worshiping a vile idol was that worshipers became like the vile gods they worshiped (Hos. 9:10, NLT). Israel had been called to worship the Lord in holiness, for He is holy, and He alone made them holy.

The "detestable things" mentioned in Daniel are condemned by Jesus as the "abomination" that brings desolation (Matt. 24:15; Mark 13:14, *bdelugma* in Greek). Babylon, the source of so much of Israel's "vile things" in the Old Testament, is destroyed in the end times as the "abomination of the earth" (Rev. 17:5). The ancient city of Babylon, a city similar to many of our cities today, didn't focus on God. Instead, the people of Babylon focused on their own military might, their own wealth, and their own pleasure. The things which the world honors—success, beauty, and wealth—are detestable in the sight of the Lord precisely because they distract people from honoring and worshiping Him (see Luke 16:15). God's people are called to worship the Lord alone. We should never seek to honor anything above the Lord.

KEY VERSES

2 Kings 23:13;
Ezekiel 5:11; 11:21;
Daniel 9:27; 11:31;
Hosea 9:10

Adversaries

Hebrew expression: *tsarim*
Pronunciation: *tsahr EEM*
Strong's Number: *6862*

Several recent books have been written about coping with difficult people. These books easily become best-sellers. The Bible has a lot to say about difficult people—specifically our "adversaries" or enemies, those people who purposefully oppose us.

When the Lord brought the Jews back to Judah from Babylonian exile, the first order of business was to rebuild the House of God (2 Chr. 36:20–21). When the returned exiles began work on the Temple, the "enemies of Benjamin and Judah" learned about the project and offered to help (Ezra 4:1–2). Zerubbabel wisely refused their help, realizing that they were "adversaries" of the Jews (Ezra 4:3). The Hebrew word used for "adversaries" is *tsarim*, a masculine plural noun that can also be translated as "enemy" or "foe." It comes from the verb *tsarar*, which means, "to be hostile" or "to distress." The use of the word *tsarim* in Ezra 4 implies that the offer of free labor by these people was suspect. These people were pagans who had been brought into Samaria and had intermingled with the Jews. They served pagan gods, but also showed some allegiance to the Lord (2 Kgs. 17:24–41). Zerubbabel refused to mingle the returned exiles with these "adversaries" of the Lord and His people (Ezra 4:3–5). For Jeshua, the High Priest, Zerubbabel, and the family heads of the Jewish community, the decision was clear. These "adversaries" were not loyal to the Lord and should have no part in the building of His Temple. With a bold refusal, this new community was willing to leave the matter in God's hands. The Lord dealt with the adversaries through King Darius, the Persian King, who supported the Israelites and used the political and military powers of the day to complete the Temple. God overcame the Israelite's enemies (Ezra 6:3–12, 15).

This story illustrates the biblical way of handling "adversaries." Let the Lord deal with them! The Lord defeated the enemies of Abraham (Gen. 14:10), David (Ps. 27:12), and Job (6:23); in fact, He defeated the foes of His people as if they were His own enemies (Num. 10:9; Deut. 32:41, 43; 33:7; Josh. 5:13). The Lord destroyed the arch adversary of the Jews in the Persian era, Haman, (Esth. 7:6) and the psalmist asked the Lord to defeat his enemies (Pss. 44:5–6; 60:11, 12; 78:42; 81:15). "Through the Lord" the psalmist says we gain victory over our enemies (Pss. 44:5, 7; 78:42, 66). Ultimately, He is our victory (Pss. 81:13, 14; 107:2). He overcame the enemies of Jesus Christ (Acts 2:35) and we are now called to love our enemies as Christ did (Matt. 5:44). Jesus will rule until He has subdued all of His enemies and ours (Acts 2:35; 1 Cor. 15:25–27; Heb. 1:13). Therefore, vengeance belongs to the Lord, not to us—and we must remember to seek God first when dealing with difficult people in our lives.

KEY VERSES

Genesis 14:20;
Numbers 10:9;
Ezra 4:1;
Psalm 44:5, 7

4

Advice

Hebrew expression: *'etsah*
Pronunciation: *'ay TSAWH*
Strong's Number: *6098*

In addition to the prophet, priest, elder, and king as leaders in ancient Israel, God recognized the place of wise men and women as leaders in Israel. The Hebrew verb *ya'ats*, "to advise" or "to counsel," gave rise to the noun *'etsah*, meaning "counselor or advisor." God's people were admonished to be a people ready to listen to the counsel of wise men and women and accept their guidance. A wise woman in the small city of Abel gave counsel to the residents to deliver the head of a man named Sheba to Joab, David's general, rather than have him destroy the whole city (2 Sam. 20:15–22). Daniel, the wisest man in Babylon, was sought out for his advice by kings (Dan. 4:27). King David realized the importance of "advice" and wise counselors when dealing with his son Absalom's conspiracy. Absalom conspired against David to take the kingship of Jerusalem and David was forced to flee for his life. He knew Absalom's "wise counselor," Ahithophel, had advised Absalom in the conspiracy. Consequently, David prayed that the advice of Ahithophel would be frustrated and turned into foolishness (2 Sam. 15:31, 34). God answered David's prayer and Absalom rejected the next advice from Ahithophel, who then hanged himself when he discovered that his advice was not followed (2 Sam. 17:23). In this particular situation, good or bad advice made all the difference in the success or failure of both Absalom and his counselor. David knew this, and was able to pray specifically and with wisdom.

The wise king Jehoshaphat advised that it was best to first seek the advice of the Lord before acting (2 Chr. 18:4). Ultimately, in the Old Testament, human counsel, without consulting God first, was considered inadequate. Job declared that counsel and understanding, as well as God's wisdom and strength, were not from human beings, but from God Himself (Job 12:13). Therefore, people should always pray and consult God before offering advice. In the New Testament, the apostle Paul offered advice to the Corinthians when he did not have a word from the Lord (2 Cor. 8:10), because he had the mind of Christ (1 Cor. 2:16). By virtue of the Holy Spirit, Paul had Christ's truth and wisdom in his heart. Paul also counseled the younger widows to go ahead and marry (1 Tim. 5:14).

KEY VERSES

2 Samuel 15:31, 34;
16:23; 17:7,
14, 23; 20:22;
Job 12:13;
Isaiah 11:2; 19:11

The branch of Jesse, the future Messiah, was given the Spirit of counsel and power (Isa. 11:2). Indeed, Jesus Christ of the branch of Jesse, is our Great counselor. In Revelation 3:18, He gave the best counsel, instructing the people in Laodicea to buy true riches and wealth from Him, including clothing to cover their shame and salve for their eyes to help them truly see.

Affliction

Hebrew expression: *'anah*
Pronunciation: *'aw NAWH*
Strong's Number: *6031*

The word "affliction" is a word that brings to mind physical and mental suffering. Someone who is afflicted is disturbed or possibly frightened because of danger, pain, or some kind of distress. Many people blame God when they experience affliction. According to the Bible, however, the Lord does not willingly afflict or grieve anyone (Lam. 3:33). The Hebrew verb *'anah*, "to be bowed down, afflicted, or humbled," can be translated in slightly different ways to reflect these basic meanings. These translations of *'anah* include "bring grief" (NJPS), "afflict" (KJV), "does not hurt" (NLT) people, and "bring affliction" (NIV). About five other nouns and adjectives are based on this root and mean things like "afflicted, humble, poverty, or affliction." *'Anah* does not describe the state of being or condition that God desires His people to be in. He desires them to be standing up straight, healthy and hopeful for things to come. As noted above, the author of Lamentations asserts that God does not afflict a person willingly. The Hebrew text says literally that He does not afflict them "from His heart." It is not in His character! Oppression and affliction come because of many other reasons, some which we cannot even fathom just as Job could not do so (Job 42:1–6).

The noun *'oni*, meaning "affliction," is used many times in Lamentations, for it is recorded in this book that God has truly afflicted His people, not because He desired to, but because He had to. The Israelites' rebellion called for their judgment and the destruction of the city of Jerusalem. God has, however, a redemptive purpose for the Israelites. He wants them, because of their affliction, to return to Him and repent so that He may forgive them. God wants their correction and healing (1 Kgs. 8:35; 2 Kgs. 17:20) and His goals are just. The psalmist said that before he was "afflicted," *'anah*, he strayed from the Lord. Through his affliction he was brought back to obedience of the Lord's word. Affliction is one of God's training grounds, but not one that He willingly chooses for us.

KEY VERSES

Ruth 1:21;
1 Kings 8:35;
Psalm 119:67, 71;
Isaiah 53:7;
Lamentations 3:33

Jesus Christ knew what it was to experience affliction and bore it with patience (Col. 1:24, *thlipsis* in Greek). Paul encourages us to be joyful in our hope in the Lord and to be patient in affliction as well (Rom. 12:12). It does not have to be our lot to suffer affliction and harsh burdens from the Lord (Lam. 1:3), but if we do, He will give us grace to endure them.

Almighty

Hebrew expression: *shadday*
Pronunciation: *shah DAH ee*
Strong's Number: *7706*

Sometimes promises cannot be kept. Good reasons often lie behind a failed prom-ise, but one reason, the lack of power or authority to keep the promise, is devas-tating. "A promise should not be made if it cannot be kept" is a familiar cliché. The Almighty God never failed to keep His promises; He had the power and the strength to see His promises through.

The name *shadday* means "All Powerful"; it occurs thirty-one times in Job and nine times elsewhere. It may come from the root *shadad*, which means "to be mighty." Or, more likely, it may come from combining *she* plus *day*, meaning "the one who is sufficient." In the Hebrew Bible, it is compounded with *'el* to form *'el shadday*, meaning "God Almighty." This name of God is used with the patriarchs six times and always in connection with the Almighty's promises of keeping His covenant with them. He promised to multiply their descendants and give them the land of Canaan (Gen. 17:1–8; 28:3; 35:11). Jacob prays that the Almighty would grant his sons success in bringing Benjamin back from Egypt (Gen. 43:14), thus, preserving the promised seed. Using "God Almighty" in these cases ensured that the promises made were kept.

As the Almighty, God provided visions to Balaam, the Mesopotamian seer (Num. 24:4, 16). God could bring destruction as only the Almighty could do (Isa. 13:6; Joel 1:15). By His might, He scattered the enemies of Israel (Ps. 68:14); His voice was like the roar of the wings of the Cherubim and other creatures in Ezekiel's visions (Ezek. 1:24; 10:5). Yet, the psalmist says that to abide under the shadow of the Almighty is to find complete rest and safety (Ps. 91:1–2). In the time of Moses it was made clear that *'el shadday* was Yahweh, the covenant God of Israel (Exod. 6:2–5). The name of the "Almighty," *shadday*, was on the lips of Job and his "friends" thirty-one times in the poetic sections of the book (Job 5:17; 40:2). Yet, the use of the name Yahweh twenty-one times in the prose sections, and six times in the poetic sections, shows that Yahweh and *'el shad-day* are one and the same God. Job appeals to the Almighty to argue his case, but ultimately he submits to the greatness and almighty power of the Lord (Job 40:1–5).

KEY VERSES

Genesis 17:1;
28:3; 35:11;
Exodus 6:3;
Job 5:17

The promise inherent in the name *Shadday* is that the Almighty can do everything He has promised. No man or other power can thwart His ways. He is an awesome God.

7

Altar

Hebrew expression: *mizbeach*
Pronunciation: *miz BAY hah*
Strong's Number: *4196*

Probably no word calls to mind sacred worship more than the word "altar." This is certainly true in the Old Testament. Immediately after the flood Noah built an altar to the Lord and worshiped there, presenting sacrifices upon it (Gen. 8:20). All of the patriarchs built altars (Gen. 26:25; 33:20). Abraham built an altar at Moriah because the Lord appeared to him (Gen. 12:7). He also built an altar to sacrifice his son, Isaac, but God provided a ram instead (Gen. 22:9, 13). God ordered Moses and Israel to build altars for use in worshiping Him: one of earth and stones (Exod. 20:24–25), one for burnt sacrifices made of acacia wood overlaid with bronze (Exod. 27:1), and one made of acacia wood overlaid with gold to offer up incense. The golden altar was placed in front of the curtain of the Holy of Holies (Exod. 30:1–6).

The Hebrew word for "altar," *mizbeach*, means "a place where sacrifices were offered." It comes from the verbal root *zabach*, "to slaughter for sacrifices." Yet "altar" was more significant in Israel's religious worship than these meanings imply. As reported above, the altar was a place of prayer, a place for calling upon the Lord. Altars are built where the Lord appeared, or built at a location where the Lord had appeared earlier (Judg. 13:20). The altar for burnt sacrifices was the first item rebuilt after Israel returned from exile so that the daily sacrifice could be offered upon it (Ezra 3:1–3). The community of God as a worshiping people was reestablished by this act.

In Numbers, *mizbeach* occurs in twenty-six verses to describe the centrality and importance that the altar held. Altars were cared for meticulously and with great respect (Num. 3:26; 4:11–26; 18:5). They were a place where truth and justice were discovered (Num. 5:25–26). They were anointed, consecrated, and set aside to use for the Lord (Num. 7:1, 84), as well as the place where the dedication offerings were received to celebrate the completion of the Tabernacle (Num. 7:10). While altars were found in all of the nations around Israel (Num. 23:2, 14), Israel's altars were set aside for worshiping the Lord only (Deut. 12; 16:21). Altars were basically places for communion with God and confession of one's total dependence upon Him (Deut. 26:4). The altar provided a "place of sacrifice," but the goal was also for the worshiper to "focus on God" in this holy spot.

KEY VERSES

Genesis 8:20; 12:7;
Exodus 20:24–25;
Numbers 5:25–26;
Deuteronomy 26:4

The New Testament indicates that there will be an altar (*thusiasterion* in Greek) in the new Temple of God (Rev. 11:1) and in the heavenly Temple (Rev. 6:9; 8:5; 9:13). In the heavenly Temple, according to John's vision, all people who are martyred for the Lord are under the altar because they kept God's Word. But the high point of the use of altars is found in Hebrews 13:10–12: Christians have the cross of Jesus, our altar, perfected by Christ's blood, from which priests who do not know God have no right to participate.

Angel

See also: *Angel, p. 224*
Hebrew expression: *mal'ak*
Pronunciation: *mahl 'AWK*
Strong's Number: *4397*

A growing number of people believe in the existence of UFO's and the extra-terrestrial life forms. Their recent motto has become "we are not alone." The Bible lends support to this claim, but not in confirming UFO sightings and verifying the existence of extra-terrestrials. The Bible does indicate, however, that we are not alone in the sense that angels—both evil and good ones—are part of the created order. There is a spiritual dimension of reality that co-exists with the physical world. The Bible records numerous stories of individuals who encountered angels. In fact, the Bible reports that at times people unwittingly entertained angels (Heb. 13:2).

The Hebrew noun *mal'ak* for "angels" may refer to human messengers, whether ambassadors or emissaries sent by a king for purposes of diplomacy (2 Sam. 5:11) or couriers carrying messages for commercial or military purposes (2 Sam. 12:27). The term is also applied to the Hebrew prophets (Hag. 1:13) and priests (Mal. 2:7) as messengers from God. The messenger was the full representative of the sender, hence the importance of the "messenger formula" ("thus says the Lord of Hosts") in the oracles of the Old Testament prophets (see, for example, Jer. 6:16; 9:17). The prophet of God spoke only those words given to the messenger by the Lord himself (compare 2 Pet. 1:21).

The word also refers to heavenly beings, spiritual creatures who comprise God's angelic host (compare Dan. 7:10). Angels are a higher order of creation than human beings (Ps. 8:5), and apparently possess or are capable of taking on human form and characteristics (Gen. 19:1–2). The classifications of angels (for example, *cherubim,* Exod. 25:19; and *seraphim,* Isa. 6:2) suggest an angelic hierarchy of sorts. The primary function of the angels is the unceasing worship of God (Pss. 103:20; 148:2). Angels are commissioned to serve God as divine messengers, bringing revelations from God about future events and interpreting the meaning of dreams and visions (Zech. 1:14; 4:1, 4; 6:4–5). At times, angels are charged to sustain and protect the people of God (1 Kgs. 19:5, 7; 2 Kgs. 6:17; Ps. 91:11). Although a mystery, it appears angels wage some kind of heavenly warfare with their fallen counterparts (compare Dan. 10:13, 20; Zech. 3:1–2).

KEY VERSES

Genesis 16:7;
Exodus 3:2;
Zechariah 2:3; 3:1

A special use of the word "angel" is the manifestation of the Godhead known as the "angel of the Lord" (Gen. 16:7; Exod. 3:2; Num. 22:35). The angel of the Lord provided guidance through the Sinai desert for the Hebrew after the exodus (Exod. 32:34), mediated divine revelation (Judg. 13:16), and was a protector of God's faithful (Ps. 34:7). The angel of the Lord had the power to forgive sins (Exod. 23:20) and accepted the worship of human beings (Judg. 13:20), works which were the prerogative of God alone. For this reason, the angel of the Lord is considered by many biblical scholars to be the pre-incarnate manifestation of Jesus Christ in the Old Testament.

Malachi mentioned a special Elijah-like messenger or angel who would announce and prepare the way for the day of the Lord (Mal. 3:1; 4:5). Jesus identified this forerunner of the day of the Lord as John the Baptist (Matt. 11:10).

The New Testament confirms the teaching of the Old in describing angels as "ministering spirits" to those who will inherit salvation (Heb. 1:14). The apostle Paul provides a further description of "spiritual warfare" that indicates a cosmic struggle between God and Satan that continues at both a national and a personal level (Eph. 6:10–13). The Christian must remember that God has already disarmed these heavenly powers and that angels are not to be worshiped (Col. 2:15, 18). Rather, the Christian is to thank God for their role in His redemptive plan as ministering spirits of revelation and protection and imitate their continual worship of God Almighty.

Anoint

See also: *Anoint, p. 225*
Hebrew expression: *mashach*
Pronunciation: *maw SHAH*
Strong's Number: *4886*

The Lord told Samuel to "anoint" David to be king in Israel (1 Sam. 16:3). At the time, David was a shepherd boy, but he turned out to be Israel's greatest king. The Hebrew verb *mashach* means "to anoint, to smear with oil." The oil used in this process was the most holy anointing oil prepared according to a special formula (Exod. 30:22–33). It was used to anoint the High Priest Aaron and his sons in Israel (Exod. 28:41). Not only kings and priests were anointed with it, but also prophets, such as Elisha (1 Kgs. 19:16).

But why anoint someone? God instructed Samuel to anoint David because He had looked at David's heart (1 Sam. 16:7). Samuel's anointing of David with oil resulted in the Spirit of the Lord entering into David's life in power from that time on (1 Sam. 16:13). The anointing merely served as an outward sign that God saw what He was looking for in David's heart and chose him to be king. Then He enabled him to fulfill his calling by "anointing" him with His Holy Spirit. The physical process of anointing Aaron as High Priest along with his sons involved the application of the holy anointing oil. They showed their dedication to the Lord in the incident concerning the Golden Calf (Exod. 32:27–29). Moses anointed them with the special oil and some blood from the altar (Lev. 8:30). God confirmed their ministry from that time forth with His own appearance and consumed their offerings (Lev. 9:23–24). Anyone who used the anointing oil, a blend of fine spices mixed with oil (Exod. 30:25), for any other reason committed sacrilege and was "cut off" from the people (Exod. 30:33). Anointing was, however, something anyone could experience in a spiritual sense, as Psalm 23:5 makes clear. The psalmist's cup ran over because God had anointed him. David had been taken from grazing sheep to being king in Israel. The physical act was symbolic of a deeper reality—the presence of God (1 Sam. 16:13; Pss. 20:6; 28:8).

In the New Testament, God instructs His people to be anointed with oil for healing, accompanied with prayer, when they are sick (James 5:14). But even more importantly, God's special anointing rested upon Jesus to preach the gospel of good news (Luke 4:18; Acts 4:27). Peter applied Psalm 2:1–2 to Jesus as the "Anointed One" who received the Holy Spirit without limitation. "Christ," which is *Christos* in Greek, means "anointed one," the one chosen by God. God has anointed each of us in Christ by His Holy Spirit. Jesus showed Himself to be our anointed King, our anointed Prophet, and our anointed Priest! John declares that we all have the Spirit, an anointing from the Holy One (1 John 2:20, 27), and are sealed as God's (Ps. 105:15). We are to continue in this holy calling from God as the Lord fulfills His work in us.

KEY VERSES

Exodus 29:7;
30:26, 30;
1 Samuel 16:3, 12,
13;
1 Kings 19:16

Ark

Hebrew expression: 'aron
Pronunciation: 'aw ROHN
Strong's Number: 727

Absalom, King David's son, had instigated rebellion against him, and David had to flee for his life. As David fled from Jerusalem with the ark of God, slowly trudging up the Mount of Olives, he hesitated, stopped, and ordered two priests to take the ark of God back to Jerusalem. David decided to depend upon the Lord to return him to the ark and the Temple (2 Sam. 15:24–29). Why was this ark so important that David could not in good faith remove it from Jerusalem?

The Hebrew word 'aron is translated "ark" most often, but it is also translated as "chest." The ark is referred to in many ways: the "ark of the covenant of God" (2 Sam. 15:24), "the ark of God" (1 Sam. 3:3), "the ark of the Lord the God of Israel" (1 Chr. 15:12), "the ark of the Lord God" (1 Kgs. 2:26), and "the ark of the testimony" (Exod. 25:22). The ark was very important because God commissioned it. Exodus 25:10 records the Lord's command and instructions to make the ark. Golden cherubim were constructed on the two sides of the covering seat of the ark (Pss. 80:1; 99:1). After its completion, the Lord promised to meet with the priests and deliver His holy laws and commandments to them over the cover of the ark between the two cherubim (Exod. 25:22). The ark housed the Ten Commandments (Exod. 25:16) and had as its lid a golden "atonement cover" (Exod. 26:34). God was in some sense "enthroned" over the atonement cover of the ark, for on the Day of Atonement and at other times He appeared in a cloud over the cover of the ark (Lev. 16:2). The ark preceded Israel when she traveled in the wilderness (Num. 10:33, 35). God's presence around the ark struck fear into the Philistines after they had captured it and it brought disease upon them (1 Sam. 5:9–10; 6:3). If a person touched the ark without proper protocol he was killed by the contact with this sacred object hallowed by God's presence (2 Sam. 6—7). The ark was the most impressive sign of God's presence in Israel, His leadership, His kingship and the focal point for His power, glory and instruction. It is also called, in fact, the "ark of His strength" (Ps. 78:61), the "ark of His might," and "His resting place" (Ps. 132:8).

KEY VERSES

Exodus 25:10, 14;
Leviticus 16:2;
Numbers 10:33, 35;
2 Samuel 15:24–25;
Psalm 132:8

In the New Testament, the writer of Hebrews records that Aaron's staff and a jar of manna were in the ark as a witness to the Lord's miraculous care for and leadership of His people (Heb. 9:4). While the ark of God was "lost" in the Old Testament (2 Kgs. 25:8–10), in the book of Revelation 11:19 it reappears within the Temple of God in heaven. The heavenly ark of God has not been destroyed. The earthly ark was merely a feeble copy of this ark. The ark of God in heaven in His Temple assures us that His presence continues to be with us, not only now, but also in the heavenly sphere of eternity.

12

Assembly

Hebrew expression: *qahal*
Pronunciation: *qah HAHL*
Strong's Number: *6951*

The "gathered church," *ekklesia* in Greek, is equivalent to the Old Testament Hebrew word *qahal*, which is translated as "assembly," "community," or "congregation." God's goal was to have a community of people gathered around Him in relationship to Him, sharing and worshiping Him. The congregation "assembled" at Mount Sinai was God's people "gathered" to hear His words (Deut. 5:19; 9:10). When Israel was gathered as an organized community, the nation was the Lord's assembly (Num. 20:4), gathered to worship Him. On the Day of Atonement, the High Priest atoned for the sins of the Lord's gathered community (Lev. 16:17; Deut. 31:30). Passover was the festival and celebration that most brought the Israelite community together and made them one. On the night of the exodus from Egypt, the *qahal* of the Lord slew the Passover lamb, witnessing together the great deliverance that the Lord was providing for them (Exod. 12:6). They would forever trace their origin as a nation to this event. *Qahal* also describes the Israelites gathered before King Solomon at the dedication of the Temple (1 Kgs. 8:14; 2 Chr. 6:3). The Lord was granting His divine presence before the people, for He was coming to fill the Temple and let His Glory abide there. The *qahal yisra'el*, the "assembly of Israel," gathered in the plains of Moab to hear Moses recite his song about the future destiny of the nation (Deut. 31:30). The most honorable and highest purpose of the "assembly" was to gather for worship. The psalmist raised his own voice to praise the name of Yahweh, along with the voice of the people (Pss. 22:22, 25; 35:18).

In the New Testament, the Greek word *eklessia*, "church," probably best continues the tradition of the *qahal* from the Old Testament. Jesus asserted that He would build or assemble His church (Matt. 16:18). God watches over His "assembly" today, just as He did in Old Testament times. In the New Testament, Jesus, Paul, Peter, James and all the other servants of God give themselves to the preservation and creation of God's true worshiping community (see Acts 15:22; Rom. 16:1; 1 Cor. 16:19; Gal. 1:13). The church is now the "assembly" of the Living God, a pillar and support of the Truth (1 Tim. 3:5, 15) made visible through Jesus Christ.

KEY VERSES

Exodus 12:6;
Numbers 16:3; 20:4;
Ezra 10:8;
2 Chronicles 6:3;
Psalm 22:22

Baal

B

Hebrew expression: *ba'al*
Pronunciation: *bah 'AHL*
Strong's Number: *1168*

Ahab, one of the most wicked kings of Israel, did many infamous acts during his reign in Israel (1 Kgs. 16:29, 874–853 B.C.). He committed all the sins of Jeroboam, married a pagan princess for a wife, and then on top of that, he built a Temple to Baal and worshiped him. The noun "baal" comes from the Hebrew verb *ba'al* which means "to rule over, or to marry." The noun can also refer to "baals" in the sense of the gods, major and minor, that the pagans of Canaan worshiped. The prophet Elijah was called by God to fight against this chief God of Canaan. On Mount Carmel, he called upon the Lord to show that the God of Israel was the one true God—not Baal! Elijah charged the people of Israel to go ahead and follow Baal if he is God, but if not, follow the Lord! (1 Kgs. 18:21). Elijah clearly showed that Baal could not or would not answer the cries of his followers (1 Kgs. 18:26).

The term "baals" as a generic term is also important, for the many baals in the land of Canaan represented all kinds of "divinities," "gods" and even "forces of nature." While the Israelites were still in the wilderness, the soothsayer, Balaam, lured them into pagan worship of the Baal of Peor. Today Baal or "baals" can stand for any number of "gods" in our modern world. Wealth, pleasure, success or religious objects are all "baals" which turn us away from God and lure us into pagan worship, just as the baals of the land of Canaan did to Israel. We, however, have the prophetic word of God in the Old Testament and an even more sure word of Christ in the New Testament that shows us the true God to follow.

The apostle Paul observed that the Lord has preserved a remnant of Jews, chosen by grace, that have not bowed the knee to Baal (Rom. 11:4; 1 Kgs. 19:18). But, not only the chosen Jews of the remnant of Israel are kept by grace, but all believers are preserved by grace (Eph. 2:8). We must make sure to not follow or worship anything other than God, teaching our children that there is only one true Lord, the God of Israel.

KEY VERSES

Numbers 25:5;
1 Kings 16:31,
    19:18;
Psalm 106:28

Banquet

Hebrew expression: *mishteh*
Pronunciation: *mish TEH*
Strong's Number: *4960*

B

There are ten banquets described in the book of Esther (Esth. 1:3–9; 2:18; 3:15; 5:1–8; 7:1–10; 8:17; 9:17–32). Significant and very important things happen at these banquets. They, in effect, provide the backdrop for the development of the key themes and plots in the story of Queen Esther. Xerxes, the Persian king, gave a banquet for his nobles (Esth. 1:3), and Queen Vashti gave one for the women of her court. When Esther was chosen to replace Vashti as queen, the king gave a banquet in her honor (Esth. 2:18). After Esther found favor in the king's eyes and he had granted her any wish up to half of his kingdom, she prepared a banquet and invited the king (Esth. 5:3). At this banquet, Esther revealed that it was Haman who had plotted to destroy all of the Jews in the Persian kingdom (Esth. 7:6). Xerxes was appalled at Haman's affront against both the Jewish informer, Mordecai, who had saved the king's life, and the Jews who had provided him with a new Queen. The Hebrew noun *mishteh* is formed from the verb *shatah* which means "to drink" or in the passive stem "to be drunk." *Mishteh* then developed into an active noun meaning "feast, banquet or drink." The *mishteh* became an occasion for drinking and evolved into a time and place for the joyous gathering of people to eat and drink. But, these "banquets" could be drunken celebrations that degenerated easily, such as the one Nabal, Abigail's husband, held where he became very drunk (1 Sam. 25:36). When Isaac was weaned, Abraham celebrated this great day with a joyful *mishteh*, "a feast." The wise writer of Proverbs used this word figuratively, asserting that a cheerful heart has a continual "feast"; that is, for a cheerful heart life is as joyous and happy as the time of a feast. Isaiah declares that the Lord will hold a banquet, a *mishteh*, for all of the peoples and nations, a symbol of the time and outpouring of the Messianic blessing for the nations.

Jesus frequented "banquets" (*gamos* is the Greek equivalent) and feasts of His people in the New Testament and He performed great things at these times of joy (John 2:8–9; *architriklinos* in Greek). Jesus' parable of the wedding banquet (Luke 14:13–14) indicates that not only the original chosen guests are invited, but also anyone who comes to the banquet that God has prepared is welcome (Matt. 22:1–14).

KEY VERSES

Genesis 21:8;
Esther 1:3;
Proverbs 15:15

Bathe

Hebrew expression: *rachats*
Pronunciation: *raw HAHTS*
Strong's Number: *7364*

It is easy to understand why people wash things that are physically dirty. The dirty, greasy hands of anyone who has worked on a car need to be cleaned. The Hebrew word *rachats*, "to bathe," "to wash off or away," or "to wash," covers this action as well as the bathing and washing of sacrificial animals. On the Day of Atonement, the High Priest and others involved were bathed (Lev. 16:4, 24, 26, 28). Aaron and his sons had to bathe their hands and feet before they could approach the altar to serve or before they entered the Tent of Meeting (Lev. 16:17–21). To bathe oneself was done before some important event (Exod. 2:5; Ruth 3:5) to not only physically clean oneself, but to prepare oneself for the event. Scripture also uses *rachats* figuratively to indicate getting rid of spiritual or ceremonial defilement, sin, and moral or ethical corruption and guilt.

Rachats is only used three times in Numbers but its use is significant. During the process of preparing the ashes of the red heifer to make the "water for cleansing" the High Priest had to bathe himself (*rachats*) after participating in the process (Num. 19:7). The person who supervised the burning of the red heifer also had to bathe himself (Num. 19:8). Even the unclean person who was cleansed by the purification water had to bathe with water to be clean (Num. 19:19). In these cases, ceremonial uncleanness was removed—that is, any uncleanness that a person might have incurred in the process of the ceremonial ritual. In the book of Isaiah, *rachats* also describes the bathing or "washing away" of sins (Isa. 1:16; 4:4). The Hebrew word *kabas*, "to wash," described the washing of clothes and garments (Num. 19:7, 8, 10, 19, 21; 31:24). Washing or "bathing" one's hands also indicated innocence in many cases (Deut. 21:6). In Jeremiah, the meanings of *rachats* and *kabas* overlap. *Rachats* is used often to refer to spiritual cleansing from sin, and *kabas* is used this way only three more times (Ps. 51:2, 7; Jer. 4:14) in the Old Testament.

KEY VERSES

Genesis 18:4;
Leviticus 16:4, 24,
26, 28;
Numbers 19:7–8,
19;
Isaiah 1:16; 4:4

The figurative use of "bathing" in the New Testament continues. Pilate washed his hands in vain as his claim to innocence in the death of Jesus (Matt. 27:24). James charges sinners to wash their hands in parallel with purifying their hearts (Jas. 4:8). And, as a sign of humility and solidarity with God's people, Jesus washed His disciples' feet (John 13:5–14). In Acts 22:16 "to baptize" is paralleled by *apolouo*, meaning "to wash away your sins." The main reference here is to the inward removal of sin and guilt signified by baptism, not the mere act of baptism. Today the "bathing and washing" necessary in the Old Testament is obsolete for believers who seek God's forgiveness. We are washed whiter than snow by the cleansing blood of Jesus Christ.

Believe

See also: *Believe, p. 234*
Hebrew expression: *'aman*
Pronunciation: *'aw MAHN*
Strong's Number: *539*

B

The people of Nineveh, the great pagan capital of Assyria, "believed God" through the word of Jonah the prophet; as a result of Jonah's warnings, they fasted, mourned and repented (Jonah 3:5, KJV, NIV, NLT, NJPS). Abraham also "believed God" and it was accounted to him as righteousness (Gen. 15:6). In both cases the biblical writer uses the verb *'aman*, "to confirm" or "to support." *'Aman* is also used to mean "to hold or stand firm," or "to believe, or to trust." Literally, the word means that the subject causes or generates confirmation or assurance that something is trustworthy or true. The common English word used to close off our prayers, "amen," comes from this Hebrew word and means "verily, truly, or surely." Abraham in his day and the Assyrians in their day both trusted in, or confirmed the word of God given to them—they "believed." They accepted the integrity of the Lord's word and responded to it in both attitude and action.

God granted miracles and signs to the Israelites and Moses in Egypt so that they would believe in Him (Exod. 4:1, 5, 8, 9). The psalmist considered "belief" in God's Word to be the same as "trust" in His deliverance (Ps. 78:22, 32), yet some Israelites still did not believe. The response of the Ninevites, therefore, is highlighted even more. The true Israelite believed and trusted, *'aman*, in God's Word and Law (Ps. 119:66). In the New Testament, the gospel is the good news and Jesus is our Jonah. It is essential to "believe" (*pisteuo* in Greek), to trust, that God has acted in Christ (Mark 1:15). Jesus urges us to not fear, but simply believe the gospel (Mark 5:36). John wrote his entire gospel to show us and help us to believe that Jesus was the promised Messiah (John 20:31). Furthermore, Paul confirms the true mark of the Christian as one who believes that God has raised Christ from the dead (Rom. 10:9). God wants us to lead the way in believing in Him, but that also means taking the message faithfully to others, even those like the Ninevites who seem destined for destruction because of their sinful ways.

KEY VERSES

Genesis 15:6;
Exodus 4:1, 5, 8–9;
Psalms 106:24;
116:10;
Jonah 3:5

Beloved

Hebrew expression: *dod*
Pronunciation: *DOHD*
Strong's Number: *1730*

In present day Israel, *dodi* rings can be purchased with Song of Solomon 2:16 inscribed on them, "My lover is mine and I am his" (Song 6:3; 7:10, NIV). The Hebrew word *dod* is often rendered as "beloved" (KJV), or "lover" (NIV). It also means "uncle," a term of endearment, and the feminine form of the word, *dodah,* means "aunt" (Exod. 6:20; Lev. 10:4; 18:14; 20:20). This forceful, delightful and tender word is found often in the Song of Solomon, which is sometimes called the Song of Songs.

The object of the young woman's affection throughout the Song of Solomon is her *dod,* her "beloved" or "lover." This book is unparalleled in world literature, secular or religious, in its powerful but delightful portrayal of love between a man and a woman. The beloved is exclusively given to the young maiden and she is exclusively devoted to him (Song 2:16; 6:3; 7:10). These ancient love songs and ballads reflect pure passionate love between two persons made in God's image. It is a picture of how good God's creation is. There is no hint of physical love bearing the blemish of "evil." In fact, the physical love portrayed in the book deepens the spiritual bond between the two persons. Love is a vital part of God's creation of male and female and this gift of love is *tob,* "good" in the sight of God.

The book presents a picture of love between two people at the right time, the right place and with the right persons—all with God's approval in a blessed ceremony of marriage. It pictures God's gift of love and intimacy to His people. It can be read symbolically as a picture of the love of Israel for God and vice-versa. It can be read as a figurative presentation of Christ's love for His church. But, those are not its primary intentions and to *only* read the narrative this way misses a message that is greatly needed for the church today. Believers need to hear that God's creation and approval of intimacy and physical love between man and woman, created in His image and united in marriage in Him, is all good. In Christ, the church finds its true spiritual intimacy. As He loved the church and died for it, so husbands are to love their wives (Eph. 5:25; Col. 3:19).

KEY VERSES

Song of Solomon
1:2, 13–14; 2:8;
Ezekiel 16:8; 23:17

Blameless

Hebrew expression: *tam*
Pronunciation: *TAWM*
Strong's Number: *8535*

B

Our critical judgments keep us from calling others blameless, yet Scripture describes a number of people as blameless—for example, Noah and David (Gen. 6:9; 2 Sam. 22:24). The book of Job is where the subject of blamelessness is explored in detail. Job is described as blameless by God, upright man who spurned evil (Job 1:8; 2:3; see also Job 31:6). Thus for the book of Job, the dilemma is: How can a blameless person suffer? Or how will this blameless person react in the face of undeserved suffering?

What exactly does the adjective *blameless* communicate about Job's character? It is instructive to look at other occurrences of the Hebrew adjective *tam* and its root *tmm* in the Old Testament. The Hebrew root *tmm* essentially refers to "completeness," whether physical or ethical. Appropriately the verb is often used in the context of something "coming to an end" (compare Gen. 47:18) or "being finished" (compare 1 Kgs. 7:22). Less often, the verb is used to describe something "being whole" (compare Ps. 19:14). Another adjective, *tamim*, is often used in a cultic setting to describe the appropriate quality of the sacrificial animal, i.e. healthy, sound, or without blemish (compare Exod. 12:5). Finally, the derived noun, *tom*, denotes "completeness" (compare Isa. 47:9), often with the connotation of innocence (compare 2 Sam 15:11) or integrity (compare Prov. 13:6). The Hebrew root *tmm* occurs eighteen times in the book of Job (1:1, 8; 2:3, 9; 4:6; 8:20; 9:20–22; 12:4; 21:23; 22:3; 27:5; 31:6, 40; 36:4; 37:16). As implied from the appearance of the adjective form *tam* in the first verse of the book, its use is far from coincidental; the concept of Job's innocence or "wholeness" lies at the heart of the book's message. Both the narrator (1:1) and Yahweh (1:8; 2:3) use *tam* to describe Job's character. Yet Job suffers. Although his friends dogmatically assert that the wicked suffer but that the righteous prosper (5:6; 8:4–7,11–20; 18:5–21; 20:26–29; 22:2–11), Job clings to his "integrity" (*tummah*), even as he sinks into despair (2:3, 9; 27:5; 31:6). Incredibly, his unwillingness to admit wrong leads him so far as to indict Yahweh for treating the blameless and the wicked alike (9:20–22; 22:3).

How is Job's ethical and spiritual wholeness reconciled with his suffering? On one level, Job is vindicated. Yahweh's appearance, as a response to Job's oath of clearance (chapter 31), establishes that Job had done nothing to deserve his suffering. The mere fact that Job survives the face-to-face encounter with the deity serves to exonerate him. However, Yahweh's message avoids the issue of Job's innocence altogether. Rather, He focuses on the order of creation. His argument can be summarized as follows: (1) I, Yahweh, am in control of the cosmos I created; (2) what you see as chaos was created as much a part of the natural order as humankind;

KEY VERSES

2 Samuel 15:11;
Job 1:8;
Isaiah 47:9;
Proverbs 13:6

therefore, (3) 'chaotic' phenomena should not be viewed as either moral or immoral events, but as amoral ones. The application of this argument to Job and his situation demands an attitude adjustment. Job has based his argument regarding his suffering on his blamelessness; Yahweh's response is that moral issues *may* have nothing to do with the suffering which Job and his family have endured. Hence, Job was mistaken when he made the connection between his suffering and his moral status.

The lesson of Job's life, blameless as it is, teaches us that as participants in the created world, we must not think that everything which befalls us, good or bad, is because we deserve it. This attitude completely denies God the prerogative to choose when and where He bestows grace. Instead, we should strive to emulate Job's life as a blameless person, holding on to a "disinterested" faith, serving God because of who He is, not because of what He gives.

Blessing

See also: *Blessed, p. 237*
Hebrew expression: *berakah*
Pronunciation: *beh raw KAWH*
Strong's Number: *1293*

B

"And the Lord blessed them" (Gen. 1:28). This was and is the normal state of people before God. Everyone wants a blessing, to be blessed or to bless others. God is portrayed as the God of blessing for His people in the Old Testament, just waiting to pour out His benefits upon His people. But in Scripture, the word means much more than just "being happy." Above all, it means having God's approval and his goodwill directed toward persons—then the covenant blessings can be granted.

The Hebrew word is *berakah* and is accurately rendered "blessing" most of the time. It comes from the verbal root *barak*, "to kneel, to bless." The noun *berek* meaning "knee" is built upon the same root and is used to indicate "kneeling in worship" to bless God (1 Kgs. 8:54; Ezra 9:5) and the congregation of Israel. Elijah put his face between his knees to pray to God—a form of blessing God (1 Kgs. 18:42).

In the Old Testament, many people granted blessings to others—parents (Gen. 49:28), Moses (Deut. 33:1). But, God is presented as the *source* of all blessing (Gen. 1:28; Exod. 32:29). He set before His people Israel the way of blessing and the way of cursing (Deut. 27: 28) and let them know that He was the one who dispensed blessings for trusting and obeying Him or curses, the opposite of blessings, to those who did not trust Him (Deut. 30:1, 19). The Israelites simply had to choose the path they would take—the path to blessings or the path to cursing (Deut. 30:19).

The famous priestly blessing, the placing of the Lord's Name upon the people to bless them by the High Priest, shows the importance of the Lord's blessing of His people. And, it shows how closely tied to the blessing of His people His Name was.

In Isaiah, the goal for God's people was to be a blessing, *berakah*, upon the earth (Isa. 19:24). Isaiah envisioned a time when God's blessing would be not only a future reality, but also a present reality for those serving God faithfully. God's blessing of His people in the Old Testament is tied to His placing His Spirit on them (Isa. 44:3). He could withdraw His blessing, but His desire was to bless His people profusely at all times (Jer. 16:5). The Lord blessed the Israelites with rain, security, the law, health, and many other things. In the future, God promised to bless them even more, more than they could hold (Mal. 3:10).

KEY VERSES

Genesis 12:2;
Deuteronomy 11:26;
Psalm 3:8;
Proverbs 24:25;
Isaiah 19:24

Blessing is available to God's people in Christ now. What was given to Abraham is now available to Christians (Gal. 3:14) through His Spirit. Not physical, but spiritual blessing are the special inheritance of God's people now (Eph. 1:3, *eulogia* in Greek). As we act as God's blessed people, we are now encouraged by Peter to return blessings upon both our friends *and* our adversaries (1 Pet. 3:9).

Blood

See also: *Blood, p. 238*
Hebrew expression: *dam*
Pronunciation: *DAWM*
Strong's Number: *1818*

"Blood that cries out" is a strange and shocking personification used by the writer of Genesis. The first mention of "blood" in the Bible is connected with the death of a human being (Gen. 4:10). It was Abel's blood, shed by his brother Cain, that cried out for justice. According to the Old Testament, the first and worst sin against another human being is to kill another person. In God's law, the punishment for murder was severe—the murderer must be executed; life for life (Gen. 9:6). The Hebrew word for "blood," *dam,* may be connected with the root *'adam* meaning "red, or mankind," and related to *'adamah,* "earth, or land." The life of a living being was believed to be in his or her blood (Lev. 17:11). When blood was shed it polluted the earth and had to be atoned for (Deut. 19:13; Prov. 6:17). Therefore, if a murder case could not be solved, a rite of atonement had to be carried out to cleanse the land (Deut. 21:1–9). God would take vengeance upon the guilty party. The only way that sin could be atoned for was by the shedding of blood, either the blood of the guilty person or the blood of a sacrificial animal. Otherwise, God's judgment would fall upon the people.

The principle of atonement by blood was established in Leviticus 17:11–12 forever. The Lord gave the blood of animals to Israel to make atonement for their sins, and the Lord declared blood sacred; Israel was not to eat or drink it (Lev. 17:11–16). The High Priest used blood several times on the Day of Atonement to cover his own sins, the sins of Israel, and to cleanse various holy items (Lev. 16:14, 16–19). Furthermore, covenants were sealed through the shedding of a sacrificial animal's blood, indicating the total commitment of the parties involved. Moses sealed the Sinai Covenant, sprinkling blood on the altar and then on the people, after the people had committed themselves to do everything the Lord had said (Exod. 24:6–8).

The Old Testament picture of atonement foreshadowed the reality of Christ's atonement for us through His own shed blood. We are redeemed from our sins because Jesus gave His life, His blood, for us (Eph. 1:7). The Israelites of the Old Testament broke their covenant with God, but Jesus established the new covenant between God and all people (Jer. 31:31–34; Heb. 8).

KEY VERSES

Genesis 4:10; 9:6;
Leviticus 17:11–14;
Exodus 24:6–8

In the Lord's Supper, we remember the value of Christ's death and His shed blood (John 6:53, 54) by "eating His flesh" and "drinking His blood." The author of Hebrews reminds us how much more Jesus' blood cleanses us from sin than the blood of bulls and goats (Heb. 9:12). Reiterating the principle from the Old Testament, the author asserts that without the shedding of blood there is no forgiveness for sins (Heb. 9:22). The blood of Jesus is indeed sacred and precious (1 Pet. 1:19).

Branch

Hebrew expression: *tsemah*
Pronunciation: *TSEH mah*
Strong's Number: *6780*

B

Plants and trees sprouting buds and putting forth new growth is an expected occurrence as winter gives way to spring in seasonal climates. The idea of a child as an "offshoot" or descendant of a particular family is still understood as an image of growth—despite the shift from a rural culture to an urban, technological one. Both understandings of the word *branch* are applied to the family tree of Jesse in the Old Testament (Isa. 11:1). A shoot or a branch sprouting from a living plant doesn't surprise anyone. A fresh branch growing from a dead stump, however, gives pause for observation and investigation. Such was the case for the Hebrews in the days of Zechariah. Jesse's family tree—Israel's royal line of David—was merely a stump after the Babylonian exile. The family wasn't flourishing. Yet, God promised to cause a branch to sprout from the stump that would one day grow into a royal tree. That sprout would begin with Zerubbabel (Zech. 3:8; 6:12).

The word *branch* occurs only twelve times in the Old Testament and refers literally to a bud or an offshoot of a plant or a tree. The term may be used in a collective sense meaning "growth" or "sprouts" (for example, Gen. 19:25; Isa 61:11) or in reference to a single plant or shoot (for example, Hos. 8:7).

More significant is the metaphorical meaning of "branch" as a figure for the land of Israel (Isa. 4:2) and as a title for the messianic king in the Old Testament prophets (Jer. 23:5; 33:15). Jeremiah forecasts a day when a branch or an offshoot from the house of David will arise as a king, bringing restoration to Israel and Judah (Jer. 23:5). This "Branch of righteousness" possesses another title in keeping with the character of His reign, "the LORD our righteousness" (Jer. 23:6). Jeremiah 33:15 describes the justice and righteousness that would characterize this king's rule.

The term "Branch" in Zechariah is used synonymously with "my Servant" (Zech. 3:8), another messianic title in the Old Testament (for example, Isa. 52:13; 53:11). It appears the prophet Zechariah understood the postexilic governor of Judah, Zerubbabel, as a partial fulfillment of the Jeremiah passages. Both the high priest Joshua and Zerubbabel were considered signs from God that He intended to make good on His promises about a Davidic king who would restore the fortunes of Israel as the people of God.

KEY VERSES

Jeremiah 23:5;
33:15;
Zechariah 3:8; 6:12

The title "Branch" is not applied to Jesus Christ in the New Testament. Rather, the emphasis is placed on the origin of Jesus as a descendant of David, fulfilling the Old Testament prophecy about the Branch (for example, Matt. 9:27; 21:9; Mark 12:35).

Build

Hebrew expression: *banah*
Pronunciation: *baw NAWH*
Strong's Number: *1129*

It is part of human nature to build things. We build toys, houses, roads, furniture—we even build nations. We build our bodies and we all try to build relationships and friendships. In the Old Testament, God was the master builder. The word "to build" in Hebrew is *banah* and it refers to the construction, new or renewed, of just about anything. Its most significant use is the Lord's "building" of His nation and people—they are the work of His hands. He made them. The Lord built, *banah*, the first woman, Eve, from a part of the first man He created, Adam (Gen. 2:22). The Lord also called His people out of Egypt and built them by multiplying them, nurturing them, and bringing them closer to Him. His further goal was to build the city of Jerusalem for His people. Before long God's ultimate goal, to dwell among His people, was made clear (Exod. 25:8); He would build a Temple in Jerusalem, through David and Solomon, in order to live among His chosen nation (2 Sam. 7:13, 27; 1 Kgs. 2:36; 2.Chr. 2:1). But God would *banah* even more, He would construct the human dynasty of David and his descendants to serve as His royal family (1 Kgs. 11:38). Only God could accomplish such a feat.

The Lord is revealed as the one who builds up or tears down His people and all the nations of the world as well. At the Lord's command Jeremiah was called to deliver the prophetic word of God to Israel (Jer. 1:10). The mercy of the Lord promised that even after He had judged His people, permitting the Babylonians to destroy them and their city, He would again build them up and not tear them down again (Jer. 24:6). The Israelites would become a nation in Judah again and He would rebuild both Jerusalem and the new Temple (Ps. 147:2; Amos 9:11; Zech. 6:12; Heb. 11:10). God was and is the builder *par excellence* of His people and nation.

Jesus is the master builder of God's people today. The church, or community of *believers in Christ, is being built upon Christ and His character* (Matt. 16:18, oikodomeo in Greek). He is preparing an eternal house—not "built" by human hands—for all believers (2 Cor. 5:1, *acheiropoietos* in Greek). The Lord challenges us to build up each other in our faith in the Lord (Rom. 15:2; 1 Thess. 5:11; Jude 20). Just like God our challenge is to help build relationships with others and to build His Church. We must never take the credit for the growth of our churches or the progress we make in relationships because the Lord is behind everything (Heb. 3:4, *kataskeuazo* in Greek).

KEY VERSES

Genesis 2:22;
1 Kings 2:36;
Psalm 51:18;
Jeremiah 1:10; 24:6;
Malachi 1:4

24

Burden

Hebrew expression: *massa'*
Pronunciation: *mah SAW'*
Strong's Number: *4853*

B

The burden of the prophet Isaiah was not physical, it was spiritual. It was a message the Lord had laid upon his heart and he was constrained to deliver—just as other true prophets of the Lord had been and would be. The Hebrew word *massa'* can mean a "load or burden," or even "tribute" in the physical sense, but its most significant use in the Old Testament was its use to describe the "message" the Lord laid upon His prophets. The word is translated as "burden, oracle, message, pronouncement, utterance" (KJV, NIV, NLT, NJPS, respectively). It is based on the root of the verb *nasa'*, "to lift, carry, take." The prophet carried the burden of the message of the Lord until he delivered it. The word is found most often in the book of Isaiah and then in the book of Jeremiah.

This word also describes an "oracle," *massa'* in the sense of wise sayings by Agar the wise son of Jakeh and by the mother of King Lemuel (Prov. 30:1; 31:1). The prophetic oracles were spoken with regard to various things: cities (Jerusalem, Ezek. 12:10), countries (Babylon, Isa. 13:1) and peoples (Arabia, Isa. 21:13).

The *massa'* delivered by the prophet was the message the Lord had put into his heart and mind. The "oracles" or "burdens" of Isaiah demonstrated His sovereignty over all of the nations of the earth (Isa. 13:1; 14:1; 17:1; 19:1, etc.). God had a divine sovereign oracle for each nation. The Lord even had an oracle of judgment for the apple of His eye, Jerusalem, in the day of the prophet Zechariah (12:1–2), and the entire book of Malachi is the burden of the prophet (1:1).

A burden, or *massa'*, from the Lord rendered both the mind and body of the speaker uneasy (Zeph. 3:18). The *massa'* or physical level of a pit of dirt, as much as two mules could carry, graphically drives home the receipt of these oracles upon the prophets. Isaiah's "heavy" judgment upon the nations was not easy for him to bear.

Christ used a Greek word equivalent to *massa'*, *baros*, "burden," "burdens" when He asserted that for those who come to Him, His burden is light (Matthew 11:30; Rev. 2:24). For Him, the burden laid upon Him by God was great; yet, He bore it gladly. If we are called to bear burdens, whatever shape they may take, we have both the Old Testament and New Testament examples to show us how to both bear and deliver them.

KEY VERSES

2 Chronicles 17:11;
2 Kings 9:25;
Isaiah 13:1;
15:1; 17:1;
Malachi 1:1

Burn Incense

Hebrew expression: *qatar*
Pronunciation: *qaw TAHR*
Strong's Number: *6999*

The Hebrew verb *qatar,* "burning of incense," was formed from the noun *qetoret* meaning "smoke of a burning sacrifice or incense." *Qatar* can also mean "incense offering" and does not indicate an inherently evil act. As a matter of fact, it was used to describe the burning of sacrifices to the Lord in worship as it ascended heavenward in honor to God (Exod. 30:7; 1 Kgs. 12:33; 1 Chr. 6:34). The burning of incense symbolized the prayers of God's people before Him. The psalmist prayed that his prayer would be like incense before the Lord (Ps. 141:2). Only priests in Israel could offer incense; Aaron had to "burn fragrant incense," *qatar,* on the altar every morning and every evening. This practice was to continue forever (Exod. 30:7, 8). The burning of incense as a sweet smelling offering before the Lord indicated the worshiper's attempt to present prayers or offerings that were pleasing to Him (1 Sam. 2:28).

The burning of incense, however, became a stumbling block to Israel when she began to worship in the pagan high places. In 1 Kings, and elsewhere, the practice of "burning incense" in the high places is condemned (1 Kgs. 22:43). Israel also began to burn incense to false deities and to useless idols (1 Kgs. 12:3; Jer. 18:15). Even after the Temple of Solomon was destroyed, Israelites continued to burn incense at forbidden high places to the Lord and in some cases to pagan deities (2 Kgs. 22:17). Pagan priests were sometimes appointed by Israelite kings to burn incense on pagan high places to pagan deities (2 Kgs. 23:5). Baal and all the hosts of heaven were "honored and worshiped" by a practice that God had established to be directed to Him alone.

This is certainly a lesson for all believers not to give anything that belongs to the Lord, such as worship, prayers, gifts, or our abilities, to something or someone other than God. The burning of incense, as God initially commanded, continued in the New Testament era (Luke 1:9). The practice continued among the Jews even after the Temple was destroyed in A.D. 70. In the New Testament, the prayers of the saints are equated with incense (Rev. 8:3, *thumiama* in Greek). Thus, in a symbolic way, the burning of incense before the Lord is replaced by the offering of "sweet-smelling" prayers (Rev. 8:3) to the Lord.

KEY VERSES

Exodus 30:7, 8;
1 Samuel 2:28;
1 Kings 22:43;
2 Kings 23:5;
Jeremiah 18:15

Burnt Sacrifice

Hebrew expression: 'olah
Pronunciation: 'oh LAWH
Strong's Number: 5930

The apostle Paul's impassioned plea to present our bodies as sacrifices to God, is especially poignant and challenging when we understand the significance of the "burnt sacrifice," the 'olah, as described in the Old Testament (Rom. 12:1–2). Paul means both our physical body and our mind and spirit as well; that is, all of us. The Hebrew term 'olah, "burnt sacrifice," comes from the Hebrew root 'alah, "to go up," or "to ascend," and means, therefore, "that which goes up." The term is also translated as "burnt offering" (NIV, KJV) or sometimes as "whole burnt offering" because the entire sacrificial animal was burnt up on the altar, except for the skin or any other part of the animal that would not be made clean (Lev. 6:8–13). The entire burnt sacrifice ascended to God from the altar, expressing both the total commitment of the person offering the sacrifice and his or her appeal and attitude toward God. The offering's heavenward ascent illustrated the individual's approach and entreaty of heaven. The offering was voluntary and therefore expressed a free and deep devotion to God. The whole burnt offering was given in integrity, but *only* when the heart of the person offering the sacrifice was right before God. Otherwise, the sacrifice became an act of deceit and hypocrisy (Ps. 51:16, 19).

Abraham was commanded by the Lord God to sacrifice his son, Isaac, on Mount Mariah as a "burnt sacrifice." Abraham's willingness to obey God, even in this matter, clearly indicated that his faith was total and complete. However, God Himself provided a lamb for the offering, instead of Isaac, just as Abraham had said He would (Gen. 22:1–19). After the flood, Noah sacrificed scarce and valuable animals and birds that pleased the Lord (Gen. 8:20–21). Israel was expected to worship the Lord with burnt offerings when they arrived at Mount Sinai (Exod. 10:25; 18:12). Neither the priests nor the person who offered the sacrifice ate the burnt offering; it was costly worship and demonstrated devotion and commitment to God.

The total dedication and costly worship of the person making an offering remains a spiritual principle in the New Testament, but now the offering is not a "burnt sacrifice" of an animal, but our total selves (Rom. 12:1–2). God no longer commands the symbolic action of worship. Instead, He wants our entire being presented to Him — our total love to God and neighbors (Mark 12:33). Christ fulfilled the goal of the entire sacrificial system, including the burnt offering, by surrendering His will totally to God's will (compare Heb. 10:5, 6; Ps. 40:6–8). Yet He also gave His whole body as the supreme sacrifice to God's will and pleasure (Heb. 10:5). As Paul beseeches us to offer our bodies as living sacrifices, we can do no less (Rom. 12:1–7).

KEY VERSES

Exodus 18:12;
Leviticus 1:3;
6:8–13;
Psalm 51:19;
Hebrews 6:2–3, 5;

Calamity

Hebrew expression: 'ed
Pronunciation: 'AYD
Strong's Number: 343

C

In the small book of Obadiah, the word 'ed occurs three times in one verse. This word is translated as "distress" or "calamity" in nearly all translations (KJV, NIV, NLT, NJPS). It may be related to an original root denoting "burden." Obadiah 13 mentions a great "calamity" which befell Jerusalem. Most likely this disaster occurred in 586 B.C. when Nebuchadnezzar destroyed the city. This was a national calamity and Israel's enemies gloated over it, including Israel's kinsmen Edom. God, however, would not let this atrocious gloating over the destruction of His people go unpunished. The oracle of judgment upon Edom, delivered through the prophet Obadiah, stated that the descendants of Esau would be wiped out (Obad. 18) and Esau would be governed by the exiles of Judah (Obad. 20–21). 'Ed also refers to the calamities of the righteous who would have to suffer. David suffered a disaster at the hands of his enemies (Ps. 18:19), but Job was permitted to suffer calamity by God Himself (Job 31:23). The word, however, also speaks of the calamity of the wicked (Job 18:12; 21:17; Deut. 32:35). In Proverbs, "calamity" describes the disasters that overtake the foolish who do not pursue wisdom diligently (Prov. 1:26–27). In Jeremiah, God says He will turn His back on the wicked and rebellious people of Judah in the time of their calamity (Jer. 18:17). The righteous, as well as the wicked, are permitted to suffer disaster and calamity; thus, God's people must remain faithful to Him during these times. God's people will receive a clearer picture of the Lord God after the clouds of the disaster have passed (Job 40:1–5; 42:5). God will come to the rescue and aid of His people (Obad. 13). Jesus' warning to His followers was that only with much trial and tribulation would they enter the Kingdom of Heaven; calamity in this Age, but blessing and deliverance in the Age to come (Acts 5:41; Rom. 5:3; 2 Thess. 1:5; 1 Pet. 4:12). Job's patient endurance during his calamitous suffering is an example for all believers (Jas. 5:10–11). We must always place our hope in the Lord. He delivered Job, and He delivers us from our suffering, trials, struggles, and discouragement.

KEY VERSES

Deuteronomy 32:35;
Job 18:12;
Psalm 18:18;
Proverbs 27:10;
Obadiah 13

Chosen

Hebrew expression: *bachar*
Pronunciation: *baw HAHR*
Strong's Number: *977*

C

In the book of Genesis, we discover that the Lord established a special covenant with Abraham, promising that the aged patriarch would be the father of many nations (Gen. 17:1–8). Out of his seed would proceed the nation of Israel. By virtue of the covenant, and not because of the merits of Abraham or Israel in particular, Israel would share a special relationship with the Lord. In fact, Scripture reminds us that Israel had little which merited God's special favor (Deut. 7:7). Rather, Israel was given a special place because God "chose" them in love.

Moses understood this truth and reminded the Israelites of it as they stood on the verge of the Promised Land:

> For thou art an holy people unto the Lord thy God, and the Lord hath chosen thee to be a peculiar people unto himself, above all the nations that are upon the earth.

> *(Deut. 14:2, KJV)*

No other nation or people could lay claim to being God's "chosen" people. Yet, what exactly is meant by the statement that God has "chosen" Israel? The Hebrew word *bachar* used by Moses denotes the process of selection and decision making common to us all. The very essence of a choice implies that there are two or more competing alternatives. The final selection is made chiefly on the basis of a careful examination. Whatever is chosen is done so because it is pleasing and desirable to the senses (Prov. 21:3), the finest specimen of its type (2 Sam. 10:9; Song 5:15), or it suits a certain purpose (Exod. 17:9). By virtue of being chosen, the object becomes precious to the one who chooses it, even if to no one else.

When God chose Israel, He placed His blessing upon them. The names of His people were given a special role in His redemptive purposes. Through them He would reveal Himself in Christ. Nevertheless, the fact that God chose Israel did not prevent His people from rebelling and turning from Him (Isa. 1:2–4). His election did not make void the will of the people to respond or to reject the love of God. Still, the Lord remained faithful to them and in love pleaded for their willing return (Jer. 3:12). Paul declares that even with the advent of the church, and salvation for the Gentiles as well as the Jews, the Israelites remain God's chosen people (Rom. 11:1–2). The Lord has special purposes in store for them (Rom. 11:26).

KEY VERSES

Deuteronomy 7:6–7;
Joshua 24:15;
Isaiah 41:8

Clan

Hebrew expression: *'elep*
Pronunciation: *'eh LEF*
Strong's Number: *504*

Today not many people value the family as much as people in ancient times did. For ancient Israelites, the family was central. It gave a person his or her identity, his or her role in life, and his or her financial, social, and emotional support.

In fact, in Exodus 40:38, it is asserted that the cloud or fire was with Israel day and night—in plain view of "the whole house" of Israel. The Hebrew word for "house" is the term for the smallest family unit in Israel, what we might call the "nuclear family." There were, however, many differences between the ancient household of Israel and the modern nuclear family. But in this verse, Exodus 40:38, God views Israel as one large household, one large family. After the "whole house of Israel," the "tribe" was the next largest unit. There were twelve tribes in Israel. Next came the clan, the kinship unit that was between the tribe and the smallest unit, "the ancestral household," which is *bayit*, or *bet 'ab*, "house of the father." The word for "clan" is most often *mishpachah*, but ten times the New International Version translates *'elep* as "clan." These two terms overlap, but are different in some ways. In Judges the word *'elep* is translated only once as "clan" (Judg. 6:15; NIV). The word can also mean "thousand," but a clan in Israel could evidently be smaller than a thousand people.

The tribes and clans were expected to supply leaders and military power in Israel (Num. 10:4; 31:5). In fact, from Bethlehem Ephrathah, one of the smallest clans of Judah, Jesus Christ would come (Mic. 5:2; Matt. 2:1–16; John 8:58). Gideon, one of Israel's greatest deliverers, makes the point that God should not choose him to deliver Israel from the Midianites (Judg. 6:15). The reason he gives is that his clan was the weakest and smallest one in the tribe of Manasseh. Bethlehem Ephrathah was, likewise, the smallest one among the tribes of Judah. God's answer to Gideon was to the point; it was the same answer the Lord gave to Moses explaining why he could serve as the human agent to lead Israel out of Egypt. The Lord asserted to both Gideon and Moses: "I will be with you!" (Exod. 3:12; Judg. 6:16).

KEY VERSES

Judges 6:15;
Numbers 1:16; 31:5;
Joshua 22:14;
Micah 5:2

God did not and does not choose people to be His servants and deliverers because of their size, political or military strength, or even family size and influence. He chooses people who will let Him be with them and let Him accomplish His work through them. With his three hundred picked men, Gideon defeated thousands of the Midianites (Judg. 7:22–24). Through submitting totally to His father's will, Jesus, one man, delivered the world (Luke 22:39–44). We too are given strength and ability to do far more than we could ever think or imagine because God is with us and He has great plans for us!

Cleanse

Hebrew expression: *taher*
Pronunciation: *taw HAYR*
Strong's Number: *2891*

Two great kings in Judah, Hezekiah and Josiah, set out to "cleanse" God's Temple during their respective reigns. Ezra used the Hebrew word *taher* in First and Second Chronicles to describe the kings' efforts. In the reign of Hezekiah (715–686 B.C.) the king ordered the Levites "to purify" the Temple of the Lord. In this case, *taher* is rendered "to purify" (NIV) and "to cleanse" (KJV). It also means "to be clean," or "to be pure," as in cleansing something physically; that is, removing whatever is causing any uncleanness. *Taher* also indicates the ceremonial or religious act of "cleansing" or "purifying" something. However, its most important use describes "moral purity" and "cleanness."

Hezekiah cleansed the Temple of the Lord by having the Levites remove all of the pagan idolatrous and unclean items (2 Chr. 29:15, 16). But, of course, it was the religious significance of these articles that polluted the Temple, not their mere physical presence or composition. This kind of cleanness and purity is referred to as "ceremonial" cleanness and was ordered by the Lord. The utensils, the altar, the skin of the priests, the garments of the priests, and anything else that took part in the Lord's service had to be cleansed to be ceremonially clean.

Moral purity and cleanness, however, superseded ceremonial purity, a fact illustrated beautifully in 2 Chronicles 30:18–20. After Hezekiah purified (*taher*) the Temple he held a great Passover. However, he allowed people from the northern tribes who had not cleansed themselves properly to take part! This was contrary to the Mosaic Law (2 Chr. 30:18). Hezekiah asked the Lord to forgive the ceremonial uncleanness of those who set their heart on seeking the Living God, even though they were not properly cleansed. God heard him; He forgave their ceremonial uncleanness, and healed them! Hezekiah's prayer showed that God looks at the heart, and not merely at formal ceremonial purity. King David prayed for the moral purity of his heart before God, realizing that he could offer acceptable sacrifices to God only once he was "clean" (Ps. 51:7, 19). It is the inward cleansing (*taher*) of the heart that mattered to God most in the Old Testament.

Indeed, in the New Testament, a pure (*kathatos*, Greek adjective) God-seeking heart is the chief thing that matters to the Lord. Through faith in Christ, God purifies the hearts of believers and sends us His Holy Spirit as confirmation that we are accepted by Him and saved from sin forever (Acts 15:9).

KEY VERSES

Leviticus 13:6;
2 Chronicles
29:15–16;
Ezra 6:20; Psalm
51:7

Close relative

Hebrew expression: *go'el*
Pronunciation: *goh 'EHL*
Strong's number: *1350*

C

The Book of Ruth is the story of Naomi's distress. However, it is Ruth's relationship with Boaz which eventually provides the resolution to her distress. The nature of Ruth and Boaz's relationship is complex and revolves around the concept conveyed by the Hebrew root *g'l*. The repetition of the root *g'l* (23 times in the 85 verses of the book) suggests that the word is essential to the message. In the book, the root occurs both as a verb, *ga'al* "to redeem," "to buy back," "to reclaim" (3:13, 4:4, 6) and as a noun, *go'el* "redeemer," "reclaimer," "close-relative" (2:20; 3:9,12; 4:1, 3, 6, 8, 14).

In the Old Testament, the root *g'l*, when used with a literal meaning, carries both legal and social implications regarding familial responsibilities. The duties of the "redeemer" fell to the closest male relative (that is, a son, brother, uncle, cousin, or other relative) of a family member who was in need. As an integral component in the social fabric of Israelite culture, the close relative, or "redeemer," carried the responsibility of protecting the property and rights of the tribal family. If property was sold in order to repay debts (see Lev. 25:25) or if a relative was forced to enter into indentured servitude for economic reasons (see Lev. 25:47), it was the redeemer's duty to provide monetary deliverance. Indeed, the redeemer even had the right to avenge wrongful death of a relative by killing the murderer (Num. 35:12; Deut. 19:6).

Figuratively, *g'l* is often used with regard to Yahweh's relationship to His people. Yahweh is described as the *go'el* of Israel in the Exodus event (Exod. 6:6), of Jerusalem from the desolation of destruction (compare Isa. 52:9, 59:20), of orphans from oppression (Prov. 23:10–11), and also of psalm writers crying out for protection or deliverance from enemies (see Pss. 19:14, 69:19, 72:14, 103:4). In these contexts, the root *g'l* indicates that Yahweh is functioning as the closest relative who takes up the cause of the wronged party, often by means of deliverance to safety.

When this Hebrew word, *g'l*, is used of Yahweh's activity with his people, the imagery is obviously meant to bring to mind Yahweh's intimate "family" relationship with His people.

In the book of Ruth, the function of the *go'el* is complicated and often misunderstood. First, Boaz is not the closest male relative to Elimelek, Naomi's deceased husband (Ruth 3:12). His role as the *go'el* is fulfilled only after a public confrontation with the closest relative at the end of the book. Secondly, Ruth's suggestive tactics at the threshing floor are often confused with the levirate responsibilities. Levirate marriage was instructed by God for the purpose of providing an heir for the deceased family member by marrying the widow (Deut. 25:5–10; compare Gen. 38). In the last scene of the book of

KEY VERSES

Leviticus 25:25, 26;
Deuteronomy 19:6;
Ruth 3:12;
Psalm 19:14

Ruth, it may be that Boaz first sets the two Israelite institutions of the *go'el* and levirate marriage in opposition (4:5). In effect, Boaz acknowledges that the closer relative may buy the land back. However, by responding with his own intention to provide offspring to Ruth, he implies that ownership of the land will someday revert to Ruth's children. The ironic result of Boaz's actions is that he himself ends up fulfilling (and hence combining) the broad functions of both the levirate and *go'el* institutions. Though the exact interplay of the *go'el* and Levirate responsibilities in Ruth 4 remain debatable, the essential nature of the *go'el* is clear: provision for unfortunate relatives.

The lesson for believers is also clear. We as God's people should be outward-looking (compare Matt. 25:31–46; Luke 6:27). We should be concerned for the welfare of those less fortunate, especially those within our "spiritual family" (compare Acts 4:32–37). Second, God Himself is the ultimate Redeemer. He fulfills the role of the closest relative for His people. The example set by God, who paid our redemption price with His own Son, should motivate us to be "close-relatives" to whomever we encounter.

Cloud

Hebrew expression: 'anan
Pronunciation: 'aw NAWN
Strong's Number: 6051

C

To most people today, including meteorologists, "clouds" are simply a natural phenomenon to be observed, studied, and analyzed. Clouds contain rain, powerful electrical forces, and are good predictors of what the weather will be. In the Old and New Testament clouds held a much loftier place. They could often be associated with God's presence, His power, and even His guidance. The Hebrew noun 'anan means "cloud, mist, or covering." It is almost always translated as "cloud" and may derive from an original root, 'anan, meaning "to cover or to appear." The verb form of 'anan means "to have something appear" or "to bring clouds."

The theological significance and figurative use of "clouds" is important in the Bible. The rain from the clouds was the source of the earth's destruction in the time of Noah; thus, the Lord set His rainbow in them to signify His covenant with humanity that He would never again destroy the earth with a flood (Gen. 9:13–16). A pillar of a cloud, with the presence of God in it, guided Israel through the desert (Exod. 13:21; 14:19; 16:10). At Mount Sinai, the Lord came in a dense dark cloud to communicate with His people and give them the Law (Exod. 19:9). He also spoke to Moses from a cloud covering Mount Sinai (Exod. 24:16). On the Day of Atonement, the Lord appeared in a cloud over the Mercy Seat in the Holy of Holies (Lev. 16:2). The cloud covered the Tabernacle when it was completed (Exod. 40:34–36) and led the Israelites through their wilderness travels (Exod. 40:37–38). When the cloud set out, Israel set out; when the cloud stopped and settled over an area, the Israelites stopped and pitched camp (Num. 9:16–23). Israel obeyed no matter how long the cloud stayed or moved (Num. 9:22). God's presence was inseparably linked to the cloud. The Lord spoke to them from the cloud, bringing judgment as well as blessing (Num. 11:25; 16:42–45).

The cloud that enveloped Jesus upon the Mount of Transfiguration and the voice from the cloud showed God's approval of Jesus as His chosen Son (Matt. 17:5). Jesus left earth in a cloud (Acts 1:9), further showing His divinity. And, based on the Son of Man figure who comes with the clouds of heaven in Daniel, Jesus will return in a cloud as the Mighty One to His people (Dan. 7:13; Matt. 24:30; 26:64). Believers will then exit the earth in a cloud just as Jesus had centuries earlier (1 Thess. 4:17).

KEY VERSES

Genesis 9:13–14;
Exodus 13:21–22;
19:9; 34:5; 40:34;
Numbers 9:15–22

Commandment

Hebrew expression: *mitswah*
Pronunciation: *mitz VAWH*
Strong's Number: *4687*

Mention the word "commandment" in any church service or Sunday school class and the thoughts of most will leap immediately to the Ten Commandments. We recall the episode in which the Lord calls Moses to the peak of Mount Sinai to meet with Him. Amidst the thundering and the thick smoke, the Lord gives Moses clear instructions as to how the people are to conduct themselves and their affairs. It may be surprising to note that the extent of the meeting at Mount Sinai yielded more commandments than just the ten most familiar. In fact, much of the books of Numbers and Leviticus contain various commands issued at that encounter.

The Hebrew term *mitswah* or "commandment" implies an injunction from someone having authority or jurisdiction. In a generic sense, it is used when one, by virtue of office or experience, gives instruction to an inferior. Examples would include the command of a king or similar ruler to his subjects (2 Kgs. 18:36; Esth. 3:3), the charge of a father to a son (Jer. 35:18), or when a teacher imparts learning and wisdom to a student (Prov. 2:1; 3:1). More often than not a command refers to the precepts of Moses (Neh. 9:14).

The concept many have of the Lord's commands is a negative one. They are seen as a burden on the people, forbidding anything that may hint of fun. Sadly, this perspective could not be further from the truth. We must understand the commandments as the loving instruction of a father to his children. The Lord's desire was to bless His people and keep them from trouble. In giving the commandments, the Lord provided Israel with a set of boundaries, which when followed brought the promise of long life (Deut. 17:20), prosperity (Deut. 30:9), and blessing (Deut. 11:27). To flaunt the commandments was to ignore the wisdom of God and bring the opposite to bear on one's life.

Of course the place of the commandments is obvious in ancient Israel, but not so to those of us on the other side of the cross. Many rightly ask, what responsibility does the Christian have to the commandments of the Old Testament? Jesus clearly responds that He did not come to destroy the law, but to fulfill it (Matt. 5:17). Moreover, when asked to summarize the commandments of God He stated that all were to love God and their neighbor (Matt. 22:36–40). It is enough that we love God and our neighbor, for if we truly obey this command we will never displease God or defraud another. As the apostle Paul states, "love is the fulfilling of the law" (Rom. 13:10). If we truly love one another, we will not covet, steal, lie, murder, commit adultery, and break the other commandments contained in God's Word. As believers, God has empowered us to obey His commandments.

KEY VERSES

Exodus 24:12;
Deuteronomy
11:27–28;
Psalm 119:21

35

Commit harlotry

Hebrew expression: *zanah*
Pronunciation: *zah NAWH*
Strong's Number: *2181*

"Thou shalt not commit adultery!" does not only apply to physical acts, but spiritual acts against the Lord as well. The Hebrew word *zanah* is used as a powerful descriptive term in the Old Testament. Most people think that "committing harlotry" refers to physical, illicit intercourse with another man or woman who is not one's husband or wife. The word *zanah* is used this way, but has a much deeper meaning when employed to describe spiritual harlotry; that is, serving or turning to false gods, thereby being unfaithful to the Lord. *Zanah* means "to commit fornication, to be a harlot, or to play the harlot." The noun "harlot" is the feminine participle, *zonah*, the word used most often to describe a harlot in the Old Testament. *Zonah* is sometimes translated as "whore" (KJV), "harlot" (KJV, ASV), and "prostitute" (NIV)—hence, *zanah* can mean "to commit prostitution."

In the Old Testament, the Lord is often thought of metaphorically as the husband of Israel. When the nations of Israel turned from the Lord to follow other gods it was described as committing harlotry or playing the harlot with other gods. The prophets especially accuse Israel of spiritual harlotry. Ezekiel uses *zanah* to describe the "adulterous," "whorish" (KJV), "faithless" (NLT) eyes and hearts of Israel since they have lusted after their idols (Ezek. 6:9). Hosea viciously describes Israel as a harlot who has both sold herself to others and also gone after other gods (Hos. 4:10–18; 5:3–4; 6:10). When God's people prostituted themselves to the idols of Canaan, they were given over to destruction (Ps. 106:39–41). The unfaithfulness of God's people is their great sin (Hos. 1:2). The Lord demanded the faithfulness of His people in order for them to be called His people.

God still does not tolerate committing harlotry of any kind. Paul asserts that neither adulterers nor prostitutes will enter the Kingdom of God (1 Cor. 6:9). They will be given over to their own selfishness and will be separated from the Lord, suffering in hell forever. In an age of sexual adultery and prostitution, God's people need to heed the warning of the Lord: God will not tolerate spiritual or physical adultery among His people (1 Cor. 6:15–16). God has never been unfaithful to His people, despite the fact that the act of adultery is the epitome of a faithless person or nation. Believers must endeavor to remain faithful to their spouses. Their faithfulness to their spouses will be an effective witness to the world of their faithfulness to God. We should take great comfort in the fact that no matter how we fail, the Lord will remain faithful to us.

KEY VERSES

Exodus 34:15;
Deuteronomy 31:16;
Ezekiel 16:15;
Hosea 3:3;
4:10–14, 18; 5:3

Compassion

Hebrew expression: *racham*
Pronunciation: *raw KHAHM*
Strong's Number: *7355*

C

It is not overstating the case to say that Israel exists because God is a compassionate God who lives and acts according to who He is. Yet, in His sovereignty and divine wisdom He will show compassion (Exod. 33:19). The word "compassion" translates the Hebrew verb *racham* in the Exodus passage. The word also means "to have compassion, to show love, or to show mercy." *Racham* is a tender word that is formed from the noun *rachamim* or *racham* meaning "womb" or "compassion." God has a motherly feeling toward His people whom He made and the "womb" is a place of compassion and deep emotion. *Rachum* is the adjective that describes God as a "compassionate" God (Exod. 34:6), and usually refers to God's compassion toward His people (2 Kgs. 13:23),

In the time of Israel's rebellion with the golden calf at Mount Sinai, the Lord showed Himself to be compassionate by forgiving His people and reestablishing the covenant on the basis of who He is, not who they were (Exod. 34). Israel's rebellion in the time of Micah had reached such proportions that again Israel was on the verge of destruction. But, Micah humbly pleaded to a God who pardons and removes the sins of His people. His plea was well informed; he knew the story of Israel's rebellion and the responses of her "compassionate"—that is, *rachum*—God. Perhaps He would again have compassion upon His people (Mic. 7:19). In Jeremiah 6:23 and 21:7 the Babylonians and their King Nebuchadnezzar are depicted as having no compassion or pity towards Israel, desiring to utterly destroy them. If it had not been for the compassion of the Lord towards His people, they would not have continued to exist. But, He rescued them and remains eternally compassionate towards them.

This marvelous aspect of God's character is exhibited clearly in the Bible. It is incarnated in Jesus Christ, the compassionate, loving, supreme, God-Man. When He saw crowds He was moved by compassion (Matt. 9:36, *splagchizomai* in Greek) for them. As a result He healed the sick (Matt. 14:14; Mark 8:2). He was also the compassionate one of Exodus (Rom. 9:15). In Christ, the Father of compassion (2 Cor. 1:3, *oiktirmos* in Greek) and God of solace dwells. There is no greater comfort than knowing that the Lord continues to show His compassion to us, working miracles of goodness and mercy out of every situation in our lives (Jas. 5:11).

KEY VERSES

Exodus 33:19;
Isaiah 13:18;
Jeremiah 21:7

Complaint

Hebrew expression: *rib*
Pronunciation: *REEB*
Strong's Number: *7379*

The prophets were precise in their accusations against the nation and people of Israel. They often presented their charges as God's "complaint." The word *rib* can be translated as "charge," "case," "complaint," or "accusation." Perhaps in our current culture, which is so familiar with the jargon of legal proceedings, the translation "case" (NIV, NLT) fits best. The King James Version employs the word "complaint" (Mic. 6:2) and "cause" (Mic. 7:9). The Hebrew verb *rib* means "to strive, contend, or argue a case." The form of the case against Israel by the Lord is presented in full courtroom form and drama in Micah 6. First, the Lord brings a case against Israel, and the people are challenged to prepare their defense (Mic. 6:1–2). Secondly, the charges brought against Israel by the Lord are presented (Mic. 6:9–16). Thirdly, the Lord points out how He has been faithful to His people and acted often on their behalf (Mic. 6:3–5). Fourthly, Israel speaks questioning how they should please the Lord. And finally, Micah reminds them of the Lord's requirements (Mic. 6:8).

Rib, in Micah's situation, is not just a fuzzy general complaint or case: the Lord is the accuser and Israel is the accused. The mountains and foundations of the earth are the jury called to hear the Lord's "complaint" (Mic. 6:2). In the book of Job, we see him taking up the "case" of the stranger, who was especially protected by God and Israel's laws (Job 23:7). The "cases" of the poor and the orphan were also of special concern to the Lord; He would care for them (Prov. 22:23; 23:11). God required integrity and honesty to prevail in cases argued by His people (Prov. 25:9). The Lord expressly challenged the cases of those who argued on behalf of their idols or false gods, claiming that they know the past and the future (Isa. 41:21). The Lord won and will win every time!

In the Old Testament, the Lord God was innocent of any charge brought against Him. In the New Testament, the same fact can be asserted of Jesus. Pilate represented the truth when he said, "I find no reason or basis for a charge or complaint against this man" (Luke 23:4, aitios in Greek; John 18:38; 19:4, 6). Likewise,

KEY VERSES

2 Samuel 15:2, 4;
Job 29:16;
Proverbs 18:17;
Isaiah 1:23;
Micah 6:2;
Hosea 4:1

Paul asserts that Christians are free of any charges (*egkaleo* in Greek) brought against us, for God justifies us and Christ has died for us (see also Rom. 8:33–34).

Confessing

See also: *Confess, p. 257*
Hebrew expression: *yadah*
Pronunciation: *yaw DAWH*
Strong's Number: *3034*

C

On the Day of Atonement the High Priest laid both of his hands on the head of a goat and "confessed," which is *yadah* in Hebrew, all the sins of Israel (Lev. 16:21). The goat was then sent into the wilderness bearing the sins of the people. This national day of confession was the high point of the Israelites' religious year—a day for "confessing" the sins of the entire nation (Lev. 16). Each year during this day the High Priest could offer sacrifices for himself and the people; he could even enter the Holy of Holies.

The Hebrew verb *yadah* means basically "to confess." Originally the word may have been closely tied to the physical and emotional body language that accompanied the lively worship that took place in the Old Testament. The meaning of the word in some cases seems to include stretching out one's hands as an accompanying gesture in praise to God, thereby "confessing" Him. The verb naturally means "to praise" in certain settings, for to confess God is to praise Him. Using *yadah,* the psalmists regularly asserted praise or confessed to the Lord (Pss. 106:1; 107:1; 136:1). The word was used about ten times to express openness to God by confessing one's sins. It describes individual confession (Lev. 5:5) or national confession (Lev. 16:21; 1 Kgs. 8:33, 35). Daniel confessed both his own sins and the sins of his people (Dan. 9:4, 20). Ezra is described as confessing his failure and the Jews failure, praying, weeping and throwing himself down in anguish before the House of God. His confession was heard by both man and God (Ezra 10:1, 2). In Nehemiah's day, the Israelites confessed their sins before God on a national day of contrition (Neh. 9:2).

It was by the confession of one's sins and the sins of the nation that God's people could be forgiven and return to the Lord (2 Chr. 6:24, 26). When David "confessed," *yadah*, his sins, he found deliverance from his anxiety and fears (Ps. 32:5). Then, using *yadah* again, he could "praise the Lord with an upright heart" (Ps. 119:7). The writer of Proverbs 28:13 declares that when he confessed his sins he found mercy and relief. One's entire being was involved in true confession and praise using the heart, the hands, the mouth, and musical instruments (Ps. 71:22). Upon confession a person was restored to a relationship with God. This spiritual principle has not changed. 1 John 1:9 exhorts us to confess our sins. Paul asserts that if we confess with our mouth and believe in our heart we will be saved (Rom. 10:9, 10). There is a search for restoration on a national and individual level today. Confession is the key to that goal, and through the Lord's forgiveness we are saved.

KEY VERSES

Leviticus 5:5; 16:21;
1 Kings 8:33;
Ezra 10:1;
Psalm 32:5;
Psalm 136:1–3

Consecrate

Hebrew expression: *qadash*
Pronunciation: *qaw DAHSH*
Strong's Number: *6942*

The Lord blessed the seventh day and "consecrated" it, making it holy (Gen. 2:3). This is the first use of the Hebrew verb *qadash*. Here it indicates that God set aside the seventh day because He rested on it. Humanity was to follow their Creator's example. They were to hallow this day, consecrating it to sacred and religious observance. The verb *qadash* means "to set aside, to consecrate, or to make holy," and can refer to people, things, times or places. The verb always carries the connotation of "setting aside for religious purposes." It comes from the Hebrew noun *qodesh* meaning "a holy thing" or "holiness." Holiness, in the absolute sense of separateness and moral and ethical excellence, is the attribute of the Lord God alone (Exod. 15:11; Lev. 20:3). For people to be consecrated they must be "set aside" to God and "be holy"; that is, reflect God's moral and ethical character. The second use of the root of *qadash* in the Old Testament declares that the ground where Moses was standing was "holy ground" because of God's presence at that spot (Exod. 3:5).

God is ultimately concerned with the creatures He created in His image, mankind (Gen. 1:26–28). His goal was "to consecrate, or set aside," a holy people unto Himself alone, bearing His ethical and moral characteristics (Exod. 19:5–6; 20:1–3). At Mount Sinai, not only the mountain was consecrated by God's presence and command (Exod. 19:23), but also the people were ordered to consecrate (*qadash*) themselves. This made them ritually and ceremonially pure, before the Lord would appear and talk to them (Exod. 19:10). Otherwise, God's holy presence would have consumed them. The Lord delivered His holy word, the law, to His people so that they could follow His will and separate themselves from the pagan and corrupt cultures around them (Exod. 23:32; Deut. 4:6; 28:1–2, 15). Various persons in the nation of Israel were consecrated to holy duties, and holy times were set aside for all Israel to hold feasts, rejoice, and worship God (Exod. 28:3, 41; Lev. 25:10). But Israel also, as an entire people, were "made holy, consecrated" by the Lord Himself (Exod. 31:13; Lev. 20:8). Because the Lord was holy, He made His people holy. They were to be like Him in His holiness with total dedication to Him (Lev. 21:18).

KEY VERSES

Genesis 2:3;
Exodus 3:5; 19:10,
23; 28:3, 41;
Leviticus 20:8; 25:10

The call of God to be a holy, consecrated people continues today. In the New Testament, the Greek verb *hagiazo*, "to sanctify, make holy," is used to continue this theme. Paul writes his letter to the Corinthians by addressing them as those who are "consecrated, sanctified" in Jesus Christ. We are called to live holy lives, putting off the wicked and immoral practices of this world (1 Cor. 1:2; 6:11). Through the word of the gospel and the indwelling Holy Spirit, we are consecrated to Him (John 17:7; 2 Thess. 2:13).

Covenant

Hebrew expression: *berit*
Pronunciation: *beh REET*
Strong's Number: *1285*

Diplomats from all over the world have gone to the Middle East in order to try to help establish a covenant of peace in the area between Israel and the Palestinians or Israel and other Arab nations. A covenant is only as secure as the integrity of the parties involved in the covenant process. The Bible talks about covenants in which God becomes one of the parties. *Berit* means "covenant," "treaty," or "agreement." It refers to covenants established between people (Gen. 31:44) or between God and people (Gen. 15:18). Several verbs are employed with the Hebrew noun *berit* to describe the creation of a covenant. Usually the verb *karat* is used with *berit* to mean "to cut a covenant," and *qum*, "to establish," *natan*, "to give," and *nagad*, "to declare," are also found.

The Lord, Yahweh, chose to relate to His creation and His people through the establishment of covenants. God initiated five main covenants in the Old Testament. The first covenant was with Noah and his descendants after the flood promising that God would not destroy the earth by water again. God also said He would maintain the seasons and cycles of nature as long as the earth would stand (Gen. 6:18; 8:21–22). As a sign of His covenant He set a rainbow in the sky (Gen. 9:12–16). This was a unilateral covenant; that is, only one party, God, had to keep its terms. God initiated a second unilateral covenant in which He promised to give the land of Canaan to Abraham and his descendants. This covenant was concluded in a complex ritual, with male circumcision as an outward sign of accepting the covenant (Gen. 15:12–17; 17:9–14). God secured the Abrahamic covenant by swearing by Himself and it was first fulfilled under Joshua (21:43–45). Thirdly, God initiated the Sinai covenant with the descendants of Abraham at Mt. Sinai in a bilateral covenant; that is, the covenant could be broken if either of the parties failed to observe its terms (Exod. 19:7–8; 24:7–8). Fourthly, God established a unilateral covenant with David asserting that He would not fail to establish a King in Israel from David's descendants (2 Sam. 7:11–16). The Davidic covenant was ultimately fulfilled in Christ (Matt. 1:1; Luke 1:32–33, 69; Acts 2:30).

Although Israel did not keep the Sinai covenant (2 Kgs. 17; Jer. 11), God promised a new covenant, the fifth covenant, in which He would enable His people to keep His laws and His commandments by writing them upon their hearts and in their minds (Jer. 31:31–34). This covenant was established by the Lord Jesus Christ and is the one to which Christians commit themselves (Heb. 8:7–13). Because God has bound Himself to His people swearing by His own nature and integrity, there is no need to fear that any of the good promises He has ever made to His people will fail.

KEY VERSES

Genesis 9:12;
15:18; 17:10;
Jeremiah 31:31–34

Create

Hebrew expression: *bara'*
Pronunciation: *baw RAW'*
Strong's Number: *1254*

It is a compliment to be told that something you have done or said is so "creative"! Michaelangelo, Vincent van Gogh, Chagall, and Yitzhak Perleman are all artists who have created new objects of beauty. Creativity in the medical field means trying to produce a new, artificial heart. All of the human "creators" involved in these projects are themselves created in God's image. God created (*bara'*) them to bear His image (Gen. 1:26–28). Their creative powers reflect the powers of the Creator. But, the Hebrew word *bara'*, meaning "to create", could not be used to describe these persons' work. There are four verbs used in the Hebrew Bible that may be translated "to create" *(bara', 'asah, yatsah, qanah)*; they can all have human or divine subjects who create—except *bara'*. *Bara'* always has a divine subject—God.

In Genesis 1:27 this verb *bara'* is used three times in a magnificent "creative" piece of Hebrew poetry that describes God's creation of humanity. God is the subject of this verb each time. This verb *bara'* is a special word, since its grammatical subject is always God. Only God's creative activity can be described by this verb. His creative activity goes far beyond human capability.

The writer used this verb to assert that God created the heaven and the earth (Gen. 1:1) and will create a new heaven and earth in the future (Isa. 65:17). God created the north and the south (Ps. 89:12), the clouds (Isa. 40:26), the wind (Amos 4:13), the darkness (Isa. 45:7), new things (Jer. 31:22), the great sea creatures (Gen. 1:21), disaster (Isa. 45:7). God has created Jerusalem, day and night, individual persons, Israel, Jacob, angels, and water (Ps. 148:1–5; Eccl. 12:1; Isa. 43:1, 15; 54:16; 65:18; Jer. 33:25). He created the rebellious King of Tyre, who also serves as the figure of Satan (Ezek. 28:13, 15). He created great unique wonders for His people Israel (Exod. 34:10).

However, he has created even more marvelous things—if that were possible. He has created (*bara'*), formed, and made His people for His own glory (Isa. 43:7) and creates praise on their lips to heal them (Isa. 57:18, 19). But, most amazingly, far surpassing modern creative medicine or psychotherapy, He creates *pure hearts*, free from guilt, for His people. David, seeking peace and freedom from his guilt, cried out to God, using this verb, to create, a *pure heart* (Ps. 51:10) within him. Who can forgive sins, but the One who can create a *pure heart* from an evil one (Gen. 6:5)? David prayed, fully aware that he was entreating the Creator God, who could do what he was asking. His God could create a *pure heart* in David and take away his guilt.

Today, David's cry can be heard and is heard on the lips of those who repent and seek Jesus Christ as their Savior (Acts 15:8, 9). Christ will replace their old heart of deceit and guilt (Jer. 17:9) with a new and clean heart.

KEY VERSES

Genesis 1:27;
Psalm 51:10;
Isaiah 45:7–8;
65:17–19

Cursed

Hebrew expression: 'arar
Pronunciation: 'aw RAHR
Strong's Number: 779

C

The normal state that God intended for the human race was one of blessedness. After He created them He blessed them and made them fruitful providing for both their physical and spiritual well-being. The book of Psalms calls the person happy and blessed who knows and walks with the Lord. Yet, the word "curse" became a reality to the human condition in the Garden of Eden when Adam and Eve transgressed against God's command not to eat of the forbidden fruit. To be cursed was clearly the opposite of being blessed.

The rebellion of people against God and His will, placed them under the curse rather than the blessing of God (Gen. 3:14, 17; 4:11). If people had not sinned, there would have been no curse. The fact that people are cursed is a religious and spiritual problem.

The Hebrew verb 'arar means "to curse." When God cursed He imposed judgment upon someone or something that changed the state or relationship of it to Himself. To be under God's curse is to be living under His judgment. By obeying God's commands in the Garden of Eden the human race would not have become cursed by the Lord. Because of Adam and Eve's disobedience, even the ground was cursed by God as well as the Devil, the Serpent (Gen. 3:14).

The book of Deuteronomy features the curses and blessings, which the Lord laid before His people Israel. Two ways were presented by God: the way of obedience to God's laws led to blessing, the way of disobedience led to being cursed. The word 'arar, meaning "to curse," is found six times in Deuteronomy 28:16–19. God warns that if His people sin, they and the land would be cursed and everything would fail. There would be no success either within the city or within the country. Fertility in the land would fail. But, chapter 27 mentions even more curses. Sandwiched in between is the theology of blessing: obey God and everything you do everywhere will be successful (Deut. 28:3–14).

This theology and outline for success or failure for God's people was the plumb line that judged them throughout their history. To be disobedient was to lie under the disapproval of God. God was faithful to Himself in every case; He blessed them and He cursed them according to their response of faithful obedience or disobedience to Him. When Israel eventually failed, it was because of the curses they deserved for their disobedience and unfaithfulness to their God (2 Kgs. 17). It is only in the New Testament that Christ removes the curses of the law and our transgressions (Gal. 3:13, *epikataratos*) by becoming a curse for us. Through Him God has removed the curse that had plagued the human race since Adam and Eve's fall.

KEY VERSES

Genesis 3:14, 17;
4:11;
Deuteronomy 27:26

Cut off

Hebrew expression: *karat*
Pronunciation: *kaw RAHT*
Strong's Number: *3772*

The Kennedy Memorial near Khirbet Sa'adim in Israel symbolizes the violent deaths of the two brothers, John F. Kennedy and Robert Kennedy. The memorial is set in a grove of trees that has been designed to resemble a truncated tree—cut off in the fullness of its growth like the sudden and premature deaths of John and Robert Kennedy. The structure is a poignant monument to the Kennedy brothers and a vivid depiction of our word study *karat*, "cut off" like a tree that has fallen in the forest.

The verb *karat* means to "cut" or "cut off" and is used in a variety of Old Testament contexts, including: the cutting of material from garments (1 Sam. 24:4–5; 1 Chr. 19:4), decapitation and dismemberment (1 Sam. 17:51; 31:9), the cutting down of trees (1 Kgs. 5:18; 2 Kgs. 19:23), the cutting down of idolatrous images (Judg. 6:30; 1 Kgs. 15:13), and the cutting off or stoppage of flowing water (Josh. 3:16; 4:7).

In some contexts *karat* signifies banishment from the covenant community as punishment for violation of the holiness code (Exod. 30:33; Lev. 7:20–21). In other contexts, the word may be translated "root out" (1 Sam. 24:21; Ezek. 25:7) or "eliminate" (Gen. 9:11; Jer. 11:19) as an expression of utter destruction. At times to "cut off" signifies the killing of an animal (1 Kgs. 18:5) or human beings (1 Kgs. 18:4).

Theologically speaking, the most signifcant use of *karat* is in covenant-making contexts where an agreement or a treaty is "cut" between two parties (Exod. 24:8; Deut. 4:23; 5:2). The Hebrew idiom "to cut a covenant" (Heb. *karat berit*) probably developed out of the treaty ratification ceremony which included the cutting up of a sacrificial animal (Gen. 15:9–18).

The prophet Zechariah uses *karat* to describe the destruction and abandonment of Philistine cities like Ashkelon and Ashod (9:6). According to Zechariah, the day of the Lord will see the destruction and banishment of idols from the territory of Israel (13:2) as well as the decimation of the population of Jerusalem and environs (13:8; 14:2). Finally, Zechariah forecasts the "striking" (Heb. *nakah*) of God's shepherd overseeing Israel (13:7). Most commentators understand this verse to refer to the death of the coming messianic king. The book of Daniel confirms this prediction by revealing that "Messiah" will be "cut off" (*karat*) after the sixty-two weeks (Dan. 9:26). Daniel also pinpoints the timing of the event, sometime after the end of the "sixty-two weeks"—most likely the date of the crucifixion of Christ. Despite the difficulty in unraveling the mystery of Daniel's "seventy weeks," it is clear that Messiah is killed before the destruction of the Temple by the Romans in A.D. 70. Thus, the prophecies of Daniel and Zechariah are key texts for Christian apologists in identifying Jesus of Nazareth as the Messiah.

KEY VERSES

Genesis 15:18;
Exodus 24:8;
Jeremiah 31:31;
Ezekiel 34:25;
Daniel 9:26

Darkness

Hebrew expression: *choshek*
Pronunciation: *khoh SHEHK*
Strong's Number: *2822*

D

Darkness even today serves as a symbol of fear and dread. Thick darkness was the ninth plague of judgment God brought upon the Egyptians. In the prophetic books of the Old Testament, darkness often described the coming Day of the Lord (Amos 5:18, 20). The Day of the Lord would be a time of judgment not merely for the nations but for a rebellious Israel as well. The Day of the Lord in Joel's era was at hand and featured "darkness and gloom" (NIV, KJV, NLT), further clouds, and deep blackness (Joel 2:2). Of course this is all-powerful figurative language used to describe what will in reality be times of war, earthquakes, oppression, and distress. Darkness was, in fact, used in a general sense to depict times of distress and suffering (Isa. 5:30; 50:3; Jer. 2:6). The great day of God's judgment that Joel envisions, however, was also a day pointing to the time of Christ and beyond—to the close of the present age (Joel 2:31). At Christ's first coming the distressing and devastating aspects of Christ's crucifixion are depicted by this prophetic utterance (Matt. 24:29; Rev. 6:12; 14:14–20; 16:4, 8–9). But the ultimate fulfillment of Joel's prophecy, when the sun will turn to darkness is still coming.

The Hebrew word *choshek* is usually translated "darkness," and as has been noted, was often used figuratively. But the word also referred to night as opposed to day which was "light" (*'or*). The noun *choshek* shares the same root as the verb *chashak,* meaning "to be or grow dark, or have a dark color." "Obscurity" was also indicated by the word as when it was used to describe "dark" sayings difficult to discern. It referred to the darkness of Sheol at death (1 Sam. 2:9; Job 10:21) or to dark, secret and hidden places (Isa. 45:3; Job 12:22). Isaiah used *choshek* to indicate the spiritual "darkness" or obscurity and situation of those who did not know Israel's God, but would know Him in the future (Isa. 9:2). In the story of creation, "darkness" covered everything until God spoke and light appeared (Gen. 1:1–3). The threat is always present that unless God upholds His creation it may return once again to a time of chaos and darkness.

The use of "darkness," *skotos* in Greek, continues in the New Testament. Matthew, quoting Isaiah, notes that in Christ those who were in spiritual darkness have seen a great light (compare Matt. 4:16; Isa. 9:2). The darkness of not knowing God has been overcome in Christ, for the light of God in Christ has shined for us into the darkness and overcome it (John 1:5). Although we were once in darkness, now we can rejoice in the moral, ethical, and spiritual light of being in Christ (Eph. 5:8). Finally, it is possible for us to know and relate to Jesus Christ in whom there is no darkness at all (1 John 1:5).

KEY VERSES

Genesis 1:2;
1 Samuel 2:9;
Job 10:21;
Isaiah 5:30; 9:2;
Joel 2:2, 31

Dedication

Hebrew expression: *chanukkah*
Pronunciation: *khah noo KAWH*
Strong's Number: *2598*

Somewhat serendipitously, the Hebrew word *chanukkah,* which means "dedication," occurs in the Old Testament eight times. This is also the number of days the Feast of Lights or Feast of Dedication lasts. It was and is observed for eight days beginning in the Jewish month of Kislev, December, on the twenty-fifth day. The great Jewish zealot and freedom fighter Judas Maccabeus instituted the Feast of Lights in 164 B.C. Three years earlier, the second Temple had been defiled and polluted by the Hellenist Antiochus Epiphanes, one of the hostile kings of Syria who threatened to destroy the Jews. During the time when the Temple was defiled, the Jews continued to meet in their synagogues to praise and worship God. In 164 B.C., Kislev 25, Judas "rededicated" the Temple to the worship of the Lord after defeating the enemies of the Jews and establishing control of Jerusalem.

The noun *chanukkah* comes from the root *chnk,* which means "to dedicate" something (Deut. 20:5; 1 Kgs. 8:63). *Chanukkah* also refers to the solemn and serious, yet at the same time joyous, presentation of something to the Lord for His use, honor, and glory. The other name for the "Feast of Dedication," "Feast of Lights," refers to eight candles that are lit, beginning with one on the first day and an additional one thereafter until eight are burning.

The "dedication" of the rebuilt wall of Jerusalem is described by the word *chanukkah,* also. This wall was not only a physical protection for Israel and Jerusalem, but also came to be a symbol of the strength and health of the Jews. To dedicate the wall anew was to consecrate the city and its people to the Lord again. Numbers records the dedication of the altar, accompanied by dedicatory sacrifices. *Chanukkah* is also used to describe Psalm 30 as a psalm of dedication for the Temple of Solomon. For believers today, *chanukkah* is a challenging word. We should "dedicate" ourselves to Christ and not permit anything to destroy that dedication or distract us from it.

KEY VERSES

Numbers 7:10–11,
84, 88;
Nehemiah 12:27;
Psalm 30:1

Deliverance

Hebrew expression: *teshu'ah*
Pronunciation: *teh shoo 'AWH*
Strong's Number: *8668*

D

Samson struck down one thousand Philistines with the fresh jawbone of a donkey and then celebrated this great "deliverance" in poetry and prose (Judg. 15:14–19). The Hebrew word *teshu'ah* is translated most often as "victory" (NASV, NIV), but is also translated as "salvation, deliverance, help, or rescue" in various other translations. This action noun comes from the root that gives us the verb *yasha'*, "to deliver, to save, or to liberate."

Deliverance was usually given by God through a human agent (1 Sam. 11:9, 13). In Judges, God used Samson to begin to deliver Israel from the Philistines. The Lord used Saul to deliver Jabesh Gilead from the Ammonites (1 Sam. 11:13). David later delivered the Israelites from the Philistines with a great "victory," a *teshu'ah* (1 Sam. 19:5). David's great military leaders also delivered Israel from the Philistines (2 Sam. 23:10). God granted victory to non-Israelites, such as the military commander Naaman from Aram (2 Kgs. 5:1). And the Lord promised Elisha that Israel would enjoy deliverance from Aram by means of the "victory arrow" of God. In 2 Chronicles 6:41, Solomon prays that even Israel's priests may be clothed with the Lord's "salvation." At the Lord's instruction, the priests blessed, anointed, and delivered God's people, granting them blessings on all sides in every area of life.

Among God's people deliverance did not depend upon military might, but upon the Lord. The psalmist considered a horse to be a hopeless thing for "salvation," because a horse did not really "rescue"; the Lord did (Ps. 33:17, 19). Those who experienced the Lord's "rescue" and "deliverance" came to love "salvation" (Ps. 40:16). King David could only break forth in jubilant singing because the Lord had delivered him from sin, for he had committed both murder and adultery (Ps. 51:14). He equated God's "love" to receiving "salvation," even though sometimes he had to wait patiently on the Lord (Ps. 119:8, 41). Isaiah broadens the concept of Israel's salvation into an eternal deliverance in which Israel would not be put to shame again (Isa. 45:17). He equated God's salvation to receiving His righteousness (Isa. 46:13).

Deliverance in the New Testament centers on Jesus Christ. When Jesus was brought into the Temple area by His parents, Simeon the priest broke out in poetry and singing, declaring that he had now seen the Lord's "salvation" and could depart in peace (Luke 2:30). The Lord's salvation centered in the person of Christ, as John the Baptist declared (Luke 3:6). The gospel, the word of truth, has become our means of eternal salvation (Eph. 1:13). Our ultimate deliverance is the salvation of our souls through Christ (1 Pet. 1:9; Rev. 7:10; 12:10; 19:1). We can sing and praise God for our salvation, like Samson, because we have already been granted eternal deliverance from sin.

KEY VERSES

Judges 15:18;
1 Samuel 11:9, 13;
Psalms 33:17; 37:39;
Isaiah 45:17; 46:13

Delivered

Hebrew expression: *natsal*
Pronunciation: *naw TSAHL*
Strong's Number: *5337*

D

Moses told his father-in-law Jethro the "gospel," the good news of the Old Testament—namely, he told him how the Lord had rescued, or "delivered," the Israelites from Egypt (Exod. 8:8). This first telling of Israel's deliverance was exactly what God desired. He wanted this great story of deliverance to be told throughout the earth (Exod. 9:16). Moses got the story started. The Hebrew verb *natsal* means "to deliver," "to rescue," or "to save" and is one of the key words used to describe Israel's release from slavery under Pharaoh. In Exodus 18:1–12, *natsal* is used five times to emphasize the deliverance God gave Israel from Egypt. The word *yatsa'*, "to go out," is used two times in these first twelve verses, so that the exodus out of Egypt is referred to seven times in all, the perfect number. This was God's consummate deliverance and rescue operation for His people in the Old Testament.

Natsal also has the connotation of "to snatch away" and God indeed "delivered" His people by "snatching" them away from the oppressive hand of Pharaoh (Exod. 14:5; 18:9, 10). The stem of the verb used to describe the deliverance of Israel indicates that God, as the subject of the sentence, "caused" or "brought about" this deliverance; Israel did not rescue themselves. *Natsal* was also used figuratively to describe "deliverance" from sin, rebellion and guilt. The psalmist cried out for God to deliver him from his rebellious sins (Ps. 39:8) and from blood-guilt (Ps. 51:16). Sin held the sinner so powerfully that he or she needed to be snatched away from it; just as the heavy hand of Pharaoh held the Hebrew slaves in bondage to corrupt pagan influences and oppression in Egypt. Sin in the world, and this separation from the Holy God, needed to be covered, or atoned for, which is *kapper* in Hebrew, "to cover" or "to atone." Jesus Christ covered our sins with His blood and delivered us by giving Himself as atonement for all humanity.

God, who rescued His people in the Old Testament, has rescued them supremely in His Son Jesus Christ. The New Testament Greek word *hruomai*, "to rescue," "to deliver," continues the tradition of the Hebrew verb *natsal*. As Colossians 1:13 says, "God has delivered us from the dominion of darkness, bringing us into the Kingdom of His Son" and delivering us from the devil (Matt. 6:13). The

KEY VERSES

Exodus 18:1–12;
Psalm 39:8

Israelites' physical deliverance through the Red Sea only foreshadows Christ's deliverance of people from death and the coming wrath of God (compare Exod. 14:21–31; Rom. 7:24; 1 Thess. 1:10). As the apostle Paul asserted, God has delivered us and will continue to deliver us (2 Cor. 1:10). We are freed from our sin through Jesus and can live with joy because of this definite, once for all, deliverance.

Dream

Hebrew expression: *chalom*
Pronunciation: *khah LOHM*
Strong's Number: *2472*

Sigmund Freud made dreams popular in this century, teaching that dreams may hold the key to some of life's problems if they could be correctly deciphered. Carl Jung felt that certain symbols in dreams had great significance for understanding mankind's collective consciousness. Dreams are certainly elusive—in fact, one popular song speaks about "my elusive dream." Indeed, dreams fascinate people and everyone has had a distinctive dream or two that they remember. Dreams fade away, fly away and are transient (Ps. 73:20). They can be brought on by anxiety and care and create fear (Job 4:13; 7:14). They can also be produced by our minds as a delusion (Jer. 23:25–27)—a charge Jeremiah hurled against false prophets.

Throughout the Bible, however, dreams were used by God to communicate His will. The prophet Joel asserted that even in the last days God would give young men visions and old men would dream dreams (Joel 2:28; Acts 2:17). *Chalom* comes from the verb *chalam*, "to dream." An appearance or vision can constitute a dream (Num. 12:6; 1 Kgs. 3:5, 15; 9:1) and it may include auditory phenomena. When God sends a dream it is authoritative, a manifestation of His will. God came to Abimelech in a dream and spoke to him, warning him to stay away from Sarah (Gen. 20:3, 6–7). Jacob, the patriarch, saw and heard the Lord speak, instructing him in dreams at Bethel (Gen. 28:12–15; 31:10–13). The Lord also warned Laban in a dream not to harm Jacob (Gen. 31:24). God often spoke to His prophets in visions and dreams (Num. 12:6). In Genesis, God used dreams as a way to communicate His will for and through Joseph (Gen. 37:5–41:32). Dreams are also featured in Daniel (Dan. 2:3–7:1).

Joseph's grandiose dreams got him into trouble; even his father warned him about taking his dreams too seriously and his brothers hated him because of them (Gen. 37:8, 10–11). Joseph's dreams implied that his family would one day bow down to him (Gen. 37:6, 9–10). In prison he accurately interpreted two dreams, one for a cup-bearer to the king and one for the chief baker (Gen. 40:12, 18). Each time he declared that his interpretations came from God, and not from his own mind (Gen. 40:8). He accurately interpreted two dreams for Pharaoh after the wise men of Egypt failed (Gen. 41: 10–40). He even asserted that the Lord presented the dreams to Pharaoh twice to emphasize that the matter was certain and the dreams would soon be fulfilled (Gen. 41:32). The dreams came to pass as Joseph said and thousands of people were saved from famine. Joseph interpreted all the events of his life from God's perspective, always giving credit to God's ultimate power (Gen. 50:19–21). The use of dreams in Joseph's life also demonstrated God's sovereignty in personal, family and national history.

KEY VERSES

Judges 7:13–15;
1 Kings 3:5, 15;
Jeremiah 23:25–28

Dreams are also mentioned in the New Testament, usually in a good sense (Matt. 2:22; 27:19; Acts 2:17), but sometimes in a bad sense (Jude 8). Today, depending on our dreams for guidance, especially when there is no divine sign that the dream came from God, takes our focus off of God and studying the Bible. The author of Ecclesiastes stated succinctly that many dreams and a lot of talk are meaningless (Eccl. 5:7). Believers should study how God used dreams in the Bible, but also realize that trusting in prayer and the Word are much more foolproof ways of discerning God's will for our lives.

Elder

Hebrew expression: *zaqen*
Pronunciation: *zaw QAYN*
Strong's Number: *2205*

Elihu, a young man in the book of Job, asserts that maturity through age should bring wisdom (Job 32:7; 12:12). The noun *zaqen*, usually translated "elder," can simply mean "old man" or "aged person," but it comes from the verb *zaqen* meaning "to be or become old." Age and experience were expected to result in wisdom and the ability to rule with prudence. In Exodus 24, the elders, along with Joshua and Moses, were allowed to see and worship God on Mount Sinai (Exod. 24:9–11). Numbers 11:16–25 records God's selection of seventy elders to rule over Israel so that they could help Moses. The Spirit of leadership and wisdom that the Lord put upon Moses was now distributed to these elders as well, and they prophesied (Num. 11:25).

Elders played an important role of leadership in Israel. Moses had to get their approval before he could lead Israel out of Egypt (Exod. 3:16; 4:29; 12:21). The elders were important during the exile of Israel in Babylon and were a major source of guidance for the community when the Jews returned from Babylon in 539 B.C. (Ezra 5:5, 9; 6:7, 8, 14; 10:8, 14). In fact, throughout Israel's history, the elders serve an important function of representation and leadership—from the Exodus, to the Jew's return from Babylonian exile, until the final redemption of God's people as described in Revelation (Exod. 3:16; Ezra 5:5, 9; Rev. 4:4; 19:4). The elders supported Moses when the rebels Korah, Dathan and Abiram challenged Moses' leadership (Num. 16:25). Elders were not only leaders within Israel, but also in the surrounding nations' social and political structures (Num. 22:4, 7). Each town within Israel also had its recognized elders (Deut. 19:12; 21:2) who usually gathered to judge important matters at the town gate (Deut. 25:7). When the elders fell into idolatry themselves, the nation was left without moral guidance, as the prophet Ezekiel demonstrates (Ezek. 8:12–13). God, however, chose to rule His people through these human leaders.

In the New Testament, the elders were as powerful as the priests (Mark 7:3, 5; Luke 22:66; Acts 5:21). Even after Christ, Paul and Barnabas continued to appoint elders for the Christian churches they founded (Acts 14:23). These elders had great influence in spiritual and religious matters, even laying hands upon persons to send them into the ministry of the gospel (1 Tim. 4:14). Even in heaven God has appointed twenty-four elders to lead the new people of God through Christ when He begins His eternal reign (Rev. 4:4, 10; 11:16; 19:4). Appointed elders today are called to pray for the sick (Jas. 5:14). Although denominations within the Church view the function and place of elders differently, the significance of spiritual leadership through mature, experienced men and women is vital in God's community.

KEY VERSES

Exodus 3:16; 4:29;
Numbers 11:16,
24–25

Equity

Hebrew expression: *meyshar*
Pronunciation: *may SHAWR*
Strong's Number: *4339*

How to realize and to live with integrity, equity, fairness in today's postmodern world where anything goes is a daunting challenge to the Christian. These three words translate the Hebrew noun *meyshar*. The word comes from the same root as the verb meaning *yashar*, "to be straight, smooth, right." Several other words come from this root, *yshr*, all intersecting with the idea of "straight, right; straightness, uprightness, evenness." Integrity, equity and fair reflect the translations of *meyshar* in the AMPLIFIED, KJV, NIV, and NLT translations respectively in Proverbs 1:3. In a world where spin masters, deceivers and the news media take pride in distorting the truth, this word in Proverbs sets forth *meyshar* as one of the benefits the book promises to those who read and study the book (Prov. 1:3). According to this verse, along with *meyshar*, equity, fairness, integrity, the reader will also get righteousness (*tsedeq*) and justice (*mishpat*), words that overlap in meaning with *meyshar*. Proverbs holds forth *meyshar* as something a person needs in order to live a life of wisdom and understanding. A person of *meyshar* is not deceptive, but, as the word indicates, is straight and level in all of their dealings. The word *meyshar* means something is level in Isaiah 26:7 (NLT, not steep and rough; KJV, uprightness; NASB, smooth), because God makes it that way.

In Proverbs, the ethical sense of the word is stressed, as already noted (Prov. 1:3). The same word is found indicating that when people do pursue wisdom, they will also understand how to do equity (Prov. 2:9, *meyshar*; NIV, NLT, fair; KJV, equity). Personified wisdom speaks only what is right, she speaks of right things (Prov. 8:6); God wants His people also to speak what is right (*meyshar*, Prov. 23:16). The Lord, according to the psalmist, will not only judge individuals according to equity and justice (*meyshar*), but He will judge the peoples of the world by His standard of equity and justice (Ps. 2:8b; 96:10; 98:9). The wicked of the earth, the deceivers, the spin masters, do not judge according to *meyshar*, equity, justice, but rather by premeditated injustice and violence

KEY VERSES

Psalms 9:9; 98:9;
Proverbs 1:3; 2:9;
8:6; 23:16;
Isaiah 26:7; 33:15

or deception (Ps. 58:1–2). The Lord, however, loves justice and He has established and ordained equity (*meyshar*, Ps. 99:4). God's people in an uneven and inequitable world should be a people who call things as they are, they should be straight and level with the truth, not deviating from it.

As Jesus said in the New Testament, wisdom is proved right by her actions (Matt. 11:19, *dikaioo* in Greek). And God continues to be set forth as the God who pays whatever is right, equitable (Matt. 20:4, *dikaios* in Greek). The apostle Paul urges us to never become weary of doing what is right (2 Thess. 3:13, *kalapoieo* in Greek). John goes so far as to say that those who do right, what is equitable, show that they are God's people (1 John 2:29; 3:7, *dikaiosune* in Greek).

Everlasting

Hebrew expression: *'olam*
Pronunciation: *'oh LAWM*
Strong's Number: *5769*

The prophet Micah describes a heralded ruler who will appear in the future, but His origin is from the distant past or literally from the "days of eternity" (Mic. 5:2). This phrase is also translated as from "ancient times" (NIV), "from everlasting" (KJV), and from "the distant past" (NLT). These are good renderings of the Hebrew word *'olam* which means "long duration, ancient times, antiquity" or even "future time or ages" depending upon its context. It is used to modify time words like *yom*, "day"; and it is modified by other words indicating past or future references. It essentially means "a long time—past or future" or "all of time."

'Olam is also used in Micah to refer to the indefinite future. He asserts that because of Israel's corrupt and rebellious behavior, God's splendor and glory were "forever," *le'olam*, taken away from Israel's descendants (Mic. 2:9). In Micah 4:7 the Lord asserts that He will rule over His reestablished nation in Zion "forever," *'ad-'olam*. The prophet Isaiah also describes the great works the Lord has done for His people "from ancient times," *me'olam* (Isa. 46:9). Isaiah notes that God's name, our Redeemer, was the Lord's name from "of old" (Isa. 63:16). The Lord, in fact, was "from eternity" (Ps. 93:2) as was His wisdom (Prov. 8:23).

The Bible describes many characteristics of God and His activity including: His eternal nature, His saving character from ancient times, His actual acts of salvation from eternity, and His coming King who will rule forever over His eternal Kingdom. These characteristics emphasize the security His people have in Him as the eternal One. Nothing preceded Him, nothing will be after Him—He is "alpha and omega"— the beginning and the end. Furthermore, all of these things are the inheritance of the believer in Christ. Christ is the King, the heralded ruler, who will rule over God's "eternal" (*eis ton aiona* in Greek) Kingdom. Christ was and is the bread of life that makes eternal life possible (John 6:58). The God of the Old Testament and the Father of Jesus Christ is God over everything. He will be praised "forever" (Rom. 9:5, *eis ton aiona* in Greek). Jesus carries with Himself all the "forever, eternal" attributes of God and He has become our High Priest forever (Heb. 7:3). God's people are cared for, not just from conception to the grave, but from "eternity to eternity."

KEY VERSES

Genesis 21:33;
Jeremiah 10:10;
Micah 2:9;
Psalm 93:2;
Proverbs 8:23

Evil

Hebrew expression: *ra'*
Pronunciation: *RAH*
Strong's Number: *7451*

The word "evil" has a broad application in English. Circumstances can be evil because they cause harm, injury, or suffering. We speak of an "evildoer" as someone who fosters or brings about these kinds of results. A situation, idea, or person can be morally evil. An "evil eye" is a "look" that forebodes harm to others. Evil always brings about negative results; that which is good does the opposite. The Hebrew word *ra'* has these many meanings and more. *Ra'* describes the tree of knowledge of good and "evil." The human heart corrupted itself and became incessantly evil. Whatever was considered evil in the eyes of God was in fact evil—there was no higher standard of appeal. Even suffering is a kind of evil. In fact, Jacob's mourning for a lost son was described as "evil," *ra'* (Gen. 44:34). By definition, a life that is full of sorrow, pain, and human loss is an "evil" life.

Jeremiah the prophet speaks of God's coming judgment upon His people as a great "evil," when they would be scattered and separated from one another (Jer. 44:7). God wanted His people to dwell together in peace. Therefore, Jeremiah's plea was for the people to cease from their wickedness and not bring this great judgment of God upon themselves. The people did not listen and to this day the judgment that came upon them, the destruction of Jerusalem, is remembered as the greatest calamity in the history of Israel.

Ra', evil, cannot be avoided in many of its forms, such as natural disasters. But some *ra'* is evil that is brought upon God's people by themselves. The irony of the situation was that by the Israelites doing as much evil as they could (Jer. 3:5), they brought destructive evil, "disaster," upon themselves (Jer. 44:7, NIV). Evil hearts are stubborn (Jer. 11:8; 16:12), but, with God, there is a remedy for every evil. If Israel would turn from her evil ways the Lord would deliver her (Jer. 23:22; 26:3).

In Christ a new offer of rejecting evil (*poneros* in Greek) and doing good has been proffered. Paul urges us to hate evil and pursue what is good; pursue that which builds up and does not destroy (Rom. 12:9). We are to repay evil with love and win over evil by that which is good (Rom. 12:21; 1 Thess. 5:22). It is in doing good and kind things for others that we are the people of God. Unfortunately, in today's society, many non-believers do not have the faintest idea of who God's followers are. We need to become conformed to God's ways, instead of the world's ways. Indeed, non-believers should know we are believers through our love that comes from the Father.

KEY VERSES

Genesis 2:9;
Deuteronomy 4:25;
Job 1:1;
Psalm 141:4;
Jeremiah 3:5; 4:14

Extol

Hebrew expression: *rum*
Pronunciation: R<u>OO</u>M
Strong's Number: *7311*

Psalm 145 is designated as a psalm of praise in its superscription. Praise involved the exaltation and "extolling" of the Lord, the Great King. The Hebrew word used in Psalm 145:1 is *rum*, which means "to be high, exalted, or to rise." In verse one of this psalm, the verb is translated as "to raise up," "to extol," "to lift up on high." *Rum* is often found in parallel with other words meaning "praise," so to extol the Lord is a form of praise (Ps. 145:1–2).

The primary salvation event that called for Israel's "exaltation," *rum*, and "praise," *nwh*, was His deliverance of the Israelites through the Red Sea. In Moses' Song of the Sea, he uses *rum* to proclaim that he would "exalt" the Lord for His great salvation (Exod. 15:2). But God reciprocated as well, for He "exalted" His faithful servant Joshua when he led the people into the land of Canaan (Josh. 3:7). God promised to "exalt" the power and strength of His anointed king even before Israel had a king (1 Sam. 2:10). The Lord caused even the pagan prophet Balaam to predict His "exaltation" of the kingdom of Israel (Num. 24:7). God in His very power is "exalted"; in fact, the Almighty *El-shaddai* is beyond human exaltation (Job 36:22; 37:23).

In the book of Psalms, of course, God is exalted in word, song, and musical instrument by His people. In the psalms it is simply the theme of praise that the Lord be exalted (Ps. 40:16). But the Lord asserts that He will be exalted among the nations of the earth as well (Ps. 46:10), even above the heavens (Ps. 57:5). And, as the New Testament says that Jesus' name alone is exalted above every name, so the Lord's Name was exalted alone in the Old Testament (Ps. 148:13). God's people from all ages have lifted up the Lord's Name, His character, His words, and His deeds to honor them. Luke asserts that the one who "exalts" himself or herself will be humbled (Luke 14:11; 18:14). The Lord has for now exalted (*hupsoo* in Greek) only Jesus to be equal with Him at His right hand to the highest place possible (Acts 2:33; 5:31; Phil. 2:9). He is our exalted High Priest, separate from sinners and exalted above the heavens just as the Lord was in the Old Testament. If God's people extolled the Father in the Old Testament above the heavens, how much more should we exalt the Son, whom God has exalted, in our worship!

KEY VERSES

Exodus 15:2;
Psalms 18:46; 30:1;
46:10; 57:11;
Ezekiel 21:26

55

Faith

See also: *Faith, p. 279*
Hebrew expression: *'emunah*
Pronunciation: *'eh moo NAWH*
Strong's Number: *530*

F

"Faith" is one of the most dynamic words in the Old Testament. Furthermore in the New Testament, Paul's assertion in Romans that "the righteous shall live by faith" (Rom. 1:17) lays the foundation stone for the gospel: the gospel of faith in Christ. The author of Hebrews defines faith as the assurance in our heart and mind of what we hope for, the certainty of what we do not see (Heb. 11:1). And the author also notes that it was "faith" that was the "basis" for the approval of the saints in the Old Testament (Heb. 11:2). The author of Hebrews was right, for without faith it is impossible to be approved by God.

Paul quotes Habakkuk 2:4. He does not make up this principle of acceptance before God through faith. The word used in Habakkuk to assert that the righteous should live by their faith was the Hebrew word *'emunah*. This word means "firmness," "steadfastness," "fidelity," "faithfulness," "faith." It is clearly a powerful and important word. This word is derived from the verbal root, *'aman*, meaning "to confirm," "to support," "to be confirmed," and "to trust." The New International Version translates the word as "faith," as does the King James Version. The NJPS, Jewish translation, renders it "fidelity," which means the same as "faithfulness." The King James Version gives "faithfulness" as an alternative rendering of *'emunah* in Habakkuk 2:4. This word describes a faithful (*'emunah*) man—and a faithful man, according to Scripture, is blessed greatly by the Lord (Prov. 28:20).

The flip side of this word is that God is faithful—He is what He expects His people to be (Deut. 32:4). God is faithful in all that He does. He does not falter or fail (Ps. 33:4). Both His love and His faithfulness reach to the heavens. The psalmist makes the Lord's faithfulness known throughout the world—as God's people also today should do (Ps. 89:1). The fact that God is completely dependable is a fact that is not bound by time or by the passing of a generation—all generations experience His faithfulness. Christ is our perfect example in faith—just as He is in other areas of our life. In the book of Revelation, Jesus Christ is called Faithful and True (Rev. 19:11, *pistos* in Greek)—the One who challenges us to not only have faith, but to live faithfully as He did.

KEY VERSES

Deuteronomy 32:4;
Psalms 33:4; 36:5;
Proverbs 28:20

Falsehood

Hebrew expression: *sheqer*
Pronunciation: *SHEH qehr*
Strong's Number: *8267*

"A witness of falsehoods who pours out lies" is one of the seven things that the Lord hates (Prov. 6:19). The American people have seen false witnesses and falsehoods corrupt the judicial system in celebrated legal cases in recent times. In the Old Testament, false witnesses and falsehoods threatened to destroy not only Israel's legal system, but also God's messages delivered through inspired prophets as well.

The Hebrew word *sheqer* translated as "lie," "lying," "deception," "falsehood," along with similar words, comes from a root word meaning "to deceive." A noun is formed from the root *sheqer* meaning "to do," "to act or to deal falsely." Of course, such deceitful actions or persons could not be permitted free rein among God's people, much less approved in principle. The ninth commandment uses this word when God orders His people "not to give falsehoods in their testimonies" (Exod. 20:16). The Lord is the God of truth and honesty, not deception. His people were to be like Him.

In Jeremiah, this word is used to describe the prophets in Jeremiah's day who spoke falsehoods, lies and deceived the people into believing things that were not true. And, they spoke their falsehoods in the Name of the Lord! In the book of Psalms, lies and lying persons are condemned roundly. The psalmist asks for their lies to be silenced (Pss. 31:18; 109:2; 120:2). The Lord detests lying lips (Prov. 12:22). The book of Jeremiah uses this word more than any other book in the Old Testament. The prophets whom God created to correct the corruption and deceit among His people were, all of a sudden, infiltrated by many false prophets—literally prophets of *sheqer*, "prophets of deception." These false prophets did not prophesy the truth as the true prophets were supposed to. Rather, these false prophets spoke false messages of hope for the people, when Jeremiah was prophesying the true message of doom and judgment to the people (Jer. 5:31; 9:3; 14:14; 27:15; 29:23). Ezekiel experienced this problem as well. As a result of all of this, God's people were confused. Isaiah's statement that those who worship false (*sheqer*) images would themselves become false was fulfilled in Habakkuk's day (Hab. 2:18).

KEY VERSES

Exodus 20:16;
1 Kings 22:22;
Psalm 119:69;
Jeremiah 23:25;
Zechariah 13:3

Falsehood should not be a characteristic of God's people, much less of His "inspired" prophets. Jesus made clear in the New Testament that the chief characteristic of the devil is that He is a liar and the father of lies—that is, he creates falsehoods and lies (John 8:44). But God's people are to speak the truth (Rom. 9:1, *pseudomai* in Greek).

Fasting

Hebrew expression: *tsom*
Pronunciation: *TSOHM*
Strong's Number: *6685*

Fasting is often a way to lose weight today—but many people still fast today for spiritual purposes. Fasting helps people practice self-control and self-discipline. In the Bible, fasting was also practiced to show the seriousness of one's religious endeavors and to remind each other that people do not live by bread alone (Deut. 8:4). The Hebrew noun *tsom* translates as "fast" or "fasting." The related verb "to fast" is *tsum*. A little used phrase *'inna napsho* meant "to oppress" or "to afflict the soul" and refers to fasting. It illustrates the fact that fasting was more of a spiritual exercise in the Bible than an attempt to punish the flesh in any way. Fasting also emphasized that the spiritual life of God's people was more important than their physical existence. There were some set religious fasts. The Israelites fasted on the solemn Day of Atonement (Lev. 16:29, 31; Num. 29:7). This day was also a special day of prayer and repentance, as well as fasting. At least four other fasts were observed after the Babylonian exile to commemorate God's deliverance of the Jews at different times in Jewish history (Zech. 8:18–19).

Fasting was often accompanied with the traditional signs of mourning—that is, wearing sackcloth (1 Kgs. 21:27). Ezra humbled himself through fasting. The prophet Joel declared "fasts" for the people and a time of religious assembly to seek God's mercy (Joel 1:14; 2:15). Fasting was always supposed to be directed toward God as a means of acquiring guidance and help from Him (Exod. 34:28; Deut. 9:9; Ezra 8:21–23). Fasting as an automatic way to get the attention of God, however, was condemned. Moreover, unless the person fasting was keeping faith with the Lord in all other areas of his or her life, that person's fasting was in vain (Isa. 58:5–12; Jer. 4:11–12; Zech. 7:4–8). The Lord was more impressed by His peoples' willingness to do justice, love mercy, and walk humbly before Him than He was with fasting (Mic. 6:7; Zech. 7:8–10). But even with all of its dangers, fasting still has a place among God's people today.

KEY VERSES

Isaiah 58:5;
Joel 1:14; 2:15;
Zechariah 8:19

The New Testament Christians regularly prayed and fasted (Acts 13:3, *nesteuo* in Greek). Jesus fasted for forty days and forty nights without food or water, just as Moses had—an impossible human feat in each case; but God empowered each one (compare Exod. 24:18; 34:28; Matt. 4:2). We see in these cases that God's presence and word was more life-giving than food. Jesus Himself indicated that the time after His ascension would properly be a time of fasting, for He would be gone (Mark 2:19). But He clearly instructed His followers to fast with the heart, in secret to God, and not as a show for other people (Matt. 6:16–18). When fasting, keep your focus on the Lord and His will for you.

Favor

Hebrew expression: *chen*
Pronunciation: *KHAYN*
Strong's Number: *2580*

God extended His favor in various ways in the Old Testament, sometimes even through pagan kings. Esther the Queen found "favor," which is *chen* in Hebrew, in the eyes of Xerxes the Persian King (Esth. 7:3). And, because of this she was able to plead with him to spare her people, the Jews. *Chen* means "favor" or "grace." It is formed from the root of the verb *chanon*, meaning "to show favor, be gracious or to extend favor." The word can be used to refer to physical grace, meaning "beauty" (Prov. 31:30), or refer to "elegant, gracious words and speech" (Ps. 45:3; Prov. 22:11; Eccl. 10:12). "Favor" or "grace" as a means of acceptance is most important.

How does one, if anyone can, find grace and acceptance before God or important people? God's dispensing of grace is dependent upon Him alone. No one deserves grace inherently. In the book of Esther, King Xerxes looked with "favor" upon Esther, the new Jewish queen. But the reader knows that God is behind the perception of King Xerxes. Mordecai said to her that she had probably come to her position in the Persian kingdom just at the right time to save the Jews from destruction. Esther's appeal to the King to recognize her and not to destroy her people was Israel's salvation because she found "favor," *chen*, in the King's eyes. Yet the reader knows that God orchestrated the entire situation because He is the one and only dispenser of His *chen*. When God finds favor with someone, He looks at him or her with appreciation and acceptance. Noah found favor in the eyes of the Lord (Gen. 6:8). By demonstrating excellence in understanding or wisdom, it is possible to find "favor" with people (Prov. 13:15; 3:3–4). God can also provide favor through other people or groups. He gave the Israelites favor and grace in the eyes of the Egyptians (Exod. 3:21; 11:3). God also gives grace to certain kinds of people. For example, He mocks those who mock Him or others, but He gives *chen*, grace and favor, to those who are humble (Prov. 3:34).

In Christ, God proclaimed the "year" of His favor (*dektos* in Greek) and extended His grace and favor to all humanity. We now live in the "era" of God's favor (*charis* in Greek). God's grace has been poured out to us, just as He caused Xerxes to extend his grace to Esther (1 Tim. 1:14). Paul asserts that by His grace we are redeemed (Eph. 2:5). Ultimately, the only way to heaven is through the grace and mercy of Jesus Christ, who died for our sins that we might have eternal life. As believers, we have found favor with God because of Jesus.

KEY VERSES

Genesis 6:8;
Esther 5:8; 7:3

Fear

Hebrew expression: *yir'ah*
Pronunciation: *yeer 'AWH*
Strong's Number: *3374*

"The fear of the Lord is the beginning of wisdom" is probably the best known verse in the Bible dealing with "fearing the Lord." Fear is not something people normally desire to have. It is an emotion we would like to do without. Yet, the book of Proverbs says that the "fear of the Lord" is a good thing.

The Hebrew word *yir'ah* may mean "fear," "reverence," or "piety." It comes from the root verb *yare'*, "to fear," or "to be afraid." The word indicates a genuine fear and respect for the Lord, but it is a fear that results in spiritual, moral and ethical health and wealth before both God and people in the book of Proverbs.

The word refers to the simple, but real fear of "briars and thorns" because of the physical damage they may cause (Isa. 7:25). The destructive judgments that God could bring upon a land or nation engendered fear among the people (Ezek. 30:30), fearing for their lives (Jonah 1:10, 16). The Lord put the fear of Israel upon the nations of Canaan so that they would not try to stand against His people—but rather stand in dread of them (Deut. 2:25).

The Lord came in an awesome epiphany at Mount Sinai to cause the people to fear Him so that they would not sin (Exod. 20:20). So from the beginning the fear of God made a moral and spiritual impression upon God's people. The fear of Him engendered obedience to Him and righteous living. It was never to engender fear for fear itself.

Proverbs features the "fear of the Lord." Those who hate knowledge are those who do not fear (*yir'ah*) the Lord. The person who fears the Lord shuns evil (Prov. 3:7)—in fact, the author says that to fear the Lord is to *hate* evil (Prov. 8:13). Because of the improvement in someone's lifestyle when he or she fears God, that person's mental and emotional condition and sometimes even his or her "length of life" improves (Prov. 10:27). The fear of God, rather than being a detriment to a full life, becomes a fountain of life (Prov. 14:27).

KEY VERSES

Genesis 20:11;
Job 6:14;
Psalm 19:9;
Proverbs 1:7;
2:5; 3:7;
Jeremiah 32:40

For the people of God, the fear of people can be detrimental. But the fear of God is always beneficial (Prov. 29:25). Paradoxically, the person who fears (*yir'ah*) God does not need to fear anything or anyone else. Jesus agreed with this Old Testament teaching. He told His disciples who they were to fear—fear God, *not* man (see Luke 12:5).

Fire

Hebrew expression: *'esh*
Pronunciation: *'AYSH*
Strong's Number: *784*

In the Old Testament, "fire," which is *'esh* in Hebrew, is often associated with the presence of God. As the Israelites gazed at the top of Mount Sinai, the Lord appeared as a devouring fire (Exod. 24:17)—a phenomenon remembered by the writer of Hebrews (Heb. 12:29). The word *'esh* signifies the visible aspect of the "fire," that is, the "flame." Fire may appear, however, without consuming anything. For example, the bush that Moses saw was not consumed (Exod. 3:5).

There are at least three areas where fire plays a significant role in the Old Testament. First of all, "fire" was often used by the Lord to bring judgment in various circumstances. Fire from the Lord consumed Nadab and Abihu because they did not approach the Lord properly (Lev. 10:2). A priest's daughter who became a prostitute was burned by fire (Lev. 21:9). And when God comes in judgment He will "consume" His foes (Ps. 21:9; 50:2-4); even in the last days He will be a refiner's fire (Mal. 3:2; Isa. 66:15-16). God's fire of judgment can destroy, or purify and refine. Secondly, "fire" was the means by which Israel offered her sacrifices to God (Deut. 18:1; 1 Sam. 2:28). Fire consumed both animal and non-animal sacrifices and caused the sacrifice "to ascend" to the Lord (Lev. 1:9; 2:10). The sacred bread or incense placed in the fire before the Lord in the Holy place was also presented to the Lord by fire (Lev. 16:13; 24:7). Lastly, and most significantly, "fire" often accompanies appearances of God: as in the bush of Exodus 3:2, as a pillar of fire (Exod. 13:21), at Mount Sinai (Exod. 24:17), and later to Elijah (1 Kgs. 19:12; Ezek. 1:5).

In the New Testament, fire is also associated with the presence of God, but through the Holy Spirit and as a "baptism by fire" that refines and converts God's people (Matt. 3:11; Acts 2:3). Jesus, God's offering, ascended to the sanctuary in heaven and was a perfect sacrifice—He needed no refinement by fire. But we are sinful; the fire of the Spirit invigorates and refines us and therefore should be cultivated (1 Thess. 5:19). Although God has opened Himself to us in a way that is inviting and joyful (Heb. 12:18-24), He is still a consuming fire (Heb. 12:29) as He was at Mount Sinai. God's angelic messengers are flames of fire (Heb. 1:7) and the present heaven and earth will be destroyed by fire. It is far worse to fall under God's fiery judgment, since it involves rejecting Jesus and God's new covenant (Heb. 10:26-31). Those who reject God will face the punishment of eternal fire (Jude 7). While all of these uses of fire in the Bible are instructive, it is the presence of God in our lives now, as a fire that refines and invigorates, that we should be aware of. This internal fire melts and molds us to be more like Jesus.

KEY VERSES

Exodus 3:2; 13:21;
Leviticus 10:2; 16:13

Folly

Hebrew expression: *'ivvelet*
Pronunciation: *'ih VEH leht*
Strong's Number: *200*

The book of Proverbs warns us not to answer a fool in the same way he addresses us, for we will become like him if we do! (Prov. 26:4). To pursue a foolish action, idea, or attitude is to do folly. "Folly" is an active noun, closely connected to the Hebrew root *'wl*. It is often translated as "foolishness" (KJV, AMPLIFIED). The adjective *'ewil*, "foolish," comes from the same root and its use in the Old Testament reflects this fact (Prov. 29:9). This adjective is also used to indicate a fool (Prov. 1:7; 15:5), and a fool's main occupation was the production of folly or foolishness (Prov. 12:23).

People who engage in folly are out of balance and arrogant, they tread boldly where people should not. They eventually end up disrespecting and mocking God. Psalms 38:5 describes a person overwhelmed by sin and guilt and under the wrath of God because of his *'ivvelet* (folly; foolishness, KJV). So folly is dangerous, it leads to sin and death—the opposite of where wisdom leads. Folly is not merely a psychological flaw, an anthropological defect or a sociological *faux pas* in the Bible. It is a serious breach of etiquette before God and man; it leads to sin and its deadly consequences. The psalmist parallels his folly or foolishness (*'ivvelet*) with his sins and guilt before God—it is a relational issue between the person and God (Ps. 69:5).

The book of Proverbs features fools and folly. According to the author, the two go together like birds of a feather! The person who commits folly willfully suffers for it because that person has no discipline (Prov. 5:23). The woman of folly (Hebr. *kesilut*, a synonym of *'ivvelet*) is contrasted with the woman of wisdom in Proverbs (9:1, 13). Proverbs is about various people who are guilty of folly: quick-tempered persons, simpletons, and children. This last group is especially interesting. Folly or foolishness is bound up in a child's heart (that is, character) the author of Proverbs 22:15 asserts. He is quick to add, however, that the rod of discipline (*musar*) will drive folly out of a child. Foolishness leads to disaster if it is allowed to develop. Once a person is a confirmed fool, it is practically impossible to drive folly (*'ivvelet*) from that person (Prov. 26:4–5; 27:22).

In the New Testament, Jesus lists foolishness in his catalogue of sins that come from within a person and defiles that person (Mark 7:22). Timothy calls folly a product of corrupt minds, faithless people and devoid of the truth of God (2 Tim. 3:8–9). A fool's folly will eventually catch up with him. But we, Christians, must turn away from folly and seek wisdom from God (Jas. 3:17).

KEY VERSES

Psalms 38:5; 69:5;
Proverbs 5:23;
12:23; 14:18, 29;
22:15; 26:11

Foreigner

Hebrew expression: *nokri*
Pronunciation: *nok REE*
Strong's Number: *5237*

One of the most significant uses of the word "foreigner" in the Old Testament is in the book of Ruth. Ruth is described as a foreigner (*nokriya*). The narrator often reminds the reader of her status as a Moabitess (Ruth 1:4, 22; 2:2, 6, 21; 4:5, 10) who married the Israelite Mahlon while his family sojourned in Moab (compare 1:4, 4:10). Why is her status as a "foreigner" repeatedly emphasized? In order to understand the dynamics of this element in the story, we must look at how foreigners (*nokri*) are viewed in the Old Testament.

The adjective *nokri*, meaning "foreign," is used in the Old Testament to describe people (compare Gen. 31:15; Exod. 21:8; 1 Kgs. 11:1), places (compare Exod. 2:22; 18:3) and things (compare Isa. 28:21; Jer. 2:21; Zeph. 1:8). The basic meaning may be "something previously unknown." However, it often modifies something which is non-Israelite (compare Deut. 17:15; Judg. 19:12; 1 Kgs. 11:1). Another usage for *nokri* is when in Proverbs the son is cautioned to avoid the seductive "foreign" woman. In this case, "foreign" does not designate the woman as a non-Israelite but rather as any woman who is "not your wife." The context makes it clear that this is a perjorative use of the adjective *nokri*, parallel to harlot (Prov. 2:16; 5:20; 7:5; 23:27) or evil woman (Prov. 6:24).

The adjective within the Book of Ruth is used to describe Ruth as a non-Israelite, not a harlot. Her status as a foreigner is stressed in order to evoke the promises of God. First, it brings to mind Yahweh's assurance to sojourning Abraham that he will both bless the nations and be blessed by them. The second promise brought to mind by the account of Ruth follows on the heels of the first. Ruth's place in Israel's history as a progenitress of David illustrates Yahweh's faithfulness in maintaining His promise to provide a king for Israel (Deut. 17:14–20). If Ruth had not given birth to her son Obed, David might never have existed. Ruth's status as a foreigner earns her a place in the company of the other interesting women in Jesus' line of descent (compare Matt. 1)—Tamar (Gen. 38), Rahab (Josh. 2; 6:17, 22–25), and Bathsheba (2 Sam. 11—12)..

There are two lessons to be learned from the story of Ruth the foreigner. First, her presence in the genealogy of both David and Jesus is a constant reminder that God accomplishes His purposes in strange and interesting ways. If history and salvation are a tapestry that God is weaving, then the twists and turns of our lives constitute the varied colors and patterns. The second lesson is based upon Ruth's actions as a foreigner. A young woman in a foreign land who demonstrates amazing courage, trust, obedience, and faithfulness should be an inspiration. Sometimes, we too are called to follow God into "foreign places." Would that our response be like that of Ruth.

KEY VERSES

Genesis 31:15;
Exodus 2:22;
Deuteronomy 17:15;
Ruth 2:10;
Isaiah 28:21

Forgive

See also: *Forgive, p. 284*
Hebrew expression: *nasa'*
Pronunciation: *naw SAW*
Strong's Number: *5375*

Even the arrogant Pharaoh pleaded, under great pressure from God, for the Lord to forgive him (Exod. 10:17). Moses entreated God to forgive the sins of the Israelites or wipe his name out of God's book (Exod. 32:32). The word "forgive" is one of the most powerful words in the Bible. A healthy life, spiritually and psychologically, is impossible without forgiveness. We need to forgive, not only others, but ourselves. Yet many fear that God will not forgive them or their sins (Josh. 24:19).

The Hebrew verb *nasa'* means "to lift up, to bear, or carry." From these meanings one can see how "to forgive" becomes a natural meaning of *nasa'*. It means to carry, bear away or lift up the faults, sins and failures of others—to consider them guilty but forgiven. The Lord has taught and commanded His people to forgive! (Exod. 34:5–7). But, can God's forgiveness be presumed upon so that He refuses to give? In 1 Samuel, Saul asks Samuel for forgiveness, but Samuel's response is an emphatic "No!" This is because Saul rejected the Lord's guidance and followed his own ways. For Israel's sake Samuel relented and helped Saul, but did not extend to him the Lord's forgiveness—he never saw Saul again (1 Sam. 15:27–35). This example illustrates that the Lord will by no means forgive those who do not truly repent of their sin (Exod. 34:7). Isaiah declared that Judah's sins were so profuse and ingrained that the Lord would not forgive them (Isa. 2:9). Hosea declared the same concerning Israel (Hos. 1:6). Yet, in both cases God's love led Him to forgiveness toward His people (Hos. 14:2). Is this because God is fickle? No! Only when Israel returned to God did He forgive them (Hos. 14:2).

Forgiveness is not cheap or easy, but it is available today to those who turn to God through Christ. Jesus has authority to forgive our sins on earth (Luke 5:24). The sick among God's people can also be prayed for and they can be healed; if sins are involved they will be forgiven (Jas. 5:15). Believers forgiven by God are to imitate God by forgiving those who ask us (Luke 17:3, 4). He forgives our wickedness and purifies us before Himself, although it cost Him His Son (Heb. 8:12; 1 John 1:9). Forgiveness for us costs very little—except perhaps our pride. For those who humbly turn to God—and not away from Him as Saul did—there is forgiveness.

KEY VERSES

Exodus 32:32;
1 Samuel 15:25;
Isaiah 2:9;
Hosea 1:6; 14:2

Forsaken

Hebrew expression: 'azab
Pronunciation: 'aw ZAHB
Strong's Number: 5800

One of the most beautiful yet tragic verses in the Bible declares that the Lord's people have "forsaken" Him—the fountain of living, running water (Jer. 2:13). The Hebrew word 'azab meaning "to forsake, abandon or loose" is used by Jeremiah in this verse. A noun formed from the same root means "forsakenness or desolation" (Isa. 6:12). To forsake someone or something also may indicate "renouncing something." Jeremiah uses 'azab often to translate Israel's "forsaking" of the Lord, His law (Jer. 9:13), and His covenant (Jer. 22:9). An inspired Moses assured Israel that the Lord would never forsake or abandon them (Deut. 31:6, 8), and the Lord told Joshua that He would never leave him or forsake him (Josh. 1:5). God assured Israel and these two faithful leaders that He would be with them always (Exod. 3:12). Solomon prayed that the Lord would never 'azab him or His people (1 Kgs. 8:57) and the psalmist issued the same powerful sentiment as well (Ps. 119:8).

God's people were supposed to forsake the idols of Egypt and the gods of the foreign nations around them in order to serve the Lord (Ezek. 20:8). Instead, they forsook the Lord to seek and serve these other gods (Deut. 31:16; Judg. 10:13; Isa. 65:11). God warned His people at Mount Sinai that if they should forsake Him, He would forsake them (2 Chr. 15:2). To be forsaken by God is a dreadful state of existence to contemplate, but it became a reality for the nation of Israel. The Israelites cried out to the Lord not to forsake them, because they bore His Name (Jer. 14:9). But, they sinned, and God forsook them because of their sins (Jer. 22:9; 23:33). In His great mercy and love, the Lord preserved a remnant of Israel and did not "abandon," 'azab, them entirely (Pss. 94:14; 119:8; Hos. 11:8–9), and the Lord never forsook those who earnestly sought Him (Ps. 9:10). David sought the Lord and He believed that even if his own parents forsook him, the Lord would never abandon him (Ps. 27:10).

Jesus' cry of despair when the Father abandoned (Matt. 27:46; egkataleipo in Greek) Him, the Holy One of God, reminds us of the fact that Jesus Christ has delivered those who are in Him from the agony of being utterly forsaken by God. He bore our feeling of abandonment so that we might be united with the Lord forever.

KEY VERSES

Deuteronomy 31:6, 8;
Joshua 1:5;
Psalms 27:10; 94:14;
Jeremiah 2:13; 12:7

Friend

Hebrew expression: *rea'*
Pronunciation: *RAY ah*
Strong's Number: *7453*

"There is a friend who sticks closer than a brother" is a proverb that shows that the natural ties of people can be superseded and surpassed by ties of willing devotion and companionship (Prov. 18:24). Human beings are not slaves to their natural ties of flesh and blood or shared environment. As moral, ethical, and deeply relational beings, they can establish lasting friendship with any other person God has created in His image!

The Hebrew word *rea'*, "friend," "companion," "neighbor," or "fellow," is a powerful word. It comes from the root of the verb *ra'ah*, "to associate with," "to be friends with," "to be a companion to." The book of Proverbs holds forth some encouraging things about friends. Offering wise instruction, it teaches that a righteous man is cautious about his friendships (Prov. 12:26).

A friend, *rea'*, loves through all times—through thick and thin, through good and bad (Prov. 17:17). They are like a brother or sister to help in difficult times—but even better. Sometimes, however, the social or financial standing of a person causes his friends to forsake him, especially if he is poor (Prov. 19:4). False friendship is a reality, especially for those who benefit others by gift giving (Prov. 19:6). Gossip was and is a deadly enemy to friendship (Prov. 16:28). It is to be avoided like the plague! Sometimes, it is better to avoid making friends—as in the case of a man who cannot control his anger (Prov. 22:24).

Proverbs records other aspects of a true friend, that should help us not only to be a friend, but also to pick friends. A true friend always shows candor and critique that can be trusted; although they wound you, you can trust them (Prov. 27:6). A faithful friend can be counted on for counsel that is pleasant to hear (Prov. 27:9). The mind of a friend sharpens one's own understanding (Prov. 17:17). A friend speaks the proper words at the appropriate time (Prov. 25:17, 20; 26:18, 19; 27:14). A person who has gracious speech and a heart of integrity will be recognized as a friend by the King (Prov. 22:11).

KEY VERSES

2 Samuel 16:17;
Job 16:21;
Proverbs 17:17;
18:24; 19:4, 6;
22:11

God wanted to be Israel's friend. He, in fact, spoke with Moses as a friend (Exod. 33:11). God spoke of Abraham as His friend (using *'oheb*, a synonym of *rea'* here; compare also Prov. 18:24; Jas. 2:23). In the New Testament, it is easy to view Jesus as the friend who is closer than a brother (John 15:15). He was a friend of even tax collectors and "sinners" (NIV, Matt. 11:19, *philos* in Greek). Since being a friend involves bonding with someone, James warns his readers not to become friends with the evil ways of this world, for to do so makes one an enemy of God (Jas. 4:4, *philos* in Greek). Constantly in the New Testament, the authors address their readers as beloved friends—all hostility has been removed in Christ.

Garden

Hebrew expression: *gan*
Pronunciation: *GAHN*
Strong's Number: *1588*

When someone hears the phrase "Garden of Eden," which is literally the "Garden of Pleasure," they think of the perfect ideal setting for human existence. The Hebrew word *gan* means "enclosure" or "garden." *Gan* possibly comes from an original verbal root that meant "to surround, to cover, or defend." God created a delightful garden setting for His first created pair, Adam and Eve. They were enclosed within it, protected from the outside beasts of the field, and covered by its physical features and environment. They were safe, living in peace and in the presence of their God (Gen. 2—3). The Lord provided food, vegetables and fruit, and water in abundance for His newly created persons, His image bearers (Gen. 1:26–28; 2:10, 16). The Lord "planted" the Garden and gave people the privilege of living in it and caring for it (Gen. 2:8). It was legendary in its beauty and its abundance of water (Gen. 13:10). In the end, it was not the environment that polluted all humanity, but human beings that corrupted their God-given paradise (Gen. 3:23).

The Garden of Eden has symbolic meaning, as well as having been a historical reality for the first people. People still love gardens. Kings of Israel tried to cultivate them (2 Kgs. 21:18, 26). Persian kings fostered them (Neh. 3:15). The great Babylonian King Nebuchadnezzar majored in them, creating the fabulously lush "hanging gardens of Babylon." When Isaiah pictures a restored Israel on Zion, her deserts are restored like "Eden" (Isa. 51:3; 58:11; Jer. 31:12). Ezekiel uses the term "Garden of Eden" to describe a renewed Israel (Ezek. 36:35; Joel 2:3). It is no wonder then that in the Song of Solomon, the Lover can describe his beloved as a "garden locked up" (Song 4:12), even a "fountain in a garden" (Song 4:15). The Lover used garden-like metaphors to describe the sensual delights of his beloved as well as her virginity and her exclusive devotion to him only, and he for her (Song 4:15, 16; 5:1; 6:2).

The delights of the Garden of Eden are exceeded today by God's promises for His people through Jesus. The writer of the book of Revelation recalls much of the imagery of the Garden in Genesis 2—3 to describe the new Heaven and Earth, the New Jerusalem, and the new "garden setting" of God's people in the eternal state (Rev. 22:1–5). Significantly, the only thing missing in the new Garden is the curse that destroyed the peace of God's original Garden of Eden (Rev. 22:3). Christians experience God's peace today when He removes the curse of death and guilt from His people through Jesus.

KEY VERSES

Genesis 2:8–10;
2 Kings 21:18, 26;
Song of Solomon
4:15–16;
Jeremiah 31:12

Gather

Hebrew expression: *'asap*
Pronunciation: *'aw SAHF*
Strong's Number: *622, 6908*

The Lord strikes a familiar theme through Micah the prophet—the regathering of His people of Israel after He has first exiled them (Mic. 2:12–13). *'Asap* is one of the main Hebrew words used to describe the gathering of God's people that will take place in the land. The verb *'asap* means basically "to gather" or "to assemble," but can imply "removal" in a proper context. A man can be "freed," or literally "removed," from leprosy (2 Kgs. 5:11); and the moon can "remove" or "gather" itself (Isa. 60:20). Several nouns are formed from this root such as "ingathering," *'asip*, "store-house," *'asop*, and "gathering," *'asepah*. A person who dies is said to have been "gathered to his people," *'asap*. It is also the word used to indicate the simple act of gathering anything: people, manna, an army, or the entire assembly of Israel (1 Kgs. 8:5). The word *qabats*, "to gather" or "assemble," is paralleled with *'asap* often, as in Micah 2:12.

Micah, however, touches upon a special "gathering" of people, when God gathered the Israelites once again after devastating judgment had befallen them. In Micah 2:12, *'asap* is used twice in a row. This construction is emphatic and asserts with conviction that the Lord will indeed regather His people. He physically "regathered" the Israelites in 539–445 B.C. after the exile to Jerusalem and Judah (Isa. 43:5), but He will also "gather" His people back to Himself spiritually in days to come (Isa. 49:5). The "gathering of Israel back to the land" sometimes refers to the return of Israel from Babylon, but ultimately to their return, *qabats*, from the ends of the earth after being scattered in A.D. 70 by the Romans (Ezek. 29:14; 31:8, 10). Micah speaks of God's "assembling" the exiles, probably implying the final regathering of God's people to the land of Palestine before the Messianic era (Mic. 4:6). In fact, God will gather all the nations for His purposes against Jerusalem in the end times (Zech. 14:2). Christians can watch with great joy and expectation as God fulfills His promises to Israel; as He "gathers" them to Himself, both spiritually in Christ and physically into the land of Israel today (Matt. 24:31, *episunago* in Greek). The Lord also gathers the nations for judgment (Matt. 25:32; Rev. 16:14, 17; 19:19). However, for the present time, the greatest "gathering" is the assembling of believers in Christ from all nations (Acts 14:27; 15:30).

KEY VERSES

Genesis 25:8;
Isaiah 11:12;
Micah 2:12; 4:6;
Zechariah 14:2

Generations

Hebrew expression: *toledot*
Pronunciation: *tah lay DOHT*
Strong's Number: *8435*

This word, *toledot*, "generations" also means "genealogies, or genealogical records." Even more representative of its use in the Old Testament is the translation "history, account, family history, or genealogical history"—words that describe a family or line of descendants. The "X" generation or the "baby boomers" are probably better described by a different Hebrew word—*dor*. *Toledot* is a noun formed from the verb *yalad*, "to bear, give birth, or beget." In Genesis 5:1 *toledot* refers to the descendants of Adam; that is, the genealogy of Adam. More importantly, "generations" was used to indicate the account or family history of Terah that lists descendants leading up to Abraham (Gen. 11:27). When Aaron and Moses were chosen to lead Israel out of Egypt the account, *toledot*, of their ancestors was given to show their right to be legitimate leaders (Exod. 6:16, 19). In 1 Chronicles, *toledot* indicates the "genealogical records" of the Israelites who were returning to Israel after being in exile in Babylon. In fact, nine chapters of 1 Chronicles are largely genealogical records. Why is this the case and why is it so important?

In order to belong to God's chosen people from the seed of Abraham, it was necessary for the Jews who returned to prove their pedigree. Priests and Levites, of course, had to be descended from the line of Levi (Ezra 2:62). Only persons from the tribe of Judah and the line of David qualified for consideration as a king. The Messiah was to be born of the line of David. Gentiles could become part of the people of Israel, such as Rahab, Ruth, or the widow of Zarephath, but they could not qualify to be a priest, a king, or the Messiah. To be a priest, a king, or a Messiah, a person had to be descended from a pure family line of Israel. Jesus was of the genealogy of King David, the tribe of Judah (Matt. 1:1). As High Priest, Jesus was also of the unique line of the high priest Melchizedek, who was "without father or mother." This unique genealogy qualified Jesus to be a priest in Israel *without* descent from the tribe of Levi (Heb. 7:3). Jesus' ultimate genealogy is traced to His generation by the Holy Spirit—a new birth and genealogical history that is shared with those who are born anew in Christ through the power of the Holy Spirit. Those who have been born not of flesh, blood or the will of men, but of the will of God through His Spirit share in the *toledot* of the Lord Himself (John 1:12–13).

KEY VERSES

Genesis 5:1; 11:27;
Exodus 6:16, 19;
1 Chronicles 5:7;
7:2, 4, 9

Glean

Hebrew expression: *laqat*
Pronunciation: *law QAHT*
Strong's Number: 3950

The Hebrew word *laqat*, "to glean," or "to collect," occurs ten times in the book of Ruth—all in chapter two (see Ruth 2:2–3, 7–8, 15–19, 23). In every occurrence, Ruth is the person gleaning. Apparently by her own initiative, she undertook the activity as a means of providing food for both herself and her mother-in-law, Naomi. As the narrative makes clear, it is strictly "by chance" and through no knowledge of her own that Ruth ends up in Boaz's field (Ruth 2:3).

On the face of it, gleaning is simply the activity by which Ruth is introduced to Boaz. If we take the whole story into account, the gleaning episode could be viewed as the innocuous initial stage in a sequence of events which reaches both its climax and conclusion in the redemption of Naomi (Ruth 4:14). However, the space given to this scene and the dialogue surrounding the issue of gleaning suggests that there is more to this scene than meets the eye. Let us consider the different occurrences of "gleaning" in the Old Testament.

Gleaning had a specific function in the social structure of Israelite society. From a secular perspective, gleaning of fields in ancient Israel might be considered analogous to welfare. This comparison should not be carried too far, however, because gleaning was both community and work centered—a social safety net of sorts. In the Pentateuch (Exod. 23:10–11; Lev. 19:9–10; 23:22; Deut. 24:19–22), God expressly commands the Israelites to leave produce in their fields during harvest for the benefit of both the Israelite poor as well as resident aliens. These passages suggest that after a normal day of harvesting was finished and the workers had moved the gathered sheaves to the threshing floor—then those in need were allowed to scavenge for what was left in the field.

In addition to the social function of gleaning, the concept also carried religious connotations in the Old Testament. The Hebrew word *laqat* is used in the description of the Exodus event (Exod. 16) As the Israelite people traveled through the wilderness towards Canaan, one of the ways in which God provided for their needs was *manna*. The Israelites were to "glean" the *manna* from the ground. In a similar way, gleaning is part of the imagery used by the prophet Isaiah in a message of future salvation for God's people, "It will come about in that day, that the Lord will start His threshing from the flowing stream of the Euphrates to the brook of Egypt; and you will be gathered [gleaned] up one by one, O sons of Israel" (Isa. 27:12).

KEY VERSES

Leviticus 19:9–10;
23:22;
Ruth 2:2–3, 7–8,
15–19, 23;
Isaiah 27:12

Finally, it is clear that gleaning is used metaphorically in the Old Testament in two ways. First, the use of *laqat* in all of the passages listed above serves to remind us that we are the poor and the resident aliens in God's creation. It is only out of His grace that the divine landowner allows us to glean from the bounty of His fields. Secondly, Isaiah reminds us that in the end we should be prepared for the great gleaning as the Harvester returns to gather the crops and dispense with the chaff.

We should keep the concept of gleaning in mind as we approach life. We should allow others to glean among the abundance of our blessings. We should recognize that we glean in God's fields by virtue of His grace. We should be in preparation for the day when God decides that the harvest is ready.

G

Glory

See also: *Glorify, p. 289*
Hebrew expression: *kabod*
Pronunciation: *kaw BOHD*
Strong's Number: *3519*

G

For most, glory is associated with personal glory—the "glory days" of one's youth, days of lost innocence, boundless energy, unfettered imagination, and uncomplicated living. The Bible, however, moves beyond "glory" in the past tense to an emphasis on glory in the present and future tenses based upon the possibility of a relationship with the God of glory.

The word "glory" is derived from a Hebrew root that may mean "heavy," "weighty," or "numerous, severe" in a physical sense (that is, severe famine, Gen. 12:10; heavy yoke, 1 Kgs. 12:4). The related term *kabod* expresses the attribute of "glory," "honor," "splendor" as a derived meaning of the primary idea of weightiness or gravity (for example, Num. 24:11; Job 19:9; Prov. 3:16, 35). In the Old Testament, glory may be applied to a finely crafted object in the sense of cleverness of design, intricacy of artistic work, and beauty (Exod. 28:40). When applied to human beings, glory signifies dignity or respect as a characteristic of inherited status (Ps. 8:5) or honor due to one's achieved status (Gen. 45:13). Glory is supremely ascribed to God as an attribute or possession, especially in the Psalms and prophetic literature (see Ps. 29:1–3; Isa. 6:3; Ezek. 3:12). God's glory is manifested especially in his moral perfection or holiness and his unrivaled power or omnipotence (Ps. 96:7–9).

The glory of God is frequently associated with His presence—especially His presence at the covenant ceremony at Mount Sinai (Exod. 24:16). Often a cloud was the tangible symbol of God's presence, shrouding the brilliance of His glory (Deut. 5:24; 2 Chr. 5:13; 7:1). God's glory is so dazzling people are permitted to experience it only indirectly (Exod. 33:18–23). Furthermore, His glory is so effulgent that it may be imparted to objects and persons that come in contact with God's

radiant presence (compare Exod. 34:33–35). God's glory is displayed publicly in His work of creation (Ps. 19:1) and is manifest to the nations in His sovereign control of history (compare Ps. 145:10–12).

KEY VERSES

Exodus 24:16;
2 Chronicles 7:1;
Psalms 19:1; 29:1;
Isaiah 42:8

Isaiah warned the Israelites that God was jealous for His glory and would not yield it to another (Isa. 42:8; 48:11). Foolishly, they failed to listen and at various times through the course of Old Testament history they exchanged the glory of God for idols (compare Ps. 106:20). Ezekiel witnessed the departure of God's glory from the Jerusalem Temple prior to the Babylonian exile (Ezek. 10:18). The prophet Haggai predicted that God's glory would return to the Jerusalem Temple if the postexilic community would apply themselves to rebuild the structure and offer appropriate worship there (Hag. 2:7). Haggai knew that true worship, not the Temple building, was the real issue because ultimately God's glory fills the earth and is above the heavens (Pss. 57:11; 72:19; 113:4).

According to the New Testament, the glory of God the Father is fully expressed in the person of His Son Jesus Christ (John 1:14; compare Heb. 1:3). Peter, James, and John had a glimpse of this unveiled glory on the Mount of Transfiguration (Matt. 17). It was after this experience that Jesus began to teach His disciples about His future return in the glory of His Father (Matt. 16:27). Jesus glorified God in His humanity by obeying His Father in all things, even death on a cross (John 17:4–5). The gospel record also indicates that the work of the Holy Spirit would be one of glorifying God (compare John 14:13; 16:14). Today the Christian may give God glory in the same way Jesus glorified His Father. First, a life of obedience to God's Word and dependence upon His Holy Spirit brings glory to God (John 15:8; compare 1 Cor. 10:31). Second, through prayer the Christian glorifies God because the prayer of the righteous through the Holy Spirit unleashes the power of God in a fallen world (Jas. 5:16). In this way, we fulfill our calling as God's creatures, since human beings were created for the praise of God's glory (Isa. 43:7; compare Eph. 1:12, 14).

God

See also: *God, p. 290 and Gods, p. 291*
Hebrew expression: *'elohim*
Pronunciation: *'ehl oh HEEM*
Strong's Number: *430*

'Elohim is "God," the Maker of the universe and the Supreme Creator of all life. Use of the Hebrew word *'elohim* emphasizes God's power and strength which is evident in creating, from nothing, the heavens, the earth and all that is in them (Gen. 1, 2; Pss. 33:6–15; 104). *'Elohim* means "deity" and is not to be considered gender specific for God is neither male nor female. He spoke and the universe was created (Gen. 1:3, 6; Ps. 22:6)! He can destroy and create a new heaven and a new earth (Isa. 65:16, 17) without changing Himself (Mal. 3:6, 8). The author of Genesis declares emphatically seven times that everything God created was good (Gen. 1:3), because God is good. And although He is unlimited in power and strength, with no need for others, He chooses to reach out and communicate with the people He created. He is a personal God who initiates a relationship with His people.

The crowning creation of God was men and women who bear His own image (Gen. 1:26–28). *'Elohim* is the "Supreme God" who graciously shares Himself in forming mankind into His own likeness. People are not divine as God is, but creatures made of the dust of the earth. We bear His image, not His divinity, in fragile vessels of clay. God prepared a perfect garden paradise for Adam and Eve, and communicated with them (Gen. 1:28–30). *'Elohim* directed them about good and evil, showing that He is the moral governor of His creations (Gen. 2:16). However, after His awesome display of wisdom, power and goodness, His people rebelled against Him. He then personally called Abraham to lead a new people to redemption. He formed them into a nation (Gen. 12:1; Exod. 3:12), so that He could be their God and they could be His people (Exod. 6:7; Jer. 31:33). Even when they were enslaved in Egypt, He suffered with them and proclaimed that He was their God (Exod. 2:25; 3:18; 5:3).

'Elohim identifies Himself as Yahweh, the personal covenant God of Israel, whose name is the "Lord" (Gen. 2:4; Exod. 3:14, 15), and the "Lord is God" (1 Kgs. 18:21). When gods are mentioned, *'elohim* is the "God of gods," the "Supreme God" (Ps. 136:2). *'Elohim* cares for and wants to relate to His creation and His people. Today, God seeks people to worship Him and relate to Him through Jesus Christ (Heb. 1:1). Jesus worshiped, trusted, and declared His total dependence upon the one true Supreme God, His Father (Matt. 4:7, 10; 27:46; Mark 11:22; 12:30). The Lord is now our Father as well (Matt. 6:7; John 5:18). He demonstrated His love for us in Jesus, coming to earth so that He could be our God (John 1:1, 12, 13; Isa. 7:9; Matt. 1:23). *'Elohim* is also in absolute control. He will exercise His power and once again create a new heaven and a new earth for all believers (2 Pet. 3:13; Rev. 21:1).

KEY VERSES

Genesis 1:1; 2:2;
Psalm 136:2;
Exodus 3:14–15; 6:7;
1 Kings 18:21

Good

Hebrew expression: *tob*
Pronunciation: *TOHB*
Strong's Number: *2896*

The first chapter of Genesis contains the Hebrew word *tob*, "good," seven times, indicating that God's creative work was good in every aspect. The last time it is used in the chapter it is modified by the adverb *me'od*, "very," to mean "very good" (Gen. 1:31). God Himself is good; He let all of His "goodness," *tub*, pass before Moses (Exod. 33:19). God is, therefore, "ultimate good," *tub*, *tob*, and the source of all that is good. If anyone or any thing is good it is because they share in His goodness. Jesus declared Him alone good (Mark 10:18, *agathos* in Greek). If God was not good, how could anyone trust in Him?

God's goodness also involved not clearing the guilty (Exod. 34:7). Consequently, He is experienced as a source of destruction and evil to those who are guilty and evil. But God shows Himself "good" to those who wait before Him and seek Him. To those who seek Him, He is found to be good; to those who abandon Him, He shows Himself "not good," for He cannot approve of their walk without Him. Jeremiah further affirms that it is "good" to wait for the Lord's deliverance in faith (Lam. 3:26). Both good things and calamities come from the Lord. To eventually receive the good, we need to wait patiently, exercising faith in Him (Lam. 3:38).

The word *tob*, then, has strong moral and religious overtones especially as used in Genesis, Exodus and Lamentations. It basically means "welfare, benefits, or good things." The verb of the same root as *tob* means "to be pleasing, or good." Several other words beside *tob* and *tub* are formed from the same root, but they all have the meaning of "good" in their usage. Names were compounded with the word to make, for example, *Tobiyyah*—a proper name meaning, "the Lord is my good" (2 Chr. 17:8).

As noted already, Jesus declared that there is only one who is totally good— God, the Father (Mark 10:18). Jesus showed Himself to be the good shepherd of the sheep, willingly dying for them (John 10:11). Paul asserted that those who persist in doing good, seeking God's glory and honor, will receive immortality (Rom. 2:7). God works for the good of those who love Him, using everything in their lives to bring them good, and not evil (Rom. 8:28). God's people are to be lovers of good, nothing else will do (2 Tim. 3:3, *aphilagathos* in Greek). We show who we are by doing good and kind things for others and doing good shows that we are children of God (Jas. 3:13, *kalos* in Greek; 3 John 11, *agathopoieo* in Greek).

KEY VERSES

Genesis 1:4, 31; 2:9;
Joshua 21:45;
Ezra 3:11;
Job 2:10;
Psalm 125:4

Governor

Hebrew expression: *pechah*
Pronunciation: *peh HAWH*
Strong's Number: *6346 (Hebrew), 6347 (Aramaic)*

"Governor" is a well-known political title in the United States and refers to the chief political officer of a state. This is a helpful parallel to the use of governor in the Old and New Testament. The Hebrew word *pechah* is nearly always translated as "governor"; only a very few times is it rendered as "official or officer." It is a loan word from Assyria through the Akkadian word *pachatu*, which indicated, in its proper noun form, the person in charge of a district. This person served under the king who appointed him. Zerubbabel and Nehemiah were appointed "governors" of Judah (Ezra 6:6–7; Neh. 12:26; Hag. 1:14). They were also called *tirshata* (Ezra 8:9; Neh. 7:65), a Persian title meaning governor or "honored person." The governor of these ancient provinces had direct access to the king or his immediate subordinate officers. Through these governors and king, God often worked His sovereign will.

The action and character of the governor Nehemiah is noteworthy. Although he had many rights and had been delegated much authority, Nehemiah did not always take advantage of these benefits. In Nehemiah 5:14 we learn that during the twelve years (445–433 B.C.) that Nehemiah served as governor of the province of Judah, he did not eat the food allotted to him as previous governors had done, nor did he permit his fellow workers to do so. Past govenors had "lorded" their power and benefits over the common people, taking money as well as food and wine from them (Neh. 5:15–16). But Nehemiah, because of the fear of the Lord, did not do so! He set an example as a servant of the Lord who is over the people just as Paul the apostle and Jesus Christ did hundreds of years later (1 Cor. 9; 2 Thess. 3:8–9). Nehemiah also did not take land as payment for his work on the wall. In fact, Nehemiah served 150 Jews and many others at his table. He recognized the burden he would place on the people if he demanded his "perks" as governor. Jesus' words and life illustrated the principle that anyone who would be "governor" over God's people must first be willing to be their greatest slave! The Gentiles ruled their people with oppressive power—but Jesus, the Son of God, liberated His people (Matt. 20:24–28). Christ came to serve, not to be served. Believers, too, should strive to follow Jesus' example by diligently serving others with joy and love.

KEY VERSES

Ezra 6:6–7;
Nehemiah 5:14–15,
18;
Haggai 1:1, 14

Hand

Hebrew expression: *yad*
Pronunciation: *YAWD*
Strong's Number: *3027*

"The kingdom was now established in the hands of King Solomon" (1 Kgs. 2:46). The writer's figurative use of "hands" is significant. The statement means that Solomon now had possession of his kingship and could proceed to rule and govern the kingdom as he saw fit. King Baasha of Israel angered the Lord by the evil works of his "hands" (1 Kgs. 16:7). The Hebrew word *yad*, or "hand," is an effective and picturesque expression. Men may think with their hearts and minds, but they accomplish things by the work of their hands. The hand represents action and function, the part of a person that accomplishes deeds and brings about results. Solomon recognized in his prayer that it was by the hand of the God of Israel that the Temple had been completed (1 Kgs. 8:15–16). Elisha was called the personal servant of Elijah because he poured water on the hands of Elijah (2 Kgs. 3:11), "hands" that had worked many wonders for the Lord's honor.

To be placed "into the hands" of someone means to be given into their power (2 Kgs. 10:24). While Israel had been delivered from the "hand," or power, of Pharaoh and the Egyptians (Exod. 18:9), the Israelites were also brought out of Egypt by God's "hand"—the supreme act of God's salvation for His people (Exod. 15:6–20). The "hand of the Lord" was His power to force Pharaoh to release the Israelites (Exod. 3:19–20). The hand of the Lord was also upon Ezra and prospered him so that the Persian king gave him all for which he asked (Ezra 7:6, 9).

This powerful imagery of the hand of God that brings salvation to His people is encountered in the New Testament as well. The Lord's hand of judgment is mentioned, "his winnowing fork is in His hand" (Matt. 3:12). But mostly God's hand, incarnated in Christ, is a hand of healing placed upon those who need salvation and healing (Mark 7:32). The "hand of God" was upon John the Baptist from conception (Luke 1:66). The "right hand of God" is the place reserved for Jesus Christ and those whom the Lord has chosen (Luke 22:69). Those who are saved are in the "Lord's hand" and they cannot be snatched out (John 10:28–29; Acts 2:33, 34). It is the "right hand" of Christ who holds the seven stars of the churches (Rev. 2:1). The Lord's question through Isaiah, "Is My hand so short that it cannot ransom?" (Isa. 50:2, NASB), is answered in Christ—the Lord who saved us from our sins. God's power is never "too short," but it redeems us perfectly according to His abundant love.

KEY VERSES

Exodus 15:9;
18:9–10;
1 Kings 2:46;
2 Kings 10:24

Hang

Hebrew expression: *talah*
Pronunciation: *taw LAWH*
Strong's Number: *8518*

The Hebrew word *talah* indicates death by hanging. The root means "to let dangle." *Talah* is found more often in Esther than in any other book of the Old Testament. The word's key subject is the death of Haman, the Amalekite man who plotted to annihilate the Jews. *Talah* is used to describe the act of hanging any object or person (2 Sam. 18:10) in a physical sense. Figuratively it means "to depend on" as in Isaiah 20:24 where it says that all of the honor of the family of Hilkiah will *talah* on him, "hang on him" (Matt. 22:40). *Talah* is first found in Genesis to refer to Pharaoh's execution of his chief baker by "hanging" on a tree or stake (Gen. 40:19–22).

The most important verse showing the significance *talah* can have is Deuteronomy 21:22–23. In this passage a criminal guilty of a capital offense is "hanged" on a tree after he had been executed. This additional exposure to public display served to further deprecate the memory and character of the criminal. This act clearly brought to light God's condemnation of the capital offense. The further humility of hanging on a tree made God's divine judgment evident to the people. From this, it is clear that Christ's willingness to hang on the cross, "a tree," indicated His full acceptance of our punishment as He became accused on our behalf and in our place (Gal. 3:13). In Esther, Haman is hanged on the gallows on which he had prepared to hang Mordecai (Esth. 7:9–10). Ironically, the enemy of God's people became God's enemy and the curse of God was placed upon him. And, not only Haman was hanged, but also his ten sons, completing God's stated curse to wipe out the Amalekites (Esth. 9:13–14) because they had threatened to destroy God's people in the wilderness (Exod. 17:8–16). Jesus was hanged on a tree (Acts 5:30; 10:39) by the people bearing *our* curse, not His own; but God justified Him and raised Him from the dead for our ultimate justification and His absolute glory.

KEY VERSES

Genesis 40:19, 22;
Deuteronomy
21:22–23;
Esther 7:9–10

Happy

Hebrew expression: *'esher*
Pronunciation: *'EH shehr*
Strong's Number: *835*

The "pursuit of happiness" is so central to human drives that it has even been written into a nation's constitution as one of the goals of its citizens. It is one of the things discussed in any good beginning philosophy course in college. It is also something that is mentioned often in the book of Psalms and elsewhere in both the Old and New Testament. *'Esher*, the word translated "happy" (KJV, NLT), can also be translated as "blessed." These two felicitous states of human beings are intimately laced together. They are at times impossible to differentiate in some biblical passages; by definition, the Lord blesses the happy person and the person blessed by the Lord is happy. The word *'esher* is used only in the plural form in the Old Testament. The noun comes from an original root, *'shr*, meaning "to go straight or advance." So the blessedness and happiness of the person of God is one who advances in understanding and in the ways of God, turning neither to the right or the left. In some cases, *'esher* also means to "be led on" (Isa. 9:15). The happiness or blessedness of the people of God is tied to God leading them forward. Happy is the person who does not live according to the counsel of the ungodly (Ps. 1:1), for God approves of his ways and makes him happy. The book of Psalms notes many reasons why the "blessed" man is indeed blessed and happy. Happiness belongs to those who: take refuge in the Lord (Ps. 2:12), have their sins forgiven (Ps. 32:1), live in a nation whose God is the Lord (Ps. 33:12), have righteous parents (Ps. 37:25–26), have regard for the poor (Ps. 41:1), have a wise king as their ruler (Ps. 84:4), trust in the Lord (Ps. 84:12), and fear the Lord (Ps. 112:1). This is only a partial list of who is happy and why, but in every case it is the Lord who is the ultimate cause and source of happiness.

Jesus' words in the beatitudes echo and reflect these Old Testament concepts. He says: happy or "blessed" are the peacemakers, the pure in heart, the merciful, and those persecuted for His name (Matt. 5:3–16; *makarios* in Greek). Jesus' words remind us that the truly blessed in this world are those who believe in Him (John 20:29). Blessings and real happiness are not and cannot be found in the things of this world, for they are merely gifts from God and come from His hand.

KEY VERSES

Job 5:17;
Psalms 1:1; 2:12;
144:15;
Proverbs 8:32;
Daniel 12:12

Hate

Hebrew expression: *sane'*
Pronunciation: *saw NAY'*
Strong's Number: *8130*

Modern medicine is ever more proactive in the promotion of a good diet, regular exercise, and an annual physical examination for a healthy cardiovascular system. Our study of the word "hate" prompts consideration of a similar "heart check-up" spiritually speaking. Such an examination is necessary because Jeremiah's declaration that the human heart as "desperately wicked" remains an appropriate "diagnosis" of our condition as fallen creatures (Jer. 17:9–10). For this reason, the law of Moses outlawed harboring hate in one's heart toward another and encouraged instead loving one's neighbor as the remedy for curing hatred (Lev. 19:17–18).

The verbal root *sn'* means "hate" in the sense of one who is an enemy. The word conveys a range of emotional responses, including: "hating," "detesting," "abhorring" something or someone; varying degrees of "disdain," "dislike"; or even "avoidance," "aversion." The term is sometimes used with its polar opposite, "love", as a poetic word pair (for example, Eccl. 3:8). The word "hate" may connote the attitude of the wicked who spurn the instruction of God (for example, Prov. 1:29) or those who are "unloved" in the sense of those rejected by God for unjust behavior (for example, Zech. 8:17).

There are forms of human hatred acceptable to God. For instance, the psalmist hated the assembly of evil doers and refused to associate with them (Ps. 26:5). Appropriately, the righteous "hate" those who worship idols (Ps. 31:6) and the works of those who have turned away from God, including: the double-minded (Ps. 119:113), liars (Ps. 119:163), and every false way (Ps. 119:104, 128). In fact, according to Hebrew wisdom tradition, "the fear of the Lord is to hate evil" (Prov. 8:13). Ultimately, the righteous "hate" or reject and avoid all who hate God with a "perfect hatred" (Ps. 139:21).

God's righteous hatred is grounded in His holiness and is sometimes expressed in terms of "jealousy" for His own name as the one true and living God (for example, Exod. 34:14; Josh. 24:19). God's hatred is directed against idolatry and idol worshipers, occultic activities and practitioners, those things destructive of persons made in his image, social injustice, and all that is false and insincere (Isa. 1:14; 61:8). The Old Testament reveals a God who both hates sin and the sinner (Ps. 5:5; Prov. 6:16), and yet does not delight in the death of anyone and desires that all sinners turn to Him and live (Ezek. 18:23, 32).

KEY VERSES

Leviticus 19:17;
Psalms 5:5; 97:10;
Proverbs 6:16;
Amos 5:15;
Malachi 1:3

The prophet Malachi uses the word "hate" in two distinct contexts. In the first, the Edomites are identified as a nation "hated" by God in contrast to the Israelites who are "loved" by God (Mal. 1:3). Here the issue is a theological one in that God rejected Esau because of his disdain for holy things (for example, his birthright; Gen. 25:34), whereas God "loved" Jacob in the sense of electing him to continue that covenant relationship established with Abraham (Mal. 1:2; compare Gen. 12:1–3). In the second, the prophet declares that God "hates" divorce because the dissolution of the marriage covenant is essentially an act of violence against a spouse (Mal. 2:16). God despises the disloyalty of broken marriage vows (compare Matt. 19:8).

Generally the Old Testament encourages separation from sin and evil and evil doers (for example, Lev. 20:26). At times, however, ancient Israel was called to act upon God's hatred of the wicked as His theocratic instrument of divine justice (whether against fellow Hebrews, Num. 15:32–36; or the idolatrous Gentiles, Num. 31). The instruction of the New Testament in response to hatred is one of non-violence and non-retaliation since vengeance belongs to God (Rom. 12:19; compare Ps. 94:1). Rather, the Christian is exhorted to overcome evil with good by loving one's enemies (Matt. 5:44; compare Rom. 12:21).

H

Heal

See also: *Heal, p. 300*
Hebrew expression: *rapha'*
Pronunciation: *raw FAW*
Strong's Number: *7495*

Moses cried out for the Lord to heal his sister from leprosy (Num. 12:13). He had good reason to do so. God had healed Abimelech after Abraham prayed for him (Gen. 20:17). And, the Lord declared to His people that He was not only their deliverer, but also their healer (Exod. 15:26). He had afflicted the Egyptians with diseases and pestilence, but He said that if His people would serve Him by doing what was pleasing to Him, keeping His commands and decrees, He would not put diseases upon them. The Hebrew word *rapha'* is consistently understood as "to heal." *Marpe'* is a noun formed from the same root of the verb meaning "healing, cure, or health" (Jer. 14:9).

The Lord wounded His people, but He also healed them (Deut. 32:39; Job 5:18). The prophet Jeremiah cried out that if the Lord would "heal," *rapha'*, him, he would indeed then be healed (Jer. 17:14). The psalmist noted that he had sinned against the Lord, but asked that he be healed (Ps. 41:4). The Lord answered those prayers. He also heals by His word (Ps. 107:20). And Isaiah noted that the way for Israel to be "healed" was to turn from her sin—then she would find "health" (Isa. 6:10). Jeremiah asks the question as to why the Lord had so afflicted His people that they could not be healed (Jer. 14:19). The Lord's answer is that He will restore His people (Jer. 30:17). God healed His people, their land (2 Chr. 7:14), and their wounds (Jer. 30:17). But most importantly, the Lord would heal the backsliding and waywardness of His people (Hos. 14:4). The Lord healed the Israelites spiritually, physically, and politically; in fact, He healed them in every area of need.

Isaiah revealed that the greatest healing instrument of the Lord would be God's suffering servant, the coming Messiah (Isa. 53:5). The Lord in Christ demonstrated His absolute ability to heal every kind of human illness, even death itself (Luke 5:15; 6:18, *iaomai* in Greek), simply by His word (Ps. 107:20; Luke 7:7). By Christ's wounds we are now healed (Jas. 5:16; 1 Pet. 2:24). Spiritual healing is available for all who believe in Jesus. He mends our broken hearts and showers us with love.

KEY VERSES

Genesis 20:17;
Exodus 15:26;
Ecclesiastes 3:3;
Jeremiah 17:14;
Isaiah 6:10

Hear

Hebrew expression: *shama'*
Pronunciation: *shaw MAH*
Strong's Number: *8085*

"Hear, Oh, Israel!" These are perhaps the most repeated words from the Old Testament. They introduce the *Shema*, the injunction of God through Moses to Israel, to love Him with all their heart, soul and strength (Deut. 6:4–5). What God wants in this injunction, however, is more than simply "hearing" the words spoken. He wants the one hearing to listen intently to what is said, understand it, and do it! The verb *shama'* can mean simply "to hear," or it can mean, according to context and according to what prepositions and words follow it, either "to listen, hearken," "to obey," or "to understand." Eli, the old priest in 1 Samuel 2:22, heard about the evil actions of his sons at the holy Tent of Meeting where they served as priests, but he did not act upon what he heard. He merely rebuked his sons, instead of removing them from their sacred positions—he paid his sons more honor than he did God! (1 Sam. 2:29). To really "hear God" means to obey what is spoken and heard or even read. Eli's sons "heard" (*shama'*) his rebuke, but they did not "listen" (*shama'*) to what he said; that is, they did not change their lives and obey God (1 Sam. 2:25).

Samuel, a young boy at the time, was told by Eli to answer God when He called by saying, "Speak, for your servant is listening" (1Sam. 8—10). Samuel listened and obeyed the word God gave to him. King Saul, however, did not fare as well. Through Samuel the Lord told Saul to "listen" (*shama'*) to His instructions about destroying the Amalakites (1 Sam. 15:1). Saul was told to destroy them, not sparing anyone or anything (1 Sam. 15:3). Saul did not "hear" the Lord in the sense of obeying His sacred command. But Samuel wasted no time telling Saul that his hearing was deficient! He did not "obey" (*shama'*) the voice (*qol*) of the Lord although he had heard God's Words (1 Sam. 15:19). Saul tried to satisfy the Lord with partial obedience. He offered the Lord sacrifices from the goods of the Amalakites which he had kept, but should have destroyed (1 Sam. 20—22). Using the word *shama'* as in "to obey the voice" of the Lord, Samuel condemned Saul's actions as rebellion and rejection of the Lord's word (1 Sam. 15:22–23). Because of this, Saul lost the kingship, and he himself admitted that he had obeyed, *shama'*, the voice of the people and not God (1 Sam. 5:24).

Hearing, listening, and understanding are all important, but God demands that we "obey" Him. In the New Testament, the one who had ears to hear, really heard (Mark 4:9). The author of Hebrews asserts that "today" is the time to "hear" the gospel and not harden one's heart against the Lord (Heb. 3:15). Hearing and, then, obeying is a difficult, but great responsibility—one which all believers should pursue out of true love and reverence for the Lord (Rev. 3:22).

KEY VERSES

1 Samuel 2:22–23; 3:10; 15:1, 4, 14, 19–20, 24

Heart

Hebrew expression: *leb*
Pronunciation: *LAYB*
Strong's Number: *3820*

Heart disease is one of the leading killers in today's world! This has been true throughout history and will probably continue to be so. A diseased heart is a major concern for the cardiologist. It was a diseased spiritual organ—the heart—that was the central concern of the inspired writers of the Old Testament.

Moses presented the Lord's desire for the human heart in Deuteronomy. Deuteronomy 6:4–5 appeals to us to love God with all of our heart (*leb*), soul, and strength. Yet, the Lord knew His people did not have the right heart to follow these instructions precisely (Deut. 5:29). Jeremiah emphasized how corrupt the human heart was (Jer. 17:9, 10). God, the healer of His people (Exod. 15:26), was the only One who could provide the solution to the dilemma of the human heart. The only solution was to circumcise His people's hearts (Deut. 30:6; Jer.4:4) and give them new hearts with His words written upon them (Ezek. 36:26; Jer. 31:33).

It is clear that the Bible is more concerned with the heart, as the location of moral, ethical and spiritual activity and attitudes than it is with the physical organ. In one sense, the heart is the center of a person's character in the Old Testament. Often the Hebrew word for "heart," *leb*, can be translated as "mind" as well as heart. *Lebab* is a synonym of *leb*, both words together occur 850 times in the Old Testament. The Old Testament authors do not focus on the physical heart. Instead, they speak of the spiritual heart—the heart that needs to be renewed and cleansed by God.

The book of Proverbs notes that the heart is the source of thoughts, words, action, and feeling—whether good or bad (Prov. 4:23). It was considered the source or "well-spring" (NIV) of life, and Jesus agreed completely with this Old Testament assessment (Mark 7:21). God knows, evaluates, tests, condemns or heals the heart (1 Sam. 16:7; Prov. 21:2; Jer. 12:3). The author of Proverbs encouraged his readers to bind their parents' teaching upon their hearts forever (Prov. 6:21), an exhortation that cries out for application today. In the new covenant of Jesus Christ, the commands of God are written upon our hearts (Heb. 8:10), as Jeremiah had anticipated.

KEY VERSES

Genesis 6:5;
Deuteronomy 5:29;
6:4–5;
1 Samuel 16:7;
Proverbs 2:10; 3:5

While Christians have the same physical hearts that others have, the Bible declares that our hearts are purified by faith in Christ (Acts 15:9)—therefore we are to walk in newness of life before God. Having a new spiritual heart, a new center of our character, is more important than having a healthy physical organ. It is the difference between eternal life and eternal death.

Heavens

Hebrew expression: *shamayim*
Pronunciation: *shaw MAH yihm*
Strong's Number: *8064*

Today, we think of the "heavens" as the vast space above and beyond the earth—the universe and its multitude of galaxies and stars. For thousands of years, this space has enthralled, challenged, and lured mankind to investigate it—and even to worship it. The Hebrew Bible uses the word *shamayim* to express the concept of "heavens." The word is plural and means "spatial expansion"—an expression that echoes the way modern astronomers describe the almost immeasurable stretch of space, sparsely populated with trillions of stars. This description also agrees with Genesis 1:8 where God calls the heavens, *raqia'*—a word meaning the "separation" or "expanse" (see Gen. 1:6–7).

H

The Bible depicts *shamayim* from several angles. First of all, "the heavens" are a creation of God, along with the earth. God made everything—the phrase "the heavens and the earth" is a *merismus*, a literary phrase indicating "everything" (Gen. 1:1; 14:19). As awesome as the heavens are, however, God is not contained in them or even in the highest heavens (2 Chr. 2:6). He overfills the heavens and the earth (Jer. 23:24). The heavens belong to Him (Deut. 10:14). Secondly, in a figurative sense, Scripture says that the heavens are God's dwelling place (1 Kgs. 8:30). In a symbolic sense, the heavens are His throne and the earth His footstool (Isa. 66:1). While mankind is awed by the heavens, God is high above them. He is not only God upon earth, but also the God of heaven (Gen. 24:3, 7; 1 Kgs. 8:39; Ps. 136:26; Isa. 66:1). Neither the King of Babylon, nor Satan himself, can assault God's throne in heaven successfully (Isa. 14:12, 13). Third of all, the heavens declare, in their orderliness and splendor, the glory of God in their own language (Ps. 19:1, 2–4).

Shamayim can also refer to the physical features of heaven that everyone can perceive. These features—such as the sun, moon, stars, clouds, rain, and all of the lights of heaven—regulate the seasons and provide light upon the earth (Gen. 1:14–19). The Lord can affect these objects in special ways to serve as special signs to His people (Ezek. 32:8; Joel 2:30–31).

The Lord has given His word about the current heavens. As awesome as they are, they will all disintegrate and disappear like smoke (Isa. 34:4; 51:6). Then, God will create a new *shamayim* and a new earth that will exist eternally for His people. The heavens may be studied and appreciated—but they shouldn't be worshiped. They do not contain the mystery of life as astrologers or some astronomers claim (Isa. 47:13)—God does (Exod. 32:32, 33). God is the One who inhabits the heavens and holds the secret of life. The heavens' greatness should remind us of how great God is. But even heaven's voice is inadequate to the task, for God is greater than anything we can imagine (Ps. 57:5, 11).

KEY VERSES

Genesis 1:1, 2:1;
Psalm 19:1–6;
1 Kings 8:27; 30;
Isaiah 65:17;
66:1, 22

High Place

Hebrew expression: *bamah*
Pronunciation: *bah MAWH*
Strong's Number: *1116*

In modern English, the phrase "high place" does not have any religious significance. But in the Old Testament, a "high place" or "high places" referred most often
to places of worship. In the early years of Israel's worship these *bamot*, "high
places," were used as places to worship the Lord. Samuel worshiped God (1 Sam.
9:12–25) at the high places and so did Saul (1 Sam. 10:14). The Hebrew word
bamah refers to: high ground, Canaanite burial sites, and especially "high places of
worship and religious significance." The word is used this way about eighty times
in the books of 1 and 2 Kings, and less often elsewhere. In these books, the plural
bamot is used to refer to "high places" where pagan worship and probably cultic
prostitution were carried out; they were not places to worship God.

Israel was taking over "high places" that the Canaanites had used when they
worshiped their pagan gods. The Canaanites had probably worshiped Baal there
and many other minor deities. Gibeon became known as the Great High Place,
because of all the pagan worship that took place at that location (1 Kgs. 3:4). The
Israelites, however, had been instructed to worship only at sites approved by the
Lord (Deut. 12:5). They were not to take over sites previously used by the pagans
(Deut. 7:5; 12:3); however, this slowly became more common. These preventive
instructions were not being followed even in the time of Solomon (970–930 B.C.)
and the improper use of *bamot* was vehemently condemned (2 Kgs. 17:7–18). Even
Solomon, prior to the building of God's Temple, burned incense in the high places
of pagan worship—but David had not (1 Kgs. 3:3). The presence of these high
places became a strong impetus for the construction of Solomon's Temple for the
Lord (1 Kgs. 3:2).

Israel's history, after the monarchy was founded, was permeated with references to this deadly worship at the high places—even after the Temple of the Lord
had been built (1 Kgs. 14:23; 2 Kgs. 16:4; 23:15). These pagan
religious practices and places of worship became a snare to
God's people in the Old Testament. Likewise, Christians should
avoid places of worship that are for any god other than the one
true God. Syncretism, the mixing of false religion with the true
religion of Christianity could be the result. God promised to
destroy these false religious shrines, and He did so (Jer. 17:3;
Lev. 26:30).

KEY VERSES

Deuteronomy 33:29;
1 Samuel 9:12;
2 Kings 12:3;
Jeremiah 17:3

Horn

Hebrew expression: *qeren*
Pronunciation: *QEH rehn*
Strong's Number: *7161*

When we think of a horn, we usually think of either a musical instrument or the horn of a ram, bull, or goat. These physical meanings are present in the Old Testament, but the use of the Hebrew noun *qeren*, which is translated as "horn," also has significant metaphorical meaning. The verb form *qaran* was formed from the noun which meant "to send out rays" (Exod. 34:29, 30, 35) or to "display or grow rays" (Ps. 69:32). In 1 Samuel, *qeren* is found twice in a figurative sense. The "horn" of Hannah is lifted up, referring to her dignity and self-respect as well as her strength because the Lord gave her the son she asked for (1 Sam. 2:1). In 1 Samuel 2:10, the horn of God's anointed one probably refers to the anointed king. It is the first reference in the Bible to the Lord's anointed, and horn here means the influence and strength of the anointed one.

The meaning of horn as strength, dignity, and influence is found often in the Old Testament, especially in the book of Psalms. David calls the Lord the "horn" or strength of his salvation (Ps. 18:3; 2 Sam. 22:3). In Psalm 22:21, the phrase "horns of the wild oxen" refers to the enemies of the psalmist from whom God will deliver him. So, "horns" came to refer to people as well as strength. The phrase "uplifted horns of animals" refers to the threatening actions of God's enemies against Him (Ps. 75:4, 5). And, the Lord cuts off the arrogant "horns" of the wicked (Ps. 75:10). *Qeren* also refers to Israel's king in Psalm 89:17, 25. The "horn" of the righteous man who fears God is exalted (Ps. 112:9). Finally, the phrase "horns of the altar" refers literally to the four horns on the altar, one at each corner. These horns stood for the strength and power of the Lord that was available to His people (Ps. 118:27).

With the Old Testament background outlined above, it is no surprise to hear Zechariah prophesy in poetry and song that the Lord has raised up a "horn of salvation" for His people referring to Jesus Christ (Luke 1:69). Satan also raised up horns to oppose the horn of God's anointed in both the Old and New Testament (Dan. 7:8, 11; Rev. 13:11). But, it is the horns of the golden altar in heaven which proclaim that God's Word will prevail. Our strength lies in the strength of Jesus Christ. We do not need to search for another source of power or deliverance because He is enough.

KEY VERSES

2 Samuel 22:3;
Psalms 22:21;
89:24; 148:14

Hosts

Hebrew expression: *sabba'ot*
Pronunciation: *tsaw baw 'OHT*
Strong's Number: *6635*

When the Hebrew word for "hosts" is used in Scripture, it doesn't refer to those who greet guests, serve as an emcee on a talk show, manage an inn, or furnish the facilities for a function. The Hebrew word for "hosts" in the Old Testament refers to the concept of an army or a great multitude of people.

The word "hosts" in the Old Testament is nearly always the translation given to the word *sabbaot*. This is the plural form of *saba'* meaning in general "army," "war," "warfare," and "hosts." The noun itself is based upon the verb *saba'*, "to wage war," and "to serve." In modern Hebrew, this noun is used to describe Israel's "army," *saba'*. The meaning "hosts," however, is the meaning most often used for the plural form, *sabba'ot*. The Lord is called Lord of *sabba'ot*, "Lord of hosts," about three hundred times in the Old Testament. This expression is found especially often in Isaiah, Jeremiah, Zechariah, and Malachi.

The phrase is translated "Lord Almighty" about 290 times in the New International Version. In the New American Standard Bible, the phrase "Lord of hosts" is preferred (over 300 times). The New Living Translation prefers Lord Almighty. Either translation is acceptable. Why? The expression is first used at the Shiloh sanctuary in the Old Testament (1 Sam. 1:3). It means first of all God's sovereignty and generalship over the armies of Israel. David went against Goliath in the name of the Lord of hosts, probably implying in the name of the army of Israel (1 Sam. 17:45; 2 Sam. 6:18). But the use of hosts (*sabba'ot*) with the Lord's name also clearly implied His command over all the hosts of heaven as well; He exercised a clear relationship to them, meaning the angelic hosts. This name was, then, not limited to the hosts of Israel's armies, but came to comprise all the heavenly powers at the Lord's command (Ps. 46:7, 11). Even in the days of Elisha, the Lord had opened the prophet's eyes to see the horses and "chariots of fire" at the Lord's command to fight for Israel (2 Kgs. 6:16–17). Since the Lord commands armies both human and divine, He is the Lord Almighty, in charge of all armed forces in heaven and on earth, spiritual and physical.

KEY VERSES

1 Samuel 1:3;
Psalm 24:10;
Isaiah 6:3; 10:16;
Jeremiah 32:18;
Malachi 1:14

Isaiah had no doubt that the Lord could and would fulfill His word, for the Lord of hosts (Almighty) had said He would do so (Isa. 14:27). His name, the Lord Almighty, guaranteed the execution of His prophetic word for God's people. This same assurance is, of course, available to God's people today. The divine forces of heaven are under God's command to serve Him and His people. The New Testament authors recognized this, describing God as the *pantokrator*, the Ruler over all (2 Cor. 6:18; Rev. 11:17; 16:7; 19:6).

House

Hebrew expression: *bayit*
Pronunciation: *BAH yiht*
Strong's Number: *1004*

Shelter providing protection from the elements is basic to human existence. The affluence of North American society has encouraged not only designer fashions but also custom homebuilding. The name and reputation of the builder in large measure determines the quality of the house constructed. The same is true in the Old Testament, as the psalmist understood: "Unless the Lord builds the house, they labor in vain who build it" (Ps. 127:1). For the Hebrews, the trademark of this divine builder was the very law of God written on the doorposts of the house, later embodied in the tradition of the mezuzah in Judaism (Deut. 6:9).

The Hebrew word for "house" is derived from a root that means "to spend the night" or "take shelter for a night." The term may refer to a family dwelling, often a single room structure for both people and animals (Judg. 11:31). At times the Hebrew word for "house" indicates a larger structure like a palace or Temple (1 Sam. 5:2; Jer. 39:8) or some portion of a larger multi-roomed building (2 Kgs. 23:7). The psalmist "loved the house" (or Temple) where God lives and blessed those who had the privilege of serving in the Temple (the priests and Levites, Pss. 26:7; 27:4; 84:4, 10).

The word "house" in the Old Testament may have the extended meaning of "family" or "household" (Gen. 7:1), or even "paternal family" (Gen. 24:38; Exod. 6:5). When modified in phrases, the word takes on special connotations—"Pharaoh's house" (the Egyptian royal palace or Pharaoh's court, Gen. 45:16), the "house of David" (the "dynasty" of David, 2 Sam. 7:16), or the Hebrew people ("house of Israel," Jer. 2:4). In a few unusual contexts, the word is a metaphor depicting a "container" of some kind (an "eternal home" is a grave, Job 17:13; Eccl. 12:5; Isa. 3:20).

Theologically, a house as a permanent structure or dwelling symbolizes safety, security, and stability in contrast to the more "unsettled" life of pastoral nomad living in a tent (Isa. 65:21; Ezek. 28:26). The Temple as the "house of God" was symbolic of the Lord's presence in the midst of His people, explaining Haggai's call to rebuild the Temple after the exile (Hag. 2:3, 7, 9; Zech. 1:16). Eventually, the Hebrews came to understand the structure of the Temple as a guarantee of God's presence and blessing, hence the prophet Jeremiah's oracle against trusting in a building instead of God himself (Jer. 7:4). This misunderstanding of the relationship between the reality of God's presence and the Temple as the symbolic representation of that presence prompted the elaborate vision of Ezekiel describing the "mobility" of the Lord's presence in view of the impending Babylonian exile (Ezek. 1:15ff).

The New Testament counterpart for the word "house" is used in much the same way. Of special interest to the Christian

KEY VERSES

Deuteronomy 28:30;
Nehemiah 13:11;
Psalm 127:1;
Proverbs 12:7

is the association of the term "house" with the church, whether the local church (Gal. 6:10) or the church universal as the body of Christ (Eph. 2:19; 1 Pet. 4:17). The household imagery applied to the church is an encouraging reminder that individual Christians are members of the family of God and that the church is both a fellowship and a haven—our "home" in this fallen world. A second concept of great significance is Jesus' reference to the many rooms in His Father's house being prepared for each believer in Christ (John 14:2). Here the emphasis is on the experience of God's presence and eternal fellowship with Christ as the ultimate destination for believers.

Idols

See also: *Idolatry, p. 307 and Idol sacrifices, p. 308*
Hebrew expression: *gillulim*
Pronunciation: *gih loo LEEM*
Strong's Number: *1544*

Worshiping idols was a major temptation for the ancient Israelites. That is the reason God allowed the Babylonians to destroy Jerusalem in 586 B.C. and take the Israelites into exile for seventy years. The prophets, especially Isaiah, railed against the pagan religious practice of making an idol out of wood, covering it with gold, and bowing down to worship it (Isa. 40—66). These idols could, however, also be made of stone and silver. Whatever they were made of, they were useless and detestable because they distracted people from the worship of the true God. Moses and other earlier writers had condemned worshiping idols as well (Deut. 29:17; 1 Kgs. 21:26; 2 Kgs. 23:24).

The prophet Ezekiel, who followed his fellow Israelites in 597 B.C. into exile, warned the exiles of the danger of worshiping idols. The Hebrew word *gillulim* is first used in Ezekiel 6:4 in a threatening prophecy, in which God declares that He will slay the people of Jerusalem and Judah in the very presence of their "idols." The word *gillulim* is used about forty times in Ezekiel. It is a derisive, almost lewd term. It comes from the root of *galal*, "to roll" or "to roll away," and literally means "dung pellets," or "dungy things." The prophets wasted no time seeking words to express their disgust of idols. "Idols" is a rather euphemistic translation of this word, for the word expresses Ezekiel's hatred and disgust for Israel's idols. They were worth no more than dung—yet Israel was worshiping *them* instead of their living God.

Paul encouraged believers to pity people who still sought worthless objects of wood and stone to worship and venerate. Paul was disheartened by the idolatry of the great pagan city of Athens (Acts 15:29; 17:16). These intelligent people of Paul's time were foolishly worshiping worthless, inanimate objects—objects that held no power over their lives. Anything that we venerate and serve—whether it is a career or money, some pleasure or a religious figurine—is an idol. It is something that distracts from the genuine worship of the true God. The Bible encourages us to guard our hearts from venerating anything but God Himself and serving Him with our whole heart (1 John 5:21; Rev. 9:20).

KEY VERSES

2 Kings 17:12;
Ezekiel 6:4–6, 9, 13;
20:7–8, 16, 18, 24,
31, 39

Image

See also: *Image, p. 309*
Hebrew expression: *pesel*
Pronunciation: *PEH sehl*
Strong's Number: *6459*

Throughout the Old Testament, the Israelites fell into idolatry again and again. The Israelites were in a habit of turning from the Lord to worship idols and images of other gods. They corrupted their own understanding of God by setting up an "image," supposedly representing the Lord, and worshiping it. In English translations of the Bible, more than eight words are rendered "idol" or "image." One of those words, *pesel* is found thirty-one times in the Old Testament, although the closely related word *pasil*, using the same root meaning is found another twenty-three times. *Pesel* can be rendered "idol or image" (Hab. 2:18–19, KJV, NLT, NIV), and was often carved out of wood or metal (Hab. 2:18–19; Judg. 17:3, 4). The verb *pasal* means "to hew, or to hew into shape." Moses "hewed out" two stone tablets (Exod. 34:1, 4; Deut. 10:1, 3). The verb was used to describe the "hewing out" of building stones (1 Kgs. 5:18). Generally one could say that an idol is the image of a god which was used as an object or focal point of worship.

The *pesel* was made in the likeness of animals or even people. God specifically forbade the use of these images for that purpose (Exod. 20:4; Deut. 5:8). Such an image neither represented His character nor His essence properly, and it confused the worshiper. This most serious spiritual problem arose for Isaiah who asserted that some even trust in idols, instead of the living God (Isa. 42:17). The worship of an image or idol was so ludicrous that God mocked with pathetic humor the Babylonians' practices and the practices of His rebellious people when they worshiped these lifeless things (Isa. 40:20; 41:7; Hab. 2:18). In Isaiah 44:10, He cast humor at the craftsman who "shapes a god and forms an idol!" The craftsmen and goldsmiths are ultimately shamed by their own idols because the idols have no life or power (Jer. 10:14; 51:17).

KEY VERSES

Exodus 20:4;
Isaiah 40:19; 42:17;
Jeremiah 10:14

Early Christians were not challenged to worship idols, but they were confused for a while about whether they could or could not eat food sacrificed to or prepared for the idols. Paul's polemic against these "false gods" was clear—the idols (*eidolon* in Greek) are nothing! (1 Cor. 8:4, 7). But, he warned to stay away from them because of what lay behind them, namely, demons (1 Cor. 10:18–22). The New Testament confirms the dangers of using images to worship God and especially the possibility of spiritual intercourse with evil spirits through their use (1 Cor. 12:2; 2 Cor. 6:16). Christians were recognized as those people who had turned from any form of idolatry to serve the living God (1 Thess. 1:9).

Inheritance

See also: *Inherit, p. 311*
Hebrew expression: *nachalah*
Pronunciation: *nah khah LAWH*
Strong's Number: *5159*

In Moses' masterpiece, "The Song of The Sea," he celebrates the victory of the Lord over Pharaoh and the deliverance of Israel from Egypt. Moses asserts that God will now take them to the mountain of His "inheritance"—to Jerusalem and the Promised Land (Exod. 15:17; 1 Sam. 26:19; Ps. 79:1). The books of Numbers, Deuteronomy and especially Joshua use the Hebrew word *nachalah*, "inheritance," many times. *Nachalah* can also be translated as "possession," "heritage," or "property." The verb *nachal* which means "to get or take as an inheritance" is formed from the noun. The Promised Land was promised to Abraham and his descendants in Genesis 15:15–21, and *nachalah* was used to describe this promised inheritance in Genesis 48:6. The promised *nachalah* was to be given to the Israelite tribes according to their size (Num. 26:52–53). Only the Levites and Priests had no share in the land itself, for their share was their ministry before the Lord in the Sanctuary (Num. 18:20).

The Lord made the nation of Israel the designated people of His special inheritance (Deut. 4:20). Moses appealed to this fact to pray for their preservation when God threatened to destroy them because of disobedience (Deut. 9:26, 29). Moses pleaded that surely God would not destroy His own inheritance! In the book of Joshua "inheritance" is found in 43 separate verses, for Joshua is the "book of inheritance" for Israel. In the time of Joshua the Israelites received the Promised Land. Joshua took the land and assigned the allotted portion to each tribe (Josh. 11:23). Even the land not yet conquered was assigned for future possession (Josh. 23:4–5). Then, Joshua was buried in the land he inherited (Josh. 24:29–30). Even Joseph's bones were buried at Shechem, which was his inherited land (Gen. 50:25; Exod. 13:19; Josh. 24:32). God kept His promises to Israel concerning their promised inheritance (Josh. 21:43–45). Even after His people rebelled and He had removed them from the land, He gave the land back as an inheritance to the remnant that He had preserved (Zech. 8:12–13).

Christ is the fulfillment of God's promises and He said He would make the nations His Son's inheritance (Ps. 2:7–8; Matt. 25:31–33). Through Jesus, believers will receive an eternal inheritance (*kleronomein* in Greek) (Matt. 25:34; Heb. 9:15). The promise of the land of Canaan is replaced with the promise of the Kingdom of God. God will fulfill all the promises to His people again just as He did for Israel in the Old Testament. The Holy Spirit is given to us as a guarantee of this inheritance in Christ (Eph. 1:14), which will never fade or grow old (1 Pet. 1:4).

KEY VERSES

Genesis 48:6;
Exodus 15:17;
Numbers 26:53;
Joshua 11:23;
24:30, 32

Instruction

Hebrew expression: *musar*
Pronunciation: *moo SAWR*
Strong's Number: *4148*

Is instruction and discipline an important issue for God's people? According to the Old Testament, it is a part of being a wise and pleasing person before the Lord and other people. The word *musar* is translated often as "discipline" or "instruction" (NIV, NLT, KJV, NASB). The word is formed from the root of *yasar* meaning "to discipline, admonish, instruct or chasten." The Hebrew word *yissor* means "one who reproves or disciplines" (Job 40:2).

The Israelites were disciplined (*musar*) in Egypt and during their experiences in the Sinai desert (Deut. 11:2). The psalmist asserts that the guilty or wicked person refuses, even hates, the *musar*, instruction or discipline, of the Lord. He, in fact, casts the words of the Lord behind him (Ps. 50:16–17). The author of Proverbs identifies one of the purposes of his book as helping a person attain wisdom and discipline (*musar*, Prov. 1:2). He is quick to note that the fool, on the other hand, despises wisdom and discipline (Prov. 1:7). The book of Proverbs invites every person into the "school of wisdom" and requires each person who would enter to get discipline, even to focus oneself on instruction and discipline (Prov. 23:12).

Again the author observes that the evil person dies for lack of discipline or instruction (compare NIV, KJV). The New Living Translation says the evil man is kept captive by his sins because of a lack of "self-control" (*musar*). Children are urged to accept the discipline of their parents (Prov. 13:1). Unfortunately, the fool appears to be the' one who resists *musar* most vehemently. According to the author of Proverbs, it is folly to try to discipline or instruct a fool (Prov. 16:22).

Discipline can become "chastisement" in more severe circumstances (Prov. 3:11, KJV). Chastisement can even become punishment (*musar*), as in the case of the Suffering Servant of Isaiah, whose chastisement or suffering brought us peace (Isa. 53:5). Tough, stern, or severe discipline awaits the one who abandons the correct path (Prov. 15:10).

KEY VERSES

Deuteronomy 11:2;
Proverbs 1:2, 7;
6:23; 10:17

It is clear from the Old Testament that God's people are to be disciplined and well instructed; when necessary they become a chastised and even "punished" people. But the Lord's goal is always the improvement of His people, not their destruction. God's instruction and discipline continues today for Christians. It may come through prophecy (1 Cor. 14:6, 26), the scriptures (Gal. 6:6), community nurturing (Eph. 6:4), or some other way, but it does come. Hardships are often discipline and instruction from the Lord (Heb. 12:5, 7, 11; Rev. 3:19).

Interpretation

Aramaic expression: *peshar*
Pronunciation: *peh SHAHR*
Strong's Number: *6591*

Egyptian writing in ancient hieroglyphs had been around for centuries, but was a mystery until someone could interpret the language. Between 1814 and 1822, Jean Francois Champollion, a brilliant young French scholar, discovered the proper interpretation of the ancient Egyptian hieroglyphs. Not only languages, but also life itself needs a proper "interpretation." Interpretations are hard to come by, especially when there is a need to interpret messages from God. The God-inspired authors of Scripture are "interpreters" of both the great acts of God in history and God's Words. God, for example, used Daniel as an interpreter to deliver His message to the kings of Babylon.

The Aramaic word *peshar* occurs thirty-three times in the Old Testament—but only in the book of Daniel's Aramaic sections (Dan. 7:4–28). *Peshar* means "interpretation" or "explanation" and comes from the verb *peshar*, "to interpret." It is used twenty-three times in Daniel 2 where there is a desperate search to find an interpretation of Nebuchadnezzar's dream (Dan. 2:45). *Peshar* is also used in Daniel 4 to describe the need for an interpretation of Nebuchadnezzar's dream of a great tree. It is used in Daniel 5 to describe the interpretation needed to decipher the handwriting on the wall (Dan. 5:12). And, in Daniel 7, it describes the interpretation given to Daniel by an angelic being concerning Daniel's dream (Dan. 7:16). In every situation, an interpretation comes through or to Daniel, but each time it is God who ultimately makes the interpretation possible. In the first case, God revealed the interpretation of the King's dream to Daniel in a vision (Dan. 2:19, 28, 45). In the second case, even the pagan King recognized that a divine Spirit was in Daniel helping him (Dan. 4:8, 18, 24). In chapter five, Daniel interpreted the handwriting on the wall because God gave him the ability to decipher languages (Dan. 1:17). When Daniel was unable to interpret his own dream about the flow of history and the Kingdom of God, God sent him an angelic interpreter.

God is the ultimate interpreter of His actions and words in history. Only He can give an accurate and certain rendering of His own mind and plans. Believers today are called to interpret the gospel to the world, much as Daniel was called to reveal God's plans to King Nebuchadnezzar, Belshazzar and his own people. By making sense of the gospel and sharing Christ's message with others, the world will know and have a sure interpretation of God's intentions and goals for all people.

KEY VERSES

Daniel 2:45; 5:12; 7:16

Jealous

Hebrew expression: *qanno'*
Pronunciation: *qah NOH'*
Strong's Number: *7072*

Jonah announced the destruction of Nineveh, but the city repented. The Lord, for a while, turned from His threats to destroy the city (Jonah 3:10). Nineveh, however, returned to her old ways and destroyed Samaria, taking northern Israel into exile in 722 B.C. (2 Kgs. 17). The Lord was "jealous" for His people and destroyed this mighty Assyrian capital through the Babylonians. The city of Nineveh fell in 612 B.C. (Nah. 2:1).

The prophet Nahum comforted the people of Israel by announcing the vengeance of the Lord upon Nineveh (Nah. 1:2). He began his message by declaring that the Lord is a *qanno'* God, a "jealous" God. This adjective is used to describe only God; it is formed from a root *qn'* meaning "intensity," and the verb *qana'*, "to be jealous or zealous." A synonym of *qanno'* is *qanna'* and means "jealous or zealous." Moses, at Mount Sinai, declared the jealousy and zeal of the Lord (Exod. 20:5). God declared that He alone was to be Israel's God. Later, Joshua made it clear to the people that they could not worship the Lord and the strange gods of Canaan or Egypt, for the Lord was a "jealous" God, or "zealous for His Name" (Josh. 24:19). His very Name is *qanna'*, meaning "Jealous," a synonym of *qanno'* (Exod. 34:14). The zealousness of God is that of a Creator and Redeemer who is intensely set on caring for, protecting, and, if necessary, avenging Himself upon the enemies of His people. He has a unique godly jealousy (2 Cor. 11:2). If the Lord burns with jealousy for His people, He is set on protecting them and His holy character of love. But, if His people are unfaithful to Him, God's jealousy and zeal for His character will cause Him to judge them. His anger will burn against those who defy Him or His people (Deut. 6:15). By serving false gods, Israel made the Lord jealous for His own reputation (Deut. 32:16, 21). His holiness parallels His jealous character. It was with a message of avenging wrath that Nahum announced the coming vengeance of the Lord. God was not only jealous for His destroyed people, but ultimately for His own Name's sake as well.

As Christians, we live under the grace of God. God does not change. He is still a jealous God. He wants our total allegiance and even more so now, since we are comforted with His sacrifice of His own Son on our behalf. Paul is our example, for he was jealous for his Christian brothers and sisters at Corinth with a "godly jealousy"—a jealousy that was ultimately for their benefit, not his (2 Cor. 11:2).

KEY VERSES

Exodus 20:5; 34:14;
Deuteronomy 4:24;
6:15;
Joshua 24:19;
Nahum 1:2

Jews

Hebrew expression: *yehudi*
Pronunciation: *yeh h<u>oo</u> DEE*
Strong's Number: *3064*

"I'm proud to be an American!" This is a common cliché, but one that expresses a truth that is a reality for millions of people. Who or what is an American? Many good descriptions could be given. But probably no ethnic term or term of nationality is better known than the term "Jew." *To Be A Jew* is the title of an important book you will find in the Judaic section of the library or large bookstores.

The Hebrew word *yehudi*, in the singular, is translated as "Jew." The term is formed from the name of the land inhabited by the tribe of Judah, *yehudah*. In the biblical use of *yehudi* it refers to the people of Judah, Southern Israel, both before and after they went into exile in Babylon (2 Kgs. 16:6; 25:25; Neh. 13:23). Judah rose in importance after Northern Israel was taken into captivity (2 Kgs. 17). It was then that the inhabitants of Judah were known as *yehudim*, "Jews."

The Judeans, or Jews, were identified with Jerusalem and when they returned from exile, they rebuilt Jerusalem to renew their identity (Ezra 4:12; 6:15). They believed that the Lord had given them the land and the city to reclaim. Even Cyrus, the Persian King, asserts that the Lord was the God who was in Jerusalem (Ezra 1:3), but He was the God of Heaven as well (Ezra 1:2). The Jews also possessed a unique set of laws, the Law God gave them at Mount Sinai which they were to pursue diligently (Ezra 3:2; 7:6). They were chosen by the Lord, Yahweh, as His "holy seed" (Ezra 9:2). They committed themselves to worship and to serve God. Haman, during the time of the Persian Empire, tried to kill all of them (Esth. 3:5–11). Daniel, a Jew, was attacked because he refused to change his religious practices. He was willing to die before he would disobey the Lord (Dan. 6:10–12, 23). There was also a fear among some of the Jews' enemies that they were indestructible (Esth. 6:13–14). Daniel was shown that God would overcome their enemies, and he prayed for God's mercy on the rebellious Jewish nation (Dan. 7:27; 9:17–19).

In the New Testament, Paul maintains that the Jews—a term he used for all Israelites—were entrusted with the revelation of God that was being realized through Christ (Rom. 3:1–3, 22, 31). The Jews were a privileged people. In Jesus, a Jew, all of the promises of God found their fulfillment. The significance of the Jews cannot be stressed too much, for through them God worked to redeem mankind. The promises to the Jews have been made available to Gentiles through Christ.

KEY VERSES

Nehemiah 4:2;
Esther 8:7

Joy

See also: *Joy, p. 314*
Hebrew expression: *simchah*
Pronunciation: *sim HAWH*
Strong's Number: *8057*

In modern Judaism, one often hears the praise of the *simchat torah,* "the joy of the Law!" Joy is a mark of God's people, both in the New and Old Testament. *Simchah* in Hebrew means "joy." Some scholars suggest that only the word *simchah,* the verb *samach,* meaning "to rejoice, be glad," and *gil* in its verb and noun forms, "to rejoice" and "rejoicing," fit the central idea behind the English word "joy." Although there are ten other words translated as "joy" in different Bible translations, this study will focus only on *simchah* and *samach*: the noun *simchah* contains the root from which the verb *samach* comes. *Simchah* was the purpose of the feasts and festivals of Israel; they fostered the joy of God's people, which the Lord wanted to be complete (Deut. 16:15). Whenever Israel worshiped before the Lord and wherever He directed the Israelites to worship, they were to rejoice constantly (Deut. 12:7, 12, 18), even when paying tithes (Deut. 14:26).

The source of Israel's joy was the Lord Himself along with His words and deeds performed on behalf of His people (Pss. 4:7; 16:11). The Lord gave joy to His chosen king through His presence (Ps. 21:6). Only the Lord could remove the sackcloth of mourning and clothe the king with *simchah* instead. "Joy" is one of the favorite words of the book of Psalms. The Lord, deserving of praise, was the psalmist's joy (Ps. 43:4); and the person who was upright in heart enjoyed the *simchah* of the Lord (Ps. 97:12). The joy of the Lord was God's goal for His people, and they were to find in Him the subject, the source, and the object of their joy. God's people were never supposed to find their joy in anything that in any way opposed the Lord. In the New Testament, the theme of the joy of the Lord continues even more strongly. The one who finds the kingdom of heaven "joyfully" sells all that he or she owns in order to obtain it (Matt. 13:44). The joy of Jesus' followers was a joy that superseded fear (Matt. 28:8). With Jesus in heaven, there will be no more suffering, as prophesized by Isaiah when he talks of a restored people of God, entering into Zion with a crown of everlasting joy (Isa. 35:10; 55:12). The inexpressible joy of believers is possible because even in the absence of the Lord, we know that we have received the salvation of our souls (1 Pet. 1:9).

KEY VERSES

Psalms 4:7; 16:11;
21:6; 43:4;
Isaiah 35:10

Jubilee

Hebrew expression: *yobel*
Pronunciation: *yoh BAYL*
Strong's Number: *3104*

Jubilee is a title assigned to the Year of Jubilee in Leviticus. *Yobel*, which means "trumpet," is translated as "jubilee" twenty times out of its twenty-seven uses in the New International Version, which is representative of other translations as well. *Yobel* literally means "a ram's horn," but the blowing of a ram's horn was so common as an introduction on special days of feasts and festivals that the term itself came to describe the joyous times and festivities it was signaling. This is especially true of the Year of Jubilee, a year of freedom, joy, and festivity that occurred every fiftieth year.

The Jubilee Year was announced by the blowing of the *shophar*, "trumpet," on the tenth day of the seventh month (Lev. 25:9), the beginning of Israel's civil year and the close of the Day of Atonement (Lev. 23:24). Each fiftieth New Year was consecrated, holy, for Israel (Lev. 25:8–13). This was an amazing year established in Israel by the Lord. During this year, people could return to the property the Lord had allotted to them; if they were in debt, their debts were canceled. Israelites who had been sold into slavery for various reasons were freed (Lev. 25:39–43), redeemed by the Lord. The Lord so blessed this year as a time of "renewal" and "festivity and hope" for His people that He commanded them not to plow and sow the land. The Jubilee Year came right after the Sabbath Year during which the land had lain fallow. But, God promised to so bless the produce of the year proceeding the Sabbath Year that there would be enough food and produce to carry over the Sabbath Year and the Year of Jubilee. The people also ate what grew from the fields naturally. In this way, the Lord protected the rights of His people and secured the preservation of family units. Israelites who had been forced to sell property because they could not pay their debts received the property back in the year of Jubilee (Lev. 25:28). This year was an unparalleled structure of social righteousness, not found among any other ancient Near Eastern nation. Because the Israelites were His people, God saw to it that each Israelite was treated fairly and not oppressed (Lev. 25:43, 53).

This amazing pattern of social justice concerning property and human rights is one that needs to inform God's people in principle today. Amos made it clear that any social oppression of the poor, the widow, the orphan, the oppressed in general, was a clear mark that God's people were not God's people (Amos 5:10–12, 24). God's proclamation of freedom for His people is not only freedom from sin, but also challenges believers to seek social justice for those oppressed by the powerful (Luke 7:22–23).

KEY VERSES

Exodus 19:13;
Leviticus 25:10–13,
15, 28, 30–31, 33,
40, 50, 54

Judge

Hebrew expression: *shopet*
Pronunciation: *shaw FAHT*
Strong's Number: *8199*

Someone who reads the title of the book of Judges will probably be quite surprised to find that the "judges" of Israel were different from our modern-day judges. The Hebrew noun *shopet*, which means "judge," comes from the verbal root *shapat*, which means "to judge," "to execute judgment, govern, or vindicate." So the *shopet* in ancient Israel was one who did all of these things.

Deborah, one of the most revered judges, delivered Israel from the Canaanite oppression of Jabin the King and Sisera his commander (Judg. 4—5). The judges of the book of Judges would perhaps be better named as "deliverers." They were the ones who were called by God to save the repentant Israelites from oppression. They did not sit behind desks and render verdicts, but carried out God's instructions when He called them. They "executed judgment" upon enemies who had oppressed Israel.

The story of Othniel is a good example of the cycle of history that Israel fell into during the time of the judges. Israel sinned and worshiped other gods, so the Lord gave them into the hands of their enemies to punish them. They repented of their sins and God raised up Othniel as their deliverer. The Spirit of God helped him and he took his place as Israel's judge, going to war with and defeating Cushan-Rishathaim of the land of Aram. God gave Othniel victory and the land had rest for forty years. This whole cycle is found in Judges 3:7–11 and is repeated under the judges Ehud, Deborah, Gideon, Tola, Jephthah and Samson.

The Judge of all the earth was, is, and will be the Lord (Gen. 18:25). He is a righteous Judge who judges His people as well as their enemies (Pss. 7:8; 9:8). He is appropriately termed "the Judge" in Judges 11:27. His standard of judgment is righteousness, not an outdated law code of mankind. His character is the standard of righteousness (Pss. 9:8,16). He judges by His ability to know the thoughts and intents of the human race (Isa. 11:3; Jer. 11:10). He is the judge for believers as well as non-believers (Isa. 33:22). Christians are charged, however, not to judge (Matt. 7:1), for God has now given all judgment into the hands of His dear Son (John 5:27). He will judge the world with justice (Acts 17:31)—and Christians must remember that the Judge, our Judge, is coming again (Jas. 5:9). We must therefore honor Him in all that we do, showing our love by following His commands.

KEY VERSES

Genesis 18:25;
Exodus 2:14;
Judges 2:18; 11:27

Justice

See also: *Justification, justify, p. 315*
Hebrew expression: *mishpat*
Pronunciation: *mish PAWT*
Strong's Number: *4941*

No society or nation can survive long without justice. The Hebrew word *mishpat* is frequently translated as "justice" (Amos 5:24, NIV, NLT, NJPS). The King James Version favors "judgment," but it must be thought of as "judgment that delivers" and is not soiled or slanted for any particular party. The noun *mishpat* is formed from the verbal root of *shapat* meaning "to settle," "to judge," "to render justice," or "to decide," depending upon its context. It can also be rendered as "justice," "law(s)," "judgment," "legal case," or "lawsuit." Micah and especially Isaiah were prophets who carried the message of God's call for justice to His people. Isaiah cried out to the Israelites to seek justice, lift up, and encourage the oppressed (Isa. 1:17, 23, 27). The Lord looked in His city, Jerusalem, looking for justice, but found oppression and violence instead.

The prophet Amos was concerned for the disadvantaged people of a wealthy, hierarchical society rich in luxuries, but all at the expense of the poor, the oppressed, the widows and orphans. Amos observed the lack of justice in the courts for the poor and oppressed (Amos 2:7; 5:12). Justice had become so corrupted that he called it poison, a poison that was destroying God's people (Amos 5:7; 6:12). God through Amos said, "But let judgment run down as water and righteousness as a mighty stream" (Amos 5:24, KJV; NIV, NLT, NJPS). The Lord is just, the ultimate judge of all people; He will eventually bring justice to the nations (Isa. 51:5). In fact, the Lord Almighty will be exalted by His justice (Isa. 5:16) and He loves *mishpat* (Isa. 61:8).

Jesus, the Lord's chosen Servant, will proclaim justice to the nations—just as God did in the Old Testament (Matt. 12:18). Through Christ, God has demonstrated His justice towards the entire world (Rom. 3:25). When the Lord comes again, He will bring both just judgment and just war (Acts 17:31; Rev. 19:11).

KEY VERSES

Exodus 23:6;
1 Kings 7:7;
Psalms 9:16;
99:4; 140:12;
Amos 5:7, 15, 24;
6:12

Keep

Hebrew expression: *shamar*
Pronunciation: *shaw MAHR*
Strong's Number: *8104*

"Keep the faith" is an expression that has become famous in the English language. It means to maintain the cause, the goals, and the purposes of a belief or a cause. "The faith" was nothing less than the instructions accompanying the covenant that God made with Israel at Mount Sinai and with Abraham, King David and the prophets. The Hebrew verb *shamar* means "to keep," but it is also translated in overlapping and similar ways: to care for, be careful, obey, guard, watch, or observe. *Shamar* is used by the Lord when He commands Adam to "take care of" the Garden of Eden (Gen. 2:15) or Eleazar "to guard" the ark of the Lord (1 Sam. 7:1). It can simply mean to keep food, that is, store it or other material objects (Gen. 41:35). In the Old Testament, "keep" is used in important religious, moral, ethical, and spiritual ways as well. God continually rescued Israel from all kinds of difficult and threatening situations. Festivals and feasts were then set up to commemorate these great acts of God. *Shamar* is used to indicate that Israel was "to keep," that is, observe and celebrate these great deeds of God for His people. For example, the Israelites were "to keep" watch on the night of the Passover to remember God's great salvation for them from Egypt (Exod. 12:42; 13:10). They were instructed "to keep" the covenants the Lord made with them (Exod. 19:5) and the commandments and stipulations in those covenants (Exod. 20:6; Lev. 18:5). If God's people did this, the High Priest prayed that the Lord would, therefore, bless and "keep," *shamar,* His people (Num. 6:24). This last use of the word means "to watch over, to protect, or to keep safe." Sadly, Israel and eventually Judah did not observe and keep the Holy Laws of the Lord (2 3. 17:13–20).

The new covenant of God with His people through Christ is to "be kept" (*heortazo* in Greek) in sincerity and love (1 Cor. 5:8). Believers are to "keep" (*tereo* in Greek) themselves in God's love until He comes again (Jude 1:21). Paul points out that the leaders of God's people today are responsible to "keep watch" (*prosecho* in Greek) over themselves and God's flock, helping all to not go astray (Acts 20:28). By pursuing the virtues of the Christian life and following God's Word, we will keep ourselves from becoming ineffective in our daily lives, enabling us to be successful and beneficial to the Kingdom of God (2 Pet. 1:8).

KEY VERSES

Genesis 2:15;
Exodus 13:10;
Leviticus 18:5;
2 Kings 17:13, 19

King

See also: *King, p. 316*
Hebrew expression: *melek*
Pronunciation: *MEH lehk*
Strong's Number: *4428*

"Set a King over us!" was the cry of the Israelites to Samuel. Yet, God was determined to be King over His people (Ezek. 20:32–33). The Hebrew word *melek* was the word used to designate the human sovereign ruler, serving under the Lord of Israel. The noun is translated consistently as "king." The verb *malak* was developed from the noun meaning "to be king," "to become king," or "to reign." *Melek* describes all kinds of kings, including kings of Egypt and all the other nations of the earth. But in the Old Testament, it is the King of Judah, from the line and tribe of Judah that is paramount and praised in song and dance.

Although Israel demanded a king to reign over them for all the wrong reasons, the Lord used their evil intentions to establish a line of Davidic kings (1 Sam. 10:17–22; 12:17). These kings would begin with the Great King David and culminate in the ideal, perfect God-Man ruler and King, Jesus Christ (2 Sam. 7). God ruled His people through chosen and inspired judges before Saul was made king (1 Sam. 10:24; 11:15). But, if Israel's king would submit to the Lord and His work, God would prosper and bless him and his people (1 Sam. 12:24–25). The king was supposed to serve God and His people, modeling the law of God in their personal and public life (Deut. 17:18–20). Without an exemplary king to guide them, the Israelites did what was right in their own eyes, not in the eyes of the Lord (Deut. 12:8; Judg. 17:6; 21:25).

The book of Psalms has what some call "kingship psalms," some of which refer to Israel's human king (Pss. 20, 21, 45), while others refer to God as King. Psalm 47:7 declares God as King of the earth and as the great divine Warrior King as well (Ps. 98). It is, of course, the inspired genius of the Bible that the concept of the King who is truly divine and truly human becomes a reality. Through Him, God reigns. In the New Testament era, Matthew declares that Jesus is the King of Israel, the greater King David (Matt. 27:42), and John agrees (John 1:49). Jesus was God incarnate and the torah and law of God was fulfilled in Him (Matt. 5:17–18). From the descendants of David God brought Jesus Christ, Israel's true, eternal King (Acts 13:23–31) who is, by virtue of His resurrection, immortal and invisible (1 Tim. 1:17). The King was supposed to be an example of men and of God—Jesus Christ is both. He reigns now as our perfect King of Kings whom we seek to follow unswervingly (Rev. 19:16).

KEY VERSES

Deuteronomy
17:14–15;
1 Samuel 8:6; 10:24;
Psalms 47:2, 6–7;
98:6

Kingdom

See also: *Kingdom, p. 317*
Hebrew expression: *mamlakah*
Pronunciation: *mahm law KAWH*
Strong's Number: *4467*

In the Bible, the word "kingdom" expresses a "sphere of influence"—not necessarily geographical boundaries. The Lord defines the Kingdom of Israel, His people, as "[My] Kingdom of Priests" (Exod. 19:6). His priests would serve Him and be under His tutelage and sovereignty, a treasure from among the nations of the earth (Exod. 19:5–6). Israel as a kingdom was, therefore, the Kingdom of the Lord. God intended to deliver all the kingdoms in Canaan into Israel's hands, and He did indeed deliver many, such as Og's kingdom in the Transjordan region (Deut. 3:4–5, 21).

God's Kingdom was the sphere of influence He had over His people. God divinely appointed a king to rule over Israel (Deut. 17:15). When this king took over his *mamlakah*, which is Hebrew for "kingdom," he was to use the Lord's Law given by God at Mount Sinai as the standard of rule for himself and the people over which he ruled (Deut. 17:20). God's Kingdom, His people and His King, were exalted by the Lord as long as they followed Him (2 Sam. 5:12). If God's Kingdom should rebel against Him, however, they would be humiliated by the Lord before the kingdoms of the world (Deut. 28:25). Israel's kings who did not obey the Lord and His covenant laws were removed from their kingship, just like the first King, Saul (1 Sam. 13:13–14). God's eternal covenant with David and his family established that God would always set a king on the throne of David (2 Sam. 7:12–13, 16). God would be the King's father and the King would be His son! In fact, the royal "dynasty" of David was established forever over the Kingdom of God through the Messiah (1 Sam. 24:21).

The New Testament continues this theme of the Kingdom of God through the permanent establishment of the final King over that Kingdom, Jesus Christ. God gave the Kingdom to Him, the last royal descendant of David and the Son of God.

KEY VERSES

Exodus 19:6;
Deuteronomy
17:18–20;
2 Samuel 5:12;
7:12–13, 16

Christ happily calls us into His Kingdom and His glory (1 Thess. 2:12), into the sphere of God's authority among His people. Christians have become, according to Peter, the "royal priesthood" of God's Kingdom (1 Pet. 2:9–10). We are now, through Christ, a Kingdom and priests to God our Father just as Israel was in the Old Testament (Rev. 1:6; 5:10). Christians live in the kingdoms of the world, but have citizenship and ownership in a Kingdom not of this world. To be in the Kingdom of Christ means to be under His influence and direction *today*. By believing in Jesus, we are promised a place in the eternal Kingdom and eagerly await the Messiah's return (Acts 1:6–7). There will be trials, but commitment to the Lord enables us to walk steadily forward as citizens in God's Kingdom (Acts 14:22).

Know

See also: *Knowledge, p. 106 and Know, knowledge, p. 318*
Hebrew expression: *yada'*
Pronunciation: *yaw DAH'*
Strong's Number: *3045*

People today spend a lot of time and money in order to "know" more: higher education, special classes, seminars and lectures. But how much time do we spend trying to "know" other people or even God? The Hebrew verb *yada'* has a root meaning of "to know," but the various ways of knowing and things to know are many. The wisdom words *da'at* and *de'ah*, meaning "knowledge," are also formed from the root meaning of *yada'*. *Yada'* can mean "to know a fact about something"—and the Israelites "knew" that God existed. In Hosea, the rebellious nature of God's people, their incessant sin of committing harlotry by going after other gods, and their detestable practices, is attributed to their lack of knowledge of the Lord. But, they did not follow God because they not only failed to know Him relationally, but also failed to understand and know His true character. After they finally "knew" His character, they needed to "acknowledge" Him, which is another important meaning of *yada'* (Hos. 6:3).

The sorry state of Israel's inability to know their God was based upon their abundant sins and hostility toward God. They were so confused that they considered the prophets God sent them to be fools, and the "men of the Spirit" given to them by God to be deranged (Hos. 9:7–8). God's people did not know Him or His requirements of righteousness (Jer. 5:4; 8:7). The Lord, ironically, "knew" all about His rebellious people (Hos. 5:3). What was it to *yada'*, "to know," the Lord? Hosea summarizes it well. The watchful person will "understand," *yada'*, the things of the Lord; that is, he or she will understand that to be righteous before the Lord is to walk in His ways (Hos. 14:9). Walking in the Lord's ways will lead to understanding and knowing His will, and that leads to knowing Him relationally.

But Hosea also used *yada'* to mean "recognize" or "acknowledge" ("know," KJV, NLT) the Lord. Without acknowledging the Lord there is no true relationship with Him. Only the Lord's work of restoring His people to Himself can lead to "truly knowing" or "acknowledging" Him (Hos. 2:20). A key feature of repentance is to acknowledge Him by returning to Him (Hos. 6:3). For Israel, the Lord asserted that they were to acknowledge no Savior but Him (Hos. 13:4). God's people are constantly called upon to truly know their God by acknowledging Him in every area of life. God wants a relationship and active acknowledgment, not passive or factual recognition, of Him. He wants to be truly known, because only then we will be able to love Him and other people.

KEY VERSES

Isaiah 42:25;
Psalm 119:125;
Hosea 2:20; 5:3;
9:7; 13:4; 14:9;
Proverbs 3:6

Knowledge

See also: *Know, p. 105 and Know, knowledge, p. 318*
Hebrew expression: *da'at*
Pronunciation: *DAH 'aht*
Strong's Number: *1847*

"The more knowledge, the more grief" (Eccl. 1:18) is a puzzling statement to a modern culture where knowledge is craved—where possession of knowledge usually gives a person power and standing. But the author of Ecclesiastes understood that knowledge was not enough; knowledge could not deliver a person from a "meaningless life" lived under the sun (Eccl. 1:3). In fact, knowledge tended to add to a person's problems, not remove them!

The word meaning "knowledge" in Hebrew is *da'at*, a noun coming from the root of the verb *yada'*, "to know," "to experience," "to acknowledge." This key word in the Old Testament includes both intellectual and experiential knowledge. The noun for knowledge, *da'at,* also has this range of meaning.

In Ecclesiastes, the author uses this Hebrew word in a particular way. The author of Ecclesiastes asserts that he had come to experience and acquire much wisdom (*chokmah*) and knowledge (*da'at*, see Eccl. 1:16), but he had noted a problem. Those who had benefited from their knowledge and wisdom might have to leave all that they had acquired to someone who had neither knowledge nor wisdom (Eccl. 2:21). He also noted that God gave knowledge to some, but not to others (Eccl. 2:26). Knowledge was advantageous to the one who had it (Eccl. 7:12). Yet the only time knowledge is useful is in this life. In the grave, it disappears (Eccl. 9:10). Since knowledge was at least important to possess in this life, the Preacher (Teacher, NIV; *qohelet*) sought with all diligence to impart it to his listeners and readers (Eccl. 12:9, 11).

Ultimate knowledge is to understand that the essence of life is to fear God and keep His word, for God will eventually judge every person for every deed—good or bad (Eccl. 12:13–14). Knowledge of God does not lead to more grief. To the *da'at* of this age ("under the sun") merely led to the discovery of more unsolvable dilemmas, more things that needed to be made right, more cares and more responsibilities. Only one thing counts in the end—knowing that life, from youth to old age, is to be lived responsibly before the Creator (Eccl. 12:1–8). In Christ, our goal is to know the love of God that surpasses any knowledge (*gnosis* in Greek) of life under the sun (Eph. 3:19).

KEY VERSES

Genesis 2:9, 17;
Proverbs 2:10;
Ecclesiastes 1:16,
18; 2:21, 26; 7:12;
12:9

Labor

Hebrew expression: 'amal
Pronunciation: 'aw MAWL
Strong's Number: 5999

What is the good life? Or, how are we to occupy ourselves in days on this earth? From the time of the Garden of Eden, the Lord had decreed that humans should work—God works and we are made in His image (Gen. 2:15). Work was a delight in the Garden of Eden. It became more toilsome after humans were driven from their ideal setting, but it remained a part of being human.

Ecclesiastes 5:18–19 affirms that the enjoyment of a person's work is a part of "the good life." God wants people to enjoy the labor of their hands and minds and to benefit from the fruits of that labor. The verb, 'amal, "to toil, to labor, to work, to make" refers to any kind of labor, such as building (Ps. 127:1) or farming (Jonah 4:10; Prov. 16:26). The noun comes from the root of this verb, but came to mean "trouble, labor, toil." Where the word means "trouble," the word is still closely related to "toil and labor" from the toils and cares of life (Jer. 20:18). It can mean activity that is bad (Prov. 24:2), including improper speech (Ps. 140:9).

Ecclesiastes, however, speaks of 'amal as legitimate, toilsome labor or as the fruit of labor. As was noted above, this is what we are to enjoy to the fullest as the gift of God (Eccl. 5:18–19). Labor is indeed humbling and can lead to oppression (Ps. 107:12), but if engaged in properly and with integrity, the laborer is amply rewarded. His work enables him to pass through life without undue thought of its monotony and cares. There is no better thing than to take a positive attitude toward the benefits of one's work (Eccl. 8:15) and to live responsibly before God. A fool is worn out by his work—the righteous enjoy their work and know what they are doing (Eccl. 10:15).

In a culture in which Gallup polls indicate that most persons do not enjoy or feel fulfilled by their work, the Preacher has some wise instruction. Labor, work, toil—these are good things. They give perspective on the rest of life and provide the benefits necessary to enjoy this life. Do good and enjoy the benefits of your toil as the gift of God. Even our Savior Jesus Christ, who was sent to finish the work of His Father (John 4:34, *ergon*), also enjoyed life with His friends. Paul the apostle continued to work hard with his hands as a sign of integrity before those to whom he ministered (1 Cor. 4:12).

KEY VERSES

Ecclesiastes 2:10, 24; 5:18–19; 8:15; 10:15

Lamentation

Hebrew expression: *qiynah*
Pronunciation: *qee NAWH*
Strong's Number: *7015*

The Hebrew word *qiynah* is a technical literary and musical term describing a musical composition. *Qiynah* is best translated as "lamentation," "lament," or "dirge." A dirge is, of course, a mournful musical composition. The *qiynah* in the Old Testament also had a fixed literary pattern, often featuring acrostic poetry. The word can be rendered as "eulogy," a poem or song created to recognize and laud a deceased person. Jeremiah composed a lament or eulogy in remembrance and praise of the great reforming King Josiah, who tried to bring Judah back to the Lord (2 Chr. 34—35). The eulogy was sung at King Josiah's funeral (2 Chr. 35:25). Jeremiah was so well known for his "lamentations," that he is considered the probable author of the book of Lamentations. His laments for Josiah continued to be a part of Israel's musical history for years.

Different people throughout the Old Testament offered lamentations to God. The Lord gave Ezekiel a scroll that contained words of "lament," "mourning," and "woe" on them. Ezekiel duly ate those words as the Lord instructed him and then spoke them (Ezek. 2:9–10). Ezekiel saw his own people lamenting the idolatry and corruption that had overtaken them. He was moved to produce a metered chant that constituted a lament for the princes of Israel (Ezek. 19). But he was not permitted by the Lord to lament the death of his own wife because of the greater catastrophe befalling Israel (Ezek. 24:16). The pride of the ancient city of Tyre caused her downfall and Ezekiel produced a lamentation for her destruction (Ezek. 26—28). Amos took up a lament over the fall of northern Israel (Amos 5:1). And, King David composed a lamentation for King Saul, refusing to take any pleasure in the death of his enemy (2 Sam. 1:17).

The pathos, emotion, and depth of feeling in the laments of the Old Testament show God's own heart. It is not merely the prophet who is lamenting, but God through them who was moved by the failure and destruction of His people. At Jesus' triumphal entry into Jerusalem, He wept and offered a lamentation for the city. He realized the devastation that would again overtake it, reminiscent of Jeremiah's lament over Jerusalem's initial destruction (Luke 19:41–44). While God's people are a people of praise, we are also to be a people of lamentation and weeping, especially over those things that threaten or befall God's people.

KEY VERSES

2 Samuel 1:17;
Jeremiah 7:29;
9:10, 20;
Ezekiel 2:10

Land

Hebrew expression: *'erets*
Pronunciation: *'EH rehtz*
Strong's Number: *776*

What is the final destiny of the earth, its land, its people, its nations? We have a global awareness and perspective of the earth that was not possible in previous centuries. We depend upon a healthy earth and its continued renewal. The Scriptures have important insights into God's special provision for and relationship to the home of humankind, the earth.

The noun *'erets* in Hebrew stands for "land," "earth," "country," "world," "inhabitants." The word comes from an original root meaning "to be firm" or "to be fruitful." The entire *'erets*, "earth," was prepared for humankind. In its first stage, it was uninhabitable, "vacant" and "desolate" (Gen. 1:2). Then God formed and prepared it for His people (Gen. 1:3–31).

The whole earth was available for the spread of humankind. God commanded them to multiply and fill the earth (Gen. 1:28–29). It was created to be inhabited, fertile in people as well as food (Isa. 45:18). In God's morally and spiritually determined world, the fertility of the *'erets* was tied to the moral behavior of humankind (Gen. 2:16; 3:11, 14–19). The rebellion of humankind caused the earth itself to become corrupt (Gen. 3:11; 6:11). The welfare of the earth is tied to the attitudes and actions of human beings (Gen. 2:15). The land itself (*'adamah*), a part of the *'erets*, was cursed; but, most significantly, the Lord considered the earth, its inhabitants and their environment, as corrupt. God destroyed both the earth and its inhabitants (Gen. 6:11–13). They stood together or fell together before the Lord (Gen. 6:12).

Yet, God preserved both the earth and a part of its inhabitants, establishing a covenant with Noah and his descendants to maintain the seasons and cycles of the earth as long as it would endure (Gen. 6:18; 8:22). From Noah's descendants, the earth and the nations developed (Gen. 9:1; 10:32).

When the word *'erets* refers to a particular area of the earth it means "land," "nation," or "country," such as the land of Egypt. God called Abraham to go to a land (*'erets*) that God would show him. God would create a nation through which He could bless the other nations of the earth (*'erets*). The nation of Israel was chosen for this task (Exod. 19:5–6). The same failure overtook Israel that had overtaken the nations before and after Noah—Israel sinned and rebelled (Ezek. 2:3; Hos. 7:13). The sin of mankind, Jew or Gentile, has continued to despoil the earth. This was not God's plan or desire. The land (*'erets*) of Israel was to draw all nations to God and His righteous laws (Deut. 4:6–8; Mic. 4:2–5). God wanted to bless the earth and renew it so that the singing of the Lord could be heard throughout the entire earth (1 Chr. 16:23).

Technology will not ultimately produce a healthy earth.

KEY VERSES

Genesis 1:1; 2:1;
10:32; 12:1, 7;
Exodus 1:7; 9:14;
19:5;
Zechariah 14:9

The secret to even ecological stability and health for the whole earth is the pursuit of morality and true spirituality, the way of biblical righteousness. God can then bless and heal His people and their land (2 Chr. 7:14). The destiny of the current earth is destruction, but God's people—true to their call—should work it and care for it (Gen. 2:15) until its end. As there will be a new heaven, so there will be a new earth for God's people in the future (Isa. 65:17–19; 66:1). But the greatest lesson for the present is to occupy the earth in righteousness until He comes.

Law

See also: *Law, p. 320*
Hebrew expression: *torah*
Pronunciation: *toh RAWH*
Strong's Number: *8451*

Everyone agrees that a civilized society should be guided by "law and order." But what is the law? In the United States, "law" is considered a man-made rule or guide by which a civilized society should govern itself. Part of this concept would agree with the understanding of law among the ancient Israelites, but part would not. The main body of laws in the Old Testament was not created by men nor did it originate with men. The law had its origin in God.

In Deuteronomy, the word *torah* occurs many times. The word *torah* is also used many times in the book of Psalms—where the longest psalm in the Bible praises God's *torah*, His law, as being a joy and delight to those who obey it (Ps. 119). The noun *torah* means basically "law," "direction," "instruction." It is formed from the root *yrh*, from the verb *yarah* meaning "to throw" or "to shoot." It also means "to teach," or "to instruct." There are many kinds of laws, but the word *torah* refers to God's laws, as opposed to the human instructions of parents (Prov. 1:8; 6:20; 4:2; 7:2) or of the great sages or poets of Israel (Ps. 78:1; Prov. 13:14).

The "laws"—that is, "instructions" or "teachings"—regarding the various feasts and celebrations of Israel were also described by the word *torah*. The "code" of laws given by God on Mount Sinai were the *torah*. The entire book of Deuteronomy is referred to as "this law (*torah*)" (Deut. 1:5). The divine origin of God's *torah* is clearly stated in Deuteronomy 32:46, for it is said that Israel's very life depended upon obeying the words of this *torah*. The religious, ceremonial, civil, and moral *torot* (plural of *torah*) of the Lord regulated the entire community life of Israel. The laws of the Lord were written down in the book of the Law by Moses. So at times, this word refers to the first five books of the Bible, the Pentateuch (see Josh. 24:26).

The key to Israel's success before the Lord lay in faithfully following His laws. But they failed (Deut. 4:29). God's law, as intended by God, was not burdensome. The psalmist said that he delighted in the Lord's law (Ps. 119:70) and loved it (Ps. 119:97). He could not separate loving God from loving His *torah* (Ps. 119:174). But people twisted God's *torah* into something it was not intended to be. They saw it as burdensome and limiting.

KEY VERSES

Deuteronomy 1:5;
29:21;
Joshua 24:26;
Psalm 119:70;
Proverbs 1:8

Jeremiah prophesied of a time when God's "law" would be inscribed upon His people's hearts in the new covenant He would make with them (Jer. 31:31–34). In other words, God's *torah* will never pass away for it is now written upon our minds and in our hearts. This, of course, has come true in the new covenant. We are the blessed bearers of His moral and ethical laws in our hearts (Heb. 8:7–12) through Christ and the Holy Spirit.

Led Away Captive

Hebrew expression: *galah*
Pronunciation: *gaw LAWH*
Strong's Number: *1540*

Using the Hebrew word *galah*, Amos asserted that northern Israel would "go into exile" (NIV), or "surely be led away captive" (Amos 7:11, KJV). To be exiled is a well understood expression today. It means to be banished from one's homeland. For Israel to be "led away captive" was especially devastating because the land of Canaan had been given to the Israelites by God as the Promised Land—theirs forever. *Galah* is used in Amos at least nine times meaning "to go into exile." The word also has meanings such as "to uncover," "to expose," or in appropriate contexts "to (cause) to go into exile" (Judg. 18:30; 2 Kgs. 17:23; Ezek. 39:28; Amos 1:5, 6). A simpler meaning of *galah*, "to remove," is closely related to God's removing Israel from the land into Babylonian exile.

God is sovereign over all the earth. In Amos, not only Israel goes into exile, but also the Gentile nation of Aram (Amos 1:5). A special emphatic Hebrew construction is used to stress God's causing Israel to go into exile. This is rendered into English by using the word "surely" or "certainly" (Amos 5:5; 6:2, 7; 7:11, 17). The exile was not the final word of judgment upon a disobedient people, for disaster would befall them even in exile (Amos 9:4). God would, however, ultimately restore them (Amos 9:11–15) and replant them in their own land. The exile of the nation from the land was the ultimate curse reiterated by Moses upon the disobedient people (Deut. 28:36). God promised the descendants of the patriarchs the land and they were to live there forever. But God's people suffered the agony of exile because they did not conduct themselves as His people.

Exile means being cut off from the land, the traditions of the land, and the feasts and festivals that were held properly only in the land. The Israelites' humiliating experience was a result of their rebelliousness (Acts 7:43, *metoikizo* in Greek). God carried His people into exile by the hand of a terrifying Babylonian king, but He also brought them back by the hand of His servant King Cyrus of Persia (Ezra 1:1–2; Dan. 1:1–2). The remnant that returned had at least learned to not worship idols, and to fear their God. Exile was not God's ultimate will for His people. It was His judgment on His people, so that they would learn to turn to Him, instead of idols.

KEY VERSES

2 Kings 17:23;
Isaiah 5:13;
Jeremiah 52:28;
Amos 1:5; 5:5, 27;
6:7; 7:11, 17

112

Letter

Hebrew expression: *nishtewan*
Pronunciation: *nish teh VAWN*
Strong's Number: *5406*

Famous letters are a part of history and lore. The New Testament is made up of at least twenty-one letters, all of which are inspired documents written by inspired authors committed to Christ as redeemer and Lord. They carry the authority of God's inspiration behind them. The Hebrew word *nishtewan*, or "letter," means " a writing." The word is probably of Persian origin through biblical Aramaic and describes a "written dispatched document." In the Old Testament, there are few letters, but three of them deserve special attention. An exchange of letters recorded in Ezra 4:7–22 and 7:11–26 reveals the sovereignty and intentions of God in an amazing way. The letters themselves are in Aramaic, possibly copies of the original royal documents.

The first letter is written to King Artaxerxes I of Persia (465–424 B.C.) by the adversaries of the Jews who were beginning to rebuild Jerusalem and the new Temple (Ezra 4:1). The letter informed the king about the activities of the Jews and appealed to him to stop the reconstruction of the city. There is no mention in the letter of an earlier decree of Cyrus the Great, which permitted the Jews to return and build Jerusalem. The adversaries' letter is biased and "inspired" by their hostility toward God's people. The letter puts into writing for all time their attempt to thwart the fulfillment of the prophecy of Jeremiah, the prophet of God (Ezra 1:1; Jer. 29:10). This letter was temporarily successful. The King stopped the rebuilding of the city (Ezra 4:21).

Ezra the scribe, an expert in the Law of Moses, was favored by God so that "the hand of God," a phrase found six times in the book, was upon him (Ezra 7:6, 9). The second letter was from king Artaxerxes to Ezra. Through this letter, the king granted Ezra permission to return to Jerusalem with other exiles—and he issued another letter, the third letter, approving the rebuilding of the city of Jerusalem! In addition, the king's treasury was made available for any supplies that might be needed (Ezra 7:20). This pagan king even instructed Ezra to set up a judicial system based on the Laws of his God to teach the people the Law and to enforce it. It was God's hand "upon the king" that caused him to issue this official document, communicating the Lord's will for the construction of Jerusalem.

KEY VERSES

Ezra 4:7, 18, 23;
7:11

God spoke through the letter of a pagan king, Artaxerxes, to communicate His will to build His city and His people. How much more has He spoken through the twenty-one letters of the New Testament, laying His hand upon the writers, declaring that all of His treasury is available to build His people and His Holy church in Christ.

Leviathan

Hebrew expression: *liwyatan*
Pronunciation: *lihv yaw TAWN*
Strong's Number: *3882*

The creature called the Leviathan (*liwyatan*) appears in the Old Testament six times in five verses (Job 3:8; 41:1; Pss. 74:14; 104:26;. Isa. 27:1). It is often suggested, based upon Egyptian reliefs, that the Leviathan was similar to a crocodile—a four-legged reptile with a long tail. However, the figure of a serpent, a limbless hissing reptile, might be more appropriate. Etymologically, the word is derived from the root *lwy*, "to twist," "to coil." Although this root does not occur in the Old Testament with this meaning, it is found in another Semitic language, Arabic. Furthermore, Isaiah 27:1 and Psalm 74:14 are the sole biblical texts providing some description, portraying Leviathan as a many-headed, fleeing, and twisting serpent. This definition is supported by thirteenth century B.C. Ugaritic texts which use nearly the same imagery to describe this sea creature.

If the picture of a large, sinuous, and many-headed serpent is not strange enough, the role of this creature in both biblical and extra-biblical literature is simply fantastic. With the Leviathan, we are dealing with an ancient and mythical personification of chaos. The biblical text makes it clear that the Leviathan represents a primordial power, sometimes at odds with Yahweh. On the one hand, these chaos monsters, the Leviathan and Behemoth (Job 40:15), were conquered by Yahweh during the creation of the world (Ps. 74:13; Isa. 51). On the other hand, we are informed that the Leviathan and Behemoth are a natural part of the created order (Job 40:15; Ps. 104:26). Although it was subdued at creation, chaos continues to exist in the world. However, it is also clear that chaos will cease existing on the "Day of Yahweh" (see Isa. 2; 27:1).

Why do Leviathan and Behemoth appear in the book of Job? The creatures are an integral part of Yahweh's rhetoric in His speech from the whirlwind. In His climactic answer to Job (40:15—41:26), the Lord asserts that He created the chaos monsters, *behemoth* and *liwyatan*. Furthermore, He is the only one who has the power to subdue the creatures. Apparently in his consistent questioning, Job had overlooked two items: (1) chaotic events are a part of life; and (2) questioning God is a shortsighted endeavor. The first item is the only substantive answer God provides in the whole book. The key is the recognition that not all suffering is a reflection upon a person's piety. Throughout the book, Job and his companions have consistently confused the realm of natural phenomena (which may result in "undeserved" suffering) with the realm of religion (such as punishment for iniquity or reward for piety).

KEY VERSES

Job 3:8; 41:1;
Psalms 74:14;
104:26;
Isaiah 27:1

Acceptance of this argument enables us to process the whirlwind of our lives. When the "Leviathan" wreaks havoc in our lives, we may conclude that it is not the result of some previously unknown sin. Rather, we may conclude that the present situation is part of the reality of the world which God created.

Levites

Hebrew expression: *Levi*
Pronunciation: *lay VEE*
Strong's Number: *3881*

The word Levite came from the name of the father of the tribe of Levi. The "ite" suffix means "a descendant of" (Exod. 1:2; 2:1). The Levites were chosen by God to perform their sacred duties because of their faithfulness to the Lord and Moses after the people had rebelled and worshiped the Golden Calf (Exod. 32:26). Compared to the rest of the tribes, they received no inheritance of land in Canaan; their "portion" was the Lord and His work (Josh. 14:4; 18:7). Aaron was a Levite and he and his descendants were to serve as High Priests and priests in various capacities (Num. 3:10). Levi's three sons, Kohath, Gershon and Merari, produced families who were in charge of specific duties in and for the Tabernacle and the Temple. Originally, they began their service at the age of twenty-five and served until fifty years of age (Num. 8:24–26). David lowered the entry age to twenty, when he established the ark of God at a permanent site. At that time, Levites no longer had to carry the ark or other materials related to the Temple (Num. 4:3; 1 Chr. 23:24–26).

The Levites were a vital part of Israel—without them, Israel could not worship properly. Many duties were assigned to them by David and Solomon when preparations to build the Temple were made and after it was completed (1 Chr. 9:22–34; 23:24–32). The Levites were involved in the sacred things of the Lord, including sacrifices, care of Temple implements, baked goods, music, and leadership in worship. The Levites represented the people on the popular level. They ministered at the Tent of Meeting and the Sanctuary under the priests, the sons of Aaron (1 Chr. 23:32). They were presented to Aaron and his sons in place of the whole people to serve them in a representative capacity. They were then presented by the priests as a special offering (Num. 8:11) and the tribal leaders most likely laid hands on them dedicating them as substitutes for the whole nation. The Levites were supported by the tithes of the people. They were, in fact, the mediators, along with the Aaronic priests, between Israel and God. When the Israelites returned from the Babylonian captivity, both Zerubbabel and Ezra were careful to take along with them a sufficient number of Levites to carry out proper worship in Israel (Ezra 8:15–20).

KEY VERSES

Exodus 2:1;
Numbers 35:7;
1 Chronicles
23:26–28;
2 Chronicles 30:17

While Jesus did not descend from Levi, He did ultimately fulfill the central duty of the Levites by presenting Himself as our sacrifice. By doing this once, He removed the need for the Levites. The Levites are, however, still a part of the twelve founding tribes, and Revelation describes that twelve thousand from the tribe of Levi are marked with the seal of God (Rev. 7:7).

Light

See also: *Light, p. 325*
Hebrew expression: *'or*
Pronunciation: *'OHR*
Strong's Number: *216*

God said, "Let there be light (*'or*)!" And so there was light. But equally important, God saw that the light was *tob*, "good" (Gen. 1:3–4), an evaluative statement. Even in the area of science, light is special, serving as an amazing constant in a universe of flux. Einstein's famous formula $E = MC^2$ depends upon the constant speed of "physical" light. The light that was pronounced "good" in Genesis 1:4 was physical light, but it was also much more. God also created the moral realms of light and darkness.

In Hebrew, the verb *'or* means "to be light" or "to become light." The high priestly prayer (Num. 6:25) implores, "May the Lord make His face shine upon you." The noun *'or* comes from this same root as the Hebrew word for "shine." The "light" (*'or*) is always considered good. There is the light of day; the light of the sun, moon, stars, lightning, a lamp; the light of the moral law of God to guide (Ps. 119:105; Prov. 6:23). The Lord is the light (*'or*) of His people, Israel (Ps. 27:1; Mic. 7:8). The Messiah, the Savior of mankind, is a light (*'or*) for the nations (Isa. 42:6). The light of the Lord will one day eclipse the physical light of the universe among His people from all nations (Isa. 60:19–20).

The book of Job uses this word at least twenty-one times. Always, light is good and attached to life and hope. Even physical light is seen representing life or the joy of life—the opposite of darkness and night. Light (*'or*) takes on a decidedly moral flavor with Job. Light as the opposite of darkness is good. Darkness is evil. God speaks and challenges Job, or anyone, to command and control the light (*'or*) as He does.

In a figurative sense, the wicked who haunt the night are dispersed by the coming of light at dawn (Job 38:15). Light brings moral and ethical order to a world that falls into debauchery, sin, and carousing during the "night" (Job 38:15). Death is associated with a lack of light and the reign of darkness (Job 10:22). Light is used in literary parallelism with life itself; without light there is no life, and a person in constant misery is said to be better off without light or life (Job 3:20). Light signifies the insight and wisdom needed by kings to rule well. Without it, they are hopelessly confused (Job 12:25). A king who rules in righteousness, however, is like the light (*'or*) of sunrise (2 Sam. 23:4) upon his people. Only God Himself knows where the abode of light is (Job 38:19).

KEY VERSES

Genesis 1:3–4;
2 Samuel 23:4;
Job 3:16, 20; 12:25;
22:28; 24:13, 16

It is no wonder that the moral, ethical, and salvific understanding of light continued into the New Testament. Jesus, the light of every person (John 1:4), is the light (John 8:12, *phos*) of life, the true light. Those who put their trust in Him also become sons of light (*phos*) and walk in the light.

Live

Hebrew expression: *chayah*
Pronunciation: *khaw YAWH*
Strong's Number: *2421*

One of the most powerful demonstrations of God's ability to restore life to what is dead is found in the book of Ezekiel. Ezekiel employs the Hebrew verb *chayah,* meaning "live," three times in one chapter to make his point (Ezek. 37). The nation Israel is pictured as a mass of dry dead bones in a desert valley—dead, very dead (Ezek. 37:1). God asks the prophet whether these bones, representing the exiled nation of Israel, can live again. Can they again be a nation and a people? When the Lord speaks in this passage He uses the verb *chayah*. The Lord Himself causes these bones to spring to life by bringing life into them (Ezek. 37:9). In a powerful metaphor the Lord "opens the graves" of His dead nation, puts His Spirit in them and they live again (Ezek. 37:14). The entire nation will again return and live in the land of Israel. In this context *chayah* means "to revive," "to quicken," or "to restore." This is a powerful word; used with God as its subject it presents Him as the One who alone can "give life" to His broken people. He not only restores national life, but also gives *spiritual life* to those who are physically alive. He rewards His faithful watchman and righteous person with life because they obey and trust Him (Ezek. 3:21).

God Himself exists as the Eternal One; He is life itself (Exod. 3:14–15). The Lord uses *chayah* to form an oath beginning, "As surely as I live," in several passages (Ezek. 5:11; 14:16–20; 16:48; 17:16). This assertion is the first part of an oath that assures that the second part will be fulfilled. For example, "As surely as I live (*chayah*)," declares the Sovereign Lord, "you will not say this proverb anymore in Israel" (Ezek. 18:3). Ezekiel uses this phrase more than any other prophet, because He needed to contrast the death of God's people in Babylon with the living God who could and would revive them. God "lives"—this is the one sure fact of reality that makes His other claims and assertions true and real. God's ultimate goal for Him and His people is that, "He will live among them forever" (Ezek. 43:9). The Lord will even cause the Dead Sea, in the reconstruction of His people, to be a source of life—everything in it will "live." *Chayah* describes the life that mankind would have had, had they eaten of the Tree of Life and lived forever (Gen. 3:22). God's purpose was to grant us life in Him—not by means of a "tree." The life of God is made available in the life of Jesus Christ, which He grants to those who come to Him. Jesus is life, and He holds the words of eternal life. The living Father lived in Christ and through Christ now lives in us (John 6:57; *zao* in Greek). True life is now given to us freely by the Lord, through our faith in Jesus (Rom. 1:17). While we must all face death, it is a comfort to know our God lives and we will live forever with Him after we leave this earth.

KEY VERSES

Genesis 3:22; 20:7;
Deuteronomy 30:19;
Isaiah 55:3;
Ezekiel 3:21

L

Lord

See also: *Lord, p. 326*
Hebrew expression: *hvhy*
Pronunciation: *YAH weh*
Strong's Number: *3068*

What's in a name? In the case of the covenant God of Israel—everything! His name is often called the tetragrammaton, because it consists of four letters transliterated into English as "yhwh" and is probably pronounced as *Yahweh*. This name is rendered in all capital letters in most Bibles as "Lᴏʀᴅ" (ɴɪᴠ, ᴋᴊᴠ, ɴʟᴛ) to distinguish it from another Hebrew word, *adonai*, which also means "Lord." "Lᴏʀᴅ," *hvhy*, is the personal and covenant name of God in the Old Testament. The Hebrew words *'elohim* and *hvhy* are found together and they refer to one and the same being. So the Lᴏʀᴅ is not just the national or ethnic covenant God of Israel, He is also the Creator of the universe, He is *'elohim* (Gen. 2:4), the Supreme God.

Hvhy is used 348 times in the book of Exodus alone and well over 6,800 times in the Old Testament. While His name is used in Genesis, its significance is revealed to Moses in Exodus 3:14, 15. His name means, "I am who I am" or "I will be who I will be." The significance of these translations show that God is the One who is there for His people, just as He promised Moses in Exodus 3:12, saying, "Certainly I will be with thee" (ᴋᴊᴠ; ɴʟᴛ, "I will be with you"). He will reveal Himself to His people. The Lᴏʀᴅ's name is formed from the verb *hayah* which means "to be, to happen." He is the God who is, who exists, and who brings things about. This amazing name of God became the name by which He was to be remembered for all time (Exod. 3:15). Although He had been known as *El Shaddai* (see Strong's Number 7706) to the patriarchs, now He wanted His people to experience His name in the redemption and deliverance He would give them from Egypt (Exod. 6:2–4).

The idea of a God "close at hand," even among us, has been realized to the greatest degree in the New Testament where the Lᴏʀᴅ Himself appeared among His people as Emmanuel, "God with us" (Isa. 7:14; 9:6–7; Matt. 1:23). Jesus was bold enough to apply the Greek equivalent to the Hebrew term, *hvhy*, Lᴏʀᴅ, to Himself. In John 8:58–59 the people tried to stone Him after He applied the statement "I am (*ego eimi*)" to Himself. He was God, the Lᴏʀᴅ, with us in the fullest sense of deity. And, just as the Lᴏʀᴅ led His people out of bondage from Egyptian slavery, so Jesus our Lᴏʀᴅ has rescued us from the slave house of sin. He continues to deliver those who declare their allegiance to Him and He is with us even to the end of this age (Matt. 28:20).

KEY VERSES

Genesis 2:4; 17:1;
Exodus 3:15; 6:2–6

Lot

Hebrew expression: *pur*
Pronunciation: *POOR*
Strong's Number: *6332*

Few books in the Old Testament contain as much irony as the book of Esther. Haman is hanged on his own gallows, the ones on which he had prepared to hang Mordecai (Esth. 7:9–10). Haman's pride leads to his abject humility (Esth. 6:12–14). On the first day of the month of Nisan, Haman and his supporters cast the *pur*, the "lot," to pick a day on which the Jews were to be slaughtered by the thousands (Esth. 3:7). This month, ironically, was also the month in which God had created His people—giving them new life by bringing them out of Egypt! The casting of the *pur* in this case is described in the Hebrew text as the casting of the *goral*. The Hebrew word *goral* means "lot," or stones placed in a pouch or garment and cast upon a surface. So *pur* is also understood as a "pebble" or "small stone" used for casting lots. The Hebrew word probably is, in fact, a loan word from the Akkadian, *puru*, meaning "small stone" or "pebble." The word "lot" takes on religious and theological significance in the story of Queen Esther. Haman's plot to destroy the Jews, and his arrogant casting of the *pur* to determine when they would be annihilated, turns back upon him and the Jews' enemies. Through Esther, the Lord changes the king's mind toward the Jews. Haman's plot to kill them is uncovered and leads to his execution (Esth. 7:9–10). The decree to destroy the Jews was lifted and ironically the fourteenth and fifteenth of the month of Adar, the supposed time of the Jews' destruction became the Feast of *Purim*. *Purim* is the plural form of *pur*. Through·God's providential care, He turned a day of destruction into a great day of deliverance (Esth. 4:12–14). As a memorial to this great deliverance of the Lord's people during the time of the Persian empire, the Jews named these days of celebration the Feast of Purim, or the "Feast of Lots" (Esth. 9:26). These days of Purim were to be remembered and celebrated forever (Esth. 9:28–32). This holiday holds the distinction of having been made possible through Esther's action and her words in the decree (Esth. 9:32), the only feast and festival established by decree of a woman in Israel.

Casting lots was also practiced in the New Testament. Esther's story shows that the casting of lots was a time-honored, legitimate way to discover God's will (see also Luke 1:9; John 19:24; Acts 1:26). As believers who have God's revealed Word, we need to consult the Bible, inquire of God in prayer, and seek the advice of wise believers before we use "lots" to determine God's will. The casting of lots never should contradict the truths that Scripture clearly reveals.

KEY VERSES

Esther 3:7; 9:24, 26, 28–29, 31–32

Love

See also: *Love, p. 328*
Hebrew expression: *'ahab*
Pronunciation: *'aw HAHB*
Strong's Number: *157*

The word "love" in the Old Testament essentially expresses an emotional experience emerging from one's perceptions of and relationship with some aspect of the physical realm (whether persons or things). The emotive emphasis of the word is underscored by its use in parallelism with its polar opposite, "hate" (for example, Deut. 5:9–10; Prov. 9:8; Isa. 61:8; Mal. 1:2–3). The term may describe an array of human feelings and relational situations, including: simple partiality or preference (for example, Isaac's taste for wild game, Gen. 27:4), carnal appetites (for example, sleep, Prov. 20:13; or wine, Prov. 21:17), political alliance (1 Kgs. 5:1), friendship (Prov. 17:17), parental affection (Gen. 25:28), kinship bonds (Ruth 4:15; 1 Sam. 18:16), romantic love (Gen. 24:67; 1 Sam. 1:5), as well as lust (2 Sam. 13:1) and sexual acts (Ezek. 16:33, 36).

This word "love" is applied to both human and divine relationships in the Bible. Although love tends to connote spontaneous feeling given its emotive nature, love is also a deliberate and carefully measured choice based upon the duration and depth of a relationship. Other Old Testament words used in conjunction with love illustrate the richness and complexity of this kind of relationship, especially the ideas of clinging to (Deut. 11:22) and seeking (Ps. 40:16) the one loved, showing faithfulness in the relationship (Jer. 31:3), and being knit soul to soul in desire and purpose (1 Sam. 18:1, 3). This kind of biblical love is described as the passionate desire to be intimately joined with another person (or God) in all of life's experiences appropriate to that particular relationship.

Naturally, the anthropomorphic expressions of God's love in the Bible remain part of the mystery of the Godhead and defy comprehensive human analysis and understanding. Yet, by analogy to human conventions of love we learn that God's love is extremely personal, like that of a parent and child relationship (Hos. 11:1). God's love is highly selective in that God chose one nation to bless all nations in his covenant with Abraham (compare Deut. 4:37). God's love is paradoxically both spontaneous and conditional. That is, His love is not motivated by any intrinsic merit in the object of his love (for example, the illustration of Hosea's love for the adulterous Gomer, compare Hos. 3:1) but the blessing of God's love is contingent upon Israel's obedience to legal stipulations of the divine covenant (Deut. 7:9, 13).

KEY VERSES

Leviticus 19:18;
Deuteronomy 6:5;
Psalm 119:97;
Isaiah 61:8;
Malachi 1:2

God's love is also exclusive in that the only appropriate response to Yahweh's covenant love is absolute loyalty (Exod. 20:6; Deut. 5:10). Interestingly, the desired human response to

God's love is a command to love God in return with one's whole being (Deut. 6:5; Ps. 31:23). This suggests the love relationship between God and his people is as much an act of the will as it is an emotion of the heart. God's love is rooted in His righteousness, not sentimentality (Ps. 11:7). Therefore God's love results in a relationship of moral fellowship with the faithful (Pss. 33:5; 37:28; 45:7). It is for this reason that the true people of God love his law (Ps. 119:47, 48, 97,113).

The prophet Malachi uses the word "love" in reference to God's election of Israel ("Jacob I have loved," 1:2) and God's rejection of Edom ("Esau I have hated," 1:3). This is in keeping with a pattern in the Old Testament prophets connecting God's love for Israel with his eternal covenant with them (Isa. 43:4; Jer. 31:3). It is God's covenant love for Israel that motivates both his judgment and deliverance of the Hebrews as his special people (compare Deut. 23:5; Prov. 3:12; Hos. 14:4). This remarkable covenant love causes God to save the righteous and even sing over them in gladness (Zeph. 3:17).

According to the New Testament, the very essence of God is love (1 John 4:16)—and this divine love is supremely demonstrated in the incarnation: "For God loved the world in this way: He gave His only Son" (John 3:16, HCSB).

Make Atonement

See also: *Reconciliation, p. 373*
Hebrew expression: *kapar*
Pronunciation: *kaw FAHR*
Strong's Number: *3722*

All of us have felt the need to atone for some wrong we have committed against another person. The problem is what to do and how to do it. The mystery of "atoning" for our offenses, or sins, against God and other persons is addressed by the Hebrew verb *kapar*, "to make atonement," "to cover over." The verb may come from an original root meaning "to wipe away" or "to cover." All of these meanings describe in different ways how God deals with our sins, for only His Son can truly "make atonement" for our sin.

The priests of Israel were ordained and set aside for God's service, by a ceremony that included the sacrificing of a bull and two rams. God chose to accept these animal sacrifices as an atonement for the priests. These sacrifices symbolically covered the priests' sins, so that they could serve as priests before the Holy One of Israel (Exod. 29:10–34). The altar of bronze was "atoned for"—that is made holy, so that sacrifices could be presented upon it (Exod. 29:38–42). Moses hoped to make atonement for Israel's sin by having the people drink the powder of the ground up golden calf (Exod. 32:20), and God "forgave" them because of Moses' intercessory prayer (Exod. 32:14; Pss. 65:3; 78:38). In this case, *kapar* carries the meaning "to forgive, to atone." Prayer, along with sacrifices, was a vital part of making atonement (*kapar*) for Israel's sins.

Kapar is used in Leviticus more than anywhere else in the Old Testament. The priests were in charge of the sacrifices and the handling of the sacrificial blood. When presenting the burnt offering, the worshiper laid his hand upon the head of the sacrificed animal and it was accepted in place of him, to make atonement for him (Lev. 1:4). *Kapar* is found 16 times in the description of the great ritual carried out on the Day of Atonement (Lev. 16). After the ceremony was over the nation was cleansed from all of its sins (Lev. 16:34). The Day of Atonement and all of its goals and purposes assured Israel of its relationship with God. The Israelites were clean before Him through the "blood of bulls and goats"— but only in a temporary way until the blood of Christ was offered to "take away sins" forever.

KEY VERSES

Exodus 29:33, 36–37; 30:15–16; Leviticus 16:6, 10–11, 16–18, 20, 32–34

The Old Testament ceremony of atonement has been fulfilled once and for all by our high priest Jesus Christ. He had no sins of His own to deal with, but was presented as a sacrifice of atonement (*hilasterion* in Greek) for the sins of His people (Heb. 2:17–18; 9:5, 11–14; Rom. 3:25). God accepted this perfect sacrifice and offered all people the gift of forgiveness. Forgiveness is one of the crucial elements of the Christian faith, and a blessing we should not only remember, but also exercise frequently in our relationships with others (Eph. 4:32; Col. 2:13, *charizein* in Greek).

Meditate

Hebrew expression: *hagah*
Pronunciation: *kaw GAW*
Strong's Number: *1897*

Most Christians have moved away from meditation because of the non-biblical connotations that other religions have emphasized. However, one of the most famous psalms of the Bible encourages us "to meditate" on God's law day and night (Ps. 1:2). The Hebrew verb *hagah*, used in this psalm and in Joshua 1:8, means "to muse," "to meditate," "to moan," "to think," or "to speak." King David says that in times of distress, trouble, or oppression, he would "think" (*hagah*) upon the Lord (Pss. 63:6; 77:12; 143:5). The word often refers to internal meditation, but also to verbal utterances or sounds. *Hagah* therefore can be used in a positive sense as when the psalmist's tongue speaks of God's righteousness all day long (Pss. 35:28; 37:30; 71:24), or when the righteous man "utters" (*hagah*) what is good and wise (Ps. 37:30). But, in a negative sense, those who "mutter" (*hagah*) senselessly are classed with wizards and mediums (Isa. 8:19). Also, while the wicked "plot" (*hagah*) violence and evil, the righteous "ponder" (*hagah*) a wise answer carefully (Prov. 24:2).

Meditation must be based on the Bible's guidelines. The object of meditation in the Psalms was the Law of the Lord. The psalmist not only meditated upon God's Word day and night, but he delighted in it as well (Ps. 1:2). The moral and ethical guidance of the Law is celebrated in Psalm 119 where the words "law," "torah," "ordinance," "commandment," or their synonyms are found 176 times! The word of God was a lamp to the psalmist's feet and a light to his path (Ps. 119:105). The one who meditates upon God's Word is righteous. Joshua encouraged the Israelites to meditate day and night, just as the psalmist did. By doing so, the people would then do everything written in the law. This was their key, not only to personal happiness before God, but also to their success in taking and keeping the land of Canaan (Josh. 1:8). God gave His laws and teachings to the Israelites to study and meditate upon, making them different from all other people of the world. Israel was to be a special people to the Lord and by meditating upon His law they would become like Him.

The value of thinking and meditating upon God and His works—and especially the moral and ethical law He has given to all people—are examples for us today. Believers should think and meditate upon things that are true, noble, pure and lovely (Phil. 4:8), but even more we should put into practice the things on which we meditate (Phil. 4:9). Our devotion is to be centered upon the Lord (2 Cor. 11:3) and by thinking upon those things that are pure, we purify ourselves (Jas. 4:8).

KEY VERSES

Joshua 1:8;
Psalm 1:2;
Psalms 63:6;
77:12; 143:5;
Proverbs 15:28; 24:2

Meek

Hebrew expression: 'anaw
Pronunciation: 'aw NAWV
Strong's Number: 6035

Jesus' statement that the "meek" would inherit the earth is justly famous and memorable (Matt. 5:5, *praus* in Greek). In our present-day world, the meek generally don't inherit wealth, prestige, money, or power. Assertive and aggressive people usually achieve these things. But, based upon God's message to His servants, we know that the meek as a group will eventually inherit the earth. The psalmist asserted essentially the same thing when he declared that the "meek" would inherit the land—that was, in his day, the land of Judah and Israel (Ps. 37:11). This courageous statement was made in spite of the fact that evil men seemed to have the upper hand in taking possession of the land. The meek were also to walk humbly before their God, a prerequisite to finding favor in His eyes (Micah 6:8). The Hebrew word *'anaw*, translated as "meek," means "to be low," "to be humble, or "to be gentle" in the sight of God. Before Christ, Moses was described as the most "meek" or "humble" (NLT, NIV) man on the face of the earth (Num. 12:3).

The prophet Zephaniah appealed to the "humble" of the land to seek the Lord (Zeph. 2:3). He knew they were the ones who would listen to him and accept God's message. God always favors the "humble" over the insolent, the prideful, or the arrogant (Pss. 18:27; 25:9). He saves the meek (Ps. 149:4) and sustains them (Ps. 147:6)—even guarding their ways (Ps. 25:9). Even Solomon in his proverbs notes that the Lord gives grace to the humble (Prov. 3:34). When Israel repented and returned to the land after being exiled in Babylon, it was the humble who returned at that time and reinhabited the land (Ezra 8:21). Ezra used the verb *'annah*, related to *'anaw*, meaning "to afflict" or "to be humble" before God.

Jesus was humble and meek in His attitudes (Matt. 11:29, *tapeinos* in Greek). Paul also urges us to be completely humble and gentle (Eph. 4:2). Humility is a part of being meek, as is being submissive and deferential toward others. Through Christ the Lord, God gives grace to the humble and rejects the proud. As Peter says, we are to humble ourselves before the Lord (1 Pet. 5:5, 6). Humility should be the mark of all believers. Believers should give God the credit for everything they do.

KEY VERSES

Numbers 12:3;
Psalms 25:9;
147:6; 149:4;
Proverbs 3:34;
Isaiah 29:19

Mercy

See also: *Mercy, p. 334*
Hebrew expression: *chesed*
Pronunciation: *HEH sehd*
Strong's Number: *2617*

Many words are used in the Bible to describe the character of the Lord. However, the single most prominent attribute revealed is His "mercy." In revealing Himself to Moses, the Lord declared His great mercy (Exod. 34:6-7). The prophets likewise take great pains to remind Israel of this facet of God's divine love. Micah in particular provides a challenging statement:

> Who is a God like unto thee that pardoneth iniquity and passeth by the transgression of the remnant of his heritage? He retaineth not his anger forever, because he delighteth in mercy.

(Mic. 7:18, KJV)

The Lord is not merely merciful, but relishes the opportunity to grant His mercy. This seminal characteristic of God, as Micah shrewdly notes, also distinguished Him from the myriad of pagan gods that had captured the fancy of many Israelites. At best the pagan gods could be described as fickle. Their goodness was contingent upon the whim of the moment as much as any inherent benevolence. Indeed, if an action could even be termed mercy, it would surely not extend to those least worthy of it.

The Lord on the other hand is free with His lovingkindness. The psalmist declares that all the ways of the Lord are merciful (Ps. 25:10). His very nature is to show continual and everlasting mercy without limit (Ps. 25:6; Isa. 54:8, 10). But what does Scripture mean in saying that God is merciful? The Hebrew word for "mercy," *chesed*, paints a beautiful picture of this aspect of love. It is not exclusively used of the Lord, though more often than not this is the case. *Chesed* is used to denote general kindness or hospitality (1 Sam. 15:6), pity on the afflicted (Job 6:14), good deeds (Neh. 13:14), and good favor when not necessarily deserved (Esth. 2:17). At its root, however, there is a more basic meaning. The Lord responds with love towards those who are afflicted or miserable; this is "mercy." This love is especially bestowed upon those who least deserve it, such as those who violate His commands (Pss. 86:5; 103:8; Lam. 3:22).

Indeed Scripture reminds us that the Lord does not deal with us as we fully deserve (Ps. 103:10). The Lord's mercy is rooted in the covenant relationship He has established with humanity. Though not deserved, God extends His mercy to us and calls upon us to receive it (compare Ps. 86:5; 2 Tim. 2:13). By trusting in the Lord, believers are surrounded by His mercy (Ps. 32:10; Hos. 10:12); likewise, we must be merciful to one another. Micah plainly reminds us that, "... the Lord has already told you what is good, and this is what he requires: to do what is right, to love mercy, and to walk humbly with your God" (Mic. 6:8).

KEY VERSES

Psalm 136:1–4;
Jeremiah 9:24;
Hosea 6:6;
Micah 7:18

Mighty Men

Hebrew expression: *gibborim*
Pronunciation: *gih bohr EEM*
Strong's Number: *1368*

Josheb-Basshebeth was one of David's "mighty men"—in fact, he was chief of the top three men. He killed eight hundred men in one encounter (2 Sam. 23:8–22)! The Hebrew word *gibborim* renders the English translation, "mighty men." The noun can also be translated as "warrior," or "mighty warrior." The noun is formed from the verb *gabar* meaning to "over power," "excel," or "be strong." Before the flood of Noah, there were "mighty men" who were famous for their exploits (Gen. 6:4). In the post-flood world, Nimrod was one such individual. He became a mighty hunter before the Lord (Gen. 10:8–9). Even God is described using this word as a mighty and awesome God (Deut. 10:17). The men of the city of Gibeon were described as "mighty men," warriors (Josh. 10:2). The fall of King Saul was the fall of a mighty man (2 Sam. 1:25, 27).

In the book of Psalms, *gibborim* refers to the mighty angels, and the Mighty God (Pss. 24:8; 45:3; 103:20). There are also mighty men who fight against God, but in the last days God invites His warriors and His people to come eat the flesh of the mighty men who war against His people and His city (Ezek. 39:18). In the Day of Judgment, even mighty men will not be able to save their own lives (Amos 2:14).

The New Testament refers to several people as "mighty." Jesus is a prophet and God's Son, who is mighty in deed and in His words with men and before God (Luke 24:19). Significantly, just as we noted that the mighty could not save themselves, Paul reminds the Corinthians that many who are mighty, rich, and influential are not being converted to the Lord (1 Cor. 1:26). In the list of men of faith, the writer of Hebrews notes that the great outstanding people of God in the Old Testament were people who put their faith in God. They had weaknesses, but became mighty and put to flight many enemies of Israel (Heb. 11:32–35). All of the mighty men and warriors of God in the Bible were powerful through *faith*, not through the power tactics and structures that this world praises (Heb. 11:39–40). Believers today need to remember, too, that it is not by our strength and ability that we accomplish great things, but through God who gives us our abilities.

KEY VERSES

Genesis 6:4; 10:8–9;
Deuteronomy 10:17;
2 Samuel 1:19;
23:8–9;
Psalm 52:1

Minister

Hebrew expression: *sharat*
Pronunciation: *shaw RAHT*
Strong's Number: *8334*

The minister of today's churches holds a prominent place in the worship of God's people. That person is especially called by God to perform his duties. In the Old Testament, the Hebrew verb *sharat*, "to minister," "to help," or "to aid," is used to describe the function of God's appointed priests and Levites who "ministered" at the altar in the Holy Place and in various other capacities (Exod. 28:43; 29:30; 35:19; Num. 16:9). The Hebrew word *mesharet*, a form of *sharat*, is used to refer to Joshua as the "aide" to Moses four times. Joshua was Moses' "ministering aide" when Moses went to the top of Mount Sinai to meet with God (Exod. 24:13). Joshua helped Moses when he conversed with God in the Tent of Meeting (Exod. 33:11). Joshua faithfully served Moses from his youth (Num. 11:28), and he was God's chosen *sharat*, "minister," to lead the people into Canaan after Moses died (Josh. 1:1). *Sharat* also means "to render service," "to serve," or "to aid." The religious leaders of the Lord aided the people in their praise and worship of God at the Tent of Meeting (Exod. 28:43). They presented offerings, burned incense, led the community in worship (Num. 16:9), and blessed the people (Deut. 10:8). But all of this was done in the Name of the Lord God (Deut. 18:7). The priesthood was to minister before the chosen kings of Israel from the line of David (1 Sam. 2:35–36). The psalmist makes clear that in the Lord's sight only those who walk blamelessly before the Lord would be able to minister effectively (Ps. 101:6). On an international level, the Israelites were ministers to the nations, since Israel was God's Kingdom of Priests (Exod. 19:5–6). This great calling of ministry has been extended to all followers of Christ (1 Pet. 2:9–10). Paul was called to be a minister of Christ (*leitourgos* in Greek) to the Gentiles as was Timothy (Rom. 15:16; 1 Tim. 4:6). Paul notes several others called with him to be special ministers of God through Christ (Col. 1:7; 4:7). Jesus came to serve, and not to be served, giving His life as a ransom for many (Matt. 29:18). Christ was the model for Paul and all believers. We too have a ministry (*diakonia* in Greek) of reconciliation, "aiding and ministering" to others to help them become reconciled to God (2 Cor. 5:18).

M

KEY VERSES

Exodus 24:13;
28:43; 29:30;
Deuteronomy 10:8;
Psalm 101:6

Mountain

Hebrew expression: *har*
Pronunciation: *HAHR*
Strong's Number: *2022*

Mountains provide some of the most majestic vistas of God's creation. The mountains themselves are monuments of beauty and power, but it is the quality of the experience on the mountain that is most important. The Hebrew term *har,* which means "mountain" or "mountain range," is a general term, but it also designates "mountains" in the Old Testament that are important because of their religious significance. Mountains can sometimes represent great age or eternity (Deut. 33:15; Job 15:7; Hab. 3:6); they also point to the power of the Creator (Ps. 65:6). Furthermore, the phrase "mountaintop experience" grew out of various scenarios in the Old and New Testament, in which God's presence and activity is directly linked with a specific mountain.

The mountains connected with God's actions in history were celebrated. Mount Sinai's exact geographical location was not important, its natural rugged beauty was not stressed, but the Presence of God and His activity at the mountain sanctified it, making it holy (Exod. 3:4–6; Num. 10:33). Mount Sinai is mentioned thirty-five times in the Old Testament as the holy place where God revealed Himself in fire, thunder, and smoke to Moses and Israel (Exod. 19:16–18:1; 20:18). Mount Sinai was also called the "Mountain of God" because it was the place where: God met with Moses and Israel, He gave His Law to Israel, and all the Israelites worshipped Him (Exod. 3:1, 12; 20:1–17; 24:13). Abraham demonstrated his faith by climbing a mountain to a place where God commanded him to sacrifice his son Isaac (Gen. 22:4). On the top of the mountain, God spoke to Abraham and provided a sacrifice in place of Isaac (Gen. 22:12–14). This mountain (Gen. 22:2) became the site of the construction of the Temple by Solomon where God was to dwell (2 Sam. 24:16; 2 Chr. 2:1; 2 Chr. 3:1). Mount Carmel, near the Mediterranean coast, was famous in the Old Testament because it was the place where Elijah defeated the prophets of Baal (1 Kgs. 18:25–39). Another mountain, Mount Zion, was celebrated as the place where the Lord dwelt (Pss. 2:6; 9:11; 74:2).

KEY VERSES

Genesis 22:14;
Exodus 3:12;
19:11; 24:16;
Isaiah 4:5; 10:12;
Zechariah 14:4

In the New Testament, Jesus was tempted by the devil on a high mountain and He was victorious (Matt. 4:8). Jesus delivered His most memorable sermon on a mountain just north of the Sea of Galilee (Matt. 5–7) and on another high mountain He was transfigured before the disciples (Judg. 4:6; Matt. 17:1–3). Jesus ascended from the top of the Mount of Olives (Acts 1:12), and He will return upon the same mountain according to Zechariah 14:4. The eternal Kingdom of God is described figuratively as "His holy mountain" (Isa. 65:24–25; 66:20), where pain and destruction will cease, and perfect worship and fellowship will reign. These mountains of the Bible are holy because of their connection to God—likewise, God's presence in our experiences and lives today makes us holy simply because He is with us.

Myrrh

Hebrew expression: *mor*
Pronunciation: *MOHR*
Strong's Number: *4753*

The three Magi presented gifts to the baby Jesus, and one was a gift of "myrrh" (Matt. 2:11). The gospel of John reports it as one of the ingredients Nicodemus brought to anoint or embalm Jesus' body (John 19:39). The Hebrew word for "myrrh" is found most often in the Song of Solomon to describe the love between the Lover and his Beloved. In this context, it is clear that the word must carry positive connotations of a sweet-smelling substance or perfume (Song 1:13; 3:6; 4:6; 5:1, 5, 13). The Lover's lips are described as lips that are like lilies, dripping with "myrrh," which is *mor* in Hebrew (Song 5:13). The Song of Solomon contains scenes from marriage ceremonies, and this aphrodisiac finds its place in this setting.

Mor was clearly some kind of perfume. The king's robes at the wedding ceremony are said to be fragrant with myrrh, aloes, and cassia (Ps. 45:8)—adding to the festive air of the banquet. Queen Esther went through a beautification processes for six months and an oil of myrrh was one of the elements used (Esth. 2:12). Part of the process of seduction used by the adulterous wife in Proverbs was perfuming her bed with myrrh (Prov. 7:17). The substance itself probably came from a tree known by its scientific name as Commiphora "myrrha" Nees found in Arabia. Other shrubs produced a similar resinous substance called "myrrh."

In Exodus 30:23, *mor* is a part of the holy anointing oil and its use would have added to the pleasant aroma surrounding the Lord's Tabernacle. This substance was used by the Canaanites in the second millennium B.C., and the Egyptians used it in their embalming ceremonies. This last fact may help explain its use on Jesus' body before His burial (John 19:39). But myrrh primarily indicated Jesus' holiness and dedication to God, for He became a sweet-smelling aroma of sacrifice to God on our behalf.

KEY VERSES

Exodus 30:23;
Esther 2:12;
Psalm 45:8;
Proverbs 7:17;
Song of Solomon
1:13

Name

Hebrew expression: *shem*
Pronunciation: *SHAYM*
Strong's Number: *8034*

Elijah challenged the prophets of the god Baal: "Then you call on the name of your god, and I will call on the name of the Lord, and the God who answers by fire, He is God" (1 Kgs. 18:24, NASB). This dynamic and bold challenge by Elijah took place on the top of Mount Carmel. The Name of Elijah's God was the key to his confidence. The Lord was, according to His Name, the God who was present for and with His people (Exod. 3:12, 14–15). The Hebrew word *shem* means "name," and it is the word used to designate the proper name for something or someone. Its most famous and sacred designation was to refer to Israel's God, "the Lord"—*Yahweh*. There was power, reputation, and respect attached to God's Name. To merely refer to "the Name" was a clear reference to the proper Name of Israel's God. When Elijah called upon the Name of the Lord, He responded at once and put the "name" of Baal to shame (1 Kgs. 18:38–39), honoring His own Name. His Name held sacred and practical significance. He was Israel's covenant God who bound Himself to His people at Mount Sinai and promised to be with them. *Yahweh*, the personal name of God, became so well known and carried such significance in Israel that by simply saying the word "Name," *shem*, everyone knew who was intended. The Lord made clear that it was by this "Name" that He would be known forever (Exod. 3:15). God's "great Name" is found in parallel with "your mighty hand" by the writer of Kings (1 Kgs. 8:42). Solomon recognized that the Name of the Lord would cause foreigners to come to the Temple of the Lord—they would hear of His Name; His mighty power, or hand, and arm stretched out to save His people (1 Kgs. 8:41–42). The Temple was built by Solomon to help spread the knowledge of the Lord's Name among the nations (1 Kgs. 8:43) and Jerusalem was chosen by the Lord to have His Name dwell in it (1 Kgs. 11:36). Elijah prayed and built the altar mentioned above in the Name of the Lord. The Lord answered his call in His Name (1 Kgs. 18:32).

KEY VERSES

Exodus 3:13, 15; 6:3;
1 Kings 8:29, 42–44;
9:7; 18:24, 32

Elisha later called down a curse, in God's Name, upon some evil youth who had dared to mock God's prophet (2 Kgs. 2:24).

Christians today realize the power in the Name of Jesus. He is called by the Name, "the Lord" (*ho' kyrios* in Greek) as was God in the Old Testament. Calling upon the Name of "the Lord God, Jesus Christ" is as valid today for God's people as was Elijah's calling upon "the Name, the Lord," in the Old Testament (1 Cor. 1:2). The Bible tells us that at the name of Jesus, every knee will bow and every tongue will confess that He is Lord (Phil. 2:9–11). Jesus is indeed the living God, almighty, wondrous, and deserving our praise.

Nations

Hebrew expression: *goyim*
Pronunciation: *GOH yihm*
Strong's Number: *1471*

The Hebrew word translated "nation" may refer to a specific people or ethnic group (the Israelites and the Edomites, Gen. 25:23) or to a sovereign state or political entity (Egypt, Jer. 46:1-2; Babylonia, Jer. 50:1-2). The term may also identify "people" in general (Josh. 3:17; 2 Kgs. 6:18). Theologically, the word "nations" signifies "Gentiles" who are "outsiders" in contrast to the nation of Israel. The Gentiles are non-Jews and distinct from the Hebrews as God's "covenant people." They are considered "heathen" or "pagan peoples" in the Bible because they engaged in polytheistic and idolatrous religious traditions (Jer. 10:2ff; Ezek. 23:30).

The "nations" (*goyim* in Hebrew) are created by God (Ps. 86:9) and genealogically are regarded as members of one large family (Gen. 10). God is sovereign over the nations (Deut. 32:8; Amos 9:7) and He works His divine purposes for both the judgment and salvation of the nations (Dan. 2:21; 4:3). The prophetic oracles against the nations indicate that they are accountable to God for biblical standards of morality and justice (Amos 1—2). Israel was divinely constituted as a nation at Sinai (*goy* in Hebrew, Exod. 19:6) in fulfillment of the covenant promise made to Abraham and Sarah (Gen. 12:1-3). God did this because He wanted Israel to bring the light of God's truth to the nations (Isa. 49:6). God responds to the repentance of nations with forgiveness characteristic of His merciful nature (Jonah 3:10; 4:2) and graciously grafts individuals of other nationalities into the "family tree" of His covenant people Israel (compare Ruth 1:16-17; Matt. 1:5).

The growth and development of Israel as an ethic, political, and territorial people group naturally heightened the polarization between the nation of Israel and the *goyim*, the non-covenant nations surrounding Israel. These nations are called the uncircumcised (Jer. 9:25) and they demonstrated their character in deeds of wickedness (Deut. 9:4-5), acts of abomination (Deut. 18:9), and idolatrous religion (2 Chr. 32:13). God stands opposed to these nations and judges them accordingly (Pss. 2:4-5; 10:16; 59:8; 110:1-2). In keeping with His justice and His holiness, the nation of Israel was subject to the same fate as the nations if they were disloyal to God and worshiped the gods of the Gentiles (Lev. 18:24-29).

KEY VERSES

Genesis 12:2;
Exodus 19:6;
Deuteronomy 32:8;
Psalm 86:9;
Isaiah 2:2

The nations have a prominent role in Zechariah's eschatology as they assemble to wage war against Jerusalem and the people of God and are defeated in that last great battle of the day of the Lord (Zech. 14:2ff). The Lord himself will fight for Israel, defeat the nations, and rule as King over all the earth (Zech. 14:9). Then the remnant of the nations will bring tribute to Jerusalem and make pilgrimages to worship the God of Israel (Zech. 14:16-17; see also Hag. 2:21-22).

The New Testament portrays a similar picture for the role of the nations in God's redemptive plan. Especially significant for the church is the commission given by Jesus to make disciples of all nations (Matt. 28:19). The outcome of this evangelistic ministry is glimpsed in the snapshot of those gathered in heaven to worship God at the end of the age—people from every tribe, tongue, and nation (Rev. 5:9; 7:9). To this end, the apostle Paul encouraged the preaching of the gospel of Christ to both the Jew and the Greek (or Gentile, Rom. 1:16–17).

One

See also: *Oneness, p. 347*
Hebrew expression: *'ehad*
Pronunciation: *'eh HAWD*
Strong's Number: *259*

The word "one" is the first of the ordinary numbers in Hebrew. As a cardinal number, the word occurs in the account of the tower of Babel when the peoples of the earth had "one" language (Gen. 11:1). As an ordinal number, the term "first" often marks significant events in biblical history (the completion of the Tabernacle, Exod. 40:2, 17; certain feast days, Num. 29:1). As an adjective, the word may mean "lone," "single," "unique," "certain" (Judg. 4:16; 13:2; 1 Sam. 1:1).

The kinship of the Hebrew tribes as descendants of Abraham and the covenant ceremony at Mount Sinai established the oneness of Israel as the people of God (Exod. 19:6; 24:3). This meant that there was only "one" law (Exod. 12:49) and that God would grant the people "one" heart to obey His commands (2 Chr. 30:12; Jer. 32:39).

The Shema of latter Judaism identifies God as "one" Lord (Deut. 6:4). The word "one" is not so much a title as an adjective of quality. God is "one" in the sense of being complete and unique. Theologically, "oneness" is a distinctive quality of the Hebrew God in contrast to the polytheism of all the other ancient religions. The Old Testament does not explicitly teach a doctrine of the Trinity. The plurality of the Godhead is implicit, however, in the language of the Old Testament and in the descriptions of worship offered to the differing manifestations of God (Gen. 1:26; Exod. 3:5–6; Judg. 13:18–22; Isa. 63:10).

The prophet Malachi argued poignantly for fidelity in the marriage covenant on the basis of the oneness of God. Since God is the sole Creator of the material world, all human beings have equal standing before him. Malachi echoes the Genesis ideal in acknowledging the "one" Father of all humanity as the God who created man and woman to be "one flesh" (Mal. 2:10; see also Gen. 2:24).

The New Testament affirms that "God is one" (Gal. 3:20) and articulates a Trinitarian understanding of the Godhead in the distinctive names and work of the three divine persons: Father, Son, and Holy Spirit (Matt. 28:19; 2 Cor. 13:14). All Christians are one in Christ Jesus and hence the church is called to a bond of unity and peace (Gal. 3:28). For there is "one Lord, one faith, one baptism, one God and Father of all" (Eph. 4:5).

KEY VERSES

Deuteronomy 6:4;
2 Chronicles 30:12;
Ezekiel 37:17;
Malachi 2:10

Passover

Hebrew expression: *pesach*
Pronunciation: *PEH sah*
Strong's Number: *6453*

Passover is a feast and festival that is still diligently observed by Jews today. Its significance is recognized by Christians as well, for Jesus Himself became our "Passover lamb." The two greatest reforming kings in Judah, Hezekiah and Josiah, each held a great Passover to mark the return of Israel to faithful worship and recognition of their Lord and God (2 Chr. 30:1–2; 35:6). The Passover recalled and celebrated the creation of the nation of Israel when the Lord freed them from Egypt and brought them through the perils of the Red Sea and the desert to their new homeland—the land of Canaan. This great festival was to continue forever throughout the history of God's people (Exod. 12:11–48) in memory of this salvation event. In addition to the great Passover feasts celebrated by Hezekiah and Josiah (2 Chr. 30:1–2; 35:1), a great Passover was held in the plains of Jericho after the Israelites returned from the Babylonian exile (Ezra 6:19–22). It was impossible for Israel to identify herself without this ritual depicting her salvation and deliverance from Egypt. The Hebrew word *pesach* means to "leave or spare by passing over." It comes from a verbal root meaning "to spare," or "to pass over," but the word may also skillfully depict the physical "passing over" in time and space of the Lord's destroying angel on the first night of the Passover in Egypt. The traditional date of the Passover was set in the first month of the year, Abib, on the fourteenth day—the name of the month was later changed to Nisan (Exod. 12:2; Deut. 16:1; Lev. 23:5). A lamb or goat, if a lamb was unavailable, was sacrificed on the night of the fourteenth and eaten. Bitter herbs and bread without leaven were eaten to commemorate the bitterness with which Israel left Egypt. The doors of the Israelites' houses had their lintels and side boards smeared with the blood of the slain lamb, for when the Lord saw this blood, He willingly "passed over" the house of that Israelite family. The houses of the Egyptians where there was a first born son experienced the death of that child in every case. The lamb in the later Passover ceremony was probably slain between 3:00 p.m. and sunset.

KEY VERSES

Exodus 12:11;
Numbers 9:12;
2 Chronicles 30:1;
35:1;
Ezra 6:19–20

The Passover is mentioned in the New Testament often. In the wisdom, mercy, and plan of God, Jesus Christ became the human Passover Lamb of God, slain on the cross for His people, including the Gentiles (1 Cor. 5:7). By faith Moses kept the first Passover (Heb. 11:28) and the firstborn of Israel were preserved from death. In fulfillment of the ancient ceremony no bone of Jesus' body was broken (Exod. 12:46; John 19:36). The Lord's Supper, for Christians, has now superseded the ancient Passover ceremony. However, many believers today celebrate a "Christian Passover" in which Jesus as the Messiah and passages from the New Testament are directly linked to the Old Testament ceremony.

Peace

See also: *Peace, p. 358*
Hebrew expression: *shalom*
Pronunciation: *shaw LOHM*
Strong's Number: *7965*

Shalom! is probably the best known and most famous word in the Hebrew language. But its meaning is broad and is translated seventy different ways in one translation alone (NIV). Today, *shalom* is used to say "hello" or "good-bye." In the Bible, it is used three different ways in one verse to mean something like "success" (NIV), "peace" (KJV, NLT) and "prosperity" (NLT)! This illustrates the fullness and richness of the word's meaning. The Hebrew translation of *shalom* is "completeness," "wholeness," "well-being," or "welfare and peace." It is derived from a root that means "to be complete" or "to be sound." When *shalom* is best translated as "peace," this peace is more than the mere absence of war or strife. It describes a peace that is positive; a time, place, and condition that features love, righteousness, calmness, political and moral uprightness and much more. It is a word reserved for those who walk with God in a positive relationship. The wicked person, according to Isaiah, does not and cannot know the way of peace (59:8). God speaks of the restoration and glory of His restored people in Zion. One feature that the new community will have is aptly described metaphorically in the words "peace [*shalom*] and righteousness will be your leaders," (Isa. 60:17, NLT) or "I will make peace [*shalom*] your governor" (NIV). King David's thirty mighty men wish "success, success, success"—*shalom* each time, upon David (1 Chr. 12:18). When God's *shalom* is upon His people they are in the highest possible state of His grace. God's coming King in Zion will proclaim "peace" to the nations (Zech. 9:10), a "peace" (*shalom*) that means well being, rest, and security will be with God's people. When Jesus stood among His disciples after His resurrection, He said "Peace be with you" (NIV, KJV). He used the Greek word *eirene*, which is the New Testament equivalent to *shalom*. He was giving the deepest level and meaning of *shalom* to His followers.

And, John reiterated that the peace Jesus gave was Jesus' own peace, not the peace of the world (John 14:27; 16:33; 20:21). Paul notes that a mind filled with the Holy Spirit has life and peace (Rom. 8:6). Finally, Paul instructs all believers who have received peace to live in peace with others (Rom. 12:18). We should aim to be true spiritual peacemakers between humanity, believers or non-believers, and God (Matt. 5:9).

KEY VERSES

1 Samuel 20:42;
2 Kings 22:20;
Isaiah 9:7; 60:17;
66:12;
Zechariah 9:10

Plant

Hebrew expression: *nata'*
Pronunciation: *naw TAH*
Strong's Number: *5193*

The Lord God Almighty was the first gardener. He "planted" the trees and other herbs in the Garden of Eden. But more than that, He planted the garden as the environment for His people (Gen. 2:8). God was a husbandman from the beginning. After the exodus, the Lord planted His people in the land of Canaan, establishing them as its permanent inhabitants (2 Sam. 7:10). Jeremiah described the Lord's construction and nurturing of His people with the image of the carpenter who "builds," *banah*, and the gardener who "plants," *nata'*. The Hebrew verb *nata'* means "to plant"; the noun *neta'* is built from the same root and means "plant," "plantation," or "setting."

Nata' is found more often in the book of Jeremiah than any other book in the Old Testament. God told him that his prophetic call was to deal with the nations, faithfully delivering God's message to them. He was assigned first "to uproot" and "to tear down" nations, and then "to build" and "to plant" them. These are beautiful metaphors from the architectural and botanical worlds (Jer. 1:10). Throughout the Bible, the metaphor of planting became a delightful picture of God caring for His people. King Solomon wisely noted that there was a time "to plant" and a time "to uproot" in the scheme of life (Eccl. 3:2). God also decreed this in His relationship with Israel. He would plant His people in the land (Exod. 15:17), but He would also uproot them if necessary.

In Jeremiah's day, a rebellious Israel was faced with the fact that the Lord, the Master Gardner, was now going to uproot His people from the land. The Lord had planted them and nurtured them, but they had turned into a wild vine (Jer. 2:21). He would now uproot His garden because they had broken His covenant and provoked Him to anger (Jer. 11:17). If Israel as a nation had only trusted their God they would have been like a tree "planted," *shatal*, a synonym of *nata'*, by the waters, just like the wise and righteous man (Ps. 1:3; Jer. 17:8). The hopeful word of God to His people was that they would again be "replanted" (Jer. 31:27) in the land and they would again "plant" vineyards and trees upon the hills (Jer. 31:5). The Lord would watch over the Israelites' planting and building, fulfilling His desire to plant and prosper them (Amos 9:14).

KEY VERSES

Genesis 2:8;
Exodus 15:17;
Ecclesiastes 3:2;
Isaiah 65:21;
Jeremiah 1:10; 31:28

Paul uses the metaphor of planting and growing God's people in the New Testament. He planted the seed, the word, and Apollos watered it (1 Cor. 3:6). Paul also talks of God's greatest planting of His people—for the Lord will plant His people at death, to raise them up with a new body and spirit at the resurrection. God, the Master Planter, cultivates and gives ultimate success to His garden. We are that garden. Daily, we are given exactly what we require to grow closer to Him and move on to the next day.

Praise

Hebrew expression: *halal*
Pronunciation: *haw LAHL*
Strong's Number: *1984*

The exclamation of praise and worship at the beginning and end of Psalm 150 forms an inclusion, a set of parentheses within which the psalmist directs the worshiper and reader to use every possible musical instrument to "praise the Lord!" The Hebrew word *halal* is translated "praise" and is sometimes translated as "boast," meaning "to boast" in the Lord and what He has done, and boast in whom He is as well. The book of Psalms closes with five psalms called "hallelujah" psalms. These psalms contain the phrase "praise," *halal*, the Lord at their beginning and end (Pss. 146—150). The verb *halal* in this phrase is in a stem, which adds the emphasis of directing or producing praise toward the Lord. Attached to the imperative verb form *hallelu*, "praise," is a shortened form of the Lord's name, *yah*. So the phrase *hallelu-yah* in both Hebrew and English translates as "give praise to the Lord." *Hallelu-yah* is a transliteration of the Hebrew into English, not a translation. The Hebrew phrase has taken its proper place in the repertoire of worship in the English language.

To praise the Lord is to do any number of things. It means: to "lift Him up" with our words, to call on Him (2 Sam. 18:28), to recognize His greatness (1 Chr. 16:25), to recognize His Name (1 Chr. 29:13), to give credit to His worthiness (Ps. 18:3), to admit proper fear before Him (Ps. 22:23), and to praise His word (Ps. 56:10). Psalm 150 concludes with the recognition that the Lord should be praised with every possible musical instrument and by every living creature (Ps. 150). But, praise to the Lord is only acceptable from an upright person (Ps. 119:12).

Writers of the Bible repeatedly praise the Lord. Jesus set an ongoing example of this for us (Matt. 11:25). Praise is directed to God and Him alone (Acts 12:23). Peter asserts with inspiration that in all things God may be praised (1 Pet. 4:11). Praise the Lord from whom all blessings flow, He is our great God and Father Almighty! Hallelujah!

KEY VERSES

2 Samuel 22:4;
1 Chronicles 29:13;
Psalms 146:1;
147:1; 148:1;
149:1; 150:1

Pray

See also: *Prayer, p. 364*
Hebrew expression: *palal*
Pronunciation: *paw LAHL*
Strong's Number: *6419*

Prayer is one of the activities that make human beings unique among God's creatures. Only human beings can pray to their Creator and Redeemer—animals and
plant life can not pray. In fact, prayer is the highest kind of human spiritual activity. In times of great joy (Ps. 136) or times of great distress, people will pray
(Ps. 107:23–28).

The Hebrew verb *palal* means "to pray," or "to intercede." It comes from the
root, *pll*, which carries the idea of "intervening" or "interposing." One who prays
"interposes" himself or herself between God and some other thing, condition, or
person. The Bible assumes that people will pray to their God, since they are
dependent upon Him for everything (our sin makes prayer even more of a necessity). The power of prayer is simply amazing because it changes not only the world,
but also the person praying. It touches not only the supplicant, but also the very
heart of God. During Solomon's dedication of the Temple, Solomon spoke of the
power of prayer (2 Chr. 7:13–16). Through prayer (*palal*), people who are called by
the Lord's Name can move God to hear them, forgive them, and heal them and also
their land. Prayer must be accompanied by humility—a serious search for God and
a genuine rejection of evil. Only if these attitudes and actions are present will
prayer be heard—and only when this kind of attitude accompanies prayer will it be
effective. Abraham prayed for Abimelech with this attitude, and God heard him
(Gen. 20:7). Moses prayed for the people of Israel (Num. 21:7), and God heard him.
Hannah prayed to have a child, and God heard her (1 Sam. 1:19, 27). Elisha prayed
for his servant, and God heard him (2 Kgs. 6:17–18).

We, the believers, are in a better situation than the Old Testament people of
faith because we have the Holy Spirit in us, moving us to prayer (*proseuchomai* in
Greek) and praise. Yet, James makes it clear that our prayers
must be accompanied by faith in God (Jas. 1:5–8). We must
believe in the Almighty God we are petitioning. He cites
Elijah's courageous prayer for rain as a model of a great prayer

KEY VERSES

Genesis 20:17;
1 Kings 8:30;
2 Chronicles 7:14

of faith (see Jas. 5:17–18). Jesus Himself took time to teach His
disciples to pray and encouraged them never to give up pray-
ing (see Luke 18:1). In summary, prayer is a precious gift from
God—a gift none of us should ignore. With it, we can enter
God's presence and present our thanks and humble requests.
God promises to hear us and answer.

Prepared

Hebrew expression: *manah*
Pronunciation: *maw NAWH*
Strong's Number: *4487*

The story of Jonah and the whale is one we've heard since we were children. Jonah's story reports an amazing record of the sovereignty and foreknowledge of God. Upon his rebellion against the Lord's word to go preach repentance to the Assyrians in Nineveh, he was cast overboard into the sea, but he did not drown. A great fish "prepared," *manah*, by the Lord swallowed him (Jonah 1:17). The Hebrew verb *manah* can be translated as "to count," "to reckon," "to assign," or "to appoint."

Suffering in God's plan for each of us has been "assigned," *manah*. The word is used to describe the simple assignment of a person to particular physical tasks (1 Chr. 9:29). It can be used to record a simple calculation of descendants (Gen. 13:16). Or, it can assert that which is lacking, in the scheme of "life under the sun cannot be reckoned or assigned" (Eccl. 1:15). In the stem in which the word was used in Jonah five times (Jonah 1:17; 4:6, 7, 8), it clearly takes on the meaning of "to prepare," "to assign," "to reckon," or "to provide." God's sovereignty and plan for Jonah is made clear. The Lord "prepared" a fish (Jonah 1:17), a gourd (Jonah 4:6), a worm (Jonah 4:7) and a strong east wind. Each time, Jonah came to know something new about God's preparation and provision; but mainly he learned that God "assigns" to His chosen servants the experience they need to drive them to Himself and to do their assigned tasks.

In the simple meaning of the verb *manah*, the Lord even "appointed," "numbered" (KJV), "destined" (NLT), His people for the sword and destruction. In Isaiah, God ironically demonstrated that He is the God of Destiny, since His rebellious people insisted upon turning to the false gods of Fate and Destiny (Isa. 65:11–12, NLT). God showed Himself totally in control of Jonah's life, a fact that is both comforting to us and also a warning. God will use His sovereign power to guide and direct us in His will, whether we are as rebellious as Jonah or as acquiescent as Isaiah (Isa. 6:1–9).

The Lord has assigned and prepared tasks for each of us (1 Cor. 3:5), including the circumstances in which we may find ourselves (1 Cor. 7:17). It is comforting above all to know that God is the God who provides. And, it is impossible to point to a greater provision for us than the fact that He "provided" and "prepared" purification and cleansing for our sins through our Savior Jesus (Heb. 1:3, *poieo* in Greek).

KEY VERSES

Genesis 13:16;
Ecclesiastes 1:15;
Isaiah 65:12;
Jonah 1:17

Pride

Hebrew expression: *zadon*
Pronunciation: *zaw DOHN*
Strong's Number: *2087*

The "pride of your heart has deceived you" (Obad. 1:3) is a statement that Jeremiah would have applauded (Jer. 17:9), for he asserted the deceitfulness and the wickedness of the human heart. The imagination of deceit produced by the heart is excessive and offensive confidence in one's self, a type of arrogance that always leads to destruction (Prov. 11:2). Fights and quarrels are a result of excessive pride—even among God's people (Prov. 13:10). The arrogance of the Edomites recorded in Obad. 1:3 is almost humorous to us today. They were a people who lived in a desert. But they took pride in their high rock fortress of Petra—a city cut out of the rocks, an impregnable stronghold in ancient times. The city is still a tourist site today. It is located about 50 miles south of the Dead Sea.

The Hebrew noun *zadon* is translated as "pride," "insolence," "presumptuousness," or "arrogance." The noun is formed from the verbal root *zud* or *zid*, meaning "to boil up," "to act proudly, presumptuously, or rebelliously." Two adjectives from this same root, *zed* and *zedon*, mean "insolent," "presumptuous," or "raging." The pride and arrogance represented by *zadon* can refer to presumptuousness toward other persons (1 Sam. 17:28), but usually it is a negative self-centered insolence directed in some way toward deity.

Pride and arrogance that puffs a person up so that they disrespect the appointed priest or judge of the Lord is an act of rebellion. The punishment in the Mosaic Law for such arrogance was death (Deut. 17:12). A prophet who speaks falsely was considered to have spoken arrogantly and insolently (Deut. 18:22). In the Bible, humility is the virtue that is the opposite of pride. Wisdom is the outcome of humility, while shame is the natural result of pride and arrogance (Prov. 11:2). Pride is a kind of presumption that does not respect others properly and lifts oneself up too readily (Jer. 49:16). Babylon and its kings are the chief examples of the prideful nations in the Old Testament that destroyed Israel and other peoples (Jer. 48:29; 49:16; 50:31, 32).

KEY VERSES

Proverbs 11:2; 13:10;
Obadiah 3

Although both the Old and New Testament warn against anything approaching pride, there is room for boasting as long as it is in the Lord, and not in oneself (2 Cor. 10:17). We have no right to take credit for anything that happens in life—everything comes from the Lord! Paul does indicate that there is a certain satisfaction Christians can take in carrying out our responsibilities well (Gal. 6:4). Unbridled pride, however, is a dangerous sin for it keeps our eyes on ourselves, instead of on the Lord God Almighty.

Priest

See also: *Priest, p. 366*
Hebrew expression: *kohen*
Pronunciation: *koh HAYN*
Strong's Number: *3548*

God asserts that Israel shall be a kingdom of "priests" and a holy nation for Him (Exod. 19:6). Peter, by the Holy Spirit, declares that Christians are now a royal "priesthood" and a holy nation (1 Pet. 2:9). God, from the time He chose Israel as His people, desired that they be a priestly people. Aaron was the first High Priest in Israel and Jesus became the last and eternal High Priest (Heb. 7:17; 9:11–14); but Jesus' priesthood extended far beyond the nation of Israel.

The book of Leviticus has more than sixty-six verses that mention the "priest" and his duties. The Hebrew noun *kohen* indicates "a person who performs the function of a priest" and has been appointed to the status of priest. The Hebrew verb *kahan*, "to function or act as priest," was formed from the noun. The Lord chose the tribe of Levi to perform the priestly functions in Israel and He picked Aaron, from the sons of Kohath, as the first High Priest (Exod. 6:17–23; 28:3). Aaron's sons were to succeed him in this duty (Exod. 28:1). All of their assignments consisted of carrying out the religious duties connected with the worship and service of God. They were set aside as holy to serve God (Exod. 29:1). They were authorized to perform and administer the religious rites, especially the sacrifices in Israel. Even their sacred garments set them aside (Exod. 31:10). God is holy and His people were sinful, therefore the chief function of the priest was to serve as an intermediary between God and His people. The High Priest performed the sacrificial ritual on the Day of Atonement to cleanse himself and the people of unintentional sins (Lev. 16:5, 9, 14, 15–16, 24). Other sacrifices were performed and atoning blood was sprinkled, according to the requirement of each particular ritual.

P

The priests of Israel in the New Testament carried out the same functions assigned to them in the Old Testament. While Jesus recognized the religious and historic continuity between the Old and New Testament, the author of Hebrews declares that Jesus has now been appointed as the new and final High Priest in Israel (Heb. 5:5–10). There is no need for another priest. Everything that the Levitical priesthood pointed to in the Old Testament is fulfilled in Christ. His own blood, as the blood of the Lamb of God (John 1:29), takes away the sins of Jews and Gentiles who follow Him (Heb. 10:4, 10; 8). Jesus' priesthood is greater than Aaron's or even Melchizedek's, for He lives forever. His priesthood is eternal. He is perfect and His atonement for us is perfect (Heb. 7:26–28). By virtue of His priesthood, the church is now the "Kingdom of Priests" that God desires (1 Pet. 2:5–9; Rev. 1:6; 5:10; 20:6).

KEY VERSES

Exodus 19:6; 31:10

Prophet

See also: *Prophecy, p. 368 and Prophet, p. 369*
Hebrew expression: *nabi'*
Pronunciation: *naw BEE*
Strong's Number: *5030*

A popular conception of "prophets" is that they foretell the future. Although the ability to foretell the future is an important role of a prophet, it is not the major function. God's prophets in the Bible spoke messages for the people in their day, including warnings and words of hope. A prophet was first of all called to speak forth the word of God as delivered to him or her—whether it referred to the past, present, future, or to all these aspects of life at the same time. The Hebrew word *nabi'* is always translated as "prophet." Two other words have a similar meaning: *ro'eh*, "seer" which is literally "one who sees," and *chozeh*, which is literally "one who sees," "envisions," or "has a vision" (Isa. 30:10; 1 Chr. 29:29). The noun *nabi'* gave rise to the verb *naba'* meaning "to prophesy."

Scholars have written many books about the meaning of *nabi'*. The Hebrew word for "prophet" means "one who is called" or "one who calls" in the name of the Lord. Prophets held their authority because they had been called and spoken to by the Lord to deliver His messages to the people. A false prophet was one who claimed to be called by God, but in reality was not called and was merely speaking his own heart or mind (Jer. 23:25–32). Another major aspect of the prophet is brought out in an amazing passage in Hosea. The prophet is said to be a "watchman" over Israel along with Israel's God (Hos. 9:8). Yet in Hosea's day these divinely inspired people were attacked, persecuted, and killed—hostility from the people awaited them at every move. A prophet was even reckoned to be a fool by the people (Hos. 9:7).

The Lord brought Israel up out of Egypt by the hand of the greatest prophet of all—Moses. So why was Israel persecuting her prophets rather than listening to them? The Israelites had become so corrupt that they caused some of their prophets to stumble with them (Hos. 4:5). Yet God's faithful prophets, His servants (Jer. 25:4), continued to speak His word. Without a prophet to proclaim God's messages, there would have been no hope for Israel. Today, however, the recorded words of God's prophets are sure words of assurance that God continues to use in our lives. The prophets' messages in the Bible are both words of hope and judgment.

KEY VERSES

Genesis 20:7;
1 Samuel 3:20;
1 Kings 18:36;
Jeremiah 28:1;
Hosea 4:5; 6:5

Luke's gospel asserts that Jesus, because He is God, was a powerful prophet when He was on earth. He moved the people with both His words and His deeds (Luke 24:19). Jesus was, in fact, the one in whom the Old Testament prophets' words were fulfilled. His prophetic words agree with the words of the Old Testament prophets and they all speak to those who follow the Lord. Because of the Bible, God's living word, we can hear a prophetic word in the midst of a dark generation that is rejecting God.

Proverb

Hebrew expression: *mashal*
Pronunciation: *maw SHAHL*
Strong's Number: *4912*

"A gentle answer turns away wrath, But a harsh word stirs up anger"—that is a proverb, a *mashal* (Prov. 15:1, NASB).

Mashal is translated several ways in the Old Testament. Most often it is translated as "proverb(s)," but it is also rendered as "oracle," especially in the case of Balaam (Num. 23:7, 18; 24:3, 15). It is sometimes rendered as a "byword," a word with negative connotations to it (Ps. 44:14; Jer. 24:9). Some translations prefer to render the word as "parable" (compare Num. 23:7, KJV, NIV). A proverb is often described as a short pithy saying, usually given in concrete terms, that captures and summarizes some aspect of life in a memorable way. This does not, however, describe adequately the *meshalim* (plural) of Balaam which are, in effect, prophecies. However, in every case, short, crisp, concrete, easily remembered language is used.

In the book of Proverbs, *mashal* is regularly rendered as "proverb." The noun came from a supposed original root *mashal* meaning "to represent or to be like." This language became a tool to teach. The entire book of Proverbs is referred to as the "proverbs," *meshalim*, of Solomon (Prov. 1:1). The proverbs are used to instruct the people in the wisdom of God and man, to help them better grasp and understand these wisdom gems of life. The wise Preacher of Ecclesiastes knew the value of a well spoken proverb to instruct his hearers, so he diligently sought them out and even composed some himself (Eccl. 12:9). The men of King Hezekiah copied out and preserved Solomon's proverbs long after he had died (Prov. 25:1). He had spoken three thousand proverbs (1 Kgs. 4:32), and they had been recorded.

Proverbs are memorable and beautiful. "As snow in summer, and as rain in harvest, so honour is not seemly for a fool" (Prov. 26:1, KJV). Or, "Like a gold ring in a pig's snout is a beautiful woman who shows no discretion" (Prov. 11:22, NIV). These are true, catchy, concrete examples. Difficult concepts are made easily accessible by the use of proverbs or parables (*meshalim*).

Proverbs can be positive or negative, complimentary or insulting. A "byword," *mashal*, is used to describe Israel, after God judges them for their unfaithfulness to Him. God makes His people a byword ("object of horror," NLT; Jer. 24:9) because of their rottenness before Him (Ps. 44:14). "Physician, heal thyself" was a proverb Jesus had directed toward himself (Luke 4:23, *parabole* in Greek). Peter described those who turn back from following the Lord with the parables or proverbs "A dog returns to its vomit" and "A washed pig returns to the mud" (2 Pet. 2:22, NLT). A healthy devotional practice is to read one chapter of proverbs a day—they will prod us on to wise living (Eccl. 12:9).

KEY VERSES

1 Kings 9:7;
Job 13:12;
Psalm 44:14;
Proverbs 10:1;
26:7, 9;
Ezekiel 12:22

P

Psalm

Hebrew expression: *mizmor*
Pronunciation: *mihz MOHR*
Strong's Number: *4210*

In ancient Israel, psalms were produced for nearly every occasion: death, life, oppression, deliverance, fear, dedications, festivals, feasts, worship, and more. Psalms of praise, remembrance, history, wisdom, confidence, penitence, confession and more are in the book of Psalms. The making of a psalm was a heartfelt, inspired production of music, prayer, and praise to God. The Hebrew word *mizmor* means "psalm." But other words help get a handle on the description of a "psalm." *Mizmor* comes from the root of *zamar*, a verb meaning "to make or produce music in praise to God." Several other nouns are formed from the root of this verb; they all refer to music in some way: *zimrah*, "melody, song"; *zamir*, "song"; *mizmor*, "song," "melody." The name *mizmor* also describes the entire book of Psalms composed of one hundred and fifty psalms. So the psalms are songs, melodies, poetic praise, and prayer to God set to music on musical instruments.

Mizmor occurs fifty-seven times in the "titles" of various psalms. It is, then, the word the Bible uses most often to describe the general content of the book of Psalms. The rabbis called the book of Psalms *tehillim*, "songs of praise" (title in Ps. 145). The psalmists wrote poetry because poetry rather than prose speaks to the whole person: heart, mind, will, emotions and soul. But the poetry was the servant vehicle through which God's inspired writers produced *mizmorim*, "psalms," and *tehillim*, "praises." They set their poetry to music for use in Israel's worship.

These timeless prayers, praises, and songs, used to honor God for His great words and deeds, come to us across time and cultures and speak God's comforting word to us today. The use of psalms as a way to praise God and encourage one another is important in the New Testament. Paul urges Christians to speak to each other with psalms (*psalmoi* in Greek) and hymns (Eph. 5:19; Col. 3:16). All of our worship through psalms is for the *tehillim*, praises of God.

KEY VERSES

Psalms 3; 4; 6;
8; 9; 12

Read

Hebrew expression: *qara'*
Pronunciation: *qaw RAW*
Strong's Number: *7121*

From Mount Sinai, God "spoke" His ten words of instruction to the people, and they all heard Him (Exod. 20:18–19). The Lord often spoke to His people. But the Bible describes God's Word as being read by a scribe to the people of Israel even more times. For instance, Moses wrote down the Ten Commandments God had given him. Moses wrote down all of God's Words in the Book of the Covenant. Then Moses read those words to the people (Exod. 24:7). This recorded Word of God was unique to Israel. No other nation had God's Word in written form. Once the Lord's words were written down, Israel was to keep His Words permanently—without adding to them or subtracting from them. Every seven years, the Law of the Lord was supposed to be read before the people (Deut. 31:10–11). *Qara'* is the Hebrew word for "read." It also means "to call," "to summon," or "to proclaim." It can mean to read aloud, literally "in the ears of" the people (Deut. 31:11). But it also refers to reading for one's own benefit and devotion. The king of Israel was to read the Law of the Lord all of his life in order to learn to love, revere, and obey the Lord and His decrees (Deut. 17:18–19). Reading, thus, became a way to learn about the Lord, a devotional and wise exercise, especially for God's leaders. Joshua read the Law to the people upon conquering Canaan (Josh. 8:34–35). After Israel returned from captivity in Babylon, Ezra the scribe read the Law of the Lord to them (Neh. 8:3–18). The reading of God's Word was accompanied with great praise and worship. Ezra read from the Hebrew text, but the people needed a translation or explanation to help them (Neh. 8:8). Consequently, an Aramaic translation was given to the people because this was the language they were able to speak and understand orally. The reading of the Law in captivity and throughout Jewish history has helped preserve the Israelites and their identity. Reading makes it possible to recall, and not to forget, the great events that the Lord has done for His people.

R

In the New Testament, Christians are encouraged to read and to study the word of God (John 5:39; 2 Tim. 2:15). Jesus expected the Jews to know the Scriptures, and believers should know them as well (Mark 12:26). We need to be prepared, for our own sakes as well as others, to be able to discuss the meaning and insights received from the Bible's teaching. The Bible is God's Living Word, and is therefore able to help us—through the power of the Holy Spirit—at any given point in our lives. There is also a special blessing for those who read and obey the words of the book of Revelation (Rev. 22:7). Knowing the Holy Scriptures makes us wise and able to receive salvation (2 Tim. 3:15). Just like the Israelites of old, Christians should read the word of God and remember what the Lord has done for us.

KEY VERSES

Exodus 24:7;
Deuteronomy 17:19;
31:11;
Nehemiah 8:3

Redeemed

See also: *Redemption, p. 374*
Hebrew expression: *ga'al*
Pronunciation: *gaw 'AHL*
Strong's Number: *1350*

The word "redeemed" most often points to something that has been recovered by paying a sum to get it back. It can also indicate something like a promissory note or coupon that has been redeemed by paying the value of the note or receiving the value of the coupon. In Exodus 15:13, the Hebrew word *ga'al* is used to indicate the supreme act of "redemption" in the Old Testament—the redemption of Israel at the Red Sea. Moses recounted the gospel of deliverance for the first time in the justly famous poem "Song of the Sea." He rejoiced at how the Lord had "redeemed," *ga'al*, the Israelites from Egypt. In this verse the word means "to remove" or "to rescue" the Israelites from the power and slavery of the Egyptians (Exod. 6:6). God redeemed His people and led them by His power to Mount Sinai to worship Him (Exod. 3:12) and then to Mount Zion (Pss. 2:6; 9:11; 76:2; 132:13).

When God freed His people from Egypt they were "redeemed." But, God Himself put forth His own efforts to redeem them. The verb *ga'al* means then "to ransom" or "to redeem" by paying a price. The price God paid was His own involvement—by His own outstretched arm He defeated the Egyptians, Pharaoh, and their gods (Exod. 12:12; 15:6, 12; Ps. 77:15). He slew the first born of the Egyptians to avenge for their attempt to destroy the Hebrew slaves (Exod. 1:15–22). In this capacity the Lord functioned as a near kinsman, "the Avenger of blood"—another meaning *ga'al* may carry (Num. 35:19, 21). In fact, "to act as a good kinsman" is a valid meaning for the verb. A good kinsman may act in various capacities to help his kinsmen who stand in need (Lev. 25:25, 48, 49; Job 19:25). Throughout the Bible, the Lord redeemed individuals from death and perilous circumstances (Ps. 103:4; Jer. 50:34), as well as His people Israel from the Babylonian captivity (Isa. 43:1; 48:20). The Lord is named the *go'el*, "redeemer," of Israel many times in Isaiah (Isa. 41:14; 43:14). He redeemed the orphan Israel (Prov. 23:10–11)—that is, He cared for and protected them. All of these scenarios depict God preparing His people for the supreme act of Jesus as the Kinsman Redeemer of the human race.

God demonstrated supreme redemption in His Son Jesus Christ who paid the price of atonement and died so that we may live (Mark 10:45; Eph. 1:7; 1 Cor. 6:19; Heb. 9:15). As Israel was God's unique redeemed possession in the Old Testament (Exod. 6:6; 19:5–6), so in the New Testament those redeemed by Christ are God's possession (Eph. 1:4). God's people are sealed and secured for the coming day of redemption at Christ's return (Eph. 4:30; Rev. 14:3). Though our sins separate us from God, Jesus is our Redeemer. He has rescued us from sin. Let us rejoice in the freedom He provides.

KEY VERSES

Exodus 6:6; 15:13;
Psalm 74:2;
Isaiah 62:12

146

Relent

Hebrew expression: *nacham*
Pronunciation: *naw HAHM*
Strong's Number: *5162*

We have probably seen anger that is "relentless"—that is, an emotion so strong it will not be abated. The God of Israel, however, is a God who relents of His anger and allows compassion to rule in place of power. The Hebrew word *nacham* means "to be sorry," "to pity," or "to repent." In the Bible, *nacham* is translated as "relent" (NIV), "repentant" (KJV), and "cancel your plans" (NLT). The people of Nineveh, capital of the great Assyrian Empire, entertained the possibility that God would not carry out His intended destruction upon them (Jonah 3:9–10). They mourn, repent, turn from evil and violence, and seek God. The Lord saw their changed attitude and actions and was pleased. He "had mercy" (NLT) on, "had compassion" (NIV) for, "repented" (KJV) from His judgment upon them (Jonah 3:10). Jonah said, "I knew that you are . . . a God who relents from sending calamity" (Jonah 4:2). Indeed, the Lord turned from His just judgment because He heard the cries of the repentant Ninevites.

In Jonah 3:9, the Ninevites hope that God will "relent" from His plan to destroy them; in verse ten the Lord "repents," or "relents," concerning His intentions and extends mercy, pity and grace to His intended victims. This passage records one of the great illustrations in the Bible where God does "relent," change His mind, and show compassion upon those who turn from evil and do good. When people repent He relents. History on a personal and national level is changed because of the moral response of human beings. Nineveh's hope that the Lord would relent by showing them compassion was accurate. Even at the beginning of Israel's infancy in the desert when she rebelled, God graciously did *nacham* and did not destroy His people (Exod. 32:14). All of this is further demonstrated again in Jeremiah: God always deals with His people mercifully if possible (Jer. 18:8; 26:3, 13, 19), but there does come a time when in the face of blatant continuous rebellion He will not "relent" (Jer. 4:28).

The Lord relents because of His great love (Ps. 106:45). It was His desire to relent and not cause calamity or destroy the Israelites (Amos 7:3, 6; Joel 2:13; Jonah 4:2). Job was a righteous man. When he catches a glimpse of the august sovereignty, power, and glory of God, he "repents" in dust and ashes (Job 42:6). The ultimate repentance that God looks for in humanity, Jew or Gentile, is the repentance that turns from sin to His Son and His gospel (Mark 1:15). Then He relents and turns from His anger toward us because of our faith in Jesus (Acts 17:30; 26:20). The people of Nineveh and their repentance is held up as an example to be followed today (Luke 11:32). To repent is to relent from the evil we have been following and to pursue the ways of the Lord (Acts 3:19). God loves us and wants us to follow Him so that we can enjoy Him and the blessings He provides.

KEY VERSES

Exodus 32:14;
Job 42:6;
Psalm 106:45;
Jeremiah 18:8; 26:3;
Joel 2:13

Remember

Hebrew expression: *zakar*
Pronunciation: *zaw KAHR*
Strong's Number: *2142*

The Lord is a God who remembers—He remembers His covenant and His promises to His people. Early in the Old Testament, the Lord "remembered" Noah and all the animals in the ark making it clear that He will remember all life that He created. (Gen. 8:1). Once God "remembered them," He proceeded to rescue them. When God remembers, He acts upon His memory. He made a covenant with Noah and declared that He would remember His covenant forever and never again destroy the world by water (Gen. 9:15–16). "To remember" is the translation of the Hebrew word *zakar*. It probably is closely related to the Akkadian word *zikaru*, which means "to name" or "to mention." From the root *zakar*, we also get *zeker* and *zikkaron* which both mean "memorial or remembrance."

God often directs His people in the Old Testament to remember their past and all that He had said and done for them (Deut. 4:10; 5:15; 7:18; 8:18; 24:9). After the Israelites had sinned with the Golden Calf, Moses prayed and sought God's mercy for Israel. He cried out to the Lord "to remember" Abraham, Isaac, Jacob and the promises He had made to them. Moses thought that then, perhaps, the Lord would not destroy the people of Israel for this grave sin (Deut. 9:27). Israel's rebellious history against the Lord was recorded for later posterity so that they would "remember" and "not forget" how they had sinned against the Lord (Deut. 9:7). David cries out for the Lord to "remember" His great mercy and love, because the Lord consistently displayed these characteristics toward His people; but he cries out for an even greater act on God's behalf concerning His memory. David asks that the Lord would "not remember" his rebellion and sins from the time of his youth (Ps. 25:6–7). God can remember His people in anger or love; David cries out for the Lord to remember him according to His love (Ps. 25:7). Solomon admonishes us to "remember" the Lord during the days of our youth (Eccl. 12:1). Isaiah also pleads that the Lord not remember the sins of His people forever (Isa. 64:9).

R

KEY VERSES

Genesis 8:1;
9:15–16;
Exodus 20:8;
Deuteronomy 5:15;
Psalm 25:6–7

God, in fact, promises a covenant, the new covenant that Jesus Christ has instituted, in which He will remember His people's sins no more (Jer. 31:31–34; Luke 22:20; 1 Cor. 11:25; Heb. 8:10–12). Israel was to remember all the things the Lord did for them. Likewise, Peter encourages us as Christians to remember the blessings Christ has made available to us (1 Pet. 1:3–15).

Remnant

Hebrew expression: *she'erit*
Pronunciation: *sheh 'ay REET*
Strong's Number: *7611*

Joseph told his father and brothers that the Lord had arranged for them to be saved by sending him to Egypt first, so that he could prepare for their safety. They were a "remnant" so to speak since they were so small in number. *She'erit,* usually translated as "remnant," also means "survivor," "residue," "remainder," or "rest." *She'erit* comes from the root of the verb *sha'ar* meaning "to be left over, or remain." "Remnant" is also a translation of a related noun *she'ar,* best rendered as "rest," "remnant," or "residue." The words *yeter* and *pelitah* are also translated "remnant" in certain contexts. "Remnant" can refer simply to something left over; a group of people left over or a surviving trace of something. But Joseph hinted at the most significant use of the term when he spoke of the Lord's leaving a "remnant" to Israel. This thought becomes a major prophetic theme. Israel became so rebellious that God threatened to annihilate her, but He relented and declared that He would preserve His people by saving a "remnant" of them from destruction. From that remnant, He would rebuild His people. This was an act of His grace alone—Israel had proven to be totally recalcitrant as a nation.

Isaiah, picturing a time after the judgment of Israel, speaks of a remnant that would come out of Jerusalem (2 Kgs. 19:31; Isa. 37:32). When God judged Israel He carried a remnant into exile in Babylon, preserved them (2 Chr. 36:20), and returned them to Jerusalem seventy years later (Ezra 1:1–2; 9:8, 13, 14, 15; Neh. 1:2). Ezra prayed earnestly that the Lord would continue to be merciful to the remnant and preserve it. Ezekiel interjected with "woe," "ah," "alas," when he dared wonder whether the Lord would actually destroy the remnant of Israel (Ezek. 9:8). Micah, however, foresees the forgiveness of their transgression (Mic. 7:18). Zephaniah also pierces the future and sees a time when the preserved remnant will not only overcome their enemies, but will do no wrong (Zeph. 3:13).

It is through this remnant (Acts 15:17, *kataloipos* in Greek) concept that we Gentiles are a part of God's people. Through Christ, we are the remnant of men and women seeking the Lord. And, even now among Israel the Lord is preserving His remnant, chosen by grace, to be delivered (Rom. 9:27; 11:5, *upoleimma* in Greek).

R

KEY VERSES

Genesis 45:7;
2 Kings 19:4;
Isaiah 37:32;
Jeremiah 44:7;
Zephaniah 2:7, 9

Renew

Hebrew expression: *chadash*
Pronunciation: *khaw DAHSH*
Strong's Number: *2318*

Chadash is a beautiful, refreshing word, which means "to renew," "to repair," or "to restore." It is one of the words that brought joy to the prophets as they spoke it, and delight and hope to the people of Israel when they heard it. Two other words are formed from the root of this verb meaning "new," "new moon," or "month"—since the moon was "restored" each month. *Chadash* can also refer to the refurbishing and restoration of buildings. Joash restored the Temple of the Lord, putting carpenters and others to work on it (2 Chr. 24:4, 12). Most often *chadash* refers to the restoration work of God. Isaiah saw the devastation God would bring upon Israel and Judah, but he also was moved to speak of a time when Israel and others would renew the ancient cities of the land and restore them to their former beauty (Isa. 61:4). The psalmist asserted that by the Lord's sending forth of His Spirit all life was created and the face of the earth was "renewed" (Ps. 104:30). There is nothing that God cannot renew; He is the God of renewal.

David cried out and implored the Lord to "restore" a faithful spirit within him, so that he could again know the joy of serving the Lord (Ps. 51:10). The physical nourishment that the Lord provides for His people "renews" their youth as the eagle's (Ps. 103:5). It is no surprise then that Jeremiah cries out to the Lord for a total restoration of himself and God's people (Lam. 5:21). The Lord had allowed the Babylonians to destroy Jerusalem and take His people into exile. Although the Israelites were taken far from Jerusalem, Jerusalem was not far from their thoughts and hearts. Jeremiah cries out for the Lord to return them to Himself and to "renew" their days as of old when they were in His good graces. The Israelites knew above all that their renewal would come from the Lord. And He prophesied through His faithful servant Jeremiah that He would renew them through His "new," *chadash*, covenant when He wrote His law on their hearts (Jer. 31:31–34).

KEY VERSES

2 Chronicles 24:4;
Psalms 51:10;
103:5;
Isaiah 61:4;
Lamentations 5:21

In the New Testament, the theme of the internal renewal of God's people is stressed, but a total renewal of the heavens and earth will also become a reality. Christians are being renewed inwardly every day by God's Spirit (2 Cor. 4:16, *anakainoo* in Greek). The very image of God is being restored in us as we grow in true knowledge of Christ (Col. 3:10). All of this is accomplished by what Titus called the cleansing of "rebirth and renewal" (Titus 3:5, *anakainosis* in Greek). Jesus taught that eventually all things would be renewed (Matt. 19:28, *paliggenesia* in Greek). We, as believers, should look forward to that spectacular day of renewal.

Repay

Hebrew expression: *natan*
Pronunciation: *naw TAHN*
Strong's Number: *5414*

To repay someone usually carries negative connotations—meaning something like "payback time," "revenge," or "settle the account." The Hebrew word *natan* has a very broad range of meanings; "repay" is only one way to translate this word. The basic meanings of *natan*, "to give," "to set," "to put," or "to present," produce many nuances according to the context. God's judgment upon Israel, one of the major themes in Ezekiel, is that He "gives back" to, or "repays" them for their wicked conduct and the lewd and detestable practices which they had followed, both religious and secular (Ezek. 7:3–4). Israel's worship of the sun, images of animals and creeping things, their pursuit of immorality, other pagan gods, and processes of nature led to her downfall. The detestable and abominable practices of God's people were not overlooked, and the Lord repaid her appropriately. Each time *natan* is translated "repay" (NIV) the reason given is to repay His people for these "detestable practices" (Ezek. 7:8–9). "Recompense," "call to account," and "complete" are other words used in Ezekiel 7:3–4, 8–9 (KJV, NLT).

The psalmist David asks the Lord to repay those who are working evil against him rather than take vengeance into his own hands. This sentiment is developed strongly in the New Testament. The person of God should ask the Lord's recompense upon his or her enemies and not undertake repayment with his or her own hands. It is clear that whether God's people are sinning or the enemies of God's people are working evil against the righteous, God eventually "gives" the proper wages for evil deeds. It was God who rendered payment upon the great world kingdoms of Babylon, Assyria and Egypt.

In the New Testament, Paul urges Christians not to repay (*apodidomi* in Greek) evil for evil, but to render good for evil! (Rom. 12:17; 1 Pet. 3:9). And, the same position is reiterated over and over in the words of Jesus at the Sermon on the Mount (Matt. 5—7). Christ's followers are even to pray for those who persecute them. The Lord will render repayment (Heb. 10:30, *antapodidomi* in Greek). The Lord will repay every person according to their deeds (Ezek. 7:3, 4, 8, 9). We are forgiven in Christ, but must seek to honor God always with faith, doing good and kind things for others.

R

KEY VERSES

Psalm 28:4;
Ezekiel 7:3–4, 8–9

Rest

See also: *Rest, p. 377*
Hebrew expression: *shaqat*
Pronunciation: *shaw QAHT*
Strong's Number: *8252*

The most important "rest" spoken of in the Old Testament is a spiritual rest—not the rest needed to gather strength in order to go on with some physical task. The Hebrew word *shaqat* means "to be at peace," "to rest," "to be quiet," or "to calm." It refers to many kinds of rests—rest from political turmoil, from war, from confusion, and in general, rest from all of one's human or spiritual enemies. In the Old Testament, God planned for the Israelites to live in peace in the Promised Land and rest in His presence. By remaining faithful and obedient to God, the Israelites would experience this "rest" because God would free them from internal and external enemies. To those who disobeyed, God declared that they would never enter the Promised Land and never enjoy rest (Ps. 95:7–11). Many Israelites did not enter God's rest because of their unbelief and disobedience. In fact, in Numbers 14:30, God asserts that not one person of that rebellious generation would enter the land. Those who eventually did enter were given God's peace (Josh. 1:13, 15) and His rest (Deut. 3:20; Josh. 11:23).

Those who entered the land experienced only intermittent rest from their enemies—sometimes they had peace for forty years, sometimes eighty years (Josh. 11:23; 14:15; Judg. 3:11, 30). Finally, the nation was removed from the land to Babylon because of disobedience and a lack of faith. Upon returning from Babylonian captivity, the nation hoped to once again enter God's rest (Jer. 30:10; 46:27)—that is, to dwell in His presence. But Israel had not yet learned that peace and rest was the fruit of righteousness (Isa. 32:17). In trust and quietness (*shaqat*) before the Lord, Israel would have been strong, but she failed to wait upon God (Isa. 30:15–17).

The writer of Hebrews asserts that there is still a "rest" for those who believe in Christ. Believers have entered that rest already—that is, they have entered it in faith, through Jesus (Heb. 4:1–3). We do not have to worry about our lives because the Lord takes care of us. He will help carry our burdens and give us the strength we need to endure (Matt. 11:28–30). Believers can also hope for and anxiously await our final "rest" which will be in Heaven with Jesus our Savior (Heb. 4:8–11). We will be free from sin and will live for eternity with our brothers and sisters in Christ.

R

KEY VERSES

Joshua 11:23; 14:15;
Judges 3:11, 30;
5:31;
Isaiah 30:15

Return

Hebrew expression: *shub*
Pronunciation: *SHOOB*
Strong's Number: 7725

Most of us have had the experience of posting a letter only to find it some days later in the mailbox marked "Return to Sender." Such is the nature of the reversal expressed in this Old Testament word "return."

The Hebrew word *shub* means literally "to turn," "to return," "to turn back," or even "to turn around." The term essentially refers to a reversal or change of direction, an "about face." For example, the border of the territory of Asher "turned" east toward Beth Dagon (Josh. 19:27). After his intercession for the city of Sodom, Abraham "returned" to his place of residence (Gen. 18:33). Naomi encouraged her daughters-in-law Ruth and Orpah to "turn back" to Moab, their homeland, after the deaths of their husbands (Ruth 1:11). The Israelites desired to "turn around" and go back to Egypt given the harshness of their experience in the Sinai desert (Num. 14:4).

This word *return* is also a key theological term in the Old Testament. It is one expression used to describe both apostasy (Josh. 22:23, 29) and repentance (Ezek. 14:6; 18:30). Apostasy implies the severance or abandonment of a relationship, while repentance implies a return to a relationship. In a religious context, the turnaround of repentance suggests God's acceptance and restoration of a penitent believer to a place of fellowship (2 Chr. 30:6–9; Ps. 85:4; Ezek. 18:32).

Repentance is an act of will (Jer. 3:22) that involves turning *away* from evil (2 Kgs. 17:13) and turning *to* God because He is merciful (Jer. 42:12). True repentance acknowledges God's lordship (Jer. 3:22), admits guilt and confesses sin (Jer. 3:13, 23, 25), sorrowfully recognizes the shame of sin (Jer. 3:25), and pledges a change in behavior (Jer. 4:1–2). Repentance is a rejection of the past and a new direction for the future based upon a willful change of heart and behavior. The Bible identifies symbols of repentance as well: Job repents in "dust and ashes" (Job 42:6), and Joel calls for repentance with "sackcloth" and "fasting, with weeping, and with mourning" (Joel 1:13; 2:12). The external symbols of repentance, however, can never substitute for internal changes produced by true repentance.

The prophets Zechariah (1:3–4) and Malachi (3:7) recognize a certain reciprocity in the act of repentance—God "returns" to those who have "returned" to Him (2 Chr. 30:9). In fact, Hosea suggests that sinners return (repent) by the help of God himself (Hos. 12:6; see also Jer. 31:18). That God returns to the penitent is a declaration of His faithfulness to the covenant relationship established with Israel and symbolizes the forgiveness He extends to all who truly repent (Jer. 31:31–34). The divine response includes full restoration to covenant relationship with God (Jer. 30:3; Amos 9:14) and may result in a stay of divine punishment should God choose to relent (Joel 2:14; Jonah 3:9).

R

KEY VERSES

Jeremiah 3:12, 14;
Ezekiel 18:30;
Joel 2:12, 13;
Zechariah 1:3, 4;
Malachi 3:7

Riddle

Hebrew expression: *chidah*
Pronunciation: *hee DAWH*
Strong's Number: *2420*

In the Old Testament, the presentation of a "riddle" was a serious and important way to communicate truth. *Chidah,* which is "riddle" in Hebrew, can also be translated according to the context as "a perplexing saying," "an allegory," "an answer," or "a puzzle." *Chidah* probably comes from a root meaning "indirect," "obscure"— and the verb *chud* means "to put forth a riddle or puzzle."

Chidah occurs only seventeen times in the Old Testament and can be translated "riddle" in at least ten of those occurrences. It occurs eight times alone in the story of Samson (Judg. 13—16). Samson presented a *chidah* to the Philistines and offered them a handsome reward if they could solve it (Judg. 14:14). The Philistines could not solve it. Thus Samson demonstrated his superiority over them by delivering a riddle they could not solve. They were only able to solve it by threatening Samson's wife to give them the answer (Judg. 14:15). The word *chidah* is also found in the passage about the Queen of Sheba's visit to Solomon. She tested Solomon's wisdom by presenting him with riddles to solve (1 Kgs. 10:1; 2 Chr. 9:1). Solomon met the challenge.

Someone who would solve riddles and "hard sayings" or "hard questions" was therefore considered a wise and discerning person. It took study and training to be able to understand the riddles of the wise. Yet, one of the purposes and promises of the book of Proverbs is the ability to do this (Prov. 1:6). The psalmist utters the deeds of the Lord to the current and future generations as "hidden things," and as "riddles," because they represent the great wisdom of God (Ps. 78:1–4). Jesus quoted Psalm 78:2 when He preached and taught about the Kingdom of God in parables (Matt. 13:35). By using these teaching methods that involved obscure sayings and stories, Jesus hid the precious truths of the Kingdom of God from the wicked and revealed them to those who humbled themselves to learn these mysteries from Him.

R

KEY VERSES

Numbers 12:8;
Judges 14:12–19;
1 Kings 10:1;
Psalm 49:4;
Proverbs 1:6

Right

Hebrew expression: *yashar*
Pronunciation: *yaw SHAHR*
Strong's Number: *3477*

"If I have wronged anyone, I will make it right," is the essence of Samuel's farewell speech to the people of Israel he had served so faithfully (1 Sam. 12:3). Samuel uses the Hebrew word *yashar*, which means "right," "straight," or "upright." It can also mean "level" if it is referring to certain things (Isa. 26:7). *Yashar* comes from a verb that means "to be smooth, right, correct, or straight." In the ethical sense of the word, "right" means to deal with another person fairly and honestly. The word is found most often in the Psalms, Job, and Proverbs and in the history books of First and Second Kings and Second Chronicles. It is a relational word, not an abstract word, for "what is right" or "righteousness." In Psalms, the writer asserts that God saves the "upright" in heart (Ps. 7:10) and it is the upright who are able to come into His presence (Ps. 11:7). A man who deals fairly and honestly with others is declared upright by the Lord (Prov. 11:6) and both his speech and life are approved by God (Prov. 12:6; 14:2). Above all, the Lord is upright in dealing with His people and His whole creation (Ps. 25:8). The good King Jehoshaphat did what was right and just in the eyes of the Lord—he was *yashar* (2 Chr. 20:32). Jehoshaphat kept the Law, judgments, and ordinances of the Lord, just like his father Asa (2 Chr. 14:2) and King David (1 Kgs. 15:5). In His laws, the Lord taught His people to be *yashar*. He taught them how to live both before Him and before their fellow human beings (2 Chr. 6:27). Many times it is asserted that the kings of Judah did what was just and upright before the Lord. They lived before and established a relationship with God and the people.

In the New Testament, Titus lists being "upright" (*dikaios* in Greek) as one of the characteristics a Christian overseer must have (Titus 1:8). An upright life is not only directed by the righteous laws of God, but the grace of God enables Christians to live controlled and upright lives, being honest and fair towards others and full of integrity. This Old Testament virtue is carried into the Christian life and is undergirded by God's Spirit and grace (Titus 2:12).

R

KEY VERSES

Job 1:8;
Psalm 7:10;
Proverbs 11:6;
1 Kings 15:5;
2 Chronicles 20:32;
34:2

Righteousness

See also: *Righteousness, p. 383*
Hebrew expression: *tsedeq*
Pronunciation: *TSEH dehq*
Strong's Number: *6664*

God had a plan for Jerusalem; His city was to be called the City of Righteousness (Isa. 1:26). Even after His city failed Him, He would not give up on her. He would work for His people and His city until her righteousness would shine like the dawn (Isa. 62:1, NIV, NLT)—to such an extent that the nations would see the city's righteousness (Isa. 62:2).

Righteousness was to characterize God's people. The Hebrew word used in these passages is *tsedeq*, correctly translated as "rightness" or "righteousness." A verb was formed from the root of this noun, *tsadeq* (or *tsadoq*), meaning "to be just, righteous." Other similar verbs using the basic root were used: *tsadiq* meant "righteous or just" and *tsedaqh* meant "righteousness." We will look more closely at *tsedeq* and *tsedaqh*, the words used in the passages above.

The writer of Proverbs said that righteousness (*tsedaqah*) exalts a nation. The word refers to doing or being "what is right, straight, just." It can refer to weights and measures, correct or straight paths (Deut. 25:15; Ezek. 45:10). It means justice and correctness in government and its rulers. God wanted His people to be a model of how people should treat one another and be faithful to their God (Lev. 19:15; Deut. 1:16). He wanted righteous laws for His people (Isa. 58:2). He Himself was a righteous king and husband of Israel (Job 36:3; Hos. 2:21). He wanted His people to recognize Him as the God of their righteousness (Ps. 4:1, NASB, KJV). God's people were to be righteous in their ethics (Job 35:2) and their speech (Ps. 52:3).

The marvelous child who was eventually to rule God's Kingdom was to reign in righteousness (Isa. 9:7). This stress upon righteousness is emphasized even more in the New Testament. We are to seek Him first and His righteousness above all of the things of this world (Matt. 6:33). We are to hunger and thirst after righteousness (Matt. 5:6). At the same time we realize that God has made Christ our righteousness. Our responsibility of righteousness is to believe God (Rom. 4:9) and to treat others righteously. Peter says that, as we live in this age, we patiently look for and await a new heaven and earth where righteousness dwells in them—where *righteousness* is at home (2 Pet. 3:13).

R

KEY VERSES

Isaiah 1:26; 11:5;
51:1; 62:1–2;
Jeremiah 23:6

Sabbath

Hebrew expression: *shabbat*
Pronunciation: *shah BAWT*
Strong's Number: *7676*

From the time of creation, the seventh day was a special day set aside by God for rest (Gen. 2:2); it was a time to celebrate, to rejoice in work accomplished, and to praise the Creator. Today, most Christians and Jews observe every seventh day as special, whether they recognize Saturday or Sunday. The Hebrew word *shabbat*, "Sabbath," is formed from the root *shabat*, meaning "to cease," "to desist," or "to rest." In the Old Testament, while ordinary work ceased on this day, sacred activities were encouraged and feasts or festivals sometimes coincided with the Sabbath. The religious high point of the year was the Day of Atonement, which was also called a *shabbat shabbaton*, "a Sabbath of complete rest," yet there was a great deal of religious activity carried out by the High Priest and other Levites (Lev. 23:32; 16:31).

The weekly Sabbath was a great gift to God's people. In Egypt, Pharaoh did not allow them to rest from their hard labors. But God gave the Sabbath to Israel in the wilderness after the Israelites left Egypt (Exod. 16:23–29). The formal command to observe the Sabbath as a day of rest and way of imitating God was given at Mount Sinai and repeated on the plains of Moab (Exod. 20:8–11; Deut. 5:12–15). The Sabbath was made for the benefit of God's people including slaves and work animals (Deut. 5:12–15). It was above all a day to proclaim the greatness of the Lord (Ps. 92).

The need for Israel to focus upon God one day a week was absolutely necessary to keep them from being totally preoccupied with work. A person who gathered wood on the Sabbath broke a command of God and was stoned to death because of the danger of leading others away from God (Num. 15:32–36). God was worshiped by the offering of additional sacrifices on the Sabbath, which further emphasized importance (Num. 28:9–10). Even the land in Israel, every seventh year, was to lie fallow and enjoy a "Sabbath" year in honor of the Lord and His bountiful provisions.

In the New Testament, Jesus and His disciples observed the Sabbath (Mark 1:21)— but Jesus declared it to be a day created by God for man's good, not man's oppression. He healed on the Sabbath and even declared Himself Lord over the Sabbath (Mark 2:23–28). He asserted that it is permissible to do good on the Sabbath, even if this involves "work" as the Pharisees defined it (Mark 3:4). Paul wrote that Christians are no longer required to keep the Sabbath (Col. 2:16), but Christians chose to keep the true meaning of the Sabbath alive by meeting together one day a week to worship the Lord. For believers today, this is a day of special focus on the Lord Jesus Christ, recognizing and praising God in the church. The true "Sabbath" of God, true rest in and with Him through Christ, is the goal and purpose of every believer. With joy, we strive to enter that rest (Heb. 3:10, 11; Rev. 14:13).

S

KEY VERSES

Exodus 16:23,
25–26, 29; 20:8;
Leviticus 16:31;
23:32;
Numbers 15:32;
28:9

Sackcloth

Hebrew expression: *saq*
Pronunciation: *SAHK*
Strong's Number: *8242*

Jacob's sons brought back the awful report: Joseph was dead! Jacob tore his own clothes as a sign of great mourning for his son and put on "sackcloth" (Gen. 37:34). He mourned for many days. The English word "sackcloth" comes from the Greek word *sakkos*, a rendering of the Hebrew word *saq*. This cloth was usually tied or wrapped around the waist and was one of the traditional signs of mourning in the ancient Near East. It was usually exceedingly coarse, made of goat's hair, and worn next to the skin. It was black in color and could be in the form of a kilt. In one case it was a robe (Jonah 3:6), and sometimes the mourner lay upon the sackcloth (2 Sam. 21:10; Isa. 58:5). This mourning garment was used not only in Israel, but also in Moab (Isa. 15:3), Damascus (1 Kgs. 20:31), Tyre (Ezek. 27:31), and in Nineveh (Jonah 3:5). Prophets often wore sackcloth because of the messages of doom and destruction they had to deliver (Isa. 20:2). In some cases, this garment was worn as a sign of submission and humility (1 Kgs. 20:31). During a time of impending national disaster, Hezekiah put on sackcloth when he sought help and deliverance from the Assyrians through the Lord (2 Kgs. 19:1). In the book of Esther, the annihilation of the Jews in the Persian Empire was pending. Haman, one of the last living Amalekites, had deceitfully negotiated to have the Jewish people destroyed on a given day. Mordecai learned of Haman's plot to destroy them and covered himself in "ashes" and "sackcloth," asserting by these signs of mourning that he was ready to die rather than see this catastrophe happen. Sackcloth and ashes are mentioned four times in Esther 4 as Mordecai is beside himself at the possible catastrophe that faces his people (Esth. 4:1-4). Ashes, put on one's head or body, are another sign of mourning that often accompanied the wearing of sackcloth.

The New Testament also speaks of sackcloth. In the end time, the sun turns black "like sackcloth" (Rev. 6:12; *sakkos* in Greek). Two witnesses of the Lord will wear sackcloth and prophesy about God's impending judgement (Rev. 11:3). Sackcloth is not used in general among Christians today—in fact, "mourning" is something we do only for the loss of a loved one. Perhaps the church ought to recognize the appropriateness of "mourning" for ourselves when we sin against God, as well as for the wayward people around us—showing our humility and submission to our holy God.

KEY VERSES

Genesis 37:34;
1 Kings 20:31-32;
Nehemiah 9:1;
Esther 4:1-4;
Isaiah 50:3

Salvation

See also: *Salvation, p. 384*
Hebrew expression: *yeshu'ah*
Pronunciation: *yeh SHOO 'ah*
Strong's Number: *3444*

In 1999, the refugees of Kosovo understood what is meant to need someone to deliver them from their oppressive war with the Serbians. They needed salvation.

The Hebrew word for salvation, *yeshu'ah*, is a powerful word with connotations of deliverance. The Hebrew verbal root *yasha'* means basically "to deliver." The noun *yeshu'ah* comes from this root and is usually translated as "salvation or deliverance" depending upon its context. The noun can be translated also as "help," "victory," "prosperity." Its basic denotation is "to rescue from danger or distress."

The word can also refer to help or deliverance given by persons (1 Sam. 14:45; 2 Sam. 10:11). It can indicate the safety or security (*yeshu'ah*) provided by fortified walls that protect people from danger. But primarily the word highlights the marvelous salvation provided by the Lord in the Old Testament and brought to light in the prophets.

God provided salvation through deliverance from the Egyptians and from physical danger (Exod. 14:13; 2 Chr. 20:17). God provided salvation for Israel from punishment because of their sin (Ps. 70:4; Isa. 33:6; 49:6; 52:7). Whether singular or plural, it could signify God's deliverance and salvation (2 Sam. 22:51; Ps. 42:5).

In the divinely guided viewpoint of the prophet Isaiah, the concept of salvation for all humanity broke through the clouds. The Servant of Isaiah's songs would not only restore the tribe of Jacob (Israel), but would take salvation to the ends of the earth (Isa. 49:6). This deliverance and salvation, *yeshu'ah*, given by the Lord would be eternal with the Lord's righteousness (Isa. 51:6). The Lord would send forth His messengers to dispense the news of His salvation (Isa. 52:7). The Lord's own "arm" would bring about His salvation and in the end even the "walls of protection" around God's redeemed universal city, Jerusalem, would be called "salvation." Ultimately, God would provide a salvation that would be effective beyond the boundaries of this life.

In the New Testament, the name of Jesus is based upon the Old Testament word for salvation. His name is *Iesous*, "Savior." He was the servant who was to bring the Lord's salvation to mankind (Acts 8:26–40). He is Himself that salvation (Luke 3:6; Rom. 11:11) which the apostle Paul proclaims in Romans 10:13.

KEY VERSES

Exodus 15:2;
Psalm 35:3;
Isaiah 12:2; 49:6;
52:7

Sanctuary

See also: *Tabernacle, p. 186 and Temple, p. 404*
Hebrew expression: *miqdash*
Pronunciation: *mik DAWSH*
Strong's Number: *4720*

"Then have them make a sanctuary (*miqdash*) for me, and I will dwell among them. Make this tabernacle (*mishkan*) and all its furnishings exactly like the pattern I will show you"—so are God's instructions to Israel (Exod. 25:8-9, NIV). The word study on "tabernacle" discusses the meaning of *mishkan*, which connotes "a place to dwell, or to tabernacle." The word *miqdash*, while used in parallel with *mishkan*, denotes more clearly a "holy place" or "a sanctuary." *Miqdash* comes from a root meaning "to separate," or "to be, or make, holy" (*qdsh*). The meaning of the root of the word, as well as the way the word *miqdash* is used in the passage emphasizes the holiness of the "sanctuary" as God's dwelling places.

The Hebrew word for "sanctuary" in Leviticus refers to the entire Tabernacle, the Tent of Meeting, or even the area around the Tent of Meeting. The word emphasizes the holiness and sacredness of the locations and structures where God dwelt. Sometimes "sanctuary" refers only to the Holy of Holies (Lev. 16:33)—the most holy room located in the western end of the Tabernacle. The dwelling place of God was to be kept holy and reverenced by His people just as they observed and reverenced His Sabbath (Lev. 19:30; 26:2). The priests were responsible for the care of the *miqdash* (Num. 3:38). To take unclean things into the sanctuary defiled it (Num. 18:1) and that was equal to defiling God's Holy Name! (Lev. 20:3). Any priest who had defects of any kind could not approach the sanctuary (Lev. 21:23). After the High Priest was anointed with the sacred oil to serve at the sanctuary, he was never to leave its service (Lev. 21:12). God's presence was in His holy dwelling, but Israel's sin could and did drive Him from His holy sanctuary (Ezek. 8:6). Daniel, in exile, pleaded with the Lord to have mercy upon His desecrated sanctuary (Dan. 9:17). But, it was Ezekiel who foresaw the time when God would put a new sanctuary among the Israelites and vindicate His holy name (Ezek. 37:26).

KEY VERSES

Exodus 25:8;
Leviticus 19:30;
26:2;
Numbers 3:38

While the High Priest entered the sanctuary, the Holy of Holies, once a year to cleanse the Israelites from sin (Lev. 16:29, 33), Jesus entered the inner sanctuary of heaven, the eternal Holy of Holies, for us as our eternal High Priest. He entered a sanctuary not made with human hands, but by God (Heb. 8:2). The old sanctuary served only as a copy, the time came for the new sanctuary—God's heavenly dwelling place—to be unveiled (Heb. 8:1-6). Through Jesus, we are cleansed from sin and can approach God the Father Almighty as beloved sons and daughters. With reverence and awe, we can enter God's sanctuary and appear before Him—something that the Israelites of the Old Testament could never do!

Satan

See also: *Satan, p. 386*
Hebrew expression: *satan*
Pronunciation: *saw TAWN*
Strong's Number: *7854*

Satan, the evil antagonist to all that is good, is a well-known figure to readers of the New Testament. Also known as the devil, he is Jesus' greatest adversary and is portrayed as the tempter (Mark 1:13), deceiver (Rev. 12:9), and ruler of this world (John 14:30). As expected though, the New Testament perspective on the figure of Satan goes well beyond what is known from the Old Testament. There is no doubt that he often functions as an adversary to God in both testaments. However, the Old Testament *satan* may not actually accord with the function and character of the *satan* in the New Testament.

The first clue to the complexity of the Old Testament *satan* is that the Hebrew root *stn*, which forms the noun *satan* is also used as a verb. The verb usage of *stn* occurs six times in the Old Testament with either the meanings of "to be at enmity with," or "hostile towards" (Pss. 38:21; 109:4) or "to indict," "to accuse" (Ps. 109:20, 29; Zech. 3:1). Likewise, the noun *satan* is often used as a common noun for a character (human or celestial) who functions as an adversary, opponent, or even a prosecutor in legal contexts (see 1 Sam. 29:4 [David]; 2 Sam. 19:23 [Abishai]).

In fact, within the Old Testament, there seems to be a developing theology of the *satan* figure. The first stage is the ten occurrences of the common noun without the Hebrew definite article, "an adversary/accuser" (see Num. 22:22, 32; 1 Sam. 29:4; 2 Sam. 19:23; 1 Kgs. 5:18; 11:14, 23, 25; Ps. 109:6). The next stage is the seventeen occurrences of the noun with the definite article indicating a specific (celestial) figure fulfilling the office of "the adversary, prosecutor" (Job 1:6–9, 12; 2:1–4, 6–7; Zech. 3:1–2). Finally, it is often suggested that the single occurrence without the definite article in First Chronicles is the sole use of the noun as the proper name, "Satan" (1 Chr. 21:1).

Satan has a prominent place in the book of Job. As the antagonist to Yahweh, Satan's presence and accomplishments set up the conflict at the heart of the entire narrative. He is the one who challenges Yahweh about the basic nature of His human servants, and he is the one who is permitted to carry out the devastating fieldwork which renders Job's life a wasteland. As the "prosecuting attorney" who suggests that there is a case to be made against Job, Satan sets himself to prove that there is no true human righteousness. Satan's sole purpose is to prove that our relationship with God is shallow. We can see the same force in our own lives, as we face pressure to abandon God for "profane" acquisitions: career, fame, leisure. Job responded with a tenacious desire to find vindication and preserve his faith. So too, we should persevere, when provoked by the 'satans' of the world.

S

KEY VERSES

1 Samuel 29:4;
1 Chronicles 21:1;
Job 2:1;
Zechariah 3:1

Scepter

Hebrew expression: *shebet*
Pronunciation: *SHAY veht*
Strong's Number: *7626*

For a ruler to rule he or she must have sufficient authority and power to carry out their responsibilities. In the Old Testament, the ruler's staff or "scepter" came to represent this authority and right to rule. The Hebrew word *shebet* means "rod," "staff," or "scepter." The word is formed from the root *shabat*, which meant "to smite" or "to slay." In Judges 5:14, the commander's "staff" (*shebet*) represents the authority and right to hold the power of a commander. Rulers in Beth Haven and Askelon were said to hold the "scepter." In Psalms, the scepter of the ruling King of Israel is mentioned and foreshadows the Kingship of the Messiah (Ps. 45:6–7). In Psalm 2:9, the King rules the nations with a "scepter of iron," which is significant because a scepter was usually made of strong wood (Ezek. 19:11, 14). The Lord will not always permit the scepter of those who are evil to rule over the righteous (Ps. 125:3; Isa. 14:5). Zechariah speaks of a time when the authority and rule, the "scepter," of Egypt will be removed by the Lord (Zech. 10:11). In Proverbs 22:8, the power (*shebet*) of the person who spreads evil will eventually be broken.

The two most famous passages using *shebet* are Genesis 49:10 and Numbers 24:17. Genesis asserts that the rulers of Israel will be through the "scepter of Judah." Judah's scepter will never pass away until the true King has come who deserves to hold it forever (Gen. 49:8–12). Numbers 24:17 prophesies that a "star," another symbol of a king or ruler, and a "scepter" will come from the descendants of Jacob. This kingship was realized first in King David and his sons, but will ultimately be fulfilled in the coming messianic ruler, Jesus Christ.

In the New Testament, the "scepter" of the Kingdom of God, while still an iron scepter of power in some passages, becomes essentially a scepter of moral righteousness. In the coming Kingdom of Jesus Christ, the scepter of His kingship will be righteousness (Heb. 1:5–9), not mere power. His moral rectitude and uprightness will be the source of His power and influence. He will then rule the rebellious nations with a rod of iron (Rev. 2:27; 12:5; 19:15; Ps. 2:9). And, as Numbers 24:17 observed, the final ruler of Jacob will be a "star"—in this case, the bright and morning star, Jesus Christ Himself (Rev. 22:16).

KEY VERSES

Genesis 49:10;
Numbers 24:17;
Psalms 2:9; 45:6;
125:3;
Isaiah 14:5

S

Sealed

See also:, *Seal, p. 390*
Hebrew expression: *chatam*
Pronunciation: *khaw TAHM*
Strong's Number: *2856*

When most of us think of something sealed, we think of a sealed legal deed or document that indicates ownership of a car, house, or some other possession. We might also think of something as "signed and sealed"—that is, settled. Or, we even think of something that has been "sealed off"—that is, kept separate. The Hebrew verb *chatam* means "to seal," "to affix a seal," or "to preserve," and was used to indicate the authenticity, ownership, permanence, authority, unchangeableness, or inviolability of something by placing a mark on it. In ancient times, a seal could even be the name of someone impressed upon clay with a stylus, ring, or other item that made an impression upon a soft surface. Sometimes, cylinders were used to roll seal impressions upon clay surfaces and sometimes seals were engraved with various tools. Whatever was sealed could not be opened or undone.

In the Old Testament, *chatam* often described a signed and sealed document—the signatures indicated that the signers had bound themselves to the words in the document (Neh. 10:1). An affixed seal indicated authenticity, as when Jeremiah sealed his purchase deed to land in Anathoth (Jer. 32:10, 11, 14), preserving it until fields and lands would once again be sold in Judah after the destruction of Jerusalem. Jezebel, King Ahab's wife, placed his "seal" on letters she composed to give authenticity to them and then used them to have a man named Naboth killed (1 Kgs. 21:8).

The word *chatam* was also used figuratively to describe the "sealing" of confirmed prophetic visions (Dan. 9:24). But, it could also mean "to seal the words" of a prophetic scroll until it was time for them to take place (Dan. 12:4, 9). This indicated that the prophetic words were fixed until their time of fulfillment. Isaiah's words were sealed and then read after they had been fulfilled, proving that they were true. Sealing things in the Old Testament also describes, metaphorically, the sins of people that are sealed before God (Deut. 32:34). Job observes that the Lord can uncover sins even in the night and thereby set His seal upon them (Job 33:16).

The concept of sealing something was carried into the New Testament in the Greek word *sphragidzein*, meaning "to seal or set a seal." God placed His seal of approval and ownership on Jesus (John 6:27). Paul called his converts the "seal," or the confirmation, of his right to be an apostle (1 Cor. 9:2). Ultimately, God is the One who has set His seal upon all believers (2 Cor. 1:22) by giving us the Holy Spirit (Eph. 1:13). We can assert, with Job, that our transgressions are separated from us (Job 14:17) by God's sovereign act of forgiveness. Jesus Christ sealed us as His own, and that will never change.

KEY VERSES

Deuteronomy 32:34;
1 Kings 21:8;
Jeremiah 32:10–11;
Daniel 9:24; 12:4, 9

Seed

Hebrew expression: *zera'*
Pronunciation: *zaw RAH*
Strong's Number: *2233*

To whom will you leave your possessions when you die? Most people want to leave the fruit of their labors to their own descendants—their "seed." But God entrusted the invaluable gift of forgiveness and salvation to His "seed"—the seed that came from Abraham's and David's line, the seed that would, in turn, offer salvation to all people.

The Hebrew noun *zera'* means "seed" both in a literal sense, such as a seed planted in the ground or as semen placed in the womb to bring about pregnancy (Gen. 47:19, 23–24; Num. 5:28)—and in a figurative sense, such as "descendants" or "offspring." The special line of inheritance God established began, of course, with the seed of the first woman. The noun comes from the verb *zara'* meaning "to plant," "to scatter," or "to sow." After God cursed the serpent for deceiving Eve, He also declared that there would be hostility between the "seed" of the serpent and the "seed" of the woman. Eventually this would result in the serpent's head being crushed by a "seed" of the woman. Christ was this "seed"—He was the One who fulfilled this prophecy in Genesis 3:15. He is the One who crushed sin once and for all in His death on the cross (Rom. 16:20).

God also established a line of inheritance in the offspring of Eve through Abraham. God promised Abraham that through his *zera'*, Isaac and Jacob, and through their seed, all the nations of the earth would be blessed (Gen. 12:3, 7, 15, 16; 15:5; 22:18; 24:7; 28:13, 14). Within the line of Abraham's descendants, God chose David. God, once again, gave David the promise of a seed from his offspring who would reign upon the throne of Israel (2 Sam. 7:12). Solomon was the first of David's offspring to reign—but ultimately Christ, the royal seed of David, would reign forever (compare Pss. 2:7; 45:6; 89:27; Matt. 1:1; Acts 2:30; Heb. 1:5). The special seed of Abraham that carried these divine promises and covenants is called the "holy seed" in the Old Testament (Ezra 9:2; Isa. 6:13; Mal. 2:15). Jesus Christ walked on this earth and taught what the Kingdom of God is like. Through His death on the cross, He destroyed the works of the devil—that is, the serpent—once-for-all. Then, after His resurrection from death, Jesus was enthroned in the heavens and today sits at the right hand of God the Father as the eternal King of kings (Rev. 19:16; 22:16).

KEY VERSES

Genesis 3:15; 12:7; 15:5; 22:18; 26:4; 2 Samuel 7:12

Believers who place their faith in Christ can become heirs to God's promises to Abraham, also. They are declared righteous, just as Abraham was declared righteous by faith (Rom. 4:13–25). Thus, believers in Christ are Abraham's true descendants because they imitate the faith Abraham had. Jesus defeated sin and death on the cross and forgave the sins of all who put their trust in Him. That is why the promise of "the seed" is so vital for believers. It is the way we become included in God's eternal family.

Seek

Hebrew expression: *darash*
Pronunciation: *daw RAHSH*
Strong's Number: *1875*

"Seek first his kingdom and his righteousness" is one of the most memorized verses in the Bible (Matt. 6:33). The precedent for Jesus' assertion, however, is found in the Old Testament. In fact, the essence of Moses' charge to Israel in the book of Deuteronomy could well be paraphrased as "Seek first the kingdom of the Lord, and all these other things will be added to you" (see also Deut. 4:6, 25–29). The Hebrew word *darash* is probably the most instructive word in the Old Testament. It means "to seek," "to resort to," or "to inquire about." It is used when a person "seeks a word from the Lord" (1 Kgs. 22:5). From this verbal root the word *midrash* is formed—the Hebrew word that refers to an expansive translation, or explanation, of a biblical text.

Certainly there are enough things to seek in the culture in which we live. Israel was likewise tempted to seek after all kinds of things that were not in her best interests. The Israelites sought: the wealth of the land of Canaan, to be like other nations (1 Sam. 8; 12), and other gods (Ps. 4:2). Amos's instructions are clear and to the point for Israel, they are to seek the Lord and then they will live (Amos 5:4–6). They were not to seek false gods at the altar at Bethel and Gilgal which had been established by Jeroboam I, the king who made Israel sin. Amos correctly noted that to seek the Lord was to seek good, not wickedness—the result again would be life (Amos 5:14). *Darash* describes the peoples' purpose in coming to Moses to "seek" God's will. In the Bible, seeking God and His will is the characteristic of God's people (Exod. 18:15). God promised to "be found" by those who would "seek" Him with their whole heart (Deut. 4:29; Jer. 29:13). Those who sought God found both vindication and blessing from the Lord (Ps. 24:6).

For believers, seeking (*zeteo* in Greek) God's Kingdom means finding it in Christ, the door to the Kingdom. God desires that all people would seek His Son (Acts 17:27), and He is "found" in Christ by those peoples and Gentiles who had not diligently sought Him before (Rom. 10:20). God rewards those who seek Him with all their heart, mind, soul, and strength (see Deut. 4:29).

KEY VERSES

Exodus 18:15;
Deuteronomy 4:29;
Psalm 24:6;
Isaiah 1:17;
Jeremiah 29:13

Seraphim

Hebrew expression: *saraph*
Pronunciation: *seh RAWF*
Strong's Number: *8314*

Seraphim and cherubim, these mysterious yet wonderfully privileged creatures, have always startled the imaginations of Bible readers. Cherubim are mentioned often in the Old Testament and once in the New Testament. Seraphim, a plural word describing two beings each with six sets of wings, were a part of Isaiah's vision and call (Isa. 6:2, 6). These magnificent creatures used two of their wings to cover their faces, two to cover their feet, and with two others they flew. These creatures were indeed privileged to be in the vicinity of the throne of the Lord. Seraphim are mentioned only twice in the Old Testament.

The word *saraph* is singular. The name *sarap* is related to the verbal root of *sarap* meaning "to burn." This root is found in other Semitic languages meaning "to burn up," "to turn," "to consume." The seraphim in Isaiah are not the same as the seraphs in other passages, where the word means venomous or fiery serpent (see Num. 21:6, 8; Deut. 8:15).

These beings are unique in the Old Testament. They are majestic servants of the living God who created them, doing His bidding. They declare the holiness, might, and glory of God (Isa. 6:3). They declare Him the Lord of hosts; that is, Lord over all heavenly beings (Isa. 6:3). They could speak in audible voices that Isaiah understood (Isa. 6:4). Fire and hot coals did not burn them. They had human hands (Isa. 6:6). They could handle hot coals. They applied the glowing coals to Isaiah's lips and his *sin* was covered and his guilt removed (Isa. 6:6–7). God had His fiery servants take part in consuming the sins and guilt of a human being—forgiveness and cleansing was realized in order to become "holy" as God was holy.

These seraphim demonstrate the ability and willingness of God to deliver and cleanse His people from their guilt, corruption, and sin. Uncleanness cannot stand before God, but God is the great Refiner who removes His people's dross and makes them righteous before Him. The seraphim are merely His flaming ministers to administer salvation and healing to His people. The author of Hebrews declared correctly that our God is a consuming *(katanaliskō* in Greek) fire. With Isaiah, God permitted His seraphim to participate in an atoning ministry, declaring His holiness, glory, and ability to cleanse His people.

KEY VERSES

Numbers 21:6, 8;
Deuteronomy 8:15;
Isaiah 6:2, 6;
14:29; 30:6

Servant

Hebrew expression: *'ebed*
Pronunciation: *'EH behd*
Strong's Number: *5650*

A servant who gives his life willingly as a sacrifice for others; a servant who obeys his Master to please Him; a servant whose labor and love and death on behalf of others effects the forgiveness of their sins and the removal of their guilt. This is a picture of an unusual servant. The servant in mind is the servant described in the "Songs of Isaiah."

The Hebrew word "servant" (*'ebed*) was used in the Old Testament to describe any kind of "servant or slave." The word comes from the root of the verb *'abad*, "to work, to serve." In the Old Testament, there were slaves who were themselves kings who served other kings; there were slaves who were worshipers of God, that is, servants of God. Israel as a nation was often called the servant of the Lord (Ps. 136:22; Isa. 41:8–9; 49:3). A famous psalm speaks of "His servant, Israel" (Ps. 136:22). Even those who served in the Temple or its choir were the Lord's servants who praised Him in a formal capacity (Ps. 113:1). The prophets are called "servants" (2 Kgs. 9:7; 17:13).

But Isaiah presents the ideal servant on the stage of world history (Isa. 42:1–6; 49:5–7; 52:13—53:11). This servant was to be anointed of the Lord. The work of this servant was unique, performed by One who was given the Holy Spirit to guide him. This servant was to be a covenant to Israel, a light to the nations, a person who would bring Jacob back and, above all, to bring salvation to the whole earth (Isa. 49:6). He would serve as a martyr and a sacrifice. He would sprinkle many and make them clean; He would heal others by His stripes. He would, in fact, serve others to the point of death. After bearing the sins of many, the Lord would exalt him greatly (Isa. 53:12).

In the New Testament there is no doubt who came as this ideal servant. The inspired interpretation of Philip to the Ethiopian eunuch applied the entire passage of Isaiah 53 to Jesus Christ (Acts 8:32–38). Jesus saw His ministry on earth as the ministry of a servant who came to serve and give His life as a ransom for others (Mark 10:45; Luke 22:26–27). Christians are to serve God as He did—with their whole heart (Rom. 1:9). In fulfillment of the second great commandment, we are to serve one another in love (Gal. 5:13). The greatest among Christians are those who are the greatest servants to others (Mark 10:43, *doulos*).

KEY VERSES

Exodus 14:31; 21:2;
Isaiah 42:1; 43:10;
44:1; 48:20; 49:3;
52:13

Sheol

See also: *Hades, p. 297 and Hell, p. 303*
Hebrew expression: *she'ol*
Pronunciation: *sheh 'OHL*
Strong's Number: *7585*

The concept of Sheol is difficult to grasp immediately. It is a Hebrew term of unknown origin. In ordinary usage it means ravine or chasm. It is used synonymously with pit, death, and destruction. Sheol swallows the wicked. When Korah rebelled against Moses' leadership (Num. 16:30), Moses foretold that Korah and his followers would descend alive into Sheol. Job said that Sheol consumes sinners in the same way that drought and heat consume snow waters (Job 24:19, NASB). Jacob spoke of going down to Sheol (Gen. 37:35; 42:38; 44:29) but his use of the term may be virtually equivalent to saying "I am going to die."

In order to begin to understand Sheol in the Old Testament, we must approach it from two perspectives: (1) other concepts used in connection with Sheol; and (2) physical descriptions of Sheol.

In the Hebrew poetry of the Old Testament, we are often given information about a particular concept through other terms used in parallel contexts. There are a number of such images meant to convey the notion of the abode of the dead that are used alongside Sheol. Sheol is the opposite of heaven (Ps. 139:8; Isa. 7:11)—and appropriately, as heaven is up, so Sheol is down (Ezek. 32:27; Amos 9:2). Sheol is described as death itself (2 Sam. 22:6; Ps. 6:5; Isa. 28:15), the pit (Ps. 16:10; Prov. 1:12), the grave (Ps. 55:15), or the place of destruction (*'abaddon*; Job 26:6; Prov. 15:11). Darkness pervades Sheol (Job 17:13). Some type of life does continue in Sheol (Isa. 14:9; Ezek. 32:21), albeit a life with significant limitations (Ps. 6:5; Eccl. 9:10).

Is Sheol identical with the Christian concept of hell? While Sheol and hell share similarities, our understanding of hell from the New Testament is a far clearer concept than of Sheol in the Old Testament. Hell is almost always used to name a place of punishment for those who have refused God's mercy in Christ. Sheol, on the other hand, often refers to a place but it is simply part of expressions that sometimes refer to death and not a place of the dead.

KEY VERSES

Job 26:6;
Psalm 16:10;
Ecclesiastes 9:10;
Isaiah 14:11

Righteous and unrighteous go down to Sheol in the sense that they all die. It is a mistake to view Sheol as an intermediate state in the sense that purgatory, in Roman Catholic teaching, is characterized as an intermediate state.

Though the overall picture of Sheol is grim, the Old Testament nevertheless affirms that God is there (Ps. 139:8; Prov. 15:11) and that it is impossible to hide from God in Sheol (Job 26:6; Amos 9:2).Moreover, God has power over Sheol. He is able to redeem His people from its depths (Pss. 16:10; 30:3;

49:15; 86:13; Job 33:18, 28–30). Most of these cases speak of restoration to physical life, although Psalm 49:15 seems to foresee the Christian understanding of eternal life with God.

Shepherd

Hebrew expression: *ro'eh*
Pronunciation: *roh 'EE*
Strong's Number: *7462*

"The Lord is my shepherd" may be the most widely known line of all the Bible (Ps. 23:1). Generation after generation, both Christian and non-Christian alike, have taken comfort and encouragement from David's portrayal of God as a faithful and compassionate Shepherd. This despite the fact that the majority of people living in urban and suburban areas have never seen a flock of sheep, let alone a shepherd tending his animals. Such is the power of the shepherd image in Scripture.

The verb *ra'ah* means to "graze, pasture" or "tend, lead" flocks and herds. The participle *ro'eh* signifies a "shepherd" or "herdsman." Metaphorically, the word refers to leading or ruling a people. Shepherding was essential to the semi-nomadic lifestyle characteristic of many clans and tribes in Bible times. Numerous biblical characters are associated with the occupation of shepherding: Abel (Gen. 4:2), Abraham (Gen. 13:7), Isaac (Gen. 26:20), Jacob and his sons (especially Joseph, Gen. 30:36; 46:32), Laban (and his daughter Rachel, Gen. 29:9), Moses (Exod 3:1), and David (1 Sam. 16:11).

The life of a shepherd tended to be silent, lonely, and at times dangerous (1 Sam. 17:34). The shepherd was responsible for leading his flock to pasture and water, providing shelter, protection, care, and healing in the case of sickness or injury. The shepherd lived out-of-doors or in a tent and apparently wore some kind of coat or blanket-like wrap (Gen. 4:20; Jer. 43:12). A shepherd's equipment consisted of a staff or rod and a leather bag for carrying supplies and food (and in David's case a slingshot, 1 Sam. 17:40).

The shepherd as a metaphor for God is especially prominent in the Hebrew exodus from Egypt, as God led Israel like a flock through the Sinai desert (Exod. 15:13, 17; Ps. 78:52–55). Human rulers are ascribed shepherd-like roles as well, especially as leaders and guides and as beneficent caretakers of their subjects. This was especially true of David whom God appointed to "shepherd Jacob His people" (Ps. 78:70–72; see also 2 Sam. 5:2). The Old Testament prophets condemned "shepherds" who selfishly fed themselves and neglected their flocks (Jer. 10:21; 23:1–4; Zech. 10:2–3; 11:16–17). God's sovereignty extends to the Gentiles as well, as even King Cyrus of Persia is a divinely appointed "shepherd" caring for the people of God (Isa. 44:28).

KEY VERSES

Exodus 3:1;
1 Samuel 17:34, 40;
Psalm 23:1;
Isaiah 44:28;
Jeremiah 10:21

The shepherd metaphor continues in the New Testament, with God depicted as a shepherd who leaves His flock and pursues His lost sheep until He finds it (Matt. 18:12–14; Luke 15:4–7). On the basis of Jesus' declaration that He is the "good shepherd" (John 10:11, 14), the New Testament ascribes to Him the titles "great Shepherd of the sheep" (Heb. 13:20), the

"Shepherd and Overseer" (1 Pet. 2:25), and the "Chief Shepherd" (1 Pet. 5:4). Perhaps the most enduring image of the Bible, and certainly the greatest example of divine love, is Jesus Christ as the "good shepherd" who gives His life for the sheep (John 10:11). This unselfish act fulfilling Isaiah's prophecy of one led to the slaughter like a silent sheep (Isa. 53:7) gives rise to that glorious title Jesus bears in the book of Revelation, "the Lamb" (Rev. 5:6, 8, 12).

Sign

See also: *Sign, p. 391*
Hebrew expression: *'ot*
Pronunciation: *'OHT*
Strong's Number: *226*

A sign guides or informs people. The Hebrew word *'ot* meant "sign" or "symbol" and was used in several ways in the Old Testament. The Israelites came to depend upon signs from God in order to know His will. In the New Testament, the Jews asked Jesus for a "sign" that He was sent from God (John 2:18). Moses requested that the Lord give him some sign to prove to the Israelites that God had sent him to them (Exod. 3:12; 4:1). God gave Moses three *'otot* (Exod. 4:8-9; 7:3) to present to the people to convince them that he was indeed sent by the Lord to rescue them from Egypt (Exod. 3:12).

The word *'ot* came from the verbal root of *'awah* meaning "to sign, mark, describe with a mark." But the noun "sign" was used in a broader sphere than writing alone. It described many ways that the Lord communicated to His people. The use of a sign (*'ot*) by the Lord was a kind of special language that He used to communicate with them. When stones were set up by twelve men in the middle of the Jordan River, they represented the twelve tribes of Israel (Josh. 4:4-7). In this case, these stones served as signs or memorials (*'otot*) that reminded later generations of what the Lord had done to allow Israel to cross the Jordan at flood time.

Among the prophets, an *'ot* indicated events that would occur as predicted or that would confirm their message. The Lord predicted that Israel's worship at Sinai would serve as a sign that God had sent Moses (Exod. 3:12). In Isaiah, this word is used often to indicate God's special involvement with His people. King Ahaz was not willing to ask for a sign (*'ot*) from the Lord, but God saw His response as a lack of faith and gave the sign (*'ot*) of a virgin (a young woman of that day) bearing a child at the time the Lord predicted (Isa. 7:11, 14). The Lord predicted a day when an altar in Egypt would serve as a *'ot* to the Lord in Egypt (Isa. 19:20). The Lord caused the shadow cast on Hezekiah's sundial to go backwards as an *'ot* to him (Isa. 38:7) that the Lord would heal him. Isaiah prophesied that the Lord would cause nature to prosper as a sign that He was restoring His people (Isa. 55:13).

KEY VERSES

Exodus 3:12; 12:13;
Deuteronomy 13:1;
Isaiah 7:11, 14;
19:20; 66:19

God was faithful in the Old Testament to give His people sufficient signs (*'otot*) to let them know what He was doing and to confirm His words. In the New Testament the Jews asked Jesus for signs to demonstrate that God had sent Him (John 2:18, *semeion*). He worked many signs and wonders to show that He was the Son of God (John 20:30). But to those who refused to believe the works He freely presented, He refused to work additional signs to convince them (Matt. 12:39). The greatest sign to Christians remains the birth of Jesus, the Messiah, and His atoning life and death—all foretold by Isaiah the prophet (Isa. 7:14).

Signet ring

Hebrew expression: *hotam*
Pronunciation: *hoh TAWM*
Strong's Number: *2368*

The technology revolution of the past two decades has made the use of passwords and PINs (personal identification numbers) commonplace in homes and the marketplace. Verification of one's personal identity is now essential for both accessing and protecting computer files, bank accounts, and credit cards. The seal served the same function in the ancient world, the equivalent of a signature or similar mark of personal identification.

The Hebrew verb *hatam* means to "affix a seal" to a letter or a document (as in Esth. 8:8; Dan. 12:4) or to "seal shut" (used metaphorically in reference to chastity, Song 4:12; or referring to God's control of the celestial lights, Job 9:7). The noun *hotam* is usually translated "seal" (1 Kgs. 21:8) or "signet ring" (Hag. 2:23). Most often the "seal" was a small cylinder of stone engraved with individual and clan symbols. Typically, a hole was bored through the stone cylinder so that it could be tied with a leather cord and worn around the neck. We read that Judah gave his "signet and cord" to Tamar as a personal pledge (Gen. 38:18). The book of Job describes the dawn of a new day like clay spread out and imprinted under the pressure of a cylinder seal being rolled over its surface (Job 38:14). Elsewhere, the seal is mentioned in connection with witnesses to a business transaction (Jer. 32:44).

The "signet ring" was associated with nobility and royalty in the ancient world. Like the cylinder seal, the signet was a metal or stone ring engraved with writing and personal symbols. Affixing the royal seal to an object was an official act that placed the object under the king's jurisdiction and the legal purview of the state (Esth. 3:12). The prophet Haggai's reference to Zerubbabel as the Lord's "signet ring" symbolizes the divine authority vested in Zerubbabel as the leader of the Hebrew community in Jerusalem (Hag. 2:23). Theologically, the signet ring hearkens back to God's rejection of King Jehoiachin as His "signet" and the curse of the Davidic line (Jer. 22:24). Haggai's blessing of Zerubbabel in this fashion has the effect of overturning Jeremiah's earlier curse upon the house of David and restoring the promises connected with the Davidic covenant (2 Sam. 7).

The cultural practice of affixing seals continued into the New Testament era, most notably in the "sealing" of the tomb of Jesus by Pilate (Matt. 27:66). Theologically, Paul uses the symbol of sealing to describe the work of the Holy Spirit in marking the Christian formally and permanently as a child of God (2 Cor. 1:22; Eph. 1:13). The book of Revelation employs the imagery of breaking seals when opening the scroll of divine judgment (Rev. 6:1, 3). The writer also mentions the "seal" of God upon the foreheads of the righteous protecting them from divine wrath during those "last days" (Rev. 9:4).

KEY VERSES

Genesis 38:18;
Jeremiah 22:24;
Haggai 2:23

Sing

Hebrew expression: *shir*
Pronunciation: *SHEER*
Strong's Number: *7891*

"I will sing a new song to you, Oh, God" (Ps. 144:9) is an expression of praise that could describe the entire book of Psalms. Singing to the Lord was the method used most often to exalt, praise, and glorify the Lord God of Israel. In the Old Testament, well over half of the total number of uses of the Hebrew word *shir*, "sing," occur in the book of Psalms. The verb "to sing" was formed from the noun *shir*, "song." This verb is used more often than other Hebrew verbs that mean "to sing." The noun *shir* occurs thirty-one times in the titles of these psalms (Pss. 18, 30, 46, 65, etc.). The title of the Song of Solomon is also given as "Song of Songs," *shir shirim*—in Hebrew, an expression meaning the "Most Excellent Song."

God's people were a singing people. Even after the nation was in exile and returned to Judah and Jerusalem, they sang songs of praise to their God as soon as Ezra and Nehemiah reestablished the choir in Jerusalem. In fact, in exile they had languished in despair because they had not been able to sing the songs of Zion in a strange land (Ps. 137). The plural participle of the verb *shir* is used to mean "singers" and it is found at least sixteen times in Nehemiah (Neh. 7:1; 10:28; 12:46) to describe the singers who sang the songs of Israel and Zion after they had returned from exile (Ezra 2:41).

The great salvation event of the Old Testament, the deliverance of God's people from Egypt, is the time and place where God's people became a "singing" people (Exod. 15:1); even Miriam's short song exhorts the people to "Sing to the Lord!" (Exod. 15:21). This historical deliverance from Egypt and the gods of Egypt became the foundation for the "songs of Israel." Later, all of the great acts of God on behalf of His people were added: the creation itself, the giving of the torah at Sinai, the entrance into the land of Canaan and the defeat of Israel's enemies, the building of the Temple, and similar events all became a cause for Israel's singing.

S

KEY VERSES

Exodus 15:1, 21;
Nehemiah 10:28;
Psalms 96:1;
144:9; 149:1

The exodus from Egypt and the deliverance of Israel from Babylon created new songs in Israel's praise of the Lord (Pss. 96:1; 149:1). While secular writers today may sing and compose songs lauding human love and beauty, God's people continue to praise the Lord through songs: "THEREFORE I WILL GIVE PRAISE TO THEE AMONG THE GENTILES, AND I WILL SING TO THY NAME" (Rom. 15:9, 11). The Greek word Paul uses in Romans 15:9 is *psallo*, "to sing a psalm." Believers sing not only with their minds, but also with their spirits (1 Cor. 14:15), for they have a reason to rejoice: They are saved from their sins and are going to heaven (Jas. 5:13).

Sing praise

Hebrew expression: *zamar*
Pronunciation: *zaw MAHR*
Strong's Number: *2167*

The psalmist could not keep from praising the Lord before all the nations and singing praises to His name (Ps. 18:49). God's people have always, in every age, been a singing people who give praises to their Lord for what He had done. In Deborah's and Barak's song of praise, the Hebrew word *zamar* was used (Judg. 5:3). The word means "to make, or produce, music" and in the Bible it is always music in praise to God. It is praise for who He is or for what He has done for His people. Several nouns were developed from this verb: *zimrah*, which means "melody or sing"; *zamir*, which means "song"; and *mizmor*, which means "melody." *Mizmor* is also a technical term used to designate melodies or "psalms."

Deborah declared that she would make music or "sing"—which is *shir* in Hebrew and sometimes a synonym for *zamar*—to the Lord for His great deliverance from Jabin and Sisera (Judg. 5:3). The significance of "singing praise" is the ability to convey the inner responses of God's people to the Lord's acts. In the great "Song of the Sea" by Moses, a synonym for *zamar* is used (Exod. 15:1) as Moses declares he will "sing" to the Lord because He is so exalted—He has defeated the enemy of Israel for His people. The great King David declares that he would "give praise" (*zamar*) to the Lord among the nations for delivering him from his enemy Saul (2 Sam. 22:50). In 1 Chronicles 16:9, he "sings praise" (*zamar*) to the Lord, thanking Him for all of His wonderful acts.

Zamar is used many times in the book of Psalms to praise God (Ps. 27:6). In Psalm 33:2 the word means "to make music" on an instrument in praise to God. In Psalm 57:7 it is coupled with *shir* again and means to make music (compare Pss. 92:1; 98:4, 5). In Psalm 108:1 the psalmist makes music with all of his soul. Various instruments are enumerated as tools for making praise to God, such as the harp, tambourine, and ten-stringed lyre. In Psalm 47:6 the word *zamar* appears four times in one verse and begins and ends both lines! The point is clear, God's people are a singing, praising, music-producing people—all aimed at His glory.

This same stress upon singing, praising and music-making carries into the New Testament. There are several references to singing with the heart or spirit, as well as the mind. Paul quotes several psalms from the Old Testament, praising the Lord for making it possible for the Gentiles to praise God through Christ just as the Israelites did in the Old Testament (Rom. 15:9–11). Paul also sings to the Lord with both his spirit and mind (1 Cor. 14:15) and praises and songs are to be in our hearts and on our lips (Eph. 5:19). James even encourages God's people to "sing"—anytime we feel like it (Jas. 5:13)! We should try singing to ourselves more often, offering praise and thanks to the Lord.

KEY VERSES

Judges 5:3;
2 Samuel 22:50;
Psalms 27:6;
47:6; 149:3

S

175

Slow to anger

Hebrew expression: *'arek 'ap*
Pronunciation: *'aw RAYK; 'AHF*
Strong's Numbers: *750, 639*

Semitic languages such as Hebrew often prefer to use concrete, figurative language to express difficult concepts. Hebrew employs two concrete idioms that refer to the nose or nostrils. "He became angry" is expressed by the phrase "his nose became hot" (used about eighty times as the phrase *wayyichar 'appo*), which translates as "he became angry." This is asserted of both God and people. The phrase found in Jonah 4:2 is *'arek 'appayim*, literally "length of nose," but translates as "slow to anger" or "patient." It was because of this characteristic of God that Jonah knew that the Lord would "forgive" and "relent" from His threatened destruction of Nineveh if the inhabitants of the city repented.

Jonah 4:2 echoes Exodus 34:6 where God is described as "slow to anger," literally *'erek 'appayim*, "longness of nose." He is very patient, as well as merciful, gracious, rich in kindness, and truth. This passage in Exodus 34:5–7 is the classic passage for describing the moral-ethical character of the Lord. It is echoed throughout the Old Testament and in the New Testament as well. Proverbs 14:29 describes a patient man as one who is *'erek 'appayim*, "long of nose." Such a man has an abundance of understanding and is like his Creator. A man who is short of spirit or "quick to anger" foments folly. A man of *'erek 'appayim*, patience, is a peacemaker (Prov. 15:18)—he is more praiseworthy than a warrior or conqueror (Prov. 16:32). The patience of a man like Daniel was able to win an audience with King Nebuchadnezzar (Prov. 25:15; Dan. 2:16).

Patience is one of the virtues lacking most in God's people. To control oneself and be "slow to anger," *'erek 'appayim*, is to tame one's tongue—something that can be done by few people, and then only by huge doses of God's grace. We are to be "slow to speak" and "slow to become angry" (Jas. 1:19, *bradus, orge* in Greek). Christians should not let a day end while still seething in anger (Eph. 4:26). Peter speaks of this Christian virtue as self-control (1 Pet. 1:6, *egkrateia* in Greek; see also Gal. 5:23).

KEY VERSES

Exodus 34:6;
Numbers 14:18;
Nehemiah 9:17;
Proverbs 14:29;
Jonah 4:2

Son of man

See also: *Son of Man, p. 396*
Hebrew expression: *ben 'adam*
Pronunciation: *BAYN 'aw DAWM*
Strong's Numbers: *1121, 120*

"Son of man" is an important phrase in the Old Testament. It is used to mean an individual person as a part of the human race, "a human being." Also, it is used to indicate a human being as opposed to a "son of God," a semi-divine being (Dan. 7:13). The phrase occurs 107 times in the Old Testament. The phrase in Ezekiel usually means "human being" in the sense of a "weak fragile being" (Ezek. 2:1–47:6). In Daniel, the phrase is used to describe Daniel himself as a mere human being (Dan. 8:17). In all of the other occurrences outside of these two books the phrase *ben 'adam* means "human being" or "man" in the normal use of the words (Num. 23:19; Job 16:21; Pss. 8:4; 80:17; Jer. 49:18). The expression is made up of two Hebrew words. The first word, *ben*, means "son" or "descendant." The second word *'adam* means "mankind," "Man" with a capital letter, or "humanity." The meaning of the phrase is, therefore, "son (of) mankind." In Ezekiel the phrase *ben 'adam* is applied to the prophet himself many times (Ezek 2:1; 3:1, 10). Ezekiel is addressed specifically as "You, oh son of man" (Ezek. 2:6, 8; 21:28); he stands as a fragile human prophet before God.

The use of *ben 'adam* in Daniel 7:13 in Aramaic, and in Daniel 10:16 in Hebrew, refers to a divine or angelic being whom Daniel says looked "like" a man. The little word "like" makes a huge difference in the meaning of the statement. Scholars debate endlessly about the origin and identification of the one "like a son of Man" in Daniel 7:13. This figure has been identified by many as an appearance of Christ. Others argue that the figure is an angel, perhaps Michael. In any case, Jesus applies His own coming in glory with the appearance of the one "like" a "son of Man" in Daniel (Matt. 24:27–39; 25:31; 27:43; Mark 14:62). However, most of the Greek equivalent phrase in the New Testament, *ho huios tou anthropou*, refer to Jesus as a "human being," a part of the human race.

Jesus is described both as a weak human being and also as the powerful end-time Son of Man mentioned in Daniel 7:13. This is not surprising, for He made it clear that He was the Suffering Servant of Isaiah (Acts 8), as well as the future conquering Messiah. In the gospel of John, Jesus claims to be the preexistent Son of Man (John 6:62). Jesus Christ is the fulfillment of all Old Testament prophecies. We, therefore, look to Jesus as the author and finisher of our salvation, the one who represents the human race because He shared our humanity, but was perfect.

KEY VERSES

Ezekiel 3:1, 3;
16:2; 20:27;
Daniel 7:13;
8:17; 10:16

Soul

See also: *Soul, p. 398*
Hebrew expression: *nepesh*
Pronunciation: *NEH fehsh*
Strong's Number: *5315*

From the beginning, people have been distinct from the animal kingdom. The creation account records that all animal life was spoken into existence. However, on the sixth day the Lord paused to personally create man. The author of Genesis eloquently records: "And the Lord God formed man of the dust of the ground, and breathed into his nostrils the breath of life; and man became a living soul" (Gen. 2:7). More than the "hand-on" approach to forming man, it is the breathing of God's breath into his nostrils which made man unique from the rest of creation. The phrase "a living soul" should not be passed over lightly, for it speaks much of humanity's essential nature. The Hebrew word *nepesh*, translated as "soul," carries tremendous theological and philosophical importance. Although "soul" can be used to mean the living essence which animates all living creatures (Gen. 1:21; Lev. 17:11), or a generic reference to individual persons (Gen. 12:5; Ezek. 18:4), it most often distinguishes mankind from all other animal life.

Any high school biology student could acknowledge that people share many aspects of life with other creatures on this planet. All require nourishment, must reproduce, and respond to their environment in some fashion. With mammals, people share even more aspects, such as breathing and live birth, but mankind alone is a "living soul." Only people have the ability to reason and investigate the world. People alone have the privilege of knowing God in a personal way, sharing His wisdom, and enjoying eternal life. Only mankind is threatened with the prospect of eternal torment for rejecting God, because all these things are made possible by God's creation of a man and woman with a soul.

Just as the body is essential to each of us as people, so too is the soul. The two are inseparable and stand as necessary parts of people's intrinsic nature. The Lord created the body to link people to the physical realm, and the "soul" was given to link people to the spiritual realm. Thus, the soul is variously understood in the Old Testament as the seat of emotions (Job 14:22; Lam. 3:51), the center of thought and reason (Prov. 23:7), the source of ambition (Eccl. 6:7; Hos. 4:8), and the arena of spiritual perception and faith (Ps. 19:7; Prov. 3:6).

KEY VERSES

Genesis 2:7;
Deuteronomy 6:5

If we properly understand the profound meaning encapsulated in the word "soul," then the greatest of all commandments carries a far deeper significance than a surface reading would allow. We are not merely called to love the Lord with all our heart and all our might, but also with all our "soul" (Deut. 6:5). We should love the Lord with the very fiber of our being, with everything that makes us human!

Spirit

See also: *Spirit (divine), p. 399 and Spirit (human), p. 400*
Hebrew expression: *ruach*
Pronunciation: *ROO ah*
Strong's Number: *7307*

Moses expressed his wish that the Lord would put His "Spirit" upon all of His people, making them prophets (Num. 11:26–30). He had not wanted the gift of prophecy to be his alone. It was the Lord's will to fulfill Moses' wish and His own sovereign plan. Joel the prophet announced in his day, ninth century B.C., that in the Day of the Lord, God would indeed pour out His Spirit upon all people (Joel 2:28–29). The sex, age, nationality, language, or the social status of a person would not make any difference. The figurative expression "to pour out my Spirit" emphasizes the abundance of the Spirit's presence and activity that would be granted by the Lord.

"Spirit" is a translation of the Hebrew word *ruach*, a feminine noun that means "spirit," "wind," or "breath." The word can refer to the natural spirit of a man, the wind as it blows or, most importantly, to the Spirit of God. God shared His image with people (Gen. 1:26–28), part of that image was His Spirit. He sent His Spirit upon persons to cause them to prophesy in the Old Testament, but in the Messianic era all of His children would be able to prophesy. The Messianic King himself would have the Spirit of the Lord rest on Him permanently (Isa. 11:2). Therefore He would be wise, understanding, full of counsel for His people and filled with power (Isa. 11:2). The Servant of the Lord would be filled with the Spirit of God (Isa. 42:1).

God's gift of His Spirit shows His kindness and love for us. The Spirit of God imparted Bezalel with the skill to build the Tabernacle (Exod. 31:3; 35:30) and even gave him the ability to teach others (Exod. 35:34). God's Spirit imparted life to the dead nation of Israel and brought it back from the Babylonian exile (Ezek. 37). In the era of the Messiah, the Lord gave His people a new spirit by means of His Spirit so that they could follow Him faithfully (Ezek. 11:19; 36:26). We are transformed by His Spirit (Isa. 59:21). It is the Spirit who writes the Law of God upon the heart of Christians today in fulfillment of Jeremiah's new covenant (Jer. 31:31–34).

It is reassuring to know that we live in the day spoken of by Joel of God's outpouring of His Spirit (*pneuma* in Greek) upon His people (Acts 2:39). The gift of the Holy Spirit makes it possible for all of us to have a direct relationship with God. The nearness of God to His people is through His Spirit; the presence of His Spirit has sealed us forever as His children (Eph. 4:30). While our spirits may languish in our frail flesh and blood bodies, God's Spirit is the breath of renewal in every time of sorrow or blessing.

KEY VERSES

Genesis 1:2;
Exodus 31:3;
Psalm 51:10–11;
Isaiah 11:2;
Joel 2:28–29

Statutes

Hebrew expression: *hoq*
Pronunciation: *HOHQ*
Strong's Number: *2706*

The pivotal event in the first five books of the Bible is when God gave the Israelites the Law at Mount Sinai. It was there that the Lord met with His people "face to face" (Deut. 5:4–5). However, more than merely providing the Ten Commandments, the Lord entered into a sacred covenant relationship with His people (Deut. 5:2). This relationship was grounded in the observance of His "statutes" given through Moses (Neh. 9:13).

Looking through the lens of the New Testament it is common for Christians to view these "statutes" as being something negative or in conflict with God's gift of grace, but the positive aspects must not be overlooked. This is clearly observed in the conception of the Hebrew word *hoq* which means "statutes." *Hoq* is rooted in the fundamental notion of a "boundary that must not be crossed" (Job 14:5; 26:10). The yellow and white lines on a road are added to keep us from trouble or danger, whether it is the oncoming cars in the next lane or the soft shoulder along the side of the road. Just as these lines serve a positive function, so do the statutes of the Lord. The boundaries set forth in the Law serve the function of setting the parameters of security and prosperity (1 Chr. 22:13). The individual who ignores their warning and goes "out of bounds" brings trouble and harm to bear (Exod. 15:26; Amos 2:4). The psalmist speaks positively of the Lord's statutes, even extolling the benefits of "walking" in them (Ps. 119:1–3). His desire was to learn the boundaries established by God and guide his life by them (Ps. 119:5, 12). Thus the statutes were his song of joy and the constant meditation of his heart (Ps. 119:23, 54, 117). Understanding the Law creates a proper reverence for the Lord, which is the hallmark of wisdom (Deut. 17:19; Job 28:28).

The very last command of the Old Testament is found in Malachi 4:4, urging the reader to remember the statutes given by Moses. For the Christian, this injunction holds value as well. Although the keeping of the law cannot save, nor can our good works merit the grace of the Father, a proper understanding of the decrees of the Lord reveal a pattern of life which is pleasing to God. Jesus has fulfilled the Law by His death and life, but He has also set a high standard for the believer's conduct. Rather than seek to satisfy the external demands of the Law, the disciple of Christ has the responsibility of fulfilling the heart of the law: "to love the Lord with all one's heart, and . . . soul, and . . . mind" (Matt. 22:37). The Bible, God's holy word, is filled with the statutes and guidelines that show us how to love as Christ loves us.

KEY VERSES

Deuteronomy 4:1,
5–6, 8, 14;
Psalm 119:5, 8,
12, 23;
Malachi 4:4

Stone

Hebrew expression: 'eben
Pronunciation: 'EH ben
Strong's Number: 68

The Hebrew word 'eben means "stone," but can sometimes be translated according to context as "rock or hailstone." Stones were used in ancient times as weights on the scales to measure out grain, wheat and other items. They were used to build altars and as weapons and tools. In Exodus, two stones served as birth stones or a delivery stool for newborn infants (Exod. 1:16). They served as well covers (Gen. 29:2) and boundary markers. But their most important theological use was figurative.

Jacob set up a memorial stone, symbolic of God's house at Bethel where God had appeared to him (Gen. 28:22). Jacob and Laban set up stones as a witness to the covenant between them (Gen. 31:48). The prophet Samuel set up a stone and named it Ebenezer, which means: 'eben, "stone" plus 'ezer, "help"; that is, "stone of help." He did this to commemorate the victory the Lord gave Israel over the Philistines (1 Sam. 7:12). After the Israelites crossed the Jordan to enter the land of Canaan, the Lord instructed them to take 12 stones from the Jordan's river bed and set them as a memorial at their camp on the western shore (Josh. 4:1–9). This memorial of twelve stones represented the twelve tribes of Israel and was a symbol for future generations. These stones would recall the time when the Lord "cut off" the waters of the Jordan so that the Israelites could cross over with the ark in front of them.

A stone also served as a witness at Joshua's covenant ceremony in Shechem (Josh. 24:26–27). Stone tablets served as the writing material for the Law of Moses (Josh. 8:31–32). Stones untouched by human tools were used to build the altars of Israel (Exod. 20:24–26). The most celebrated stone or "rock" in some versions of the Old Testament is the stone of Daniel (Dan. 2:34, 35, 45). This stone represents the Kingdom of God that destroys the kingdoms of the world and fills the earth. The imagery of a stone is used several times to describe the Lord as the "rock" and "refuge" of His people (Pss. 18:2; 19:14; 31:2; 42:9).

The powerful imagery of a stone (lithos in Greek) is used in the New Testament to assure Christians that Jesus Christ is the stone rejected by men which has become the chief cornerstone of His people (Mark 12:1–11; Acts 4:11; 1 Pet. 2:4–8).

S

KEY VERSES

Genesis 28:22;
31:45;
Joshua 4:6;
1 Samuel 7:12

Christ is the New Testament "Ebenezer," or "stone of help." He is the cornerstone (akrogoniaios in Greek, compare 1 Pet. 2:6; Isa. 28:16) who makes us "living stones" along with Him as He builds the new living Temple of God (1 Pet. 2:4–8). Paul recognizes Christ as the spiritual rock that the faithful Israelites and Christians drink from for their new life (1 Cor. 10:4).

Strength

Hebrew expression: *chayil*
Pronunciation: *KAH yihl*
Strong's Number: *2428*

The word "strength" usually reminds us of the physical strength of popular wrestlers and weightlifters on sports television. In a culture where athletes are nearly deified, it is difficult for many of us to imagine the word "strength" describing anything other than physical strength. But in the 264 times the Hebrew word for "strength" is used in the Old Testament, the majority of time the word refers to spiritual strength—to the strength of the Lord.

Habakkuk ties together two important concepts—faith and strength—in his prophetic message in Habakkuk 3. The Hebrew word *chayil* is translated "strength" (Hab. 2:19, NIV, KJV, NLT). It can also be translated as "efficiency," "wealth," "army," "warrior," or "influence." It comes from the same root as the verb *chil*, which means "to be strong," or "to be firm." Habakkuk used *chayil* to assert that his strength came from the Lord (Hab. 3:19). This strength from the Lord is what enabled the prophet to live by faith, not by sight (Hab. 2:4). He asserted that even if he had to wait for the Lord to deal with Babylon, even if there were no fig trees blooming, no grapes, no olives, no food, no cattle or sheep, he would wait on God (Hab. 3:16–17). In the face of God's judgment and seeming failure to act, he would still live by faith, rejoicing in the Lord (Hab. 3:18). For, as has been noted, the Lord would be his *chayil*. The "secret" of living by faith is not finding the power within ourselves to believe, but instead lies in the fact that the Lord invests His strength in us (Hab. 3:19). Habakkuk was looking for inner strength from the Lord for his victory, while the Babylonians were trusting in the strength of their "armies."

In beautiful poetry Hannah asserts that those who have fallen are now armed with "strength." David declares that the Lord supplied him with strength (Ps. 18:32, 39). It is not physical strength, but the strength that comes from God, that delivers His people so that they can keep doing God's will (Ps. 84:7). Not even the great strength of the warhorse—or the strength of military technology—can save us (Ps. 33:17). What strength we do have is from God. And we should not abuse this strength (Prov. 31:3; Eccl. 10:10), but use it to establish the glory of God's kingdom on this earth (Matt. 12:30, is*chus* in Greek). God now works in us giving us strength to walk in His ways (Eph. 1:19; Phil. 4:13, *endunamoo* in Greek). Economic power, nuclear weapons, and even computer technology—all these will fail to deliver us. But God's strength will deliver us completely and will empower us to do good.

KEY VERSES

1 Samuel 2:4;
Psalms 18:39;
33:17; 84:7;
Proverbs 31:3;
Habakkuk 3:19

Stumble

Hebrew expression: *kashal*
Pronunciation: *kaw SHAHL*
Strong's Number: *3782*

"Like mother, like daughter" is a famous proverbial saying in many cultures. But the prophet Hosea adds an interesting twist to the phrase, saying, "like people, like priests!" (Hos. 4:5). Hosea's assertion that the priests were as wicked and guilty as the people reflected the confusion and error that was rampant among the Lord's people in his day. No one could really accuse anyone else, because no one had a true knowledge of God. They had all failed to pursue an understanding of God that would lead them to truly know Him (Hos. 4:6). Because of this the people and the priests stumbled day and night along with the prophets (Hos. 4:5). Could anyone expect otherwise of a people who would seek divine guidance from an idol, expecting a piece of wood to answer them (Isa. 4:10)?

The Hebrew word *kasha,* "to stumble," "to stagger," "to reel, or "to totter," can also mean "to be feeble" or "to cause to stumble." Failing to continue on a true path, to be sidetracked, or to find offense and turn away from a true path is the root idea. Israel in Hosea's day was sidetracked by their morally culpable refusal to know God the way they should have. They set up "stumbling blocks" for themselves; the word "stumbling block" is a noun formed from the root verb *kashal.* A person was openly rebelling against God if he or she did not recognize the true knowledge of God that He had made known. Because of Israel's refusal to know God, He Himself put a stumbling block in their way—His divine judgment (Jer. 20:11). The rebellious people, because of their attitude, "stumbled" *kashal* over that which was to light their path (Hos. 14:9). Malachi warned that the false teaching of the priests, the spiritual leaders of the people, was also causing God's people to stumble. But God was also ready to help the unrighteous person who turned from his or her wicked ways, assuring them that they would not fall (Ezek. 33:12).

The chief stumbling block that caused people to stumble in the New Testament was Jesus Christ and His claims (Rom. 9:33, *proskomma* in Greek). Those who willingly walked in His light, however, did not stumble (John 11:9). But, just as in the Old Testament, when a believer stumbles due to disobedience, it is ultimately his or her responsibility (1 Pet. 2:8, *proskopto* in Greek). Paul's charge to Christians individually is not to put or become a stumbling block in anyone's path (2 Cor. 6:3). We should live a life that leads people to Christ, not away from Him.

S

KEY VERSES

Leviticus 26:37;
Proverbs 4:12;
Hosea 4:5; 14:9

Sun

Hebrew expression: *shemesh*
Pronunciation: *SHEH mesh*
Strong's Number: *8121*

"There is nothing new under the sun" is a well-known proverb from Ecclesiastes (1:9). God created the sun, designating it as the "greater light to rule the day" (Gen. 1:16). The sun is the life-giving luminary for the earth and is studied as an object of science. The sun was also a god who was worshiped by the ancient cultures of Egypt, Babylon, and Assyria under various names.

But no book features the sun, *shemesh*, as much as Ecclesiastes. In this short book of twelve chapters, the word *shemesh* occurs thirty-five times. The noun comes from a root *shmsh*, but its meaning is unknown; however, the meaning of the word in the Old Testament is clear. It refers to the object God created on the fourth day (Gen. 1:14–19).

In Ecclesiastes, the sun controls the rhythm of life as it rises and sets (Eccl. 1:5). All of life is lived "under the sun" (Eccl. 2:18–19). The key to understanding Ecclesiastes is to understand the significance of this little, but all encompassing, phrase. If life consists merely of the things under the sun, no wonder the author despairs of ever finding any ultimate meaning for his existence.

The sun does not give meaning to life; it merely marks time and seasons and gives warmth and energy to all biological life on earth. It provides a framework in which life is lived out. This world and its biorhythms are not equal to the eternity that God has placed in mankind (Eccl. 3:11). Life under the sun can only be enjoyed because God gives good gifts (Eccl. 2:24; 3:13; 5:19). Life, true life, consists in recognizing God and His gifts and the joy of keeping His moral and ethical commandments. Life "under the sun" has an end—at the end of which stands God who made it all (Eccl. 12:13–14). Without Him, this life is meaningless (Eccl. 1:2; 12:8). In the new heaven and the new earth, there will be no "life under the sun," but only under the Son (Rev. 21:23; 22:5).

KEY VERSES

Deuteronomy 4:19;
2 Kings 23:5, 11;
Psalm 19:4;
Ecclesiastes 1:3,
5, 9; 2:18

Swear

Hebrew expression: *shaba'*
Pronunciation: *shaw VAH*
Strong's Number: *7650*

During the proceedings of a court trial a witness preparing to give testimony is asked a familiar question, "Do you swear to tell the truth, the whole truth, and nothing but the truth, so help you God?" Answering "I do" places the witness taking the oath under a special obligation to tell the truth. Violating the terms of the oath is an action that brings penalties enforceable by the judge. Outside the courtroom the same principle holds true. When one "swears" to do something, he or she is bound to carry out that task. Simply put, he or she enters into a solemn promise that cannot be broken without bringing harm. It is interesting to note that the Hebrew word for swearing such an oath, *shaba'*, conveys a sense of being bound to one's word by seven cords. Moreover, Ezekiel 16:8 declares that swearing enters one into a covenant relationship (1 Sam. 20:16–17).

A survey of the Old Testament yields a number of instances in which individuals made sacred pledges. Jacob made Joseph swear to bury him in his own Canaan (Gen. 50:5). Likewise Ezra urges the people to swear an oath of allegiance to uphold the Law (Ezra 10:5). There are sacred promises, more significant than those above, that the Lord swears to uphold, such as the pledge made to the Patriarchs concerning the Promised Land (Exod. 13:5; Deut. 1:8). The authority God appeals to in upholding His promises is His own. He swears by Himself (Gen. 22:16), by His name (Jer. 44:26), by His right hand (Isa. 62:8), and by His holiness (Amos 4:2). Any pledge made by the Lord and backed by His omnipotent guarantee is a sure promise indeed.

Individuals swearing an oath undertake an awesome responsibility. An oath sworn falsely, or broken knowingly, is roundly condemned in Scripture (Lev. 19:12; Jer. 7:9–10; Zech. 5:3–4). Any oath sworn before God must be kept without violation (Num. 30:2; Josh. 9:19–20). It is for this reason that Jesus warned of swearing rashly (Matt. 5:34–37). Nevertheless, if an oath or vow is sworn, it must be done properly. Jeremiah gives us two principles that must be heeded. First, an oath must be sworn to by the Lord alone (Jer. 5:7–11; Deut. 6:13). Second, it must be sworn in truth and with a pure heart (Jer. 4:2).

KEY VERSES

Genesis 26:3;
Leviticus 19:12;
Numbers 30:2;
Psalm 110:4

Tabernacle

See also: *Sanctuary, p. 160 and Temple, p. 404*
Hebrew expression: *mishkan*
Pronunciation: *mish KAWN*
Strong's Number: *4908*

"But will God indeed dwell on the earth?" the wise King Solomon asked (1 Kgs. 8:27). A reasonable question since neither heaven nor the heaven of heavens can contain Him! Although God had not dwelt on the earth since He drove Adam and Eve from the garden He prepared for them, He announced that Moses and the Israelites should build a Tabernacle for Him in the desert at Sinai. He was going to dwell among them (Gen. 3:23–24; Exod. 25:8, 9). This *mishkan* or "dwelling place" was to be a portable tent so that the Lord God could accompany His people in their travels to the land of Canaan and as they moved about in the wilderness (Exod. 40:36–38). God desired to make "contact" with the human race by settling among them, something He had not done with the patriarchs or with the Israelites in Egypt (Exod. 25:8, 9).

Mishkan designates the dwelling that the Lord ordered for Himself and is translated as "dwelling," or "Tabernacle," and sometimes as "sanctuary." The noun *mishkan* is formed from the verbal root meaning "to settle," "to dwell," "to stay," or "to inhabit." The verb is used in Exodus 25:8 when God tells His people that He will "dwell" (*shakan*) among them, while Exodus 25:9 states that He will dwell in the *mishkan*, or "dwelling place." God wanted to relate to His people, and have them know He was with them, even while they were on the move. He wanted a holy people (Exod. 19:5–6) and His presence among the Israelites was what made them holy (Exod. 3:5; 33:15–17). The Tabernacle served as a pattern and forerunner of the Temple that Solomon would build. Solomon's Temple was a permanent dwelling compared to the Tabernacle and was usually described as a "House," hardly ever as a *mishkan.*

God dwelt in the Holy of Holies of the Tabernacle, enthroned above the Mercy Seat (Lev. 16:1–2). The Tabernacle was also called the Tent of Meeting because the Lord met with His people in it at appointed times (Exod. 28:43; 29:42, 44). God's purpose was to dwell in His Tabernacle among His people so that He could be their God and they could be His people (Exod. 6:7; 29:44–46).

God's persistent presence among His people in the Old Testament paved the way for His supreme appearance in the New Testament through Jesus. Jesus "tented"—that is, "lived"—among His people, for His presence was again not a permanent residence. Christ descended in human flesh to dwell among us (John 1:14). Yet, since Jesus returned to the Father, we have become God's new Temple of flesh inhabited by God Himself in the person of the Holy Spirit. As Temples for the Holy Spirit, we have a great responsibility to keep our bodies holy and worthy of God.

KEY VERSES

Exodus 25:9; 39:32; 40:2, 34–38

Take away

Hebrew expression: *sur*
Pronunciation: *SOOR*
Strong's Number: *5493*

Through the prophet Nathan, God assured David that His lovingkindness would never be "taken away" from him and his descendants (2 Sam. 7:15). David's dynasty would last forever. With Saul the situation had been different. The Hebrew word *sur* means "to turn aside," in its most simple definition. But in 1 Chronicles 17:13, the word means "to take away," "to remove," or "to depart." God "took away" his lovingkindness from Saul (2 Sam. 7:15; 1 Chr. 17:13), which literally means He "caused it to go away." This happened to Saul because he totally rebelled against the Lord and set his own policies over the Lord's (1 Sam. 15:22–23). The Lord's rejection of Saul and His act of taking His lovingkindness from him was preceded by Saul's repudiation of the Lord. When the Lord gave His love to David, however, the Lord's unchangeable promise to him assured Israel that they would always have a king from Judah to rule over them. The good King Asa later "deposed" Maacah from being queen mother because of her lewd and idolatrous practices in making an Asherah image (1 Kgs. 15:13–15). The word translated "deposed" in some translations is *sur*.

God's actions against Saul and with the line of David show that He can both "set up" or "take away" His lovingkindness as He in His divine wisdom deems proper. Saul's failure hastened God's rejection of Him. Likewise, the Christian church in Ephesus was instructed to repent because they had forsaken their first love for the Lord and had fallen. They were charged to do their first repentance over. If they would not repent, the Lord would remove (*kinein* in Greek) their lampstand from them—that is, they would experience judgment and the church, as a lighthouse to other Christians and the world, would be lost (Rev. 2:4–6). The Greek word translated "remove" is equivalent in this context to the Hebrew word *sur*. Saul refused to truly repent in time and lost his kingship. The church at Ephesus was warned to repent, or they would be removed by the Lord.

KEY VERSES

2 Samuel 7:15;
1 Kings 15:13–14

T

Thanksgiving

Hebrew expression: *todah*
Pronunciation: *toh DAWH*
Strong's Number: *8426*

A thorough study of the use of this word in the Hebrew Bible can lead to one con-clusion: Everywhere and in every situation, God's people should continually give thanks to God, the One who has created and redeemed them.

The giving of thanks in the Old Testament is indicated most often by the Hebrew word *todah,* which is translated "thanks," "thankfulness." *Todah* is the noun that is formed from the verb *yadah,* which means "to throw" or "to cast." In the causative stem of the verb, its most used stem, the word means "to give thanks," "to praise," or "to lead." This meaning possibly arose because of the ges-tures and physical involvement of the people toward God as they gave thanks. The verb also has the meaning of "affirming" or "confessing" the Name of the Lord (1 Kgs. 8:33, 35).

As might be expected, the word *todah* is found most often in the book of Psalms, the praise book of God's people in which thanksgiving to the Lord domi-nates. Thanksgiving was accompanied with cries and shouts of joy, music, and singing (Pss. 42:4; 95:2; 100:4). In the time of Nehemiah, formal thanksgiving was rendered by two large choirs (Neh. 12:31, 40). The word *todah* is even used to describe an entire psalm as "A Psalm of Giving Thanks" (see Ps. 100, title). Most often thanks was rendered to God for His acts and words on behalf of His people (Ps. 119:62), but many times the psalmist calls for thanks to be given to the Lord "because He is good" (Pss. 106:1; 107:1; 118:1, 29; 136:1). He is good in His very nature as well as in the expression of that nature through His works.

In Leviticus 7:12 and 22:29, a thank offering was even provided for the person who wanted to express his appreciation to the Lord for deliverance from illness (Ps. 116:17), troubles of various kinds (Ps. 107:22), death (Ps. 56:12), or any blessing he may have received. It is evident that all of Israel's thanksgiving was a serious but joyous form of praise.

KEY VERSES

Leviticus 7:12;
Psalms 42:4;
50:14; 95:2

Thanksgiving permeates the New Testament as well. Jesus gave thanks to the Father to model true thanksgiving to us (Matt. 11:25; John 11:41). Most references to thanksgiving in the New Testament are found in the letters of Paul. The goal of God's people is to honor God through their thanks to Him, for what He had done in Christ (2 Cor. 4:15). The rendering of thanks should characterize the Christian's life in every circum-stance, marking the individual's life and even corporate wor-ship (1 Cor. 4:16–17; Phil. 4:6).

T

Throne

Hebrew expression: *kisse'*
Pronunciation: *kih SAY*
Strong's Number: *3678*

The "throne" in Israel's day was the chair of state. Pharaoh sat on a throne in Egypt (Gen. 41:40) and the kings of Assyria and Babylon occupied their throne chairs. Solomon prepared a great throne, inlaid with ivory and overlaid with pure gold (2 Chr. 9:17–19). According to Ezra, no such elaborate throne had been made for any other king or kingdom (2 Chr. 9:19). The Hebrew word for throne was *kisse'* meaning "throne, chair, or seat." Solomon received the throne from his father David; God promised David that a king from his line would always be on the throne (1 Chr. 17:12, 14). This throne was to last forever (1 Chr. 22:10) and God promised David that Solomon would not only be David's son but also the Lord's adopted son. David readily acknowledged the Lord's appointment (1 Chr. 28:5) which was in agreement with the Lord's word through Moses (Deut. 17:15). Consequently, Solomon sat on the throne established by the Lord (1 Chr. 29:23). The throne chair itself was symbolic of the power which God, the King of the Universe, had vested in the office He created. The "throne" (*kisse'*) was and continues to be a sign of authority, majesty and exalted rule by God's chosen rulers in Israel (Pss. 9:7; 45:6; 94:20; Prov. 16:12). God delegates His authority from His heavenly throne (Pss. 11:4; 45:6; 47:8; 132:12). In Isaiah, the Lord is the picture of Majesty, seated upon His throne high over the universe (Isa. 6). Heaven itself is the Lord's throne and even it does not contain Him. In Daniel's picture of God, He sits on His throne of judgment as judge over all the nations (Dan. 7:9).

In the New Testament, Jesus Christ, the descendant of David and Solomon, inherited the "throne" of power and majesty forever (Acts 2:30). The Son of God has been given the scepter of Judah permanently and He now reigns over His Church (Heb. 1:8). Daniel's vision of the great white throne is reiterated in Revelation 20:11. After God's judgment from this eternal throne, the Lord God and His Lamb, Jesus Christ, will rule forever. Scripture makes it clear that ultimately all creation will bow before the throne of God and His Son, Jesus Christ.

KEY VERSES

2 Samuel 7:13;
1 Chronicles 17:12, 14; 22:10; 28:5;
2 Chronicles 9:17–18

Time

Hebrew expression: 'et
Pronunciation: AYT
Strong's Number: 6256

"To every thing there is a season, and a time to every purpose under the heaven." This proverb captures the orderliness and repetition of the seasons of life, the points in the passing of time when certain events, happy or unhappy, will occur. Seven more verses follow that present the assured inevitable seasons and times of our lives.

The word for time used here is 'et. The root is 'anah, possibly meaning "to answer, respond," but this is uncertain. This word usually marks the time of an *event*, as in Genesis 21:22 where it means "at that time." It can refer to near or distant times, or to continuous times, according to its context (Esth. 5:13; Ezek. 12:27). It can refer to the quality of time, such as a time of anger (Ps. 21:9) or a time of difficulty (Pss. 9:9; 10:1). It points to an appointed time (1 Sam. 18:19; Ezek. 7:12). The author asserts that there is a proper time and activity "for everything" (Eccl. 8:6).

In Ecclesiastes 3, this word takes center stage as a way to describe all of life under the sun. In verses 2–8 the word is used 27 times. Time is not empty—it is filled with events. Simply "marking time" is not how the author understands the significance of the flow of life. Events mark time, while time is the conduit within which events occur. But one thing is clear—time progresses from birth (3:2) to death (3:2). For humans encased in time and under the sun, all other events take place within these two fixed parameters.

The writer mentions the major experiences of existence between life and death: planting, harvesting, killing, healing, tearing down, building up, weeping, laughing, mourning, dancing, getting, losing, silence, speaking, loving, hating, war, peace. The challenge of life is to learn to manage these events in their proper times and places. It is what we do "with" time ('et) and "in" it that counts. The author asserts that we should "do good."

KEY VERSES

Genesis 18:10;
Psalms 21:9;
145:15;
Ecclesiastes
3:1–11; 8:6;
Ezekiel 21:25

Time is a gift of God and should be spent remembering our Creator, especially in our youth (Eccl. 12:1). It should be a time of doing something, "casting our bread upon the waters," or nothing will return to us. Outside of the boundaries of "time" stands God, who will judge us for how we spent our time (Eccl. 12:13–14).

Tithe

Hebrew expression: *ma'aser*
Pronunciation: *mah 'ah SAYR*
Strong's Number: *4643*

Words tend to have meaning at two levels; that is, a word may have a literal meaning (denotation) and an implied meaning (connotation). The English word "tithe" denotes "a tenth part paid as a voluntary contribution"; but it has come to connote "a tax" or "a levy." Since the offering of the tithe was a duty prescribed by Moses' law in the old covenant, it is often understood by the modern reader in terms of a tax or levy. This word study should help us unlearn the mistaken definition of a tithe as a penalty paid and learn the proper meaning of the word "tithe": It is a gift to God. The issue is ultimately one of ownership versus stewardship.

The term translated "tithe" is derived from the Hebrew word for the number "ten" (*'eser*). The tithe is a measure consisting of a "tenth-part" or "one-tenth" of some whole object. According to Moses' law, the Hebrews were to set aside a tenth of their agricultural produce as an offering to the Lord (Deut. 14:22–27). The tithe was to be taken to the Lord's sanctuary as a type of thank offering—and then a portion of it was to be eaten as a fellowship meal before the Lord (Deut. 14:23). The giving of the tithe was an act of worship and served as a tangible reminder that it was God who gave them the produce or increase.

The giving of a tenth as a thank offering has its precedent in Abraham's presentation of a tithe of his wealth to the priest-king Melchizedek (Gen. 14:20). Once given to the Lord, the tithe was considered holy (Lev. 27:30–33). The tithe became the means of both affirmation and economic support for the ministry of the priests and Levites because they received no inheritance of land (Num. 18:21–24). Every third year, the tithe was not taken to the sanctuary, but was set aside to aid disadvantaged groups within Hebrew society—especially the widows, orphans, and resident aliens (Deut. 14:28–29). On the more practical side, these stipulations for the use of the tithe helped ensure both the good stewardship of perishable resources and the redistribution of those resources with a view toward social justice.

For the prophet Malachi, the act of offering the tithe was the external sign of the internal attitude of reverence desired by God (Mal. 1:6). The prophet's call for the tithe should not be construed as a mechanistic formula for material blessing from God (Mal. 3:10). The people's return to God had to begin somewhere, and Malachi said that the formal act of offering the tithe was symbolic of a change of heart. Failure to offer the tithe was tantamount to robbing God because God owns everything (Mal. 3:8–9; see also Job 41:11). Theologically, the offering of the tithe was a demonstration of the essence of the Mosaic law, love for God and love for one's neighbor (Lev. 19:18; Deut. 6:4–9; 26:10–15).

Jesus rebuked the religious leaders of His day for failing to

KEY VERSES

Leviticus 27:30;
Numbers 18:21;
Malachi 3:10

offer their tithe with a sincere heart (Matt. 23:23). He encouraged the kind of giving that went beyond the law—beyond merely counting a tenth to a generosity that gives all (see the story of the widow in Mark 12:42; see also Matt. 6:1–4). The rest of the New Testament teaches cheerful and generous giving (Rom. 12:8; 2 Cor. 9:6–9). Theologically, the principle of the tithe as the first fruits is applied to the resurrection of Jesus Christ as the first fruits of the dead (1 Cor. 15:20–23).

Transgression

Hebrew expression: *pesha'*
Pronunciation: *peh SHAH'*
Strong's Number: *6588*

"For three transgressions of Damascus and for four . . ." (NASB). Eight times, Amos reiterates this charge against eight separate nations—the last two nations, Judah and Israel respectively (Amos 1:3–13; 2:1–6). *Pesha'* is the Hebrew word translated "transgression," a noun that is also rendered as "sins," "offenses," or "rebellion," depending upon its context. It is rendered with at least six Greek words in the Septuagint, a Greek translation of the Hebrew Bible. *Pesha'* is formed from the verbal root *pasha'*, "to transgress," "to rebel," "to revolt," or "to sin." "Transgression" tends to be an activity done in open rebellion against God (2 Kgs. 24:1, 20).

Amos records various nations that have rebelled against the Lord's international laws of humanity. Israel rebelled and transgressed the sacred laws the Lord had imparted to that nation at Mount Sinai. Israel would especially be punished for its rebellion (Amos 3:14; 5:2). "Transgression" is a good translation of this Hebrew word, for the English word combines *trans* and *egere* (Latin), meaning to "to go over" or "to go beyond"—in this case, to go beyond God's sacred laws. So, trangression amounts to rebellion and is well-stated in the word *pesha'*, which also carries the connotation "to commit a legal offense." This meaning is clear in Amos' assertions: the offending parties have transgressed, by taking away the rights of various other peoples. Stealing from one's parents is considered *pesha'*—a blatant disregard of natural responsibilities toward other people (Prov. 28:24). *Pesha'* is also associated with a wicked person (Ps. 36:1), and in Amos, with a wicked nation (Amos 1; 2).

In the Old Testament, Israel could only accept that her "offenses," *pesha'*, were always before her. The Lord knew how numerous they were (Amos 5:12). Yet Isaiah uttered the wonderful news of God's grace for His rebellious people— just like the morning mist which dissipates, the Lord had swept away their *pesha'im*, "transgression," (Isa. 44:22). David asserted in more than one psalm the marvel of the Lord's forgiving, or blotting out, of his transgressions and offenses (Pss. 32:1; 51:1). Paul echoes David by declaring the blessedness of the persons whose sins have been forgiven (Rom. 4:7, *anomia* in Greek). Transgressions are serious before God; until they are forgiven and removed we are considered dead (Eph. 2:1, 5); we cannot enter the Lord's presence because of them. The good news is that Jesus Christ "swept away" our sins and offenses (*hamartias* in Greek). Jesus died for us, even when we were dead in our transgressions, to bring us back to life in Him (Isa. 53:5; Eph. 2:5). His absolute, unconditional love saved us all.

KEY VERSES

Psalms 32:1;
51:1, 3; 65:3;
Isaiah 43:25; 53:5

T

Trumpet

Hebrew expression: *shopar*
Pronunciation: *shoh FAHR*
Strong's Number: 7782

"When the priests blew with the trumpets . . . and the people shouted with a great shout, the wall fell down flat" (Josh. 6:20, KJV). The Hebrew word *shopar* is translated "trumpet." In this case, it is clear that the trumpet was not used as a musical instrument, but to signal the time when God would bring down the walls of Jericho. Today the *shopar* is still used to signal the beginning of the New Year and the commencement of the Day of Atonement. *Shopar* is the name of the material from which the instrument was made—the horn of a ram or wild goat (Josh. 6:4–6). The Hebrew word *yobel*, "jubilee" is used as a synonym of *shopar* (Exod. 19:13; Josh. 6:5; Lev. 25:13). *Shopar* is also translated as "horn" (1 Chr. 15:28).

The *shopar* is the most mentioned musical instrument in the Old Testament. In Joshua, *shopar* is used fourteen times in connection with the fall of Jericho. The number seven is significant in this chapter: seven priests each carried a trumpet (*shopar*) around the city of Jericho for seven days, and on the seventh day they marched around the city seven times blowing the trumpets. At the sound of a long trumpet blast by the priests the people mingled their shouts with the trumpets' sound and the fortified walls of Jericho fell down (Josh. 6:3–5, 20).

Besides being a musical instrument, the *shopar* announced the presence and action of the Lord. In Exodus an extra loud trumpet blast announced God's proclamation of the Ten Commandments and His epiphany to the people of Israel at Mount Sinai (Exod. 19:16, 19; 20:1–17). *Shopar* was also used to call the people to war (Judg. 6:34; Neh. 4:18–20) or to announce war (Jer. 4:19–21; 6:1). It even alerted the enemy to Israel's attack (Judg. 7:8). It is also used in connection with the final Day of Judgment (Isa. 27:13; Zeph. 1:16).

The call of a trumpet continued to be a signal of momentous events in the New Testament. Paul and Jesus said trumpets would sound to mark the end of the age and the beginning of God's Kingdom. *Shopar* announces the Day of the Lord, when the Lord said He would send His angels to gather His elect at Jesus' second coming (Matt. 24:30–31). In the book of Revelation the seventh angel blows the seventh trumpet (Rev. 11:15, 17) to announce the beginning of the reign of our Lord over the kingdoms of this world. We are told that at the last trumpet sound all Christians will be changed into incorruptible beings (1 Cor. 15:51–52; 1 Thess. 4:16).

KEY VERSES

Exodus 19:16;
20:18;
Leviticus 25:9;
Joshua 6:20;
Judges 3:27;
2 Samuel 15:10

T

Truth

See also: *Truth, p. 410*
Hebrew expression: *'emet*
Pronunciation: *'EH meht*
Strong's Number: *571*

Pilate asked probably one of the most remembered lines in the Bible, "What is truth?" (John 18:38). Truth defines Christ and is, therefore, at the heart of the Old and New Testament. The Hebrew expression most often translated "truth" is *'emet*. The word comes from the root meaning of *'aman*, "to confirm," or "to support." It is also often translated as "faithfulness." Several other key words in the Old Testament fall into the semantic range of this root: *'emunah*, which means, "faithfulness," or "steadfastness"; and *'amen*, which means, "truly," "verily," "amen."

The Hebrew word *'emet* indicates something is true when it "conforms to the facts," but this is not its most significant use in the Old Testament. The truth for the biblical writers was the reliability, dependability, and trustworthiness of a person—and, specifically, of God. When Scripture speaks of truth, it is a moral matter—a way of thinking and acting—not merely an intellectual or scientific matter. The Israelites were expected to reflect God, the One who is perfectly reliable and trustworthy. The psalmist asserts his desire and willingness to walk in the truth of the Lord (Ps. 86:11). This "truth" includes God's instructions and laws that were constructed to lead a person to Him. The "way of truth" was a manner of life in accord with God's revealed paths of righteousness and holiness (Ps. 119:30, 43). God's people were to always speak the truth to one another (Zech. 8:16). In other words, the concept of truth encompasses who we are—whether we approach God in honesty and humility (Ps. 145:18). In other words, truth is more than skin deep. God demands *'emet* in the center of our being, in our heart (Ps. 51:6), so that we can approach God and be reconciled to Him.

Daniel and the prophets revealed that the truth, *'emet*, had been cast down by the people—and this had led to the Lord's judgment of His people (Dan. 8:12; 9:13). Since God is the God of truth, He will judge mankind from what is recorded in His book of truth (Dan. 10:21). No one in the Bible can dispense God's truth, except God Himself. But Jesus says, "I tell you the truth (*amen*)" using the Greek word that comes from the Hebrew word *'aman*! He makes this claim dozens of times (Matt. 5:18; Mark 14:25; Luke 21:32; John 16:23). Ironically, Pilate asked Jesus, the dispenser of God's truth, "What is truth?"—in fact, Pilate was interacting with God's incarnate Truth. Jesus is still the Way, the Truth (John 14:6, *aletheia* in Greek), and the Life. He leads us to the Father.

KEY VERSES

Exodus 34:6;
Psalms 15:2; 86:11;
Zechariah 8:16

195

Utterly destroyed

Hebrew expression: *charam*
Pronunciation: *haw RAHM*
Strong's Number: *2763*

God said, "Totally destroy them and all their property!" But Saul disobeyed God by sparing Agag's life and letting the best of his flocks and herds live. So afterwards, Saul lost his kingship because of his disobedience (1 Sam. 15:3–11). Why would this happen? The key lies in the meaning of the verb *charam*. *Charam* means "to exterminate," "to destroy completely," "to devote to destruction, or "to ban." The verb spawned a noun translated as "devoted thing, set aside for destruction." These were strong words commonly used to designate people and things set aside for destruction for a religious reason. For instance, all of the inhabitants of Canaan were supposed to be annihilated and their property and cities destroyed (Deut. 7:2, 16, 25–26). But it was really the Lord who would annihilate these pagan peoples and their heathen influences completely (Deut. 31:3). God ordered His people to destroy everything connected with these people, because He knew that they, with their false gods, altars, and Temples would lead the Israelites astray. Their inequity had reached its peak, and God ordered them destroyed so that their contagious evil would not corrupt His people (Gen. 15:16).

God uses the word *charam* to describe the divinely ordained destruction of things. To lie under the *herem*, "ban for destruction," was to be doomed by God. It was a holy rejection. King Saul explicitly refused to carry out the ban on the Amalakites—thereby rebelling against God's command (1 Sam. 15:9, 22–23). The word *charam* is found often in Joshua where places such as Jericho fell under the ban and were destroyed at the Lord's command (Josh. 6:18–21). The Lord devoted the city to destruction. Achan took a "devoted" item and by this act became devoted to destruction himself (Josh. 6:18; 7:15–26). Isaiah depicts God as placing His wrath upon the nations to totally destroy them (Isa. 34:2). Babylon, the bane of Israel, is finally totally destroyed (Jer. 51:3). It is impossible to think of anything being worse than *charam*—that is, coming under the ban of God and being set aside for His absolute destruction.

God will ultimately destroy those who do not believe—they are appointed to holy destruction (Jude 1:5). Yet God assures us that the threat of destruction can be removed if we believe in Jesus, the Son He sent to us. Satan held the power of destruction and death, but Jesus at the cross triumphed over Satan (Heb. 2:14; 1 John 3:8). Those who believe in Christ are set aside—not for destruction—but for everlasting life (Phil. 1:28–29).

KEY VERSES

Deuteronomy 7:2;
Joshua 6:21; 11:11;
1 Samuel 15:3;
Isaiah 34:2

Vanity

Hebrew expression: *hebel*
Pronunciation: *HEH behl*
Strong's Number: *1892*

Few Bible books start off so shockingly—"Vanity of vanities . . . Vanity of vanities! All is vanity" (Eccl. 1:2, NASB). So begins the book of Ecclesiastes and the author continues to use this highly charged word throughout his book—in fact, thirty-six times, over half the times it is used in the entire Old Testament.

The Hebrew word used is *hebel,* which properly means "vapor," "breath," or "nothingness." Something with this quality or nature perishes quickly—its activity or significance is mere "vanity." The New International Version translates *hebel* as "meaningless"; the NJPS Bible, the Jewish version, renders it "futility." The noun spawned a verb, *habal,* meaning "to act emptily" or "to become vain." *Hebel* could be translated as "emptiness." The word also serves as the name for Abel, whose life did not come to full fruition (Gen. 4:25).

Job used this word to describe the vain and meaningless advice that his friends were offering (Job 27:12). The prophet Jeremiah described idols as *hebel,* nothing more than "vapor" (Jer. 10:8, 15; 14:22; 16:19). The people who followed these worthless objects became worthless themselves (2 Kgs. 17:15; Jer. 2:5). Paul the apostle asserted this as well (Rom. 3:12). In both the Old and New Testaments, God's people must turn from worthless (*hebel*) idols (Acts 14:15).

In Ecclesiastes, however, the word refers to all of life lived "under the sun" (Eccl. 1:3). Every human accomplishment is seen as useless. The end of life is the end of it all. Both good and bad people die. In fact, there really is no distinction in a world where there is nothing more than life lived under the sun.

In modern philosophy, this view of life would be called nihilism—the belief that nothing is ultimately of any value. The Preacher in Ecclesiastes was correct. Everything amounts to vanity—that is, if there is no God. When God enters the picture, however, there is purpose. Life is meant to be enjoyed, for it is God's gift to us (Eccl. 2:24–25; 3:12–13; 4:9, 12; 5:12, 19). Ultimately, there *is* meaning in life if we understand that there is a God to whom we must give account (Eccl. 12:13–14).

KEY VERSES

Deuteronomy 32:21;
Jeremiah 2:5; 10:8;
Job 27:12;
Ecclesiastes 1:2;
3:19

V

Vengeance

Hebrew expression: *naqam*
Pronunciation: *naw QAHM*
Strong's Number: 5358

Vengeance is generally considered a negative term, something in which Christians should not take part. The prophet Nahum, however, declared that God "takes vengeance." Unlike mankind, God is righteous and holy; so His vengeance is just. Nahum says He takes vengeance because He is a God who is "jealous" or zealous for His people; therefore, He will destroy their enemies (Nah. 1:2). In one verse Nahum uses the Hebrew word *naqam*, "vengeance" three times: twice he says that the Lord takes vengeance, and once that He takes vengeance against His adversaries. Nahum employs the participle of the verb *naqam* meaning "to avenge" or "to take vengeance" in its simplest meaning. In other stems of the verb it can mean "to avenge oneself or be avenged." English translations regularly use the words "avenge," "vengeance," "take vengeance" to render the word. As Nahum 1:2 indicates, God takes divine or godly vengeance upon His enemies and the enemies of His people. He repays them for breaking His laws, abusing His character, and threatening His people (Num. 31:2–3).

According to Isaiah, the Lord has appointed a day when the Lord God will come in vengeance, not only upon the nations but also upon His rebellious Israel as well (Isa. 34:8; 35:4; 61:2). His revenge will be complete, for He will spare no guilty person (Isa. 47:3). Vengeance is appropriate to God—for His revenge is just, righteous, and perfect. It is not for people to take revenge upon each other. Moses charged the Israelites not to pursue revenge or even to maintain a grudge against anyone (Lev. 19:18). Israel can justly cry for revenge against her human enemies, but not take the matter into her own hands (Ps. 44:16). God again sides with His people when He takes vengeance upon Edom for helping the Babylonians devastate His people. The Lord states His operative principle clearly in Deuteronomy 32:35, "I will avenge, I will repay."

KEY VERSES

Leviticus 19:18;
26:25;
Jeremiah 51:36;
Nahum 1:2

Paul asserts the same principle in the New Testament. Christians are to have mercy, not vengeance, upon enemies and pray for them. Paul and the writer of Hebrews teach that the Lord will take care of any vengeance that is to be taken (Rom. 12:19; Heb. 10:30; *ekdikesis* in Greek). The book of Revelation assures God's people that He will finally avenge His followers (Rev. 6:10, *ekdikeo* in Greek). We should not even attempt to take revenge. God alone is able to properly avenge His cause and His people, for only He can dispense justice in a perfectly equitable way.

V

Vision

Hebrew expression: *chazon*
Pronunciation: *khaw ZOHN*
Strong's Number: *2377*

Captive in the Babylonian exile, Daniel needed guidance from God. Jerusalem was in ruins, Judah was scattered, and the Gentile nations were ruling the world with a rod of iron! He needed a new "vision" or revelation to expand upon what he was diligently studying in the Holy Scriptures (Dan. 9:2). He was puzzled about the outcome of the tragic state of affairs in which he found himself and his people. But God gave him what he needed, a "vision" of His plans for His servant and Israel. God used visions to communicate to His people in both the Old and New Testament. In the Old Testament, the Hebrew noun *chazon* meaning "vision" or "revelation" comes from the verb *chazah* meaning "to see" or "perceive." Visions may refer to the distant future or the present (Ezek. 12:27–28). A vision was valid for guidance when used along with the Law and the counsel of the elders for God's people (Ezek. 7:26).

Daniel received more visions than any other person in the Bible except John, the author of Revelation. Daniel received instruction concerning the future of his people through visions that taught things that he could have learned no other way (Dan. 8; 9; 10; 11). Although Daniel was an expert at interpreting (Dan. 1:17), the Lord had to provide divinely communicated understanding for him to know what his visions meant (Dan. 8:16; 9:22; 11:2). The Lord's plans for Judah and Jerusalem were given to Isaiah in a *chazon* (Isa. 1:1). God also used a vision to reveal His plans for David and the construction of His Temple (2 Sam. 7:17; Ps. 89:20). We learn from the practical wise man who authored many proverbs, that where there is no vision—no presence of God, and no guidance—the people cast away restraint (Prov. 29:18; 1 Sam. 3:1). Visions were indeed important in the Old Testament, because when God ceased to give visions to instruct His people, confusion resulted (Lam. 2:10).

The use of "visions" in the Old Testament often referred to the future, but often impacted the present. This rich tradition is taken up and used in the New Testament in several pivotal situations. In a "vision" (*optasia* in Greek) God announced the birth of John the Baptist to Zechariah; the immediate impact was John's birth, the future impact was his role as "Elijah" the prophet who made way for the Messiah (Luke 1:22). God used visions (*horama* in Greek) to reveal the truth of the gospel to Peter, that God had given repentance to life not just to the Jews, but also to the Gentiles. Even Gentiles could be saved and become God's children with a promise of heaven (Acts 10:1–34; 11:5). At crucial points in time, God intervened to give us the sure knowledge that He is in control of history and our salvation.

KEY VERSES

1 Samuel 3:1;
Proverbs 29:18;
Isaiah 1:1;
Daniel 8:17;
Habakkuk 2:2, 3

Vow

Hebrew expression: *neder*
Pronunciation: *NAY dehr*
Strong's Number: *5088*

A vow is often thought of as a human act alone, but in the Bible a vow is made before God alone. The Hebrew noun *neder* comes from the verb *nadar* meaning "to vow" or "to dedicate." A vow may be one in which a person promises to perform an act (Gen. 28:20–21; 31:13; Num. 21:2–3) or to refrain from something (Ps. 132:1–4). No one needed to make a vow, but once made, it was binding. While a person could swear to a person or to God, they could vow only to God. In the Old Testament, the Lord saw and heard all vows; not honoring a vow was therefore a grave sin. Both the wise man of Proverbs (Prov. 20:25) and the wise Preacher in Ecclesiastes warned against making a vow rashly or delaying its fulfillment (Eccl. 5:4–5).

Vows played an important part in Israel's worship, especially with regard to individual commitment to the Lord. In Isaiah 19:21, the prophet envisions a time when Egypt will show allegiance to the Lord not only by offering sacrifices and offerings, but also by making and keeping "vows" to Him as their God (Isa. 19:21). Vows were made in times of distress, but also in times of blessing and rejoicing (Lev. 23:38; 1 Sam. 1:21). When God performed an action described in a vow, not only sacrifices were promised to God, but also public praise and thanks could be offered (Pss. 40:6; 50:12–15; 69:30–31).

Of the thirty-three verses in the Pentateuch where *neder* occurs, nineteen are in the book of Numbers. In the Nazarite vow, while there were certain prohibitions, the stress was upon the individual's consecration to the Lord during the time of the vow (Num. 6:2–8). Vows were part and parcel of Israel's worship (Num. 15:3). Numbers 30 is solely about "vows" and *neder* is mentioned in twelve of the sixteen verses. As stated earlier, the person who makes a vow must not break his or her word (Num. 30:2). Failing to honor one's vows was a sin (Deut. 23:22). It was considered better not to make a vow than to make it and not keep it (Eccl. 5:4–6); simply saying, "I made a mistake by making the vow" was no excuse.

KEY VERSES

Genesis 28:20;
Numbers 6:2, 5, 21;
15:8; 30:2–9,
11–14;
Acts 18:18

The seriousness of taking a vow is as significant today as it was in the time of the Old Testament. In the New Testament, Paul made a vow and considered it binding upon himself to keep it. He may have carried out the vow as thanks to God for being delivered from mortal dangers. He then had his head shaved at Cenchrea marking the end of the vow (Acts 18:18). Paul later joined in the rites necessary for four Jews who had made vows. He accompanied these Jewish Christians to demonstrate that he had not rejected the essence of the Law of Moses.

V

Wait

Hebrew expression: *chakah*
Pronunciation: *khaw KAWH*
Strong's Number: *2442*

Waiting takes patience, but the prophets indicate that God's people will have to wait on Him at times. They will have to wait whether they are anticipating judgment or whether they are hoping for blessing. The verb *chakah* in Hebrew means essentially "to wait," "to await," "to delay," "to tarry," or "to long for." In many contexts the connotation of the word is "to have patience" (Zeph. 3:8). In other contexts, the word simply marks time as when men lie "in wait" to ambush someone (2 Kgs. 7:9; Job 32:4; Hos. 6:9). But the most significant use of the word is when it indicates patient waiting upon the Lord (Ps. 33:20; Isa. 8:17).

The psalmist declares that we "wait and depend," *chakah*, upon the Lord for His deliverance and salvation (see Ps. 33:20, KJV, NLT). Deliverance is assured because His people are willing to depend on Him. Israel found themselves in serious trouble when they refused to wait patiently on the Lord in the wilderness of Sinai and at Mount Sinai (Exod. 32:1–2), therefore the Lord dealt with them in judgment. The psalmist recalls this event as the time when the people would not wait for the Lord's counsel (Ps. 106:13).

Remaining in expectation, or waiting for the Lord, in our lives is necessary, according to the Scriptures, to receive the Lord's blessing. The prophet Isaiah practiced what he preached as he waited for the Lord to act in his life and the life of the nation (Isa. 8:17). Blessed, or "happy," are these who go through the waiting period the Lord decrees for each of us (Isa. 30:18). The nine months of waiting for a child to be born is more than repaid at the child's birth. The same is true for those who wait upon the Lord—for Isaiah says He acts on their behalf (Isa. 64:4, NIV, KJV, NLT). In this light, Zephaniah delivers the Lord's message to His people Israel to wait for the Lord (Zeph. 3:18). His charge is double-edged in this case, for the people are to wait for the Day of the Lord when the Lord will judge Israel and the nations. But, also, He gives them a glimpse of a time of future restoration. First, God will come in judgment—but then He will renew His people and restore their fortunes (Zeph. 3:20). All of this is applicable to believers today— both at the individual and national level. We, as believers, must wait patiently for the Lord Jesus to correct injustices in this world when He returns in glory (1 Cor. 1:7, *apekdechomai* in Greek). On another level, we must "wait" on God when we are praying for guidance or making tough life decisions. Sometimes, it seems as if the Lord is not answering our prayers. But during those times, we need to remind ourselves that He is our Living God. He is with us at every moment. He is in control of all life, and He is working for our own good. He does all this because He loves us. Be patient and trust the Lord.

KEY VERSES

2 Kings 7:9;
Job 32:4;
Psalms 33:20;
106:13;
Isaiah 8:17; 30:18;
Daniel 12:12

Walk

Hebrew expression: *halak*
Pronunciation: *haw LAHK*
Strong's Number: *1980*

For Christians, "walk the talk" has become a cliché. The thought is also thoroughly biblical. The Hebrew word *halak*, "to walk," "to go, or "to come," is used over fif-
teen hundred times in the Old Testament. It literally describes physical movement,
but its metaphorical use is much more significant. *Halak* often describes dying, as
when someone "goes the way of all the earth" (1 Kgs. 2:2). In a more general sense,
it refers to the normal "process of living," such as walking in a valley of deep darkness (Ps. 23:4). But even more importantly, it describes "walking before the Lord"
or "living a moral, ethical and religious life" that pleases God. The Israelites, being
a part of God's chosen people, were supposed to "walk" before the Lord in truth
and integrity (1 Kgs. 2:4; 3:6). The blessing of the Lord is upon the person who does
not "walk" in the counsel of the wicked (Ps. 1:1). The kings of Israel were declared
righteous if they "walked" in God's ways; that is, in His decrees, commands, laws
and ordinances. David did so (2 Chr. 7:17) and he charged Solomon to do the same
(1 Kgs. 2:3). Rehoboam and his faithful followers walked in the ways of David and
Solomon three years and were blessed during this time (2 Chr. 11:17), but then they
abandoned the Lord.

God's people are characterized by their walk in His name (Mic. 4:5). The "walk"
of a person is all-important, for only the person whose walk is blameless can enter
the Temple of the Lord (Pss. 15:1; 84:11). Before the Law was given, Abraham
"walked in faith" before God and the Lord considered him blameless (Gen. 17:1).
The apostle Paul asserts that Abraham is also the father of faith to those who walk
in Abraham's steps (Rom. 4:12). Christians now "walk in the light" of the Lord
because He is light (1 John 1:7). In the New Jerusalem, those who know Christ will
walk by the light of the glory of God and the light of the Lamb (Rev. 21:23–24). As
we await Christ's return, we must strive to live a life that honors God—not veering
from the path, but walking with Him every step of the way.

KEY VERSES

Genesis 17:1;
Deuteronomy 10:12;
Joshua 22:5;
Psalm 119:3

Wall

Hebrew expression: *chomah*
Pronunciation: *khoh MAWH*
Strong's Number: *2346*

Solomon built his palace, the Lord's Temple, and the "wall" of Jerusalem. The wall was standard fare for a strong city in the ancient Near East. It protected the people, keeping the enemy out and securing the people inside. The wall of Jerusalem was totally destroyed in 586 B.C., however, by the Babylonians (2 Chr. 36:19). In the days of Ezra and Nehemiah the wall of the city of Jerusalem was rebuilt. These walls had lain in ruins for almost 150 years! Nehemiah and his workers finished the wall of Jerusalem in fifty-two days on the twenty-fifth of Elul (October 2, 445 B.C.). The finished wall was celebrated with great fanfare in which both Ezra and Nehemiah took part (Neh. 12:27–47). The Hebrew word *chomah*, "wall," is found thirty times in the small book of Nehemiah and twenty-nine times in the book of Ezekiel. In Nehemiah, *chomah* always refers to the wall of Jerusalem. But in Ezekiel, the word refers to a wall around the new Temple which Ezekiel envisions (Ezek. 40:5; 42:20). *Chomah* is also used figuratively to refer to the wall of water the Lord created in order to rescue Israel (Exod. 14:22, 29). The wall of Jerusalem kept unwanted people out, while once again making the city a safe, desirable place to live. Nehemiah brought the leaders of the people to live in the new walled city, as well as one-tenth of the rest of the common people (Neh. 11:1–2). Nehemiah's completion of the wall made the resettlement of the city possible. It also fulfilled the ancient prophecies that foretold a day when the streets and market places of the city would once again resound with the sounds of happy voices. In order to keep the merchants of the city from profaning the Sabbath, Nehemiah ordered the gates of the walls to be shut when the sun set on the Sabbath. They remained closed until the Sabbath was over (Neh. 13:15–22).

David used the phrase "build up the walls of Jerusalem" to indicate God's blessing of prosperity for the city (Ps. 51:18). The prayer for the "peace of Jerusalem" asked for peace within the city's walls (Ps. 122:2, 7). The walls that would provide security and peace in God's restored Jerusalem are called the "walls of salvation" (Isa. 60:10,18). In the New Jerusalem of Revelation, the walls of the city are high walls decorated with all kinds of precious stones.

KEY VERSES

1 Kings 3:1;
2 Chronicles 36:19;
Nehemiah 1:3;
6:15; 12:27

Inside the walls are God's people, those who have accepted Jesus Christ as Savior. Outside the walls are those who have rejected the Lord (Rev. 21:12, 19; 22:14–15).

Watchman

Hebrew expression: *tsaphah*
Pronunciation: *tsaw FAWH*
Strong's Number: *6822*

An ancient Israelite city often had a watchman who guarded the city and kept his eyes open for approaching enemies (2 Sam. 13:34). The noun meaning "watchman" in Hebrew is *tsaphah*. It means to "look out," "to spy," or "to keep watch," and is more literally translated as "one who watches" (Ezek. 3:17). In certain contexts, *tsaphah* can be translated as "to spy on" (Ps. 37:32) or "to lie in wait for." The *tsaphah*, also rendered "scout" or "lookout," was aware of any approaching friends or enemies. There are many references in the Bible to these watchmen of physical threats. Ezekiel, however, was appointed by the Lord to be a watchman for God's people in a spiritual sense.

God made Ezekiel a spiritual watchman, watching over the lives and souls of his own people (Ezek. 3:16–21). The Lord said to Ezekiel, "I appointed you a watchman for the house of Israel" (Ezek. 33:7, NASB). Ezekiel's responsibility was twofold: he was to warn the righteous of the danger in falling away from God and doing evil, and he was to warn the wicked about the ultimate fate awaiting them if they did not turn from their wicked ways. Ezekiel's charge as watchman was to either warn the people to turn from wickedness to the Lord, or encourage them to continue to live righteously. The consequence of the watchman's failure to be faithful to God was mortally dangerous to him. If he did not faithfully warn others as God had charged him to do, they would die in their sin. The watchman would then be responsible for a grave sin of omission and rebellion against the word of the Lord and their deaths would be charged to him! He would be guilty of their failures (Ezek. 33:2–6). When Israel's watchmen were blind, the nation itself suffered (Isa. 56:10). Obedience to the Lord's word is the only path for the true watchman of God to follow (Ezek. 33:9). The prophet Hosea was also God's watchman, along with God, over the people—an awesome privilege for a human being (Hos. 9:8).

God's charge to Ezekiel and Hosea is also a charge to every Christian. Christ warned His followers to "watch" for His return and to keep their lamps burning and trimmed. Servants of the Lord, who are found watching (*gregoreo* in Greek), will be given special favor for being ready (Luke 12:35–40). Jesus, the faithful watchman of His sheep, has instructed us to follow Him (John 10:3, *thuroros* in Greek). In so doing, believers keep themselves focused on the Lord, constantly growing in their relationship with Him.

KEY VERSES

2 Samuel 13:34;
18:24–27;
Ezekiel 3:17;
33:2, 6–7;
Hosea 9:8

Water

Hebrew expression: *mayim*
Pronunciation: *MAH yihm*
Strong's Number: *4325*

Bread and water are the basic substances needed for maintaining physical life (1 Kgs. 18:13). The Hebrew word *mayim,* which means "water," is dual in form, indicating water above and below the earth (Gen. 1:6–7). Water is a source of life, composing eighty percent of our bodies and the earth, given by God to sustain us. Modern science affirms that it is the major means of internal cleansing for the human body as well. God, however, could turn water into a destructive force; during the flood, life-giving water ironically killed everything that had life (Gen. 7:21–24). God often withheld rains from crops in order to discipline His people (Deut. 28:24). But He also delivered His people from Pharaoh's army by taking them through the waters of the Red Sea (Exod. 15:1–21).

Water was used to cleanse and purify. It purified the Levites when they were set apart for God (Num. 8:5–7). Weapons taken from the Midianites were cleansed by the "water of cleansing" and passed through fire before the Israelites could use them in battle (Num. 31:23–24). Water was used to test whether a wife had been unfaithful to her husband. The woman had to drink the "bitter water"; if she was guilty it would become evident by physical signs (Num. 5:16–28). Anyone who touched a dead body had to be bathed and washed to become clean.

The figurative use of water stands out in the Old Testament. The "flowing" of justice and righteousness like "water" was a key simile of Amos (Amos 5:24). The Lord was described as the "spring of living waters" (Jer. 2:13; 17:13), the source of true spiritual life. In Numbers, water was the life-giving element that God supplied for Israel in the desert (Num. 20:8–11). Water was so precious that the Israelites told the Amorites and Edomites that they would not drink any water from their wells if they would permit them to pass through their land (Num. 20:17; 21:11).

Water is also one of the greatest sources for similes and metaphors in the New Testament. Birth by "water and the Spirit" was necessary for one to be saved (John 3:5). Baptism was truly sacramental, indicating an external sign of inward spiritual grace. Jesus asserts that those who believe in Him would have wells of "living water" springing up in them (Isa. 12:3); these people would have eternal life and would not thirst again (John 4:10–14). Naaman's dipping in the Jordan seven times for cleansing from leprosy tied faith, obedience, water, and renewal together in anticipation of the spiritual cleansing available through Jesus (2 Kgs. 5:1–14). The river of "the water of life" in Revelation, available to all those who need and want it (Rev. 22:1, 7), is a final picture of life reminiscent of the Garden of Eden's river flowing with living water (Gen. 2:10).

KEY VERSES

Genesis 1:2, 6–7;
Numbers 5:17; 19:7;
2 Kings 5:12;
Ezekiel 36:25;
Amos 5:24

Weeps

Hebrew expression: *bakah*
Pronunciation: *baw KAWH*
Strong's Number: *1058*

The book of Lamentations deals with one bitter, mournful theme, a theme the rabbis said was the saddest theme since God created the world—the fall of the city of Jerusalem. The devastated city of Jerusalem is portrayed weeping over her own misfortune. With great pathos and personification the city is pictured not only in ruins, but also with no comforter and no friends. In fact, her friends have become her enemies and she is a city who has lost her children (Lam. 1:16). When Jesus foresaw its destruction again in the New Testament, He wept over it (Luke 19:41, *klaio* in Greek). The Hebrew word *bakah* is an emotional verb meaning "to weep" and in some contexts "to bewail," or "to wail."

In the book of Judges, a location near Bethel was named *Bokim*, or "weepings," for there the Lord withdrew His promises to drive Israel's enemies out of the land because His people had betrayed Him (Judg. 2:1). No prophet wept as Jeremiah did for His people, their land, and for the chosen but devastated city of God, Jerusalem (Jer. 9:10; 22:10; Lam. 1:16). Weeping was graphically and humanly portrayed in Jeremiah. His emotions expressed grief and anguish by shedding tears. His weeping expressed great mourning for his people. Weeping was an appropriate response for many of the saints. Abraham wept for Sarah (Gen. 23:2) and Joseph wept over his brothers (Gen. 42:24). Weeping is a part of the cycle of human life, according to the author of Ecclesiastes, for there is a time to laugh, but also a time to weep (Eccl. 3:4). If one can weep over a single person, it is understandable that God, through Jeremiah, could weep over His entire people and their chosen capital, Jerusalem. The psalmist had hope that his weeping would continue only through the night—joy would come in the morning (Ps. 30:5). This was also God's plan for His people. Indeed, Jeremiah saw hope of restoration for Jerusalem and her people (Jer. 31:9). Again the Lord would treat His people as a father to His firstborn son. Jesus wept over the rebuilt, but again rebellious, city of Jerusalem just as Jeremiah had (Luke 19:4, *klaio*), and like His Father He wept over His own people (John 11:35). A God and a Savior who weeps deserves a people who feel and love deeply. Jeremiah's eyes failed from so much weeping (Lam. 2:11). We have hope, however, for eventually all weeping and sadness will turn to joy (Luke 6:21).

KEY VERSES

Genesis 23:2; 42:24;
Ecclesiastes 3:4;
Jeremiah 22:10;
Lamentations 1:2

W

Wine

Hebrew expression: *yayin*
Pronunciation: *YAH yihn*
Strong's Number: *3196*

In the Old Testament, wine, grain, and oil made up a trio of blessings that God would bestow upon His people if they were faithful to Him (Deut. 7:13). Of these three items, wine was a special blessing from the Lord that gladdened the hearts of His people in times of blessing and prosperity. The Hebrew word *yayin* has a broad meaning and refers to various kinds of "wine" according to its contextual usage. Wine is mentioned often in the book of the Song of Solomon, where it is a fitting drink for the lover and his beloved. Wine, along with milk, honey and honeycomb, and myrrh and spices, are the ingredients of love making between the lovers (Song 5:1). The mouth of the beloved is like the "best wine" and the sharing of "spiced wine" is an indication that the beloved would offer to her lover the delights of her love when they were properly united (Song 7:9; 8:2). But there is more to their relationship than wine. In three verses (Song 1:2, 4; 4:10), it is the love between the two that is compared most favorably with wine. Their love is more delightfully to be praised and more pleasing than any wine could be. In the end, it is the love, not the wine that is to be desired.

Wine is a sign of blessing, joy, and prosperity in the Old Testament. Scripture makes it clear, however, that wine wrongly used is a dangerous, potent drink and aphrodisiac. It is personified as a mocker and a brawler when improperly used (Prov. 20:1) and the "love of wine and oil" will keep a person from prosperity (Prov. 21:17). God's people should not join those who drink too much (Prov. 23:20). Wine is not recommended for those who need to give guidance to others, such as kings or other leaders; it is rather used in strong dosages for those who need relief from their anguish (Prov. 31:6). In Hosea's day, the misuse and abuse of God's gift of wine as a blessing to His people led to His people's turning from Him (Hos. 2:8; 7:5, 14). Too much wine even caused people to praise idols, made of gold and silver, as gods (Dan. 5:4).

In the New Testament, Jesus turned water into wine at the marriage ceremony in Cana of Galilee, a clear sign that He was able to provide joy and happiness to His people as the Lord's Messiah (John 2:3–10). One of the things that would mark the Messianic age, figuratively speaking, was a full supply of wine (Gen. 49:11). Paul directed Timothy to take a little wine for his stomach ailments (1 Tim. 5:23). Yet, the joy of God's people in the New Testament comes not from wine, but from the fullness of God's Spirit (Eph. 5:18)—not engaging in much wine (1 Tim. 3:8; Titus 2:3), but enjoying the presence of God.

KEY VERSES

Genesis 49:11–12;
Proverbs 20:1;
21:17; 31:6;
Song of Solomon
1:2, 4; 4:10

Wisdom

See also: *Wisdom, p. 418*
Hebrew expression: *chokmah*
Pronunciation: *khohk MAWH*
Strong's Number: *2451*

The author of Proverbs asserts that the man who finds wisdom (*chokmah*, Prov. 3:13) is blessed; that is, not only happy, but fruitful in all His ways because true wisdom is God's wisdom. But long ago, Job had asked where wisdom could be found (Job 28:12), for to find biblical wisdom is also to find life (Prov. 8:35).

The word *chokmah* comes from the root of the verb *chakam*, "to be wise," "to act wisely." An adjective, *chakam*, "wise" also was formed from the same root. But *chokmah* is the parade word for the various words clustering around the idea of wisdom, understanding, discretion, and prudence. In a secular world, wisdom can be a dangerous thing to have for absolute wisdom breeds absolute power—and power is often a corrupting influence. But in the Old Testament, wisdom was to be pursued because it led one to know how to live successfully before God. Wisdom led to humility, respect, and service toward others.

The most discussed group of people in the book of Proverbs, however, are the fools—so called because they reject, despise, and mock *chokmah*. Because the Lord gives wisdom, the fools' rejection is tantamount to rejecting one of God's good gifts (Prov. 2:6). Wisdom, however, has many practical consequences. Biblical wisdom is not the same as having a high I.Q.—it has, above all, ethical, moral, and religious implications.

Proverbs teaches that wisdom is accessible to all who want it. Wisdom even calls out to people to come and learn from her (Prov. 1:20). King Solomon asked for wisdom, and God granted it to him (1 Kgs. 5:12). In the New Testament, James echoes this Old Testament concept, urging Christians to pray for wisdom and God will gladly give it (Jas. 1:5). Wisdom saves the wise from wicked persons (Prov. 2:12). The Lord created all things by wisdom (Prov. 3:19). Wisdom is priceless, and the fear of the Lord is the beginning of wisdom (Prov. 8:11; 9:10). A wise person seeks out advice from others—and that is a mark of *chokmah* (Prov. 13:10). Self love, in a good sense, is a reward for those who pursue wisdom (Prov. 19:8). The model wife and mother of Proverbs is a woman who has learned to speak with wisdom (Prov. 31:26).

KEY VERSES

Deuteronomy 4:6;
1 Kings 3:28;
Job 28:12; 32:7;
Psalm 104:24

The wisdom of God in the Old Testament and in the New Testament leads to an understanding of life and a true knowledge of God (1 Cor. 1:17–30). The world cannot and does not know God through its misguided and secular wisdom (2 Cor. 1:12; *sophia* in Greek). Christians are to seek the wisdom from God to truly know Him and live wisely in this life (Jas. 3:13–18).

Witchcraft

Hebrew expression: *keshep*
Pronunciation: *KEH shehf*
Strong's Number: *3785*

In today's drug-saturated culture, it is useful to know that sorcery and witchcraft, which is condemned in the Old Testament, were closely associated in ancient times with the use of herbs. The Hebrew word used for "sorceries" as well as "witchcraft" is *keshep* (NJPS "sorceries"). The noun spawned the verb *kishshep*, "to practice scorcery or witchcraft." The root meaning of this word is "to cut"—and the word possibly refers to cutting herbs for charms and spells.

The pagan nations that inhabited the land of Canaan before God drove them out and gave the land to Israel practiced sorcery. In fact, it was because of this sorcery that the Lord drove them from the land. The Babylonians, also, used magic, sorcery, and witchcraft to protect themselves from their enemies (Isa. 47:9, 12). Nineveh, the capital of Assyria, was considered a source for all kinds of witchcraft. In Israel's history, Queen Jezebel was the principal person who introduced sorcery to the Israelties (see 2 Kgs. 9:22). But the attempt by the ancient Israelities and others to use black magic, sorcery, and witchcraft to control people, events, and the spiritual world was useless. God Almighty sovereignly controls all these realms. In the end, the Babylonians, the Ninevites, and evil Jezebel were all destroyed by the Lord because they sought to control their world with sorcery and black magic, instead of humbly turning to God and submitting themselves to His purposes.

In the New Testament, the Greek word *pharmakos* conveys the idea of witchcraft. Its root meaning refers to drugs—and from it we get the English word "pharmacy" (Rev. 9:21; 18:23). The apostle Paul soundly condemns all kinds of "witchcraft" (Gal. 5:19–21, *pharmakos* in Greek). People who practice black magic and consult spirits will not, according to Paul, inherit the Kingdom of God. It is God Himself who should be sought out. He can't be manipulated with drugs or any other kind of magic. Instead, we are to meditate on His good works and pray that He will empower us to do His will.

KEY VERSES

2 Kings 9:22;
Isaiah 47:9, 12;
Micah 5:12;
Nahum 3:4

Woe

Hebrew expression: *hoy*
Pronunciation: *HOH ee*
Strong's Numbers: *1945*

Hoy!!! is an interjection. It is a short utterance, usually only one word that more or less comes forth with great force. It expresses great emotion and can be an interjection of warning or distress. It represents a thought transformed into a feeling and expressed in a word—*hoy*, "woe!" The word can also be translated "alas, ah," or even "ha!" *Hoy* is used regularly in lamentations, songs, and poems written to remember or commemorate a tragic personal or national event (Jer. 22:18). The entire book of Lamentations "laments" the fall of the city of Jerusalem and *hoy* is used to warn the city of its impending judgment (Jer. 13:27). *Hoy* can be used to introduce a prophetic declaration of judgment, as when Isaiah announced the coming destruction of Assyria (Isa. 10:5). It conveys a note of certainty about what is said and an atmosphere of finality—such as in, "Woe unto you, the end has come!" The word is also applied to groups of people and individuals who are wicked (Isa. 5:8, 11, 18, 20–22).

The prophet Habbakuk delivers five "woes" to the city and kingdom of Babylon. These five woes announce God's judgment upon the city and its imminent fall. Babylon is condemned for confiscating the goods of other peoples, accumulating unjust gain, building an empire by bloodshed, abusing her neighboring countries, and especially for the folly of worshipping gods of wood and stone (Hab. 2:6, 9, 12, 15, 19). These "woes" make up a Taunt Song which the prophet delivers (Hab. 2:6–20). The woes will come to pass because the Lord already rules the earth from His holy heavenly Temple and God's Kingdom will rule on earth when the Messiah comes again (Hab. 2:14, 20).

Sins, which deserve God's judgment of "woe," encompass religious, moral, ethical, political, military, and economic issues. Jesus delivered "woes" regularly in His teaching and preaching to cities, classes of people, nations, Jerusalem, and even His own followers (Luke 6; 10; 11; 17; 22; *ouai* in Greek). Paul delivers a woe to himself, saying how terrible it would be if he did not faithfully preach the gospel (1 Cor. 9:16). Revelation takes up the announcement of woes at the consummation of this age (Rev. 8; 11; 12; 18). The end of the kingdoms of this world and the beginning of the rulership of God's Kingdom is heralded by the deliverance of three final woes (Rev. 8:13; 9:12; 11:14).

KEY VERSES

Numbers 21:29;
Isaiah 5:8;
Jeremiah 13:27;
Habakkuk 2:14

Wondrous Works

Hebrew expression: *pala'*
Pronunciation: *paw LAW*
Strong's Number: *6381*

In Psalm 71, King David is in the later stages of his life. He declares unequivocally that the Lord has faithfully instructed him since the days of his youth and, now in his old age, he can continue to declare the "wondrous works" of the Lord (Ps. 71:17). The word *pala'* means "wondrous works" and in some translations it can render "marvelous deeds" (NIV) or "wondrous deeds" (NJPS). Both in the Old and New Testament, God's wondrous works for His people never cease. "Wondrous works" contrasts with the Hebrew word *zakar,* "to remember," because *pala',* the word for "wondrous works," describes *what* God's people are to remember. The verb *pala'* comes from the noun *pele',* which means "wonder," or "marvel," and is used in some forms to describe "wonderful acts," "wonderful deeds," or "wonderful works"—in other words, things beyond human ability and power. The word also describes the characteristics of intangible things, such as love, which is said to be "wonderful" (2 Sam. 1:26). Job speaks of things "too wonderful" for him to comprehend—things that God easily sets in place and fully comprehends (Job. 42:3). The great acts of God that He has performed for His people in word and deed are the centerpieces of His glory. These "wondrous works" provide redemption for His people. A central theme of the Israelites' worship was, as the psalmist said, the recounting of the wonders of the Lord (Ps. 9:1), for even the heavens praise His marvelous works. The Israelites realized that, ultimately, it was the Lord alone who did these amazing things.

The Lord promised His people that He would be with them (Exod. 3:12) and that He would create His wonders before the nations around them (Exod. 34:10). No better word could be used to describe God's ultimate salvation event. Isaiah describes God's coming King as the One who would be called "Wonderful Counselor" (Isa. 9:6). He would provide light for His people.

In the New Testament, Peter observes that the Lord, in Christ, has called us out of darkness into His wonderful (*thaumastos* in Greek) light. Luke continues to see God's people praising the great wonders (*megaleios* in Greek) of God among them (Acts 2:11; 5:12). God testifies of Himself by signs and wonders as He did in Egypt and throughout the history of His people. His wonders among us have not ceased.

KEY VERSES

Exodus 3:20; 34:10;
1 Chronicles 16:12;
Psalms 9:1; 119:27

Wooden Image

Hebrew expression: *'asherah*
Pronunciation: *'ah shay RAWH*
Strong's Number: *842*

In ancient times, the Israelites were surrounded by people groups—Canaanites, Phoenicians, and Egyptians—who worshiped idols. They carved images that represented the false gods, who they believed controlled their lives. The common Hebrew expression for "wooden image" was *'asherah*. The word specifically referred to a "wooden image" that symbolized the Canaanite mother goddess, Asherah. The name *'asherah* has been found in some texts from the ancient city of Ugarit in Syria. It refers to a goddess who was the female counterpart, the consort, of the Canaanite god El.

In the Old Testament, *'asherah* is the name of a goddess who was also the female consort of the chief Canaanite god, Baal—the false god with whom Elijah and Elisha had to contend. Manasseh, the most wicked King in Judah, carved a "wooden image" of *'asherah* and put it inside the Temple of the Lord. Ahab did the same thing in Israel in the north (2 Kgs. 21:3). These wooden images of Canaanite religion and worship were supposed to be burned by Israel upon their entrance to the Promised Land (Exod. 34:13; Deut. 7:5). Gideon cut one down, but his life was threatened because he did so (Judg. 6:25–30). Both Hezekiah and Josiah cut down Asherah poles. Josiah even destroyed the places where women did weaving for the goddess Asherah (2 Kgs. 23:6, 7). All during Israel's history this symbol of the goddess, which probably had fertility and seductiveness attached to its religious use, was a snare that eventually helped destroy her. It angered the Lord. The Lord Himself destroyed these Asherot when He finally delivered His people (Isa. 27:9; Mic. 5:14). To Israel's credit they were not mentioned again after the Lord judged them by turning them over to the hands of the Babylonians. The last reference to them is in Jeremiah 17:2.

The Lord's anger with these wooden images is a lesson for people today who would, unwisely, covet or use any image, idol, or symbol in a religious way to worship the Lord. The Lord's command is clear—we are to have no other gods with Him or in His presence (Exod. 20:1–4, 23). We are to get rid of any signs or symbols of wood, gold, silver, or mental entities that compete in any way for our attention with the Lord. To not do so is to invite disaster and fail to learn from the history of Israel.

KEY VERSES

Exodus 34:13;
1 Kings 14:15;
2 Kings 18:4; 23:4;
Jeremiah 17:2;
Micah 5:14

Word

See also: *Word, p. 422 and (The) Word, p. 423*
Hebrew expression: *davar*
Pronunciation: *daw VAWR*
Strong's Number: *1697*

The common understanding of the Hebrew word *davar* depicts a "word" as a vocable spoken by a person—that is, a word considered as a combination of letters which communicates a concept. The words of men and women often mean very little, since they alone do not reflect the real character of the speaker. The "word" of the Lord, however, is a sure indicator of who He is and what He will do. *Davar* can be translated many different ways, but it essentially means "word or speech," "command," "deed," or "thing." It is a noun formed from the root letters of the verb *davar*, "to speak," but can also mean "to promise" or "to command." Moses uses *davar* to refer to the "command" of the Lord to His people to love Him supremely, and keep all His commands (Deut. 30:14–16). God gave Israel His "words," *devarim* the plural of *davar*, and by obeying them the Israelites would be choosing life, not death (Deut. 30:15). The Word of God was powerful, it was as effective as an act of God. God makes sure that the events spoken by His word come to pass (Jer. 1:12), and His dynamic prophetic "word" always accomplishes its goal.

The Ten Commandments spoken by God at Mount Sinai were actually described as the "ten words" by Moses (Exod. 20:1; Deut. 4:13; 10:4; 34:28). The words were the "covenant stipulations" of the Sinai Covenant, the guidelines for God's people in their relationship to Him and to one another. God's Words became the foundation for the entire personal and national life of His people. When God spoke, the entire universe was created by His word (Gen. 1:2). Israel's life and success lay in obeying His word (Deut. 32:46–47) and all of the covenants of the Old Testament were formed by the words of God (Exod. 24:8). God spoke and things happened; the New International Version of the Bible translates *davar* fifty-one times as "event(s)" and twenty-seven times as "things" (1 Sam. 12:16; 2 Chr. 9:29). Strikingly enough, the Old Testament writers used the word *davar* regularly to mean the "deeds" and "acts" of God as well as His "words."

While man's word may fail us many times, God's Word is something we can count on, for what He says represents Him. The promises He has given to His people are as sure as His very existence. His words are His deeds for us. When we obey them, we live abundantly.

KEY VERSES

Genesis 15:1;
Exodus 20:1;
Deuteronomy 11:18;
Psalm 33:6;
Jeremiah 1:9

Worship

See also: *Worship, p. 426*
Hebrew expression: *shachah*
Pronunciation: *shaw HAWH*
Strong's Number: *7812*

What does it mean to worship God? Jesus states to the woman at the well that the worship of God must be in "spirit and truth" (John 4:24). How is this accomplished? As one attempts to describe true worship, our answers tend to confuse external ritual with the more basic internal truth of worship. Our experience at church on Sunday is only the outward expression of worship. The singing of hymns, responsive readings from Scripture, corporate or private prayer, and the preaching of a sermon are all parts of worship, but true worship begins in the heart. A proper understanding of the Hebrew word *shachah*, translated "worship," will help convey this fundamental principle.

If we had occasion to ask an ancient Israelite about his worship experiences, he may tell of sacrifices given at the altar, singing the songs of David, or the celebration of the feast days. If we asked about the word "worship," he would give a simple response—that literally, the word means "to bow down." The basic notion is common enough, crouching down or prostrating oneself. Proverbs uses the word to convey the image of one stooping under a heavy load. In the ancient world, as in some Near Eastern cultures, when entering the presence of one to whom reverence was due, bowing was the proper sign of respect. Therefore, *shachah* came to express homage or obeisance to a higher authority; the act of bowing was enough, no sacrifices or other outward expressions of worship were needed.

The Old Testament contains numerous references to such honor paid to a monarch (1 Kgs. 1:31; 2 Chr. 24:17) or some other superior figure (Gen. 27:29; 49:8). From this point, the link between "bowing down" and "worship" can be easily discerned. In worship, one comes into the presence of the Lord. Above all, He is deserving of supreme reverence and humility. Greater homage than what is paid to an earthly ruler must not be denied the Lord. Thus, the image of bowing down, both physically and mentally, is used to convey worship and allegiance to God. On occasion, worship would involve physically bowing the face to the ground (Neh. 8:6), but it also involved any general act of worship (Gen. 22:5). Since bowing down expressed special reverence and allegiance, it was reserved for the Lord alone. The Israelites were forbidden from "bowing down" to any idol or false God (Exod. 20:5; Num. 25:2).

KEY VERSES

Deuteronomy 26:10;
Joshua 5:14;
Nehemiah 8:6;
Psalm 95:6

Our attitude, and not the external trappings of worship, is central to praising God. The heart must always be "bowed down" and humble before the Lord for worship to be in "spirit and truth" (Ps. 51:17; Isa. 57:15). As the psalmist proclaims, "O come, let us worship," but he is quick to add, "and bow down" (Ps. 95:6). The two are inseparable.

Write

Hebrew expression: *katab*
Pronunciation: *kaw TAHV*
Strong's Number: *3789*

God's decision to "write" His law on the hearts of His people and to put it into their minds was a revolutionary concept (Jer. 31:33). Yet the Law was as old as Mount Sinai. The new covenant was refreshingly new because God's people would be able to internalize His Law. No more would the Law remain written on stone, Jeremiah said, but it would be written on tablets of flesh, upon the hearts of God's people (Exod. 24:4; 31:18; 34:28, 29). The verb *katab* is simply the Hebrew verb that means "to write." The kind of writing varied greatly. The writing could be done with a pen, a stylist, or it could be an instrument used to inscribe words on stone or to engrave words upon wood. As noted the object receiving the writing could vary. It could be stone tablets, a papyrus scroll, wood, bronze, other metals, or even the ground. But the Lord spoke to Jeremiah of writing His Law upon hearts of flesh, upon the hearts of His people. How can that be done?

Jeremiah had earlier called upon the people of Judah to circumcise their hearts to the Lord (Jer. 4:4)—that is, dedicate their hearts to God, make their hearts pure and centered only upon Him. Their hearts were utterly corrupt (Jer. 17:10). Circumcising their hearts was the same as washing the evil from their hearts so that they could be saved (Jer. 4:14). The Lord had promised to give them a "new" heart so that they would know Him (Jer. 24:7). The question was "how" would He give them a new heart and renew their corrupt heart? The Bible tells us that God can write His moral, ethical, and religious laws upon the human heart, thereby renewing it (Jer. 31:31–34). He can cause them to know Him by doing this miraculous work.

God's new covenant with His people was established through the blood of Jesus Christ (Luke 22:20; 1 Cor. 11:25; 2 Cor. 3:6; Heb. 9:15). Hebrews 8:10; 10:16 repeats Jeremiah 31:33 twice. The "writing" of the law on Christians' hearts at the new birth is the reception of God's gift of a new heart so that they may know Him—a heart infused with the Holy Spirit. The Spirit of God "writes"—that is, impresses God's ways upon His people. God has radically altered our predicament. We are no longer slaves to sin, for Christ has freed us from sin and death and the Holy Spirit has written God's law on our hearts. We know God's ways, and God has empowered us to resist temptation. As believers, our responsibility is to depend on God for the power to do what is good and live in obedience to His ways.

KEY VERSES

Exodus 24:4; 34:28;
Jeremiah 31:33;
Deuteronomy 5:29

New Testament Words

Abide

Greek expression: *menō*
Pronunciation: *MEHN oh*
Strong's Number: *3306*

In our fast-paced society, who has the time to stay put or sit around? But that is exactly what Jesus commands his followers to do in order to be productive: "Abide in Me, and I in you" (John 15:4, NKJV). In Christ's well-known vine illustration in John 15:1–8, Jesus tells believers "to stay put"—"don't go anywhere." The Greek word here is *menō*. It means "to abide," "to remain," or "to stay."

According to Jesus' illustration, each branch—that is, each believer—has been positioned in the vine—that is, Christ. Jesus orders each branch to "remain" in union with him, not to "attain" that union. In John 15:4, the Greek word for "abide" is an imperative (Gk. *meinate*). It is constative; it encompasses the entire act of abiding and views the act as a single event. Then, in the following verse (John 15:5), the Lord uses present tense verbs to describe the continual activity involved in maintaining this "organic" union with Christ. Each branch that continues to remain in the vine will keep on bearing fruit (John 15:5). Some commentators say that the fruit is new converts; while others assert it is "the fruit of the Spirit" (Gal. 5:22). The devotional writer, Andrew Murray, says "the essential idea of fruit is that it is the silent natural restful produce of our inner life." This fruit is the practical expression of the indwelling Holy Spirit in our lives. This should attract others to Christ.

Each branch that does not continue to abide in the vine is cut off from the vine (John 15:6). What did Jesus mean by that statement? When Israel failed to be a profitable fruit-bearing vine, when it didn't yield the good fruit of righteousness, God said He would destroy that vine (see Ps. 80:8–16; Isa. 5:5–7; Ezek. 15:2–7; 19:10–14). Yet such destruction did not mean eternal perdition for all Israelites; it meant a withdrawal of God's blessing so that a remnant of Israelites would seek the Lord again. On the positive side, Jesus assures His disciples of the fruitfulness of each branch that continues to abide in Him—the vine.

But since abiding in the vine can be so subjective, Jesus quickly defines what He means by abiding in the vine. Abiding in the vine means abiding in God's Word and keeping Jesus' commands (John 15:7, 10; see also 1 John 2:6). Every believer who remains in Jesus, who is careful to learn from God's Word and to obey His commands, will be fruitful (John 15:7–10). It is God's design that believers should live in union with His Son and become fruitful—that is, express the effect of their union with Jesus in their daily lives. This is what glorifies the Father— a changed heart and a changed life.

KEY VERSES

John 15:4–7, 9–10;
1 John 2:24, 27–28

219

Abomination of desolation

See also: *Abomination, p. 3*
Greek expression: *bdelugma tēs emoseōs*
Pronunciation: *BDEHL oog muh; TAYSS; eh ray MOH seh ohss*
Strong's Numbers: *946, 2050*

Say the name "abominable snowman," and one immediately thinks of a huge, terrifying creature traipsing through the snow looking for victims to devour. The word abomination is potent; it makes us shudder in fear. In the Bible, the Greek word for abomination is used to describe God's reaction to things He detests. More than anything, He hates idolatry; it makes Him shudder out of disgust.

The Greek word for "abomination" is used only a few times in the New Testament (Luke 16:15; Rom. 2:22; Titus 1:16; Rev. 17:4–5; 21:8, 27). It is translated by several different English words—including detestable and sacrilegious object. Yet, the word "abomination" is most well-known by Jesus' use of it in the expression "abomination of desolation" (see Matt. 24:15; Mark 13:14, KJV). In these Gospel passages, Jesus repeated Daniel's prophecy that an "abomination of desolation" would be set up in the temple in Jerusalem (Dan. 11:31). In 1 Maccabees, it is recorded that the Antiochus Epiphanes invaded Palestine (around 167 B.C.) and erected this abomination of desolation—probably a statue of Zeus—upon the altar of burnt offering in the temple (1 Macc. 1:54). Jesus predicted a similar "abomination of desolation" being erected in the temple when His disciples asked about the events that will take place prior to his return from heaven (Matt. 24:1–31; Mark 13:1–27; Luke 21:5–28). Alluding to the Daniel passages, Jesus predicts that something like the destruction produced by Antiochus would reoccur. Some commentators believe Jesus' prediction was fulfilled when the Romans destroyed the temple in A.D. 70. But many scholars agree that the "man of lawlessness" will be responsible for another detestable sacrilege. He will set up an idol of himself in a rebuilt temple and demand to be worshiped as God (2 Thess. 2:3–4). A similar incident is predicted in the book of Revelation, where the beast from the sea demands obedience and submission from all people (Rev. 13:1–10). In God's sight, this is detestable. Stealing the worship that is rightfully due Him is the greatest abomination—the most hideous sacrilege.

KEY VERSES

Matthew 24:15;
Mark 13:14;
Luke 21:21

Adoption

Greek expression: *huiothesia*
Pronunciation: *hwee aw theh SEE uh*
Strong's Number: *5206*

Most people would rather have been born into a loving family than adopted into one. But with respect to God's family, both—birth and adoption—happen to believers at once. Anyone who believes in Jesus is born of God and is also adopted by God into His family.

The Greek word for "adoption" comes from two words put together: *huios,* meaning "son," and *thesis,* meaning "a placing." Thus, the word means "placement into sonship." The Greek word is a legal term that indicates that believers have been given all the legal privileges of being sons in God's family. When God adopts believers as His children, He places the Spirit of His Son into their hearts so that they become, in effect, His natural-born children. As such, they are not merely "adopted" (in the sense the word now conveys) but genuinely "begotten" by God. God makes "sons of God" out of "sons of men." The term "sons of God," a common King James expression, includes believers of both sexes (see 2 Cor. 6:18; compare Isa. 43:6).

According to the New Testament, all persons are sinners by nature and, therefore, are called "children of wrath" (Eph. 2:3, KJV). But through God's grace, those whom God loves become children of God (1 John 3:12). It is out of God's love and also the work of the Son of God that believers can be adopted into God's family. While believers are called sons of God in the Scriptures (see Matt. 5:9; Rom. 8:14, 19; Gal. 3:26), the title "Son of God" when used for Jesus Christ refers to Christ's deity (Matt. 11:25–27; 16:16–17). Jesus Christ is one in substance and glory with God the Father. As the second person of the Trinity, Christ is distinguished from the Father as "the only begotten Son." Believers in Christ, although "adopted" as God's sons, are not equals with the uncreated, divine Son. Nevertheless, through the Son's work, God has adopted sinners into his family (Eph. 1:4–6). Through His death and resurrection, Jesus destroyed sin and its death penalty and has covered believers with the righteousness needed for the status of being sons of God. Believers are beneficiaries of Christ's work. They are transformed into God's heirs and become joint heirs with Christ (Rom. 8:17). And as sons of God, they receive the Spirit who assures them that they are indeed God's children (Rom. 8:15; Gal. 4:6). They can rightfully call God: "Father" (Rom. 8:15–16). Though Christians are already adopted into God's family (1 John 3:1), they won't experience what it really means to be God's sons until they are raised from the dead (Rom. 8:21–23). Only then will believers receive their full inheritance from their divine Father—only then will they enjoy living constantly in His presence.

KEY VERSES

Romans 8:15;
Galatians 4:5;
Ephesians 1:5

Allegorize

Greek expression: *allēgoreō*
Pronunciation: *ahl lay gaw REH oh*
Strong's Number: *238*

When most of us think of allegory, a classic work of literature comes to mind: John Bunyan's *Pilgrim's Progress.* In his book, every person and place represent a specific spiritual reality in a Christian's life. Readers who ignore the allegories in *Pilgrim's Progress* are missing Bunyan's point.

Interpreting literature in an allegorical manner first began among the ancient Greeks, who enjoyed assigning life principles to the various elements in the epic poems of Hesiod and Homer. Hellenistic Jewish teachers used allegory to make the Old Testament relevant to the Greco-Roman world. Later, a group of Christian interpreters centered around Alexandria used allegory as their primary method of interpreting the Bible. Allegory was the dominant interpretative method of medieval Christian teachers.

As a method of interpretation, allegorization seeks to find a deeper moral or spiritual meaning behind the literal words of a text. Since allegorizing is a highly individualized interpretative method, each commentator can find a different allegorical meaning from a single text. An allegorical interpreter views the individual parts of a story, such as persons, places, things, numbers, and colors, as clues pointing to deeper spiritual realities. For example, the writer of the so-called Epistle of Barnabas (which is actually an anonymous writing composed around A.D. 120–130) allegorized the number 318 in Genesis 14:14. He stated that the 318 servants of Abraham symbolized Jesus' death on the cross because 300 is the numerical value of the Greek letter *T,* which is cross-shaped, and 18 is the value of the first two letters of the Greek word for "Jesus." This interpretation isn't accepted by Christian commentators today.

Allegory is only mentioned once in the New Testament (Gal. 4:24), but in several places Paul states that the Hebrew Scriptures have a typical meaning, besides their literal meaning (compare Gal. 4:22–26 with Rom. 5:14; 1 Cor. 10:1–4). In Galatians 4:22–26, Paul uses the allegorical method to identify Ishmael and Isaac as types of the old and new covenants, respectively. For example, Ishmael typifies members of the old covenant because he was born to the slave woman, Hagar. In a similar way, the Israelites were born into slavery to the Law. In contrast, the new covenant is typified

KEY VERSES

Galatians 4:24

by Isaac, who was born to Sarah—a free woman and the wife of Abraham. Likewise, believers who have embraced the new covenant are born anew into true freedom and are free citizens of the heavenly Jerusalem (Gal. 4:24–26). God inspired the apostle Paul to write down this allegorical interpretation of the story of Isaac and Ishmael. It contains spiritual truths that cannot be ascertained by interpreting the Genesis story literally. We, however, should be careful to test all allegorical interpretations of the Bible to see if they are consistent with God's Word.

Alpha and Omega

Greek expression: *Alpha kai Ōmega*
Pronunciation: *AHL fuh; KIGH; oh MAY guh*
Strong's Numbers: *1, 5598*

Have you heard the expression, "He knows everything from A to Z?" "A to Z" in this context connotes comprehensiveness. In the Greek alphabet, *Alpha* is the first letter and *Ōmega* is the last. The expression "A to Z" in Greek would therefore be "Alpha to Ōmega." The New Testament gives both God and Jesus the title *Alpha* and *Ōmega*, as well as "the Beginning and the End" and "the First and Last" (Rev. 1:8,17; 2:8; 21:6; 22:13). According to these passages, God in Christ is not only the First and the Last, but is also comprised of everything in between. Thus, God expresses and affirms His fullness, comprehensiveness, and all-inclusiveness; He is the Source of all life and will bring all things to their appointed end.

Such affirmations, which have their counterpart in the Old Testament (see Isa. 41:4; 44:6; 48:12), stress the unique and faithful sovereignty of God and his Son, Jesus. Christian readers are reminded that the creation and the end of all human history are under control of the living God.

In the book of Revelation, God is called the *Alpha* and *Ōmega* because all revelation begins from Him and ends with Him. He is the Creator and Terminator of all life. Christ also bears this title because He is the source and the goal of life. If we have anxiety about how the world will end and what it will be like after this life is over, we can rest assured that the same God who began this world (as the *Alpha*) will be there in the end (as the *Ōmega*). The Lord presents Himself many times as the *Alpha* and *Ōmega* in the final book of the Bible. The knowledge that He is in complete control of every aspect of our lives is a source of assurance and comfort during times of trial.

KEY VERSES

Revelation 1:8;
21:6; 22:13

Angel

See also: *Angel, p. 9*
Greek expression: *angelos*
Pronunciation: *ANG gehl awss*
Strong's Number: *32*

In our culture, angels are en vogue. Bookstores and television shows popularize the stories of people who have encountered angels, and it is difficult to discern truth from falsehood. As Christians, we have the Bible to direct and guide our understanding of who angels are and their purpose under God. The English word "angel" comes directly from the Greek word *angelos* which means "messenger." In Luke 9:52, Jesus sent "messengers" ahead of him. Usually the same word is translated to "angel" and is understood to mean a spiritual messenger from the Lord.

Angels were created by God and for God (Ps. 148:2, 5–6; Col. 1:16), and the Bible even suggests that they witnessed the creation of the world (Job 38:7). As wholly spiritual creatures, they are free from many human limitations, such as death (Luke 20:36). They appear throughout the Bible in human form and were perceived to be men, never women or children. But, Matthew writes that they do not marry and so they could be regarded as sexless. Their power and awesome appearance (Matt. 28:2–4) sometimes tempted people to fear or worship them, but the New Testament does not condone such worship (Col. 2:18; Rev. 22:8–9). Angels are stronger and wiser than human beings, but their power and knowledge are limited by God (Ps. 103:20; Matt. 24:36; 1 Pet. 1:1–12), plus they share the status of "created being" with humankind.

Angels' ability to communicate in human language and to affect human life in other ways is essential to their role in the Bible. They appeared to many of God's people to announce good news (Judg. 13:3), warn of danger (Gen. 19:15), guard from evil (Dan. 3:28; 6:22), instruct (Acts 7:38), and guide and protect (Exod. 14:19). When Christ came to earth as the Savior, angels heralded His birth (Luke 2:8–15), guided and warned His parents (Matt. 2:13), strengthened Him when he was tempted (Matt. 4:11), fortified Him in His last distress (Luke 22:4–44 in some manuscripts), and observed His resurrection (Matt. 28:1–6). Angels are also mentioned in the following passages: Jesus spoke about the guardian angels of little children (Matt. 18:10); Philip was guided by an angel (Acts 8:26); the apostles were rescued from prison by an angel (Acts 5:19; 12:7–11); and Paul was encouraged by an angel in a frightening situation (Acts 27:2–25). Angels throughout the Bible offered continual support, guidance, wisdom, and other messages of love and justice from the one Almighty God.

KEY VERSES

Matthew 28:2;
Revelation 22:8

Anoint

See also: *Anoint, p. 11*
Greek expression: *aleiphō, chriō*
Pronunciation: *ah LAY foh; KREE oh*
Strong's Numbers: *218, 5548*

The Greeks had two words for anointing: *aleiphō* and *criō*. *Aleiphō* was commonly used in Greek literature to describe a "medicinal anointing," while *chriō* was used to describe a "sacramental anointing." The distinction is still observed in modern Greek, with *aleiphō* meaning "to daub," or "to smear," and *chriō* meaning "to anoint."

The medicinal definition of "anoint," *aleiphō*, has historical significance. Both the Egyptians and the Syrians anointed people for medical reasons. Among the Greeks, oil, as well as perfume, was used to "anoint" people who were sick. In the New Testament, anointing of the sick accompanied by prayer for healing by local church elders is recommended when requested (Jas. 5:1–16). Anointing with oil was also a part of the apostles' healing ministry (Mark 6:1–13). Furthermore, on two occasions two different women anointed Jesus with well-scented perfume—a precious oil (Luke 7:38; John 12:3).

The sacramental description of "anoint," *chriō*, is most clearly seen in the New Testament, where Jesus Christ is portrayed as fulfilling the three offices of prophet, priest, and king. He is, supremely, God's Anointed One—the Messiah. "Messiah" means "anointed one" and is derived directly from the Hebrew word for anointed; "Christ" is the same title derived from the Greek word *chriō*. A king's anointing is physical, performed with oil or a crown, but the Messiah's anointing is spiritual (Ps. 2:2; Dan. 9:2–26); He is anointed by and through the Holy Spirit (Luke 4:1, 1–19; compare Isa. 61:1). Jesus of Nazareth was indeed the Anointed One (Messiah) of Old Testament prophecy shown in His anointing by the Holy Spirit and through the miracles that He performed (John 1:3–51; Luke 4:3–37). As Christians, now filled by the Holy Spirit, we are joined to the Anointed One and share in Jesus' anointing (2 Cor. 1:2–22). Therefore, because the Spirit lives within us, we know the difference between truth and falsehood. Christ, the Anointed One, gives us all that we need to know in order to resist the temptations of false teachers and live godly lives in this world (1 John 2:20, 27).

KEY VERSES

Matthew 6:17;
Mark 6:13;
Luke 7:38;
John 11:2; 12:3;
James 5:14

Antichrist

Greek expression: *antichristos*
Pronunciation: *ahn TEE kree stawss*
Strong's Number: *500*

Most of us think the antichrist is a bloodthirsty, slightly mad ruler—someone like Hitler or Mao Tse Tung. The biblical image, however, is somewhat different. Several places in the Bible define the antichrist as the deceiver, the false Christ, the man of lawlessness, and the beast. The "antichrist," according to the apostle John (who was the only writer to use the term *antichristos*), is anyone who denies that Jesus is the Christ, the unique Son of God who has come to this world in the flesh.

The Greek word *antichristos* occurs only four times, all in John's letters (1 John 2:18, 22; 4:3; 2 John 7). John assumed that his Christian readers knew about the antichrist and had been taught to expect his coming (1 John 2:1–27). He reminds them that "many antichrists" had already appeared, thus indicating that the end time had arrived. But John also warned that a final antichrist had yet to make an appearance. He defines the antichrist as a "deceiver" and writes that there are many deceivers—that is, antichrists—already in the world who do not believe that Jesus Christ came to earth in a real body (2 John 7). John further described that a person (or message) can have the spirit of the antichrist if they do not "confess Jesus" (1 John 4:3).

John's concept of the antichrist comes from the teachings of Jesus in the Gospels. A lengthy passage (Mark 13, paralleled in Matt. 24–25 and Luke 21) records the instruction Jesus gave His disciples about the tragic events and persecution that they could expect before His return. Jesus says that His coming will be preceded by the appearance of many "deceivers" and "false Christs." The term "false Christs" is found only twice in the New Testament (Matt. 24:24; Mark 13:22).

Another probable reference to the antichrist is "the man of lawlessness" (2 Thess. 2:3). While instructing the church at Thessalonica about Christ's second coming, Paul stressed that the appearance and rebellion of the man of lawlessness must occur beforehand. This antichrist would oppose the worship of any gods or God and would even proclaim himself to be God.

KEY VERSES

1 John 2:18, 22; 4:3; 2 John 7

In Revelation, John's symbol for the antichrist is "the beast" (Rev. 13:1–18; 17:3, 7–17). The beast is described not only as a challenger of Christ, but also as a satanically inspired Christ-counterfeit. John writes that although the beast (antichrist) is clearly distinguishable from the Lamb (Christ), he will receive worship from everyone except God's elect. These events are set in the final days of history when Christ will destroy the antichrist forever (2 Thess. 2:4–8).

Apostasy

Greek expression: *apostasia*
Pronunciation: *ah paw stuh SEE uh*
Strong's Number: *646*

Originally, apostasy in Greek meant rebellion against government. For example, *apostasia* described the Jews as "rebels" against King Artaxerxes in 1 Esdras 2:23. The term was then applied to "one who rebels from God." Apostasy, therefore, is serious business. People who commit apostasy abandon their faith and repudiate their former beliefs. It is not heresy (denial of part of the faith), or the transfer of allegiance from one religious body to another within the same faith. Apostasy is a complete and final rejection of God.

The Greek word *apostasia* from which the English word *apostasy* is derived appears in only two biblical passages. The apostle Paul was accused of apostasy for teaching others "to forsake Moses" (Acts 21:21, NASB), and Christians are warned not to be deceived by the widespread apostasy that will come in the end times before the Lord's return (2 Thess. 2:3). The apostasy of the end times is directly linked to the rise of the antichrist (2 Thess. 2:3–12; compare 1 Tim. 4:1–3).

Many New Testament passages, using different words, convey warnings against apostasy. In the last days, tribulation and persecution will cause people to reject Christ, and false prophets will lead many others astray (Matt. 24:9–11). Paul pointed to Hymenaeus and Alexander as examples of those who had rejected the faith (1 Tim. 1:20). The apostle Peter warned that believers in Christ who knowingly turn away are "worse off than before" (2 Pet. 2:2–22). The writer of Hebrews referred to those who had believed and then departed from the faith as being in a hopeless state—with no possibility of further repentance (Heb. 6:1–6). He was speaking specifically of Jewish Christians who returned to the practice of offering animal sacrifices for forgiveness of sins. This was tantamount to profaning the blood of Christ which was shed on the cross for us (Heb. 10:2–31).

KEY VERSE

2 Thessalonians 2:3

Apostle

Greek expression: *apostolos*
Pronunciation: *uh PAW stuh lawss*
Strong's Number: *652*

The Greek word for "apostle" is derived from the verb *apostellō*, or "to send." The noun was often used in the language of sea travel, with respect to a particular "ship" or a "marine expedition." The Greek word was almost always used in an impersonal and thoroughly passive way. Later on, the Greeks used *apostolos* to mean "bill," "invoice," or even a "passport"—continuing to reflect the vocabulary of maritime affairs.

In the New Testament, apostle was used to designate a special group among the disciples. Out of Jesus' seventy-two disciples, he selected twelve to be His apostles. These were the men who were sent by Jesus to take his message to the world and then raise up churches (Matt. 10:1–4; Mark 3:13–19; Luke 6:12–16). They maintained a particularly close relationship with Jesus, received private instruction, and witnessed His miracles and controversy with the Jewish authorities. On one occasion, Jesus sent these men out to preach the message of repentance, to cast out demons, and to heal the sick—that is, to minister in ways that were characteristic of His own work (Matt. 10:1–15; Mark 6:7–13, 30; Luke 9:1–6). This relationship between Jesus and His apostles is best expressed in the saying, "The one who listens to you listens to Me, and the one who rejects you rejects Me; and he who rejects Me rejects the One who sent Me" (Luke 10:16, NASB). Jesus makes it quite clear that the purpose of the twelve disciples is not merely to share Jesus' teachings with others, but to also represent His very person. After the resurrection, Jesus commissioned the Twelve to proclaim the gospel. Only those who had been with Jesus from the beginning of His ministry to His resurrection were qualified to be His apostolic witnesses (Acts 1:21–22). Paul qualified because he had seen the risen Christ (1 Cor. 15:4–10). His apostleship was accompanied by a great deal of suffering, including false teachers in the Corinthian church who doubted his authority.

Thus, in 2 Corinthians, Paul had to repeatedly defend the genuineness of his apostleship.

Paul's writings demonstrate two characteristic uses of the word "apostle." On occasion, it refers to persons authorized by local congregations and entrusted with the safe delivery of specific gifts for other members of the Christian community (2 Cor. 8:23; Phil. 2:25). The other meaning is far more common and refers to those who are the "sent ones of Jesus Christ" (Rom. 16:7; 1 Cor. 9:1, 5; 12:28; Gal. 1:17–19). Apostles are the chosen vessels of Christ's message and love.

KEY VERSES

Matthew 10:2;
Acts 2:37;
Romans 1:1;
Hebrews 3:1

Appearing

Greek expression: *epiphaneia*
Pronunciation: *eh pee FAH nay uh*
Strong's Number: *2015*

Superman. He appears as a normal man and then reappears as a hero with super-natural power. Everyone knows that he is a myth, but there is a wonderful corre-lation between Superman and the event, when God "showed up" as a man.

The Greek word *epiphaneia* literally means "a shining forth" and was used in Greek literature to denote a divine appearance. The English word *epiphany* is a close equivalent. The New Testament writers used *epiphaneia* to refer to Jesus' first coming, the time when he entered this world as a man, but they also used the word to speak of Jesus' second coming. In the pastoral epistles, Paul used the word to refer to both of Christ's comings. In 2 Timothy, Paul said:

> Therefore do not be ashamed of the testimony of our Lord, or of me His prisoner; but join with me in suffering for the gospel according to the power of God, who has saved us, and called us with a holy calling, not according to our works, but accord-ing to His own purpose and grace which was granted us in Christ Jesus from all eter-nity, but now has been revealed by the *appearing* of our Savior Christ Jesus, who abolished death, and brought life and immortality to light through the gospel.

> *(2 Tim. 2:9–10, NASB, emphasis added)*

According to God's eternal purpose, we were predestined to experience the grace of His beloved Son—even before the world began. This is the gospel in a nut-shell. This was done in hiding, in secret. Then, God revealed His design by sending His Son into the world. When Jesus "appeared" or "shown forth," He defeated death, thus confirming that life and freedom from sin was purposed by God from eternity. Before the revelation of the gospel, man had only a glimmering idea of the soul, but not the faintest idea of the resurrection of the body (Acts 17:18, 32).

In writing to Titus, Paul used the Greek word for "appearing" in two different ways when speaking of Christ's second coming:

> For the grace of God has appeared, bringing salvation to all men, instructing us to deny ungodliness and worldly desires and to live sensibly, righteously and godly in the present age, looking for the blessed hope and the appearing of the glory of our great God and Savior, Christ Jesus.

> *(Titus 2:11–13, NASB)*

Interestingly, Paul used the verb form, "to appear," in speak-ing of God's grace appearing in the first coming of Christ, and then he used the noun form, "appearance," to speak of Christ's hoped-for second coming. Notice, also, that Paul called Jesus our great God and our Savior. We await this wonderful coming, when Jesus will reveal all His glory to us. He will appear in all His splendor, and there will be nothing that could weaken Him.

KEY VERSES

2 Thessalonians 2:8;
1 Timothy 6:14;
2 Tim. 1:10; 4:1, 8

Armageddon

Greek expression: *harmageddōn*
Pronunciation: *hahr muh geh DOHN*
Strong's Number: *717*

When we hear the word "Armageddon," we usually think of a violent war or a cataclysmic event that will end the world. This isn't too far from the truth as presented in the Bible.

The Greek term appears only once in the New Testament (Rev. 16:16). It is derived from the word *har*, which means a mountain, and the word *Megiddo*, a name of a city in Manasseh. The town of Megiddo was strategically located between the western coastal area and the broad Plain of Jezreel in northern Palestine. The area of Megiddo was the scene of many important battles in Israel's history. In this area, Sisera was defeated by armies of Deborah and Barak (Judg. 4–5). Gideon was victorious over the Midianites and Amalekites (Judg. 6). Saul and his army were defeated by the Philistines (1 Sam. 31), and Josiah was killed in battle by the Egyptian army of Pharaoh Neco (2 Kgs. 23:29). Because of that history, the name seems to have become symbolic of a battlefield.

Such is the depiction in the book of Revelation. Revelation 15 and 16 describe seven angels who pour out seven bowls of God's just anger upon the earth. The sixth angel pours out his bowl upon the great river Euphrates, and its waters are dried up, preparing the way for the "kings of the East." Also three demonic spirits cause the kings of the whole world to gather for a battle of the great day of God the Almighty (16:13–14). Their gathering takes place at Armageddon (16:16).

How do we interpret this? Whereas most interpret this as referring to a literal battle on earth, some see it as symbolic of God's destruction of all the forces of evil. But no matter how it is interpreted, it describes a final battle in which Christ is victorious. God comes out the winner, and so do His people.

KEY VERSE
Revelation 16:16

Ascend

Greek expression: *anabainō*
Pronunciation: *ahn uh BIGH noh*
Strong's Number: *305*

The Greek word *anabainō* was typically used in the New Testament to describe the way in which a traveler in Judea approached Jerusalem. Because Jerusalem was elevated and because it was the holy city, people "went up" to Jerusalem (see, for example, Matthew 20:17–18). It was also used by the New Testament writers to speak about ascending to heaven. Most specifically, it was used to describe Jesus' ascension to heaven after His resurrection (John 20:17; Eph. 4:8–10).

Among the New Testament writers, only Luke actually described Jesus' ascension. Acts 1:9–11 pictures a scene in which Jesus was "taken up" and disappeared into a cloud. Luke 24:50–51 and Acts 1:12 locate that final event near Bethany, east of Jerusalem on the Mount of Olives. Matthew concluded his history before Pentecost, but John suggested the ascension in Jesus' own comments (see Matt. 20:17). Thus, the Gospels and Acts indicate that Jesus appeared to His disciples in resurrection for a period of forty days. After this, He ascended into heaven (Acts 1:1–11). Now, though He is physically absent, Jesus is spiritually present in His church.

Other New Testament writings affirm Christ's ascension. The apostle Paul wrote that God raised Christ from the dead "and seated Him at His right hand in the heavenly places" (Eph. 1:20, NASB). The writer of Hebrews said that Christ is now "at the right hand of the Majesty on high" (Heb. 1:3, NASB). For the author of the book of Hebrews the ascension is also proof of Christ's superiority to angels (Heb. 1:13). Angels, authorities, and powers are all subject to the ascended Christ (1 Tim. 3:16; 1 Pet. 3:22).

KEY VERSES
Ephesians 4:8–10

Atonement

See: *Make Atonement, p. 122 and Reconciliation, p. 373*

Baptize

Greek expression: *baptizō*
Pronunciation: *bahp TEE dzoh*
Strong's Number: *907*

Christians have had a long history of debate as to how a person should be baptized: should a Christian be sprinkled with or completely immersed into the water. The Bible does not focus on this debate, but does point to the importance of the act. The Greek word *baptizō* means "to dip" or "to immerse." In the Jordan River, John the Baptist immersed Jews who had decided to repent of their sins and ready themselves for the coming of the Messiah. The Messiah would then baptize them with the Holy Spirit and with fire (Matt. 3:11). John's baptism symbolized moral purification and prepared the people for God's coming kingdom (Matt. 3:2; Luke 3:7–14).

Acts 2:38 shows that baptism was practiced from the very beginning of the church. It was understood and expected to follow repentance as a confession of the change that had taken place in the believer. Acts 10:44–45 shows that water baptism wasn't a condition for receiving the Spirit. There was most likely a question-and-answer period in which the believer confessed his faith and dedicated himself to Christ. The result was reception into and identification with the community of Christians. Baptism signified that the believer's sins had been forgiven (see Acts 2:38; 5:31; 10:43; 13:38; 26:18) and that he had received the Holy Spirit (see Luke 3:16; Acts 2:38, 41; 9:17; 10:47–48; 11:16–17; 19:5–7).

Paul used baptism to speak about the believer's identification with Christ. His basic statement is found in Galatians 3:27, "baptized into Christ." This is clarified further by Romans 6:3–8, which indicates that a believer joins Christ in His death and resurrection through baptism. Baptism is also related to the Spirit; 1 Corinthians 12:13 connects "baptism by the one spirit" with being "given that same Spirit." Many Christian commentators think that baptism is the outward testimony of the inward possession of the Spirit (2 Cor. 1:21–22; Eph. 1:13; 4:30).

KEY VERSES

Matthew 3:6;
Mark 1:5;
Acts 2:38;
Romans 6:3

Barbarian

Greek expression: *barbaros*
Pronunciation: *BAHR bahr awss*
Strong's Number: *915*

B

Have you ever listened to a person speak who is from a different country and not understood a word he or she was saying? As far as you were concerned, they might as well have been saying, "Blah, blah, blah, blah." To the ancient Greeks, it seemed that all foreigners were saying, "Bar, bar, bar, bar." As a result, they called a foreigner *barbaros*, which is transliterated into English as "barbarian." In the English language, a barbarian connotes one who is uncivilized. The Greeks held to the same view. Considering themselves as the only truly cultured people in the world, the Greeks tended to refer to everything non-Greek as barbarian. The Romans adopted Greek culture, considered themselves equals of the Greeks, and also regarded other languages, customs, and people as barbarian.

The word *barbarian* has several shades of meaning in the New Testament. The source of *barbaros* and its relationship to language is evident in Paul's statement about speaking in tongues through the Holy Spirit (1 Cor. 14:11). He said that if a Christian's spiritual language were not understood, the person speaking would be a barbarian to Paul and vice versa. Luke's account of Paul's shipwreck on Malta refers to "barbarous people" and "barbarians" (Acts 28:2–4). Obviously, nothing derogatory was intended, since the kindness of the natives was being described.

Elsewhere, Paul indicated that he felt obligated to take the gospel to the Greeks and to the barbarians (Rom. 1:14). This is significant because it shows that Paul was not culture-bound. He shared Christ's message with all groups of people—even those considered uncivilized. In a statement about the unity of the church, Paul said, "A renewal in which there is no distinction between Greek and Jew, circumcised and uncircumcised, barbarian, Scythian, slave and freeman, but Christ is all, and in all" (Col. 3:11, NASB). All these kinds of people not only became members of the church, but their differences were also dissolved by virtue of their unity in Christ. Believers today should also not make distinctions between other believers because of race, cultural, or economic background, but should try to see one another as Christ sees us. We are all His children saved by His grace.

KEY VERSES

Acts 28:2, 4;
Romans 1:14;
1 Corinthians 14:11;
Colossians 3:11

233

Believe

See also: *Believe, p. 17*
Greek expression: *pisteuō*
Pronunciation: *pee STEW oh*
Strong's Number: *4100*

"Believe me, you don't want to go down that road," is a common statement which all of us have heard at one time or another. The message is clear: though you can't see what is down the road, the other person has knowledge of danger. That person is telling you to trust his word rather than experience the danger for yourself and suffer the consequences. If you don't "go down that road," you trusted the person. There was belief that what he said was true. The Greek word for believe, *pisteuō*, literally means "to place one's trust in another." It occurs over 90 times (always as a verb) in the Gospel of John alone. Quite often the verb denotes that one must accept that something is true—that is, simple credence or belief. For example, Jesus said, "Believe me that I am in the Father and the Father in me" (John 14:11) and, "If you had believed Moses, you would believe me" (John 5:46).

Even more significant is the special expression for *pisteuō*, "to believe into," in the sense of putting one's trust into another. The particular form of the expression is found only in the fourth Gospel. It expresses the strong sense of personal trust in the eternal Word made flesh. In John 3:16 whoever puts trust in Him has eternal life. "Believers" are given power to become sons of God—to be born of God (John 1:12). They will never thirst—they will live, even though they die (John 6:35; 11:25).

In other places, John speaks of belief or trust as an absolute, without referring to the one in whom trust is placed. In John 11:15 Jesus arrives after the death of Lazarus and He is glad ". . . so that you may believe." Similarly in the prologue, John the Baptist bears witness to Jesus in order that through him all might have faith and believe (John 1:7). As Jesus satisfies the doubt of Thomas concerning the resurrection, he says, "Because you have seen Me, have you believed? Blessed are they who did not see, and yet believed" (John 20:29, NASB).

KEY VERSES

John 1:7, 12;
2:23–24; 3:15–16,
36; 6:47; 11:25;
14:1; 20:31

Belief and knowledge are closely related. In John 6:69, Peter says, "We have believed and have come to know that You are the Holy One of God." In His priestly prayer, Jesus says that eternal life is that believers "may know Thee, the only true God, and Jesus Christ whom Thou hast sent" (John 17:3, NASB). The Bible says that he who has seen Jesus has seen the Father (John 14:9). No one has ever seen God and lived, but since Jesus has revealed the Father to us, we can see God through the eyes of faith (John 1:18). To believe is also expressed in the verb *receive*. Those who receive Christ are given power to become the sons of God (John 1:12). Trust is that form of knowing or seeing by which the glory of God (John 1:14; 17:4) is made present.

Bind and Loose

Greek expression: *deō kai luō*
Pronunciation: *DEH oh; KIGH; LOO oh*
Strong's Numbers: *1210, 2532, 3089*

B

For almost two thousand years, Bible students have debated what Jesus actually meant when He told Peter:

> And I also say to you that you are Peter, and on this rock I will build My church, and the forces of Hades will not overpower it. I will give you the keys of the kingdom of heaven, and whatever you bind on earth will have been bound in heaven, and whatever you loose on earth will have been loosed in heaven.
>
> *(Matt. 16:18–19 HCSB)*

Peter has just made the confession of all times. He had told Jesus, "Thou art the Christ, the Son of the living God" (Matt. 16:16). In clear and uncertain terms, Peter was proclaiming Jesus as God. Jesus applauded Peter for his confession, indicating that Peter could not have known this if it hadn't been revealed to him from heaven. Then Jesus went on to give Peter the authority to "bind" and to "loose"—a saying that has puzzled Bible readers ever since. Later, Jesus gave the same authority to bind and to loose to all of His disciples (Matt. 18:18). To understand what authority Jesus was giving to the disciples, we have to understand how the Greek words for "bind" and "loose" were used in Jesus' day.

"Bind" and "loose" are translations of two Greek words, which were themselves translations of two words in Aramaic—the language spoken by Jesus and his contemporaries. The two Aramaic words were often used as technical rabbinic terms. They referred to the verdict of a teacher of the Law who, on the basis of his authority as an expert in the interpretation of the Mosaic Law, could declare some action "bound"—that is, forbidden—or "loosed"—that is, permitted. Among the greatest Jewish rabbis, Shammai bound many actions that the more liberal rabbi Hillel loosed. These terms also referred to the imposition or the removal of a ban, or judgment, by a judge. In this legal context, the Aramaic word for "bound" meant "to condemn" or "to imprison" and the Aramaic word for "loose" meant "to absolve" or "to set free."

According to Matthew 23:13, the scribes were supposed to be the guardians of the kingdom since the knowledge of God had been entrusted to them (Luke 11:52). But they had not fulfilled their trust. They had shut the doors of the kingdom to those who wanted to enter. Therefore, Jesus was transferring their authority to Peter, the spokesman for the twelve disciples, who were representatives of a new Israel, the church (see Matt. 21:43). As those entrusted with the keys to the kingdom, Peter and the disciples were given the task to open God's kingdom to all seekers and to protect it against the forces of evil.

KEY VERSES

Matthew 16:19;
18:18

Bishop

See: *Overseer, p. 354*

Blasphemy

Greek expression: *blasphēmia*
Pronunciation: *blahss fay MEE uh*
Strong's Number: *988*

The popular thought about blasphemy is that it is a horrible, unforgivable sin. This is not far from the truth. However, *blasphēmia* in general use referred to any kind of "slander." In Greek literature the term was used for insulting the living or deriding dead persons; it was also used to denote insults against the gods.

In the Old Testament, "blasphemy" always means to insult God, either by attacking Him directly or mocking Him indirectly. In the New Testament, blasphemy takes on the wider Greek meaning, for it includes slandering a human being as well as God (Matt. 15:19; Rom. 3:8; 1 Cor. 10:30; Eph. 4:31; Titus 3:2). It even includes mocking angelic or demonic powers (Jude 8–10, 2 Pet. 2:1–12). In other words, slander, derision, and mocking of any kind are totally condemned in the New Testament.

In the New Testament, the most common form of blasphemy is blasphemy against God. Jesus was accused of blasphemy by the Jewish leaders because He claiméd to have the power to forgive sins (Mark 2:7). On another occasion, the Jewish leaders wanted to stone Jesus to death because, as they said to Him, "You, being a man, make Yourself out to be God" (John 10:33, NASB). Jesus was condemned by the highest Jewish court, the Sanhedrin, on the charge of blasphemy, because He claimed to be the Son of Man (the Messiah). The Sanhedrin found no evidence that Jesus was such an exalted personage—thus He appeared to be mocking "the Messiah" and, by extension, God Himself (Mark 14:64). But Jesus told the Jewish leaders that they had committed blasphemy against the Holy Spirit because they had said that Jesus' miracles (really done by the power of the Holy Spirit) were performed by the power of the devil (Beelzebub). This was true blasphemy! (See Matt. 12:31; Mark 3:28–29; Luke 12:10.)

KEY VERSES

Matthew 12:31;
Mark 3:28;
Luke 12:10

Jesus, pointing out that the charge of demon possession was illogical, also stated strongly that blasphemy against the Holy Spirit can never be forgiven. Jesus was saying that to slander the Holy Spirit is even worse than insulting Christ or God Himself, which was a crime punishable by death in the Old Testament (Lev. 24:16). Jesus said that blasphemy against Himself can be forgiven (Matt. 12:31–32). Consequently, when Jesus called blasphemy against the Holy Spirit "an eternal sin," He was making it serious indeed.

Blessed

See also: *Blessing, p. 21*
Greek expression: *makarios*
Pronunciation: *mah KAH ree awss*
Strong's Number: *3107*

B

Makarios in Greek means "fortunate" or "happy" and is derived from the root *mak*, which means "lengthy." Perhaps the Greeks saw blessedness as related to the idea of "length of life"—a long life was a blessed one.

Makarios was frequently used in Greek literature, the Septuagint (a Greek translation of the Old Testament), and the New Testament to describe the kind of happiness that comes from receiving divine favor. Consequently, the word can also be rendered "favored." In the New Testament it is usually a divine passive; this means that people are blessed by God. The Lord God is the One who is blessing or favoring the person.

The most well-known "blessings" are described in the Beatitudes, wherein we see the various kinds of blessings God gives to those who are worthy of these graces. The Beatitudes are written in two different forms: one in Matthew 5:3–12 and the other in Luke 6:20–23. The pronouncement of the blessings in Luke is done immediately after the selection of the twelve disciples (Luke 6:12–16). Yet, the sermon is addressed to the crowd generally and speaks of the advent of God's kingdom. Luke balances four blessings with four woes—changing from the present tense to the future tense—to heighten the contrast of the impending reversal of social conditions.

In Matthew's account, the kingdom has already begun, indicated by the use of the present tense. These Beatitudes are addressed to the disciples particularly and are not a general proclamation. They are more concerned with the interior life of the disciple—to activate here and now the kind of life Jesus communicates in those who follow Him. The eight Beatitudes reflect on the traits of those who belong to that kingdom and who therefore reflect Christ's own life. Read, for example, the following blessings:

> Blessed are the poor in spirit, because the kingdom of heaven is theirs.
>
> Blessed are those who mourn, because they will be comforted.
>
> Blessed are the gentle, because they will inherit the earth.
>
> Blessed are those who hunger and thirst for righteousness, because they will be filled.
>
> *(Matt. 5:3-6, HCSB)*

KEY VERSES

Matthew 5:3–11;
Luke 6:20–23;
James 1:12, 25

The people and situations described may seem bad by our human standards. Yet, because of God's presence in our lives, we are actually blessed by God through these trying situations.

Blood

See also: *Blood, p. 22*
Greek expression: *haima*
Pronunciation: *HIGH muh*
Strong's Number: *129*

Blood is precious; lose too much of it and you lose your life. Blood is also life and as the source of life, it takes on a special significance in animal sacrifices. On the day of Atonement (Lev. 16), the blood of a bull and of a goat was sprinkled upon the altar as an atonement for the people's sin. Animal life was given up on behalf of the life of the people. Judgment and atonement were carried out through a transfer of the people's sin to the animal sacrifice (Lev. 16:20–22). In the first Passover the *haima* or "blood" of a lamb had the same meaning. It was put on each door as a sign that a death had already taken place (death of the animal sacrificed), so the Angel of Death passed over (Exod. 12:1–13).

In the New Testament, the primary reference to the Greek word *haima* is to the blood of Christ—with constant reference to the Old Testament sacrifices. In the first three Gospels, Jesus spoke of His blood at the Last Supper with reference to a new covenant; that is, His sacrificial death and its redemptive significance (Matt. 26:28; Mark 14:24; Luke 22:20). The Gospel of John expresses the same thought in a different context: "Truly, truly, I say to you, unless you eat the flesh of the Son of Man and drink His blood, you have no life in yourselves" (John 6:53, NASB). Jesus' death is the means by which believers can have life.

The apostle Paul's writings likewise associate blood with Christ's death. The word "blood" becomes, like the term "cross," synonymous with the death of Christ, as in these two verses: "having made peace through the blood of His cross" (Col. 1:20, NASB); and "you who formerly were far off have been brought near by the blood of Christ" (Eph. 2:13, NASB).

Peter reminded his readers that they had been redeemed by the blood of Christ (1 Pet. 1:2, 19). In calling Christ the "spotless lamb of God," he may have had in mind either the servant of Isaiah 53 or the Passover Lamb, both of which had redemptive significance in his readers' minds. Finally, the writer of Hebrews argued that the whole Old Testament system of sacrifices found its ultimate fulfillment in the blood of Christ through His sacrificial death (Heb. 9:7–28; 13:1–12). Christ took our sins upon Himself, sacrificed Himself on the cross, poured out His blood for all people, and then rose again in final victory over death—thus, He eliminated the need for animal sacrifices once and for all. We now have forgiveness and hope of eternal life through Jesus Christ our Savior.

KEY VERSES

Matthew 26:28;
Mark 14:24;
John 6:53;
1 Peter 1:2, 19;
Hebrews 9:7

Body

See also: *Body of Christ, p. 240 and Body of Jesus Christ, p. 241*
Greek expression: *sōma*
Pronunciation: *SOH muh*
Strong's Number: *4983*

In the Bible, the Greek word *sōma*, or "body," is used in several different ways, including metaphorical and theological expressions. In its most basic definition, the Greek word for "body" denotes the physical entity that encases our soul. For example, Jesus said not to fear those who kill the body but cannot kill the soul; rather fear those who can destroy both soul and body in hell (Matt. 10:28).

The term "body" is also used metaphorically. Jesus spoke of His own body with reference to the bread of the new covenant: "This is My body." And then he added—with the cup of wine in His hand: "This is My blood" (Mark 14:22–24). These terms, derived from the Old Testament sacrificial system, were intended to underscore the sacrificial significance of Jesus' death. Under both the old and new covenants, a real, physical life was offered to God in death.

The apostle Paul made the term "body" a fundamental reference in the understanding of Christian experience. Most of the New Testament references to "body" are found in his letters. For example, in Romans 6:6, Paul spoke of a "body of sin." The phrase does not mean that the body itself is sinful, as though sin is in some way connected to physical matter. Rather, the phrase refers to the physical life of human beings—life on earth—which is dominated by sin's influence. To link sin with the body is only to recognize that human beings in their earthly life are inherently sinful.

When unbelievers convert to a belief in Christ, Paul said that they experience not only the "saving of the soul" but also the transformation of their lives. They have died to sin and have been freed from sin's bondage. He wrote, "Therefore do not let sin reign in your mortal body that you should obey its lusts" (Rom. 6:12, NASB). Righteousness, not sin, is to govern a Christian's physical experience. The lives of believers are to be characterized by holiness. Believers are in the world (John 17:11) and are to live for God in the world (that is, in their bodily existence); but they are not to be indifferent to the world.

Physical, earthly life takes on new significance when people become believers in Christ. Paul told Christians to present their bodies as a "living sacrifice" to God (Rom. 12:1). Paul did not deprecate earthly existence, but saw that in Christ the body had new potential. Jesus said, "Your body is a temple of the Holy Spirit who is in you, whom you have from God, and that you are not your own" (1 Cor. 6:19, NASB). "Body" means one's whole physical, earthly existence. Paul also anticipated an ultimate transformation of life in the body through Christ. We will be redeemed and physically transformed—given new bodies to be like Jesus' glorious body (Rom. 8:23; Phil. 3:21).

KEY VERSES

Mark 14:22;
Romans 6:6, 12;
8:23;
Philippians 3:21

Body of Christ (the Church)

See also: *Body, p. 239 and Body of Jesus Christ, p. 241*
Greek expression: *sōma tou Christou*
Strong's Numbers: *4983, 3588, 5547*

The phrase "body of Christ" is used as a metaphor for the whole church—the unity of believers connected with and dependent on Christ. God's people are thus said to be members of Christ's "mystical body" (1 Cor. 12:27), in fellowship with Christ, and spiritually nourished by Him (Eph. 5:25, 29). A number of other metaphors are also used for the whole people of God, such as: the vine (Ps. 80:8), the temple of God (1 Cor. 3:16–17), the building (1 Pet. 2:5), the chosen people (1 Pet. 2:9), and the family of God (Eph. 3:14–15). Such metaphors amplify the interrelatedness, communion, and dependence of the "body of Christ" upon the living God.

The Greek expression *sōma tou Christou*, or "body of Christ," was often used by Paul to remind a local church that it was a vital part of the larger body (Rom. 12:4–5). Paul taught the Corinthian Christians that they, individually and collectively, were part of the body of Christ (1 Cor. 12:27)—all baptized by one Spirit into that one body (Eph. 5:30). In a number of passages, the church is called the "body" and Christ the "head" (Col. 1:18). Paul writes that Christ has been made "head over all things to the church, which is His body, the fulness of Him who fills all in all" (Eph. 1:22–23). As head of the body, Christ is its Savior (Eph. 5:23), and the body grows by holding fast to the head (Col. 2:19). The head-body metaphor stresses the organic dependence of the church on Christ and His lordship over the church. Life flows from and is sustained by the head, and the church finds its self-understanding in terms of its head. The relationship is immediate, direct, and complete.

The Bible tells us that each member of the body of Christ has been given spiritual gifts with which to serve Christ in the body (Rom. 12:6; 1 Cor. 12:11). The gifts are given "for the equipping of the saints for the work of service, to the building up of the body of Christ; until we all attain to the unity of the faith, and of the knowledge of the Son of God, to a mature man, to the measure of the stature which belongs to the fulness of Christ" (Eph. 4:12–13, NASB). The goal is "to grow up in all aspects into Him, who is the head, even Christ" (Eph. 4:15–16, NASB). Christ sustains all of us, and we are given gifts to sustain other members of the Church. We should continue growing as we strive together to be unified in our head and Lord, Jesus Christ.

KEY VERSES

Romans 12:15;
1 Corinthians
12:12–20, 22–25;
Ephesians 4:12, 16

Body of Jesus Christ

See also: *Body, p. 239 and Body of Christ, p. 240*
Greek expression: *sōma tou Iēsou Christou*
Pronunciation: *SOH muh; TOO; yay SOO; kree STOO*
Strong's Numbers: *4983, 3588, 2424, 5547*

B

The Greek expression, *sōma tou Iēsou Christou*, which means the "body of Jesus Christ," has three meanings in the New Testament: (1) the physical body of Jesus Christ; (2) Jesus' broken body and shed blood viewed symbolically in the bread and wine of the Lord's Supper; and (3) both the local and universal church viewed metaphorically (for this, see Body of Christ, the Church).

1. The Physical Body of Jesus Christ. The New Testament indicates that the Son of God had a human body prepared for Him by God the Father (Heb. 10:5). The earthly body came into being through the miraculous power of the Holy Spirit through the virgin Mary (Matt. 1:20). The apostle John emphasized that the body of Christ was truly physical, not something ethereal as some people in John's day were already beginning to argue (1 John 4:2–3). John said that God "became flesh and dwelt among us" (John 1:14, NASB). Jesus' earthly body possessed ordinary human characteristics and limitations. As a real human being, Jesus Christ experienced sorrow (Heb. 5:7–8; John 11:35), weariness (John 4:6), thirst (John 19:28), and pain (John 19:1–3). When Jesus gave up His spirit, His physical body died on the cross (John 19:30, 33). While on the cross, the New Testament proclaims that He bore the sins of the world in His body (1 Pet. 2:24; 1 John 2:2). Christ's physical body was prepared in the normal way for burial (Matt. 27:59; Mark 15:46; Luke 23:53, 56; 24:1; John 19:39–40) and placed in the rock tomb of Joseph of Arimathea (Matt. 27:57–60; John 19:41). On the third day, Jesus' body experienced a real physical resurrection, as He had predicted (John 2:19–22). He was seen in His physical, resurrected body (Matt. 28:9; Luke 24:31, 36; John 20:10–19, 26). He was heard, touched, and held on to (Matt. 28:9; Luke 24:39; John 20:17; 1 John 1:1). He even offered His body, wounded by the crucifixion, to be touched (Luke 24:39; John 20:17). Plus, the fact that He ate demonstrates that His resurrected body was a physical one (Luke 24:42–43). Christ's body was also glorified; it was not restricted as ordinary bodies are and He entered and left rooms in a remarkable way (Luke 24:31, 36; John 20:19, 26).

2. The Body of Christ in the Lord's Supper. During Jesus' Last Supper (Matt. 26:26–29; Mark 14:22–25; Luke 22:15–20; 1 Cor. 11:23–26), which accompanied the Passover celebration, Jesus held up a loaf of bread and said, "This is My body." Then He picked up a cup of wine and said, "This is My blood of the covenant" (Matt. 26:28). While the wine symbolized Jesus' life sacrifice, the bread symbolized Jesus' body, which would be broken when He was crucified (Luke 23:33; John 19:1–2). For Christians, the body of Christ is viewed sym-

KEY VERSES

Matthew 26:26;
Mark 14:22;
Luke 22:19;
Hebrews 10:5

241

bolically as a broken body (Matt. 8:17; 1 Pet. 2:24; see Isa. 53:4–5) in the breaking of the bread at the Lord's Supper. The cup is a sign of His blood poured out, viewed as the central factor in God's covenant of grace with His people. Jesus referred to "the new covenant in My blood" (Luke 22:20). The Lord's Supper reminds believers that Christ died for the forgiveness of the sins of many (Matt. 26:28). It shows the Lord's death until He comes again.

The body of Christ offers Christians hope. In the Lord's Supper, it reminds us of Christ's broken body sacrificed for us. And Christ's resurrected body strengthens our belief that we, too, will receive resurrected bodies, in which we can live forever in God's presence.

Book of Life

Greek expression: *biblos tēs zōēs*
Pronunciation: *BEE blawss; tayss; dzoh AYSS*
Strong's Numbers: *976, 3588, 2222*

B

In ancient times, as in modern, people have depended on books to keep records and to write literature. A book is a set of written sheets—whether composed of wood, parchment, papyrus, or paper. Throughout history, there have been many kinds of books: scrolls, codices, or a collection of books such as the Bible. Prior to the first century A.D., people wrote larger works on scrolls, which were rolls of papyrus, parchment, or leather used for writing a document or literary work. The papyrus scroll of Egypt can be traced as far back as 2500 B.C. Jews used leather scrolls for writing the books of the Old Testament and most of the scrolls discovered from the Dead Sea area were written on leather, with a few written on papyrus. In the first century A.D., the codex was developed. A codex was constructed much like our modern books by folding sheets of papyrus or vellum (treated animal hide) in the middle and then sewing them together at the spine. This kind of book was advantageous because it enabled the scribe to write on both sides. The codex facilitated easier access to particular passages (as opposed to a scroll, which had to be unrolled). It also enabled Christians to bind together all four Gospels, or all Paul's letters, or any other such combination. With respect to the Bible, each individual composition is called a "book" because that was what the document was before it became part of the biblical collection. As such, the Bible has 66 books, such as Genesis, Isaiah, Matthew, John, and Revelation.

The Greek terms *biblion* and *biblos* were used by the New Testament writers to denote: a scroll (Luke 4:17, 20); a specific book of the Old Testament such as the book of Psalms (Luke 20:42) or the book of Isaiah (Mark 1:2); a New Testament book such as John's Gospel (John 20:30) or Revelation (Rev. 22:18); and perhaps a codex (Rev. 5:1–9; note how there is writing on both sides of this book, thereby indicating a codex, not a scroll). The term *biblos* was used in the special expression *biblos tēs zōēs* or "the book of life." The phrase appears seven times in the New Testament (Phil. 4:3; Rev. 3:5; 13:8; 17:8; 20:12; 21:27). In Philippians 4:3, Paul uses "book of life" to affirm that his coworkers have eternal life. The book of life in Revelation refers to a heavenly record of the names of persecuted Christians who remain faithful to the Lord. If a person's name is found in the book, admittance is granted to New Jerusalem (Rev. 20:15; 21:27). If one's name is not written there, they are cast into the lake of fire.

KEY VERSES

Luke 4:17, 20;
John 20:30;
Philippians 4:3;
Revelation 1:11;
5:1–5, 8–9; 20:12

Born again

Greek expression: *gennaō anōthen*
Pronunciation: *gehn NAH oh; AHN oh thehn*
Strong's Numbers: *1080, 509*

Have you ever wished that you could start life all over again? Who hasn't? At one time or another, we have all had regrets. But starting over in our physical life will not solve our problems. Our real need is to be born again spiritually. This is why Jesus told the teacher Nicodemus, "You must be born again" (John 3:7). The Greek word *gennaō* means "to be born" and *anōthen*, meaning "again," can also be rendered "from above" or "anew." The birth that Jesus spoke of was therefore a new birth, a heavenly birth, or both. He was most likely speaking of a heavenly birth because He later used an analogy of the wind coming from some unknown, heavenly source, to depict spiritual birth. But Nicodemus clearly understood that Jesus was speaking of a second birth—that is, being born again. Jesus explains this new or heavenly birth in John 3:6-8, contrasting being born "of the flesh" with being born in "the Spirit."

The believer possesses a new life from God through the process of spiritual birth. Christians are born of God (John 1:12-13) and it is only through this spiritual birth that one may participate in the Kingdom of God and receive His Spirit. Those born into God's family reflect His righteous character (1 John 2:29) and they are freed from habitual sin (1 John 3:9; 5:18). In James 1:18 this process of birth is attributed to the power of the Word of God. Those who are reborn possess a living hope (1 Pet. 1:3). Again, this new birth is brought about through the power of the Word of God (1 Pet. 1:23). The initial experience of being born again is followed by a continuing renewal in the life of the Christian. The newborn are to desire the pure milk of the God's Word in order to grow (1 Pet. 2:2). Paul encourages an ongoing transformation in all believers by commanding us to renew our thoughts and attitudes (Rom. 12:2; Eph. 4:23).

Contrary to what many people think, Christian life is not boring, stagnant, or uneventful. The believer's inner self is renewed daily (2 Cor. 4:16), and all of us are constantly in the process of becoming the men and women God wants us to be (Col. 3:10). The Lord loves us so much, that He has something exciting for us to know, learn, and experience every day. He wants us to become more like Him every day.

KEY VERSES

John 3:3, 7

Bread of life

Greek expression: *artos zōēs*
Pronunciation: *AHR tawss; zoh AYSS*
Strong's Numbers: *740, 2222*

B

One of the most simple, yet profound statements Jesus ever made was, "I am the bread of life" (John 6:35). The Greek words Jesus used were simple enough. *Artos* simply referred to bread in contrast to meat and could also designate the shew-bread, consecrated bread, in the temple (Matt. 12:4). Jesus said this to a multitude of people who were following Him after He miraculously fed them with five loaves and two fish. They followed Jesus because He had satisfied their appetites, and not because they had seen a sign from God (John 6:26). To those caught in the drudgery of sustaining life, Jesus said "Do not work for the food which perishes, but for the food which endures to eternal life, which the Son of Man shall give to you" (John 6:27, NASB). In other words, Jesus told the people that the food they were striving and working for would not give them eternal life. But if they believed in Him, they would have eternal life. The people would not believe in Him, however, until they saw a sign. They even quoted the Scriptures to Jesus: "HE GAVE THEM BREAD FROM HEAVEN TO EAT" (John 6:31; compare Ps. 78:24; 105:40, NASB). But Jesus told them, "Moses has not given you the bread out of heaven, but it is My Father who gives you true bread out of heaven. For the bread of God is that which comes down out of heaven, and gives life to the world" (John 6:32–33, NASB). The manna that had been given to the Israelites in the wilderness had no present effect on the Jews of Jesus' day. Their boast in the ancient miracle could not give them life. Jesus was the real "bread of God," who came to be the ever-present manna—the ever-present life-giving supply.

Jesus' listeners, of course, wanted this bread. But when Jesus kept telling them that He Himself was the "bread of life," even the bread that came down from heaven, they became more and more offended. How could Jesus, a mere man, be the bread of God? How could Jesus, the son of Joseph and Mary—people the Jews knew—come from heaven? The offense increased even more when Jesus told the people that He had come to give His flesh for the life of the world—that is, He had come to sacrifice His life so that the world could have eternal life (John 6:51). He instructed that the people eat His flesh and drink His blood. If they didn't, they would have no life in them. This was a repulsive thought to the Jews. Mosaic law prohibited the drinking of blood (see Lev. 3:17; 7:26, 27; 17:10–14). But His death—the shedding of blood—enables people to have eternal life. To eat His flesh and drink His blood is to appropriate, by faith, the meaning of Jesus' death. The blood separate from the flesh evidences a death—and what a glorious death, a death that has enabled millions to receive eternal life. To all who believe in Him and receive Him, He is the bread of life.

KEY VERSES

John 6:35, 48

Bride

Greek expression: *numphē*
Pronunciation: *NOOM fay*
Strong's Number: *3565*

"Here comes the bride!" These are such joyful words, and we picture her radiant, beautiful, and adorned in pure white, walking expectantly towards her husband-to-be. In the Bible, the church is called the *numphē*, or the "bride" of Christ; the imagery evoked by this relationship shows the love, devotion, and unity God intended between His Son and the unified body of believers.

Addressing the church at Corinth, the apostle Paul referred to himself as the one who gave the church to Christ, presenting her as a pure bride to her one husband (2 Cor. 11:2–3). In ancient Near Eastern culture, the father gave his daughter in marriage to the bridegroom, assuring him of her purity. To Paul, understanding that he was the church's spiritual father (1 Cor. 4:15), the thought of the church as his daughter sprang readily to mind. To be Christ's pure bride requires the church to have pure and simple devotion. Like a concerned father, Paul was worried that the young bride (the church) might commit adultery by her willingness to accept "another Jesus," "another Spirit," or "a different gospel" (2 Cor. 11:4).

In Ephesians 5:22–33, the relationship between Christ and His church is compared to the relationship between a husband and wife. The image is taken from the common understanding of the husband-wife relationship in Roman society at that time. The church's submission to Christ is compared with the wife's submission to the husband, but the stress of the passage is on the role of the husband: he is to love her as Christ loved the church and gave Himself up for her. The metaphor of the church as the Messiah's bride is further developed in Revelation 19:7–8 where the prophecy announces the marriage of the Lamb (Christ) to the bride (church). In Revelation 21 the vision depicts the New Jerusalem coming down from heaven, "made ready as a bride adorned for her husband" (Rev. 21:2). Then the apostle John is invited to look at "the bride, the wife of the Lamb" (Rev. 21:9). The New Jerusalem, the bride of Christ, is identified as the people of God among whom and with whom God will live forever. Christian believers past, present, and future can rejoice that this marriage will take place and can look forward expectantly to an eternal celebration with God.

KEY VERSES

Revelation 21:2, 9

Bridegroom

Greek expression: *numphios*
Pronunciation: *noom FEE awss*
Strong's Number: *3566*

B

In a wedding, all eyes focus on the beautiful bride. The bridegroom doesn't get the glory. In the kingdom of heaven, however, it is much different. The Bible shows us that Christ is the bridegroom and He is the glorious focal point of all His admirers.

The Greek word *numphios*, or "bridegroom," is found in both the Old and New Testaments. In the Old Testament, God is likened to a bridegroom and His people to a bride (Isa. 62:5; Jer. 3; Ezek. 16; Hos. 2). In the New Testament, John the Baptist, Jesus' forerunner, was the first one to recognize that Jesus was the Bridegroom. John, speaking of Jesus said, "The bride belongs to the bridegroom" (John 3:29, NIV). As such, Christ is the attractive One, the charming One, the lovely One—to whom all God's people, as His bride, should be attracted. John pictured himself as being the bridegroom's friend, or, as we would say in modern parlance, "the best man." As the best man, John enjoyed being with his friend, did not expect to receive any attention, and would rejoice with Him. John also implied that Jesus was the divine husband of God's people, as written in the Old Testament, and all of God's people belonged to Him. John was not the first to attribute the term and imagery of "bridegroom" to Jesus. John first heard Jesus use the term Himself. The text shows Jesus referring to Himself as the "bridegroom":

> Now John's disciples and the Pharisees were fasting. People came and asked Him, "Why do John's disciples and the Pharisees' disciples fast, but Your disciples do not fast?" Jesus said to them, "The wedding guests cannot fast while the groom is with them, can they? As long as they have the groom with them, they cannot fast.

> *(Mark 2:18-19, HCSB)*

When Jesus, the bridegroom, was present on earth, He considered it a time of great celebration—as in a wedding. No one fasts at a wedding. But the day would come when the bridegroom would be taken away. Then people would be sad and they would fast. The church today is glad to have the Bridegroom's spiritual presence. But we long for Jesus' actual, physical return. In that final day, we will meet our bridegroom and live with Him forever.

KEY VERSES

Mark 2:19–20;
John 3:29

Brothers

Greek expression: *adelphoi*
Pronunciation: *ah dehl FOY*
Strong's Number: *80*

Siblings of the same family have a right to call each other "brother" and "sister." Members of the same religious groups have assumed the same right. Jews at the time of Jesus frequently referred to themselves as brothers (Acts 2:29, 37; 7:2; 22:5; 28:21; Rom. 9:3), and from the beginning it seemed natural for Jewish Christians to call each other "brothers" (Acts 1:15–16; 9:30; 11:1). Members of Gentile religious communities also called each other brothers, so the name found a home in the Gentile churches as well (Acts 17:14; Rom. 1:13; 1 Cor. 1:1, 10). Along with the terms "disciple" (in Acts) and "saints," it was one of the most popular names for Christians and the only one used in James and 1 John. Each Christian was called "brother," and the Christians collectively were "the brothers." The name stressed the intimacy of the Christian community—that is, the relationship of believers to one another was as close as that of kin.

When *adelphoi* is used in the New Testament, it is often used to stress the equality among members of the Christian community. In the New Testament letters, when the apostles addressed their readers as "brothers," they were not speaking only to the male believers. In the early church, it is apparent that both male and female believers gathered together for fellowship (Acts 1:14; 12:12–13; 16:13; 17:12; 1 Cor. 11; Col. 4:15). It is also clear from a close reading of the epistles that Paul was speaking to both the men and women in the church (1 Cor. 7; 11; 14; Phlm. 1:1–2). At certain points in his letters, he would give specific admonitions to husbands or to wives (Eph. 5:22; Col. 3:18) and Peter did the same (1 Pet. 3:1, 7). This indicates that both men and women were included in Paul's audience, as well as Peter's. At other times, Paul would make direct appeals in his writing to certain female believers, such as Euodia and Syntyche (Phil. 4:2), or he would pass along his greetings to various female Christians, such as Priscilla, Junia, and Julia (Rom. 16:3, 7, 15). Thus in many biblical contexts, *adelphoi* should be understood as referring to both male and female believers within a Christian community.

KEY VERSES

Acts 1:15–16;
9:30; 11:1;
Romans 1:13;
1 Corinthians 1:1, 10

Calvary

See: *Golgotha, p. 293*

Chiefborn

See: *Firstborn, p. 281*

Christ

Greek expression: *Christos*
Pronunciation: *kree STAWSS*
Strong's Number: *5547*

Many say the name Jesus Christ without realizing that the title means Jesus "the Anointed One." The Greek word is *Christos*, which is a translation of the Hebrew word, *Messiah* (John 1:41). Both terms come from verbs meaning "to anoint with sacred oil"; hence, as titles they mean "The Anointed One."

In the Old Testament, *Messiah* was applied to prophets (1 Kgs. 19:16), priests (Lev. 4:5, 16), and kings (1 Sam. 24:6, 10). All of them were anointed with oil, which was the symbol that God had specifically chosen them for their respective offices. But the preeminent Anointed One would be the promised Messiah, for He would be anointed by God's Spirit to be the ultimate Prophet, Priest, and King (Isa. 61:1; John 3:34). In the New Testament, *Messiah* is used in combination with His "birth" name (Jesus) or with other titles: "Jesus Christ" (Matt. 1:1; Mark 1:1; Rom. 1:4), "Christ Jesus" (Rom. 1:1; 1 Cor. 1:1), with the article "the Christ" (Rom. 7:4), or with another title "Lord Christ" (Rom. 16:18). It is also used alone as the one favored substitute name or title for Jesus (John 20:31; Rom. 15:3; Heb. 3:6; 5:5; 1 Pet. 1:11, 19).

The Gospels portray Jesus as accepting the title and role of "Christ the Messiah." At His baptism by John, Jesus received the outpouring of the Spirit and God's mandate to begin His ministry (Matt. 3:16—4:17). Jesus' baptism should be understood as His anointing to the threefold office of Prophet, Priest, and King. John himself denied being the anointed one and identified Jesus as "the Christ" (John 1:20; Luke 3:14–17). Jesus' first disciples followed Him because they knew He was the Messiah (John 1:41). Though the crowds followed Jesus as the Prophet (John 6:14, 32), they deserted Him when they understood that His kingdom was a spiritual and not a political realm (John 6:66). The Twelve remained loyal, saying, "We believe . . . you are the Holy One of God" (John 6:69, NIV). The confession of the disciples voiced by Peter and approved by Jesus as a divine revelation is: "You are the Christ, the Son of the living God" (Matt. 16:16, NIV). Further proof of Jesus as the Messiah was during His trials before the crucifixion; the decisive factor in His condemnation was His claim to be "the Christ" (Matt. 26:63–64, 68; 27:11, 17, 22, 37).

KEY VERSES

Matthew 1:1; 16:16;
John 1:41;
Romans 1:1, 4

The title "Christ" occurs about 530 times in the New Testament; Paul used the title more than any other writer (about 380 times). Since Paul used this title so profusely in his letters, which are all dated between A.D. 50–65, it stands to reason that "Christ" was a very popular title for Jesus in the early years of the church. Thus, believers in the early church confessed their belief that Jesus was the Messiah the Old Testament prophesied about by calling Him the Christ.

Christian

Greek expression: *Christianos*
Pronunciation: *kree stee ah NAWSS*
Strong's Number: *5546*

Today, the name "Christian" means one who professes Christianity as their religion. It is even used to mean one who is "commendably decent or generous" (see *Webster's Ninth*). But the English word "Christian" comes from the Greek word *Christianos* and really means "one who belongs to Christ." It was first used as a term of contempt against the believers at Antioch (see Acts 11:26).

In the early days of the church, the believers did not have a distinctive name. They called each other "brothers" (Acts 6:3), "disciples" (Acts 6:1), "believers" (1 Tim. 4:12), followers of "the Way" (Acts 9:2), or "saints" (1 Cor. 1:2). The Jews who denied that Jesus was Christ, the Messiah, would never call believers "Christians," so they called them "the Nazarenes" (Acts 24:5). In Antioch, many Gentiles were converted and missionary work beyond the Jewish community began in earnest. The believers were consequently no longer considered a Jewish sect, and since members of the group constantly talked about Christ, the Gentiles in Antioch began calling believers "Christians."

Some satire may have been intended in the name. "Christ" was an unusual and meaningless name to Greeks, but *Chrestos*, which meant "good" or "kind," was a common name. Some Greeks therefore called the new sect *Chrestians*. Thus, Suetonius wrote of the Jews being expelled from Romanse in A.D. 49 on account of *Chrestus* (Christ). The believers themselves apparently did not appreciate the name, but, like many other nicknames, *Chrestian* or *Christian* stuck. *Christianos* appears only three times in the New Testament: Acts 11:26 describes its origin in Antioch; Acts 26:28 records Herod Agrippa II saying satirically to Paul, "In a short time, you will persuade me to become a Christian"; 1 Peter 4:16 instructs believers not to be ashamed if they suffer because the name "Christians" has been applied to them. No further record of the name appears until the second century, when Ignatius of Antioch became the first Christian to call believers by the title "Christians."

KEY VERSES

Acts 11:26; 26:28;
1 Peter 4:16

Church

Greek expression: *ecclēsia*
Pronunciation: *ehk klay SEE uh*
Strong's Number: *1577*

In the New Testament, the Greek word *ecclēsia*, usually translated "church," is primarily used in two ways: to describe a meeting or an assembly, and to designate the people who participate in assembling together (whether they are actually assembled or not). The New Testament contains a few places which speak of a secular Greek assembly (Acts 19:32, 41); everywhere else it depicts a Christian assembly. Sometimes the word *ecclēsia* is used to designate the actual meeting together of Christians. This is certainly what Paul intended in 1 Corinthians 14:19, 28, and 35, in which the expression *en ecclēsia* must mean "in a meeting" and not "in the church." It would be misleading to translate this phrase "in the church," as is done in most modern English versions, because most readers will think it means "in the church building." The New Testament never once names the "place" of assembly—a "church." Aside from the few instances where the word clearly means the actual meeting together of believers, *ecclēsia* most often is used as a descriptor for the believers who constitute a local church (such as the believers of the church in Corinth, the church in Philippi, and the church in Colossae), or all the believers (past, present, and future) who constitute the universal church—the complete body of Christ.

Thus, when reading the New Testament, Christians need to be aware of the various ways in which the word "church" is used. On the most basic level, the *ecclēsia* is any gathering of believers. On another level, the *ecclēsia* is an organized local entity, comprised of all the believers in any given locality. The *ecclēsia* is also the universal church whose constituents are all the believers who have ever been, are now existing, and will ever be. The New Testament writers used all of these various meanings of *ecclēsia*.

When the church first began in Jerusalem the believers met in homes for fellowship and worship. Acts 2:42–47 tells us that the early Christians met in homes to hear the apostles' teachings and to celebrate communion, which is called "the breaking of bread." During such gatherings the Christians often shared meals with one another in what was called a lovefeast (2 Pet. 2:13; Jude 12). They recited Scripture, sang hymns and psalms, and joyfully praised the Lord (Eph. 5:18–20; Col. 3:16–17). Christians also gathered together to pray (Acts 12:12) and read the Word. Small groups of believers met in homes for worship quite regularly; and in a city where there were several such *ekklēsiai*, all the believers would gather together for special occasions. Scripture tells us that they would often come together to hear an epistle from the apostles read out loud (Acts 15:30; Col. 4:16). According to Scripture, the church is fundamentally a gathering of believers dedicated to worship God and support each other in the Christian faith.

KEY VERSES

Acts 8:1;
Romans 16:1,
4–5, 16;
1 Corinthians 14:19,
28, 35

Circumcision

Greek expression: *peritomē*
Pronunciation: *peh ree toh MAY*
Strong's Number: *4061*

C

Circumcision today is nothing more than a medical procedure performed shortly after birth for hygienic reasons. In ancient times, however, circumcision, or *peritomē* in Greek, signaled a male's membership in the Jewish religion. The first Christians continued to participate in the Jewish rites and customs, even attending the services of the temple (Acts 3:1; 5:21, 42). As Gentiles came to Christ, controversy arose between those who said that circumcision was unnecessary, and those who believed that circumcision was necessary in order to participate in the covenant community. Some people argued that since the covenant promise of the Messiah was given to the Jews, Gentiles must first be circumcised and become Jews before they could receive salvation in Christ. Consequently, not all the Jewish believers were willing to accept Gentiles into the church.

Many Jews in Christ's day misunderstood the significance of circumcision, believing that the physical act was necessary for and a guarantee of salvation. Thus, observing the rite of circumcision became not only a symbol of religious privilege, but also a source of racial pride (Phil. 3:4–6). These Jews associated the ceremony with the Mosaic law rather than the promise to Abraham (John 7:22; Acts 15:1; Gen. 17:10–11). Because Greeks and Romans did not practice circumcision, Jews were called "the circumcision" (Acts 10:45; 11:2; Rom. 15:8; Gal. 2:7–9; Eph. 2:11), and Gentiles were called "the uncircumcision" (Gal. 2:7; Eph. 2:11).

While visiting Caesarea, Jewish believers were amazed to realize that uncircumcised Gentiles received the purifying gift of the Holy Spirit (Acts 10:44–48). When Peter returned to Jerusalem after his visit to Caesarea, "the circumcision party" criticized him; but after telling how the Spirit had fallen upon the Gentiles, Peter declared that he could not stand against God. At this, the Jewish believers were silenced and glorified God that repentance unto life had been granted to Gentiles (Acts 11:1–3, 15:18). But certain Judaizers of the Pharisaic party taught the Christians in Antioch that circumcision was necessary for salvation (Acts 15:1, 5). After debating these persons, Paul and Barnabas went to Jerusalem to consult with the other apostles and elders (Acts 15:2). Peter argued that God had given the Spirit to Gentiles and cleansed their hearts by faith, affirming that "we believe that we are saved through the grace of the Lord Jesus, in the same way as they also are" (Acts 15:11, NASB). Therefore, James and the other Jerusalem leaders agreed that circumcision should not be imposed on the Gentiles (Acts 15:13–21). It was decided that Peter, James, and John would be entrusted with the gospel to the circumcised, while Paul and Barnabas would preach to the uncircumcised (Gal. 2:7–9).

KEY VERSES

Romans 2:26–29;
Galatians 2:7–9

The teaching of the New Testament affirms that a faithful believer, though physically uncircumcised, is regarded by God as spiritually circumcised (Rom. 2:26–29). Both Jews and Gentiles are saved by grace (Acts 15:11) and circumcised and uncircumcised alike are justified on the ground of their faith, apart from obeying the law (Rom 3:28–30). People of the Old Testament were reminded of God's covenant through circumcision. Christians today have the knowledge of the Holy Spirit as well as the Bible to remind us that God's love for us is eternal.

Comforter

Greek expression: *paraklētos*
Pronunciation: *pahr AH klay tawss*
Strong's Number: *3875*

C

The Greek word *paraklētos* literally means "one who is called to our side." This could be a comforter, someone who consoles, or a defense attorney. The word denotes one who acts on someone else's behalf as a mediator, an intercessor, or an encourager. In John 14:26 and 15:26, the Holy Spirit is called our *paraklētos*, our "Comforter." While the Holy Spirit works within us to comfort and help us, Christ represents us before the Father in heaven. The two *Paraclētes*, or Comforters, work together in perfect harmony (Rom. 8:26, 27, 34). In 1 John 2:1, Christ is called a *paraclēte* because He represents people to God—similar to His ministry as High Priest (Heb. 7:25–28).

The most numerous uses of *paraclēte* come in John's Gospel which all refer to the work of the Holy Spirit (John 14:16, 26; 15:26; 16:13). In these passages Jesus declares that the Holy Spirit will come from the Father when He departs. The *paraclēte*, or Comforter, also called "the Spirit of truth," will lead them into all truth and aid them in their ability to recall Jesus' message correctly.

The crucial passage for understanding the identity of the "Comforter" is John 14:16–18. Jesus said that the Father would give the disciples "another Consoler," or "another Comforter." This expression, *allon paraklēton*, means "another comforter of the same kind as the first." This, of course, implies that Jesus was the first *Paraclēte* (1 John 2:1), and the Spirit would be the same kind of *Paraclēte*. In John 14:17, Jesus identifies the Comforter as the Spirit of truth, or even better, the Spirit of reality. Jesus declares, "you know Him because He abides with you, and will be in you." This statement indicates that the Spirit embodied in Jesus was not only then and there abiding with the disciples, but would also, in the future, abide "within" the disciples. In other words, the One who was with them would be in them. Notice the shift of pronouns from John 14:17 to John 14:18: "He abides with you, and will be in you . . . I will come to you." Who is the "He"? The Comforter, the Spirit. Who is the "I"? Jesus, the Son. Who would be coming to them, the Spirit or Jesus? Clearly, the answer is not either or—but both as One. Notice that further on, in John 14:20, the Lord says "I in you." Compare this to verse 17 where Jesus said that the Spirit "will be in you." When we put all these statements together, it should be clear that the Comforter is none other than the Lord Jesus in His spiritual form.

KEY VERSES

John 14:16, 26;
15:26; 16:7;
1 John 2:1

The Comforter who was with the disciples was the Spirit abiding in Christ, and the Comforter who would be in the disciples was Christ in and as the Spirit. From now until Christ physically returns, we are not alone. The Holy Spirit is by our side as a Comforter to direct and guide us, helping us to follow Jesus.

Coming

Greek expression: *parousia*
Pronunciation: *pahr* <u>oo</u> *SEE uh*
Strong's Number: *3952*

In the past century, thousands of papyrus manuscripts have been discovered in Egypt, many of which contain the Greek word *parousia* or "coming." The word literally means "presence" and is derived from *para*, meaning "with," and *ousia*, meaning "being." The word was commonly used in these Egyptian writings, which date in the era of Christ, to describe the visit of royalty or of some other important person. Thus, the word signaled an extraordinary "coming." The New Testament writers used the word to describe Christ's second coming when He would return to earth in His last and glorious visitation as the King over all.

Parousia can be translated in a number of different ways, depending on the context. It can mean "presence," "arrival," "appearance," or "coming." In the New Testament, we see its ordinary use, with reference to people going somewhere to be present with others (1 Cor. 16:17; 2 Cor. 7:6; 10:10; Phil. 1:26; 2:12). It was also used by Paul to speak of the coming of the antichrist (2 Thess. 2:9). Other than these occurrences, *parousia* was used with reference to Christ's second coming, but never His first coming (Matt. 24:3, 27, 37–39; 1 Cor. 15:23; 1 Thess. 2:19; 3:13; 4:15, 16; 5:23; 2 Thess. 2:1, 8). Consequently, the *parousia* now denotes the second coming of Christ at the end of the ages. Paul was most responsible for fleshing out the details of this "coming." While affirming that the exact time of Jesus' return is unknown (1 Thess. 5:1–2; 2 Thess. 2:2–3; Matt. 24:4–36), he otherwise painted a vivid picture of Jesus' second coming (1 Thess. 4:13–18; 2 Thess. 1:7–2:8; 1 Cor. 15:20–28, 50–55). According to Paul's teaching, it will be a visible, sudden, and glorious coming (1 Cor. 15:23; 1 Thess. 2:19; 3:13; 4:15–17).

At first, Paul felt he would experience Christ's return during his lifetime (Rom. 8:23; 13:11; 1 Thess. 4:15). But his approaching martyrdom caused him to moderate his thinking (Phil. 1:23). James also called for patience (Jas. 5:7–8), and Peter cautioned against allowing Christ's delay to create doubt (2 Pet. 3:8–10). A lot of time has passed since Jesus first came to earth, but we must not doubt or grow weary of following Christ—the Lord's day will come. Meanwhile, we must ready ourselves for His glorious arrival by reading God's Word and continuing to seek the Lord and His will for our lives (1 John 2:28).

KEY VERSES

1 Thessalonians
3:13; 4:15; 5:23;
2 Thessalonians
2:1, 8;
1 John 2:28

Confess

See also: *Confessing, p. 39*
Greek expression: *homologeō*
Pronunciation: *haw maw law GEH oh*
Strong's Number: *3670*

"Confess, confess!" Sounds like an interrogation scene, doesn't it? The word does have this negative connotation, but it also has a positive one. Confess means to declare affirmatively what one believes in. The Greek word *homologeō* literally means "saying the same thing"—that is, affirming one's agreement with a particular spiritual reality. We confess that we are sinners, and we confess (affirm) that Jesus is the Savior. These two kinds of confession occur in the Bible. First, individuals confess that they have sinned and are therefore guilty before God. Second, they confess that Jesus is Lord. One confession often leads to the other.

In the first kind of confession, one agrees or acknowledges that he has broken God's law and therefore deserves punishment (Rom. 6:23). Those who were baptized by John the Baptist publicly confessed their sins and repented (Mark 1:4–5). All Christians, in fact, must agree with God that they are sinners (1 John 1:8), and they are encouraged to confess their sins to God (1 John 1:9). James said that when a Christian is sick, the elders are to visit that person and give him an opportunity to confess any sins. In the same passage, James urged Christians to confess their sins to one another (Jas. 5:13–16).

The second, more positive meaning of the word, occurs frequently in the New Testament with respect to affirming one's faith in Christ. When Christians confess, they declare as a matter of conviction and allegiance that Jesus is the Christ and that they belong to Him. Jesus said, "Whosoever therefore shall confess me before men, him will I confess also before my Father which is in heaven" (Matt. 10:32, KJV). Refusal to confess Christ is the same as denying Him (Matt. 10:33; Luke 12:8; 2 Tim. 2:11–13; Rev. 3:5). The Christian life therefore begins with a confession of faith, a public declaration before witnesses (Rom. 10:9–10; 1 Tim. 6:12). An additional dimension of the Christian's confession is provided in 1 John 4:2. One must confess that "Jesus Christ has come in the flesh." A person must not only acknowledge that Jesus "has come" and confess belief in Jesus' divinity and preexistence as the Son of God, but also that He has come "in the flesh"—that is, confess belief in Jesus' incarnation.

KEY VERSES

Mark 1:4–5;
Romans 10:9–10;
1 Timothy 6:12;
1 John 1:9; 4:2

In the world today there are religions based on false prophets, the Bible tells us this is so, but some believers find it difficult to ascertain truth when the values and morals being taught by these religions seem to be in accordance with the Bible. However, as shown above, we can discern whether people have the spirit of God or not depending on their ability to proclaim that Jesus is indeed the Son of God (1 John 4:15).

Conform

Greek expression: *summorphizō*
Pronunciation: *sọọm mohr FEE dzoh*
Strong's Number: *4832*

Remember kindergarten, when we used to take a piece of clay, turn it into a particular shape by squishing the clay into a plastic mold, and then taking out the newly formed object? The clay was "conformed" from shapeless mass to a formed object. The Greek word for conform, *summorphizō* means "to take the form as another." The word is used in the writings of Paul to describe the spiritual process of molding the believer into the image of Jesus. In Romans 8:28–30, Paul writes:

> We know that all things work together for the good of those who love God: those who are called according to His purpose. For those He foreknew He also predestined to be conformed to the image of His Son, so that He would be the firstborn among many brothers. And those He predestined, He also called; and those He called, He also justified; and those He justified, He also glorified.

> *(Rom. 8:28-30, HCSB)*

Since it is God's desire and plan to have many sons and daughters, each believer has to be conformed to the prototype, Jesus. Note how the words "predestined," "called," "justified," and especially "glorified" in Romans 8:29 and 30 are in the past tense. The past tense is used because God, from His eternal perspective, has already seen this completed process. From God's perspective, believers have been glorified already because He sees them like His Son. But during their time on earth, believers must undergo the process of being conformed to the image of Jesus. God is working all things together in the lives of those who love Him and are called according to His purpose. His goal is to conform each son and daughter to the image of His beloved Son.

God will apply outward pressure to work the image of Christ into His children. It is quite evident throughout the rest of Romans 8 that He uses various kinds of suffering to conform Christians. Conformity to the image of Jesus necessitates learning what it means to share in His death (Phil. 3:10–11). To know Jesus, as far as Paul was concerned, was to know both the power of His resurrection and the fellowship of His sufferings (Phil. 3:10). The Lord Jesus, the pioneer of salvation, left His followers a pattern of suffering that cannot be avoided. God perfected Jesus through this path of sufferings (Heb. 2:10). Christians should expect to suffer, at least in part, some of the trials Jesus endured. Eventually, all the sufferings will be over and we will be glorified, even receiving a body that is conformed to Jesus' glorious body!

KEY VERSES

Romans 8:29;
Philippians 3:10, 21

Cornerstone

Greek expression: *gōnia, akrogōniaios*
Pronunciation: *goh NEE uh; ah kraw goh nee IGH awss*
Strong's Numbers: *1137, 204*

The most significant stone in important buildings is the cornerstone. Usually it is the first stone laid at a formal ceremony. Often it is engraved with the date of the building and perhaps some other ascription, honoring a person or an event. Thus, it should come as no surprise that Jesus is called the *gōnia* or "cornerstone" of the church. In fact, Jesus used this title for Himself. In the parable of the wicked tenants, which symbolizes Jesus' approaching death, He calls Himself the cornerstone that the builders had rejected (see Matt. 21:42; Mark 12:10; Luke 20:17). The setting for this parable was Jesus' final ministry in Jerusalem after He had cleansed the temple. In the parable, the tenants who were caring for the vineyard represented the Jewish leaders, and the vineyard symbolized God's people. The tenants wickedly refused to honor the owner, who represented God, ultimately putting the owner's son to death. Jesus concluded the parable by referring the Jewish leaders back to their own Scriptures, Psalm 118:2–23 (see also Isa. 28:16), which He understood as speaking of His rejection and exaltation. Jesus knew that although the Jewish leaders would reject Him, God would exalt Him as the cornerstone.

The term "cornerstone" is also used in Acts 4:11 by Peter in his defense before the Jewish rulers in Jerusalem. Peter explained to them that the lame beggar by the temple gate was healed by the name of Jesus Christ, the Nazarene whom they crucified but whom God raised from the dead (Acts 4:10). He then quoted Psalm 118:22 to confirm the events as being according to Scripture. It seems clear that Peter intended the rejection of the stone to refer to Jesus' death and the placing of the stone as the cornerstone to refer to Jesus' resurrection and exaltation. Peter combines the idea of the rejection of the stone in Psalm 118:22 with the idea of the chosen and precious stone in Isaiah 28:16 (1 Pet. 2:4, 6–7). Peter encouraged the believers to come to Jesus, that they may be built up as a spiritual house to God. This imagery is compatible with Ephesians 2:20, where Paul also declares that Christ Jesus is the cornerstone upon which the church is built. How wonderful it is to have a sure foundation for our faith, one that will never crumble!

KEY VERSES

Matthew 21:42;
Mark 12:10;
Acts 4:11;
Ephesians 2:20;
1 Peter 2:6–7

Cross

Greek expression: *stauros*
Pronunciation: *stow RAWSS*
Strong's Number: *4716*

C

We shudder when we look at the hangman's noose or an electric chair. They are modern symbols of execution. In ancient times, the symbol for execution was the cross or *stauros* in Greek. In the era of Jesus Christ (first century B.C. to first century A.D.), the cross was used to execute criminals and rebels. Crucifixion was a widespread form of execution and was used in most places in the Roman Empire, including India, North Africa, and Germany. Between 4 B.C. and A.D. 70, the number of people crucified at one time sometimes reached into the thousands.

Three types of crosses seem to have been used: a cross with the crossbar below the head of the upright bar (Latin cross); a T-shaped cross (St. Anthony's cross); and an X-shaped cross (St. Andrew's cross). At Jesus' crucifixion, Matthew records that the inscription, "This is Jesus the King of the Jews," was placed over Jesus' head (Matt. 27:37). This indicates that for Jesus' crucifixion a Latin cross was used, as artists have traditionally depicted. In crucifixions, the victim was most likely affixed to the cross while it was still lying flat on the ground. Then the cross was raised into position and dropped into a hole. The hands were either nailed or bound to the cross. It is uncertain whether the feet were nailed with one or two nails. The weight of the body was supported by a piece of wood at the feet and possibly by another that was like a spike between the legs. If the executioners wished a particularly slow, agonizing death, they might drive blocks or pins into the stake for a seat or a step to support the feet. Death came about through loss of blood circulation followed by coronary collapse. The process could take days. Often, the victim's legs would be broken below the knees with a club, causing massive shock and eliminating any further possibility of easing the pressure on the bound or spiked wrists. After death, the body was usually left on the cross to rot, but in some instances was given to relatives or friends for burial.

KEY VERSES

Matthew 27:32;
Mark 15:21;
John 19:17, 19

The crucifixion of Jesus combined Roman and Jewish elements. The Gospel writers, for their own polemical purposes, stressed that the Jewish religious leaders were guilty of Jesus' crucifixion. They were especially careful to distinguish between the leaders and the common people. It was the Jewish leaders who initiated Jesus' arrest (Mark 14:43) and His trial by the Sanhedrin (Mark 14:53–64). Though Pilate seemed to vacillate and in the end surrendered weakly to the crowds by "washing his hands" of any guilt (Matt. 27:24), Rome was also implicated in the crucifixion. Since the Sanhedrin did not have the power to inflict capital punishment, Pilate's decision was necessary before crucifixion could occur. Furthermore, the Roman authorities actually carried out the execution. So in the end, both Jew and Roman, both leaders and common people were guilty of murdering the Son of God.

For Christians, the cross became a symbol of adoration instead of horror because the cross represents Jesus' sacrificial death for humanity's sins. The cross has meaning because of the significance of Jesus who was put to death on it and because of what His death accomplished. The message of the cross was also central in the proclamation of the salvation message (see 1 Cor. 2:2). Above all, the event of the cross was God's principal saving act in history—hence the cross, though a past event, has present significance. Christ crucified and risen is the core of the church's message (Gal. 3:1).

C

261

Crucify

Greek expression: *stauroō*
Pronunciation: *stow RAW oh*
Strong's Number: 4717

The noun "cross," or *stauros* in Greek, and the verb "crucify," or *stauroō* in Greek, appear many times in the New Testament. Interestingly, there is no noun for the act of execution, or what we call "crucifixion." In all the accounts, the wording is either "the cross of Christ" or "Christ was crucified."

The four Gospels describe Jesus' crucifixion in great detail because it is the central theme of the Christian faith. Matthew and Mark show the horror of the Messiah being put to death by human beings. The first half of Mark's scene contrasts the taunts of the crowd with the true significance of Jesus' death. The second half of his description stresses the horror of the scene, progressing from a darkness motif, to the cry of abandonment, and then to further taunts (Mark 15:33–36). The Gospel of Matthew extends Mark's imagery, adding that Jesus refused the stupefying drink (a drugged wine to alleviate pain) (Matt. 27:34), as well as adding "yielded up His spirit" at the death scene (Matt. 27:50, NASB). Matthew emphasized that Jesus voluntarily faced His death fully conscious and in complete control of Himself. Matthew also stressed the disparity between Jesus' suffering and His vindication by alluding to two events: the ripping of the temple veil (Matt. 27:51) and the centurion's testimony (Matt. 27:54).

The account in Luke's Gospel has two major thrusts. First, Jesus is portrayed as the perfect example of the righteous martyr who forgives His enemies and by His attitude converts some of His opponents. The taunts of the rulers and soldiers are reversed when the crowd returns home "beating their breasts" (Luke 23:48) and the centurion cries, "Certainly this man was innocent!" (Luke 23:47). Second, in Luke the entire setting has an atmosphere of reverence and worship.

In the Gospel of John one finds a change of theological focus. John shows Jesus' sovereign control of His situation, as the crucifixion virtually becomes a coronation procession. John alone states that the inscription on the cross was written in Hebrew, Latin, and Greek—the charge thus becomes a worldwide proclamation of Christ's enthronement. The inscription, "Jesus of Nazareth, King of the Jews," continues Pilate's dialogue on kingship beyond Jesus' trial. John thus adds to Matthew's emphasis; Jesus had not only become King but had been Sovereign all along.

KEY VERSES

Matthew 27:35, 38;
Mark 15:24–25, 27;
Luke 23:33;
John 19:18, 20, 23

The apostle Paul considered himself to have been co-crucified with Christ. In spiritual union with Christ, Paul died when Christ died, "I have been crucified with Christ; and it is no longer I who live, but Christ lives in me" (Gal. 2:20). He considered this to be a spiritual reality in which all the believers have participated. Our old life of sin ended when Christ was crucified, for in His death He took us with Him (Col. 2:20).

Death

Greek expression: *thanatos*
Pronunciation: *THAHN uh tawss*
Strong's Number: *2288*

D

All of human life is lived under the shadow of death. The devil, who rules the world, is the lord of *thanatos*, which is the Greek word for "death" (Heb. 2:14). But Satan met his match: Jesus Christ conquered death once and for all on the cross (1 Cor. 15:26–27; Rev. 6:8; 20:13–14). Christ died, was buried, and rose again on the third day (Rom. 4:25; 1 Cor. 15:3–4; 1 Thess. 4:14). Through that historic event, the power of death was broken. The New Testament in various ways expresses Christ's subjection to death in payment for sin. He became obedient to death (Phil. 2:8); He died as a sacrifice for the sins of all (1 Cor. 5:7; 2 Cor. 5:15); and He descended into Hades, the place of the dead (1 Pet. 3:1–19). The major point of these passages is that Jesus did not remain dead. Instead, He defeated the devil on the cross, took the power (keys) over death, and ascended to heaven in victory (Heb. 2:14–15; Rev. 1:17–18).

Through God's eyes, the believer dies with Christ. The paradox is that through Jesus' death on the cross, believers are granted eternal life (2 Cor. 4:10). The apostle John expressed this death-life paradox somewhat differently. Jesus came into the world to give life to the dead, and all who put their trust in Jesus pass immediately from death to life (John 5:24). In other words, those who obey Jesus' teachings will never see death (John 8:51–52). Those who are outside Christ are already dead, and those trusting in Christ are already enjoying eternal life.

Believers who experience physical death are not separated from Christ—that is, they are not really dead. All the powers of death and hell cannot separate believers from Christ (Rom. 8:38–39). For them, death is not a loss but a gain; it brings them closer to Christ (2 Cor. 5:1–10; Phil. 1:20–21). What is more, believers will share in Christ's victory over physical death as well. Jesus is the "firstfruits" of those rising from the dead (1 Cor. 15:20; Col. 1:18) and those "in Christ" will rise on the last day to be with Him. However, for those who do not belong to Christ, there is a final, total separation from God. At the last judgment, all whose names "were not written in the book of life" are consigned to a lake of fire, in the company of death itself and Hades. The first death is when they leave their earthly bodies—that final separation from God on Judgment Day is called the "second death" (Rev. 20:14).

KEY VERSES

Hebrews 2:14–15;
Revelation 1:17–18

Demon

Greek expression: *daimonion*
Pronunciation: *digh MOH nee awn*
Strong's Number: *1140*

Cartoons typically depict demons as small, red, horned beings with a pointed tail and a pitchfork. But what does the Bible say about who and what demons are? Surprisingly, the Bible does not spend a lot of time on demons. The English word "demon" comes from the Greek word *daimon*. In Greek literature, this word depicts a god or deity. But in the Greek New Testament, such entities are considered false deities (see 1 Cor. 10:20). Any deity other than the one true God is a spirit opposed to Him—therefore, such a demon is an evil spirit. In fact, in the New Testament the titles "evil spirit" and "demon" can be used interchangeably. The word "demon" does not appear in the King James Version, which translates *daimon* as "devil." Yet according to the Greek text, there is only one devil (which in Greek is *diabolos*), who is known by a variety of names, titles, and epithets in the Bible.

We know that Satan is the ruler of all demons, who are subject to him (Matt. 12:24–27). It is believed that these demons may be fallen angels, but this is never explicitly said in the Bible. Ephesians 6:12 suggests an order or rank of demons: "against the rulers, against the powers, against the world forces of this darkness, against the spiritual forces of wickedness in the heavenly places" (Eph. 6:12, NASB). Their allegiance is to the devil, whom they serve out of fear and delusion. Their purpose is to carry out the schemes of Satan and to oppose God. They tempt, deceive, and delude people so as to bring them to eternal damnation. In opposing God, they attack, oppress, hinder, and accuse the people of God. They also can possess people (demon-possession) so as to incapacitate them in one fashion or another—whether in body or in mind.

In the end, demons will be eternally punished. Jesus spoke of the eternal fire prepared for the devil and his angels (presumably demons), into which the cursed among men and women are also to go (Matt. 25:41). Eventually, Satan and his host will be thrown into the lake of fire (Rev. 20:10), which is also the place of eternal torment for all whose names are not written in the book of life (Rev. 20:12–15).

KEY VERSES

Matthew 12:24, 27;
1 Corinthians 10:20

Descend

Greek expression: *katabainō*
Pronunciation: *kah tuh BIGH noh*
Strong's Number: *2597*

D

The Greek word *katabainō* means simply to "go down." Anyone departing from Jerusalem was said to "go down," just as anyone visiting Jerusalem was said to "go up." This reflects the geography of the holy lands. Christ made two significant descents in His lifetime, and He is yet to make a third. First, Jesus descended from heaven to earth. Second, He descended from earth to Hades (the place of the dead) after His death and burial. Third, He will descend from heaven a second time when He returns.

The first descent, from heaven to earth by becoming incarnated in human flesh, was questioned and doubted by the Jewish leaders who encountered Jesus. They wondered how He could have claimed to come down from heaven when they knew who Jesus' parents were (John 6:42). Only those who knew His true Father knew His heavenly origin and that Jesus had "come down" from heaven. The second descent was made when Jesus visited the underworld after His death and burial, prior to His resurrection. This descent is based on Ephesians 4:8-10. Some scholars see this passage as indicating that Christ descended into Hades (the place of the dead), liberated souls from death, and led them to heaven. The "lower, earthly regions" is identified with Hades and the "captives" with the throng of Old Testament believers whom Christ released from their waiting stance and triumphantly conducted into full fellowship with God. A related passage is 1 Peter 3:18-20, in which Christ is said to have gone and "preached to the spirits in prison—those who disobeyed God long ago" in the time of Noah.

The third descent of Christ is made very plain in the Scriptures. We are told that Jesus Christ will physically descend from heaven in His *parousia* or second coming (see "Coming"; 1 Thess. 4:16). Those of us who are alive today did not witness His first or second descent, but we may see His third. Jesus exhorts us to be prepared for it (see Luke 12:40).

KEY VERSES

John 6:42;
Ephesians 4:9–10;
1 Thessalonians
4:16

Destroy, destruction

Greek expression: *apōleia, olethros*
Pronunciation: *ahp OH lay uh; AWL eh thrawss*
Strong's Numbers: *684, 3639*

It is not uncommon to hear a football team say to another team, "We're out to destroy you!" Destroy in this context does not mean "annihilate," but rather "do some serious damage." Yet, if a general of the army says, "We must destroy the enemy," he intends to "annihilate" the enemy. Both these meanings for destroy can be found in the Greek New Testament.

The stronger Greek term, akin to "annihilate," is *apōleia*. It is frequently used in the New Testament to denote eternal destruction, or what is called perdition—a term used in the King James Version to express the eternal aspect of the destruction of life and self. In Philippians 1:28, "perdition" is the opposite of "salvation." Hebrews 10:39 contrasts it with "preserving one's soul." Second Peter 3:7 links perdition with the Day of Judgment, while 1 Timothy 6:9 implies both present and future destruction. The term "son of perdition" is a label affirming the destiny of both the betrayer Judas (John 17:12) and the antichrist (2 Thess. 3:2). In Revelation 17:8, 11, perdition designates the final abode of the beast, which is the "lake of fire," a place of everlasting torment (Rev. 19:20; 20:10). Furthermore, the verb form of *apōleia* (*apōllumi*) is found quite frequently in the New Testament and has traditionally been translated as "perish." For example, John writes in the famous Gospel verse: "For God loved the world in this way: He gave His only Son, so that everyone who believes in Him will not perish but have eternal life" (John 3:16, HCSB). From this verse, it is clear that perishing is the opposite of enjoying eternal life.

The other Greek word for destroy, *olethros*, does not mean annihilation, but the loss of everything worthwhile. In 1 Corinthians, Paul used the word to speak of the temporal and devastating consequences of sin (1 Cor. 5:5). In 1 Timothy 6:9, Paul used the same word to refer to the eternal consequences of sin. Although the penalty for sin is not annihilation, it is severe—namely, eternal ruin and eternal separation from Christ. Just as endless life belongs to Christians, endless ruin belongs to those who are opposed to Christ.

KEY VERSES

1 Corinthians 5:5;
1 Thessalonians 5:3;
1 Timothy 6:9

Disciple

Greek expression: *mathētēs*
Pronunciation: *mah thay TAYSS*
Strong's Number: *3101*

In the New Testament, the Greek word *mathētēs*, which means "disciple," is found exclusively in the Gospels and the book of Acts. Although Paul never uses the term, he often describes those who had the characteristics of being disciples. In the Gospels the immediate followers of Jesus are called "disciples" and include the twelve in His inner circle, plus the other seventy-two.

During Jesus' time on earth, other teachers had disciples—most notable were the Pharisees (Mark 2:8; Luke 5:33) and John the Baptist (Matt. 9:14). It is evident from the practice of John the Baptist that different teachers called for different disciplines from their followers. John's way was considerably more ascetic in character than that of Jesus (Matt. 9:14). John's teaching not only covered conduct and manner of life, but also a distinctive pattern of praying (Luke 11:1).

The disciples of Jesus had a unique experience. They benefited from the immediate teaching of Jesus (Mark 10:21), but were also witnesses of the unfolding drama of God's plan of salvation. They followed a teacher who embodied the substance of His teaching. Christ taught the first disciples little by little—not only because He had to remove their misconceptions (Matt. 16:21), but also because the full significance of what Jesus said could not be fully appreciated until after the events of His death and resurrection (Matt. 28:9).

Groups of Jesus' first disciples—both the twelve disciples and the seventy-two disciples (Matt. 26:20; Luke 10:1)—received Jesus' teaching, taught others (Luke 10:1–11), were given power to heal (Matt. 10:1), and were sent to other cities to proclaim the message of salvation. Yet, the twelve were given special prominence and with the exception of Judas Iscariot (whose place was taken by Matthias, Acts 1:26), they became the primary teachers of the newly emerging Christian church after Jesus' death. Their authority in the church, given by Christ (Matt. 16:19; 28:16–20), was characterized by a unique style of self-giving service (Luke 22:24–30). To this group of disciples, who came to be known as "the apostles," Saul of Tarsus was added. At Saul's conversion on the road to Damascus, Christ Himself appeared and commissioned Saul (later renamed Paul) as the apostle to the Gentiles (Acts 9:15; Gal. 1:12, 16).

KEY VERSES

Matthew 10:1;
28:16;
Acts 6:2, 7

At the time of Jesus' ascension, Christ commissioned the first disciples to "make disciples of all nations" (Matt. 28:19)—hence, the term *disciple* is also used in the book of Acts to describe believers. Though Christ has not directly called believers, we are called by Christ's Spirit through the message delivered by the first disciples. We too are to "make disciples of all nations," spreading the gospel so that no one can claim they "never knew about Jesus."

Divine, divinity

Greek expression: *theios*
Pronunciation: *THAY awss*
Strong's Numbers: *2304, 2305*

The word *God* (*theos*) saturates the writings of the New Testament. Two other related words connote the nature of God—what we call in English "divine" or "divinity." The word first appears in the book of Acts, in Paul's speech to the Athenians, who had erected a monument to an unknown God. This God, whom Paul called "deity," is not far from any of us, human beings. Paul proclaimed that God has placed within each one of us the sense to worship and seek Him. We grope for Him by creating images to worship—whether it be a piece of stone or personal pleasures. Without revelation from God, we would always be worshiping an unknown God. Paul's whole point is that God is not far away. He wants to fellowship with us. In fact, every day we are absolutely dependent upon him for our existence (see Acts 17:22–33).

Paul, again speaking about God's manifest presence in the world, said, "For since the creation of the world His invisible attributes, His eternal power and divine nature, have been clearly seen, being understood through what is made, so that they are without excuse" (Rom. 1:20, NASB). No one can look at creation and deny the presence of a divine Creator because His divine power and nature are revealed in what He has made.

While unbelievers should recognize God's divinity through His creation, believers can actually partake of the divine nature and power. Peter clearly states this in his second letter (2 Pet. 1:3–5). The divine power is the power God used in raising Christ from the dead and that same power is available to the church (Eph. 1:19–20). This divine power has provided us with the spiritual dynamo to live a godly life. The divine nature is the nature that characterizes God—the nature that is expressed in holiness, virtue, righteousness, love, and grace (see 2 Pet. 1:5–7). By being regenerated with the divine nature, believers can exhibit these same characteristics. Any failure to live a godly life is due to our weakness or folly and not to God's lack of supply. According to Peter, this power is meted to us as our experiential knowledge of God and Jesus increases, and we thereby become a partaker of God's divine nature.

KEY VERSES

Acts 17:29;
Romans 1:20;
2 Peter 1:3–5

Divorce

See also: *Marry and Divorce, p. 332*
Greek expression: *apostasion*
Pronunciation: *ah paw STAH see awn*
Strong's Number: *647*

D

In the account of creation in Genesis, marriage is defined as the "one flesh" union established by God (Gen. 2:24). During His ministry, Jesus affirmed this aspect of God's original design for marriage (Matt. 19:6). Jesus said that God's original design preceded and preempted Moses' law, wherein there was allowance for "divorce," or *apostasion* in Greek. According to Moses' law, a man could give his wife a certificate of "divorce" (Matt. 5:31; 19:7; compare Deut. 24:1–4). The certificate of divorce protected the woman's rights by providing evidence of her freedom and ensuring that her husband could not claim her dowry. Jesus spoke against this certificate by stating that "from the beginning it has not been this way" (Matt. 19:8).

In Matthew 5:31–32, Jesus explicitly abolished the Mosaic legislation that allowed men to divorce their wives. He viewed the practice as a violation of the integrity of women. Adulterous men who divorce their wives reduce them to the status of adulteresses. By marrying a woman discarded from a previous marriage, a man perpetuates the demeaning process and becomes guilty of adultery. Jesus deliberately withdrew from men the right of discarding a wife at will and reinstated the original pattern of the lifelong "one flesh" union. His disciples understood His intent accurately. But the principle of male privilege was so deeply ingrained in their mentality that they declared that the freedom available in celibacy was preferable to a commitment to lifelong monogamous marriage (Matt. 19:10).

Despite such strong sanctions for the permanency of the marriage bond, the New Testament permits divorce, but only as an exception intended to protect the innocent spouse in the case of immorality and desertion. Jesus made exceptions that established the right of a spouse wronged by an unfaithful mate (Matt. 5:32; 19:9). The wronged spouse has the option of maintaining the marriage bond, despite the breach of commitment by the unfaithful mate. The other exception that justifies divorce, according to the New Testament, is desertion. Although the provisions of 1 Corinthians 7:15 refer primarily to desertion by an unbelieving spouse, it should be noted that a believer guilty of desertion is to be treated as an unbeliever (1 Tim. 5:8). Abandonment of the marriage relationship constitutes a breach of conjugal commitment.

KEY VERSE

Matthew 5:31

In either case, adultery or desertion, the aggrieved spouse has the right to seek divorce from the offending spouse and, having obtained it, becomes a single person again. According to Scripture, a person who is not bound to the marriage is free to remarry, but only "in the Lord," meaning to another Christian (1 Cor. 7:39).

Down payment, pledge

Greek expression: *arrabōn*
Pronunciation: *ar-hrab-OHN*
Strong's Number: *728*

In ancient times, people showed their intent to purchase a property or land by providing a down payment. In the Greek language, this was called an *arrabōn*. At the same time, the word was used to designate a sampling of what was purchased. Thus, in the purchase of a property the buyer could make a down payment for the land and the seller could give the buyer a sampling of the soil he was about to buy. Both were called an *arrabōn*. The word was also used to designate an engagement ring, whereby a man could show a woman his intentions to marry her.

Paul used this word three times to describe God's gift of the Holy Spirit to the believers. In 2 Corinthians 1:21–22, Paul tells the believers that God has anointed them, sealed them (that is, marked them as his own), and given them the Holy Spirit as an earnest or down payment. The Holy Spirit is a gift from God that demonstrates his earnestness to give us full salvation. The presence of the Holy Spirit is also a foretaste of what we will receive from God in eternity.

In 2 Corinthians 5, Paul goes on to explain what God has prepared for us in the future: he will give us a new, glorified body to experience a new spiritual life in eternity. And how do we know that he will give us this: we know it because we have the down payment, the earnest—the Holy Spirit whom God has put into our hearts.

In Ephesians 1:13–14, Paul tells us this: "after listening to the message of truth, the gospel of your salvation—having also believed, you were sealed in Him with the Holy Spirit of promise, who is given as a pledge of our inheritance, with a view to the redemption of God's own possession, to the praise of His glory" (NASB). These verses tell us that our faith in Christ was compensated by a wonderful gift: the promised Holy Spirit. This Spirit, given as God's down payment, is a pledge from God indicating that we will receive the full inheritance of all God's riches. The best is yet to come—and we know it will come—because we have the down payment, the Holy Spirit.

KEY VERSES

2 Corinthians
1:21–22; 5:5;
Ephesians 1:13–14

Elect

Greek expression: *eklektos*
Pronunciation: *ehk lehk TAWSS*
Strong's Number: *1588*

Every year or so American citizens have the right to participate in elections. This is the process whereby votes are cast by a group of people to select one representative. An element of choice is involved, since usually there are several candidates out of whom one must be chosen. When the Greek verb *eklektos*, which means "elect," is used in the Bible, it usually has God as its subject. He is the one making the selections.

In Old Testament times, God selected the children of Israel to be His people (Acts 13:17). They became His people not because they decided to belong to Him, but because God took the initiative and chose them. The same thoughts are found in the New Testament. God's people are described as His "elect" or "chosen ones." Jesus used this term when speaking of His future return when, as the Son of Man, He will gather God's people together (Mark 13:20, 27). Jesus will vindicate them for their sufferings and for their patience in waiting for His coming (Luke 18:7). In 1 Peter 2:9, God's people are called an "elect nation."

In Romans 9—11, Paul discusses why the Gentiles have accepted the Gospel, while the people of Israel, as a nation, have rejected it. He states that in the present time there is a "remnant" of Israel as a result of God's gracious choice of them. This group is called "the elect." They are the chosen people who have obtained what was meant for Israel as a whole, while the greater mass of people have failed to obtain it because they were hardened as a result of their sin (Rom. 11:5–7). Nevertheless, God's choice of Israel to be His people has not been canceled. Most Jewish people have aligned themselves against the gospel, and Gentiles may receive God's blessings in their place; but Jews are still loved by God, and God will not go back on His original calling of them (Rom. 11:28). Consequently, Paul is confident that in due time there will be a general return to God by the people of Israel.

Eklektos is generally found in the plural and refers either to the "members of God's people as a whole" or to "those in a particular local church." The singular form of the verb is found only in Romans 16:13 and 2 John 13. The use of the plural may partly be explained by the fact that most of the New Testament letters are addressed to groups of people rather than to individuals. More probably, however, the point is that God's election is concerned with the creation of a collective people rather than the calling of isolated individuals.

KEY VERSES

Romans 8:33;
Colossians 3:12;
2 Timothy 2:10;
Titus 1:1;
1 Peter 1:1

271

Element

Greek expression: *stoicheiōn*
Pronunciation: *stoy KAY awn*
Strong's Number: *4747*

"Elementary principles" in English is a phrase used to describe the building blocks for further development of a given subject. The Greeks used the word *stoicheia* to mean "elementary or rudimentary principles," but the word can also be used for the "physical elements" of the world: earth, water, air, fire, or it could even mean "elemental spirits." All three meanings are found in the New Testament writings, but it is not always clear which meaning is intended.

In three passages, the meaning of *stoicheiōn* is clearly "physical elements" (Heb. 5:12; 2 Pet. 3:10–12). In antiquity, the word also commonly referred to the letters in a word, notes in music, the "elementary" rules of politics, or the basic principles in science, art, or teaching. "Elementary principles" clearly was the meaning of the word in the letter to the Hebrews, which describes people's need to have someone teach them the elementary truths of God's Word (Heb. 5:12).

However, the meaning of *stoicheiōn* in four other passages, all in Paul's writings, have caused considerable debate. The difficult phrase "the elements of the world" appears in three of the four passages (Gal. 4:3; Col. 2:8, 20). The meaning of "elements" in the fourth passage (Gal. 4:9) is probably the same as in the other three because of its similar context. The difficulty with Paul's use of "elements" is that any of the three possible meanings makes sense. One can understand "elements" to mean spiritual beings and view Paul's reference to "elements" as similar to his mention of the principalities and powers (that is, in Eph. 6:12). Translating Galatians 4:3 according to this view (as in RSV), Paul would be saying that before conversion a person is enslaved to evil spiritual forces. Thus, in Galatians 4:9, he asks how the Galatians could ever want to be enslaved to these forces again. Paul's references in this passage to "beings that by nature are no gods" (Gal. 4:8) and to angels through whom the law was mediated (Gal. 3:19) are both used to substantiate the meaning of "elemental spirits." Similarly, Colossians 2:8 would be warning Christians against being led captive through the philosophical speculations and empty deceit that are perpetrated by human traditions and elemental spirits. It is only two verses later in which Paul declares that Christ is the head of every principality and power (Col. 2:10). But other biblical scholars understand "the elements of the world" to refer to elementary religious teaching (as in Heb. 5:12). Thus, Paul may have been appealing to the "ABC's of religion," or perhaps to the elementary character of the Law (Gal. 3:24; 4:1–4), or to pagan religious teaching (Gal. 4:8). Similarly, in Colossians "the elements of the world" seem to be parallel to mere human traditions (Col. 2:8).

KEY VERSES

Galatians 4:3, 9;
Colossians 2:8, 20;
Hebrews 5:12;
2 Peter 3:10

Whether *stoicheia* refers to spiritual elements, human traditions, or basic religious teaching—the bondage Paul warned against is bondage to elementary religious thinking, which comes from people or spiritual forces against God. Bondage to such thinking would be equivalent to remaining at a kindergarten level of thought, instead of learning the advanced teaching of Christ. As mature believers, we ought to always be on guard for false teaching. We need to filter what we hear and experience with what we know for certain from the Bible.

Epistle

Greek expression: *epistolē*
Pronunciation: *eh pee stawl AY*
Strong's Number: *1992*

We write each other letters, so did people in the days when Jesus walked the earth. They called these letters "epistles." The Greek word *epistolē* has transferred into English as "epistle." It signifies a "written letter," whether a personal correspondence, as in the small epistles of 2 and 3 John (2 John 12; 3 John 13), an official correspondence (as in Acts 15:30; 22:5; 23:25, 33), or a formal treatise as in Romans (Rom. 16:22). Sometimes letters of recommendation were sent along with emissaries in order to establish their credentials among those they were visiting. In 2 Corinthians, Paul called the believers in Corinth his "epistles," or his living letters of recommendation from God (2 Cor. 3:1–3).

The usual procedure for a dictated epistle was for the amanuensis, or scribe, to take down the speaker's words in shorthand. Then, the scribe would produce a transcript, which the author would then review, edit, and sign in his own handwriting. Two New Testament epistles provide the name of the amanuensis: Tertius for Romans (Rom. 16:22) and Silvanus for 1 Peter (1 Pet. 5:12). Four of Paul's epistles indicate that he provided the concluding salutation in his own handwriting: 1 Corinthians 16:21, Galatians 6:11, Colossians 4:18, and 2 Thessalonians 3:17. He said that he did this at the end of all his epistles to authenticate them and guard against forged letters circulating (2 Thess. 3:17). At any rate, the only epistles that might have been initially produced in multiple copies were Ephesians (written as a letter for circulation among many churches) and Revelation (Rev. 1:11). Each of the other books was probably produced as one original manuscript, which was later reproduced in multiple copies.

Paul observed, with some care, the forms of letter writing common in his day. There is an opening word of salutation, followed by thanksgiving and prayer for the person or company addressed. Then, he explains the special subject he wants to communicate to his readers, greets friends, and perhaps a closing word of prayer. John's two short epistles (2 John and 3 John), and especially the third, follow the pattern of letter writing in the first century.

KEY VERSES

2 Corinthians 3:1–3;
2 Thessalonians
2:2, 15;
2 Peter 3:1, 16

Eternal

Greek expression: *aiōnios*
Pronunciation: *igh OH nawss*
Strong's Number: *166*

E

The desire to live eternally is not merely modern desire—it's as old as the Egyptian pharaohs, who built pyramids to secure eternal significance, and Ponce de Leon, who looked for the elusive fountain of youth. Who doesn't want to live forever? But what does it mean to have eternal life?

The Bible's concept of eternity stands in contrast to that of other ancient cultures. The ancients typically thought of eternity in cyclical terms. For example, many Greeks thought time was an ever-recurring, circular sequence of events. Consequently, salvation meant finding an exit from that vicious cycle and freeing oneself from time in order to experience timelessness. The biblical concept of time is not a circle—but a line with a beginning and an end guaranteed by the eternal God.

The contrast between Greek and biblical ways of viewing time raises the question of the exact nature of "eternity." Is it to be understood as merely unlimited time? Or should it be understood in direct contrast to present time, simply as timelessness? The biblical view seems to be that eternity is not timelessness. Eternity does not stand in contrast to present time as its opposite, because present time and eternity share certain basic qualities. The New Testament uses the Greek words for "eon" or "age" to divide time into "this present eon," and *aiōnios* which means "the eon that is about to be" or "the coming eon." The contrast is not simply between time and timelessness, for the "eon that is about to be" is future and shares a specific and identifiable character. Eternity, or "the new age," is not simply restoring time to the primitive innocence of an earlier stage, but a consummation of how time is meant to be according to the purposes of Him who is and who was and who is to come (Rev. 1:4). Thus, eternal time, or *aiōnios*, is designated as a new creation—something "about to be." The New Testament clearly teaches that the "age that is to be" already began in the life and ministry of Christ, although there is a definite overlap in the two ages. For example, the believer can enjoy the blessings of the future age even now, as portrayed by the writers of Hebrews 6:5: "who have tasted the word of God and the powers of the coming age" (NIV).

KEY VERSES

John 3:15–16;
1 Timothy 1:16;
1 John 5:11, 13

The concept of eternity, then, does not stand in opposition and in contrast to time as timelessness. Eternity is the unlimited and incalculable space of time bounded at its beginning by the introduction of the kingdom of God in Christ and stretching out into the unlimited future. Both time, or "the present evil age" (Gal. 1:4), and eternity are governed by God as the Lord of all time—the one who gives content and meaning to both. As believers in Christ, we have eternal life and will indeed live forever with Him.

Eternal life

Greek expression: *aiōnios zoē*
Pronunciation: *igh OH nee awss; dzoh AY*
Strong's Numbers: *166, 2222*

"I wanna live forever" are lyrics in many rock songs. Who doesn't? Ever since the beginning of time men and women have wanted to find a way to live forever. But there is only one way: Jesus Christ, who is the Way, the Truth, and the Life. The Greek word *aiōnios* which is translated "eternal" is derived from the Greek word for "age" or "eon" (*aiōn* or *aiōnios*). The Greeks thought of eternity as continuous, successive, unending ages. A modern English idiom close to this idea is "forever and ever."

The Greek word for "life" is *zoē*. In classical Greek, the word was used for life in general. There are a few examples of this meaning in the New Testament (Acts 17:25; James 4:14: Rev. 16:3), but in all other instances the word was used by the New Testament writers to designate the divine, eternal life—the life of God (Eph. 4:18). This life resided in Christ, and He made it available to all who believe in Him. Human beings are born with the natural life which is called *psuchē* in Greek (translated "soul," personality," or "life"); they do not possess the eternal life. This life can be received only by believing in the one who possesses the *zoē* or "life," namely, Jesus Christ.

This theme is thoroughly developed in the Gospel of John. John's purpose in writing his Gospel was explicitly stated at the end of his work: "But these are written that you may believe that Jesus is the Christ, the Son of God, and that by believing you may have life in His name" (John 20:31, NASB).

The central emphasis of John's Gospel on "eternal life" is that the life of the age to come is already available in Christ to the believer. The metaphors with which Jesus defined His own mission emphasize the present new life: living water that is a spring of water welling up to eternal life (John 4:10–14); living bread that satisfies the world's spiritual hunger (John 6:35–40); the light of the world who leads His followers into the light of life (John 8:12); the good shepherd who brings abundant life (John 10:10); the life giver who raises the dead (John 11:25); the way, the truth, and the life (John 14:6); and the genuine vine who sustains those who abide in him (John 15:5).

KEY VERSES

John 3:15–16, 36

Jesus was very careful to note that the accomplishment of His mission did not rest in His own nature and ability, but in the Father who sent Him. Jesus' submission to the Father highlights again the fact that life is a gift of God. Those who believe in the Son of God are recipients of the life that God alone gives—eternal life.

Example

Greek expression: *tupos, hupogrammos*
Pronunciation: *TOO pawss; hoo paw grahm MAWSS*
Strong's Numbers: *5179, 5261*

E

In our day and age, we expect public officers and professional athletes to be role models. Anticipating that they will be good examples, we look up to them. The Bible presents the same concept. Paul told the Thessalonians that he set an example for them (2 Thess. 3:9). He also told the Philippians to follow his example of life (Phil. 3:17). Peter told church leaders that they should be exemplary models for the church members in their care (1 Pet. 5:3). The Bible also tells us that we should follow Jesus' model of suffering and thereby become a model to others. Nobody likes to suffer, but suffering is good for us. God uses it to make us like Jesus. In fact, Jesus Himself suffered greatly, and thereby became a model for us.

There are two Greek words, which pertain to being a model or "example" for others. The first Greek word, *hupogrammos,* means "model" and occurs only once in the New Testament. First Peter 2:21 says, "For you have been called for this purpose, since Christ also suffered for you, leaving you an example for you to follow in His steps" (NASB). The Greek word underlying "example," *hupogramma,* designated a tracing tablet that contained the entire Greek alphabet. Students would have to learn each letter, from alpha to omega, by tracing the letters one by one. The life of Jesus, a life of suffering, is a tracing tablet as well. Those who learn to follow Jesus will be those who know what it is to suffer, for suffering is the means by which God conforms us to the image of Jesus.

The other Greek word for "example" is *tupos.* It appears sixteen times in the New Testament and is derived from the root *tup* meaning "a blow." Thus, the word depicts the impression from a blow and came to mean "type," "example," or "model." In 1 Thessalonians 1:7, Paul tells the church in Thessalonica: "you became an example to all the believers in Macedonia and in Achaia" (NRSV). Collectively speaking, the church at Thessalonica was a model to the other churches in the region. Thessalonica was not only the largest city in Macedonia and the capital of the province, but also the center of evangelistic activity in the region. The extraordinary perseverance in the faith of the members of that church, while being persecuted by Jews, made their church an example for others.

KEY VERSES

1 Corinthians 10:6;
1 Thessalonians 1:7;
2 Thessalonians 3:9;
1 Peter 2:21

Unbelievers are always watching us, curious as to what makes us different, or eager to point out our mistakes and shortcomings. In Luke 12:48, Jesus says, "to whom they entrusted much, of him they will ask all the more." We have been given much—Jesus Christ, eternal life, and the message of salvation. We must, therefore, respond to this higher calling, by embracing our responsibility to be Christ-like role models for others.

Exodus, departure

Greek expression: *exodos*
Pronunciation: *EHKSS aw dawss*
Strong's Number: *1841*

In English, we have several euphemisms for death. After someone dies, we say, "he passed away," "she's gone to the other side," "he's gone to heaven," "she's with the Lord now," and so on. The Jews had an interesting euphemism: "he's gone to be with his fathers." The New Testament writers also had a particular euphemism for death and would frequently say, "he fell asleep." In a few rare occurrences, however, the New Testament writers spoke of death as "an exodus." The Greek word *exodus* literally means "the way out" or "the road out." The exodus is a picturesque euphemism for death because it depicts a road leading from this life to the next.

The word *exodus* is used only three times in the New Testament: once to speak of the Israelites' exodus from Egypt (Heb. 11:22), and twice to speak of death—Jesus' and Peter's. When Jesus was transfigured before three of His disciples (James, John, and Peter), Elijah and Moses appeared with Jesus and spoke with Him about His upcoming "exodus" or "departure." Having already made their own exodus from earth to heaven, they were anticipating Jesus' exodus via His death and resurrection. Jesus was about to make a great transition—from His existence on earth in a human body to an existence in heaven.

Peter also used the Greek word *exodus* in speaking of his own "departure" from this earth (2 Pet. 1:13–15). He used two images drawn straight from the Old Testament. First, he said that he must "put off his tabernacle"; then he spoke of his death as an "exodus":

> I think it right, as long as I am in this body ["tabernacle" in Greek] to refresh your memory, since I know that my death ["the putting off of my tabernacle" in Greek] will come soon, as indeed our Lord Jesus Christ has made clear to me. And I will make every effort so that after my departure ["exodus" in Greek] you may be able at any time to recall these things.

(2 Pet. 1:13–15)

KEY VERSES

Luke 9:31;
Hebrews 11:22;
2 Peter 1:15

In the Israelites' journeys across the desert, they often had to take down their tents and the tabernacle in order to travel on. Thus, putting the tabernacle up and taking it down became associated with "departure" imagery. Paul used the same image in 2 Corinthians 5:1–4. Death is described as a journey, an "exodus." Jesus made this exodus, as well as Peter. And each one of us will make this exodus, when we depart this world to the next. In this regard, death as an exodus is not just a euphemism; it's a promise.

Faith

See also: *Faith, p. 56*
Greek expression: *pistis*
Pronunciation: *PEE steess*
Strong's Number: *4102*

F

Faith is one of those words that Christians use often. Even so, it is one of the most difficult words to define. Just what is faith? The writer of Hebrews wrote, "Now faith is the assurance of things hoped for, the conviction of things not seen" (Heb. 11:1, NLT). As such, faith involves believing that someone else will do something that is not yet visible or that has not yet happened. Thus, to have faith is to relinquish trust in oneself and to put that trust in another. For example, in the Gospels, we read of a woman with a hemorrhage problem. She had put her trust in physicians, but to no avail. Then, she put all her trust in Jesus, believing He could cure her. According to Jesus, it was her faith that made her well (Luke 8:43–48). This was a proclamation Jesus made many times (Matt. 8:10; 9:22, 29; 15:28; Luke 7:50; 8:48).

The writers of the epistles sometimes used the Greek word *pistis* to refer to "what one believes," the content of "faith," which is God's revelation in the Scripture (Gal. 1:23). But the overall emphasis is placed on the active, responding faith of the hearer to the gospel. Both verb and noun regularly describe the adequate response of people to Jesus' word and to the gospel.

Faith is the medium by which the power of God is made visible. It moves mountains, heals the sick, and is the means of entrance into the kingdom of heaven. Faith may be mingled with doubt, as with the father who sought healing for his son: "I do believe; help my unbelief" (Mark 9:24, NASB), or as with John the Baptist in prison, who, even with his doubts, was confirmed by Jesus as the greatest of the offspring of woman (Matt. 11:2–15). In Paul's letters, he writes about faith from a number of angles. He sets faith over and against works of the law as the only and true basis for being made right with God (Rom. 1—4; Gal. 1—4) and appeals to Abraham to prove his point: "Abraham believed God, and it was reckoned to him as righteousness" (Gal. 3:6; see also Rom. 4:5). Salvation is entirely apart from the law (Rom. 3:21)—righteousness is the gift of God through faith in Christ.

Faith, then, is belief in Jesus Christ as the Son of God who saves. It is by faith that believers are justified (Rom. 5:1), reconciled (2 Cor. 5:18), redeemed (Eph. 1:7), made alive (Eph. 2:5), adopted into the family of God (Rom. 8:15–16), recreated (2 Cor. 5:17), and set free (Gal. 5:1). James speaks of faith as being perfected by works (Jas. 2:22). He rejected the concept of faith without resulting action—that is, believing something is true without founding one's life on it and acting upon it. Faith apart from works is not real faith. It is barren and, thus, not genuine faith at all (Jas. 2:20).

KEY VERSES

Matthew 8:10;
15:28;
Luke 7:50; 8:48;
Romans 4:5;
James 2:20;
Hebrews 11:1

Fellowship

Greek expression: *koinōnia*
Pronunciation: *koy noh NEE uh*
Strong's Number: *2842*

The Greek term *koinōnia* means "that which is shared in common." In secular Greek literature, *koinōnia* was used to describe the marriage bed and communal meals. In the New Testament, the word was used to denote the believers' common participation, or "fellowship," with the Triune God—the Father, the Son, and the Holy Spirit. The Father and Son have enjoyed communion with each other since before the creation of the world. When Jesus entered into time, His fellowship with the Father also entered into time. During the days of His ministry on earth, Jesus was introducing the Father to the disciples and initiating them into this fellowship. The unique fellowship between God and Jesus began in eternity, was manifested in time through the incarnation of Jesus, was introduced to the apostles, and then introduced to each and every believer through indwelling of the Holy Spirit (2 Cor. 13:14; Phil. 2:1).

The richness of fellowship among the first Christians is portrayed in the early chapters of Acts. The believers met together daily in house groups for teaching, fellowship, the Lord's Supper, and prayer (Acts 2:42, 46). So profound was their sense of togetherness that the Christians pooled their possessions and distributed them to brothers and sisters in need (Acts 2:44–45; 4:32–35). The dominant characteristic of this early Christian fellowship was the love among the believers (1 Thess. 4:9; 1 Pet. 1:22). Motivated by love, Paul organized a collection for poor believers in Jerusalem. In Romans 15:26, which speaks of the gifts of the churches in Macedonia and Achaia, the Greek word for "contribution" is also the common Greek word for "fellowship." Similarly, the fellowship that the Philippian church shared with Paul was in the form of gifts which supported the apostle's ministry (Phil. 1:5; 4:14–15).

Scripture uses several images to describe the spirit of togetherness that characterized the early church. The first is "the household of God" (Eph. 2:19; 1 Tim. 3:15), or "the household of faith" (Gal. 6:10). In God's household, love and hospitality are to be the rule (Heb. 13:1–2). Further, the church is depicted as the family of God on earth (Eph. 3:15). God is the Father and believers are His faithful sons and daughters. The life of God's family is to be governed by love, tenderness, compassion, and humility (Phil. 2:1–4). Finally, Christian fellowship is represented as the "one new man" or the "one body" (Eph. 2:15–16). In spite of great natural diversity, the Holy Spirit binds believers together into a single organism (Eph. 4:4–6). In this fellowship of love, no believer is insignificant. Each member has been endowed with gifts for the spiritual edification of the entire body.

KEY VERSES

Acts 2:42;
1 Corinthians 1:9;
Philippians 2:1;
1 John 1:3, 6–7

280

Firstborn

Greek expression: *prōtotokos*
Pronunciation: *proh TAW taw kawss*
Strong's Number: *4416*

Many cultures still value the firstborn child. This dates back thousands of years to Old Testament times. The firstborn was given priority or preeminence, as well as the best inheritance, by their parents. "Firstborn" can also be used figuratively to denote the most or best of something. For example, the expression "firstborn of the poor," (Isa. 14:30, NRSV) means one who is supremely poor, or the poorest of the poor.

Prōtotokos, the Greek word for "firstborn," is used eight times in the New Testament, usually with reference to Jesus. He is called Mary's firstborn son (Luke 2:7), the firstborn of all creation (Col. 1:15), the firstborn of the dead (Col. 1:18; Rev. 1:5), the firstborn of God's family (Rom. 8:29), and simply the "firstborn" (Heb. 1:6; 12:23). The intent of all these references is to show Jesus' priority and preeminence. He had preeminence in Mary's family as the oldest son, and He has preeminence in the church as the firstborn from the dead and firstborn of all God's family.

Jesus also has preeminence over all creation as the firstborn of all creation. This last expression has troubled interpreters for hundreds of years. From the Armenians to the present day Jehovah Witnesses, there have been those who used "the firstborn of creation" to teach that Christ was a creation of God and therefore not coequal with God. This needs to be refuted.

Let's begin with an analysis of the word. The first part of the Greek word *prōto* can indicate "first in time" (temporal priority) or "first in place" (preeminence). In the context of Colossians 1:15, the second meaning is in the forefront. Thus, the Son of Man is the "chiefborn" among all God's creatures (compare Exod. 4:22; Deut. 21:16, 17; Ps. 89:27, wherein the Greek Old Testament *prōtotokos* is used to express the idea of preeminence). Jesus is the foremost of all creation. The title "chiefborn" or "firstborn" as a description of the Son of Man indicates that the Son in His humanity is now the foremost creature of all creation. The designation in no way indicates that Christ is the first creature created by God, for the next verse asserts that all things were created in, through, and for Christ (Col. 1:15–17). As a co-participant in the creation of all things, Christ cannot be a created being. Instead, He is the Son of God, the Second Person of the Godhead, who has existed from eternity.

KEY VERSES

Romans 8:29;
Colossians 1:15, 18;
Revelation 1:5

As the firstborn of all creation, He has priority over creation. As the firstborn of the dead, He has preeminence in the church. Thus, Paul concludes in Colossians 1:18, "so that He Himself might come to have first place in everything." As believers, Jesus should occupy the "first place" in our hearts and nothing should consume us more than Him who has suffered everything to give us life.

Flesh

Greek expression: *sarx*
Pronunciation: *SAHRKSS*
Strong's Number: *4561*

In Greek literature, the word *sarx* usually meant nothing more than "the human body." It was also used this way in the New Testament (John 1:14; Rev. 17:16; 19:18, 21). In many places, "flesh" is synonymous with the "body"; Paul spoke either of being absent in the "body" (1 Cor. 5:3) or in the "flesh" (Col. 2:5). Paul also writes that the life of Jesus may be manifested in our body or our mortal flesh (2 Cor. 4:10–11).

However, Paul often used *sarx* to denote the entire fallen human being—not just the sinful "body," but the soul and mind which are affected by sin as well. Thus, Paul often pitted the "flesh" against the "Spirit" as being two diametrically opposed forces. The most vivid passage is the first part of Romans 8, where Paul sharply contrasts those who are in the "flesh" with those who are in the "Spirit." "To be in the Spirit" in this sense does not mean to be in a state of ecstasy, but to be living one's life in that spiritual realm that is controlled by the Spirit of God. Those who are in the "flesh," that is, not renewed by the spirit or unregenerate, cannot please God. In Romans 7—8 Paul makes it clear that the unregenerate person cannot please God because human beings are unable to love and serve God as He requires. Indeed, the Law was unable to make mankind truly righteous, because the flesh is weak (Rom. 8:2). And, to live according to the flesh is death (Rom. 8:6). Elsewhere Paul says, "For I know that in me [my flesh] dwelleth no good thing" (Rom. 8:18, KJV). "Flesh" in this context cannot be the physical flesh, for the body of flesh is also called the temple of the Spirit (1 Cor. 6:19). Paul, therefore, means that in his unregenerate nature there dwells none of the goodness that God demands.

While Paul makes a sharp and absolute contrast between being in the flesh (unregenerate) and being in the Spirit (regenerate), when we become renewed in the Spirit (regenerate), we are no longer in the flesh (unregenerate). However, the flesh is still in us. In fact, there will always be a struggle between the flesh and the Spirit in each believer. Because the Christian life is the battleground of these two opposing principles, it is impossible to be the perfect people that we wish to be. But, Paul repeatedly encourages believers to overcome the deeds of the flesh by living in the Spirit.

KEY VERSES

Romans 7:5, 18, 25;
8:3–9, 12–13

Foreknowledge

Greek expression: *prognōsis*
Pronunciation: *PRAW gnoh seess*
Strong's Number: *4268*

Though fortune-tellers and psychics pretend to know the future, only God has foreknowledge. The Greek term *prognōsis*, which means "foreknowledge," indicates "knowledge beforehand." The English term "prognosis" is derived from this Greek word. In the New Testament, *prognōsis* and its verbal form indicate "advanced knowledge" (Rom. 11:2; 1 Pet. 1:2; 2:23).

Scripture teaches that God is aware of events before they happen. This sets Him apart from pagan idols who lack the ability to foresee the future (Isa. 44:6–8; 45:21; 48:14). It is God's "foreknowledge" that provides the basis for the predictions of the prophets. In many places of the New Testament, Christ's ministry and the establishment of the Christian church is seen as the fulfillment of predictions made beforehand by the Old Testament prophets (Matt. 1:22; 4:14; 8:17; John 12:38–41; Acts 2:17–21; 3:22–25; Gal. 3:8; Heb. 5:6; 1 Pet. 1:10–12).

Peter also tells that God had foreknowledge of His Son's death on the cross long before the event occurred (1 Pet. 1:20). This is also the implication of Revelation 13:8, "everyone whose name has not been written from the foundation of the world in the book of life of the Lamb who has been slain" (NASB). Jesus' death for our redemption was not an afterthought; it was part of God's eternal plan. Paul declared that all the children of God were selected according to God's foreknowledge (Rom. 8:28–29). This statement has puzzled theologians for generations. Theologians of the early church denied that foreknowledge implied any predetermination of events. Justin Martyr, for example, said, "What we say about future events being foretold, we do not say it as though they come about by fatal necessity." In other words, although God knows what is going to happen before it happens, He has not necessarily caused it to happen.

By contrast, Calvin insisted that God knows all events precisely because He sovereignly determines what is to happen in human history right down to the tiniest detail. Here "foreknowledge" is closely tied to, if not identified with, "foreordination." At the same time, most Calvinistic theologians assert that human beings are nonetheless responsible for their choices—not victims of a blind fate.

Arminius distinguished "foreknowledge" from "foreordination" of events. While the plan of salvation for the world and humanity are predetermined in broad outline by God, Arminius argued that each individual's response to God is not predetermined because each person has free will. Yet, God knows us intimately. Hence, God can foreknow an event without directly decreeing that event to take place.

KEY VERSES

Acts 2:23;
1 Peter 1:2

Forgive

See also: *Forgive, p. 64*
Greek expression: *aphiemi, charizomai*
Pronunciation: *ah FEE ay mee; kahr EE dzoh migh*
Strong's Numbers: *863, 5483*

We have all heard the expression, "To err is human; to forgive is divine." The cliché contains some truth. Forgiveness really is a divine attribute, for it is only God who can forgive sins. Forgiveness is an act of God, releasing sinners from judgment and freeing them from the divine penalty of their sin—death. It makes sense that the only one who could forgive sin is someone who is without sin—that is, someone who is holy. Since only God is holy, only God can forgive sin (Mark 2:7; Luke 5:21). Forgiveness is also a human act extended toward one's neighbor—a manifestation of one's realization and appropriation of God's forgiveness. Hence, forgiveness is a uniquely Christian doctrine.

The Greek expression for "forgiveness" is *aphiemi*. In the New Testament, the concept of the unmerited "forgiveness" of God is intensified by the fact that God forgave our sins when His Son died for us. Each human is a debtor (Matt. 18:23–35) who has no hope of repaying God. As sinners, we cannot keep the Law or save ourselves (Mark 10:26–27). This highlights the New Testament teaching that it is in the person of Christ Himself that there is forgiveness. He alone has the power to forgive sins (Mark 2:5–10). Once forgiven, we can enter through Him into a living experience with God (Heb. 9:15, 22).

There is another New Testament word for "forgiveness." The Greek word *charizomai*, meaning "to extend grace," is distinctively developed by Paul in terms of God's gracious pardon of our sins (2 Cor. 2:7; 12:13; Eph. 4:32; Col. 2:13; 3:13). The full teaching on forgiveness in the New Testament insists not only on repentance as a condition for forgiveness (2 Cor. 7:10), but also on the need to forgive others (Matt. 6:14–15). If in the midst of receiving forgiveness one does not forgive others, it is a clear sign that repentance is not complete. Several times in His parables, the Lord insisted that the readiness to forgive others is a sign of true repentance (Matt. 18:23–35; Luke 6:37). Christ taught that to forgive is a duty, and no limits can be set on it. Forgiveness must be granted without reserve, even to seventy times seven (Matt. 18:21–22). Forgiveness is part of the mutual relationship of believers: since all are dependent upon God's forgiveness, all are required to forgive one another. "Just as the Lord forgave you, so also should you" (Col. 3:13).

KEY VERSES

Mark 2:5, 7, 9–10;
Ephesians 4:32;
Colossians 3:13

Greek expression: *morphē*
Pronunciation: *mohr FAY*
Strong's Number: *3444*

The Greek word *morphē* is found only three times in the New Testament, but each time it is extremely significant because it is used to describe Christ's "form of existence." According to these three verses, Jesus has existed in three different "forms": first, in "the form of God" from all eternity (Phil. 2:6), then in "the form of a slave" after His incarnation (Phil. 2:7), then in a special resurrection "form" after He rose from the dead (Mark 16:12). Let us look at these meanings one by one.

Morphē was generally used to express the way in which the being of any living thing appears to our senses. Thus, when this word is applied to God, His *morphē* must refer to His deepest being—to what He is in Himself (see Phil. 2:6). The expression "form of God" may be correctly understood as the essential nature and character of God. To say, therefore, that Christ exists in the "form of God" (Phil. 2:6) is to say that Christ possesses all the characteristics and qualities belonging to God because He is, in fact, God. This somewhat enigmatic expression, then, appears to be another way for the writer to say that Christ was God. He possessed the very nature of God.

The Son of God, however, emptied Himself and took on another "form"—that of a slave (Phil. 2:7). He did this at the time when He took a body, as is explained by the next phrase: "but emptied Himself, taking the form of a bond-servant, and being made in the likeness of men" (NASB). It seems that Christ divested Himself of His divine state, or mode of existence, when He relinquished His "position," but not His "disposition," of equality with God. By giving up His place next to God, Jesus assumed a subservient role to the Father, resulting in His being sent to earth to assume a new "form of being" as a man. In this form, Jesus accomplished redemption by His death on the cross for the sins of the world (Phil. 2:8).

The other "form" that Jesus took on was a new resurrected body and new existence in resurrection (Mark 16:12, NASB). When Jesus arose from the dead, three significant things happened to Him. He was glorified, transfigured, and He became spirit. All three happened simultaneously. When He was resurrected, He was glorified and His body was transfigured into a glorious one (Luke 24:26; Phil. 3:21). Simultaneously, and quite mysteriously, He became life-giving spirit (1 Cor. 15:45). Paul did not say Jesus became "the Spirit," as if the second person of the Trinity became the third. Instead, Jesus' mortal existence and form were metamorphosed into a spiritual existence and spiritual body. Jesus' person, or essence, was not changed through the resurrection. His "form" merely changed. In this new resurrected body, He appeared to His disciples on this earth (Mark 16:12).

KEY VERSES

Mark 16:12;
Philippians 2:6–7

Full of the Spirit

Greek expression: *plētho tou pneumatos*
Pronunciation: *PLAY thoh; TOO; PNEW muh tawss*
Strong's Numbers: *4130, 3588, 4151*

The Greek word *plētho* is used for describing the "filling" of everything from a sponge to a boat (Matt. 27:48; Luke 5:7). Luke uses this common term to describe how the Holy Spirit influences a person. He uses the expression *plētho tou pneumatos,* which means "filled with the Holy Spirit," eight times in his writings. It is used three times in the first chapter of Luke to describe: John the Baptist (Luke 1:15), Elizabeth when she met Mary (Luke 1:41), and Zechariah when he proclaimed the prophecies about his son, John the Baptist (Luke 1:65).

Being "filled with the Spirit," according to Acts, is associated with the baptism of the Holy Spirit. At the beginning of Acts, Jesus repeated John the Baptist's prediction that the Messiah would baptize people in the Holy Spirit (Luke 3:16; Acts 1:5). This prophecy was fulfilled on the day of Pentecost, when all the assembled believers were baptized in the Holy Spirit and thereby "filled with the Holy Spirit" (Acts 2:4). Once saturated with the Holy Spirit, this Spirit-effusion gave them the boldness to speak out for Jesus. Through the Spirit, the disciples were constantly empowered to speak for Jesus. Acts 4:8 says that Peter, when full of the Holy Spirit, spoke boldly to the rulers and elders. At the end of the same chapter, it says that all the church was filled with the Holy Spirit and thereby "spoke the word of God with all boldness" (Acts 4:31). Later in the book of Acts, we hear of Saul of Tarsus (Paul) being converted to Christ. He was filled with the Spirit and empowered to rebuke the false prophet, Bar-Jesus (Acts 9:31; 13:6–12).

In nearly every case, the effusion of the Holy Spirit enables the person to speak or preach for God. Thus, the filling of the Spirit is directly related to the prophetic ministry—the revelation or explanation of God's Word. The Holy Spirit is the gift Jesus gave us to lead us and guide us in truth and understanding of God's Word.

KEY VERSES

Luke 1:15, 41, 67;
Acts 2:4; 4:8, 31;
9:17; 13:9

Fullness

Greek expression: *plērōma*
Pronunciation: *PLAY roh muh*
Strong's Number: *4138*

In ancient Greece, the word *plērōma*, which means "fullness," was a common and ordinary word. It simply meant "that which fills." *Plērōma* is found in reference to the cargo or crew that fills a ship, the people that make up a crowd, and the years that fill a person's life. The philosopher Aristotle used the term to denote the population that fills a city. In the New Testament, however, *plērōma* is a word pregnant with meaning. The apostles John and Paul used the term to describe Jesus' deity. The prologue to John's Gospel states that the "fullness of Christ" is received by all believers (John 1:16). The exact nature of this "fullness" is defined in verse 14: "the Word became flesh, and dwelt among us, and we beheld His glory, glory as of the only begotten from the Father, full of grace and truth."

In the Greek New Testament, *plērōma* or "fullness," indicated "plenitude" and "totality." The heretical Gnostics used the word to describe the totality of all deities. John, as with Paul, used the word to describe Christ as the fullness or the plenitude of God—for, as Paul put it in Colossians 1:19 and 2:9, all the fullness of the Godhead dwells in Jesus bodily. Since all of God's fullness resides in Christ, every spiritual reality is found in Christ. In Christ, we lack nothing. The Greek word *theotetos* for "Godhead" is used only in the New Testament and designates the totality of God's nature and person. *Theotetos* could also be translated as "Deity," but not as "divinity," which is *theiotes* in Greek, because *theiotes* emphasizes only the divine nature. The Godhead encompasses God's nature and person. All the fullness of the Godhead "dwells" or "permanently resides" in the body of Jesus, the God-man. Is it any wonder, then, that Paul declares in the very next sentence, Colossians 2:10: "and you have come to fullness in him". (Col. 2:10, NRSV).

In Christ, believers lack nothing. Of course, no single believer could receive all that Christ is. It takes the body of Christ, the church, to appropriate Christ's fullness and to express it (Eph.1:23). Nevertheless, each believer receives in measure the same content of that fullness. Christ is continually full; He is never depleted. No matter how much the believers receive of Him, He keeps on giving. Believers do not need to seek any other source, but Christ.

KEY VERSES

John 1:16;
Ephesians 1:23;
Colossians 1:19; 2:9

Futility

Greek expression: *kenōs, mataiotēs*
Pronunciation: *KEHN awss; mah tigh OH tayss*
Strong's Numbers: *2756, 3152, 3153*

Futility is best pictured in Greek mythology. Doomed to Tatarus (hell) forever, Sisyphus is given the endless task of trying to roll a huge stone up to the top of a mountain. But just when he gets within sight of the pinnacle, the weight of the stone pushes him and the stone all the way down to the bottom, where he begins again the futile attempt to push the stone to the top. Complete futility!

In the New Testament, especially in Paul's writings, there are two Greek words that convey the idea of futility: *kenōs* and *mataiotēs* (in adjectival form, *mataios*). *Kenōs* was used by Paul to signify that which is "empty and hollow"—hence, pointless and futile. *Mataiotēs* was employed by Paul to signify that which is "vain and useless"—hence, ineffective and futile.

In Paul's writings, *kenōs* expresses the emptiness of all that is not filled with spiritual substance. Nothing comes from this nothingness; it is futility. Paul also used *kenōs* to describe the hollow utterances spoken by Judaizers and Gnostics trying to entice the believers with philosophy (1 Tim. 6:20; 2 Tim. 2:12) and empty deceit (Col. 2:8). In contrast, Paul claimed that his preaching was not futile, but purposeful and effective (1 Cor. 15:14). He made the same claim for his labor among the believers (1 Thess. 2:1).

Paul's use of the word *mataiotēs* was influenced by teachings in Ecclesiastes. In the Greek translation of Ecclesiastes (Eccl.1:2, 14; 2:1, 11, 15, 17), the expression appears again and again in the refrain, " Meaningless! Meaningless! Utterly meaningless! Everything is meaningless," *mataios ton mataion, pantas estin mataiotēs* (Eccl. 1:2). The idea of this phrase focuses on ideas like "meaninglessness" (NIV), "emptiness" (NEB), and "uselessness" (TEV). Nowhere in the New Testament is the kind of futility described in Ecclesiastes so characterized as in Romans 8:20: "For the creation was subjected to futility, not of its own will, but because of Him who subjected it, in hope." When Paul said that the creation was subjected to futility, he was focusing on the inability of creation to function as it was originally designed to do. But eventually, all creation will be liberated from *mataiotēs* by our Savior Jesus.

KEY VERSES

1 Corinthians 15:14;
Titus 3:9

Paul also used *mataiotēs* to depict the "meaninglessness" that has its source in the thought-life of fallen human beings. Paul characterized the "thoughts of the wise" as being futile (1 Cor. 3:20), and he described the Gentiles as living "in the futility of their mind, being darkened in their understanding," because they are "excluded from the life of God" (Eph. 4:17–18, NASB). The ideas of the unregenerate produce a life of purposelessness and ineffectiveness. Salvation from "futility" comes from the indwelling Spirit of Christ in believers (Rom. 8:10–11, 26–27). Thank the Lord for the meaning and purpose which He alone brings to life.

Glorify

See also: *Glory, p. 72*
Greek expression: *doxazō*
Pronunciation: *dawkss AH dzoh*
Strong's Number: *1392*

The Greek term *doxazō* means "to give glory" or "to make glorious." The New Testament gives us glimpses of when Jesus Christ was glorified. The transfiguration of Christ brought His glory out into the open (Matt. 17:1–8). The apostle Paul called Jesus the "Lord of glory" (1 Cor. 2:8) and wrote that the "glory" of God radiated from His face (2 Cor. 3:18).

G

John's Gospel is uniquely the Gospel of glory. In the incarnation, the Son of God showed the glory that was His as the only begotten Son of the Father (John 1:14). The raising of Lazarus was a manifestation of the glory of God in Christ (John 11:40). Jesus' prayer in John 17 is filled with comments on the glory of Christ, including the affirmation that the disciples of the Lord would share in that glory. John said that Jesus would be fully glorified as the result of His crucifixion and resurrection (John 7:39; 12:23, 24). These events would show the world that Jesus was no ordinary man. The resurrection, especially, would show that He was the glorious Son of God worthy of all honor. In His final prayer, Jesus asked the Father to be glorified alongside of Him—that is, in the Father's presence by means of the glory He had with the Father before the world existed. In other words, Jesus was praying to enter into that pristine state of coequal glory with the Father, a position He possessed from eternity as God's only Son (John 1:1, 18). He would enter into that glory in a new way—as the God-man, the crucified and risen Lord Jesus Christ.

The believer will also experience glorification. In 2 Corinthians 3:18, spiritual transformation is described as a changing from glory to glory. Glorification is implied as the last event in the change from glory to glory. In the process of salvation, Paul lists glorification as the last and final event (Rom. 8:28–30). Just as the inner person undergoes glorification, so does the believer's body. Paul calls the resurrection of the body the redemption of the body (Rom. 8:23). In Philippians 3:21, Paul speaks of the transformation of bodies of humiliation—that is, humiliated by sin and mortality—into bodies of glory identical to that of Christ (1 Cor. 15). Just as Christians have borne the image of the mortal clay of Adam, we shall one day bear the image of the immortal Son of God. What a glorious future we have.

KEY VERSES

John 7:39; 12:23;
13:31–32; 17:5;
Romans 8:30

God

See also: *God, p. 74 and Gods, p. 291*
Greek expression: *theos*
Pronunciation: *THEH awss*
Strong's Number: *2316*

The Caesars, beginning with Augustus Caesar, were all called "god," which is *theos* in Greek. Although we don't have an explicit example of a Caesar being called "god" in the New Testament, there is an event in which Herod is called a "god." After giving a speech to the people of Tyre and Sidon, they shouted, "the voice of a god and not of a man!" Shortly thereafter, Herod died a violent death because he had taken all the glory to himself and given none to God (Acts 12:20–23, NASB).

The only person worthy of being called "God" is Jesus. His deity is explicitly asserted in several New Testament passages, many of which are found in John's writings. It is John who tells us that "the Word was God." Not only was the Word with God from eternity, He was God from eternity (John 1:1, NASB). This is asserted at the beginning and at the end of John's prologue, where the Son is called "God" again (John 1:18). In the Gospel narrative, Jesus declares that He existed before Abraham even came into being (John 8:58), and He asserts that He and the Father are one (John 10:30). The Jewish leaders understood this assertion as a claim to deity (John 10:31–33). At the end of John's Gospel, Thomas saw the risen Christ, believed in Him, and proclaimed, "My Lord and my God" (John 20:28). Furthermore, at the end of John's first letter, he said that Jesus is "the true God and eternal life" (1 John 5:20).

Paul and Peter also affirm the deity of Jesus—each of them calling Him "God." In the book of Romans, Paul praises Jesus Christ, saying, "Christ according to the flesh, who is over all, God blessed forever" (Rom. 9:5). In Philippians 2:6, Paul says that Jesus Christ was in the very form, or substance, of God, and in Colossians 1:19 and 2:9 he says that "For in Him all the fulness of Deity dwells in bodily form" (NASB). In Titus 2:13, Paul identifies Jesus as "our God and Savior." Peter also named Jesus as "God and Savior" in 2 Peter 1:1; and in the next verse, he says Jesus is "our God and Lord."

The Jewish leaders of Jerusalem considered it blasphemous for Jesus to claim equality with God. On more than one occasion, they wanted to stone Him for His claims. Jesus told the Jewish leaders, "I and the Father are one" (John 10:30, NASB). These leaders immediately understood that He was claiming deity for Himself; they wanted to stone Jesus for His blasphemy, because He, a mere man, made Himself God. Actually, it was the other way around: Jesus was God who became a man!

KEY VERSES

John 1:1, 18;
Titus 2:13;
2 Peter 1:1

Gods

Greek expression: *theoi*
Pronunciation: *theh OY*
Strong's Number: *2316*

In the Greek language the term for "a god" and "God" is the same: *theos*. In English we differentiate between the two by using a small letter "g" or a capital letter "G." Ancient Christian scribes differentiated between the two by always writing the sacred name of the true God.

In New Testament times, most people believed in many gods—that is, they were polytheists. At least three Greco-Roman deities are mentioned in the New Testament: the Greek goddess Artemis (Acts 19:24–28, 34–35), known as Diana by the Romans, and the Greek gods Zeus and Hermes, known as Jupiter and Mercury, respectively, by the Romans (Acts 14:12–13). Diana was worshiped by the Ephesians, who built a temple in her honor. This temple was one of the wonders of the ancient world. The Ephesians also made and sold small wooden images of the goddess Artemis (Diana). Like other famous idols, it was believed to have fallen from heaven (Acts 19:35). Paul's proclamation of the truth—that "gods made with hands are not gods" (Acts 19:26)—stirred the pagan-worshipers of Artemis to fever-pitch. For two straight hours they chanted, "Great is Artemis of the Ephesians!" (Acts 19:28, 34, NASB). Jesus' deity challenged Artemis' deity, and the sale of images was declining in proportion to the apostles' proclamation of the gospel. Consequently, the Ephesian pagans strongly opposed the preaching of the gospel.

Paul spoke of these various "gods and lords" in his letter to the Corinthians. In contrast to the multitude of deities worshiped by the pagans, Paul asserted in 1 Corinthians that there is only one true God and one true Lord, Jesus Christ (1 Cor. 8:5–6). So the early Christians soundly rejected polytheism of the ancient world. Only one, true God was worthy of worship and adoration.

KEY VERSES

Acts 12:22; 19:26;
1 Corinthians 8:5

God-inspired

Greek expression: *theopneustos*
Pronunciation: *theh AW pnew stawss*
Strong's Number: *2315*

We often hear people say, "That song was inspired" or "He was inspired to write that book after the death of his wife." Human inspiration, however, as good as it may be, cannot compare with divine inspiration. Great literary works were inspired by their authors: Shakespeare, Dostoevsky, C. S. Lewis, and so on. But, no work of literature can compare with the Bible on this count: it was inspired by God.

The Greek expression for "God-inspired" is one word *theopneustos*, meaning "God-breathed." It is derived from *theos* (God) and *pneustos* (breath or spirit). Although it is difficult to fully recreate this Greek expression in English, we are fairly certain that Paul meant to say that all Scripture was breathed out from God. This is the primary meaning. But the expression could also mean that the Word was breathed into others (that is, inspired) by God. The first definition affirms the Bible's divine origin; the second speaks of God's spiritual presence in the Word. Thus, God not only inspired the authors who wrote the words of the Bible, but also inspires those who read it with a heart of faith.

The words of the Bible came from God and were written by men. The apostle Peter affirmed this when he said that "no prophecy of Scripture came about by the prophet's own interpretation. For prophecy never had its origin in the will of man, but men spoke from God as they were carried along by the Holy Spirit" (1 Pet. 1:20–21, NIV). Peter writes "men spoke from God." This short sentence is the key to understanding how the Bible came into being. Thousands of years ago, God chose certain men—such as Moses, David, Isaiah, Jeremiah, Ezekiel, and Daniel—to receive His words and write them down. What they wrote became books, or sections, of the Old Testament. Nearly two thousand years ago, God chose other men—such as Matthew, Mark, Luke, John, and Paul—to communicate His new message of salvation through Jesus Christ. What they wrote became books, or sections, of the New Testament.

Before Jesus left this earth and returned to His Father, He told the disciples that He would send the Holy Spirit to them. Jesus told them that one of the functions of the Holy Spirit would be to remind them of all the things He had said, and then the Spirit would guide them into more truth (John 14:26). Those who wrote the Gospels were helped by the Holy Spirit to remember Jesus' exact words, and those who wrote other parts of the New Testament were also guided, and even taught, by the Spirit in teaching Christ's message and explaining His principles (1 Cor. 2:12–15). The next time you read the Holy Bible, remember that you are reading the book that is God-inspired. The Bible is God's Word to us. His living Word is breathed into us as we read and therefore has the power to speak to us no matter where we are in our faith-journey with God.

KEY VERSE

2 Timothy 3:16

Golgotha

Greek expression: *Golgotha*
Pronunciation: *gawl gaw THAH*
Strong's Number: *1115*

Golgotha would have faded away into history as some obscure place of execution (just outside Jerusalem) had not it been the place where Jesus Christ was crucified. The term *Golgotha* appears in the New Testament only in the accounts of the crucifixion. Three of the Gospels use the Hebrew or Aramaic term, which is transliterated into Greek as *Golgotha* (Matt. 27:33; Mark 15:22; John 19:17), while one uses the Latin equivalent, *Calvary* (Luke 23:33, meaning "skull" or "cranium").

The exact location of the site is unknown. The Bible gives us only general indications: It was outside the city proper (John 19:20; Heb. 13:12). It may have been on an elevated site since it could be seen from a distance (Mark 15:40). It was perhaps near a road since "passersby" are mentioned (Matt. 27:39; Mark 15:29), and John's account places Golgotha near a garden that contained the tomb in which Jesus was buried (John 19:41). The use of the definite article, "the place of the skull," would indicate that it was a well-known place.

Why is this place called "the skull"? Again, no one knows for sure. An early tradition, apparently originating with Jerome (A.D. 346–420), said that it was a common place of execution and that the skulls of many who had been executed were left around the site. Some suggest that since it was a place of execution that "skull" was used figuratively, simply as a symbol of death. Origen (A.D. 185–253) mentioned an early, pre-Christian tradition that the skull of Adam was buried in that place. This is probably the oldest explanation of the name, and is referred to by several writers after Origen. Others said that the name resulted from the fact that the place of the crucifixion was a hill that had the natural shape of a skull. None of these viewpoints, however, can be historically validated.

In 1842 Otto Thenius posited the hypothesis that Golgotha was a rocky hill about 250 yards northeast of the Damascus Gate. He based his opinion on the assertions that it had been a Jewish place of stoning, lay outside the city wall, and was shaped like a skull. Later, General Charles Gordon also advocated this spot, and it has come to be known in many circles as "Gordon's Calvary." No matter what Golgotha's original origin, it has significance because "Golgotha," or "Calvary," is the place in which our Savior Jesus died for our sins. In the place of skulls, Jesus gave us life.

KEY VERSES

Matthew 27:33;
Mark 15:22;
John 19:17

Good news, gospel

Greek expression: *euangelion*
Pronunciation: *ew ang GEHL ee awn*
Strong's Number: *2098*

Interestingly, the Greek word for "gospel," *euangelion*, was originally used to describe the "good news" of military victory brought from a messenger to his commander. It then came to mean simply a "good message." The New Testament writers chose this word to describe the "Good News" of Jesus Christ and His salvation.

According to Mark 1:1–4, the gospel begins with John the Baptist's proclamation. The promised birth of John the Baptist is good news (Luke 1:19), not only for his parents (Luke 1:7, 24–25) but for all the people. John is sent to prepare them for the Messiah's coming (Luke 1:14–17, 67–79). John's own preaching is "gospel" (John 3:18) for the same reason. The Messiah would be coming to execute judgment, a process that involves both condemnation and salvation (Luke 3:3–17). John's message is gospel for sinners in that they are warned of impending doom and urged to repent before the ax falls (Luke 3:7–9). It is also gospel for the repentant in that they are promised forgiveness (Luke 3:3) and membership in Messiah's community (Luke 3:17). The birth of the Savior Himself is announced as "good news" bringing great joy (Luke 2:10–11).

After John the Baptist baptized Jesus, Jesus was authorized by God and anointed by the Spirit to proclaim the gospel (Mark 1:14; Luke 4:18). At the heart of His preaching stands the announcement, "The time is fulfilled, and the kingdom of God is at hand; repent and believe in the gospel" (Mark 1:15, NASB). Jesus' gospel message focuses on the coming of God's kingdom. With the coming of the kingdom, God's rule will be completed. Wrong will be judged, righteousness established, and His people will be glorified.

After the resurrection of Jesus, the gospel was proclaimed by His eyewitnesses. The contents of this gospel are recorded in the book of Acts and Paul's letters. Having risen from the dead, Jesus Christ again evangelizes (Eph. 2:16–18), doing so now through His appointed representatives (Rom. 15:16–18). More than that, Christ became and is the central theme of the gospel—the Proclaimer is now the Proclaimed. This is repeatedly affirmed by Luke (Acts 5:42; 8:4–5, 35; 11:20; 17:18) and by Paul (Rom. 1:1–4; 10:8–17; 15:19–20; Phil. 1:15–18). Christ Himself is the central theme of the gospel message that has been entrusted to us to share to the world.

KEY VERSES

Mark 1:1, 14;
Romans 1:1, 9, 16;
Philippians 1:16

Grace

Greek expression: *charis*
Pronunciation: *KAHR eess*
Strong's Number: *5485*

The Greek word for "grace," *charis*, is equivalent to the Hebrew word *hesed*, which means "loving kindness"—a word frequently used by the psalmists to describe God's character. In the New Testament, the word *charis* usually means "divine favor" or "goodwill," but it also means "that which gives joy" and "that which is a free gift."

Grace is the gift of God. It is expressed in God's actions of extending mercy, loving-kindness, and salvation to people. Divine grace is embodied in the person of Jesus Christ (John 1:14, 17). God's grace manifested in Jesus Christ makes it possible for God to forgive sinners and to gather them in the church. During His ministry, Jesus repeatedly offered forgiveness to a great number of sinners and extended God's succor for a variety of desperate human needs. Through teachings such as the father's forgiveness of the prodigal son and the search for the lost sheep, Jesus made it clear that He had come to seek and save those who were lost. But ultimately, it was His redemptive death on the cross which opened wide the gate of salvation for repentant sinners so that they have access to God's forgiving and restorative grace.

This simple truth is formulated in the doctrine of "justification by faith through grace" (Rom. 3:23; Titus 3:7). According to this teaching, God graciously provides life, through the death of Christ, to sinners who believe in Jesus. Jesus' substitutionary death for all people enables God to pronounce a verdict of "not guilty" on repentant sinners and to include them in His eternal purposes. God's grace manifested in Jesus also makes it possible for God to bestow undeserved benefits on believers. These benefits enrich our lives and unite us together in the church. God's acceptance of believers on the basis of grace gives us a new status: we are children of God, members of the household of God, and can relate to Him as our heavenly Father (Gal. 4:4–6).

God's disposition to exercise goodwill towards His creatures is another essential meaning of "grace" in the Bible. This favorable disposition of God finds its supreme expression in Jesus Christ. By its very definition, this grace is rendered fully accessible to all humans with no precondition other than a repentant desire to receive it (Titus 2:11–12). The tragic alternative to receiving God's grace is to remain in hopeless alienation from God (Rom. 1:21). Therefore, let us accept God's gift of grace granted to us in Christ Jesus.

KEY VERSES

Romans 3:24; 5:15;
Ephesians 2:5;
Titus 2:11

Guardian

Greek expression: *paidagōgos*
Pronunciation: *pahee-dahg-oo-GOS*
Strong's Number: *3807*

In Greco-Roman times, the *paidagōgos* was not really a teacher (as in the KJV). He or she was usually a slave who served a household by being a companion to the children—accompanying them to school and making sure that they did their studies and stayed out of trouble. There are several examples of the use of this word in ancient Greek papyri. In all of them, the *paidagōgos* (literally "child leader") was responsible for taking care of the children—that is, leading them around. The guardian had significant authority over the children, including giving out discipline. But when the child reached maturity, the entire situation changed and the slave-guardian served his or her former supervisor.

Paul used this word in Galatians 3:23–25 to show how the law had only temporary authority over God's children—until they were led to Christ, who is the real teacher and master:

> Before faith came, we were kept in custody under the law, being shut up to the faith which was later to be revealed. Therefore the Law has become our tutor [guardian] to lead us to Christ, that we might be justified by faith. But now that faith has come, we are no longer under a tutor [guardian].

(Gal. 3:23–25; NASB)

Once a person is brought to Christ, he or she no longer needs the guardian. For those who have experienced Christ, the guardianship of the law has ceased. The temporary services of the law are, therefore, no longer needed because God has provided something better.

As Paul indicated in Galatians 3:19–22, the function of the law was not to provide a way for people to become acceptable to God but to exhibit God's standard whereby people might recognize their sinfulness and seek God's salvation—and thereby become justified by faith. Since the old era (the law) has come to an end, Paul dismissed the guardian as no longer needed (Gal. 3:25). Therefore, for anyone to turn to the law, after receiving Christ, is to return to a child-like disciplinary way of life, which is tantamount to turning away from the grace of Christ.

KEY VERSES

1 Corinthians 4:15;
Galatians 3:25

Hades

See also: *Sheol, p. 168 and Hell, p. 303*
Greek expression: *hadēs*
Pronunciation: *HAH dayss*
Strong's Number: *86*

Although many people think that *hadēs* and hell are synonymous, there is actually a big difference between saying "he's in hell" and "he's in *hadēs*." The Greek term *hadēs* means "the place of the unseen." It designates the invisible world of the dead, as does the Hebrew word *sheol*. All people who die go to *hadēs* because all pass from the visible world to the invisible.

Originally the Greeks thought that being in *hadēs* was a shadowy, ghostlike existence that happened to all who died, good and evil alike. Gradually, they and the Romans came to think of it as a place of reward and punishment. The Roman poet Virgil, 70–19 B.C., described *hadēs* as an elaborately organized and guarded realm where the good were rewarded in the Elysian Fields and the evil were punished. *Hadēs* became important to the Jews as the typical term used by the translators of the Septuagint (the Greek Old Testament) to render the Hebrew name *sheol* into Greek. This was a very suitable translation for the Hebrew term because both words can signify the "physical grave" or "death" (Gen. 37:35; Prov. 5:5; 7:27), and both originally referred to a dark underworld (Job 10:21–22). Later, Jews spoke of the idea of reward and punishment after death in this place. In other Jewish literature, *hadēs* is the place of torment for the wicked, while the righteous enter Paradise (see Wisdom of Solomon 2:1; 3:1).

Thus, by the beginning of the New Testament period, *hadēs* had three meanings: (1) death, (2) the place of all the dead, and (3) the place of the wicked dead only. Context determines which meaning an author intends in a given passage. In Matthew 11:23 and Luke 10:15, Jesus speaks of the descending of Capernaum to *hadēs*. He simply means that the city will be destroyed. In Acts 2:27, quoting Psalm 16:10, *hadēs* is referred to as the place of the dead. Christ did not stay among the dead in *hadēs*; unlike David, He rose from the dead (see Acts 2:27). In Revelation 20:13–14, *hadēs* refers to the place of the dead, because *hadēs* is emptied of all who are in it at the end of the world. When the wicked are judged and cast into the lake of fire (see Hell), *hadēs* is also thrown in the lake of fire. Luke 16:23, however, clearly refers to *hadēs* as the place of the wicked dead. There, the rich man is tormented in flames, while the poor man Lazarus goes to Paradise.

KEY VERSES

Luke 16:23;
Acts 2:27, 31;
Revelation 20:13–14

Unfortunately, the word *hadēs* was often translated as "hell" in the King James Version. But there is a different Greek word for "hell"; it is *gehenna* (Mark 9:43–45). We cannot avoid *hadēs*, "the grave" or "the place of the dead"; but we can avoid "hell" by believing in Jesus and receiving eternal life.

Hallelujah

Greek expression: *hallēlouia*
Pronunciation: *hahl lay loo ee AH*
Strong's Number: *239*

Around Christmas time every year, people will hear bits and pieces of Handel's "Messiah"—especially the lines from the Hallelujah chorus:

> Hallelujah! Hallelujah! Hallelujah! Hallelujah!
>
> Hallelujah! Hallelujah! Hallelujah! Hallelujah!
>
> For the Lord God Omnipotent reigneth!

Most people know that Hallelujah is an exuberant word, but very few people know what the word actually means. Hallelujah is a transliteration from the Greek expression *hallēlouia,* which comes from two Hebrew words, which mean "praise Jah." "Praise Jah" is short for "praise Yahweh." *Yahweh* is God's personal, self-revealed name. Unlike the general Old Testament word for God (*elohim*), this essential name conveys a dynamic personality. In Exodus 3:14, God tells Moses, "I AM WHO I AM." These words denote one whose absolute uniqueness requires His defining Himself by Himself. The expression conveys the sense of a vitally real being, as if God had said to Moses, "I really am!" The Jews were explicitly commanded not to take the name *Yahweh* in vain (Exod. 20:2, 7; Lev. 24:16). Consequently, when reading the Old Testament, the Jews substituted *Adonai,* meaning "Lord," for *Yahweh.* The closest they came to uttering His name was when they said, "Praise Jah," which is translated as "Hallelujah" in English translations.

In the Septuagint version of Psalms 113—118, each psalm is headed with *Allelujah.* Through the Vulgate, the Latin translation of the Bible by St. Jerome at the end of the fourth century, this form of the word "Hallelujah" came into use among believers. "Hallelujah" does not appear anywhere in the New Testament, except in Revelation 19:1–6. There it is used in an acclamation of praise from the believers in heaven for God's destruction of Babylon. Like another famous Hebrew praise term "Amen," the word "Hallelujah" passed from the Old Testament to the New Testament, and thence to the Christian church. Believers in the early church used the word Hallelujah in their songs and hymns at an early date. It became the characteristic expression of joy, and was therefore sung at Christmas and Easter time. At Christmas time, we sing the Hallelujah chorus. At Easter, we often sing:

KEY VERSES

Revelation 19:1,
3–4, 6

> Christ the Lord is ris'n today, Alleluia!
>
> Sons of men and angels say: Alleluia!
>
> ("Christ the Lord Is Risen Today," Charles Wesley)

We should remember that every time we sing "Hallelujah," or "Alleluia," we are praising the Lord Most High, Yahweh, with absolute respect and love—and if we casually use "Hallelujah," or "Alleluia," we are essentially taking the name of our Lord in vain.

Head

Greek expression: *kephalē*
Pronunciation: *keh fah LAY*
Strong's Number: *2776*

The President of the United States is called the "head of state." Likewise, Jesus Christ is called "head of the church" and "the head of creation" in the Bible. *Kephalē* is the Greek word for "head" and is used in the Bible several times. Describing Jesus as the *kephalē* means, in part, that Jesus is the "ruler" and "authority" over the church and creation. But there is far more richness to the metaphor about Jesus being the "head" than just being the authority.

The expression "head of the body" is found only in the writings of Paul when he describes the relationship between Christ and the universe (Eph. 1:21–22; Col. 2:10), as well as Christ and the church (Eph. 4:15; 5:23; 1 Cor. 12:12–27). Where did Paul get this image? It is possible—indeed very likely—that he borrowed it from Greek philosophers who used the image of the head and body in their writings. They considered their "head," which was called "Zeus" or "Reason," as responsible for the creation and sustenance of the celestial beings, humans, animals, and plants. The universe or "body" owed its existence to the "head."

Between 450 B.C., the time of Hippocrates, and A.D. 150, the time of Galen, Greek medical science came to understand the "head" as the seat of intelligence. The Greek scientists realized that the body was able to operate efficiently only because the brain was capable of interpreting data received from the body (eyes, ears, skin, and so on). They also realized that the brain was able to send out appropriate impulses to the various members of the body based upon the data received. The ability of the brain to interpret and direct made the existence of the body completely dependent upon it. Paul drew upon the philosophical and medical writings of the Greeks to show that Christ is the dynamic force that provides the body with direction and unity. The focal point of the church's activity and its ability to exist are rooted in the work of its "head," Jesus Christ. In this light, various modern commentators have indicated that "head-ship" does not merely mean "authority," it also means "source"—as in the term "fountainhead." Thus, He who is the head is the source or the supplier. Jesus is our Source of life, the Supplier of all our needs, and has authority over all creation. Because He is sinless, as our Head, He is also our link to perfection and our Father in heaven.

KEY VERSES

1 Corinthians 12:21;
Ephesians 4:15;
5:23;
Colossians 2:10

Heal

See also: *Heal, p. 82*
Greek expression: *therapeuō, sōzō*
Pronunciation: *thehr uh PEW oh; SOH dzoh*
Strong's Numbers: *2323, 4982*

It is common these days to hear people say, "He needs some therapy." Actually, our English word "therapy" comes from the Greek word *therapeuō* which means "to heal" or "to cure." *Sōzō* is another Greek word for healing. Most frequently, *sōzō* is used with respect to "saving" people, but it also was used to denote "healing" because healing brings deliverance.

The greatest healer of all times was Jesus. All four Gospels portray Him as such, but each Gospel also reveals a different aspect of Jesus through the healings described. Mark's Gospel has the most complete list of the people Jesus healed. In his opening account of Jesus' ministry in Capernaum, we read about the healing of the demoniac, Peter's mother-in-law, the sick brought to Jesus in the evening, and the leper (Mark 1:21–45). Then, Mark presents in rapid succession Jesus' healing of the paralytic (Mark 2:1–12), the man with the withered hand (Mark 3:1–6), the multitudes by the sea (Mark 3:7–12), the Gerasene demoniac (Mark 5:1–20), the woman with a hemorrhage, and Jairus' daughter (Mark 5:21–43). Mark writes that Jesus then commissioned the twelve to proclaim repentance, to cast out demons, and to "heal" the sick (Mark 6:7–13). Meanwhile, Jesus continued healing people at Gennesaret (Mark 6:53–56). These healings expressed not only Jesus' compassion for those suffering but also constituted a revelation of His person—that He was indeed the Messiah of Old Testament prophecy.

The Gospel of Matthew portrays Jesus' healings as directly fulfilling the Old Testament, as is stated in Matthew 8:17. Luke also portrays Jesus preaching and healing. He focuses on the power of the Holy Spirit which anointed Jesus to proclaim good news, to announce release for the captives, and to recover sight for the blind (Luke 4:18). Luke has all the healing incidents noted by Mark, except for those in Mark 6:45—8:26. John's Gospel, however, has only four healing incidents: the official's son (John 4:46–54), the man who was sick for thirty-eight years (John 5:1–18), the man born blind (John 9:1–41), and the raising of Lazarus from the dead (John 11). The special purpose of John's Gospel indicates that the healings listed were intended as signs that revealed the person of Jesus.

KEY VERSES

Mark 1:34; 5:34

The Acts of the Apostles portrays the continuation of Jesus' ministry through the Spirit at work in His disciples. The healing of the lame beggar in Jerusalem indicates that the disciples were able to exercise the power of healing in the name of Jesus (Acts 3:12–16; 4:8–16). These healings were clearly intended to glorify the person of Jesus and lead people to faith in Him (Acts 3:12–26). In contrast to the Gospels' emphasis on the healing miracles of Jesus, the letters of the New Testament focus on the gift of healing given to some believers (1 Cor. 12:9, 28). First Corinthians implies that such gifts are intended to be part of the ministry of the church, but not all believers are given such gifts (1 Cor. 12:30).

Throughout the New Testament, we see the gradual progression of Christ's healing message: first, we are told of many of Jesus' healing miracles, each with a different emphasis on the character of Jesus. Then, we are shown how the Holy Spirit gave the disciples the ability to heal others in order to glorify Jesus and lead others to Him. For believers in need of healing, the Lord's message is clear: He is sovereign and heals, cures, and saves people today in the same loving, eternal capacity conveyed throughout the New Testament.

Heir, coheir

Greek expression: *klēronomos, sugklēronomos*
Pronunciation: *klay raw NAW mawss; soong klay raw NAW mawss*
Strong's Numbers: *2818, 4789*

Though we all might dream of becoming heirs of a millionaire, God has given us something better. We, who believe in Jesus Christ, are heirs of all God's promises! As we all know, an heir is one who inherits something or who is entitled to a future inheritance. The heir receives the property of a deceased person, particularly on the basis of law and usually by means of a will. In both the Old Testament and New Testament, the Hebrew and Greek words for "heir" encompass these ideas.

In a number of references in the New Testament, the Greek word *klēronomos* is used to refer to "the believer in Christ" who has an inheritance from God because of being a child of God the Father. The believer is consequently a joint-heir with Christ (Rom. 8:16–17). The inheritance received by believers from God is referred to in different sections of the New Testament. In Hebrews 6:17, Christians are called "heirs of the promise." This promise occurred when God said to Abraham, "I will certainly bless you richly, and I will multiply your descendants into countless millions" (Heb. 6:13–14, NLT). In Hebrews 11:7, Noah is described as "an heir of the righteousness which is according to faith" (NASB). In James 2:5, the poor in the world who are rich in faith are said to be "heirs of the kingdom which He promised to those who love Him" (NASB). Paul writes that those who are justified by God's grace are made "heirs" according to the hope of eternal life (Titus 3:7).

In Hebrews 1:2, the word "heir" is used with a singular reference to God's Son, who is said to have been appointed "heir" of all things by His Father. Believers, as sons and daughters of God, will share this inheritance with Christ. They will be "coheirs" which is *sugklēronomos* in Greek. Paul uses the same Greek word to describe Christians' participation with Christ in glory (Eph. 3:6). For Christian couples to be "fellow heirs" is for them to have an equal share and joint-participation in the Father's kingdom (1 Pet. 3:7). What a wonderful thing to be an heir of God's eternal kingdom! We are God's children and will one day receive an eternal inheritance.

KEY VERSES

Romans. 8:17;
Ephesians 3:6;
Hebrews 11:9;
1 Peter 3:7

Hell

See also: *Sheol, p. 168* and *Hadēs, p. 297*
Greek expression: *gehenna*
Pronunciation: *GEH ehn nah*
Strong's Number: *1067*

The translators of the King James Version caused much confusion by translating two different Greek words (*hadēs* and *gehenna*) with one-in-the-same English word, "hell" (see Hades). *Hadēs* almost always denotes the "grave" or the "place of the dead." Only one New Testament passage definitely describes *hadēs* as a place of evil and punishment of the wicked and may appropriately be translated "hell" (Luke 16:23). In all other instances, *hadēs* indicates nothing more than the place of the dead. *Gehenna*, a much rarer expression in the New Testament, denotes the "eternal fires." Thus, "hell," as most people think about it, is really *gehenna*, not *hadēs*.

The Greek word *gehenna* is used in a number of New Testament texts to designate the fiery place for punishment of sinners and is often translated "hell" or "the fires of hell" (Matt. 5:22, 29–30; 10:28; 18:9; 23:15, 33; Mark 9:43, 45, 47; Jas. 3:6). *Gehenna* is also usually used in connection with the final judgment and its use suggests that the punishment spoken of is eternal. The word is derived by transliteration from the Hebrew phrase of the Old Testament, "valley of Hinnom" or the "valley of the son of Hinnom," a ravine on the south side of Jerusalem. This valley was the center of idolatrous worship in which children were burned by fire as an offering to the heathen god Molech (2 Chr. 28:3; 33:6). In the time of Josiah, this valley became a place of abomination, polluted by dead men's bones, the filth of Jerusalem, and by garbage and rubbish dumped there (2 Kgs. 23:10–14). A fire burned continuously in this valley. It thus became a symbol of the unending fires of hell, where the lost are consumed in torment, and a symbol of judgment to be imposed on the idolatrous and disobedient (Jer. 7:31–34; 32:35). Another Greek word used to designate "hell" or "the lower regions" is *Tartarus*, a classical word for the place of eternal punishment. Peter used the word *Tartarus* in 2 Peter 2:4 to describe the place where fallen angels were thrown: "For if God did not spare angels when they sinned, but cast them into hell and committed them to pits of darkness, reserved for judgment" (NASB).

KEY VERSES

Matthew 5:22,
29–30; 10:28; 18:9;
23:15, 33;
Mark 9:43, 45, 47

The most descriptive and conclusive utterances about hell come from the lips of Jesus. He spoke of hell in terms of a furnace of fire, eternal fire, eternal punishment (Matt. 13:42, 50; 25:41, 46); outer darkness, the place of weeping and torment (Matt. 8:12); the lake of fire, the second death (Matt.21:8); and a place for the devil and his demons (Matt. 25:41). Those in hell experience everlasting separation from the Lord (2 Thess. 1:9). Separation from the Lord, for all people, would mean existing without meaning, hope, love, or anything good—there is nothing worse than separation from God.

Holiness

Greek expression: *hagiasmos*
Pronunciation: *hah gee ahss MAWSS*
Strong's Number: *38*

We've all heard the expressions "Holier than thou," and "holy-rollers." These pejorative comments have made the words "holy" and "holiness" quite unpopular in recent times. However, "holiness" is actually a wonderful word.

In the New Testament, the Greek word *hagiasmos* means "holiness" and denotes "separation from everything ceremonially impure." It was normally used to describe the priesthood and everything involved with worship. Because God is distinct from everything common, He demanded that nothing common or impure taint the worship of Him. Jesus affirmed this distinct nature of God when He taught His disciples to pray in a way that the Father's name might be esteemed for what it is: "Hallowed [Holy] be thy name" (Matt. 6:9, KJV). In the book of Revelation, the Father's moral perfection is extolled with the threefold ascription of "holiness" borrowed from Isaiah: "HOLY, HOLY, HOLY, is the Lord God, the Almighty, who was and who is and who is to come" (Rev. 4:8, NASB; compare Isa. 6:3).

Similarly, the "holiness" of Jesus Christ and the Holy Spirit is asserted in the New Testament. Luke (Luke 1:35; 4:34), Paul (Acts 3:14; 4:27-30), the writer of Hebrews (Heb. 7:26), and John (Rev. 3:7) ascribe "holiness" to both the Father and the Son. Since the Spirit comes from God, discloses His holy character, and is the dynamo of God's holy purposes in the world, He also is absolutely holy (Matt. 1:18; 3:16; 28:19; Luke 1:15; 4:14). The common title "Holy Spirit" emphasizes the perfection of the third person of the Godhead (John 14:16-17, 26).

In the New Testament, "holiness" also characterizes Christ's church. The apostle Paul taught that Christ loved the church and died for it, "... that He might sanctify her, having cleansed her by the washing of water with the word" (Eph. 5:26, NASB). Peter addressed the church as a "holy" people in language borrowed from the Old Testament. Separated from the unbelieving nations and consecrated to the Lord, the church is "a holy nation" (1 Pet. 2:9; compare Exod. 19:6). But the New Testament more often discusses "holiness" in relation to individual Christians. Believers in Christ are frequently designated as "saints," literally meaning "holy ones," because through faith God justifies sinners, pronouncing them "holy" in His sight. However, the God who freely declares a person righteous through faith in Christ commands that the believer progress in holiness of life. God graciously provides the spiritual resources to enable Christians to be partakers of the divine nature (2 Pet. 1:4). Thus, our journey as believers is one of holiness—learning about and becoming more like Jesus and casting off any "unclean or impure" impediment in walking the way of Christ.

KEY VERSES

Romans 6:19, 22;
1 Timothy 2:15;
Hebrews 12:14;
1 Peter 1:2

Hope

Greek expression: *elpis*
Pronunciation: *ehl PEESS*
Strong's Number: *1680*

Today the word "hope" usually means nothing more than wishful thinking. We often hear people say, "I hope I get an 'A' on that paper," "I hope my team wins," or "I hope it doesn't rain today." In all of these statements, hope is nothing more than a wish for something good to happen.

Of course, people need to have hope—it keeps them going. Present hurts and uncertainty over what the future holds create the constant need for hope. Worldwide poverty, hunger, disease, terrorism, and destruction create a longing for something better. Historically, people have looked to the future with a mixture of longing and fear. Many have concluded that there is no reasonable basis for hope—therefore, "to hope" is to live with an illusion. This viewpoint is partially correct; Scripture tells us that those who do not have God in their lives do not have hope (Eph. 2:12).

The Greek term *elpis* denotes "confident expectation" or "anticipation"—not "wishful thinking." Hope is consequently an expectation or belief in the fulfillment of God's promises. Biblical hope is hope in what God will do in the future. At the heart of Christian hope is the resurrection of Jesus. Paul discusses the nature, certainty, and importance of the resurrection in 1 Corinthians (1 Cor. 15:12–28). Paul is certain that Christian hope points to the future, "If we have hope in Christ only for this life, we are the most miserable people in the world" (1 Cor. 15:19). The significance of Christ's resurrection is not only that it points to His victory over death, but it also extends that victory to those who are His: "Christ was raised first; then when Christ comes back, all his people will be raised" (1 Cor. 15:23, NLT).

The apostle Peter said, "Blessed be the God and Father of our Lord Jesus Christ, who according to His great mercy has caused us to be born again to a living hope through the resurrection of Jesus Christ from the dead" (1 Pet. 1:3, NASB). In that passage, Peter attributes living hope to the resurrection of Christ and points to God's future blessing upon those who belong to Christ. This future hope empowers us to live without despair through the struggle and suffering of the present age.

KEY VERSES

Romans 8:24;
1 Corinthians 13:13;
1 Peter 1:3

I AM

Greek expression: *egō eimi*
Pronunciation: *eh GOH; ay MEE*
Strong's Numbers: *1473, 1510*

Descartes said, "I think, therefore I am." Jesus said, "I am." Who of the two is greater? Of course, Jesus is the greater because He was making a proclamation about His divine being, whereas Descartes was speaking about how he knew he existed. The Greek expression *egō eimi* means "I am" and denotes "self-identity in self-sufficiency."

When Jesus declared, "Before Abraham was born, I am," He asserted His eternal preexistence and His absolute deity (John 8:58). Abraham, as with all mortals, came into existence at one point in time. The Son of God, unlike all mortals, does not have a beginning. He is eternal; and He is God. This is evident in Jesus' use of the words "I AM" for Himself. This statement recalls the Septuagint (the Greek Old Testament) translation of Exodus 3:6, 14, in which God unveiled His identity to Moses as the "I AM WHO I AM." Thus, Jesus was claiming to be the ever-existing, self-existent God. No other religious figure in all of history has made such claims to deity.

The Gospel of John records other "I am" statements that Jesus made. These statements begin with the words "I am" and then continue to express a deep theological thought in terms of metaphorical statements. The "I am" statements found in the Gospel of John are: the Bread of life or the living bread (John 6:35, 48, 51), the light of the world (John 8:12, 9:5), the gate (John 10:7, 9), the Good Shepherd (John 10:11, 14), the resurrection and the life (John 11:25), the way, the truth and the life (John 14:6), and the vine (John 15:1, 5).

These "I am" statements are often linked with Jesus' miracles. The statement and a miracle each contribute to the understanding of the other. Thus when Jesus proclaims that He is the light of the world, He proceeds to bring sight to the blind man. Before Jesus raises Lazarus from the dead, He tells Martha that He is the resurrection and the life. The raising of Lazarus is intended to show Jesus' power to give life now and to demonstrate His power to do what He proclaimed He was able to do. After Jesus had fed the five thousand, He declared that He was the living bread that came down from heaven. Each of these miracles is interpreted by the "I am" statement. All in all, the "I am" statements in John's Gospel help us identify Jesus as divine. He is the ever-existing God.

KEY VERSES

John 6:35; 8:58;
10:7, 14; 15:1; 18:5

Idolatry, idolater

See also: *Idols, p. 91* and *Idol sacrifices, p. 308*
Greek expression: *eidōlolatria, eidōlolatrēs*
Pronunciation: *ay doh law luh TREE uh; ay doh law LAH trayss*
Strong's Numbers: *1495, 1496*

"Idolatry," or *eidōlolatria* in Greek, is "the worship of false gods," usually by doing homage to images—called idols. God's people in the Old Testament were constantly tempted to participate in idolatry and often gave in. By the time of Jesus, however, the Jews had basically abandoned the worship of man-made idols. Thus, there is no mention in the Gospels of Jesus ever speaking about idolatry—except in a specialized sense concerning the worship of *mammon*, Aramaic for "wealth" or "riches" (Matt. 6:24).

Outside of Palestine, however, idolatry was pervasive. Throughout the Greco-Roman world, idols were venerated in temples dedicated to the traditional Gentile gods, in popular magic and superstition, as well as in mystery religions. Thus, when Paul went out on his missionary journeys into the Gentile world, he encountered those who participated in idolatry and idols of every sort. For example, when Paul went to Athens, he was "greatly distressed to see that the city was full of idols" (Acts 17:16, NIV). Athens was typical of other Hellenistic cities that were committed to many forms of idolatry. Ephesus was given over to the worship of Artemis, and Corinth was plagued with idolatry and its accompanying evils.

The fullest discussion in the New Testament on idolatry (*eidōlolatria*) and the idol-worshiper (*eidōlolatrēs*) is found in 1 Corinthians. In an earlier letter, Paul had told the Corinthians not to associate with those who called themselves believers, but were still idol-worshipers (1 Cor. 5:9–11). In that letter from the Corinthians to Paul, they must have asked for clarification on this matter. Thus, 1 Corinthians provides a response to their question. The kind of idolatry that Paul condemns is that which involved Christians offering sacrifices to idols and then partaking of the food that had been sacrificed to them. The participants are called "idol-worshipers" because their involvement in idolatrous sacrifices was perceived as having fellowship with demons (see Idol sacrifices).

In Paul's other letters, Paul speaks out against actual idolatry and what we might call figurative idolatry—that is, idolatry in the sense of desiring something above God. For example, in Romans 1:18–32, sexual licentiousness and other sins are ultimately traced to idolatry. Idolatry is included in Paul's list of what he calls "deeds of the flesh" (Gal. 5:19–20, NASB). And those who are idol-worshipers are included in the catalog of all those evil people who will not inherit the kingdom of God (1 Cor. 6:9). Believers today must take special care not to desire or value anything more than God: whether it be family, a job, success, money, and even depression, self-image, or loneliness. All we need is the Lord, and He is to be first in our lives.

KEY VERSES

1 Corinthians 5:10;
6:9; 10:14

Idol sacrifices

See also: *Idols, p. 91 and Idolatry, p. 307*
Greek expression: *eidolothutos*
Pronunciation: *ay doh LAW th<u>oo</u> tawss*
Strong's Number: *1494*

Idolatry is uniformly condemned in Scripture. We aren't to place anyone or anything above God. The kind of idolatry that Paul specifically condemned in 1 Corinthians is the kind that involved Christians offering sacrifices to idols and then partaking of the food that had been sacrificed to them. The participants are called idol-worshipers, which is *eidolothutos* in Greek. Paul prohibited the eating of sacrificial food at the pagan temples in the presence of "idol-demons." He shared the same view of idols as most Jews in his day did. For the Jews, idols showed that the heathen worshiped mere images, not the true God. This is made clear in 1 Thessalonians 1:9, where Paul contrasts "idols" with "the living and true God." To Paul, idols in and of themselves were nothing (1 Cor. 8:4)—yet, behind every idol was a demon (1 Cor. 10:20).

The eating of sacrificial food at the meals in pagan temples was censured by Paul because the believers understood participants in these meals to be united to demons (1 Cor. 10:19–21). Paul had no problem, however, with those who purchased food that had been left over from these events and was later sold in the marketplace. They could eat this food with a good conscience—unless, of course, in doing so they would be the means of destroying a weaker believer. For the sake of such believers, Paul said they should abstain. This was a matter of conscience. But going to pagan festivities and eating meals offered to idols was not permitted in any form.

The Corinthians had participated in these meals regularly before they became Christians and apparently had continued to do so after their conversion. In Corinth, such meals were the regular practice both at national festivals and private celebrations. The "gods" (whom Paul considered "demons") were thought to be present at these events because the sacrifices were made to them. Thus, to participate in these events was to join oneself to demons and thereby become an "idol-worshiper." The ancient Israelites had been carried away into idolatry by their pagan neighbors on several occasions by participating in such pagan celebrations (Num. 25). These festivities often involved all sorts of licentiousness. In 1 Corinthians 10, Paul referred to this apostasy of the Israelites and used it as a negative example for believers. The Israelites' worship of idols had led to God's wrath and had brought destruction.

KEY VERSES

1 Corinthians 8:1, 4, 7; 10:19

There are still cultures today that worship man-made idols and offer gifts of food and grain; most common are Buddist or Indian idols. Believers know these are not images of God, nor do they represent our Father in heaven—but according to Paul, there are demons behind these man-made images.

Image, likeness

See also: *Image, p. 92*
Greek expression: *eikōn*
Pronunciation: *ay KOHN*
Strong's Number: *1504*

In recent years, a famous tennis player, Andrew Agassi, advertising for a camera company, was fond of saying, "Image is everything." The Bible also has its "image" motto: "People are created in God's image." Whereas the advertisement promotes physical image, the Bible promotes people's spiritual image.

Human beings are unique among all creatures in that they were created to be like God. Genesis 1:26–27 teaches that God determined to create man and woman in His own "image" and "likeness" and that they would have dominion over the animal creation. Both male and female shared this "likeness" to God, which is expressed as *eikōn* in Greek (Gen. 1:27). While the fall of mankind damaged this "image," it was not damaged completely. There is still enough in our make-up to hint at what we once were like and what we can become again through the work of Christ.

Yet, Jesus Christ is preeminently the image of God (2 Cor. 4:4; Col. 1:15; Heb. 1:3). Frequently, this is understood exclusively as a reference to the deity of Christ. To see Christ is to see the Father (John 14:9). However, in the passages cited, Jesus is the incarnate God—the last 'Adam' who is all that God intended the first Adam to be. Incarnation means that Jesus is truly a man; and because He is truly a man, He shows us what being made in the image of God should mean.

Jesus Christ is also the prototype for all God's children. Believers need to be recreated into the image of Christ to regain the image they lost in the Fall. Ephesians 4:24 and Colossians 3:10 describe the recreation of the believers in the likeness of God—in righteousness, holiness of the truth, and true knowledge. In other words, Paul declares that the redeemed are recreated into the image of God as they are transformed into the image of Christ. Just as Adam's fall affected the image of God in mankind, so also redemption from sin affects mankind.

Jesus brings His people into conformity with His own image—that is, the image of the Son of God (Rom. 8:29). People are changed into the same image, from glory to glory, by the Spirit of the Lord (2 Cor. 3:18). Conformity to the image of Jesus Christ is achieved through the process of sanctifica-tion, which was ultimately completed at the resurrection. Thus, as we grow in our relationship with God, we begin to reflect the "image" of Christ more and more. And, when Jesus returns, our bodies will be changed to be like His glorious body (Phil. 3:21). Restoration to the image of Christ moves us beyond the sinful body. All believers will be transformed—the "image" of the earthly will then be exchanged for the "image" of the heavenly (1 Cor. 15:49).

KEY VERSES

Romans 8:29;
1 Corinthians 15:49;
2 Corinthians 3:18,
4:4; Colossians 3:10

Immanuel

Greek expression: *Emmanuēl*
Pronunciation: *ehm mahn <u>oo</u> AYL*
Strong's Number: *1694*

Messiah, Christ, I AM, and Immanuel are some of the names used to describe Jesus of Nazareth. Immanuel, however, appears only three times in the Bible, and is charged with meaning because it means "God with us." Indeed, the title "Immanuel" is appropriate for Jesus—He is "God with us."

The title "Immanuel" appears twice in the Old Testament (see Isa. 7:14, 8:8) and once in the New Testament (Matt. 1:23), where it is transliterated into Greek as *Emmanuēl*. In the Old Testament, the name was given to a child born in the time of Ahaz as a sign to the king that Judah would receive relief from Syrian attacks. The name symbolized the fact that God would demonstrate His presence with His people by delivering them. But, this prophecy also foretold the birth of the incarnate God, Jesus the Messiah, as illustrated in the Gospel of Matthew (see 1:23).

More than seven hundred years passed after Isaiah's prophecy until Jesus was born. Matthew cites Isaiah 7:14 as being fulfilled in the birth of Jesus (Matt. 1:23). The Scripture is very explicit in stating that Mary had no sexual contact with her husband prior to the birth of Jesus (Matt. 1:25). The same precision is seen in the Gospel of Luke. When the announcement of this child's conception was made to Mary, she asked, "How shall this be, since I have no husband?" (Luke 1:34, NIV). The angelic messenger explained that this conception would be brought about by the Holy Spirit coming upon her and by the overshadowing power of the Most High (Luke 1:35). For this reason, the child would be called Holy, the Son of God, God manifest in the flesh (John 1:18). The child would be unique, being both God and man.

The concept of "God with us" was often reiterated by Jesus in Matthew's Gospel. He told His disciples that where two or three gathered in His name He would be present with them (Matt. 18:20). At the very end of the Gospel, just before His ascension, Jesus assured them that He would be with them until the end of the age (Matt. 28:20). Though the exact title "Immanuel" does not appear again in Scripture, the book of Revelation concludes with an affirmation that the one called "God with us" will be with us forever: "The tabernacle of God is among men, and He shall dwell among them, and they shall be His people, and God Himself shall be among them" (Rev. 21:3).

KEY VERSE

Matthew 1:23

Inherit

See also: *Inheritance, p. 93*
Greek expression: *klēronomia, klēronomos*
Pronunciation: *klay raw naw MEH uh; klay raw NAW mawss*
Strong's Numbers: *2818, 2817*

The New Testament speaks of inheritance in terms quite similar to modern notions of inheriting property from one's parents or grandparents. In modern English, the word "inherit" means that a beneficiary receives various possessions once the will of a deceased person is put into effect. Christ's redemptive death enables all believers to become recipients of God's gifts, or His "inheritance" (Heb. 9:16–17).

The New Testament tells us that the believers "inherit" the age to come, the kingdom, and eternal life (Matt. 19:29; 25:34; Luke 10:25; 18:18; 1 Cor. 6:9–10; 15:50; Gal. 5:21; Eph. 5:5; Titus 3:7; Jas. 2:5; 1 Pet. 3:7–9). The most significant feature in the New Testament is its emphasis that, as a result of the death of Christ, His people begin even now to receive the promised "inheritance," which is *klēronomia* in Greek. The Gospel of John frequently stresses the present reality of eternal life (John 6:12–17; 9:15; 11:13, 39–40).

This contrasts sharply with the Old Testament view of inheritance, which included God's gift to His people, but did not necessitate anyone's death. Furthermore, the Jews considered themselves to be the "only" heirs of God's promises, which thereby excluded the Gentiles. Paul addressed this whole matter thoroughly in Galatians 3:7—4:7. In response to the Judaizers, who claimed that the Abrahamic inheritance is restricted to those who become Jews through circumcision, Paul argued that Abraham's true children are those who believe—whether Jew or Gentile (Gal. 3:7; Acts 26:16–18; Eph. 3:6). They become heirs of God's promise, for they receive the Spirit (Gal. 3:14). The principle of inheritance is promise, not the Law (Gal. 3:18). Those who believe are brought into union with Christ (Gal. 3:27–29)—but then they are not merely Abraham's children but God's (Gal. 3:26). Christ is the Son of God and God has determined to send the Spirit of His Son to believers so that they too may call God the Father (Gal. 4:4–7). By His grace all who become Christ's brothers and sisters through faith are joint-heirs with Christ, the heir of all God has created (Rom. 8:15–17; Heb. 1:3).

KEY VERSES

Romans 8:17;
Galatians 3:18, 29;
4:1, 7

Intercession, intercede

Greek expression: *enteuxis, entugchanō*
Pronunciation: *EHN tew kseess; ehn toong KAH noh*
Strong's Numbers: *1783, 1793*

In our day, we often hear of mediators, or intermediaries, working to establish peace in the Middle East or in a terrorist crisis. These intermediaries engage in the work of intercession—that is, they represent one person trying to establish peace with another party. The New Testament concept of "intercession" is not far from this concept. The Greeks used the verb *entugchanō* to express "meeting," "approaching," or "making an appeal." In the Jewish literature written between the Old and New Testaments, the word was employed in the sense of personally petitioning an official to gain a favor (2 Maccabees 4:8).

The New Testament writers borrowed the Greek term *enteuxis* to describe Christ's heavenly ministry of "intercession." After Christ offered Himself on the cross as the sacrifice for sins, He ascended to the Father and entered the heavenly sanctuary where He now represents His people (Heb. 7:25). The letter to the Hebrews depicts Christ as a Priest engaged in His continuing ministry of intercession. Christ's heavenly intercession is a sequel to His earthly sacrifice accomplished once for all (Heb. 10:10–18). Jesus said, "Everyone therefore who shall confess Me before men, I will also confess him before My Father who is in heaven" (Matt. 10:32, NASB). His continuing intercession is recognized in such New Testament phrases as "through Jesus Christ" (Rom. 1:8; 16:27; 1 Pet. 2:5) and "through Him" (Col. 3:17; Heb. 13:15).

The doctrine of Christ's heavenly "intercession" is explicitly affirmed in four New Testament texts. The apostle Paul spoke of Christ, "at the right hand of God, who also intercedes for us" (Rom. 8:34, NASB). The writer of Hebrews affirmed that Christ "is able to save forever those who draw near to God through Him, since He always lives to make intercession for them" (Heb. 7:25, NASB). Further, Christ has entered "into heaven itself, now to appear in the presence of God for us" (Heb. 9:24, NASB). The apostle John also described that ministry: "If anyone does sin, we have an Advocate with the Father, Jesus Christ the righteous" (1 John 2:1, NASB). The Greek word for "advocate" meant a legal counselor who appeared before a magistrate to plead a client's cause. John thus pictured the ascended Lord as appearing before God on behalf of His people.

KEY VERSES

Romans 8:34;
1 Timothy 2:1;
Hebrews 7:25

The noun form of the Greek word for "intercede" is translated in the New Testament both as "intercession" (1 Tim. 2:1) and as "prayer" (1 Tim. 4:5). Paul exhorts believers to intercede on behalf of all people, so that all might come to know Jesus Christ as their Savior (1 Tim. 2:4). We should pray—and pray often about all things for God is the source of our effectiveness in this life.

Jesus of Nazareth

Greek expression: *Iēsous tou Nazariou*
Pronunciation: *yay SOOSS; TOO; nah dzuh RIGH oo*
Strong's Numbers: *2424, 3588, 3480*

In modern times, many people name their children according to how the name sounds, or sometimes children are named after a caring relative. Our names become our identity, but not necessarily because the name itself describes us; we define the name. In ancient times, however, a name signified one's identity. A name described the person and was not just a tag or a label. In keeping with this ancient tradition, Joseph was told by an angel that he should name his son "Jesus" because "it is He who will save His people from their sins" (Matt. 1:21). The name "Jesus" signifies two important aspects of our Lord and Savior: first, it means that He is *Yahweh*; second, it means that He is "the Savior." This is not our Lord's first name. It is His primary name. He is Jesus; He is *Yahweh*, the Savior. *Iēsous* is a Greek transliteration of the Hebrew name *Yeshua* meaning "Yahweh shall save." Although *Yeshua* was a common name among the Jews (Luke 3:29; Col. 4:11), the name uniquely expresses Jesus' work on earth: to save and to deliver.

Jesus was known by His contemporaries as *Iēsous tou Nazariou* or "Jesus of Nazareth." This name created problems for Jesus because Old Testament prophecies predicted that the Messiah would come from Bethlehem, the city of David (Mic. 5:2). Yet, most Jews thought that Jesus was born in Nazareth. Jesus was, in fact, born in Bethlehem, but His parents had to flee to Egypt and later return to Galilee, where Jesus was raised in the obscure town of Nazareth. This gave Jesus the reputation of being a Galilean—specifically a Nazarene, from the hill country of Nazareth. Nazareth was not an esteemed place, as seen in the book of John shortly after Jesus began His ministry. A man named Philip told his friend Nathaniel that he had found the Messiah predicted by Moses and the prophets. But when Philip named Him "Jesus of Nazareth," Nathaniel retorted, "Can any good thing come out of Nazareth?" (John 1:45–46). Since Jesus rarely told people about His birth in Bethlehem—that He did indeed come from Bethlehem—many Jews continued to believe that He was reared from birth as a Galilean and Nazarene. Throughout His ministry, many Jewish leaders refused to believe that Jesus was the Messiah because He was called "Jesus of Nazareth."

After Jesus was crucified for the sins of His people and raised from the dead, the early apostles proclaimed Jesus as the one and only Savior (Acts 5:31; 13:23). Thereafter, the whole world eventually came to know the name Jesus as a name exalted by God above all other names (Phil. 2:9–11).

KEY VERSES

Matthew 1:21;
Luke 1:31;
Acts 2:36; 4:18;
13:23; 17:3;
Philippians 2:10–11

Joy

See also: *Joy, p. 98*
Greek expression: *chara*
Pronunciation: *kahr AH*
Strong's Number: *5479*

Being filled with joy is far better than having sorrow. Joy makes us feel good and uplifted; sorrow makes us feel down. Joy is a feeling called forth by well-being, success, or good fortune. A person automatically experiences it because of certain favorable circumstances. *Chara*, which is Greek for "joy," usually comes after great sorrow because the contrast heightens the sense of happiness. This dichotomy is depicted in the three stories told by Jesus as recorded in Luke 15. In each story, something is lost and then found, thus bringing great joy to the finder. The finder feels joy because the initial loss made the finder appreciate what he or she found. This was the case for the shepherd finding one lost sheep, the woman finding one lost coin, and the father welcoming back his lost, prodigal son. In each case, there was tremendous joy experienced in the recovery of that which was lost.

This sorrow-turned-to-joy is also depicted in Jesus' final words with the disciples before His death. In His final discourse with them (John 14—17), Jesus told His disciples that they would not see Him for a little while, but then they would see Him. On that day, that is the day of resurrection, the disciples would have great "joy." Following Jesus' explanation of the interim between His going and coming, He used an allegory to depict how quickly the disciples' grief would turn to joy, and to convey a spiritual truth about His death and resurrection: "You will be sorrowful, but your sorrow will be turned to joy. 'Whenever a woman is in travail she has sorrow, because her hour has come; but when she gives birth to the child, she remembers the anguish no more, for joy that a child has been born into the world'" (John 16:20–21).

There is more to the allegory of the woman giving birth than depicting grief turned to joy—especially for the disciples. The woman's hour of travail corresponds to the "hour" Jesus constantly referred to throughout His ministry, which would be the hour of His glorification through His crucifixion and resurrection (John 2:4; 7:30; 8:20; 12:23, 24,27; 13:1). The "man born into the world" represents Christ who was raised from the dead (Acts 13:33, 34; Col. 1:18). The travailing woman, according to the context, depicts the grieving disciples who, in a greater sense, represent God's people and their expectation of being delivered from their sorrows and travails by virtue of Christ's victory over death (Rev. 12:1–5; compare Isa. 26:16–19). Jesus is the man born into the world—as such, He is the hope and joy of all mankind. Christ was consequently offering His disciples comfort and hope to fortify them during the period leading up to His crucifixion. Jesus also knows exactly how to comfort us during times of trial and remind us of the joy we will experience and can experience through Him.

KEY VERSES

Luke 15:7, 10;
John 16:20–21;
Galatians 5:22

Justification, justify

See also: *Justice, p. 101*
Greek expression: *dikaiōsis, dikaioō*
Pronunciation: *dee KIGH oh seess; dee kigh AW oh*
Strong's Numbers: *1347, 1344*

The people in the courtroom are filled with anxiety as the jurors bring back their verdict. Then, the judge makes the pronouncement: "Not guilty!" Everyone lets out a sigh of relief. The pronouncement, "not guilty," is what it means to "justify" someone. In common Greek, outside of the New Testament, "justification" and "justify" were frequently used terms in the court of law to describe the act of acquitting or vindicating someone.

The Greek noun for "justification," *dikaiōsis*, is derived from the Greek verb *dikaioō*, meaning "to acquit" or "to declare righteous" (Rom. 4:2, 5; 5:1). It is a legal term used for a favorable verdict in a trial. The word depicts a courtroom setting, with God presiding as the Judge, determining the faithfulness of each person to the Law. In the first section of Romans, Paul makes it clear that no one can withstand God's judgment (Rom. 3:9–20). The Law was not given to "justify" sinners, but to expose their sin. To remedy this deplorable situation, God sent His Son to die for our sins, in our place. When we believe in Jesus, He credits His righteousness to us, and we are declared righteous or "not guilty" before God. In this way, God demonstrates that He is both a righteous Judge and the One who declares us righteous, our Justifier (Rom. 3:26).

Almost all discussion of "justification" in the New Testament is found in the letters of Paul, primarily in those letters to the Romans and the Galatians. In these two letters, "justification" is one of the fundamental terms, by which Paul seeks to set forth the consequences of the work of Christ for sinful humanity. Justification by faith is set primarily against the background of Jewish legalism, and its attempts to make the Law the basis of salvation. Justification is the gift of God and is entirely apart from the Law (Rom. 3:21). The Law, in fact, is not capable of leading one to righteousness nor was it given to bring about righteousness.

God is the one who justifies. God now makes it possible for people to have a personal relationship with Him because our sin was dealt with directly in the death of our sinless Christ, who became sin for us that we might in Him become the right-eous of God (2 Cor. 5:21). We are thus proclaimed "not guilty" before the God of Heaven and allowed into eternity with Him.

KEY VERSES

Romans 3:4, 20, 24, 26, 28, 30; 4:2, 5, 25; 5:1

315

King

See also: *King, p. 103*
Greek expression: *basileus*
Pronunciation: *bah see LEWSS*
Strong's Number: *935*

When the thirteen colonies formed the United States of America, they rejected the idea of having a king and renounced their subjugation to the King of England. There is a King, however, whom we should never reject. He is the King of kings and Lord of lords. The prophets of the Old Testament spoke of a coming Messiah who would establish God's kingship on earth. They spoke of another "king," or *basileus* in Greek, who would be a descendant of David and would rule permanently. Through Him, the reign of God would extend to the ends of the earth (Isa. 9:2–7; 11:1–9; Jer. 33:14–16; Ezek. 34:22–31; Mic. 5:2–5). The Messiah King would put down all opposition to God's rule, remove all enemies, and bring in an era of universal peace and righteousness. The Messiah-King would reveal the perfection of divine rule, as the Spirit of God would be upon Him. His kingship would be marked by service to the people of God, so that they would be a well-cared-for flock—He would serve them as their shepherd.

Jesus came as that messianic King. Jesus is the "King" of whom the angels said, "The Savior—yes, the Messiah, the Lord—has been born tonight in Bethlehem, the city of David" (Luke 2:11, NLT). This magnificent proclamation shows the fulfillment of the prophetic words of the Old Testament. Jesus is the Savior, whose role included not only our deliverance from sin, but also deliverance from all causes of adversity and evil. His mission pertained to both forgiveness and to the establishment of peace on earth (Luke 1:77–79). In this light we must look at Jesus' ministry of healing, feeding, opposition to the forces of evil, suffering, and teaching as the establishment of God's kingdom on earth. He was the "King" who served, fought against the demonic powers, and overcame death. His resurrection marks His victory; He was crowned with glory by being seated at the right hand of the Father (Acts 2:33–36; 1 Cor. 15:25).

KEY VERSES

Matthew 25:34, 40;
27:37;
John 18:33, 37, 39;
19:14–15

Throughout the book of Revelation, Jesus is viewed as "King" over the church as well (Rev. 4:2, 9–11; 5:1, 9–13). At His return, His kingship will be established and enemies of the cross will see whom they have rejected and will bow before Him (1 Cor. 15:25–28). "After that the end will come, when [Jesus] will turn the Kingdom over to God the Father, having put down all enemies of every kind" (1 Cor. 15:24, NLT). Jesus taught His disciples that at His second coming He would be seated on His throne and all mankind would pay Him homage. The enemies of God will be cast out from His presence, and the people of God will fully inherit the kingdom (Matt. 25:31–46).

Kingdom

See also: *Kingdom, p. 104*
Greek expression: *basileia*
Pronunciation: *bah see LAY uh*
Strong's Number: *932*

There are two phrases that appear again and again in the New Testament: "the kingdom of God" and "the kingdom of heaven." You would think that there is a difference between these two concepts—but actually "the kingdom of heaven," used almost exclusively in Matthew's Gospel, is simply a Jewish way of saying "the kingdom of God." Jews avoided saying the name of God out of respect for Him. Therefore, they used the word "heaven" as an alternative way to refer to God. The word "heaven" also points to the heavenly nature of Jesus' "kingdom," which is translated from the Greek word *basileia*. Jesus' kingdom did not involve a political restoration of the nation of Israel as many Jews had hoped. Instead, He brought a heavenly kingdom with a spiritual domain—the hearts of people.

According to the testimony of the first three Gospels, the proclamation of the kingdom of God was Jesus' central message. Matthew summarizes Jesus' ministry with the words, "And Jesus was going about in all Galilee, teaching in their synagogues, and proclaiming the gospel of the kingdom" (Matt. 4:23, NASB). The Sermon on the Mount is concerned with the righteousness that qualifies people to enter the kingdom of God (Matt. 5:20). The collection of parables in Mark 4 and Matthew 13 illustrate the mystery of the kingdom of God (Matt. 13:11; Mark 4:11).

The key to an understanding of the kingdom of God is that the basic meaning of *basileia* is "rule," "reign," or "dominion." Jesus proclaimed the kingdom of God as an event taking place in His own person and mission because He brought God's rule, reign, and dominion to earth. No first-century Jew had any idea that the kingdom of God would come into history in the person of an ordinary man—a teacher who was meek and lowly. But Jesus demonstrated that the kingdom had come by healing the deaf, the blind, and lepers. He cast out demons and preached the Good News of the kingdom to the poor (Matt. 11:5).

Though Jesus brought the kingdom of God to earth, it will not be fully manifested until Jesus returns a second time. This is why Jesus taught us to pray: "Thy kingdom come on earth as it is in heaven"(Matt. 6:10). It is a prayer for God to manifest His reign so that His will be done on earth as it is in heaven. This will ultimately happen at Christ's second coming, but we can experience a foretaste of that kingdom here and now (Matt. 6:33). The kingdom of God in Jesus' person is like a hidden treasure or a pearl of great price, whose possession outranks all other goods (Matt. 13:44–46). We must seek it now, in anticipation of that one day, at the end of this age, when the kingdom of the world will become the dominion of our Lord and Jesus Christ (Rev. 11:15).

KEY VERSES

Matthew 3:2; 4:17;
5:3, 10; 6:10, 33;
John 18:36;
Revelation 11:15

Know, knowledge

See also: *Know, p. 105 and Knowledge, p. 106*
Greek expression: *ginōskō, gnōsis, oida*
Pronunciation: *gee NOH skoh; GNOH seess; OY dah*
Strong's Numbers: *1097, 1108, 1492*

The Greeks had two words for knowing, *oida* and *ginōskō* (the noun form of which is *gnōsis*). *Oida*, related to the Greek word for "seeing," denotes "perception" and "absolute knowledge." Once something is known, it is known for good—nothing can be added to it. *Ginōskō* denotes "inceptive and ongoing knowledge." It designates ongoing, personal knowledge, which implies a relationship between the person who knows and the person who is known. This knowledge can grow and mature. By way of illustration, we can "know" (*oida*) someone's name immediately, but it will take a lifetime to really "know" (*ginōskō*) that person.

The New Testament encourages us to grow in our actual, personal knowledge of Jesus Christ. This is one of the prominent themes in Peter's Second Epistle. As an antidote to false teachings, Peter exhorted the believers to attain a fuller, more thorough knowledge of Jesus Christ (2 Pet. 1:8; 2:20; 3:18). To know God involves relationship, fellowship, concern, and experience. This kind of knowledge is also presented in the Gospel of John. The knowledge of God is mediated through Jesus who has a perfect knowledge of God's purpose and nature and reveals it to His followers: "If you had known Me, you would have known My Father also; from now on you know Him, and have seen Him" (John 14:7, NASB). The identification of Jesus' own relationship with the Father as a model for the relationship of the disciples indicates that knowledge signifies a personal relationship which is intimate and mutual. The definition of eternal life in John 17:3 adds further content to this concept: "And this is eternal life, that they may know Thee, the only true God, and Jesus Christ whom Thou hast sent" (NASB). This concept is vastly different from that of Hellenistic mysticism, in which contemplation and ecstasy are consummated in gradual merging of God and the person who knows. In John, by contrast, the result of knowledge is having a personal relationship with God through His Son.

KEY VERSES

John 17:3;
1 Corinthians 2:12,
14, 16;
2 Peter 1:5; 3:18

Paul also says that the source of knowledge is the revelation of God in Christ. God has made known the mystery of His will to the one who is "in Christ." The spiritual person is taught by the Spirit of God (1 Cor. 2:12–16) and responds to the truth as it is revealed in Jesus Christ. Again, there is emphasis on relationship and encounter as essential elements in the concept of "knowledge." Christian knowledge of God is not based simply on observation or speculation, but is the result of experience in Christ. We can have this experience through daily prayer and studying of God's living Word in the Bible.

Lamb, Lamb of God

Greek expression: *amnos, amnos tou theou*
Pronunciation: *ahm NAWSS; ahm NAWSS; TOO; theh OO*
Strong's Numbers: *286, 3588, 2316*

How would you like to be announced to the world the way Jesus was? Right after Jesus was baptized and about to begin His ministry, John the Baptist declared, "Behold, the Lamb of God who takes away the sin of the world!" (John 1:29). To every listening Jew, *amnos tou theou*, which is Greek for the title "Lamb of God," would have been pregnant with meaning. It would have reminded them of the lambs used in the daily sacrifices for the sin offerings (Lev. 14:12, 21, 24; Num. 6:12), and of the Messianic lamb led to the slaughter (Isa. 53:7). More than anything, Lamb of God would have recalled the Passover lamb (Exod. 12; John 19:36) and evoked the image of Israel's deliverance from bondage.

In saying that Jesus was the "Lamb of God," John was declaring that Jesus was the substitute sacrifice provided by God. What a way to be announced to the world! John was also intimating that the announced Messiah came not to be a conqueror, but a suffering Savior and a Deliverer. Jesus came to do what we could not do for ourselves—take away sin. As the fulfillment of what the Passover lamb represented, Jesus would provide all believers with the means for being delivered from sin. And, just as the eating of the Passover lamb marked the beginning of Israel's journey, so the reception of Jesus as the Lamb of God marks the beginning of every believer's journey. The Israelites celebrate the Passover annually in order to remember God's faithfulness when He delivered them from slavery—the time when a lamb was sacrificed to protect the firstborn of each family and Moses led them on their journey through the desert. Likewise, Christians remember Christ's sacrifice at the time of communion. In this light, Paul declares, "Christ, our Passover lamb, is sacrificed for us; therefore, let us keep the feast" (1 Cor. 5:7).

The slain lamb also symbolizes the first step in the worship of God. Without the shedding of blood, the priests could not approach God's presence. For Jesus to be initially presented as the Lamb of God shows that God wanted to provide a way for believers to approach Him. The shed blood of the Lamb takes care of the sin that separates people from God. With the separation removed, we can approach God to worship and commune with Him.

KEY VERSES

John 1:29, 36;
1 Peter 1:19

Law

See also: *Law, p. 111*
Greek expression: *nomos*
Pronunciation: *NAW mawss*
Strong's Number: *3551*

Among the many definitions of law in the English language, two are prominent: (1) a rule of conduct or action which is prescribed, formally recognized as binding, or enforced by a controlling authority; and (2) a statement of an order or relationship between phenomena that so far as is known is invariable under the given conditions (*Webster's Ninth New Collegiate Dictionary*). The first definition can be applied to the laws of this country; the second to a law such as the law of gravity. In the Bible, the first definition is primary; it speaks of God's law, or *nomos* in Greek, for His people. The best known law is the law of God, as revealed through the Ten Commandments. The law revealed at Mount Sinai was intended to lead Israel closer to God. He used the law as His righteous instrument to teach, in a very specific way, the nature of sin (Rom. 5:20; 7:7–8). God also used the law to show the Israelites how to walk on a path that kept them undefiled by sin and holy to the Lord. But all failed; all are sinners worthy of the just punishment for not having kept the law—and this punishment is death. But Jesus paid the price for the penalties of our sins by His substitutionary death on the cross.

In the early chapters of Romans, Paul describes the "law" of God and peoples' failure to keep it. Then, in Romans 7—8 Paul speaks of other laws, which fit the second definition noted above; that is, they are governing principles of action. The first is called "the law of sin," which Paul says was operating through his flesh causing him to sin. But Paul, as with all believers, needed another law to overcome "the law of sin." This is "the law of the Spirit of life in Christ Jesus," which makes us "free from the law of sin and death" (Rom. 8:2). By following this law, believers can actually fulfill the righteous requirements of God's law or rule (Rom. 8:4). Sin always operates in our flesh to cause us to commit sins; it is an invariable law, like the law of gravity. But there is a stronger law, a stronger principle: "the law of the Spirit of life in Christ Jesus." If we cooperate with His Spirit, He can empower us to overcome sin.

KEY VERSES

Romans 6:14;
7:21–23, 25; 8:2–4

Leader

Greek expression: *archēgos*
Pronunciation: *ahr kay GAWSS*
Strong's Number: *747*

Every team needs a leader. Every country needs a leader, and the family of God needs a leader. Jesus Christ is that leader. The Greek word for "leader" literally means "the first one to lead the way." It is derived from *archē* which means "the first," and *ago* which means "to lead." To express this idea of leadership, *archēgos* is typically translated in Acts 3:15; 5:31 as the "Prince," and as "the author" in Hebrews 12:2.

The best description of our leader Jesus Christ—and what He went through to become our leader—is found in the book of Hebrews. The second chapter of Hebrews tells us that the Son of God joined the human race in order to participate in our humanity, to experience our sufferings, and even to taste death on our behalf. In so doing, He is the one who pioneered the way for all other believers to follow. Hebrews 2:10 calls Him "the captain of our salvation," which could easily be rendered "the pioneer of our salvation" or "the leader of our salvation." As a man, Jesus pioneered the way for all the other sons and daughters of God to follow. He, who was the express image of God's substance and the effulgence of His glory (Heb. 1:3), relinquished His place of glory and took a human body for the sake of accomplishing the Father's will. In that body, Jesus suffered and died for our salvation (Heb. 10:5–10). He did this because He loved the Father and because He anticipated the joy set before Him (Heb. 12:2). His joy would be to return, through His resurrection and ascension, to His Father. Jesus knew that He would again be in glory, but now as a man.

After Jesus Himself entered into glory, He did not just stay there awaiting our arrival. Indeed, after having entered into glory, He came back to God's children to be in their midst and confirm for them His path to glory. The verses following Hebrews 2:10 tell us that Jesus is in the midst of the church. He is dwelling with all those whom He is not ashamed to call His brothers and sisters. Jesus, therefore, is leading us to where He has already gone—into the glorious presence of the Father. The path to that glorious destiny cannot be different than the one the Lord Himself traversed. He left a pattern for us to follow—that is, a mold to which we are conformed. Each believer, if we are to grow and mature, must be conformed to the image of God's Son. And, while following Jesus' way, we have the hope of eternal glorification through Christ.

KEY VERSES

Acts 3:15; 5:31;
Hebrews 2:10, 12:2

Leaven

Greek expression: *zumē*
Pronunciation: *DZOO may*
Strong's Number: *2219*

Physically speaking, "leaven," or *zumē* in Greek, is any substance that produces fermentation when added to dough. This became an excellent metaphor for explaining how one substance (bread dough) was entirely affected by another (yeast). Among the Jews and other peoples as well, it was common knowledge that leaven represented decay and corruption, as did other fermented things. This view of leaven made it inconsistent with the concept of God's perfect holiness. Plutarch also expressed this long-held belief when he wrote, "Now leaven is itself the offspring of corruption and corrupts the mass of dough with which it has been mixed." The apostle Paul quotes a similar proverb in 1 Corinthians 5:6 and Galatians 5:9.

The significant aspect about leaven is its power, which may symbolize either good or evil. Usually, though not always, leaven was a symbol of evil in rabbinical thought. Jesus referred to leaven in the adverse sense when He used the word to describe the corrupt doctrine of Pharisees, Sadducees (Matt. 16:6, 11–12), and of Herod (Mark 8:15). Like leaven that works its way into fresh dough, spreading out through the bread until its effects are evident in the entire batch, the ideas of Herod, the Pharisees, and Sadducees were gradually infiltrating people's minds. These ideas "spread" until they had penetrated and permeated every part of the people's thinking. Paul applied the same concept to moral corruption, warning that "a little leaven leavens the whole lump." He admonished his readers to clean out the old leaven—that is, any evidence of their unregenerate lives—and to live the Christian life with the "unleavened bread of sincerity and truth" (1 Cor. 5:6–8, NASB).

There is only one instance in the New Testament where leaven is used as a positive metaphor. Christ used the concept of leaven's effect upon dough to provide His disciples with a brief, but memorable parable (Matt. 13:33; Luke 13:20–21), wherein leaven illustrates the cumulative, pervasive influence of the kingdom of God on the world. In this case, leaven illustrates how a mere spark of God's Spirit, love, and hope can work through an entire community, society, and people to catalyze spiritual growth.

KEY VERSES

Matthew 13:33;
16:6, 12;
1 Corinthians 5:6–8;
Galatians 5:9

Liberty

Greek expression: *eleutheria*
Pronunciation: *eh lew thehr EE uh*
Strong's Number: *1657*

Patrick Henry exclaimed, "Give me liberty or give me death." To this man, liberty was as precious as life itself. The Greek word *eleutheria* means "liberty" or "freedom." Jesus came to give us liberty (Luke 4:18). But what kind of liberty? The Jews in Jesus' day thought of this liberty in terms of freedom from foreign domination. But the Messiah is concerned with setting people's spirits free. The freedom that matters is the freedom Christ gives. Jesus says plainly that people are really free when the Son sets them free (John 8:36). Paul exults in this freedom that Jesus Christ brings (Rom. 7:24–25). The same idea can be expressed in terms of "the truth" setting people free (John 8:32); of course, these words must be understood in light of the fact that Jesus is Himself "the truth" (John 14:6). This is not, however, the philosophical concept which states that ignorance enslaves people, while truth (as knowledge) has a liberating effect. Truth here is that truth which comes from knowing Jesus and experiencing His Spirit. Paul says, "Now the Lord is the Spirit, and where the Spirit of the Lord is, there is freedom" (2 Cor. 3:17, RSV).

The New Testament is insistent that people left to themselves cannot defeat sin. We may earnestly desire to do good, but evil is too powerful for us. We cannot do the good we wish to do (Rom. 7:21–23), but because of Christ's Spirit in us, we can overcome the power of sin: "For the law of the Spirit of life in Christ Jesus has set me free from the law of sin and death" (Rom. 8:2, RSV). Does this mean that the Bible says nothing about freeing people from actual slavery or freeing this physical world from the corruption of the fall? On the contrary, the New Testament addresses both issues. As to slavery, Paul encouraged Christian slaves to get their freedom if they could (1 Cor. 7:21), and he personally advocated for the freedom of Onesimus, a slave who had run away from his master Philemon (Phlm. 10-17). But Paul did not advocate freedom from slavery as part of the Christian gospel.

As to all of creation, Paul anticipated that the whole creation would be liberated from the bondage of decay (Rom. 8:21). Creation will in some way share in the liberty of the glory of God's children. This points to a wonderful destiny for creation. In the meantime, we should enjoy our freedom in Christ.

KEY VERSES

Romans 8:21;
2 Corinthians 3:17

Life

Greek expression: bios, zōē, psuchē
Pronunciation: BEE awss; dzoh AY; psoo KAY
Strong's Numbers: 979, 2222, 5590

The Greek language is rich. It has three different words to describe three different aspects of life: zōē, psuchē, bios.

The word zōē in classical Greek was used for "life in general." There are a few examples of this meaning in the New Testament (Acts 17:25; Jas. 4:14: Rev. 16:3), but in all other instances zōē was used to designate "divine, eternal life"—the life of God (Eph. 4:18). This life resided in Christ, and He has made it available to all who believe in Him. Human beings are born with the "natural life"—called psuchē in Greek. Psuchē is translated "soul," "personality," or "life." Indeed, human beings have "natural life," but they do not possess "eternal life." This life can be received only by believing in the one who possesses the eternal life—namely, Jesus Christ. Human beings have another life, which is called bios in Greek. Although we get the word biology from bios, it does not mean our physical body. Rather, the Greeks used bios to denote a person's "physical sustenance" or "livelihood." For example, when the widow put her one small coin into the offering box at the temple, Jesus said she gave her entire bios or "means of livelihood."

Interestingly, all three words are used in one passage in 1 John:

> We know that we have passed from death to life [zōē] because we love one another. Whoever does not love abides in death. All who hate a brother or sister are murderers, and you know that murderers do not have eternal life [zōē] abiding in them. We know love by this, that he laid down his life [psuchē] for us – and we ought to lay down our lives [psuchē] for one another. How does God's love abide in anyone who has the world's goods [bios] and sees a brother or sister in need and yet refuses help?
>
> (1 John 3:14–17, NRSV)

As mentioned above, the word zōē in the New Testament is used to designate "the life of God." This life resides in Christ, and He made it available to all who believe in Him (John 1:4; 1 John 3:15). Human beings are born with the natural life or psuchē ("soul" or "personality"); so Jesus also had a soul. He gave up His soul in death so that we might have the zōē-life, the eternal life of God. John then asks us to sacrifice our psuchē-life by giving our bios-life to those in need. The Greek word bios or "livelihood" can also be translated as "that which is necessary to sustain our physical life." A believer demonstrates that he or she has eternal life (zōē) by giving up part of their livelihood (bios) to sustain the soul and life (psuchē) of another believer. This is the true and best manifestation of love.

KEY VERSES

John 1:4;
10:10–11, 15;
Ephesians 4:18;
1 John 3:14–17

324

Light

See also: *Light, p. 116*
Greek expression: *phōs*
Pronunciation: *FOHSS*
Strong's Number: *5457*

John Milton begins the third book of his poem *Paradise Lost* with these lines:

> Hail holy light, offspring of Heave'n first-born, Or of th'Eternal Coeternal beam May
> I express thee unblam'd? since God is light, And never but in approached light Dwelt
> from Eternity, dwelt then in thee, Bright effulgence of bright essence increate.

In these lines Milton captures three aspects of light, which is *phōs* in Greek, that are revealed in Scripture. The first is that God has been "light" forever; He has always lived in unapproachable light (1 Tim. 6:16). The second is that the Son of God (the co-eternal beam) has also been "light" forever—He has always been the bright effulgence of God's glory (Heb. 1:2–3). The third aspect is that which is spoken of in the first line: the "light" that God created on the first day of creation —"offspring of Heav'n first-born" (Gen. 1:3).

The light of creation is enjoyed by all living beings, especially human beings. But this light is only a picture of the real Light, or God. We cannot comprehend this light for it is God Himself. This is why Paul says that God dwells in "light unapproachable" (1 Tim. 6:16), the psalmist says that the eternal God is "clothed in light" (Ps. 104:2), and John says that "God is light" (1 John 1:5). Mortals would die instantly if they came into the very presence of the radiant God; it would be like coming into direct contact with the sun. But there is good news: the Son of God brought this light to people in a way that they could receive God as light. The Son of God is the effulgence of God's glory; He is like the beams of the sun reaching earth and humanity (Heb. 1:2). This is why John says, "in Him was life, and the life was the light of men" (John 1:4, NASB).

To experience God is to experience being illumined, enlightened, and even exposed by Christ. As the psalmist said, "in thy light shall we see light" (Ps. 36:9, KJV). We see God in all His goodness and righteousness, and we see ourselves with all our faults and sins. This is the normal experience of those who live in the light by having close fellowship with God—and miraculously, He loves us despite our faults.

KEY VERSES

John 1:4, 5;
1 Timothy 6:16;
1 John 1:5

Lord

See also: *Lord, p. 118*
Greek expression: *kurios*
Pronunciation: *KOO ree awss*
Strong's Number: *2962*

Among the many titles attributed to Jesus, none is more frequently used than "Lord." The title appears over 700 times in the New Testament. This title is significant in several ways. First, it equates Jesus with "the Lord" of the Old Testament, translated in the Greek Old Testament as *kurios*. Second, it attributes to Jesus a title that was also (in those days) being attributed to the Caesars. Third, it attributes to Jesus a title that was frequently given to pagan gods.

In the Greek Old Testament, the term *kurios* appears over 9,000 times. In about 3,000 occurrences, it is the equivalent for *adonai*. In the other 6,000 occurrences, it is a roundabout way for saying *Yahweh*. The Jews who first followed Jesus would have been aware that God was repeatedly called "Lord" in the Greek Old Testament. Thus, they knew what they were saying when they called Jesus "Lord." To call Him Lord was to call Him "God." When Thomas encountered the risen Christ, he proclaimed to Jesus, "My Lord and my God" (John 20:28, NASB).

In the first century, many people worshiped the Roman emperor, Caesar. Certain cities even built temples for Caesar-worship as was the case in Smyrna. Because they had been an ally of Rome, the people of Smyrna thought it would be to their advantage to build (in A.D. 26) a temple in which the Roman emperor would be honored. It became a crime punishable by death to refuse to worship the image of the Roman emperor as "Lord." Hence, many Christians were compelled to choose between "Caesar as Lord" or "Jesus as Lord." To choose Jesus was to choose martyrdom.

During the same time period, pagan deities were also given the title "Lord" (*kurios*). The gods and goddesses of the national and mystery religions, especially in the east, were addressed as *kurie* ("Lord," masculine) or *kuria* ("Lord," feminine). In the literature of that era, we see that gods such as Isis, Serapis, and Osiris were addressed as "Lord." Paul referred to these "gods and lords" in his letter to the Corinthians. In contrast to the multitude of deities worshiped by the pagans, Paul asserted that there is only one true God and one true "Lord," Jesus Christ (1 Cor. 8:5–6). The early Christians rejected polytheism—the belief in many lords and gods. Interestingly, from the ancient Greek's perspective, these Christians were "atheists" because they did not believe in the gods and lords of the surrounding peoples. As a consequence, in addition to martyrdom, Christians were persecuted for refusing to believe in these gods (1 Cor. 12:3). Christ tells us to expect persecution for our belief in Him (Matt. 10:22–25). As true believers, we need to be ready to face suffering in order to confess that there is one Lord, one Way, and one Truth.

KEY VERSES

John 20:28;
1 Corinthians
8:5–6; 12:3

Lord's day

Greek expression: *kuriakos hēmera*
Pronunciation: *koo ree ah KAWSS; hay MEHR uh*
Strong's Numbers: *2960; 2250*

Although the "Lord's day" is mentioned only once in the New Testament (Rev. 1:10), it is a very significant term. The "Lord's day" was most likely the first day of the week, a day on which Christians gathered to worship and celebrate the Lord's Supper because Jesus rose from the dead on that day (1 Cor. 11:20). The earliest reference to Christian activity on Sunday comes in a brief allusion Paul makes to "the first day of the week" (1 Cor. 16:2). He instructed the church in Corinth to remember their poverty-stricken fellow believers in Jerusalem by setting aside a sum of money each Sunday. Paul made it clear that this observance was not merely local (1 Cor. 16:1), Sunday was the day when special church meetings took place everywhere.

In Acts 20:6–12, Luke describes a church meeting that took place on the first day of the week. This was not a special meeting convened to hear Paul who had already been in town six days, but a regular weekly event. The main purpose behind the church's Sunday meeting at Troas was "to break bread" (Acts 20:7) which was the New Testament's term for eating the Lord's Supper. The Lord's Supper probably included the less formal table fellowship of the love feast (1 Cor. 11:17–34) and very quickly became a focal point of the early church's Sunday worship.

In Revelation 1:10, John describes how he was worshiping on the Lord's day when he received his great vision. The immediate context of Revelation 1:10 makes it clear that John saw Sunday as the Lord's day because on it Christians expressed together their total commitment to Jesus as Lord and Master (Rev. 1:8). It was Jesus' resurrection on the first day of the week that demonstrated His lordship most clearly (John 20:25–28; Rev. 1:18). One day the whole world will have to acknowledge that He is "King of kings and Lord of lords" (Rev. 19:16; Phil. 2:11), but in the meantime it is in the church that His lordship is recognized. Thus, Christians make a commitment to worship God on the first day of the week, Sunday, in preparation of Jesus' final return.

KEY VERSE

Revelation 1:10

Love

See also: *Love, p. 120*
Greek expression: *agapē, phileō*
Pronunciation: *ah guh PEH; fee LEH oh*
Strong's Numbers: *26, 5368*

We use the word *love* to describe all kinds of feelings—from adoration to lust. But the ancient Greeks had four words to express different kinds of "love": (1) *eraō* for "sexual passion," a word not found in the New Testament; (2) *storgeō* for "family devotion," a word used in a negative sense in 2 Timothy 3:3 as "unloving"; (3) *phileō* for "friendship," a word appearing frequently in the New Testament; and (4) *agapaō* for "loving-kindness."

The first three Greek words were used abundantly in Greek writings, but the fourth word *agapaō* (the noun form is *agapē*) was rarely used in Greek literature prior to the New Testament. When *agapaō* was used, it denoted showing kindness to strangers, giving hospitality, and being charitable. In the New Testament, the word *agapē* took on a special meaning. It was used by the New Testament writers to designate a "volitional love" as opposed to a purely emotional love, a "self-sacrificial love," and a "love naturally expressed by God," but not so easily by men and women. It is a word that speaks of compassion, regard, kindness, and true love. It is an unselfish love that transcends natural affinities. In short, it is a love that we don't naturally have. It is divine.

John made a wonderful proclamation when he said, "God is love" (1 John 4:8). This means that God creates and sustains all things in love. Love is the very essence of God. No one could possibly be described as being "love" itself. Only God is completely loving because love is His very entity, nature, and character. When John writes, "God is love," he is giving the reader the clearest, briefest, most comprehensive expression possible of the nature of God. This divine love motivated God to give His Son to this world to die for our sins. God loves and as a natural consequence of this love, He gives us: His Son, forgiveness, salvation, fellowship, and eternal life. Believers can see the love of God most clearly in the crucifixion and resurrection of Jesus Christ.

KEY VERSES

Romans 5:5, 8;
1 John 4:7–8

Agapē-love comes from the divine nature. When we are born again through the Spirit, we too can express *agapē*-love (2 Pet. 1:3–9; 1 John 3:9). With this love that God gives us, it is possible for us to truly love our friends, co-workers, and neighbors.

Mammon, money

Greek expression: *mamõnas, argurion*
Pronunciation: *mah mohn AHSS; ahr GOO ree awn*
Strong's Numbers: *3126, 694*

Money, money, money. How many hours do we waste worrying about money? In Aramaic, the language Jesus spoke, the word for *money* or *wealth* is called mammon. Instead of translating this word into Greek, the writers of the Gospels simply transliterated the word into Greek letters. Some English translations preserve the Greek form of the word in English as "mammon" (KJV, RSV, NASB); others translate it with the words "wealth" or "money" (NEB, TEV, NIV, NLT). In Matthew 6:24 and Luke 16:13, "mammon" is personified as a rival to God for the loyalty of the disciples. Jesus asks us—who will we obey: God or money? It is impossible to serve this god called "mammon" and the true God at the same time. According to the story in Luke 16, there can be no doubt that this word is used for "riches." Jesus considers riches as an idol, master, or god of the human heart—something in direct conflict with worship of the true God.

In Jesus' day, Roman coins were inscribed with the Emperor's image. Since the emperor was worshiped in the Roman Empire, these coins represented a form of idolatry. In Matthew 22:19–21, Jesus asked the Jews, who were trying to trick Him with a question, to show Him a coin used to pay the government tax. They handed Him a denarius bearing the portrait and inscription of Caesar. That coin could have been a denarius of Caesar Augustus, who had died some sixteen years before, or of Caesar Tiberius (A.D. 14–37), who was then on the throne. The silver denarius of Tiberius read "Tiberius Caesar Augustus, son of the divine Augustus." By asking Jesus whether Jews should pay taxes, these Pharisees were trying to get Jesus to either (a) say it was wrong—and then they could accuse Jesus as traitor before the Roman authorities; or (b) say that taxes should be paid—and then they could accuse Jesus of opposing God (because the inscription on the coin acknowledged Roman gods). Ironically, these Jews were carrying Roman coins with them—coins, which they themselves considered idolatrous. Jesus aptly responds to them with, "You, hypocrites!"

In fact, the Jews refused to accept Roman coins as offerings to God in the temple because these coins had a graven image of a god. Therefore, these coins broke one of the Ten Commandments (Exod. 20:4). The Jews, therefore, instituted the business of exchanging Roman currency for temple currency in the temple courts. The moneychangers converted Roman money into "orthodox coins" for the temple half-shekel (Matt. 17:24; 21:12; 25:27; Mark 11:15; Luke 19:23; John 2:14–15). This system became a means for certain Jews to become rich. This hypocritical system infuriated Jesus, who overthrew the moneychangers' tables, and then proclaimed,

KEY VERSES

Matthew 6:24;
Luke 16:13

"My Father's house is a place of prayer, but you have turned it into a den of thieves" (Matt. 21:13).

We need to listen to Jesus' warning and beware of the power of money in our lives. We have a dual citizenship with Christ; we must pay for services we receive from our government. But we also are citizens of God's kingdom and must therefore honor Him with our God-given gifts, obedience, and commitment. We have to use money, but we must not serve it or value its accumulation more than our Holy Father.

Greek expression: *anthrōpos, anēr*
Pronunciation: *ahn throh PAWSSS; ah NAYR*
Strong's Numbers: *444, 435*

The Greek language has two words that can be translated "man"—*anthrōpos* and *anēr*. *Anēr* designates a "male person," as opposed to a female, an "adult," or a "husband." It is also used to specify certain people groups. In most instances, it should be translated as "man," "husband," or "the people of such and such a place." The word *anthrōpos*, on the other hand, primarily designates a "human being," regardless of sex. It can also be used for a male individual—as in John 1:6, which says, "there was a man sent from God named John." The context makes it clear whether the word is referring to people in general or males. There are hundreds of verses in the Bible where the reference is to "human beings" in general, and not to "males." The King James Version and other literal translations (RSV, NIV, NASB), however, use the word "man" or "men"—instead of "human being" in these verses. Here are a few sample passages:

> Man shall not live by bread alone, but by every word, that proceedeth out of the mouth of God.
>
> *(Matt. 4:4, KJV)*

> In him was life; and the life was the light of men.
>
> *(John 1:4, KJV)*

> For there is no other name under heaven given to men by which we must be saved.
>
> *(Acts 4:12, NIV)*

Clearly, the intent of these passages is that God has some wonderful things—His word, life, and salvation—to offer to all people—not just males. What we must realize is that *mankind* was created by God as male and female (Gen. 1:27), meaning that what is said generally of man must be said of both the male and the female. The truest picture of what it means to be human being will be found in the context of man and woman together. Furthermore, it is mankind—as male and female—that bears the image of God. God's command to multiply and exercise sovereignty over the earth was given to both sexes as shared responsibility. Similarly, it is mankind as male and female that rebelled against God and bears the consequences of original sin; and it is to mankind—as both male and female—that Christ came to redeem (Gal. 3:28).

KEY VERSES

Matthew 4:4;
John 1:4, 6;
Acts 4:12;
1 Timothy 4:10

Marry and divorce

See also: *Divorce, p. 269*
Greek expression: *gamizō, apoluō*
Pronunciation: *gahm EE dzoh; ah paw LOO oh*
Strong's Numbers: *1060, 630*

Many, today, lament the fact that approximately half of all marriages end in divorce. Did ancient peoples, such as the Greeks, respect marriage more than we do? Unfortunately, not much more. The Greek verb for marry is *gamizō*, and the Greek word for the verb divorce is *apoluō*.

In Greek society, a man could divorce his wife fairly easily. If he found fault with her in any small matter, he had the right to divorce her. If a bride was found to have committed adultery, the husband was entitled to a divorce. A man could divorce his wife, even if he merely suspected her of infidelity. He could also divorce his wife if he felt that she had violated normal morality, had abandoned her faith in God, or had been less than efficient in the management of her household. If a woman refused her husband his conjugal rights for a period of at least one year, he could also divorce his wife. Other grounds for divorcing a wife included insulting behavior to a husband or his relatives, contracting an incurable disease, or refusing to accompany her husband when he moved to a new area. In general, wives were not protected by the law in ancient times. Despite the fact that she gave advice to her husband, managed the household, educated the young children, and worked alongside her husband when necessary, her husband was still her master.

This general attitude towards women was not only prevalent in Greek society, but was also prevalent among the Jews of Jesus' day. But Jesus challenged the popular view of divorce by affirming the importance of marriage in God's eyes. Jesus affirmed that God had originally made one woman for one man. Therefore, a man shouldn't divorce a woman (Mark 10:2–9). Further, He stated if a man does divorce his wife and marries again, "he commits adultery against her" (Mark 10:11). With this statement, Jesus made man and woman equal when it came to adultery. An unfaithful husband is just as adulterous as an unfaithful wife.

KEY VERSES

Matthew 19:3,
7–10;
Mark 10:2, 4, 11;
1 Corinthians 7:10

There is a slight difference in Matthew's account of Jesus' teaching. According to Matthew 19:9, a wife's "unchastity"—that is, some sexual misconduct—allows an aggrieved husband to divorce her and marry again. Paul basically affirmed Jesus' view on marriage (1 Cor. 7:10–11) and then added that divorce was permissible if an unbelieving partner found it objectionable that the other spouse was a Christian (1 Cor. 7:12–16). Despite the fact that people throughout history have not honored the ties of marriage, Jesus and the New Testament writers uphold the importance of keeping one's marriage vows.

Mediator

Greek expression: *mesitēs*
Pronunciation: *mehss EE tayss*
Strong's Number: *3316*

In recent years, United States presidents have played various intermediary roles in trying to achieve peace in the Middle East. Intermediaries are necessary because the Palestinians and Israelis are long-time enemies, estranged from one another. Because of original sin, all people are estranged from, or enemies of, the Holy God. Humanity thus needs an intermediary to "make peace" with God. Our intermediary is Jesus Christ.

The Greek word *mesitēs* is comprised of the words *mesos*, meaning "middle," and *eimi*, meaning "to go." Thus, *mesitēs* literally means "a go-between" and connotes a "mediator" between two parties. The world's premier mediator is Christ, for He made peace between God and humanity, and He provides access to God.

The New Testament declares that people's knowledge of God, salvation, and hope come through Christ alone. No one knows the Father except the Son and those to whom the Son reveals Him. No one comes to the Father but through Jesus—neither is there salvation in any other person or god. This is made explicit by Paul in 1 Timothy 2:5: "There is one God, and also one mediator between God and men, the man Christ Jesus" (NASB).

Paul described Moses as a "mediator" of the first covenant: he acted as a liaison between God and the Israelites, communicating the obligations of the covenant to Israel and pleading the Israelites' case before God (Gal. 3:19–20). In a similar way, Jesus is the "mediator" of the new covenant. He established the new covenant through His own death, which removed the enmity between God and humanity. Now He sits at the right hand of God and intercedes for us (Heb. 7:25).

Christ's mediation is the fulfillment and end of all mediation. The book of Hebrews opens with the assertion that Christ surpasses all other mediators—angels, Moses, and the priests of the Aaronic priesthood. Christ's priesthood is a timeless priesthood, like Melchizedek's. The new covenant He established between God and believers offers better promises, a better sacrifice, a better sanctuary, and a better hope (Heb. 7:19; 8:6; 9:1, 11–15). Christ's mediation excels all others and can never be superseded. He is the only way to God; there is no other way—no other "go-between."

KEY VERSES

Galatians 3:19–20;
1 Timothy 2:5;
Hebrews 8:6; 9:15

Mercy

See also: *Mercy, p. 125*
Greek expression: *eleos*
Pronunciation: *EHL eh awss*
Strong's Number: *1656*

"Mercy" is a word we use to describe various kinds of compassion. When we ask people to "have mercy on" someone—whether that person is homeless or simply rebellious—we are asking people to have compassion. We also use the word to describe the compassionate treatment of those in distress—showing "mercy" to another. The Greek word *eleos* has the same connotations in the New Testament, but its primary meaning is "a blessing that is the act of God's favor."

We see the first use of "mercy" in the story of the tax collector who calls out to God, "Be merciful to me a sinner," while praying in the synagogue (Luke 18:13, KJV). *Eleos* here means "to be propitious" or "to be favorably inclined to." The Greek term is used only one other time as a verb in the New Testament, and there it describes how Christ acts mercifully as our high priest (Heb. 2:17). Jesus, as our sacrifice, propitiated God concerning our sins—that is, He appeased God. The tax collector, well aware of his sinful condition, was asking God for propitiation—for mercy.

The other connotation of this *eleos* focuses on "demonstrated compassion" or "sympathy" that expresses itself in helping a person in need instead of remaining completely passive. We often see this word used when those in need cry out to Jesus for help. For example, the two blind men call out to Jesus, "Have mercy on us, son of David!" (Matt. 9:27).

Finally, the Greek word *eleos* is closely associated with the Greek word *charis*, meaning "grace" (Eph. 2:4–5; 1 Tim. 1:2; 1 Pet. 1:2–3). Both "mercy" and "grace" are similar in meaning to the Hebrew word *hesed*, a term that is often translated "loving-kindness" or "goodness" in the Old Testament. *Hesed* speaks of the "loyal love" that God freely showed the Jews.

The ultimate expression of God's mercy is His voluntary offering of His only Son for our sins—even when we were still His enemies (Eph. 2:4–5). Since Jesus, our Intercessor at the right hand of God (Heb. 7:25), has experienced every kind of temptation we endure (Heb. 4:15), we can approach Him with boldness, knowing that He will shower us with sympathy, grace, loving-kindness, and mercy. We who have experienced God's mercy and forgiveness should, in turn, show mercy to our friends, neighbors, co-workers, and even our enemies (Col. 3:12).

KEY VERSES

Ephesians. 2:4;
Titus 3:5;
1 Peter 1:3

Messiah

See: *Christ, p. 249*

Mind

Greek expression: *dianoia, nous*
Pronunciation: *dee AH noy ah; NOOS*
Strong's Numbers: *1271, 3563*

When we speak of someone's "mind," we are really speaking about the thoughts produced by their brain. Old Testament writers understood the mind as the inner being of a person—much like a person's heart. When the Gospels speak of a person's mind, it is mostly in connection with a person's heart as well ("in the thoughts of their heart"; see Luke 1:51, NASB). The only other significant occurrence of the word *mind* comes in Jesus' statement of the great commandment: "You shall love the Lord your God with all your heart, and with all your soul, and with all your strength, and with all your mind" (Matt. 22:37; Mark 12:30; Luke 10:27, NASB). The Gospel writers are unanimous in their agreement that Jesus quoted Deuteronomy 6:5 and added "with all your mind" to the quote.

In the writings of Paul, we enter the Greek world's understanding of the *mind*. Paul used two words for the *mind: dianoia*, meaning "understanding" or "mind," and *nous*, meaning "mind" or "intellect." Paul understood the *mind* as distinct from the *spirit* and the *heart* of a person. The mind possesses the ability to understand and to reason (1 Cor. 14:14–19); it is the seat of intelligence. In other places, Paul used the Greek word for *mind* to refer to the entire mental and moral being of a human. A person's actions flow from the inclinations of his or her mind; whether a person is good or evil depends on the state of that person's mind. Paul makes it clear that a person's condition depends upon how that person controls his or her mind. Romans 8:6–7 speaks of a person's mind being controlled either by the flesh or by the Spirit. The person whose mind is controlled by the flesh is evil and the mind controlled by the Spirit leads to good. Other passages refer to the inclination of a person's mind being controlled by the god of this world (2 Cor. 4:4). People whose minds are controlled by the god of this world will have their minds darkened and will not be able to understand the world as it really is (2 Cor. 3:14). It is like a veil over one's understanding; but it is the Lord who can open peoples' minds.

When we are born again, we can experience God's renewing of our minds (Rom. 12:2; Eph. 4:23). It is our responsibility to renew our minds by regularly reading God's Word; but only the Holy Spirit can make us spiritually-minded (1 Cor. 2:15–16). Through Christ, we can live in the Spirit and follow God's ways (Rom. 8:2–6).

KEY VERSES

Matthew 22:37;
Romans 12:2;
Ephesians 4:23

M

335

Miracle

Greek expression: *dunamis*
Pronunciation: *DOO nah meess*
Strong's Number: *1411*

"It's a miracle!" Of course, reports of miracles span from, "It's a miracle that my car started," to "It's a miracle that I didn't die when I was hit by that car."

According to the Bible, a miracle is a divine act. Through miracles, God reveals His power to people on the earth. The Greek word for "miracle"—*dunamis*, literally meaning "power"—indicates that a miracle is an act of God's power. Miracles often defy, or overpower, natural law—but not always. God can also use nature to perform a miracle. For example, God used the wind to part the Red Sea (Exod. 14:21).

The greatest miracle is that the Son of God became mortal and then overcame mortality, death itself, through the resurrection. In between these events, while on earth, Jesus performed miracles, especially exorcisms—the casting out of demons. The exorcisms demonstrated that Jesus Christ was binding the forces of evil and instituting the reign of God (Mark 3:23–27). Jesus' miracles signified the dawning of the age of salvation (Luke 4:18–21). Yet, these miracles were not irrefutable evidence of God's actions. They had to be interpreted through the eyes of faith. Jesus was well aware of the presence of other miracles in His day (Matt. 12:27) and so stressed the presence of faith when He healed (Mark 5:32; 10:52). A person's faith had to be directed towards Jesus Himself.

Among the four Gospels, Mark records the most miracles. The first of the five groups of miracles in Mark centers on Jesus' authority over demons (Mark 1:21–29). The second concerns Jesus' authority over the Law and the conflict with the religious leaders (Mark 1:40—3:6). The third group contains exorcisms and the Beelzebub controversy, centering around Christ's power over Satan (Mark 3:7–30). The fourth group contains especially powerful miracles, such as Jesus' stilling of a storm, His exorcism of the Gerasene demoniac, and the raising of Jairus' daughter. It is through these miracles that Jesus reveals the power of God's kingdom to His disciples and seeks to overcome their spiritual dullness. The fifth and final group of miracles prepares the disciples for Jesus' crucifixion (Mark 6:30—8:26).

KEY VERSES

Mark 6:2, 5, 14;
Acts 8:13

The miracles in Mark center on conflict—first with Jesus' opponents and then with His own disciples. While they are harbingers of God's kingdom, their purpose is to challenge people with God's awesome power. They do not show Jesus as a "wonder worker"—in fact, miracles lead only to amazement or disbelief in those who don't believe. Jesus can only be understood in light of His death on the cross. The miracles are not proofs, but powers—God does not authenticate Himself through them, but shows Himself to those with eyes to see. Even as the apostles and other Christians have continued to perform miracles, they always point to God and glorify Him.

Mystery

Greek expression: *musterion*
Pronunciation: *moo STAY ree awn*
Strong's Number: *3466*

In modern times, "mysteries" are detective thrillers or incomprehensible phenomena. In ancient times, the Greek word *musterion* was a "revealed secret." This is how "mystery" is used in the New Testament. It signifies that which was formerly hidden, but now is made clear by God's revelation (Rom. 16:25; Col. 1:26–27). In New Testament times, the term was often used with reference to the mystery religions. Adherents to the mystery religions used the term to speak of the secret knowledge of their religion revealed only to the initiated ones. In contrast, Paul used the Greek word for "mystery" to speak of a secret that had been openly revealed to all the believers.

Jesus occasionally used the word "mystery" in some of His parables about the kingdom of heaven because He wanted to emphasize that those who understand the message will know its meaning, while those who don't understand it will not enter into the kingdom (Matt. 13:12–15). The apostle Paul used the Greek word *musterion* frequently. He used it to describe Israel's disbelief in the Messiah and their eventual salvation (Rom. 11:25). In Romans 16:25, Paul connects the "revelation of the mystery which has been kept secret for long ages past" with the gospel message of Jesus Christ (NASB). Then, God's secret wisdom is mentioned in 1 Corinthians 2:7 in connection with Paul's proclamation of Jesus' crucifixion. Those who understand the mystery realize that Jesus' death was not foolish—it was God's way of saving the world. Later, in the same book, Paul uses the word "mystery" to speak about the resurrection of the believers and the new bodies they will receive (1 Cor. 15:51–52).

M

In Ephesians, Paul speaks about God's purpose in history culminating in the universal authority of Christ as a "mystery of His will" (Eph. 1:9–10, NASB). Part of God's purpose was to form a body of believers, reconciled to Himself and to each other through the cross (Eph. 2:14–18). Jewish and Gentile believers have been made members of one body and share together in the promise of Christ Jesus—a new phase of God's revealed plan, which Paul also calls a "mystery" (Eph. 3:6). Paul had a responsibility to minister the truth of this mystery faithfully (Eph. 3:2–5).

Colossians continues to show Paul's sense of responsibility regarding this mystery (Col. 1:25–29). Once again, the span of history is linked with God's "mystery" known only by revelation: "the mystery that has been hidden from the past ages and generations; but has now been manifested to His saints" (Col. 1:26). As in Ephesians, Paul declares that the church—the hearts of believers everywhere—is the place where God works out this mystery, "which is Christ in you, the hope of glory" (Col. 1:27, NIV). What a privilege to be part of the revelation and outworking of God's mystery in history!

KEY VERSES

Romans 11:25;
16:25;
1 Corinthians 2:7;
Ephesians 1:9;
3:3–4, 9;
Colossians 1:27

337

Natural

Greek expression: *psuchikos*
Pronunciation: *psoo kee KAWSS*
Strong's Number: *5591*

The Greek term *psuchikos*, usually translated "natural," is literally "soulical" in Greek. In 1 Corinthians, where all four occurrences of *psuchikos* are contrasted pointedly with the "spiritual," this adjective signifies "that which is natural." For example, in 1 Corinthians 2:14, Paul says the "natural man" is one who does not accept or understand the things that come from the spirit of God. Rather, these things are "foolishness" to him. He cannot understand them because they are spiritually discerned. This foolishness is the foolishness of unbelief (1 Cor. 1:21), and the discernment these people don't have is insight given only by the Holy Spirit. Plainly, Paul is describing someone utterly opposed to the Holy Spirit and God's revealed truth.

In 1 Corinthians 15:44–46, the contrast between "spiritual" and "natural" occurs in a different context—that of the "body" in death compared to the "body" in resurrection. In verses 44 and 45, the "natural body" is traced back to Genesis 2:7, to Adam before the fall, at creation. Thus biblically, what is natural refers to what God has created. Originally, what God had created was "very good" (Gen. 1:31). But subsequently, the "natural" creation has been subjected to corruption and perversion because all humanity has sinned against God. The sinful rebellion of natural man, measured by God's original creation, is thoroughly unnatural and abnormal. The opposing work of the Holy Spirit now, in Christ, not only removes this abnormality, but also fulfills the original purposes of creation (Rom. 8:19–22; 2 Cor. 5:17). The bodies of believers laid in the grave—that is, "sown"—are natural bodies. But when believers' bodies are raised from the dead, they will be raised as spiritual bodies—that is, bodies transformed by the Holy Spirit, suitable for spiritual life beyond the grave (Rom. 8:11).

The Greek word for "natural" was also used by James to describe natural wisdom, which is a worldly wisdom as opposed to divine wisdom (Jas. 3:15). And *psuchikos* was also used by Jude to describe those people who didn't have the Spirit and thus were completely "natural" or "worldly" (Jas. 3:19). These New Testament verses should serve as a reminder to us that we should live according to "the Spirit" and not according to our natural, selfish tendencies.

KEY VERSES

1 Corinthians 2:14;
15:44;
James 3:15;
Jude 19

N

New commandment

Greek expression: *kainē entolē*
Pronunciation: *kigh NAY; ehn tawl AY*
Strong's Numbers: *2537, 1785*

God gave the people of Israel Ten Commandments starting with, "You shall have no other gods before Me" and ending with "You shall not covet your neighbor's house" (Exod. 20:3–17). But Jesus gave His people one commandment; He called it "the new commandment." On the night of His arrest, Jesus said: "I am giving you a new commandment: Love each other. Just as I have loved you, you should love one another" (John 13:34, NLT). John, in his letters, refers to this commandment three different times (1 John 2:7, 8; 2 John 5). The same command occurs elsewhere in the New Testament (John 15:12, 17; Rom. 13:8; 1 Peter 1:22; 1 John 3:11, 23; 4:7, 11–12), but is not called "new."

Jesus had already commanded His disciples to love their enemies (Matt. 5:43–45) and to love their neighbors as themselves (Luke 10:25–37). With the "new commandment," which is *kainē entolē* in Greek, Jesus directed Christians to love each other. In no sense did these new commandments overrule the other two love commands. Jesus' command to love those within the church was intended to produce a compelling testimony to unbelievers outside the church. It would offer them demonstrable proof that His followers were becoming Christ-like.

The apostle Paul thought of love as the "law of Christ" (Gal. 6:2), and James called the command to love "the royal law" (Jas. 2:8) and "the perfect law of liberty" (Jas. 1:25; 2:12). When the apostle John talked about this in his letter, he said "I am not writing a new commandment to you, but an old commandment which you have had from the beginning" (1 John 2:7, NASB). Why does John indicate that the new commandment is not new, but old? The phrase "from the beginning" (1 John 2:24; 3:11; 2 John 6) refers to the beginning of the readers' Christian experience—that is, when they first heard the word of the gospel. Thus, John meant that he was not teaching anything beyond the original message that Jesus had given them—which was the message to love one another.

The new commandment of love is also the all-embracing, single requirement of all born-again believers (Rom. 13:8, 10; Gal. 5:14). We obey this commandment because we have been born of God and love God—as John said, "love is from God; and every one who loves is born of God" (1 John 4:7, NASB).

KEY VERSES

John 13:34;
1 John 2:7, 8;
2 John 5

New covenant

Greek expression: *kainē diathēkē*
Pronunciation: *kigh NAY; dee ah THAY kay*
Strong's Numbers: 2537, 1242

A "covenant" is an arrangement between two parties involving mutual obligations. In ancient times, nations would enter into covenants with each other—a stronger nation would promise to protect the weaker nation, while the weaker promised some sort of service to the stronger. In the Bible, the covenant, which is *diathēkē* in Greek, is the arrangement that establishes the relationship between God and His people. The "old covenant" stipulated a relationship with God based on keeping God's law. This covenant failed because the people failed to keep God's law. The new covenant is based on what God has promised to do in the hearts of believers. This is expressed clearly in the book of Jeremiah:

> "Behold, days are coming," declares the Lord, "when I will make a new covenant with the house of Israel and with the house of Judah, not like the covenant which I made with their fathers in the day I took them by the hand to bring them out of the land of Egypt, My covenant which they broke, although I was a husband to them," declares the Lord. "But this is the covenant which I will make with the house of Israel after those days," declares the Lord, "I will put My law within them, and on their heart I will write it; and I will be their God, and they shall be My people."
>
> *(Jer. 31:31–33)*

The quotation of Jeremiah 31:31–34 in Hebrews 8:8–12 is the longest Old Testament quotation found in the New Testament. This quotation explains that the new covenant will one day supersede the old covenant. The theme of the new covenant dominates the book of Hebrews, which was written to encourage faltering Christians by demonstrating the superiority of the Christian faith over older Jewish beliefs and practices. The writer compares the new covenant to a person's "will" throughout the book of Hebrews, tying the two different meanings of the word *diathēkē*—"covenant" and "will"—together. Just as the stipulations of a will go into effect when a person dies, so Christ died to initiate the new covenant—the covenant that frees us from bondage to the law of God, or the "old covenant."

KEY VERSES

Hebrews 8:8; 9:15;
1 Corinthians 11:25;
2 Corinthians 3:6

The expression "new covenant" is found at least six times in the New Testament (1 Cor. 11:25; 2 Cor. 3:6; Heb. 8:8, 13; 9:15; 12:24) and perhaps a seventh (Luke 22:20 according to some manuscripts). Jesus saw the Lord's Supper as instituting a different, and therefore, new covenant. The covenant was sealed by His own sacrificial death, and the cup of the Lord's Supper symbolizes the blood of Christ's sacrifice. Every time we gather to celebrate the Lord's Supper, we are celebrating the new covenant—the wonderful truth that Christ died to save us from our sins and give us new life.

New creation

Greek expression: *kainē ktisis*
Pronunciation: *kigh NAY; KTEE seess*
Strong's Numbers: *2537, 2937*

God's first creation was good, in the beginning. All of creation, however, was ruined when Adam and Eve fell into sin. But God did not leave humanity to die with sin. He gave us salvation, freedom from sin and an open door to being in His presence, through Jesus Christ. Once we accept Jesus, our sins are forgiven and we become *kainē ktisis*, which means a "new creation" in Greek. Thus, salvation is the distinguishing factor between God's original creation and our life through Christ as God's "new creation."

Salvation, according to the New Testament, is from beginning to end a matter of being united with Christ and sharing in all the benefits resulting from His once-for-all redemptive work. Accordingly, because Christ died and was resurrected, anyone who has accepted Jesus and received the Holy Spirit is already a participant in God's "new creation" (2 Cor. 5:15–17). Resurrection is not only a future hope for believers, but also a present reality. We have already been raised with Christ (Eph. 2:5–6; Col. 2:12–13; 3:1). Consequently, we are "created in Christ Jesus for good works" (Eph. 2:10). The church is also God's "new creation," seen as "the one new person" made up of both Israelites and Gentiles (Eph. 2:15; Gal. 6:15). As such, members of God's church are already being renewed inwardly by the Lord, who is the Spirit, according to the glorified image of Christ (2 Cor. 3:18; 4:4–6, 16; Rom. 8:29; Eph. 4:24; Col. 3:10). Believers will bear this same image bodily when Christ returns (1 Cor. 15:49). Therefore, one of the deepest desires of the believer should be to live as a new creature, as God's holy child.

As we are a new creation in Christ, this is not only a present reality, but also a future hope. We should be looking to Christ's return so He can establish "new heavens and a new earth, in which righteousness dwells" (2 Pet. 3:13, NASB). We look forward to getting new, spiritual bodies when we are raised to eternal life. Our present body—sown in corruption, dishonor, and weakness—will be raised incorruptible, glorious, and powerful. And what holds true for our bodies is also true for all of creation. The anxious longing and groaning of the entire creation will be set free from decay, not annihilated, and will share in the glorious freedom of the children of God (Rom. 8:19–23).

KEY VERSES
2 Corinthians 5:17;
Galatians 6:15

Furthermore, the "new creation" is not merely a return to the conditions of "the beginning," when God created Adam and Eve, but a "renewed creation"—the fulfillment of God's saving purposes in history. Those who believe in Jesus will know what it is like to be this new creation.

New man

Greek expression: *kainos anthrōpos*
Pronunciation: *kigh NAWSS; ahn throh PAWSS*
Strong's Numbers: *2537, 444*

The Greeks had two different words for "new." The word *neos* was used to denote "new in time." The word *kainos* was used to denote "new in quality"; that is, something that has a new quality or different nature. In the New Testament, *kainos anthrōpos*, "new man," is used to describe the "new humanity" created in Christ, of which all believers participate—both individually and corporately. The church, the collective group of regenerated people, is the "new humanity" (Eph. 2:14–15; 4:24; Col. 3:9–11).

The "new man" is a "new humanity" made up of Jewish Christians and Gentile Christians. When we understand that the two groups were absolute enemies in New Testament times, this creation is truly amazing. According to Ephesians 2:14–15, Christ made peace with God on behalf of both Jews and Gentiles which, in turn, made the way for peace between them. Then, Christ made "both groups one" by taking them into Himself, reconciling them to God, and uniting them. God healed the breach between Jews and Gentiles, as well as the breach between all people and Himself. By His death, Christ destroyed the enmity between these two groups. Then, He created the "one new man" by reconciling the two parties and incorporating them in Himself into a new unified humanity.

Although Christ created the "new man" through His death and resurrection, each believer needs to appropriate—or put on—this new man through a spiritual renewal of the mind (Col. 3:9–11). According to Paul, the opposite of the new man is the "old man." The old man is humanity in its sinful, fallen condition. Human beings were created in the image of God (Gen. 1:26–27), but the sin of Adam and Eve was passed on to all humanity. In Colossians 3:9–10, Paul tells believers that since they are united with Christ, they are in the process of putting off the old man and putting on the new man. Putting off the old man means putting away sinful habits and living a holy life dedicated to God. Let us live this holy life and cast off anything that takes us away from worshiping the Lord.

KEY VERSES

Ephesians 2:15, 24

New heaven and new earth

Greek expression: *kainos ouranos kai kainē gē*
Pronunciation: *kigh NAWSS; oo rah NAWSS; KIGH; kigh NAY; GAY*
Strong's Numbers: *2537, 3772, 1093*

Since God is the Creator of the heavens and the earth, it is entirely appropriate that once they have served their purpose God may do with them what He wishes. Speaking of the heavens and the earth, the psalmist said, "Even they will perish, but you remain forever; they will wear out like old clothing. You will change them like a garment, and they will fade away" (Ps. 102:26, NLT). The old earth and heavens will pass away, but the Lord has told us He will create *kainos ouranos kai kainē gē*, which is the Greek expression for "a new heaven and a new earth."

The New Testament (quoted below from NLT) gives considerable attention to the passing away of the old creation; it speaks of a future time when heaven and earth will disappear (Matt. 24:35; Rev. 21:2). A number of related phrases portray the same idea: "And this world is fading away" (1 John 2:17); "They [the heavens and earth] will wear out like old clothing" (Heb. 1:11, quoting Ps. 102:26); "But the day of the Lord will come as unexpectedly as a thief. Then the heavens will pass away with a terrible noise, and everything in them will disappear in fire, and the earth and everything on it will be exposed to judgment" (2 Pet. 3:10). This consummation by fire will take place at the time of final judgment. It will be "the day when God will set the heavens on fire and the elements will melt away in the flames" (2 Pet. 3:12).

N

This judgment opens the way for God to create new heavens and a new earth. Peter continues, "But we are looking forward to the new heavens and new earth he has promised, a world where everyone is right with God" (2 Pet. 3:13). The heaven that will be renewed is probably not the heaven of God's presence, but the starry expanse that constitutes the universe. In the book of Revelation we learn that the new Jerusalem comes down from heaven to earth (Rev. 21:2, 10) and forms the eternal dwelling place of God and His people.

This recovery or renewal is eagerly awaited by all creation. Paul writes, "For all creation is waiting eagerly for that future day when God will reveal who his children really are," (Rom. 8:19) because "all creation anticipates the day when it will join God's children in glorious freedom from death and decay" (Rom. 8:21). One day, we will be free from sickness, death, and the worries of this world; we will have joy, fellowship, and everlasting unconditional love.

KEY VERSE

2 Peter 3:13

New Jerusalem

Greek expression: *kainos Hierousalem (and Ierosoluma)*
Pronunciation: *kigh NAWSS; hyehr oo sah LAYM (hyehr aw SAW loo mah)*
Strong's Numbers: *2537, 2414, 2419*

Of all the places on earth, Jerusalem is the most sacred to Jews and to Christians. The city was considered holy because it was the habitation of God's holy temple. In fact, the name itself signifies that it was a holy city. Jerusalem is translated from two Greek words *Ierousalem* and *Hierosoluma*. The former is the Greek transliteration of the Old Testament Aramaic form; the latter reflects the Greek word *hieros* (holy)—a Hellenistic paranominen.

The city of Jerusalem was considered to be an earthly archetype of the eternal, heavenly city. In most Christian's thinking, the eternal Jerusalem is equivalent to heaven. This is not exactly Scriptural. The "new Jerusalem," according to the book of Revelation, is said "to come down out of heaven from God" and thereby become the eternal habitation of God with His redeemed people on the new earth (Rev. 21:1-4).

There are five passages elsewhere in the New Testament which help to fill in the background to Revelation 21—22. In Galatians 4:26, Paul speaks of "Jerusalem above," the mother city of all who receive salvation by faith, as opposed to the "old Jerusalem," where those who belong seek to please God by trying to obey the law (Gal. 4:25). In Ephesians 5:25-32 Paul speaks of the bride of Christ, by which he means the church; in John's vision the "bride" is the "holy city, Jerusalem" (Rev. 21:9-10). In Philippians 3:20, we are told that the heavenly city is not simply the future home of believers, but also the place of their present "citizenship." Hebrews 12:22 makes the same point: those who believe have already arrived at the "heavenly Jerusalem." In other words, this Jerusalem is the home of all God's believing people, Jew and Gentile, from Old Testament and New Testament times, and it seems not only to be in the future, but also exists already, in some sense, in the present. The fact remains, of course, that everything John records in the last two chapters of Revelation belongs to a world that will appear only after the first heaven and the first earth have passed away—a world which is (to us, at any rate) still in the future.

KEY VERSES

Galatians 4:25–26;
Hebrews 12:22;
Revelation 3:12;
21:2

Taking into account all these Scriptures, we may come closest to understanding the New Jerusalem if we see it as the community of Christ and His people, which will appear in its perfection only when this age has come to an end. Yet in another sense, Christians belong to it already, and it gives them both an ideal to strive for in this world and a hope to anticipate in the next.

Obedience

Greek expression: *hupakoē*
Pronunciation: *h<u>oo</u>p ah kaw AY*
Strong's Number: *5218*

How often have parents wished that they had obedient children. All too frequently, children won't listen to their parents or do what they ask. The Greek word for "obedience," *hupakoē*, means "to hear what someone in authority is requesting and then act upon it." In other words, to obey is to submit to the command of one in authority; it is to be compliant with the demands or requests of someone over us.

Jesus Himself set the example for what true obedience means. On the night of His betrayal, He told His disciples that His love for the Father was evidenced by His obeying the Father's commands (John 14:31). That command meant that Jesus took on human form to live in subservience to His Father, and to eventually die on the cross. Jesus emptied Himself, taking the form of a bond-servant; He humbled Himself and became obedient to death, even death on a cross (Phil. 2:7–8). In other words, Jesus was compliant with the requirements of a human death, even though He was and is God.

Jesus also told His disciples that love for Him is measured by obedience to His commandments (John 14:15, 21, 23–24; 15:10). Therefore, a person who claims to be a child of God demonstrates this by showing continued obedience to the commandments of God (1 John 2:3–5). Christians are called upon by God to be obedient to a variety of people: believers to the Lord (John 14:21–24; 15:10), wives to their husbands (Eph. 5:22–24; Col. 3:18; Titus 2:5; 1 Pet. 3:1, 5), children to their parents (Eph. 6:1; Col. 3:20), citizens to their governmental officials (Rom. 13:1–7; Titus 3:1; 1 Pet. 2:13–14), and servants to their masters (Eph. 6:5; Col. 3:22; Titus 2:9; 1 Pet. 2:18).

O

In spite of the emphasis on obedience in the Bible, such obedience is not the grounds for justification before God. Paul declares that salvation is a gift of God that will produce good works (Eph. 2:8–10). In the same way, James speaks of works of obedience as flowing from faith (Eph. 2:14–26). Thus, our obedience to God is the result of putting our faith in Him (Rom. 1:5).

KEY VERSES

Romans 1:5,
5:19, 15:18;
Hebrews 5:8;
1 Peter 1:2

Offend

Greek expression: *skandalizō*
Pronunciation: *skahn dahl EE dzoh*
Strong's Number: *4624*

When we talk about someone "getting tripped up," we mean they were caught in some error. This English idiom is similar to the Greek meaning behind the word "offend." This word *skandalizō* means "stumbling block" or "snare." The term refers to the trigger that springs a trap; therefore, "offend" in the New Testament means anything that hinders someone from doing what is right, causes one to sin, or causes someone to fall away from the faith.

According to the New Testament, there are three ways in which people stumble.

(1) There may be something bad in an individual that causes him or her to stumble. Jesus expressed the seriousness of this, and, though speaking metaphorically, indicated some steps for cure (Matt. 5:29–30; 18:8–9).

(2) There may be something in a person that causes offense to others. Jesus said, "Woe unto the world because of offenses! For it must needs be that offenses come; but woe to that man by whom the offense cometh!" (Matthew 18:7, KJV). There are, in fact, many New Testament passages which insist that one should live in a way that does not cause others to stumble (Rom. 16:17). The apostle Paul says, "Don't tear apart the work of God over what you eat. Remember, there is nothing wrong with these things in themselves. But it is wrong to eat anything if it makes another person stumble. Don't eat meat or drink wine or do anything else if it might cause another Christian to stumble" (Rom. 14:20–21, NLT; 1 Cor. 10:32; 2 Cor. 6:3).

(3) People may be offended at the truth through no fault of the person who presents it. In the time of Jesus' ministry, there were those who were offended by Him—by His lowly birth and by what He said and did (Matt. 13:57; 15:12). Even some of Jesus' disciples were offended and stopped following Him (John 6:61). In the end, all were offended and fled from Him (Matt. 26:31, 56).

Isaiah predicted that people would be offended by the Messiah. Jesus was "a stone that causes people to stumble and a rock that makes them fall" (Isa. 8:14, NLT). The New Testament writers, Paul and Peter, applied Isaiah's words to people who were offended by the gospel of Christ (Rom. 9:32–33; 1 Pet. 2:8). Paul wrote that

KEY VERSES

Matthew 5:29;
13:21;
John 6:61;
1 Corinthians 8:13

people were offended by anyone, including himself, who spread the message of the Gospel. He could have chosen to preach a popular message and thus avoid persecution (Gal. 5:11). He chose, however, to preach about Jesus even though it was a stumbling block to Jews and would cause persecution (1 Cor. 1:23).

Oneness

See also: *One, p. 133*
Greek expression: *henotēs*
Pronunciation: *hehn AW tayss*
Strong's Number: *1775*

The Greek word *henotēs* appears only twice in the New Testament—in Ephesians 4:3 and 4:13, where Paul speaks of the "unity" of the Spirit and the "unity" of the faith. According to Paul, the unity among believers is based on the fact that we all share the same Spirit. In other words, "oneness" already exists. All born-again Christians are "one" in the Spirit. It is our duty to keep or observe that unity, recognize it as real, and act upon it. Unity of faith is another matter; it comes as the result of the body of Christ being built up and then being unified in the basic elements of the Christian faith.

The concept of "oneness" between believers is more thoroughly expressed in Jesus' final prayer, where He asked the Father for oneness among the disciples. From eternity, the Father loved the Son and the Son enjoyed equal glory with the Father. The two were, and are, essentially and inherently "one." The disciples, He asked, should be brought into "oneness" by virtue of being in the triune God and the triune God being in them. Oneness "among" the disciples was to issue from each disciple's oneness "with" God. What a lofty petition!

After praying for His disciples, Jesus prayed for all those who would believe in Him through their word (John 17:20). Since the apostles' word became the New Testament Scriptures, for the most part, and the very foundation of the faith (Eph. 2:19), everyone who has become a believer has done so through the apostles' words. Therefore, Jesus was praying for all the believers that would ever be. This includes you and me and every genuine believer. How good it is to know that Jesus prayed for me! First, Jesus prayed for the apostles to be one (John 17:11) and then He prayed for all the believers, including the apostles, to be one. This is included in the petition, "that they all may be one" (John 17:21).

Let us look closely at the three things Jesus requested in John 17:21–23 (NASB). Each request begins with the word *that:* (1) "that they may all be one, even as Thou, Father art in Me and I in Thee"; (2) "that they also may be in Us"; and (3) "that the world may believe that Thou didst send me." All the requests are subsequential: the second depends upon the first, and the third depends on both. In the first request, the Lord asked that all the believers may be one. This universal and all-encompassing petition includes all the believers throughout time. Then the first request is qualified by an astounding fact: the oneness among the believers is to be the mutual indwelling of the Father and the Son. In other words, as the Father and Son's oneness is that of mutual indwelling (John

KEY VERSES

Ephesians 4:3, 13

347

10:30, 38; 14:9–11), so the believers are to have this oneness as theirs (John 17:11–22). Since the believers cannot indwell each other, their oneness is not exactly the same as the Father and Son's, but in the same principle as their oneness—that is, the principle of mutual indwelling. The oneness of the believers would be realized by virtue of the mutual indwelling between each believer and the triune God—much like each and every branch in the vine is one with all the other branches by virtue of their common participation of abiding in the vine. We are magnificently interconnected with our Lord, who sustains us and gives us the strength to sustain others based solely and perfectly on the three-way unity of the Son, the Father, and the Holy Spirit.

Only begotten Son

Greek expression: *monogenēs huios*
Pronunciation: *maw naw gehn AYSS; hwee AWSS*
Strong's Numbers: *3439; 5207*

People have a mistaken idea about the term "only-begotten" because the English term "begotten" connotes a birth. By contrast, the Greek word *monogenēs* denotes a "one and only son"; it does not convey the idea of a birth. *Monogenēs* appears nine times in the New Testament; in five of these occurrences, it makes references to Jesus. Three of the other occurrences refer to an only son or daughter (Luke 7:12; 8:42; 9:38). Because of the word's frequent use for referring to an "only child," it often conveys the idea of something especially favored or precious. In Hebrews 11:17, *monogenēs* is used to refer to Isaac as Abraham's "favored" or "unique" son. Isaac was not Abraham's "only-begotten" son since he had other children, but Isaac was his favored and unique son—the son that fulfilled God's promise.

Where *monogenēs* is used to refer to Jesus, its meaning is likewise not "only-begotten," but "only" or "unique." The word is used with "son" and should be understood as "God's only Son," indicating both God's favor toward Him and His uniqueness (John 3:16, 18; 1 John 4:9). The statement at the baptism and transfiguration of Jesus in the Synoptic Gospels, "This is my beloved son," expresses virtually the same idea. In John 1:14, the word "only" is used by itself to stress that the incarnate Word comes as a unique One from the Father.

The Son of God was the Father's "one and only" unique Son. Although the Father has "begotten" many sons (John 1:12, 13), none of these sons are exactly like Jesus Christ, who is the unique Son of God. His role and title as "Son" is from eternity. As the unique Son of God, He has had a special glory and an unrivaled place of honor. Because of the confusion related to the idea of the "Son of God" being "begotten," the early Christians had many debates. The issue was finally solved by the beginning of the fourth century and formalized in the creed from the Council of Nicaea (A.D. 325). This creed speaks of the Son of God as "begotten not made, of one substance with the Father." This wording of the creed completely rejected the heresy that the Son of God was the first created being. It unambiguously proclaimed that Jesus was fully God and fully man—the only One who could truly take our sins on Himself on the cross, the only One who can invite us in God's kingdom to live with Him forever.

KEY VERSES

John 3:16, 18;
1 John 4:9

One and only God

Greek expression: *monogenēs theos*
Pronunciation: *maw naw gehn AYSS; theh AWSS*
Strong's Numbers: *3439, 2316*

Among the most unique titles for Jesus is one found in John 1:18: *monogenēs theos*, which translates as "one and only God." Many readers are not aware of this expression because the King James Version, a long-time favorite, has a different reading in John 1:18: "only begotten Son."

The discovery of two ancient manuscripts (P66 and P75) in the middle part of this century, both of which have the reading *monogenēs theos*, has convinced modern translators to go with "one and only God" over and against "only begotten Son." Their decision is helped by the fact that other early manuscripts (Codices Vaticanus, Sinaiticus, Ephraemi Rescriptus) and some early versions (Coptic and Syriac) support the text, as do many church fathers (including Irenaeus, Clement, Origen, Eusebius, Didymus).

Furthermore, the reading "one and only God" is the preferred reading because it is the most difficult of the two readings to translate. This difficulty best explains why scribes might write the variation—"only begotten Son." Scribes would not be inclined to change a common wording "only begotten Son" to an uncommon wording "only begotten God." Whatever the rendering, the reading in all the earliest manuscripts indicates that Jesus is here called "God," as well as "the one and only." This perfectly corresponds to the first verse of John's prologue, where the Word is called "God" and is described as the Son living in intimate fellowship with the Father.

In John 1:18, John tells us that no man can see God—that is, know God as God. But there is One who has come to explain Him to us, not just in words but in His very person. This One is uniquely qualified to be God's "explainer" because He is (1) the one and only Son, (2) God, and (3) the One in the bosom of the Father. As the one and only Son, He alone has a unique position with God the Father. He alone can communicate the Father's message to mankind. And, since Jesus is also God, He is the very expression of God manifest in the flesh. Furthermore, His intimate relationship with the Father enables Him to share the heart of God and the love of God with all of humanity.

KEY VERSE

John 1:18

Oracle

Greek expression: *logiōn*
Pronunciation: *LAWG ee awn*
Strong's Number: *3051*

Anyone who has read about ancient Greece and Rome has heard about the "oracles." Two famous oracles were the oracles of Apollos at Delphi and Zeus at Dodona. The Greeks and Romans believed that the gods took a personal interest in their lives, so they would go to these places to seek advice from the gods about their lives. The gods were supposed to answer them through these oracles. But the oracles were often very difficult to interpret, even for the priests of the temples.

The expression "oracle of God" shares some of the same denotations, with one major exception: it is the one and only God who speaks—and He does so clearly. The Greek term *logiōn* is a form of the word *logos*. This is not "the Word of God," but a "word from God," a "divine communication." An oracle is a "divine revelation communicated through God's prophet," usually pronouncing blessing, instruction, or judgment.

Two New Testament writers, Luke and Paul, recognized that God's direct messages to His prophets of old were oracles. In the book of Acts, we read that God instructed Moses through "living oracles" (Acts 7:38). Paul tells us that the Jewish people had been entrusted with God's oracles (Rom. 3:2). When we turn to the pages of the Old Testament we realize that they are filled with oracles. For example, oracles of judgment were uttered against King Joram of Israel (2 Kgs. 9:25) and Joash of Judah (2 Chr. 24:27). The prophets often delivered oracles against evil nations. For example, Isaiah proclaimed God's oracles against Babylon (Isa. 13:1), Moab (Isa. 15:1), Philistia (Isa. 14:28), Damascus (Isa. 17:1), Egypt (Isa. 19:1), Jerusalem (Isa. 22:1), and Tyre (Isa. 23:1). Nahum gave oracles against Nineveh (Nah. 1:1); Habakkuk against Judah (Hab. 1:1); and Malachi against Israel (Mal. 1:1).

When we come back to the New Testament, we see that Christian teachers, functioning as prophets, also spoke the "oracles" of God. Peter said, "Whoever speaks, let him speak, as it were, the oracles of God" (1 Pet. 4:11, NASB). The author of Hebrews also used the word *oracles* to describe the words of God that had originally been communicated to the believers (Heb 5:12). God still speaks His oracles to us today—we can hear His voice through the Bible and through the Spirit.

KEY VERSES

Acts 7:38;
Romans 3:2;
1 Peter 4:11;
Hebrews 5:12

Ordain

Greek expression: *kathistēmi, tithēmi*
Pronunciation: *kah THEE stay mee; TEE thay mee*
Strong's Numbers: *2525, 5087*

We have all heard of ordained ministers. But what does it mean to be ordained? It means that the person has met certain qualifications to be appointed a position in the church. Thus, ordination is the act of officially investing someone with religious authority. This act signifies selection and appointment to God's service.

The original twelve apostles were selected or "ordained" by Jesus Christ. This means they were "put" or "placed"—from the Greek words *kathistēmi* and *tithēmi,* which mean "to place"—into these positions by Christ. When Jesus ordained the twelve apostles, He called those whom He desired. Later, He told them, "You did not choose me, but I chose you and appointed you" (John 15:16, RSV). The only apostle not directly chosen by Jesus was Matthias, who replaced Judas. But, the disciples chose him through God by praying and casting lots (Acts 1:24–26).

There are several verses in the New Testament that indicate that God, through the Holy Spirit, is the prime mover in selecting men and women for service in the church. Paul declared that he had been set apart by God before he was born, and did not receive his apostleship from or through men (Gal. 1:1, 15). Paul and Barnabas were commissioned and sent to Cyprus by the Spirit during worship, through a Christian prophet (Acts 13:1–5). Similarly, Timothy was first chosen as assistant to Paul through prophetic words spoken about him (1 Tim. 1:18; 4:14). At Corinth, various ministries of speaking, teaching, healing, and administration were directly conferred as gifts of the Spirit (1 Cor. 12:8–11, 28; Eph. 4:11). In addition, elders of the church at Ephesus were appointed as shepherds of the flock by the Holy Spirit (Acts 20:28).

There are other verses in the New Testament that indicate that the church also had a hand in the selection process. For example, the church "nominated" Barsabbas and Matthias before submitting the final choice to God (Acts 1:15, 23).

KEY VERSES

John 15:16;
Titus 1:5

The believers chose the seven deacons and then presented them to the apostles (Acts 6:2–6). An assembled church, at the Spirit's command, commissioned and sent off Paul and Barnabas as mentioned in the above paragraph (Acts 13:3). The congregation's selection of leaders could have involved prayer, fasting, and casting lots (Acts 1:26; 6:6; 13:2–3; 14:23); selection by group choice (Acts 1:15, 23; 6:2–5; 13:3; 16:2; 1 Tim. 4:14); and sometimes leaders were chosen through "selection-by-hands," which is *cheirotonein* in Greek and originally meant "election by raising hands," and later "selection by pointing to" (2 Cor. 8:19; Acts 14:23). Paul and Barnabas themselves appointed elders and Paul instructed Titus to do the same (Acts 14:23; Titus 1:5). Paul and elders at Lystra and

Iconium, obeying a Christian prophet, appointed Timothy to leadership (1 Tim. 4:14; 2 Tim. 1:6).

In due course, Paul knew what kind of believers were best qualified to serve the church, so he provided Timothy with a list of qualifications required for church leaders (1 Tim. 3:1–13; 2 Tim. 2:2). Churches today use these guidelines, and prayer, to select elders, deacons, and other church leaders.

Overseer

Greek expression: *episkopos*
Pronunciation: *eh PEE skaw pawss*
Strong's Number: *1985*

The English term "episcopal" is based on the Greek term *episkopos*, which means "one who oversees" or "overseer." In New Testament times, there were several elders in positions of responsibility in every given church (Acts 14:23; Titus 1:5–7). After New Testament times, it became the custom to appoint one elder as the presiding elder and to give him the title of "bishop." But actually, the title *bishop* is the Latin equivalent of the Greek term *episkopos*; both mean "overseer."

Thus, in the New Testament, overseer, bishop, and elder refer to the same office. This is shown by the fact that Paul told Titus to appoint "elders in every city" and then he referred to those same individuals as "overseers" (Titus 1:5, 7). While at Miletus, Paul summoned the elders from the church at Ephesus and then addressed them as "overseers" (Acts 20:17, 28). Then, in his letter to the Philippians, Paul greeted the "overseers and deacons" (Phil. 1:1). The fact that there were numerous overseers (or bishops) at Philippi, as well as in Ephesus, shows that the episcopal office had not yet developed into what it later became: a single bishop governing one or more churches.

Overseers obviously had positions of authority, but the duties of the office are not clearly defined in the New Testament. One task was to combat heresy (Titus 1:9) and to teach and expound the Scriptures (1 Tim. 3:2). In addition, there is evidence that economic matters and the care of the poor were primary concerns, as well as a general overseeing of the congregation. The lists of qualifications in Paul's letters to Timothy and Titus indicate that an overseer had a good reputation in the world and was considered a leader in the congregation. An overseer's primary task was to shepherd the flock of God—to make sure it was fed spiritually and to guard it against danger. Jesus, the shepherd and overseer of our souls, is the prime example (1 Pet. 2:25).

KEY VERSES

Acts 20:28;
Philippians 1:1;
Titus 1:7;
1 Peter 2:25

Parable

Greek expression: *parabolēs*
Pronunciation: *pahr ah bawl AY*
Strong's Number: *3850*

Do you know that over one-third of Jesus' recorded sayings are parables? He was the master of the parable. But what are parables? Some have said that a "parable" is a heavenly story with an earthly meaning. Others have said "parables" are comparisons or illustrations of what Jesus wanted to say. The latter is closer to the truth. Not being able to tell us exactly what the kingdom is, He used "parables" to tell us what it is like.

The Greek term *parabolēs* means more than just a comparative story. It was used for anything from a proverb to a full-blown allegory including a riddle, an illustration, a contrast, or a story. For example, the word *parabolēs* is used in Luke 4:23 with reference to the saying "Physician, heal yourself" and most translations render it as a "proverb." In Mark 3:23 "parables" is used with reference to the riddles Jesus asks the scribes, such as "How can Satan cast out Satan?" Similarly Mark 13:28 uses a "parable" for a simple illustration. In Luke 18:2–5 the unjust judge is contrasted with God who brings justice quickly. The broad meaning of "parable," then, can refer to "any unusual or striking speech"; that is, any saying intended to stimulate thought. One of the specific uses of the parable is that it is a story with two levels of meaning—literal and figurative.

Jesus taught in parables because they are both interesting and compelling and therefore one of the most effective means of communicating. His parables also contained biblical "mystery," which is "a hidden secret revealed only by God." When one reads Mark 4:10–12, it seems that Jesus taught in parables in order to keep ordinary people, who were not chosen by God, from understanding profound, spiritual truths. It seems as well that there is a mystery given to the "in-group," which the "out-group" is prohibited from learning. Herein lies the biblical meaning for the term "mystery." It doesn't mean "unknown" or "not understood" as "mystery" means today. Instead, it means that which has been revealed by God and would not have been known had God not revealed it.

In short, Jesus' parables focus on God and His kingdom. They reveal what kind of God He is, by what principles He works, and what He expects of humanity. Those who have ears to hear do hear what He is saying—those who aren't given ears, don't understand God's message.

P

KEY VERSES

Matthew 13:3;
Mark 4:2;
Luke 15:3

Paradise

Greek expression: *paradeisos*
Pronunciation: *pahr AH day sawss*
Strong's Number: *3857*

Everyone on earth would love to find "paradise"—a place of natural perfection, comfortable ease, and endless provision. In the very beginning of history, Adam and Eve lived in paradise. At the end of history, there will be another paradise, the New Jerusalem. The word "paradise" was borrowed from a Persian word, which means "Garden of God." The Greek word *paradeisos* literally means "garden" or "park"; and it was used in the Greek Old Testament in Nehemiah 2:8, Ecclesiastes 2:5, and Song of Songs 4:13 to express that meaning. The Septuagint (Greek Old Testament) also used *paradeisos* for the "Garden of Eden" (Gen. 2:8).

In later Jewish thought, writers would speak of "paradise" as the place of the righteous, departed dead in *Sheol* (Hebrew for "place of the unseen"). This parallels Greek and Roman mythology, where "paradise" was called "the Elysian Fields," a pleasant part of Hades inhabited by the deserving dead. By New Testament times, the picture of God's "paradise" had developed in various ways. Paradise is the place into which Paul was mysteriously "caught up" during his lifetime (see 2 Cor. 12:4). It is also the place where the repentant thief on the cross went to be with Christ—immediately after his death (Luke 23:43). The last New Testament reference in Revelation 2:7 tells us that paradise is where the tree of life grows, and so identifies it both with the original world of Genesis 2 and with the future world of Revelation 22, complete with the life-giving tree and living river.

Paradise will be restored to the new earth when the new Jerusalem will be established. The blessed participants will experience eternal joy in the presence of their Savior, Jesus Christ. Since Satan and all evil will be eliminated, there will be no fear of the devil ruining this paradise, as he did the first one.

KEY VERSES

Luke 23:43;
2 Corinthians 12:4;
Revelation 2:7

Patience

Greek expression: *makrothumia, hupomonē*
Pronunciation: *mah kraw th<u>oo</u> MEE uh; h<u>oo</u> paw mawn AY*
Strong's Numbers: *3115, 5281*

There is an old maxim, "patience is a virtue, which all admire, but few attain." The translators of the King James Version used one English word, "patience," to translate two different Greek words. The first Greek word, *makrothumia*, literally means "long-suffering." It speaks of having "long-spirited-ness" or "calmness of spirit"— the ability, even under severe provocation, not to lose one's temper. The other word, *hupomonē*, literally means "to remain under" and "to stay put under." It has the idea of "remaining firm under" tests and trials. *Hupomonē* is better translated "endurance" or "steadfastness." Both words speak of the ability to take a great deal of punishment from evil people or circumstances without losing one's temper, without becoming irritated and angry, or without taking vengeance. It includes the capacity to bear pain or trials without complaint, to forbear under severe provocation, and to have the self-control that keeps one from acting rashly even though suffering opposition or adversity.

The greatest biblical illustration of patience is found in God Himself. According to the New Testament, it is God's kindness, forbearance, and patience that lead people to repentance (Rom. 2:4). God was patient in holding off the flood for the sinners of Noah's day while the ark was being built, thereby giving more time for repentance (1 Pet. 3:20). Probably the greatest of the New Testament references to God's patience is in 2 Peter 3:9. The delay in Christ's return is not an indication of slowness on God's part, says Peter, but of His long-suffering and unwillingness to have anyone perish.

Patience, which is an attribute of our God and of our Lord Jesus Christ, should also characterize each Christian. Paul's prayer for the Colossians is that they might demonstrate this quality (Col. 1:11). It is one of the fruits of the Spirit (Gal. 5:22), an attribute of love (1 Cor. 13:4), and a virtue (Col. 3:12). In addition, Christians are exhorted to be patient (1 Thess. 5:14). Most particularly, Christians are commanded to be long-suffering until the coming of the Lord (Jas. 5:7). The image James presents is that of a farmer waiting patiently for the crop to come. In due season, the harvest will come. Jesus will return. Let us be patient until then, and endure our trials for the glory of God.

KEY VERSES

Romans 2:4;
Galatians 5:22

Peace

See also: *Peace, p. 135*
Greek expression: *eirēnē*
Pronunciation: *ay RAY nay*
Strong's Number: *1515*

Peace means many things to different people. To those in war, peace means the cessation of battle and enmity. To those living hectic lives, peace means calm. To those with troubled minds, peace means inner tranquillity. The Greek term for peace, *eirēnē*, was used for all of these meanings, both in Greek literature and in the New Testament. The word *eirēnē* could be used as a greeting or farewell, as in "peace be with you" (Luke 10:5; Gal. 6:16; Jas. 2:16; John 20:19). *Eirēnē* could also signify the presence of domestic tranquillity (1 Cor. 7:15) or the "cessation of conflict"—national conflict (Luke 14:32; Acts 12:20) or interpersonal conflict (Rom. 14:19; Eph. 4:3).

Jesus came to bring peace on earth. When Jesus was born, the angels proclaimed: "Glory to God in the highest, and on earth peace among men with whom he is well pleased" (Luke 2:14, NASB). This means that Jesus as the Messiah would usher in God's reign of peace. This peace was Jesus' farewell gift to the disciples (John 14:27); it was given to them when He breathed His Spirit into them (John 20:19–22). The greatest "peace" Jesus achieved for us is that He took away the enmity between us and God by His death on the cross to absolve our sin. Those who accept Christ's salvation have peace with God (Rom. 5:1–2).

This gift of peace with God, made available through Christ, means that Christians in the community of faith need to live in peace with each other (Rom. 12:18; 14:19; Heb. 12:14). This concept of peace alters the meaning of the common greeting "go in peace" to "go, and live in peace." As used by the Christian community, the expression "grace and peace be with you" conveys total well-being, prosperity, and security—all emanating from God's presence with His people (1 Cor. 1:3; 2 Cor. 1:2; Gal. 1:3; Eph. 1:2; 1 Peter 1:2; 2 John 3; Jude 2; Rev. 1:4). When we say or hear the phrase above, it is not a mere wish for peace, but a reminder of the peace given through Christ.

KEY VERSES

Luke 2:14;
John 20:19, 21;
Romans 5:1;
Philippians 1:2; 4:7

Perfect

Greek expression: *teleiōs*
Pronunciation: *TEHL ay awss*
Strong's Number: *5046*

We think of "perfect" as being "flawless and immaculate," but the Greeks had a different definition. They thought of "perfect" as being "mature and complete." The Greek word *teleiōs* is derived from the word *telos*, meaning "the end," "the limit," or "the fulfillment." Paul used this word to speak of Jesus Christ as "the complete fulfillment" of God's law (Rom. 10:4). In his letter to the Colossians, Paul uses *teleiōs* to speak of "the end"—that is, the completion or "perfection"—of Christians (Col. 1:28; 4:12). Paul himself was always pressing toward the goal of Christian "perfection," or "complete maturation" in Christ-likeness (Phil. 3:12–14). We, too, should make perfection in Christ our goal—a goal that will be completely achieved when "that which is perfect," Jesus Christ, comes again (1 Cor. 13:10).

One of the most important facets of perfection is in our love for God and for others. The apostle John said, "as we abide in God, our love grows more perfect" (1 John 4:17). This perfection develops our relationship with God, who is love. By growing in our relationship with God, we will not be afraid on the day of judgment, but will be able to face Him with confidence (1 John 4:18). As we mature in love, we will be motivated by love to please God. If we feel afraid and are motivated by fear of God's punishment, we have not yet matured in our walk with Him. John affirms that it is love—not fear—which should motivate us. We are in a new era— the era of the new covenant—where God is the initiator and supplier of love. As He supplies the love, we receive His love, and in that receiving, fear is cast out. Eventually, we will have "perfect" love.

Remember, we must not think of "perfect" as meaning "flawless." A fully developed apple is mature, "perfect," even if it has bumps, scabs, and bruises. None of us will be flawless and faultless in this lifetime, but we can mature in our love for God and His people.

KEY VERSES

Colossians 1:28;
4:12;
Romans 12:2;
Philippians 3:15;
James 1:4;
1 John 4:18

Persecution

Greek expression: *diōgmos*
Pronunciation: *dee ohg MAWSS*
Strong's Number: *1375*

Just as Jesus was persecuted—even pursued to death—He predicted that His disciples would be "persecuted." On the Mount of Olives, Jesus predicted the time of the beginning, the extent, and the end of tribulation (Matt. 24—25; Mark 13; Luke 21). Jesus told the twelve disciples that they—and all who believed in Him—would experience great tribulation and *diōgmos* which means "persecution"—even to the death—for His name's sake (Matt. 24:9).

The persecution against Christians commenced almost as soon as the church began in A.D. 30. Then it became intensified throughout the Roman world as people began to distinguish the "followers of Jesus" from "the Jews." Nero was the first Roman emperor to instigate a vile and violent persecution against those who espoused to be Christians. The Roman historian Tacitus left us a record of how Nero blamed the Christians for the great fire of Rome in A.D. 64 and how Nero persecuted them:

> All human efforts, all the lavish gifts of the emperor, and the propitiation of the gods, did not banish the sinister belief [among the Romans] that the fire was the result of an order [from Nero]. Consequently, to get rid of the report, Nero fastened the guilt and inflicted the most exquisite tortures on a class hated for their abominations (flagitia), called Christians by the populace. Chrestus [Christ], from whom the name had its origin, suffered the extreme penalty [crucifixion] during the reign of Tiberius at the hands of one of our procurators, Pontus Pilate, and a deadly superstition, thus checked for the moment, again broke out not only in Judea, the source of the evil, but also in Rome, where all things hideous and shameful from every part of the world meet and become popular. Accordingly, an arrest was first made of all who confessed; then, upon their information, an immense multitude was convicted, not so much of the crime of arson, as of hatred of the human race. Mockery of every sort was added to their deaths. Covered with the skins of beasts, they were torn by dogs and perished, or nailed to crosses, or were doomed to the flames. These served to illuminate the night when the daylight failed.

(Annals 15.44.2–8)

KEY VERSES

Acts 8:1;
2 Thessalonians 1:4;
2 Corinthians 12:10

During this period of the church, to be called a "Christian" (one belonging to Christ) was to ask for persecution and suffering. During this period of persecution, Peter wrote a letter to many Christian churches throughout the Roman Empire (1 Pet. 1:1–2) to prepare them for what might happen to them just because they were Christians. What he told them is a message for unbelievers in all ages. None of us is exempt from persecution: Be happy if you are insulted for being a Christian, for then the glorious Spirit of God will come upon you . . . [I]t is no shame to suffer for being a Christian" (1 Pet. 4:14, 16, NLT).

Persevere

Greek expression: *proskartereō, proskarterēsis*
Pronunciation: *prawss kahr tehr EH oh; prawss kahr TEHR ay seess*
Strong's Numbers: *4342, 4343*

We tell people who are going through hard times "hang in there," or "keep your chin up." To persevere means to "persist in something," in spite of persecution, opposition, or discouragement. Among several Greek expressions, the usual word, *proskartereō*, has the root meaning "to adhere steadfastly" (Mark 3:9; Acts 8:13; 10:7; Rom. 13:6), and is translated "to be devoted," "to continue [in something]," "to be constant," "to be steadfast," and "to persevere."

Throughout the New Testament, Christians are urged to "perseverance" (*proskarterēsis*). It is called for in prayer (Col. 4:2); in Christian teaching (Acts 2:42; 2 Tim. 3:14); in doing well (Rom. 13:6); in standing firm (1 Cor. 16:13; 2 Thess. 2:15); in abiding in Christ (John 15:4–10; 1 John 2:28); in running with patience (Heb. 6:12; 12:1); in not falling away (Heb. 3:12; 4:1–10); and in being zealous to confirm our call and election (2 Pet. 1:10).

Jesus said, "He who endures to the end will be saved" (Matt. 10:22; 24:13). The pressures of society, the danger of persecution, and the emotional "high" after the wonderful initial salvation experience, make it imperative for Christians—both today and during New Testament times—to understand that they need to persevere in their faith (Luke 21:19; Rom. 5:3; Col. 1:11). Readers of the New Testament can't help but be struck by several warnings against losing the faith or falling away. We are warned not to neglect our salvation (Heb. 2:3) and not to commit apostasy (Heb. 6:1–8).

Fortunately, our perseverance does not depend entirely on our efforts. Christ assured His believers that He would raise them from the dead on the last day and that no one would pluck them from His hand or the Father's. Christ will keep us from falling (John 10:27–30). God is faithful; He works in us to will and work for His good pleasure, and He will not allow us to be tempted beyond our strength. Nothing, in heaven or earth, present or future, shall separate us from divine love (Rom. 8:28–39). We are already sealed by the Holy Spirit as a guarantee of eternal salvation (2 Cor. 1:21–22). Let us persevere in Christ, remembering that God promises to give us the strength to resist temptation and endure persecution.

P

KEY VERSES

Acts 2:42, 46;
Romans 12:12; 13:6

Peter, rock, stone

Greek expression: *petros, petra, lithos*
Pronunciation: *PEH trawss; PEH truh; LEE thawss*
Strong's Numbers: *4073, 4074, 3037*

God specialized in making name-changes at critical moments in biblical history. For example, He changed Jacob's name to Israel, which means "He who struggles with God" (Gen. 32:18). When Jesus first saw Simon, the son of John, He immediately changed his name. Addressing him, Jesus said: "You are Simon, the son of John; you shall be called Cephas (which is translated Peter)." When Jesus saw Peter, He saw him for what he would become—*Cephas,* which is Aramaic for "stone." Peter would become a "stone" in the building of Christ's church (Matt. 16:16–18). Throughout his days with Jesus it appears that Simon was anything but a stone, but after Christ's resurrection and Pentecost, Simon Peter was strengthened and fortified. He became a pillar and a foundation stone in the building of the first century church (Gal. 2:9; Eph. 2:20). Jesus not only sees what is in us, He sees what we can be through God's power and transformation.

A few years later, Peter made a remarkable, history-changing proclamation. He declared that Jesus was "the Christ, the Son of the living God," to which Jesus responded, "Blessed are you, Simon, son of Jonah, because flesh and blood did not reveal this to you, but my Father in heaven. And I also say to you, that you are Peter, and upon this rock I will build my church" (Matt. 16:16–18). As "Peter" and "rock" are one word in the dialect spoken by Jesus (Aramaic), the wordplay in this verse can be seen only in languages that have one word for both. In the Greek, the word for "Peter" is *petros* meaning "stone" or "fragment of a rock"; the word for "rock" is *petra* which is more specifically "rock mass." Some commentators have indicated that though the two words are nearly synonymous, Jesus intended a distinction—Peter is but a fragment of the whole, while Christ Himself is the entire rock. Thus, it could be said that the church would be built on Christ, the Rock. Others have maintained that Jesus is saying in this passage that the church will be built on Peter's confession that Jesus is the Son of God.

KEY VERSES

Matthew 16:18;
John 1:42;
1 Peter 2:5

However we interpret this passage, it is clear that Peter himself never declared that he was the single rock upon which the church was built. Rather, he told the believers: "you also as living stones are being built up a spiritual house" (1 Pet. 2:5). The word "also" shows that he put all other believers in the same category as he: We all are living stones in the church God is building.

Power

Greek expression: *dunamis*
Pronunciation: *DOO nah meess*
Strong's Number: *1411*

The Greek word for power is *dunamis*; it speaks of "potential power" and "actual power." Our English word "dynamite" is a derivative. Everyone knows that dynamite is powerful, but God is more powerful. He can create things, while dynamite can only devastate.

Everything in creation has a certain amount of "power," but God's power is immutable. Animals have power. There is power in nature: the wind and storms, the thunder and lightning. People have the power to do good and evil. Rulers have God-given power and authority (Rom. 13:1). The Bible also speaks of the power of angels (2 Pet. 2:11) and of spiritual beings known as "principalities and powers." Satan has also been given certain powers (Job 1:6–12; 2:1–6). But God is all-powerful (Eph. 1:19). In fact, "Power" is a name for God. Jesus said that the Son of man would be seen "seated at the right hand of Power" (Matt. 26:64, NASB).

God's power was manifested in Jesus. This power was shown through Jesus' miracles (Matt. 11:20; Acts 2:22); in His works of healing and exorcism (Luke 4:36; 5:17; 6:19; Acts 10:38). God's power is shown supremely in His resurrection. Jesus speaks of His power to give up His life and the power to take it again (John 10:18), but the New Testament speaks most frequently of the power of God the Father shown in the raising of His Son from the dead (Rom. 1:4; Eph. 1:19–20). During the Second Coming, Jesus will be seen coming on the clouds of heaven with "power" and great glory (Matt. 24:30).

Meanwhile, Jesus is able to deliver people from the power of sin and death, from Satan, and from all the spiritual forces of evil (2 Cor. 10:4; Eph. 6:10–18). Since the ruler of this world, Satan, had no power over Christ (John 14:30), he cannot have power over those who rely on Him. Those who believe in God receive power from the Holy Spirit (Acts 6:8), inner dynamo to live in His service (Eph. 3:16), power to be His witnesses (Luke 24:49; Acts 1:8), and power to endure suffering (2 Tim. 1:8).

KEY VERSES

Matthew 26:64;
Ephesians 1:19;
2 Timothy 1:8

Prayer

See also: *Pray, p. 138*
Greek expression: *proseuchē (verb proseuchomai)*
Pronunciation: *prawss ew KAY; prawss EW kaw migh*
Strong's Numbers: 4335, 4336

All believers want to know how to pray effectively. The place to begin is with Christ's teaching and example. Christ's dependence on His Father expresses itself in repeated prayer, culminating in His prayer after the last supper and the agony of Gethsemane, followed by His prayer from the cross (John 17). The parables on "prayer" (*proseuchē* in Greek) are another important source of Christ's teaching. These parables emphasize persistence (Luke 18:1–8), tenacity (Luke 11:5–8), simplicity and humility (Luke 18:10–14). A significant source of teaching about prayer is the Lord's Prayer (Matt. 6:9–13). The requests given in the Lord's Prayer are concerned first with God, His kingdom and His glory, and then with our need for forgiveness and for daily support and deliverance.

Christ stated that when the Holy Spirit came, the disciples would pray to the Father in the name of Christ (John 16:23–25). Accordingly, we find that after the coming of the Spirit on the day of Pentecost the early church is characterized by prayer (Acts 2:42). The Spirit enables all Christians to come to God with all their needs. Prominent among these needs, in the mind of the apostle Paul, are a deepening of faith in Christ, love for God, and a growing appreciation of God's love in turn (Eph. 3:14–19). Prayer is also part of the Christian's armor against satanic attack (Eph. 6:18). Furthermore, believers are encouraged to pray for all sorts of things, with thanksgiving (Phil. 4:6), to be free from anxiety.

The Christian's prayer is rooted, objectively, in Christ's intercession; subjectively, in the enabling of the Holy Spirit. The church is a kingdom of priests, offering spiritual sacrifices of praise and thanksgiving (Heb. 13:15; 1 Pet. 2:5), but Christ is the great High Priest. Nowhere in Scripture is it suggested that there is any other mediator between God and people except Christ (1 Tim. 2:5). Nowhere in either the Old Testament or New Testament is there any encouragement to pray to individuals other than God. Thus, the church is encouraged to come to God boldly in prayer, receive God's mercy through Jesus Christ, and be reassured that grace will be provided when it is needed (Heb. 4:14–16; 9:24; 10:19–23).

KEY VERSES

Matthew 6:9;
Acts 2:42;
Philippians 4:6

Predestine

Greek expression: *prohorizō*
Pronunciation: *praw ohr EE dzoh*
Strong's Number: *4309*

To predestine means "to mark out beforehand," and "to establish one's boundary, or one's limits, beforehand." Our English word "horizon" is a derivative of this Greek word, *prohorizō*. The Christian's ultimate "destiny" or "horizon" has been fixed by God from all eternity: to be made like His Son.

The impetus of God's eternal purpose came from His heart's desire to have many sons and daughters made like His only Son. In love, He predestined many people to be His honored children—not by their own merits, but by virtue of being in the Son (Eph. 1:4–5). Notice how often in Ephesians 1 Paul speaks of the believer's position "in Him." Outside of Jesus the Son, no one could be a son or daughter of God and no one could be pleasing to the Father. These many children owe all their divine privileges to Jesus, as children graced in Him (Eph. 1:6).

Paul provides the best explanation on "predestination" in Romans 8:28–30, quoted as follows:

> And we know that God causes all things to work together for good to those who love God, to those who are called according to His purpose. For whom He foreknew, He also predestined to become conformed to the image of His Son, that He might be the first-born among many brethren; and whom He predestined, these He also called; and whom He called, these He also justified; and whom He justified, these He also glorified.

Note how the words "predestined," "called," "justified," and especially "glorified" in Romans 8:29 and 30 are in the past tense. That is because God, from His eternal perspective, sees this process as having been completed already. From God's perspective, believers have already been glorified because He sees them like Jesus. But still, in the reality of time, believers must undergo the process of being conformed to Christ's image. God is bringing all things together for good in our lives, we are called according to His purpose, and His goal is to conform each believer to the image of His beloved Son. What a destiny!

KEY VERSES

Romans 8:29–30;
Acts 4:28;
Ephesians 1:5, 11

Priest, priesthood

See also: *Priest, p. 141*
Greek expression: *hiereus, hierateuma*
Pronunciation: *hyehr EWSS; hyehr AH tew mah*
Strong's Numbers: *2409, 2406*

To the modern person, the word "priest" connotes a clergyman with a black robe in a Catholic church. During biblical times, *hiereus*—which is Greek for "priest"—was "one who served in the temple" to aid people in worship. The pagan temples had their priests, and God's temple in Jerusalem had its priests.

In the New Testament church, things are different because there is no physical temple. But there are still priests. The first and preeminent priest is Jesus Christ, the "high priest." The writer of Hebrews has much to say about Him. He was appointed high priest by God Himself (Heb. 5:4–6) with a "priesthood," or *hierteuma* in Greek, superior to that of Aaron (Heb. 7:1–28). He is able to care for God's people because He has faced the same temptations they experience, yet without sin (Heb. 4:15; 7:26). He offered Himself, as the sinless lamb, to take away all sin forever (Heb. 7:27; 9:24–28; 10:10–19). Having risen from the dead He is a priest forever, and part of His high priesthood is to offer intercession for His people (Heb. 7:17, 25). Only through Jesus are sinful human beings able to enter the holy presence of God to be accepted as children of God (John 14:6; 2 Cor. 5:18–20; 1 Tim. 2:5).

The church is also described as a group of priests—a "priesthood." The New Testament describes believers as "a royal priesthood, to offer spiritual sacrifices acceptable to God through Jesus Christ" (1 Pet. 2:5); "priests to his God and Father" (Rev. 1:6); "a kingdom and priests to our God" (Rev. 5:10); and "priests of God and of Christ" (Rev. 20:6). The priesthood of Christians involves spiritual worship and love for God, as well as compassionate activity and prayer for their fellow human beings. Paul wrote: "Present your bodies as a living sacrifice, holy and acceptable to God, which is your spiritual worship" (Rom. 12:1, RSV). Each Christian offers his or her whole body to Christ and each local church offers itself wholly to Christ.

Thus, in and by Christ, the priesthood of believers is exercised and made effectual.

KEY VERSES

Hebrews 7:11, 17,
21, 24;
1 Peter 2:5;
Revelation 1:6;
5:10; 20:6

Proclamation

Greek expression: *kerygma*
Pronunciation: *KAY roog mah*
Strong's Number: *2782*

The Greek word *kerygma* is taken straight from a well-known practice in ancient times. A king publicized his decrees throughout his empire by means of a *kerux*, "a town crier or herald." This person, who often served as a close confidant of the king, would travel throughout the realm announcing to the people whatever the king wished to make known. In English, we know him as a "herald."

Each New Testament apostle considered himself to be exactly like the *kerux*—a "herald" of the Good News. In fact, Paul called himself "a herald and an apostle" (1 Tim. 2:7; 2 Tim. 1:11), for it was his function as an apostle to travel throughout the "earthly realm" announcing to people what Jesus, the King, wished to make known.

Paul and the other New Testament apostles had a common "proclamation" (*kerygma*) to take to the world. This proclamation is a proclamation of the death, resurrection, and exaltation of Jesus, seen as the fulfillment of prophecy and involving human responsibility. This proclamation exalts Jesus as both Lord and Christ, and it is a call to repent and receive forgiveness of sins.

Above all, the *kerygma* always focuses on the resurrection. This supernatural act of God in history authenticates the words and works of Jesus and constitutes the basis for the Christian hope of immortality. Without the resurrection, the church would be no more than a group of well-intentioned, religious people who had placed their faith in the superior philosophical and ethical teachings of an unusually fine man. The resurrection is proof positive that Jesus is who He said He was. Essentially, the *kerygma* is a declaration that Christ is risen from the dead, and by that great act God has brought salvation to those who believe in God's Son.

P

The apostles proclaimed the risen Christ because it is the resurrection that validates the claims of Christ. Who can resist the compelling logic of the resurrection as it leads irresistibly to the conclusion that Jesus of Nazareth is the living Lord? Indeed, this message is good news to all those who believe! We have been saved from our sins through Christ's death on the cross; and Christ has risen from the grave to defeat all of God's enemies—sin, death, and the devil. We have been saved!

KEY VERSES

Romans 16:25;
1 Corinthians 1:21;
2:4; 15:14;
Titus 1:3

Prophecy

See also: *Prophet, p. 142 and p. 369*
Greek expression: *prophēteia*
Pronunciation: *praw fay TAY uh*
Strong's Number: *4394*

The Greek word for "prophecy," *prophēteia*, denotes two ideas: that of "forth-telling," or speaking for God, and that of "foretelling," or predicting future events. Both aspects of the word are found in the New Testament. The beginning of prophetic activity in early Christianity, according to Acts, coincided with the out-pouring of the Holy Spirit upon the earliest Christians on the day of Pentecost (Acts 2:1–21). Peter's sermon on the day of Pentecost indicates that the outpouring of the Spirit fulfilled Joel's prophecy (Acts 2:4, 17–21; Joel 2:28–32). Furthermore, since the Spirit, which is inherently a Spirit of prophecy, had been poured out upon all early Christians, all believers are actual or potential prophets. Christian prophets were leaders in early Christian communities (1 Cor. 12:28; Eph. 4:11) who exercised their gift in church gatherings (Acts 13:1–3; 11:27–28; 1 Cor. 12—14). Since the Spirit of God was particularly active in Christian worship, prophecy was a major means whereby God communicated with His people.

Unfortunately, we know only a little about the content of prophecies uttered in the first-century church. Prophetic utterance occasionally provided divine guidance in making important decisions in the early days of the spread of Christianity. Through some kind of prophetic utterance, Paul and Barnabas were selected for a particular mission (Acts 13:1–3; 1 Tim. 1:18; 4:14), and Paul and Timothy were for-bidden to preach the gospel in Asia (Acts 16:6). The most frequent use of prophe-cy is in the prediction of the future. Agabus predicted a universal famine and the imminent arrest of Paul. Other prophets predicted his impending imprisonment as well (Acts 11:28; 20:23; 21:11). The prophecies contained in the Revelation of John contain the unveiling of events in the last days (Rev. 1:3; 19:10; 22:18–19).

According to Paul, the primary purpose of prophecy is to build up the church. In 1 Corinthians 14:3 he says, "... one who prophesies is helping others grow in the Lord, encouraging and comforting them." Again, in 1 Corinthians 14:4, Paul states that the "... one who speaks a word of prophecy strengthens the entire church." Paul discussed the subject of spiritual gifts, particularly tongues-speaking and prophecy, because the Corinthians had placed an excessive emphasis on speaking in tongues. Prophecy, which consisted of comprehensible speech inspired by the Spirit, con-tributed to the mutual edification and encouragement of all present (1 Cor. 14:20–25, 39).

KEY VERSES

1 Corinthians 14:22;
Revelation 1:3;
19:10; 22:18–19

P

Prophet

See also: *Prophet, p. 142 and Prophecy, p. 368*
Greek expression: *prophētēs*
Pronunciation: *praw FAY tayss*
Strong's Number: *4396*

The Greek word *prophētēs*, or "prophet" in English, evokes thoughts of Elijah, Isaiah, Jeremiah, Ezekiel, and Daniel. Indeed, these words should remind us of these men—who were the great prophets of the Old Testament era. But the word "prophet" should also evoke thoughts of New Testament prophets—namely John the Baptist, Jesus, other prophets in the early church (such as Agabus), and the apostle John.

John the Baptist is remembered in the New Testament primarily as Jesus' forerunner, whose coming was predicted by Malachi (Mal. 4:5–6). Yet in his own right, John was also a prophet, proclaiming the imminent judgment of God. Indeed, John was regarded as a prophet by people everywhere (Matt. 14:5; 17:10–13; Luke 1:76; 7:26). According to Jesus, John was the last representative of the Old Testament prophetic tradition (Matt. 11:13; Luke 16:16).

Jesus was considered to be a prophet, as is clear from all the Gospels (Matt. 16:14; Mark 6:14–15; Luke 7:16, 39; John 6:14; 7:40, 52). This assessment was based as much on the miracles Jesus performed as on His prophetic speeches and predictions. Jesus Himself claimed prophetic status, a claim implicit in Mark 6:4: "A prophet is not without honor except in his home town," and Luke 13:33: "Nevertheless I must journey on today and tomorrow and the next day; for it cannot be that a prophet should perish outside of Jerusalem" (NASB). In Acts, Jesus is regarded "as the prophet like Moses" predicted in Deuteronomy 18:18 (Acts 3:22; 7:37).

Among the many prophetic predictions of Jesus, three are most noteworthy: predictions of His betrayal, crucifixion, and resurrection; predictions about the destruction of Jerusalem with its temple and the end of the age are woven into a lengthy discourse to the disciples; and predictions of His second coming. The longest prophetic section in the Gospels is Jesus' eschatological discourse—His discussion of the end times in Mark 13:1–32 (see also Matt. 24:1–36; Luke 21:5–33).

P

God gave the church other prophets. In the church, according to 1 Corinthians 12:28, God has appointed first apostles, second prophets, and third teachers. The names of several early Christian prophets have been preserved. These include Agabus (Acts 11:27–28; 21:10–11), Judas and Silas (Acts 15:32), Barnabas, Simeon Niger, Lucius of Cyrene, Manaen, Paul (Acts 13:1), and the four unmarried daughters of Philip the Evangelist (Acts 21:8–9). John, the author of Revelation, was a prophet as well (Rev. 1:3; 22:9, 18). He recorded the visions of the end times given to him while he was in exile on the island of Patmos.

KEY VERSES

Matthew 11:13;
Mark 6:4;
1 Corinthians 12:28;
Revelation 22:9

Propitiate

Greek expression: *hilaskomai, hilasmos*
Pronunciation: *heel AHSS kaw migh; heel ahss MAWSS*
Strong's Numbers: *2433, 2434*

"Propitiate" and "propitiation" are not commonly used in the English language. We must look to an age long gone in order to discern their meaning. In ancient times, many polytheists thought of their gods as unpredictable beings, liable to become angry with their worshipers for any trifle. When any misfortune occurred, it was believed that a god was angry and was therefore punishing his worshipers. The remedy was to offer the god a sacrifice to appease his anger. This process was called "propitiation."

A few of the New Testament writers used exactly the same word, but the meaning was slightly different. Instead of seeing God as one whose mood needs to be appeased, "propitiation" focuses on the sacrifice of Jesus by death on the cross which brought the resultant peace between God and sinful humanity. The Greek term for "propitiation," *hilasmos,* occurs in some important passages: Romans 3:25; Hebrews 2:17; 1 John 2:2; 4:10. The message we get from these passages is that propitiation (also called "expiation") pertains to Christ's sacrifice for sins in order to bring about a peaceful relationship between God and humanity.

Whenever God's children sin, they provoke His anger. Of course, His anger is not an irrational lack of self-control, as it so often is with humans. His anger is the settled opposition of His holy nature to everything that is evil. Such opposition to sin cannot be dismissed with a wave of the hand. It requires something much more substantial, and the Bible states that it was only the cross that did this. Jesus is "the propitiation for our sins; and not for ours only, but also for the sins of the whole world" (1 John 2:2, KJV). This is not the only way of looking at the cross, but it is an important way. If God's anger is real, then it must be taken into account in the way that sin, which caused that wrath, is dealt with. When the New Testament speaks of "propitiation," it means that Jesus' death on the cross for the sins of mankind appeased God's wrath against His people once and for all. First John 4:10 states that God demonstrated His love to us by sending His Son to become "the propitiation for our sins." Just as in the Old Testament God met with His people when the blood of the sin offering was sprinkled on the altar, so Christ's death brings us into fellowship with God.

KEY VERSES

Hebrews 2:17;
1 John 2:2; 4:10

Punishment

Greek expression: *kolasis*
Pronunciation: *KAWL ah seess*
Strong's Number: *2851*

Webster's Dictionary defines "punishment" as "an imposed penalty for a fault, offense, or violation." Punishment, *kolasis* in Greek, is retribution for a crime or an offense. For example, in most states in the United States, murder can be punished by taking the murderer's life. This same law—and retribution for breaking it—is mandated in the Ten Commandments. But God's commandments far exceed the laws of the United States and most other countries. These commandments call for compliance on matters of one's relationship with God, spouse, and neighbors in ways that cannot be measured by any national law. The penalty for breaking these laws was severe punishment.

There is no way around it: sin demands judgment and must be dealt with. The penalty of sin against God is death. Because we are born with original sin, we are all sinful, we all sin against God and must therefore pay the penalty—death. However, Jesus paid this penalty for us. In His substitutionary death He bore the guilt of all humanity. His death on the cross was a vicarious offering to His Father; it removed the sinner's guilt by satisfying divine justice (Rom. 5:8; Gal. 3:13).

It may be difficult for us to understand the righteous judgment of a holy God who hates all sin yet loves sinners enough to sacrifice His only Son for our salvation. But the fact remains: those who accept His offer of salvation are free from God's eternal judgment; they will not suffer eternal punishment. Those who don't accept His offer will accept the consequences of His judgment against sin. Ultimately, that means that a person will go to "the eternal lake of fire"—commonly known as "hell." Hell was not originally prepared by God for people; it was prepared for the devil and his angels (Matt. 25:41; Rev. 20:10). However, those who reject God's offer of salvation will receive the same fate as the devil.

While the duration of punishment in hell is eternal for all who have chosen that destiny for themselves, there are degrees of punishment proportional to the sins of each individual. Only God is able to determine what those degrees are, and He will assign the consequences with perfect justice according to the responsibility given to each individual (see Matt. 11:20–24; Luke 12:47–48; Rev. 20:12–13).

KEY VERSES

Matthew 25:46;
1 John 4:18

P

Ransom

Greek expression: *antilutron, lutrōn, lutrōsis*
Pronunciation: *ahn TEE loo trawn; LOO trawn; LOO troh seess*
Strong's Numbers: *487, 3083, 3085*

In the news we sometimes hear of high-profile kidnapping cases, in which the kidnappers have demanded exorbitant ransom fees in exchange for the release of the person kidnapped.

The word "ransom" in Greek, as found in 1 Timothy 2:6, is *antilutron* made up of *anti*, signifying "substitution," and *lutrōn*, which is the word used for the ransom of a slave or prisoner. The *antilutron* is "a payment given instead of the slave or prisoner"—that is, in substitution for the slave or prisoner. The person holding the slave accepts the payment as a substitute for the slave. Two other words for "ransom" are *lutrōn* and *lutrosis*. A related word is *apolutrosis*, but this is usually translated as "redemption." In the New Testament, ransom denotes releasing, or liberating on payment of the ransom price. The translation "ransom" is restricted to approximately eight instances where there is a clear reference to the payment of some sort of price: Matthew 20:28; Mark 10:45; Luke 1:68; 2:38; Hebrews 9:12 where the word is also translated as "redemption"; 1 Timothy 2:6; and 1 Peter 1:18.

Jesus described His entire ministry as one of service in giving His life as "a ransom for many" (Matt. 20:28; Mark 10:45). Three features stand out in Jesus' words: His service is one of ransom, His self-sacrifice is the ransom price, and His ransom is substitutionary in character: "He gave his life to purchase freedom for everyone" (1 Tim. 2:6). Jesus Christ "gave his life to free us from every kind of sin" (Titus 2:14). The ransom price was "the precious blood of Christ" who was a lamb without blemish (1 Pet. 1:18–19).

To whom did Christ pay the ransom? One early church father, Origen, thought the ransom was paid to the devil. Origen theorized that Christ cheated the devil by escaping through His resurrection. However, although Jesus Christ defeated Satan and liberates believers from Satan's bondage, Scripture does not teach that the ransom was paid to Satan. Rather, the ransom was paid to God—or to be more precise, to the law of God. According to Galatians 3:13, Christ redeemed (or ransomed) us from the curse of the law. The law held us captive to its demands, and no one but Christ could pay the price to release us from this bondage.

KEY VERSES

Matthew 20:28;
Mark 10:45;
1 Timothy 2:6

Reconciliation

See also: *Make Atonement, p. 122*
Greek expression: *katallagē, katallassō*
Pronunciation: *kaht ahl lah GAY; kaht ahl LAHSS soh*
Strong's Numbers: *2643, 2644*

When two parties are at war with each other and then decide to make up their differences, that is called "reconciliation"—in modern understanding. Estranged husbands and wives are asked to "reconcile," as are warring countries. The Greek word *katallagē* basically means "change" or "exchange." When used in relationships between people, the term implies a change in attitude on the part of both individuals—a change from enmity to friendship. When used to describe the relationship existing between God and a person, the term then implies the "change of attitude" on the part of both a person and God. The need to change the sinful ways of a human being is obvious; but some argue that no change is needed on the part of God. However, inherent in the doctrine of justification is the changed attitude of God toward the sinner. God declares a person who was formally an enemy to be righteous before Him.

The King James Version translators used the word "atonement" to translate the Greek word *katallagē* in Romans 5:11. The term is derived from Anglo-Saxon words meaning "making at one." The word presupposes a separation, or alienation, that needs to be overcome if human beings are to know God and have fellowship with Him. Modern translations generally, and more correctly, render the word "reconciliation" (NASB, NIV).

The idea of reconciliation fills the New Testament. God is seen as taking the initiative in man's salvation; thus, reconciliation is the work of God, who opens the possibility for sinful human beings to receive pardoning grace. Humans are so sinful it is impossible for them to take the initiative in reconciliation. Paul summed up the human condition when he said, "All have sinned and fallen short of the glory of God" (Rom. 3:23). Elsewhere Paul described people as "enemies of God" (Rom. 5:10), as "hostile to God" (Rom. 8:7), as estranged and hostile in mind, and doing evil deeds (Col. 1:21). Adam's race is just like Adam: "Therefore, just as through one man sin entered into the world, and death through sin, and so death spread to all men, because all sinned" (Rom. 5:12, NASB). People are lost and helpless, standing under the awful judgment of God. They cannot justify themselves before God and cannot merit God's concern. The possibility of reconciliation, then, rests entirely with God.

Throughout the New Testament it is made clear that the work of Christ, primarily on the cross, is what provides reconciliation (Eph. 2:13). When we accept Christ's salvation, we can be reconciled to God (Col. 1:20). Indeed, we can now function as God's ambassadors to spread the message of reconciliation to the world (2 Cor. 5:18–20).

KEY VERSES

Romans 5:10–11;
11:15;
2 Corinthians
5:18–20

Redemption

See also: *Redeemed, p. 146*
Greek expression: *apolutrōsis, lutrōsis*
Pronunciation: *ah paw LOO troh seess; LOO troh seess*
Strong's Numbers: *629, 3085*

When we speak of "redemption" today, it is in the context of "redemption stamps." These are coupons that enable people to redeem merchandise. The word "redeem" is also frequently used to speak of an action that someone does in order to re-establish or recover himself or herself from some error. For example, the pitcher who lost the game last week redeems himself by winning the next two games.

The English word "redemption" is derived from a Latin root, meaning "to buy back." Thus, it means "the liberation of any possession, object, or person, usually by payment of a ransom." In Greek, the root word means "to loose" and so "to free." It is used to mean freeing from chains, slavery, or prison. Two cognate words in the New Testament, *lutrōsis* and *apolutrōsis*, are both typically translated "redemption" in various versions. *Lutrōsis* indicates the act of "freeing or releasing" by paying a ransom price; *apolutrōsis* indicates the act of "buying back" by paying a ransom price. Christ paid the ransom price with His own blood (1 Pet. 1:18–19) and thus freed us from the demands of the law, and its curse on sin, to become children of God (Gal. 3:13; 4:5). When payment seems to be the main point in a passage, the term "ransom" is a good English equivalent. When the point seems to be more related to buying something back—hence, recovering someone from sin— the word "redemption" is a better choice.

Jesus, the Son of man, came to give Himself as a ransom for many (Matt. 20:28; Mark 10:45). The work of the Messiah was vicarious and substitutionary. The same thought occurs especially in the writings of Paul where Christ is the sin offering to the Father (Rom. 3:25). In other words, Jesus purchased and redeemed us with His life (Acts 20:28; 2 Cor. 5:14–17). All who believe in Jesus Christ—by accepting His payment for us to the Father—are freed from the bondage of sin.

R

KEY VERSES

Romans 3:24;
Ephesians 1:14;
Colossians 1:14;
Hebrews 9:15

Regeneration

Greek expression: *paliggenesia*
Pronunciation: *pahl eeng gehn eh SEE uh*
Strong's Number: *3824*

Anyone who experiences any kind of winter looks forward to springtime, for that is a season of "regeneration." Flowers bud and bloom, birds return and sing. Unfortunately, it never lasts. Spring goes into summer, summer into autumn, autumn into winter.

People throughout the ages have longed for an eternal spring, a "regeneration" of the pristine earth. Secular writers spoke of such a regeneration. For example, the Stoic philosophers considered regeneration to be a return to a former state of existence. For the biblical writers, however, regeneration means a renewal on a higher level. It is a "radically new beginning," rather than a mere restoration of previous conditions. This renewal is twofold: it occurs within people's spirits and it will occur when God recreates a new heaven and a new earth.

The regeneration of a person is spoken about in Titus 3:5. Paul said, "He saved us, not on the basis of deeds we have done in righteousness, but according to His mercy, by the washing of regeneration and renewal of the Holy Spirit." The Greek word for "washing" can signify the receptacle of washing (the *laver*) or the act of washing itself. In Ephesians 5:26, the only other New Testament occurrence of *paliggenesia*, the natural meaning is "washing." Quite simply, the text says that "regeneration" is characterized by, or accompanied by, the action of washing. The regenerative activity of the Holy Spirit is characterized elsewhere in Scripture as "cleansing and purifying" (Ezek. 36:25–27; John 3:5). The Greek term for regeneration, *paliggenesia*, literally means "birth again"—indicating a new birth effected by the Holy Spirit (John 3:6; Rom. 8:16; Gal. 4:6). Thus God saves people through one process with two aspects: the washing of regeneration and renewing of the Holy Spirit.

Regeneration is not just a nice idea or a good philosophy. The Bible insists that regeneration is absolutely necessary. Apart from it, all persons are dead in trespasses and sin (Eph. 2:1–3). An unregenerated person is unable to understand the things of God, and no amount of good works can change him or her (1 Cor. 2:14; Titus 3:5). This is why Jesus insisted, in His dialogue with Nicodemus, "You must be born again" (John 3:7, NASB). God's first plan is to regenerate people. Then, He will regenerate the universe, in that He will establish a new world order at His return (Matt. 19:28). The ultimate goal of regeneration is the creation of a new heaven and earth that will be totally righteous and without sin (2 Pet. 3:13; Rev. 21:1). The present working of the Holy Spirit in the believer is a foretaste of this future cosmic regeneration (Eph. 1:13–14).

KEY VERSES

Matthew 19:28;
Titus 3:5

375

Repentance

Greek expression: *metanoia*
Pronunciation: *meht AH noy ah*
Strong's Number: *3341*

The Greek word for "repentance" is a compound word derived from *meta*, meaning "after," and suggesting "some type of change," and *nous*, meaning "mind." Thus, *metanoia* strictly denotes "a change of mind"—a rejection of past sinful ways. But it also connotes remorse for sin, accompanied by a desire to turn away from one's sin and to God for salvation. Such repentance accompanies faith in Christ (Acts 20:21).

It is inconsistent and unintelligible to suppose that anyone could believe in Christ and yet not repent. Repentance is such an important aspect of conversion that it is often stressed more than faith, as when Christ said that there is joy in heaven among the angels over one sinner that repents (Luke 15:7). The apostles described the conversion of the Gentiles to Christ as God granting them "repentance unto life" (Acts 11:18). Both John the Baptist and Jesus began their ministries with a call to repentance (Matt. 3:2; 4:17)—a call which many of the social outcasts and "sinners" of that day answered (Luke 19:1–10), while the religious people of that day rejected it (Luke 11:39–44; 18:9–14).

Repentance, however, is not just a one-time experience. Recognition of daily sins and shortcomings provides the occasion for renewed acts of repentance. A good example of this is found in the book of Revelation in Jesus' address to the church in Ephesus (Rev. 2:1–7). The basic problem with this church was that even though they had stood fast against evil and false teaching, they had left their "first love"—their basic love for Christ and for one another. Consequently, Jesus told them they had to repent: "Remember the height from which you have fallen! Repent and do the things you did at first. If you do not repent, I will come to you and remove your lampstand from its place" (Rev. 2:5). They needed to repent of their lack of love, and love as they had originally loved, with enthusiasm and devotion. If they refused to repent, however, Christ said that He would come and remove the church's lampstand from its place—which meant that the church would cease to be a witness for Christ.

R

KEY VERSES

Acts 11:18, 20:21;
2 Corinthians 7:9–10

Second Corinthians 7 provides another example of how a group of Christians repented after being confronted with their sins. Their repentance shows elements of sorrow for sin, and a determined resolve to forsake old sinful ways and to behave properly. These examples serve as reminders to all of us that repentance is not just a one-time occurrence. As God enlightens us, we need to repent.

Rest

See also: *Rest, p. 152*
Greek expression: *katapausis*
Pronunciation: *kaht AH pow seess*
Strong's Number: *2663*

The Old Testament tells us that "by the seventh day God completed His work which He had done; and He rested on the seventh day from all His work which He had done" (Gen. 2:2, NASB). This rest by God on the seventh day was the basis for the Hebrew Sabbath—God's command to the Hebrews to rest on the seventh day. But this Sabbath rest really didn't give God's people a peaceful cessation from all of the hardships of life—so God promised another day of rest in Psalm 95:7–11. These two different rests are important for our understanding of how the concept of *katapausis*, the Greek word for "rest," is developed in the New Testament—specifically by the writer of the book of Hebrews.

Quoting Psalm 95:7–11, the writer of Hebrews rehearsed the tragic experience of Israel under Moses during the desert wanderings (Heb. 3:7–19). Throughout the forty-year wilderness experience, the people hardened their hearts and rebelled against God. In turn, God was provoked by their stubbornness and swore that those who sinned would never enter "the rest" He was going to provide (Heb. 3:10–11, 18). The writer thus argued that if disobedience to God under Moses had serious consequences, forsaking Christ will be much more perilous. Hence, the wavering Christians were urged to be careful in case they should fall away from the living God due to an evil, unbelieving heart (Heb. 3:12). Although Joshua was regarded as a great leader of Israel, the Israelites under Joshua's leadership failed to enter "the rest" that God had planned because of the people's disobedience. The "rest" spoken of in this passage is related to the Sabbath rest of God (Heb. 4:3–4); but, it is more closely related to the concept of salvation. It is a spiritual reality that is achieved by turning from our own empty works and trusting in the finished work of Christ (Heb. 4:10). The author of Hebrews reminded his readers that "there remains therefore a Sabbath rest for the people of God" (Heb. 4:9, NASB), one that only Christ can provide. Christians not only benefit from this Sabbath rest in the present age, but anticipate its full realization in the age to come.

It is God's "rest" into which all persons are encouraged to enter. The weekly day of rest is a reminder and a reflection of that rest. The "rest" of the Israelites in the Promised Land after their wilderness wanderings is a symbol of God's eternal rest that His people will share. The rest that Christ gives to those who come to Him (Matt. 11:28) is a foretaste and a guarantee of "the divine rest" that awaits them. The rest after death of believers who have fallen asleep in Christ is a blissful intensification of the reality of this experience: "Blessed are the dead who die in the Lord . . . They may rest from their labors" (Rev. 14:13, NASB).

R

KEY VERSES

Hebrews 3:11, 18;
4:1, 3, 5, 10–11

377

Resurrection (of Christ)

Greek expression: *anastasis*
Pronunciation: *ahn AH stah seess*
Strong's Number: *386*

The Bible records that several people were raised from the dead. Elijah raised a widow's son from the dead, another widow's son was raised by Jesus, and Lazarus was also raised by Jesus. However, their revitalization (or resuscitation) is absolutely not the same as Christ's "resurrection," which is *anastasis* in Greek. They arose only to die again; He arose to live forever. They arose still doomed by corruptibility; He arose incorruptible. They arose with no change to their constitution; He arose in a significantly different form. When Jesus arose from the dead, He was glorified, transfigured, and became life-giving spirit. All three happened simultaneously. When He was resurrected, He was glorified (Luke 24:26). At the same time, His body was transfigured into a glorious one (Phil. 3:21) and became a life-giving spirit (1 Cor. 15:45).

Prior to the Lord's crucifixion and resurrection He declared, "The hour has come for the Son of Man to be glorified. 'Truly, truly, I say to you, unless a grain of wheat falls into the earth and dies, it remains by itself alone; but if it dies, it bears much fruit' " (John 12:23–24). This declaration provides the best picture of resurrection. Paul also used this illustration. He likened the glory of Christ's resurrection to a grain being sown in death, then coming forth in life. Actually, Paul used this illustration when answering two questions the Corinthians posed about resurrection: (1) How are the dead raised? and (2) With what sort of body do they come? (1 Cor. 15:35).

To the first question Paul responded, "Foolish man, what you sow is not made alive unless it dies" (1 Cor. 15:36). This follows perfectly the Lord's saying in John 12:24, and the two mutually explain each other. The grain must die before it can be quickened. Paul devotes more explanation to the second question; and the Spirit inspired him to unfold this mystery. Using the same natural example of the grain of wheat, Paul revealed that the body that comes forth in resurrection is altogether different in form from that which had been sown. Through an organic process, the single, bare grain is transformed into a stalk of wheat. In essence, the grain and the stalk are one and the same—the latter simply being the living growth and expressed expansion of the former. In short, the stalk is the glory of the grain or the glorified grain.

KEY VERSES

Romans 1:4;
1 Corinthians 15:42

This illustration shows that Jesus' resurrected body was altogether different from the one that was buried. In death, He had been sown in corruption, dishonor, and weakness; but in resurrection, He came forth perfect, in glory and power. The natural body that Jesus possessed as a man became a spiritual body. And at the same time Christ became "life-giving spirit."

Resurrection (of Christians)

Greek expression: *anastasis*
Pronunciation: *ahn AH stah seess*
Strong's Number: *386*

The resurrection of Christ is the central point of Christianity. So important was the resurrection for Paul that he hinged both preaching and faith upon its validity. He considered that Christianity without the resurrection would be empty and meaningless (1 Cor. 15:12–19). The resurrection of Christ is the presupposition of all New Testament truths and experience. Rebirth to a living hope is based upon the resurrection (1 Pet. 1:3). Resurrection and regeneration are closely linked in the Scriptures in the same way that crucifixion and redemption form an inseparable unity. As redemption was not possible without Christ's crucifixion, so regeneration of all people and creation is not possible without Christ's resurrection. The Scripture plainly says that we have been born again through the resurrection of Christ (1 Pet. 1:23).

After Christ was raised from the dead, He called the disciples His brothers (Matt. 28:10; John 20:19), and He declared that His God was now their God, and His Father their Father. Through resurrection, the disciples had become the brothers of Jesus, possessing the same divine life and the same Father. As the firstborn from among the dead (Col. 1:17; Rev. 1:18), Jesus Christ became the firstborn among many brothers and sisters (Rom. 8:29). The Scriptures even tell us that all believers were included with Christ in His resurrection. Paul declared: "For since by a man came death, by a man also came the resurrection of the dead" (1 Cor. 15:21, NASB). This shows that Christ's resurrection included "the resurrection of believers" to eternal life. When He arose, many arose with Him, for they were united with Him in His resurrection (Rom. 6:4–5; Eph. 2:6; Col. 3:1).

The previous verses speak of the spiritual gains of resurrection. Christians are also counting a physical resurrection. Paul looked for the day of the Lord when the dead in Christ would be raised and those who were still alive would join the dead in final victory over death and sin (1 Thess. 4:15–18). There was no doubt in his mind that this resurrection was a glorious expectation, that it involved some type of a personalized body, and that this body would not be a natural, finite body, but spiritual and eternal (1 Cor. 15:35–44).

Paul's teaching on the resurrection of a physical body ran counter to current Greek thinking. The Greeks developed a doctrine of the immortality of the soul. The body was thought to be a disposable physical outer garment, whereas the soul was related to the immortal forms and sustained from age to age. It is no wonder that Paul had a difficult time preaching to the Athenians (Acts 17:16–32).

R

KEY VERSES

Romans 6:5;
1 Corinthians
15:12–13, 42

Revelation

Greek expression: *apokalupsis*
Pronunciation: *ahp aw KAHL oop seess*
Strong's Number: *602*

The New Testament Greek term *apokalupsis* (apocalypse) means "unveiling," "uncovering," or "making someone or something known." It designates God's own self-disclosure or manifesting of Himself or things concerning Himself; it may also mean the word that conveys such "revelation." Revelation is essential for people to know God. People have knowledge of God because of God's initiative and activity. God is always the Initiator and Author of revelation; people are the recipients. God discloses what otherwise would be unknown; He uncovers what would otherwise be hidden (Gal. 1:12; Eph. 3:3).

God draws back the veil in a twofold manner. There is first of all what has come to be called "general revelation." God reveals Himself in nature, in history, and in all people made in His image. The association of God's revelation with nature, by which people have an intuitive knowledge of God's existence, is of long standing and is a truth supported throughout the New Testament (Acts 14:17; 17:22–29; Rom. 1:19–21). The fact that there is a God, that God is the Creator with almighty power, that God deals justly as the supreme Judge—these things are known and recognized by many people. Paul could expect agreement from the Athenians when he asserted that it is in God, the one and only true God, that all people live and move and have their being (Acts 17:38). Knowing God through nature, however, is not the full revelation. "Full and complete revelation" comes when people encounter the person God.

To know God from His revelation in nature still leaves Him and His gracious purposes completely unknown. But, fortunately for us all, God intends the salvation of all people—that all could come to be known and thereby have eternal life. Mankind would know nothing at all of God's purposes had God not revealed His heart and purposes through Jesus Christ and through Scripture. Therefore, the zenith of God's revelation came with the incarnation of His beloved Son, Jesus Christ (John 1:14–18; Gal. 4:4–5; Heb. 1:1–2). Those who experienced the incarnate Word and those who saw the risen Christ provided eyewitness testimony (2 Pet. 1:16–21; 1 John 1:1–4). We have this word, contained in the New Testament, as God's revelation for all to read and understand.

R

KEY VERSES

Romans 16:25;
Ephesians 1:17; 3:3;
Revelation 1:1

Reward

Greek expression: *misthos*
Pronunciation: *meess THAWSS*
Strong's Number: *3408*

When we think of reward, we usually think of favorable compensation. However, in the Scriptures the Greek word *misthos* is used as payment for both evil and good deeds. Thus, Peter uses *misthos* when he says that wicked people "suffer wrong as the wages [*misthoi*] of doing wrong" (2 Pet. 2:13), while Luke uses the word to speak of the disciples' reward for having followed Jesus (Luke 6:35). The underlying concept is that of "being paid for doing work"—whether good or evil.

In Jesus' day, the Jews recognized the merit of good works and, therefore, exhorted each other to accumulate a store of merit on a basis by which God would bless them. The Pharisees believed that accurate and conscientious observance of the Law would oblige God to recompense them for their performances. The individual who did much was to expect reward from God, while every transgression was met with punishment.

The concept of reward was a significant part of Jesus' teaching, especially in the Sermon on the Mount (Matt. 5—7). Jesus proclaimed that the blessing of God would come upon all people who exhibit certain moral characteristics (Matt. 5:1-12). The individual who acts to receive the praise of others shall receive that and nothing more, but the one whose motives call him or her to please God will be rewarded by God (Matt. 6:1, 4, 6, 18). But lest people think they could count on God to operate on a purely economic basis—that is, commensurate pay for time of labor—Jesus presented the parable of the laborers (Matt. 20:1-16). In this parable, each laborer was paid the same amount no matter how long he had worked. In the end, Jesus calls us to work for motives higher than reward. In the discourse on the good shepherd, the hireling who only works for wages is contrasted with the shepherd who is willing to lay down his life for the sheep (John 10:11-14).

Beginning with Paul, the idea of reward especially as it relates to salvation is seen in a drastically different light. No longer is salvation considered to be the result of an individual having done more good than evil in life. Salvation is an act of divine favor which no one can earn; given by a loving, beneficent God (Rom. 4:4). After one's salvation, he or she is rewarded for his or her work. First Corinthians 3:8-14 teaches that the quality of a person's works will be examined and rewarded, but that salvation does not hinge upon good works. Believers are saved and guaranteed a place in heaven by the grace of God. But out of love for our God, we should urge each other to act and interact with others, according to Jesus' example.

R

KEY VERSES

Matthew 6:1; 20:8;
1 Corinthians
3:8, 14;
2 Peter 2:13, 15;
2 John 8

Riches

Greek expression: *ploutos*
Pronunciation: *PLOO tawss*
Strong's Number: *4149*

In the Bible, the word "riches" describes two opposing ideas. Sometimes riches, or material wealth, is a sign of God's blessing and approval. At other times, the word virtually identifies the rich with the wicked.

The Bible clearly states that God made all things for people to enjoy (1 Tim. 6:17). Every possession that a person can possibly own comes from the Creator, so all wealth can rightly be counted as a blessing from God. Nowhere, then, does the Bible say that having possessions and becoming wealthy are wrong in themselves. However, Jesus warned that *ploutos*, which means "riches," could keep a person out of the kingdom: "How hard it will be for those who are wealthy to enter the kingdom of God" (Mark 10:23, NASB). Affluence, Jesus taught, can: destroy peace (Matt. 6:24–34), blind people to the needs of others (Luke 16:19–31), stand between individuals and the gateway to eternal life (Mark 10:17–27), and even bring God's judgment (Luke 12:16–21). He told His disciples not to accumulate personal wealth and praised those who gave up their possessions (Matt. 6:19; 19:29).

Jesus' warnings against wealth are not, in fact, directed against "riches" in themselves. What He condemns is the wrong attitudes many people have toward acquiring wealth and the wrong ways in which they use it. Longing for riches chokes the spiritual life like weeds in a field of grain (Matt. 13:22). The greedy desire to have more wealth doomed the unforgiving servant (Matt. 18:23–35). And the rich man's selfishness, not his wealth, sealed his fate (Luke 16:19–26). Paul captured the main theme in these parables when he said "the love of money is at the root of all kinds of evil" (1 Tim. 6:10).

The greatest danger of all arises when riches master a person's life. The whole Bible warns against this idolatrous attitude to material things (Luke 14:15–24). Satan tempted Jesus to put material wealth and power in place of worshiping God (Matt. 4:8–9), and Jesus delivers the clearest warning against making money one's master (Matt. 6:24). In this light Jesus instructs the rich young ruler to sell everything (Mark 10:17–22). Here was a wealthy man who had allowed his possessions to posses him. Jesus' aim was to make him recognize his bondage so he could enter the kingdom. In Jesus' view, the truly rich are those whose main aim in life is to serve Him as King (Matt. 13:44–46).

KEY VERSES

Matthew 13:22;
Luke 8:14;
1 Timothy 6:17

Righteousness (righteousness of God)

See also: *Righteousness, p. 156*
Greek expression: *dikaiosunē*
Pronunciation: *dee kigh aw S<u>OO</u> nay*
Strong's Number: *1343*

The great reformer Martin Luther defined the "righteousness of God" as a righteousness valid before God, which a man may possess through faith. In other words, the "righteousness of God" is the righteousness that comes from God; it is God's way of making a sinner "right" before Him. Luther said that this righteousness is the first and last need of any sinful individual.

The "righteousness of God," as discussed in Paul's letter to the Romans, carries a double meaning and may be labeled both legal and moral. In other words, the Greek word *dikaiosunē* refers to the legal action God takes in declaring believers righteous—that is, "without guilt or sin"—but it also refers to "perfect righteousness," a characteristic that can only be attributed to God Himself in Scripture. This characteristic is the lofty standard for human behavior, which cannot be achieved by anyone apart from God's provision.

In short, righteousness is a gift from God (Rom. 3:21—5:21). There is no righteousness apart from Jesus Christ, for we could not be declared "without sin" except through Jesus' sacrifice for us on the cross. In the proclamation of the gospel of Jesus we discover that, "it is through faith that a righteous person has life" (Rom. 1:17). Therefore the Father requires acceptance of His Son as His appointed means of justification (Rom. 3:25–26; 5:9). God declares people to be righteous when they put their trust in Jesus (Rom. 8:33–34; 2 Cor. 3:8; 11:15). God pardons sins, is reconciled with sinners, and grants His peace to them because of Christ (Rom. 5:1, 9–11; Eph. 2:14–17). Those who have been declared righteous now enjoy a new relationship. They are "children of God." The Father relates to His children righteously and expects them to relate righteously to Him.

R

The fullness of righteousness will be manifest at the second coming of the Lord Jesus, when all those who have been justified will also be glorified (Rom. 8:30). History moves toward the final glorious manifestation of God's kingdom, when all creation will be renewed in "righteousness"—that is, all creation will be right with God, without sin, forever (2 Pet. 3:13).

KEY VERSES

Romans 1:17; 3:21, 22; 10:3

Salvation

See also: *Salvation, p. 159*
Greek expression: *sōteria, sōzō*
Pronunciation: *soh tay REE uh; SOH dzoh*
Strong's Numbers: *4991, 4982*

In classical Greek the verb *sōzō*, "to save," and the noun *sōteria*, "salvation," are used for the concept of "rescue," "deliverance" or "salvation," and even "well-being" or "health." The Septuagint (the Greek translation of the Old Testament) most frequently uses *sōzō* to render the Hebrew word *yasha'* ("to save") and the New Testament primarily employs *sōzō* and its derivatives for the idea of "salvation."

In the Gospels, "salvation" is clearly connected with the Old Testament concept of "bringing deliverance." It is applied to the coming of Christ in Zechariah's prophecy (Luke 1:69, 71; Ps.106:10; 132:17) and in Simeon's hymn of praise (Luke 2:30). While *sōteria* does not occur frequently in the Gospels, the concept of salvation is implied in Jesus' statement about entrance into the kingdom of God (Matt. 19:24–26) and His miracles of healing (Luke 17:19; 18:42). Luke sees salvation as that which delivers people from disease and from sin.

The New Testament teaches that salvation has its source in Jesus Christ (2 Tim. 2:10; Heb. 5:9) who is the author and mediator of salvation (Heb. 2:10; 7:25). Salvation is God's work (1 Thess. 5:9) and is offered by His grace (Eph. 2:8–9). The message of salvation is contained in the Scriptures (2 Tim. 3:15) and is carried by those who proclaim the word of truth (Eph. 1:13). The appropriate response to salvation is repentance and faith (2 Tim. 3:15; 1 Pet. 1:9). This was the preaching of the early church as it proclaimed the Savior Jesus (Acts 4:12; 13:23–26). Paul especially proclaimed the universality of God's offer of salvation (Rom. 1:16).

Within the Scriptures, there are many other terms associated with the concept of "salvation"—especially justification, redemption, and reconciliation. Justification is one's legal standing before God, while redemption speaks more of the means of salvation—the payment or price required to bring one back to God. Reconciliation speaks of a change in relationship and appeasing God, which evokes the Old Testament sacrificial system and the turning away of God's wrath. These terms and others share some common ground with the biblical concept of salvation, but they all point to the person and work of Jesus Christ the Savior. He has saved us from our sin and will rescue us all someday from this finite, sin-filled, world.

S

KEY VERSES

Luke 1:69, 71;
Romans 1:16;
2 Timothy 2:10;
Titus 3:5;
Hebrews 5:9

Sanctification

Greek expression: *hagiasmos, hagiazō*
Pronunciation: *hah gee ahss MAWSS; hah gee AH dzoh*
Strong's Numbers: *37, 38*

The Greek term for sanctify, *hagiazō*, means to "set apart" for God's special use, or "to make distinct from what is common." Hence, sanctification is to be made like God who is distinct from all else and therefore holy. The Greek word for "sanctify" refers to a process which is perfect in principle, though not yet attainable. Though we are not yet completely holy, we stand in relation to God as though we are. This is indicated in Hebrews 10:10 where the verb "sanctified" is a perfect participle, literally "having been sanctified," indicating the present result of a past action. Sanctification is something that has been done once for all, but its effect still continues—as stated in Hebrews 10:14, "those who are being sanctified."

A comprehensive definition of sanctification is found in the New Hampshire Baptist Confession (1833), which states: "We believe that Sanctification is the process by which, according to the will of God, we are made partakers of His holiness; that it is a progressive work; that it is begun in regeneration; and that it is carried on in the hearts of believers by the presence and power of the Holy Spirit, the Sealer and Comforter, in the continual use of the appointed means—especially the Word of God, self-examination, self-denial, watchfulness, and prayer" (Article X). This definition helps us to distinguish sanctification from regeneration in that the regeneration speaks of the beginning of the Christian life. Sanctification is also distinguished from glorification, which focuses on the consummation of God's work in the believer. Put quite simply, then, regeneration refers to the beginning of salvation, sanctification to the middle, and glorification to the end of salvation.

The distinction between sanctification and justification calls for more detailed attention, both because it is somewhat subtle and even more fundamental. In the first place, justification, like regeneration, refers (though not exclusively) to the beginning of the Christian experience, whereas the above definition in the New Hampshire Baptist Confession emphasizes the progressive character of sanctification. Second, justification refers to a judicial act of God whereby believers are at once absolved of all their guilt and accounted legally righteous; whereas sanctification, like regeneration and glorification, calls attention to the transforming power of the Holy Spirit upon the character of God's children. In short, justification is a once-for-all, declarative act of God as Judge. Sanctification is a progressive change in the character of the person justified—making the believer become a partaker of God's holy nature. Thus, God's salvation of believers includes a continual process of sanctification. A believer's walk is a path of continual growth—and a process that brings us closer to God.

S

KEY VERSES

Romans 6:19, 22;
1 Corinthians 1:30;
2 Thessalonians
2:13;
Hebrews 12:14

Satan, devil

See also: *Satan, p. 161*
Greek expression: *diabolos, satanas*
Pronunciation: *dee AH bawl awss; sah tahn AHSS*
Strong's Numbers: *1228, 4567*

The Greek word for devil is *diabolos*. The Greek word signifies a "slanderer" and an "accuser"—one who accuses another (Rev. 12:10). The devil's other name in Hebrew is *Satan*—the Greek word is *Satanas*, a word signifying "an adversary," one who lies in wait for or sets himself in opposition to another. These and other names of the same fallen spirit that tempted Eve in the Garden point to different features in both his evil character and his deceitful operations. Satan is seldom mentioned in the Old Testament. When he is mentioned, he is pictured as an angel who acts as the heavenly prosecutor (Job 1:6–12; 2:1–7; Zech. 3:1–2). As such, he is called "the satan" or "the accuser," and there is nothing in the context to indicate that this angel is evil. It is not until the late Old Testament period that Satan appears as "a tempter." In 1 Chronicles 21:1, the story of 2 Samuel 24:1 is retold with Satan (the Hebrew word used for the first time as a proper name) pictured as the sinister instigator behind David's sin. The Old Testament, then, doesn't have a developed doctrine of Satan.

In contrast to the Old Testament, the New Testament has a well-developed portrayal of Satan. He comes with a whole list of names: Satan (Hebrew for "accuser"), devil, Beliar, Beelzebub, the Adversary, the Dragon, the Enemy, the Serpent, the Tempter, and the Wicked One. Satan is pictured as the ruler of a host of angels and the controller of the world, who especially governs all who are not believers (Matt. 25:41; 2 Cor. 4:4; John 8:44). Satan is opposed to God and seeks to alienate all people from God. Therefore, he is an especially dangerous foe of Christians who must steadfastly resist him and beware of his trickery (1 Pet. 5:8; Eph. 6:11). Satan works his evil will by tempting persons (John 13:2; Acts 5:3), by hindering God's workers (1 Thess. 2:18), by accusing Christians before God (Rev. 12:10), and by controlling the evil persons who resist the gospel (2 Thess. 2:9). But Christians must not fear Satan because he will always be under God's control, who will eventually destroy him (Rom. 16:20; Rev. 20:10).

S

KEY VERSES

Matthew 4:1, 10;
Romans 16:20;
Revelation 20:2, 10

Savior

Greek expression: *sōtēr*
Pronunciation: *soh TAYR*
Strong's Number: *4990*

A Savior is a "deliverer," "protector," or "preserver." In ancient Greek society, the term was applied not only to gods but also to people whose significant actions brought some type of benefit to others. In Luke 1:47, Mary rejoices in God her Savior, referring to the Lord's mighty acts of protection and deliverance on behalf of Israel. In Luke 2:11, the angel announces to the shepherds the birth of "a Savior, who is Christ the Lord," one who would offer Himself as a sacrifice to provide redemption for all. Luke's emphasis on Jesus as Savior can be seen in the summary of Jesus' mission in Luke 19:10: "to seek and to save that which was lost" (NASB). In New Testament times, the Greek term for Savior, *sōtēr*, was used for military heroes and Caesars. The Romans used the word to refer to the divine status of their emperors. Thus, for Jesus to be called "Savior" by His believers was tantamount to being called "God." It is no wonder, then, that two New Testament writers, Paul and Peter, call Jesus, "our God and Savior." In Titus 2:13, Paul identified Jesus as "our God and Savior." Peter also named Jesus as "God and Savior" in 2 Peter 1:1. And in the next verse, he says Jesus is "our God and Lord."

Jesus is God, who came as a man to save us. In fact, Jesus' name means "Yahweh the Savior" or "Yahweh who saves." Matthew points this out in Matthew 1:21: "you shall call His name Jesus, for it is He who will save His people from their sins" (Matt. 1:21). Christians believe that Yahweh, God Himself, became man. He became incarnate. He is Jesus (Yahweh the Savior), the Christ, the Son of God—even God Himself. His greatest act of salvation was not to set the Jews free from Roman rule—as many expected of their Savior. Rather, He came to save the whole world from sin. This salvation cost Him death on the cross. This salvation costs us nothing, but to accept Jesus' gracious act of salvation on our behalf.

S

KEY VERSES

Luke 1:47; 2:11;
John 4:42;
Titus 2:13;
2 Peter 1:1

Scribe

Greek expression: *grammateus*
Pronunciation: *grahm mah TEWSS*
Strong's Number: *1122*

In New Testament times, the scribes were a class of scholars who taught, copied, and interpreted the Jewish Law for the people. They appear in the Gospels primarily as opponents of Jesus. They continually accused Him of violating the Law on numerous occasions: in forgiving sins (Matt. 9:1–3; Luke 5:17–26), in breaking their notion of Sabbath observance through work and healing (Luke 6:1–2, 6–11), in not following their accepted ceremonial washings (Mark 7:2–5), and in ignoring their practice of fasting (Luke 5:33–39). Not surprisingly, they especially disapproved of Jesus' practice of mingling with the unclean and outcasts of Jewish society (Mark 2:16–17; Luke 15:1–2).

Although there is evidence that a minority of the scribes accepted Jesus (Matt. 8:19; 13:52; Mark 12:32), their primary attitude toward Jesus was one of hostility. As previously suggested, this was partly due to Jesus' differing expression of fidelity to the Mosaic law and His openness toward the outcasts. It was also partly due to the rising popularity of Jesus among the people, which posed a threat to their own authority and to the safety of the city (Mark 7:29; 11:18).

Another contributing factor of their opposition to Jesus was His open exposure of their hypocrisy and corruption. In His rebukes of the scribes and Pharisees, Jesus openly accused them of catering to public approval (Matt. 23:5–7). While appearing to be outwardly correct and holy, they were inwardly corrupt (Matt. 23:25–28; Luke 11:39–41). Jesus also attacked the principle of oral law taught by the scribes, which they demanded the people to follow. Jesus charged that the oral law was a "heavy burden," which the scribes themselves did not even bother to follow (Matt. 23:2–4, 13–22). While emphasizing the minor points of the Law, the scribes were also guilty of ignoring the weightier concerns of justice, mercy, and faith (Matt. 23:23–24). Contrary to being the descendants of the prophets, as the scribes held themselves to be, Jesus claimed that the scribes would have killed the prophets if they had lived in their day (Matt. 23:29–36; Luke 20:9–19).

KEY VERSES

Matthew 23:2, 13, 15, 23, 25, 27, 29, 34; 27:41

Therefore, it is not surprising that the scribes were anxious to get rid of Jesus (Mark 14:1; Luke 11:53). The scribes joined forces with their normal opponents (the high priesthood) to engineer Jesus' arrest (Mark 14:43). When Jesus appeared before them and the rest of the Sanhedrin, they worked with the other leaders to construe a case against Him worthy of death (Matt. 26:57–66). When taking Jesus before Herod, they stood by and shouted their accusations with the others (Luke 23:10). Finally, they participated with other members of the Sanhedrin in mocking Jesus on the cross (Matt. 27:41–43).

Scriptures

Greek expression: *graphai*
Pronunciation: *GRAHF igh*
Strong's Number: *1124*

The Scriptures are the writings contained in the Bible. Jesus referred to the books of the Old Testament as "the Scriptures" (Matt. 21:42), and Paul spoke of them as "the holy Scriptures" (Rom. 1:2). Furthermore, Paul declared that the Old Testament Scriptures are inspired by God and therefore profitable for reading in church meetings (2 Tim. 3:15–16). The writings of the New Testament are also "Scriptures." In Peter's second letter, he said:

> Regard the patience of our Lord to be salvation; just as also our beloved brother Paul, according to the wisdom given him, wrote to you, as also in all his letters, speaking in them of these things, in which are some things hard to understand, which the untaught and unstable distort, as they do also the rest of the Scriptures, to their own destruction.
>
> *(2 Pet. 3:15–16)*

In this statement, we discover that the author unequivocally indicates that Paul's letters are on the same par as "the other Scriptures." Thus, both the Old Testament and New Testament are "Scriptures."

The Old Testament was written almost entirely in Hebrew, with a few isolated passages in Aramaic in the latter books. If one accepts the view that Moses wrote the first five books of the Old Testament which is the position the Scripture itself takes, the earliest books of the Old Testament were written by about 1400 B.C. provided one accepts the early date proposed for the exodus. If the last book written was Malachi (before 400 B.C.), composition took place during a thousand years of time. All the writers, about thirty in number, were Jews: prophets, judges, kings, and other leaders in Israel.

The New Testament was probably written entirely in Greek. If James was the first to write a New Testament book before the middle of the first century and if John was the last, composing Revelation about A.D. 90, the New Testament was written during a fifty-year period in the latter half of the first century. All the writers, approximately nine, were Jews, with the exception of Luke who wrote Luke and Acts—and they came from a variety of walks of life: fishermen, doctor, tax collector, and religious leaders.

KEY VERSES

Matthew 21:42;
Romans 1:2;
2 Timothy 3:16

In spite of great diversity of authorship in the Old Testament and New Testament, and composition spanning over 1,500 years, there is unity in the total message. The two Testaments complement each other remarkably well. As Augustine said more than 1,500 years ago, "The New is in the Old contained; the Old is in the New explained." Christians believe that God superintended the production of a divine-human book that would properly present His message to humanity, for all time and for all generations.

Seal

See also: *Sealed, p. 163*
Greek expression: *sphragizō*
Pronunciation: *sfhrahg-ID-zoo*
Strong's Number: *4972*

One of the most colorful words in the New Testament is "seal." It may mean nothing more to us than what we do to an envelope. But to the ancients, it carried significant meaning because a seal had many uses.

In ancient times, seals were produced in many shapes and sizes, the earliest being the stamp seal, a flat engraved stone that produced a replica of itself by pressing it against soft clay. Eventually, the flat seal was replace by a cylinder seal, which was better adapted for sealing papyrus documents. Symbols or designs were carved on the outside of the cylinder, which left their imprint when the seal was rolled over the wet clay. Another type of seal was the jar handle seal. Cloth was placed over the neck of a bottle, soft clay was smeared on top of the binding cord, and then the seal was pressed into the wet clay. The unbroken seal showed that the merchandise had not been opened before delivery.

In time, people used a seal with their name written on it. They used it to mark their authorship of documents and ownership of products. Nearly everyone carried his or her seal around with him or her. It was held by a cord about the neck or the wrist or attached to some part of the owner's clothing. There are some examples of this in the Old Testament (see Song 8:6; Jer. 22:24). Seals also served as signals of protection. An unbroken seal proved that the contents had not been tampered with, whether on a document, a door of a granary, or a wine jar. Jesus' tomb was secured by sealing the stone (Matt. 27:66).

When the New Testament writers used this word, the readers would have immediately thought of the various connotations of "seal"—as being an impress, as marking ownership, and as signaling security. For the most part, the word was used symbolically in the New Testament to designate God's personal ownership.

KEY VERSES

John 3:33; 6:27;
2 Corinthians 1:22;
Ephesians 1:13; 4:30

For example, the Gospel of John says that God's seal is on Jesus, His Son (John 3:33; 6:27). This means that Jesus exhibits God's personal name because He is God's personal expression. The Scriptures also say that the Holy Spirit seals each believer (2 Cor. 1:22; Eph. 1:13; 4:30). This means that the Spirit is God's mark of ownership on the believers—it also means that the Spirit protects and preserves the believers.

Sign

See also: *Sign, p. 172*
Greek expression: *sēmeion*
Pronunciation: *say MAY awn*
Strong's Number: *4592*

The Greek word for "sign," *sēmeion*, means a visible event intended to convey meaning beyond that which is normally perceived in the outward appearance of the event. The word *sēmeion* is very prominent in John. In Matthew, Mark, and Luke, Jesus' miracles are not called "signs," but many deeds of "power" (Greek *dunamis*). They are seen as acts of mercy and divine power. In the Gospel of John, however, the miracles of Jesus are seen in a strikingly different light and are considered "signs." Beginning with the changing of water into wine (John 2:1–11), these "signs" are intended to lead those who see them to faith (John 2:23). Jesus even laments that the people will not believe unless they see signs (John 4:48). John's purpose in writing his Gospel is to present the signs of Jesus so that those who come to faith may do so through seeing these signs (John 20:30). The signs in the Gospel are expressly chosen because they lend themselves to the development of true faith.

In the Gospel of John, the miracles of Jesus confirm the teaching of Jesus. They are carefully selected to demonstrate what Jesus has to tell the world about Himself. In this respect, they are a bit like the symbolic actions of Isaiah and Ezekiel in that the action of the speaker dramatizes the message. After Jesus feeds the 5,000 with the five loaves of bread and the two fishes, He announces in the synagogue at Capernaum, "I am the bread of life which came down from heaven" (John 6:51). He tells them not to labor for the bread of this world that perishes. In much the same way, the healing of the man born blind is bound up with Jesus' teaching that He is the light of the world (John 9:5). The resurrection of Lazarus prepares the way for Jesus to proclaim that He is the resurrection and the life (John 11:25).

In John's Gospel the signs are not only a demonstration of divine power but also a revelation of Jesus' divine character. In addition to confirming His divine message, they also proclaim His personhood and mission. Thus, to understand a sign is to believe in the person who performed the miracle—Jesus.

KEY VERSES

John 2:11; 3:2;
4:54; 10:41; 11:47;
12:37; 20:30

Sin

Greek expression: *hamartia*
Pronunciation: *hah mahr TEE uh*
Strong's Number: *266*

As defined by the Bible, sin is a violation of God's standard for human behavior. The most frequent biblical words for "sin" speak of violating that standard in some fashion. The Greek equivalent, *hamartia* meant, originally, "to miss the mark, fail in duty" (Rom. 3:23). As Lawgiver, God sets limits to humanity's freedom; another frequent term (Greek *parabasis*) describes "sin" as "transgression," which means overstepping those set limits. A similar term is *paraptoma* (Greek); it denotes "a false step" or "a trespass on forbidden ground." Two other New Testament words are *anomia*, which means "lawlessness," and *paranomia*, which means "lawbreaking."

Jesus said little about the origin of "sin," except to trace it to the human heart and will (Matt. 6:22–23; 7:17–19; 18:7; Mark 7:20–23; Luke 13:34), but He significantly redefined sin's scope. Where the Law could assess only people's actions, Jesus showed that anger, contempt, lust, hardness of heart, and deceitfulness are also sinful. He also spoke of sins of neglect, good deeds left undone, the barren tree, the unused talent, the priest ignoring the injured, and love never shown (Matt. 25:41–46). He especially condemned sins of unkindness, implacable hostility, selfishness, and insensitivity (Luke 12:16–21; 16:19–31).

Paul argued strongly from observation and from Scripture that "all have sinned" (Rom. 1—3). To him, sin is a force, a power, a "law" ruling within people (Rom. 7:23; 8:2). Sin produces all kinds of evil behavior, the hardening of the conscience (Rom. 7:21–24), alienation from God, and subjection to death (Rom. 5:10; 6:23; Eph. 2:1–5). And, humans are helpless to reform themselves (Rom. 7:24). The solution to sin is through the believer's death with Christ—death to sin, self, and the world. Concurrently, new life is given through the invasive, effusive Spirit which transforms one's life from within, making each person a new creation by sanctifying their personality into the likeness of Christ (Rom. 5:6–9; 8:1–4, 28–29).

The apostle John, in his first epistle, also deals with sin. 1 John affirms 15 reasons why sin cannot be tolerated in the Christian life and emphasizes again that sin is both ignorance of the truth and lack of love (1 John 3:3–10). Yet, God forgives those who confess their sins, and Christ makes atonement for their sins and intercedes for them (1 John 1:7—2:2).

KEY VERSES

Romans 8:2, 3;
1 John 1:7, 9; 2:2;
3:4, 9; 4:10; 5:16

Slave

Greek expression: *doulos*
Pronunciation: *DOO lawss*
Strong's Number: *1401*

Slavery is often our worst nightmare. Who would want to be a slave? Amazingly, the apostles boasted that they were bond-slaves of Jesus Christ.

The Greek word *doulos* means "bond-slave"—literally "one tied to another." The Greek word speaks of one who is subject to the will of his or her master. Slavery was widespread in the ancient Near East, although the economy was not dependent upon it. From at least 3000 B.C., captives in war were the primary source of slaves. Slaves could be purchased locally from other owners, or from foreign traveling merchants who sold slaves along with cloth, bronze-ware, and other goods.

During the era of Roman rule, a large portion of conquered foreigners were bond-slaves to the Romans (Rev. 6:15; 13:16; 19:18). Slavery was so extensive that in the early Christian period one out of every two people was a slave. This would mean, of course, that many Christians were slaves. When the number of slaves increased dramatically, household slaves remained the best treated. Many became servants and confidants; some even established good businesses to their own and their masters' benefit.

The New Testament does not sanction slavery, nor does it promote a political crusade against it. Instead, Paul encouraged slaves to get their freedom if they could (1 Cor. 7:21), and it seems that Paul was asking Philemon to set Onesimus free (Phlm. 15–16). In general, the apostles admonished slaves and servants to serve their masters faithfully and that masters should treat their slaves humanely and fairly (Eph. 6:9; Col. 4:1; 1 Tim. 6:2; Phlm. 16; 1 Pet. 2:18–21).

To express their complete submission to Jesus Christ, Paul, James, Peter, and Jude declared that they were "bond-slaves" of Jesus Christ (Rom. 1:1; Gal. 1:10; James 1:1; 1 and 2 Pet. 1:1; Jude 1). "Bond-slave" expresses the apostles' absolute subjection and devotion to the Lord Jesus. In the New Testament, all the believers are pictured as being Jesus' bond-slaves because they all accept His lordship (1 Pet. 2:16; Rev. 1:1).

The term also carried with it a sense of honor. Often the title "slave of the king" meant that the person was an officer in the king's service; it was a title of honor. The term "bond-slave" was thus a title both of honor and of subjugation.

KEY VERSES

Romans 1:1;
1 Corinthians 7:21;
Philemon 16;
1 Peter 2:16;
Revelation 1:1

Sleep

Greek expression: *hupnos*
Pronunciation: *HOOP nawss*
Strong's Number: *5258*

The Greek word for "sleep," *hupnos*, is where we get the English word "hypnosis"—that is, the act of putting someone to sleep. In both the Bible and in modern English, sleep is used in three ways: (1) natural sleep, (2) moral or spiritual inactivity, and (3) death. We say, "I had a good sleep." We also tell a sluggish worker: "Stop sleeping. Get to work." And we speak of someone's death euphemistically when we say, "he went to sleep."

The first definition of sleep refers to a natural sleep. The sleep that the human body needs is seen as a precious gift of God (Ps. 4:8; 127:2). During a person's sleep God may make His will known by dreams or visions (Matt. 1:20–24).

Secondly, in a figurative way, sleep is used as a symbol of laziness, carelessness, or inactivity. In the New Testament those who are the Lord's servants are called to watch and to be sure that when their Master comes He will not find them sleeping (Mark 13:35–37; Matt. 25:1–13; 26:40–46). Likewise, the challenge to spiritual alertness and to refrain from sleep comes in a number of places in the epistles: "So be on your guard, not asleep like the others. Watch for his return and stay sober" (1 Thess. 5:6, TLB).

Finally, the Bible speaks of "death" as "sleep." Commonly in the Old Testament when a person dies, he is said to go to sleep with his fathers (2 Sam. 7:12). Jesus spoke of death as sleep (Matt. 9:24; John 11:11), as did the apostle Paul (1 Cor. 11:30; 15:20, 51; 1 Thess. 4:14). In some of these references, it would seem that it is the temporary nature of death that is the reason why it is spoken of as "sleep." Even in the Old Testament passage, Daniel 12:2, it is said that death is a sleep. This is made more specific in many passages in the New Testament, especially 1 Thessalonians 4:14, which speaks of "those who sleep in Christ" as being deceased Christians.

KEY VERSES

Matthew 1:24;
John 11:13;
Acts 20:9;
Romans 13:11

Son of God

See also: *Sons of God, p. 397*
Greek expression: *huios theou*
Pronunciation: *hwee AWSS; theh OO*
Strong's Numbers: *5207, 2316*

In New Testament times, each Caesar considered himself to be a "son of God." For example, coins depicted Augustus as the incarnate Zeus or "worship-worthy son of God," and altars were erected in his honor. Augustus encouraged the cult as a unifying element in his diverse empire and as a type of patriotism. After his death temples were built in his honor, and the symbols of divinity were transferred to succeeding emperors. For decades, all new temples were made for the imperial cult.

Jesus' identity as *huios theou*, which in Greek means "the Son of God," startled His Roman world. Even more so, this title startled Jesus' fellow Jews because they considered it blasphemous for any mortal to assume deity. At one point in the Gospel narrative (John 10), we are told that the Jewish leaders encircled Jesus and demanded that he give them a plain answer about His identity. He asserted that He had already told them—of course, He had not done so with plain words. After further prompting, He told them, "I and the Father are one." This could mean that the Father and Son are one in nature and in position; that is, the two mutually indwell each other (John 10:38). Furthermore, Jesus' statement could also mean that the Father and Son are numerically one. Whichever meaning the Lord intended to convey, the Jews understood that He was claiming deity for Himself, because they were about to stone Him for blasphemy. How could He, a mere man, make Himself God?

Jesus argued that it was not blasphemous to call Himself the "Son of God" when, in fact, He was the One the Father consecrated and sent into the world. Furthermore, on occasion God had called the judges of Israel "gods," inasmuch as they were His representatives. These "gods" were the official representatives and commissioned agents of God. If God called them "gods," why was it blasphemous for Jesus, the One consecrated by the Father and sent into the world, to say, "I am God's Son." The Jews could not argue against this because it stands written in "the Scriptures." But Jesus was greater than those men who received messages from God, for He Himself was the very message from God to men. And whereas they were earthly men selected by God to represent Him, the Son of God came from heaven as the consecrated one, dedicated to do God's will on earth.

KEY VERSES

Matthew 16:16;
Romans 1:4;
1 John 5:10

S

Jesus was therefore justified in calling Himself the "Son of God," equal with the Father. Thereafter, others called Him "the Son of God"—such as Peter (Matt. 16:16), Paul (Rom. 1:3–4) and John (1 John 5:10–12). Anyone who wants to become a Christian must do the same (1 John 5:10–12).

Son of Man

See also: *Son of Man, p. 177*
Greek expression: *huios anthrōpou*
Pronunciation: *hwee AWSS; ahn THROH poo*
Strong's Numbers: *5207, 444*

When Jesus spoke of Himself, He used the enigmatic title, "the Son of Man." This was His way of saying He was the Messiah without coming out directly and saying, "I am the Messiah." If He told the Jewish people directly, "I am the Messiah," they would have thought He was claiming to be the next "Maccabean" revolutionary leader and deliverer, come to set them free from Roman military rule.

Consequently, Jesus used a title borrowed from Ezekiel and Daniel. In the book of Ezekiel, the prophet was referred to as "Son of Man" 90 times. Often, God addressed Ezekiel as "son of man"; in the same breath, God called him "son of dust." As such, it pointed to Ezekiel's humanity, as well as to his position as a servant. Thus, when Jesus adopted *huios anthrōpou*, which is the Greek expression for "Son of Man," for Himself, He was emphasizing that He had become a man to carry out service to God (Phil. 2:5–11). This is one side of the coin. The other side shows that "Son of Man" is a divine title, taken from Daniel 7:13–14. This passage describes a vision of one "like a son of man" who "comes with the clouds" into the presence of "the Ancient of Days," who gives Him the universal and eternal kingdom of God. Jesus repeatedly quoted parts of this text in His teachings (Matt. 16:27; 19:28), especially about His second coming:

> Then the sign of the Son of Man will appear in the sky, and then all the tribes of the land will mourn; and they will see the Son of Man coming on the clouds of heaven with power and great glory.

(Matt. 24:30, HCSB)

Then again, Jesus quoted this passage in His trial before the Sanhedrin:

> Then the high priest said to Him, "By the living God I place You under oath: tell us if You are the Messiah, the Son of God!" "You have said it," Jesus told him. "But I tell you, in the future you will see 'the Son of Man seated at the right hand' of the Power, and 'coming on the clouds of heaven.'" Then the high priest tore his robes and said, "He has blasphemed! Why do we still need witnesses? Look, now you've heard the blasphemy!"

(Matt. 26:63-65, HCSB)

KEY VERSES

Matthew 16:27;
24:30; 26:64

Clearly, Jesus understood the passage in Daniel about "the Son of Man" to be a title for the "Christ," the "Son of God." Evidently, the high priest also understood the passage in this way, for he considered it blasphemy for Jesus to have applied the passage to Himself.

Sons of God

See also: *Son of God, p. 395*
Greek expression: *hiuoi theou*
Pronunciation: *hwee OY; theh OO*
Strong's Numbers: *5207, 2316*

According to Ephesians 1, it was the Father's love for His Son that first inspired God to want to have many more sons—like His first Son Jesus. God's one Son brought Him so much satisfaction that He decided to have many more. The opening verses in Ephesians resound with this note: the heart's desire of God was to obtain many sons in and through His Son. In union with His unique Son, these many sons would bring great glory and satisfaction to the Father.

The impetus of God's eternal purpose came from His heart's desire to have "many sons," which is *hiuoi theou* in Greek, made like Jesus (Rom. 8:26–29). In love, God predestined many people to become His sons—not by their own merits but by virtue of being in the Son (Eph. 1:4–5). Notice how often in Ephesians 1, Paul speaks of the believers' position "in Him." Outside of Jesus (the Son), no one could be a son of God and no one could be pleasing to the Father. The many sons of God owe all their divine privileges to the beloved Son, as people given grace and mercy through Jesus (Eph.1:6). If it were not for God's satisfaction in Jesus, there would not have been the inspiration for the creation of mankind in the first place. People exist because God wanted to obtain many more sons, each bearing Christ's image. People are well-pleasing to God and bring Him satisfaction by being united to the One who always satisfies. Apart from the Son, we have no access, no right to the title of "sons of God" or "children of God." He is our unique way to the Father.

Thank God that it was His good pleasure to include us in His Son—to impart to all believers the divine, eternal life, and to extend to us an opportunity to participate in the fellowship that He and Jesus have enjoyed from eternity. God is calling people to enter into this fellowship—even as Paul told the Corinthians: "God is faithful, through whom you were called into fellowship with His Son, Jesus Christ our Lord" (1 Cor. 1:9).

KEY VERSES

Romans 8:14, 19,
9:26;
Galatians 3:26

S

Soul

See also: *Soul, p. 178*
Greek expression: *psuchē*
Pronunciation: *psoo KAY*
Strong's Number: *5590*

The Greek philosopher Plato (fourth century B.C.) perceived the soul as the eternal element in human beings: whereas the body perishes at death, the soul is indestructible. According to Plato, at death the soul enters another body; if it has been wicked in this life, it may be sent into an inferior human being, or even an animal or bird. By means of transmigration from one body to another, the soul is eventually purged of evil. In the early centuries of the Christian era, Gnosticism also taught that the body was the prison house of the soul. Redemption comes to those initiated into the Gnostic secrets, leading to the release of the soul from the body.

Biblical thought about the soul is different. In the Old Testament the "soul" signifies that which is vital to humans in the broadest sense. The Hebrew and Greek words for "soul" often can be translated as "life"; occasionally, they can be used for the life of creatures (Gen. 1:20). "Soul for soul" means "life for life" (Exod. 21:23). In the New Testament the Greek word for "soul," *psuchē*, is synonymous with "life" itself. Followers of Jesus are said to have risked their lives (souls) for His sake (Acts 15:26). As the Son of Man, Jesus came not to be served, but to serve and to give His life (soul) as a ransom for many (Mark 10:45). As the Good Shepherd, He lays down His life (soul) for the sheep (John 10:14–18). In Luke 14:26 the condition of discipleship is to hate one's "soul," that is, to be willing to deny oneself to the point of losing one's life for Christ's sake.

Frequently "soul" can mean "person" (Acts 2:43; 1 Pet. 3:20). The expression "every living soul" (Rev. 16:3, KJV) reflects the vital aspect of living beings. It denotes the person himself or herself, the seat of his or her emotions, one's inmost being. For example, when Jesus was agonizing about His death, He spoke of His soul being crushed (Matt. 26:38). In an entirely different setting, Jesus promised rest to the souls of those who come to Him (Matt. 11:29). Here, as elsewhere, "soul" denotes the essential person.

KEY VERSES

Mark 10:45;
Luke 14:26;
John 10:15, 17

Spirit (divine)

See also: *Spirit, p. 179 and Spirit (human), p. 400*
Greek expression: *pneuma*
Pronunciation: *PNEW muh*
Strong's Number: *4151*

The Greek word for "Spirit" is derived from the verb *pneo*, meaning "to breathe." Thus, *pneuma* is sometimes used to refer to "the wind" or to "life" itself (John 3:8; Rev. 13:15)—and sometimes even refers to angels, demons, and the spirit of human beings (Heb. 1:14; Luke 4:33; Luke 7:59). Yet, *pneuma* is also used for the "Spirit of God" (1 Cor. 2:11); that is, the Holy Spirit, the third Person of the Trinity, the One who lives inside believers (Matt. 28:19; Jas. 4:5; 1 John 4:13). The Spirit was extremely important to the early believers because they considered the Spirit to be the Spirit of the risen Christ; that is, the Spirit of Jesus making Himself real to the believers in His spiritual form. From the writings of the New Testament, which are explained below, we gather that the early Christians considered Jesus to be present with them and in them via His Spirit. Thus, they honored the title "Spirit" by writing it as a *nomen sacrum*, which means "Holy Spirit."

In his letter to the Corinthians, Paul described Jesus, after His death, as being raised as a life-giving spirit (1 Cor. 15:45). Paul did not say Jesus became "the Spirit"—as if the second person of the Trinity became the third, but that Jesus became spirit in the sense that His mortal existence and form were metamorphosed into a spiritual existence and form. Jesus' person was not changed through the resurrection, only His form. With this changed spiritual form, Jesus regained the essential state of being He had emptied Himself of in becoming a man. Before He became a man, He subsisted in the form of God (Phil. 2:6), whose form is Spirit, and thereby was united to the Spirit, the third of the Trinity, while still remaining a distinct person of the Godhead.

The Scriptures assert this threefold relationship. On one hand, there are numerous verses that certify the fact that the Spirit and Jesus are united: "the Lord is the Spirit" (2 Cor. 3:17); "the Lord, who is Spirit" (2 Cor. 3:18); "the Spirit of Christ" (Rom. 8:9); "the Spirit of Jesus Christ" (Phil. 1:19), and "the Spirit of his Son" (Gal. 4:6). On the other hand, there are many Scriptures that substantiate the truth that the Son and the Spirit are distinct: "I [the Son] will send you another Comforter, the Spirit of truth" (John 15:26); "having received from the Father the promise of the Holy Spirit, he [Jesus] has poured forth this" (Acts 2:33); "for through him [the Son], we both have our access in one Spirit to the Father" (Eph. 2:18). God is one and three at the same time. As Christians, we believe in God the Father, Christ His Son, and the Holy Spirit. We have a threefold relationship with God, which is similar to a triple-braided cord that cannot easily be broken.

KEY VERSES

Acts 16:7;
Romans 8:9–11;
Philippians 1:19;
1 Peter 1:11

Spirit (human)

See also: *Spirit, p. 179 and Spirit (divine), p. 399*
Greek expression: *pneuma*
Pronunciation: *PNEW muh*
Strong's Number: *4151*

The Greek word *pneuma* can denote "wind," "breath," an "evil spirit," the "human spirit," or the "divine Spirit." The context mandates the particular sense. In the previous article, we discussed the divine Spirit, especially the Spirit of Jesus Christ. In this article, we will focus on the "human spirit."

The "human spirit" is the innermost being of the human person, corresponding with the nature of God, which is Spirit. Some scholars think the "spirit" is the same as the "soul"; others see a distinction. As such, some believe in the tripartite, or threefold, nature of a human— spirit, soul, and body—compared to a bi-partite or twofold nature—material and immaterial. 1 Thessalonians 5:23 clearly speaks of a tripartite design for mankind. Other Scriptures seem to present them as the same. A clear case of the synonymous use of soul and spirit is in Mary's Magnificat. She says, "My soul magnifies the Lord, and my spirit has rejoiced in God my Savior" (Luke 1:46–47, NKJV). Rather than divide the soul and spirit as "parts," some have suggested that a human "has a spirit" and "is a soul." Usually "spirit" indicates the vitalizing, energizing, empowering agent; it is that essence of the human being which corresponds with God's nature and can commune with God who is Spirit.

People who are united to Christ experience spiritual union with Him—His Spirit with their spirit. This is what Paul meant when he said, "He who joins himself to the Lord is one spirit" (1 Cor. 6:17). Note that Paul does not say, "he who joins himself to the Spirit is one spirit"; he uses the word "Lord" as synonymous with "the Spirit." It is generally understood to indicate spiritual union between the believer and Christ. As two bodies join to become one through sexual union, two spirits join to become one in spiritual union. Union with the Lord is a union of the human spirit with His Spirit.

Since the day of regeneration—when a person accepts Christ into his or her life—a believer's human spirit is united to Christ's Spirit. Look at John 3:6, "that which is born of the Spirit is spirit," and Romans 8:16, "his Spirit bears witness with our spirit that we are the children of God." These Scriptures show that one's union with Christ is based upon the regeneration of one's spirit by the divine Spirit.

S

KEY VERSES

John 3:6;
Romans 8:16;
1 Corinthians 6:17;
1 Thessalonians
5:23

Spiritual gifts

Greek expression: *pneumatikos, charisma*
Pronunciation: *pnew mah tee KOHSS; KAHR ees mah*
Strong's Numbers: *4152, 5486*

There are two Greek expressions for "spiritual gifts" in the Bible. A "spiritual gift," *pneumatikon* in Greek, is a thing, event, or individual which serves as an instrument of the Spirit, manifests the Spirit, or embodies the Spirit. The other expression for "spiritual gift," *charisma*, is an event, word, or action which is a concrete expression of grace or serves as a means of grace. *Pneumatikon* is the more general Greek word, *charisma* is more specific. Moreover, *charisma* is probably Paul's own word in preference to the more ambiguous *pneumatikon* (Rom. 1:11; 12:6; 1 Cor. 7:7; 12:4), which seems to have been relied upon by those causing difficulty for Paul in Corinth (1 Cor. 2:13–3:4; 14:37; 15:44–46). Consequently, this word study will focus mostly on *charisma*. Not forgetting those passages where Paul uses this word in broader terms for the direct act of God (Rom. 5:15,16; 6:23; 11:29; 1 Cor. 1:11), concentration will be on the passages where Paul speaks in more precise terms of particular manifestations of grace mediated through one individual to others.

The Greek term *charisma* is closely akin to the word *charis*, which means "grace" or "favor"; *charisma* denotes "that which is graciously given." Paul used the term *charisma* synonymously with the Greek term *ton pneumatikon*—literally "the spiritual things"—because the word describes the endowment of spiritual gifts. These gifts were given by the Lord to various individuals in the church so as to enliven the meetings and to edify the believers in the church body. Each and every member has been gifted with at least one kind of *charisma*—whether it be the "gift of teaching," "prophesying," "exercising faith," "healing," "performing miracles," "discerning spirits," "speaking in tongues," "interpreting tongues," or other gifts. The lists of *charismata* are found in Romans 12; 1 Corinthians 12; Ephesians 4; 1 Peter 4. A "spiritual gift" is essentially "an act of God's Spirit," a concrete manifestation in word or deed of God's grace through an individual for the benefit of others.

Whoever has the Spirit and is being led by the Spirit (Rom. 8:9,14) will inevitably manifest the grace of God in some way. They should also be open to the Spirit's power coming to expression in particular words and deeds within the community of the Spirit. For Paul, the church is the body of Christ. The functions of that body's members are expressions of the spiritual gifts (Rom. 12:4–6; 1 Cor. 12:14–30). As the body is many different members functioning as one body, so the unity of the church grows out of the diverse functions (gifts) of its members. It follows that a spiritual gift is given primarily with the community in view. It is given "for the common good" (1 Cor. 12:7). Do you know what your spiritual gift is and how to use it for the common good of the body of believers?

KEY VERSES

Romans 12:6;
1 Corinthians 12:1,
4, 9, 28, 30–31;
1 Peter 4:10

S

Suffering

Greek expression: *pathēma*
Pronunciation: *PAH thay mah*
Strong's Number: *3804*

According to the Bible, "suffering" began when sin entered into the world. Both mankind and all creation were afflicted with "thorns and thistles," sin, death, and decay (Gen. 3:16–19; Rom. 8:18–21). Because of sin, misery is a common human experience, and our short life is full of trouble (Job 14:1–6). It is impossible for human beings to avoid natural calamity, physical injury, and interpersonal conflict.

Jesus Christ bore the grief and sorrows of humanity as the culmination of the "sufferings," which is *pathēma* in Greek, begun by Adam's sin (1 Pet. 2:24). This is called Jesus' "passion"—a derivative from Latin meaning "suffering." It is used in some translations (KJV and RSV) in Acts 1:3 to refer to the sufferings of Jesus. Throughout the centuries Christians have referred to Jesus' sufferings as His Passion. Each of the four Gospels has what is called a "passion-narrative," which is the section recording the sufferings of Jesus on the night of His arrest and the following day leading up to His death. Matthew includes it in chapters 26—27, Mark in 14—15, Luke in 22—23, and John in 18—19. These passages describe Jesus' agonizing prayer in the garden of Gethsemane, His arrest, His trials, His scourgings, and His crucifixion. He did this for our sakes—as Peter said, "He Himself bore our sins in His body on the cross, that we might die to sin and live to righteousness; for by His wounds you were healed" (1 Pet. 2:24, NASB).

Before Jesus experienced His "passion," He told His disciples that they would encounter many trials and sorrows for His sake (John 16:33). Paul taught that entrance to the kingdom of God comes with many tribulations (Acts 14:22), which must not shake a Christian's faith (1 Thess. 3:3). They are to be understood rather as a finishing up of the remainder of Christ's suffering for His body, the church (2 Cor. 4:10–11; Col. 1:24). The Bible says affliction will grow more intense as "the end" approaches (Matt. 24:9–14; 2 Tim. 3:13). The forces of Satan will attack in an effort to deceive and destroy the "elect" (Matt. 24:24; 2 Thess. 2:9–12). But when Jesus Christ is revealed from heaven in flaming fire, God will afflict those who have afflicted believers and will bring vengeance upon those who have not obeyed the gospel of Jesus Christ (2 Thess. 1:5–10; 2:7–8). As we patiently endure suffering and trials, we have hope in God's divine justice when Jesus returns.

KEY VERSES

Romans 8:18;
2 Corinthians 1:6–7;
Hebrews 2:10;
1 Peter 5:9

Teach, Teacher

Greek expression: *didaskō, didaskalos, katēcheō*
Pronunciation: *dee DAH skoh; dee DAH skaw lawss; kaht eh KEH oh*
Strong's Numbers: *1320, 1321, 2727*

In New Testament times, the "teacher" of religion and Scripture was known as a "rabbi." Because Jesus was a great teacher, the term "Rabbi" was used as a respectful address when others were speaking to Him. In John's Gospel, the title "rabbi" meant "teacher"; John explicitly states this in 1:38 and implicitly says this in 3:2. It was used by Nathaniel (John 1:49), by Peter and Andrew (John 1:38), by Nicodemus (John 3:2), and by the disciples as a group (John 9:2; 11:8).

In the New Testament, the Greek noun for "teacher" and verb "to teach" are widely used. John the Baptist was called a "teacher" (Luke 3:12). The term is used more than 30 times to refer to Jesus (Matt. 4:23; 5:2; 7:29; 9:35; 11:1; Mark 1:21; 2:13; 4:1,2; 6:2, 6, 34; Luke 4:15, 31; 5:3; 6:6; John 6:59; 7:14, 28). People recognized Jesus' teaching as authoritative (Matt. 7:29; Mark 1:22; Luke 4:32). And then, in the early church, the "teacher" was widely recognized as one of the most important members (Acts 13:1; 1 Cor. 12:28–29; Eph. 4:11; 2 Tim. 1:11; Jas. 3:1).

In most instances, the common verb for "teach" in Greek, *didaskō*, was used by the New Testament writers. However, in a few places, the less common verb *katēcheō* was used. *Katēcheō* means "to instruct by oral recitation" or "to learn by recitation." The English word "catechism" is derived from this term. We first see this word in Luke's preface to his Gospel (Luke 1:1–4), which was addressed to a Christian called Theophilus. This believer was typical of most Christians in that era in that he had received the "sayings," or *logia*, of Jesus through the preaching of the apostles. But Luke felt that he needed a written affirmation of what he had been taught orally. Luke didn't say that his written account would improve the oral account in any way; rather, the written account would affirm or substantiate the oral sayings. As such, the written Gospel became an accurate extension and continuation of the oral teachings of the apostles (Acts 18:25; 21:21; 1 Cor. 14:19; Gal. 6:6). As the Living Word, the Bible continues to teach us on a continual basis—and Jesus our great Rabbi continues to instruct us as we grow closer to Him.

T

KEY VERSES

Luke 1:4;
John 1:38;
1 Corinthians
12:28–29;
Ephesians 4:11

Temple

See also: *Sanctuary, p. 160 and Tabernacle, p. 186*
Greek expression: *hieron, naos*
Pronunciation: *hyehr AWN; nah AWSS*
Strong's Numbers: 2411, 3485

The New Testament writers used two different Greek words to describe the "temple": *naos* and *hieron*. *Naos* refers to the actual "sanctuary" of the temple, the place of God's dwelling. *Hieron* refers to the "temple precincts" as well as to the "sanctuary." Generally speaking, *naos* was used to designate the inner section of the temple known as the "holy place" and the "holy of holies," whereas *hieron* would designate the outer court and the temple proper.

In the Gospels, these words are usually used to describe the two parts of the temple in Jerusalem. In Paul's Epistles, *hieron* and *naos* also carry a spiritual significance. The word *naos* appears six times (1 Cor. 3:16–17; 6:19; 2 Cor. 6:16; Eph. 2:21; 2 Thess. 2:4) and *hieron* once (1 Cor. 9:13) in Paul's writings. When speaking of the actual physical temple, he uses the word *hieron* to indicate the place where the priests offered up animal sacrifices on the altar (1 Cor. 9:13), which was situated in the outer court (Exod. 27—29, 40). He uses the word *naos*—the word that designates the place of God's presence—when referring to the abominable act of the man of lawlessness usurping God's place in the temple (2 Thess. 2:3–4).

In all of Paul's other passages, *naos* is used metaphorically—to depict a human habitation for the divine Spirit. In one instance the sanctuary image describes the individual believer's body (1 Cor. 6:19); in every other instance the sanctuary depicts Christ's body as "the church" (1 Cor. 3:16–17; 2 Cor. 6:16; Eph. 2:21). In arguing for sexual purity Paul asked the Corinthians, "Do you not know that your body is a temple [sanctuary] of the Holy Spirit within you, which you have from God, and that you are not your own?" (1 Cor. 6:19, NRSV). Each person who has been spiritually united to the Lord is His sanctified dwelling place; his or her body belongs to the Lord. Those now sanctified by the Lord are now His holy temple (as contrasted to a pagan temple) joined to the Lord (not to a prostitute) by virtue of the indwelling presence of the Holy Spirit. 1 Corinthians 6:19 is the only passage that describes the individual believer as God's temple. Mistakenly, many readers think 1 Corinthians 3:16–17 also speaks of the individual. According to the Greek text, it is unquestionably clear that Paul was not speaking about the individual in 1 Corinthians 3, but the local church in Corinth when he said, "... do you [plural] not know that you [plural] are God's temple."

In Ephesians, the local churches are portrayed as living, organic entities which are all growing, "into a holy sanctuary in the Lord" (Eph. 2:21). Paul pictured each local church as providing God with a spiritual habitation in that locality (Eph. 2:22) and as growing together with all the other churches into one holy, universal sanctuary for the Lord's indwelling.

KEY VERSES

1 Corinthians 3:16;
6:19;
2 Corinthians 6:16;
Ephesians 2:21;
Revelation 21:22

Tempt, test

Greek expression: *peirazō*
Pronunciation: *pehr AH dzoh*
Strong's Number: *3985*

The Greek word, *peirazō*, has been translated two ways in English Bibles. It is often rendered "test" in the sense of meaning "to try" or "to make proof of." When ascribed to God in His dealings with people, it means, and can mean, no more than this. But for the most part in Scripture, *peirazō* is used in a negative sense and means "to entice," "solicit," or "provoke to sin," that is, "to tempt." Hence, the name given to Satan is "the tempter" (Matt. 4:3).

When Jesus was led by the Spirit out into the wilderness for forty days, He was both "tested" and "tempted." His faith was "tested" by the "temptations" of the wicked one, whose whole object was to seduce Jesus from His allegiance to God. Both Matthew and Luke record the details of the temptations to which Jesus was subjected by the devil. All these temptations presented short-cuts which, if pursued, would have deflected Jesus from His calling. The record leaves us in no doubt that Jesus gained the victory. Both Gospels show that He accomplished this by appealing to Scripture. Jesus is also seen in this event as a genuine man who, like all other men, was subject to temptation. Yet Jesus did not give in to "temptation"; He passed the "test" (2 Cor. 5:21; Heb. 7:26). He proved His allegiance to God and was not enticed by Satan.

The writer of the letter to the Hebrews notes that all of Jesus' trials qualified Him to become our high priest who intercedes on our behalf (Heb. 2:18; 4:15). Jesus came to earth as a human being to experience our trials; therefore, He understands our weaknesses and shows mercy to us. Because He was fully human, Jesus "himself was tested by what he suffered" (Heb. 2:18). This "testing" refers to Jesus' exposure to conflicts, tensions, and suffering. The testing was not to show that He might fail, but to show His real power and strength under fire. This suffering refers not only to the cross, but to the testing Jesus experienced throughout His life—from Satan's temptations in the wilderness to the drops of blood He shed in prayer before His crucifixion. Having undergone all the tests and temptations of human life, Jesus "is able to help those who are being tested" (Heb. 2:18). No temptation is too great for the Lord who helps us resist. We will be put to the test—but with God's strength, we will be victorious!

KEY VERSES

Matthew 4:1, 3;
Hebrews 2:18; 4:15

T

Tongues

Greek expression: *glōssa*
Pronunciation: *GLOHSS sah*
Strong's Number: *1100*

The Greek term *glōssa* means "languages." When the early believers were empowered with the Holy Spirit on the Day of Pentecost, they were given the ability to speak in many different "languages," so that those visiting from all around the Greco-Roman world could hear the glories of God being uttered in their native tongue (Acts 2:4–11). The household of Cornelius also spoke in different languages when they were baptized in the Holy Spirit (Acts 10:46). The same phenomenon happened with the new disciples from Ephesus (Acts 19:6).

But not all spoke in "tongues" when they received the Spirit (Acts 8:15–17); so it wasn't the unique sign for having received the Holy Spirit. The Scripture teaches that all believers are baptized by the Spirit as they become integrated into the body of Christ (1 Cor. 12:13). The genuine evidence of the work of the Holy Spirit is the "fruit of the Spirit" as defined in Galatians 5:22–23. In any event, some members of the early church regularly spoke in different languages as a way of praying to God, and others spoke in different languages in church meetings. When these languages were spoken in private, interpretation was not needed; when they were spoken in the meetings, Paul required interpretation so that the others could understand and be edified (1 Cor. 14:2–27).

In order to establish firmly the public practice of tongue-speaking as a ministry to the church and to prevent its abuse as a quest for personal fulfillment, Paul put forth a set of rules designed to control its corporate exercise. These are explained in 1 Corinthians 14:27–33. Those people speaking in tongues must always have their utterances interpreted for the benefit of others. Persons participating in worship should be in control of their conduct at all times. They may not appeal to ecstatic states to excuse disorderly conduct or infractions to the rules of worship.

Finally, Paul taught that the gift of tongues is not to be sought after. Only the "higher gifts" involving communication through directly intelligible speech are to be earnestly desired (1 Cor. 12:31; 14:1, 5).

KEY VERSES

Acts 2:4, 11;
10:46; 19:6;
1 Corinthians 12:10;
14:2, 4–6, 9, 13–14,
18–19, 27

Transfigure

Greek expression: *metamorphoō*
Pronunciation: *meh tuh mohr FAW aw moo*
Strong's Number: *3339*

The Greek word *metamorphoō*, which means "transfigure," is used in the New Testament to describe three significant events: the time Jesus was completely glorified in His bodily appearance in the presence of James, Peter, and John; the time Jesus arose from the dead and was transfigured; and the time when all believers will also receive a new, transfigured body when they rise from the dead.

According to the Gospel accounts (Matt. 17:1–8; Mark 9:2–8; Luke 9:28–36; 2 Pet. 1:16–18), Jesus' transfiguration was quite spectacular: "his face shone like the sun, and his garments became white as light" (Matt. 17:2). This transformation is described in Matthew and Mark by the Greek verb *metamorphoō*, the root for the word "metamorphosis." This indicates that a tremendous change occurred.

At the "transfiguration" God spoke to Peter, James, and John about Jesus. He declared: "This is my beloved Son" (Mark 9:7). God appeared to affirm, at the transfiguration, what Peter had previously confessed at Caesarea Philippi: Jesus is indeed the Christ, the Son of God. In 2 Peter 1:16–18, Peter recounts that he was an eyewitness of the transfiguration. John seems to have done the same thing, when he wrote the prologue to his gospel and said, "… we have beheld his glory" (John 1:14). At the transfiguration the true form (Greek, *morphe*) of the Son of God temporally broke through the veil of His humanity and the disciples saw His preexistent glory. In this transformation of Jesus, the three disciples witnessed something of Jesus' pre-incarnate glory, as well as His future glory which He received at His resurrection and which all will see when He returns to judge the world.

When Christ returns in His glory, all believers will also be transfigured and thereby receive a glorious, resurrected body. Thus, Christ's transfiguration is the preview of every believer's own transfiguration (1 Cor. 15:42–45; Phil. 3:20–21; Col. 3:4).

KEY VERSES

Matthew 17:2;
Mark 9:2

Transform

Greek expression: *metamorphoō*
Pronunciation: *meh tuh mohr FAW aw moo*
Strong's Number: *3339*

The Greek word *metamorphoō* means "to change form," as in the English derivative "metamorphosis," in addition to meaning "transfigure" in Matthew 17:2. In Paul's letters, this word is used to describe an inward, metabolic-like renewal of a Christian's mind through which an inner spirit is changed into the likeness of Christ. Paul told the Romans believers: "Do not be conformed to this world; but be transformed by the renewing of your mind" (Rom. 12:2, NASB). The best way to escape conforming to this world is not by trying to be unlike the world, but by allowing ourselves to become like Christ. Furthermore, this change is not effected by a change in outward behavior, but by a change in one's thinking. Transformation begins in the mind and continues in the mind. A transformed mind produces transformed behavior.

As one's Christian life progresses, he or she should gradually notice that one's thought life is being changed from Christ-less-ness to Christ-likeness. Transformation does not happen overnight. People are transformed to Christ's image gradually, as they spend time in intimate fellowship with Him (2 Cor. 3:18). Eventually, they will begin to mirror the one they behold. Paul said, "But we all, with unveiled face beholding as in a mirror the glory of the Lord, are being transformed into the same image from glory to glory, just as from the Lord, the Spirit" (2 Cor. 3:18, NASB).

This kind of transformation does not come from conscious imitation, but from spiritual communion with the Lord. One cannot decide to imitate Jesus and then do so perfectly. One must spend time with the Lord and then gradually one will mirror Him. The result will be beyond expectation and imagination. The apostle John said it well: "Beloved, now we are children of God, and it has not appeared as yet what we shall be. We know that, when He appears, we shall be like Him, because we shall see Him just as He is" (1 John 3:2, NASB).

KEY VERSES

Romans 12:2;
2 Corinthians 3:18

Tree of life

Greek expression: *xulon zōēs*
Pronunciation: *KSOO lawn, dzoh AYSS*
Strong's Numbers: *3586, 2222*

Some people wish they had a tree which grew money, but there is an even better tree—the "tree of life." The term in Greek, *xulon zōēs*, denotes "a tree that gives life"—that is, eternal life (John 20:31). This tree symbolizes the eternal life God has made available to humanity. We see this tree in the very beginning of the Bible and at the very end.

The "tree of life" was placed by God in the midst of the garden of Eden (Gen. 2:8–9). God told Adam that he could eat from every tree of the garden except the "tree of the knowledge" of good and evil (Gen. 2:16–17). When Adam and Eve disobeyed God by eating from the tree of the knowledge of good and evil, they were expelled from the garden lest they "take also of the tree of life, and eat, and live for ever" (Gen. 3:22). The Genesis narrative suggests that God intended the "tree of life" to provide Adam and Eve with a symbol of life in fellowship with and dependence on Him. Human life, as distinguished from that of the animals, is much more than merely biological; it is also spiritual—it finds its deepest fulfillment in fellowship with God.

The book of Revelation contains the only references to the "tree of life" in the New Testament (Rev. 2:7; 22:2, 14, 19). The Bible begins and ends with a Paradise in the midst of which is a "tree of life." The way to the "tree of life," which was closed in Genesis 3, is open again for God's believing people. This was made possible by the second Adam, Jesus Christ. He died on the cross for the sins of all humanity—from Adam to you and me. Those who have washed their robes in the blood of Christ (Rev. 7:14) and have sought forgiveness of their sin through the redemptive work of Christ, receive the right to the "tree of life" (Rev. 22:14), but the disobedient will have no access to it. This tree will give constant, continuous life to all who partake of it, for it symbolizes the eternal life of God made available to redeemed humanity.

KEY VERSES

Revelation 2:7;
22:2, 14, 19

T

Truth

See also: *Truth, p. 195*
Greek expression: *alētheia*
Pronunciation: *ahl AY thay uh*
Strong's Number: *225*

The Greek word for truth, *alētheia*, means "reality" and "verity"; in John it is usually connected with the idea of "divine revelation" (John 8:32; 17:17; 18:37). Those who have been enlightened by God realize that Christ is the divine reality. The prologue to John's Gospel (John 1:1–18) tells us that Jesus is "full of grace and truth." This means that He is the full reality of God.

Later in the Gospel, Jesus declares, "I am the way and the truth and the life; no one comes to the Father except through me" (John 14:6). The goal of Jesus' mission, according to the Gospel of John, was to express the Father to mankind and to bring the believers to the Father. Jesus repeatedly indicated that He was in the Father (John 10:38, 14:10, 11), and He prayed in John 17 that the disciples would also be with Him in the Father (John 17:21–24). Jesus came to provide believers with a way to approach and live in the Father here and now (Eph. 2:18). To live in the Father through the Son brings spiritual reality.

Jesus is not only the way to the Father; but He is also the "truth," or the reality, of the Father. To see Jesus was to see the Father; to experience Jesus was to experience the reality of the Father. Furthermore, truth is the opposite of falsehood and that which is shadowy and insubstantial. Jesus Christ, who is absolute truth, is constant, as opposed to the unreality that holds mankind in bondage. He is also true life. Apart from Jesus, every person is spiritually dead—that is, they are little more than a walking corpse. No one has life and no one has experienced life until they have received, by faith, Jesus Christ who is eternal life. As we live our life in Christ Jesus, we know the truth and advance in the way. Or turning it around, as we follow the way, we learn the truth and are filled with the life. He who is life and truth is the only way to the Father.

KEY VERSES

John 1:17; 14:6;
Galatians 2:5;
Ephesians 1:13;
Hebrews 10:26;
2 John 1–4

In order to have this real experience, we need the Spirit. Fortunately, Jesus said He would send us "the Spirit of truth" to guide us into all truth (John 14:26). We could also call Him "the Spirit of reality" because He is the Spirit who reveals the reality about God (compare with TEV). The world cannot receive, or appropriate, this Spirit of reality because the world does not see Him or know Him. But all of Jesus' disciples saw and knew Him. After Jesus left this earth and sent His Spirit, this Spirit was to guide the apostles as to what constituted true doctrine and what was false. Under the guidance of the Spirit, they established the truths of the faith. These were recorded in Scripture, and left for us to study and to live by (Gal. 2:5; Eph. 1:13; Heb. 10:26; 2 John 1).

Vessel

Greek expression: *skeuos*
Pronunciation: *SKEW awss*
Strong's Number: *4632*

In ancient times, people used "vessels" or jars for many purposes—especially to contain liquids and food. Most of these were made of clay, which is *ostrakinos* in Greek. In ancient times, it was also a common practice to bury treasures or valuable items inside of clay jars. Two recent discoveries of biblical manuscripts—the Chester Beatty Papyrus, containing many portions of the Greek Old Testament and Greek New Testament, and the Dead Sea Scrolls—reveal that these manuscripts were hidden away in jars for nearly two thousand years. In addition to the dry climate, the jars helped to preserve the treasures within for over two millennia!

Paul drew upon this image when he spoke of Christians as being "vessels," which is *skeuos* in Greek, that contain a treasure. In 2 Corinthians 4:6–7 Paul said:

> God . . . is the One who has shone in our hearts to give the light of the knowledge of the glory of God in the face of Christ. But we have this treasure in earthen [clay] vessels, that the surpassing greatness of the power may be of God and not from ourselves (NASB).

The treasure in Christians is the divine revelation of Jesus Christ. What irony: the glorious Christ lives in inglorious people. He dwells in clay pots! The purpose for God putting such a valuable treasure in such a lowly vessel was so that it would be apparent that the great power of the gospel is God and not the vessel.

Paul uses this image in 2 Corinthians 4 to explain how the vessel will be "beat up" by life's experiences—yet not destroyed—and thereby preserve the glorious treasure within. All the experiences believers have and endure teach us one valuable lesson: we know without a doubt that the surpassing greatness of power, goodness, and life is from God and not from ourselves. Paul says that the vessel will be pressed, oppressed, and distressed. We, as the *skeuos*, or "vessel," experience affliction (2 Cor. 4:8). Yet the believers are not crushed. The believers are also "perplexed" which comes from two Greek words: "no" plus the word for "way." It means to be at a loss. One is perplexed when he or she sees "no way out," yet believers are "not despairing," which means not "utterly at a loss." Paul was "at a loss" but "not utterly at a loss." Believers will also be persecuted, but not forsaken by the Lord; they will be struck down, but not destroyed (2 Cor. 4:9). All these experiences teach Christians that they are weak, vulnerable earthen vessels, who are empowered by God to carry a treasure, the glorious Christ.

KEY VERSES

2 Corinthians 4:7;
1 Thessalonians 4:4;
2 Timothy 2:20

V

Vine

Greek expression: *ampelos*
Pronunciation: *AHM pehl awss*
Strong's Number: *288*

The vine is a very significant image in the Bible from the Old Testament to the New. From God's perspective, the final goal of Israel's journey, from Egypt to Canaan, was to be planted as a vine in the good land of Canaan. This was predicted in the song of Moses and Israel, where the prophecy is exclaimed, "You will bring them and plant them in the mountain of your inheritance, the place, O Lord, which you have made for your dwelling, the sanctuary, O Lord, your hands have established" (Exod. 15:17). The habitation of God in Jerusalem was supposed to be like a fruitful "vine," which is *ampelos* in Greek, glorifying both God and men. But Israel failed to bear the proper fruit (Isa. 5:1–7; Jer. 2:19–21). With this background, we can better appreciate Jesus' statement in John 15:1, "I am the true vine." This does not mean that He, in contrast to the physical vine tree, is the real one. It means that He, in contrast to Israel, who should have been God's vine but failed, is the true vine—the true fulfillment and actualization of the vine. This, then, becomes the fulfillment of Psalm 80, in which "the Son of man" is said to be the vine planted by God.

The whole race of Israel sprang from the patriarch Jacob-Israel; the new race of God's people are viewed in John 15:1–8 as originating from Christ, organically united to Him, as branches emanating from the vine—the entire economy being under the care of the Father, the vine dresser. The union between the vine and the branches is characterized by the expression "in me" and "in you" in John 15:4. But some of the branches need to be cut off. This reminds us of Paul's exposition of Israel's rejection in Romans 11, wherein he speaks of Israel being cut off from the olive tree so that the Gentiles could be grafted in their place. Israel had failed to bear the fruit God required, so there was a need for a removal of the old, dead branches. As such, the branches that are cut off are the Israelites who did not join themselves to Jesus "the vine" and therefore died. But the new, grafted-in branches—if they did not bear fruit—could also be cut off. So, the warning applies to Jews and Gentiles alike (Rom. 11:17–23).

KEY VERSES

John 15:1, 4–5

Each branch that continues to remain in the vine will keep on bearing fruit (John 15:5). Some commentators say the fruit is new converts (Rom. 15:6), and others believe that it is "the fruit of the Spirit" (Gal. 5:22). The devotional writer, Andrew Murray said, "... the essential idea of fruit is that it is the silent natural restful produce of our inner life." The fruit is the practical expression of the indwelling divine life. This expression in our lives should attract people to Christ and thus make them new members of God's vine.

Virgin

Greek expression: *parthenos*
Pronunciation: *pahr THEHN awss*
Strong's Number: *3933*

The word "virgin" is very important to Christians because it pertains to the miracle of Jesus' birth. According to Matthew, Jesus was born of the "virgin" Mary (Matt. 1:23–25). Matthew quoted Isaiah 7:14 as showing that this "virgin" birth fulfilled prophecy. Isaiah 7:14 says that a "virgin," or "young woman," shall "conceive and bear a son . . . Immanuel." This passage has been greatly debated, especially since the Revised Standard Version changed the King James Version of "virgin" to "young woman." The term in the original Hebrew is ambiguous. The Hebrew word *'almah* refers generally to "a young girl who has passed puberty and thus is of marriage-able age." Another Hebrews word, *bethulah*, specifies "a woman who is a virgin"— that is, she has not had sexual intercourse. The Greek Old Testament (Septuagint) translators, nevertheless, translated *'almah* as *parthenos*, which does denote a "vir-gin." And Matthew used the word *parthenos* when describing Mary.

Both Matthew and Luke agree that a "virgin," Mary, conceived through the Holy Spirit and bore a son, Jesus. Matthew's account is simpler and more direct, attributing the birth of the Messiah to divine origins and highlighting the signifi-cance of this birth—that Jesus is the Son of God. Jesus is called the "Christ [or Messiah]," the son of David (Matt.1:1), who comes to inaugurate the kingdom of God. As evidenced both by the fulfillment of Isaiah's prophecy and by the nature of His conception, Jesus is "God with us"—now come to "save his people from their sins" (Matt.1:18–23). The scene where Joseph decides to privately divorce Mary is added to give even greater stress to the miraculous conception.

Luke told the nativity story from the perspective of Mary. The angel Gabriel vis-ited her and announced that she would give birth to the Messiah (Luke 1:26–38). She conceived miraculously by the Holy Spirit, as was foretold by the angel Gabriel: "The Holy Spirit will come upon you, and the power of the Most High will over-shadow you. So the baby born to you will be holy, and he will be called the Son of God" (Luke 1:35). Mary was portrayed by Luke as being devoutly submissive to the purposes of God.

KEY VERSES

Matthew 1:23;
Luke 1:27

From the very beginning of the church, the doctrine of the virgin birth became the foundation of the Christian belief that Jesus is the Son of God. Some of the earliest church fathers stressed this more than any other event in Jesus' life as proof of the incarnation and deity of Christ. This truth is summarized in the Apostles' Creed of the fifth century, which declares "I believe in God the Father almighty . . . and in Jesus Christ, His only Son, our Lord, conceived of the Holy Ghost, born of the Virgin Mary."

Virtue

Greek expression: *aretē*
Pronunciation: *ahr eh TAY*
Strong's Number: *703*

We have all heard it said, "he is a virtuous man" or "she is a virtuous woman." Such comments are praises of a person's moral character. The Greek word for "virtuous" is *aretē*; it was used all the time in Greek literature, but only rarely in the New Testament.

Though "virtue" is said to have been possessed by various people, it is a quality that comes from God. In his first letter Peter used *aretē* to describe the excellent nature or "excellencies" of God (1 Pet. 2:9). In his second epistle, Peter uses "virtue" three times in the opening chapter. The first instance is in 2 Peter 1:3, where there is a significant textual variant. Some manuscripts indicate that the believers are called "by" God's glory and virtue; others indicate that they are called "to" God's glory and virtue. The first reading denotes that we are attracted by God's glory and virtue as expressed in Jesus Christ to follow Christ and become like Him. This reading suggests the means by which the divine call is exercised in our lives. The "virtues" refer to the qualities in Jesus which attracts believers to Him. The glory (*doxa*) which John saw in Jesus (John 1:14) was His authority and power; that which Peter saw probably refers to the Transfiguration, described in 2 Peter 1:16–18. Jesus' virtue (*aretē*) is that moral excellence which so continually awed His disciples.

The second reading means that we are called by God to participate in His very own glory and virtue. The rest of the passage in 2 Peter 1 primarily affirms the second reading—because this section tells us that we have been given God's divine power so that we can become partakers of His divine nature. One significant feature of the divine nature is "virtue." It is plain that Christians cannot produce this from themselves; it comes from the divine nature, of which we can partake by means of the Spirit of God.

Furthermore, we have been given great and precious promises. These promises are the offers of divine provision found in the Scriptures. They offer the glory and virtue of Christ to us as the basis for growing participation in the divine nature. We have Him within us, as He promised (John 14:23), to enable us to become increasingly Christ-like (2 Cor. 3:18). Because we have become new creatures in Christ, we have already escaped, by new birth, the moral ruin that is in the world through lust, or perverted desire. With God's strength, we can truly become "virtuous."

KEY VERSES

Philippians 4:8;
1 Peter 2:9;
2 Peter 1:3, 5

V

414

Wash

Greek expression: *louō, niptō*
Pronunciation: *LOO oh, NEEP toh*
Strong's Numbers: *3068, 3538*

The Greeks had two different words for "washing." *Niptō* was used to denote the "washing of the feet and hands"; *louō* was used to denote a "complete bathing." The difference between the two words is illustrated in the Last Supper scene, as described by John, where Jesus washed the feet of His disciples.

In between the act of rising from His place at the meal and then returning, Jesus washed the disciples' feet and thereby demonstrated His servanthood. In ancient times, the task of washing guests' feet was a job for a household servant. All the disciples accepted the washing, perhaps reluctantly but without voicing any protest, until Jesus came to Peter, who questioned Jesus: "Lord, are you going to wash my feet?" Jesus did not respond to Peter's question; instead, He assured Peter that he would understand the significance of the washing some time in the future. Indeed, after Jesus' crucifixion and resurrection, the disciples understood the significance of what Jesus had said and done. But at the time, Peter refused to let Jesus wash his feet. Jesus told him, "If I do not wash you, you have no part with me." Then Peter wanted a bath! But a bath is not necessary for one who had been bathed, for that person is completely clean except for his feet. What a bathed person needs is a foot-washing.

In speaking to Peter, Jesus used both *niptō* and *louō* to convey these two different kinds of washings. The two washings, one initial and the other continual, are very important to the Christian life. *Niptō*, appearing in John 13:5, 6, 8, and in the last part of John 13:10, is used throughout the Greek Old Testament and New Testament to indicate the "washing of the hands and feet." *Louō*, from which is formed the perfect participle *lelouomenos* in John 13:10, specifically means "bathing." According to the customs of those times, once a person had "bathed" his body, he needed only to "wash" his feet before partaking of a meal. Jesus was going around to all the disciples washing their feet until Peter protested. In His response to Peter, Jesus appropriately used both words in order to advance a precious truth: as he who has been "bathed" needs only to "wash" his feet daily, so he who has been "bathed" by the Lord, needs only to "wash" himself day by day from the filth and defilement which he accumulates by his contact with the world. All the disciples except Judas, the betrayer, had been cleansed by Jesus. This cleansing probably indicates the washing of regeneration through Jesus' Spirit and word (John 15:3; Titus 3:5; Eph. 5:26). All true believers have received the same cleansing.

KEY VERSES

John 13:5–6, 8, 10

Way

Greek expression: *hodos*
Pronunciation: *haw DAWSS*
Strong's Number: *3598*

The Greek term *hodos* means "road" or "way." In the Bible, it was used in both the literal sense and in the spiritual sense—especially in the Gospel of John. This Gospel tells us that it was Jesus' mission, as the Word of God, to express and communicate God to humanity and then bring believing humanity into a relationship with God through Him. This is characterized by Jesus' famous statement: "I am the way, the truth, and the life; no one comes to the Father except through me" (John 14:6). Jesus had come to provide a "way," a road, for the believers to travel on. Thus, the Gospel of John is not just a record of Jesus' journey, but of His believers' journey as they followed "the way."

In John's Gospel, Jesus presents "the way" to God by providing the reality of God and the eternal life of God (John 14:6). The spiritual journey takes the believers through Jesus the Son, to God the Father. The original disciples had followed Jesus on a journey; His goal was to reveal to them God's true identity through Himself, the incarnate God-man, via numerous signs and oracular revelations. The purpose of the journey was also to introduce the disciples into the divine fellowship of the Father and the Son through the Spirit.

John's Gospel, unlike the synoptic Gospels and even unlike any other book in the Bible, gives the fullest presentation of the interpersonal relationships in the Trinity. No other book of the Bible reveals the intimate fellowship and eternal union between the Father and the Son so completely; no other book presents such detail about the functional relationship between the Father, Son, and Spirit. John's unveiling of the Triune God is superb, precious, and matchless. Yet even better, for our sakes, John shows how it was Jesus' primary aim to reveal the Father to those who believe, bring them to know the Father, and participate in His enjoyment of the Father—as well as enjoy their union with the Son through the Spirit.

KEY VERSES

John 14:6;
Acts 9:2; 18:26;
19:9, 23; 22:4;
24:14, 22

Once the disciples followed this "way," they were convinced that it was the only "Way" to God. This was their spiritual reality and their proclamation to the world. Indeed, the early Christians called their movement "The Way"—and that is how they were first known by outsiders (Acts 9:2; 18:26; 19:9, 23; 22:4; 24:14, 22).

W

Will

Greek expression: *boulē, thelēma*
Pronunciation: *boo LAY, THEHL ay muh*
Strong's Numbers: *1012, 2307*

When speaking of God's "will," the New Testament writers used two words, which are nearly synonymous: *boulē* and *thelēma*. In Ephesians 1, Paul explains the "will" of God from all eternity. The primary Greek word he used was *thelēma* which conveys the idea of "desire," even heart's desire (Eph. 1:5, 9, 11). *Thelēma* is usually directly translated as "will"—"the will of God"—but the English word "will" sublimates the primary meaning. *Thelēma* is primarily an emotional word and secondarily volitional. "God's will" is not so much "God's intention" as it is "God's heart's desire." God does have an intention, a purpose, and a plan, "In him we were also chosen, having been predestined according to the plan of him who works out everything in conformity with the purpose of his will" (Eph. 1:11). Plan is called *prothesis* in Greek and it literally means "a laying out beforehand" like a blueprint. This plan was created by God's "counsel," which is called *boulē* in Greek (Eph. 1:11). But behind the "plan" and the "counsel" was not just a mastermind but a heart of love and of good pleasure. Therefore, Paul talked about "the good pleasure of God's heart" (Eph. 1:5). Paul also said, "He made known to us the mystery of his heart's desire [will], according to his good pleasure which he purposed in him" (Eph. 1:9). Indeed, God operated all things according to the "counsel" of His heart's desire or "will" (Eph. 1:11).

The impetus of God's eternal purpose and plan came from His heart's desire to have many sons and daughters made like His only Son (Rom. 8:26–28). In love, He predestined many people to participate in this—not by their own merits but by virtue of being in the Son (Eph. 1:4–5). Notice how often in Ephesians 1 Paul speaks of the believers' position "in him." Outside of Him (the Son), no one could be a son or daughter of God and no one could be pleasing to the Father. The many sons and daughters owe all their divine privileges to the Beloved, as ones graced in Him and selected in Him (Eph. 1:6). Thus, predestination and election are the results of God's will.

KEY VERSES

Ephesians 1:1, 5, 9, 11

Wisdom

See also: *Wisdom, p. 208*
Greek expression: *sophia*
Pronunciation: *saw FEE uh*
Strong's Number: *4678*

The Greek word *sophia* means "wisdom" and is used in the New Testament both as the "wisdom of God" and the "wisdom of humans." Usually, the New Testament speaks negatively of human wisdom. Thus, Paul describes his message as being "not in the plausible words of wisdom, but in demonstration of the Spirit and of power" (1 Cor. 2:4). Human wisdom alone has no ultimate merit of its own, and Paul quotes the Old Testament to demonstrate that God would destroy human wisdom (1 Cor. 1:19–21; Isa. 29:14). The Lord also made sure that the world would never find Him through human wisdom; that none may boast except for in His name.

God's wisdom is most clearly seen in the gospel of the crucified Christ, as conveyed in the New Testament. In Paul's first letter to the Corinthian church, he vividly contrasted the positive and negative senses of wisdom in proclaiming the death of Jesus Christ. The world did not know God by their own wisdom (1 Cor. 1:21). In other words, the true revelation of God and His redemption of mankind were not revealed to those who sought such truth through worldly wisdom alone, which was typified in the Greek approach. From the Greek perspective the gospel was a kind of foolishness. And yet the gospel of Jesus Christ was both the power of God and the wisdom of God (1 Cor. 1:24). Jesus, for those who believed, became the ultimate source of that wisdom which could come from God alone (1 Cor. 1:30).

Since wisdom is rooted and grounded in God, true and spiritual wisdom is God's gift. It could be seen in the lives and words of the servants of God such as Stephen (Acts 6:10) and Paul (2 Pet. 3:15). Spiritual wisdom, which provided the knowledge to enable a person to fully live the life given by God, was to be desired for oneself and prayed for in others (Col. 1:9). A clear distinction between good and evil wisdom is provided in the letter of James (Jas. 3:13–18). A person whose life reflects jealousy and selfish ambition does not have the true wisdom of God, but is earthly-minded and not spiritual. But true wisdom is God-given; this wisdom is "first pure, then peaceable, gentle, open to reason, full of mercy and good fruits, without uncertainty or insincerity" (Jas. 3:17). Seeking God's wisdom, and not our own, will surely lead to blessing and contentment in Jesus.

KEY VERSES

1 Corinthians
1:19–22, 24, 30, 2:4;
James 3:13, 15, 17

W

Wise Men

Greek expression: *magoi*
Pronunciation: *MAH goy*
Strong's Number: *3097*

Just who were the wise men, technically called "magi," that followed the star and worshiped the baby Jesus? The Bible doesn't tell us, so we have to look in other sources.

The historian Herodotus mentioned "magi" as "a priestly caste of Media or Persia." As the religion in Persia at the time was Zoroastrinism, these magi were probably Zoroastrian priests. Herodotus, together with Plutarch and Strabo, suggested that magi were partly responsible for ritual and cultic life, supervising sacrifices and prayers, and partly responsible as royal advisers to the courts of the East. Believing the affairs of history were reflected in the movements of the stars and other phenomena, Herodotus said the rulers of the East commonly utilized the magi's knowledge of astrology and dream interpretation to determine affairs of state. The magi were, therefore, concerned with what the movement of the stars, as signs and portents, might signify for the future affairs of history. Such an interest could account not only for the magi's interest in the star in Matthew, but also their conclusion, shared with Herod, that the star's appearance signified the birth of a new ruler of great importance.

According to Matthew 2:1–12, these magi followed a star, came to Jerusalem and then to Bethlehem in order to worship the newborn "king of the Jews." Matthew's account forms a significant introduction to his Gospel by drawing attention to the true identity of Jesus as King and by foreshadowing the homage paid by the Gentiles to Jesus throughout that Gospel. From the beginning it reveals the true identity of the infant as the long-expected and prophesied royal Messiah of Israel.

In addition to confirming that Jesus is the long-awaited Messiah, the account of the magi's visit, as part of the introduction to Matthew's Gospel, introduces several prominent themes which reappear in subsequent chapters. First, the account establishes that Jesus' title as Messiah has bearing not only on the Jews, but on the Gentile world as well, symbolized in the fact that "wise men from the East" visited the baby Messiah. A second theme, which surfaces later, is the surprising faith of the Gentiles, a faith which is lacking among Jesus' own people (Matt. 8:5–13; 15:21–28; 27:19, 54).

KEY VERSES

Matthew 2:1, 7

Witness

Greek expression: *martureō, martus*
Pronunciation: *mahr toor EH oh; MAHR tooss*
Strong's Numbers: *3140, 3144*

Martureō and *martus* mean "to bear witness" (verbal form) and "witness" (noun). The Greek word *martus* is the origin of the English word "martyr," inasmuch as one who witnesses for his or her faith in Christ would often die for making that testimony. The first Christian witness and "martyr" was John the Baptist. As the forerunner of the Messiah, his mission was to bear "witness" to the light and to identify the Lamb of God (John 1:7–8, 19–36).

The issue of "witness" was very important in Jesus' ministry on earth because the Jewish leaders questioned the validity of His claims. According to the Jewish law, truth or validity has to be established by two or three witnesses (Deut. 17:7; 19:15). Jesus made His defense to the Jewish leaders by providing them with a five-fold witness: (1) the Father Himself (John 5:31–32, 37), (2) John the Baptist (John 5:33–35), (3) Jesus' miracles and teachings (John 5:36), (4) the Scriptures (John 5:39–40), and (5) Moses (John 5:45–47). All these witnesses were accessible to the Jews. They had heard John the Baptist, that burning and shining lamp who pointed the way to the Light. They had seen the miraculous works of Jesus. They also had the Father's testimony—had they been receptive to Him (John 8:47). They researched the Scriptures daily, thinking they could gain eternal life by this endeavor. The Scriptures attested to the kind of Messiah Jesus was, but the Jews were too focused on the kind of Messiah that was yet to be. Jesus came as the suffering Lamb, while they were looking for a conquering King. Nevertheless, the Scriptures abound with testimony to Him. And Moses himself wrote of Him (Deut. 18:15–18).

The Jewish leaders who criticized Jesus did not have God's word residing in their hearts. If that word had been abiding in their hearts (John 8:31; 15:7), they would have recognized the One to whom the Scriptures gave testimony (John 5:39). Even more so, they had the greatest of all God's manifestations standing right before their eyes—Jesus, the Word, the visible expression of God to all people. But the Jewish leaders did not, or could not, believe in Jesus, their Messiah from Old Testament prophecy.

KEY VERSES

John 5:31–33,
36–37, 39;
Acts 1:8;
1 John 1:2

After Jesus' departure from earth, the followers of Jesus, and particularly the twelve apostles, were "witnesses" to the person and character of Jesus. Indeed, at the time of His ascension, the disciples were specifically commissioned to be His witnesses (Acts 1:8). They knew Him intimately, heard His teachings and observed His miracles; three were witnesses of His transfiguration (Matt. 17:1–2; 2 Pet. 1:17–18) and many were witnesses to His resurrection (Luke 24:48; 1 Cor. 15:4–8). Believers today are witnesses to others, by our actions and love, and witnesses for Christ in sharing the Gospel with unbelievers.

Woman

Greek expression: *gunē*
Pronunciation: *goo NAY*
Strong's Number: *1135*

Genesis 1:26–28 is the opening portrayal of the creation of the first man and woman. God created humans in His image, as male and female. Hence, the "female," or *gunē* in Greek, shares with the male the image of God, reflects God's power and majesty on earth, and is commanded to multiply and bring dominion to the earth. From Genesis 1:26–28 there is no suggestion of inferiority of the female to the male, nor is there any suggestion of her submission to his dominance. Rather, they are pictured together, the male and the female, as the representation of their Maker. A woman is a person in every respect as a man; she shares in the image of God and has the potential of varied ranges of response to culture, community, and life about her.

It is a fact of Scripture that women are regularly associated with, and find their sense of worth in, childbearing. Yet the same Scriptures show that the nature of woman is not exhausted by associations with childbearing: she has her own identity in the community, in the church, and before the Lord in the whole of her life, not just when (or if) she bears and nourishes a child. Further, the biblical concept of childbearing always involves the husband, who is her partner at conception, at her side during delivery, and partner with her in the ongoing task of nourishing the child.

The image of the woman as the childbearer begins with the promise of God in Genesis 3:15, where he announced the ultimate victory over the evil one, Satan, by the offspring of the woman. This promise respecting the offspring of the woman became the universal blessing of God upon woman as the childbearer. Ultimately, through one born of a woman, there would come the final deliverance. Mary, mother of Jesus, is the preeminent woman because through her the ancient promise to Eve, that she would one day be the great victor over the enemy of mankind, is fulfilled. And there is a sense in which each birth experience is a participation in the continuity of this promise (1 Tim. 2:15), and its possible relationship to this continuity of women, salvation, and childbearing.

After Mary, other women in the New Testament were noted for their significant ministries: Phoebe, Priscilla, Junias, Tryphena, Tryphosa, Persis, Euodia, Syntyche, and the daughters of Philip. These women mark the beginning of the fulfillment of Joel's prophecy of a day in which women as well as men would be the instruments of the outpouring of the Holy Spirit (Joel 2:28–29).

KEY VERSES

Luke 1:42;
Acts 5:14;
Ephesians 5:25

Word

See also: *Word, p. 213* and *(The) Word, p. 423*
Greek expression: *logos, rhēma*
Pronunciation: *LAW gawss; HRAY muh*
Strong's Numbers: *3056, 4487*

There are two terms in the Greek New Testament that are used for the term "word": *logos* and *rhēma*. The first term, *logos*, was used primarily to denote the "written word" or "total message"; the second term, *rhēma*, was used to denote the "spoken word." However, these distinctions are not always maintained throughout the entire New Testament.

One passage where the distinctions are maintained is 1 Peter 1:23–25, where Peter says:

> For you have been born again . . . through the living and abiding word [*logos*] of God. For, all flesh is like grass, and all its glory like the flower of the grass. The grass withers, and the flowers fall off, but the word of the Lord abides forever. And this is the word [*rhēma*] which was preached to you (NASB).

In 1 Peter 1:23, the Greek expression for "word" is *logos*, referring primarily to the written message. In 1 Peter 1:25 the Greek term is *rhēma*, referring primarily to the "spoken word." The spoken word is the gospel preached and proclaimed (see the use of *rhēma* in Rom. 10:17–18). "The word of the Lord" is the gospel message about the Lord Jesus Christ. This "word" can regenerate men and women. Peter adapted the Old Testament text which says "the word of our God" in Isaiah 40:6–8 to its New Testament context.

God's "word" has power to execute His will. It will not return to Him empty but accomplish that which He purposes (Isa. 44:23; 55:11). By His speech alone, God created the world, and His word upholds it (Gen. 1; Ps. 33:6; Heb. 1:3; 11:3; 2 Pet. 3:5). Eventually, this divine revelation was put into writing, which makes it also "the word of God" (Mark 7:13; Luke 16:29–31; John 5:39).

Jesus spoke "the word of God." He was "mighty in word" (Luke 24:19); He taught with authority (Mark 1:22, 27), exercising power over the sea, disease, demons, and death (Matt. 8:8,13). His "word of the kingdom" is the living seed, which bears fruit for God when planted in the good soil of receptive hearts (Matt. 13:19; Mark 4:14). The "word" that Christ gives to His disciples cleanses them and frees them (John 8:31; 12:48; 15:3; 17:14). The words *of* Christ, combined with the word *about* Christ, constitute "the word of Christ." This is the "word," or the message, that the church preaches (Rom. 10:8–9, 17).

KEY VERSES

John 8:31; 12:48;
15:3; 17:14;
Romans 10:17;
1 Peter 1:23, 25

(The) Word

See also: *Word, p. 213 and Word, p. 422*
Greek expression: *ho logos*
Pronunciation: *haw; LAW gawss*
Strong's Number: *3056*

In the opening verse of John's Gospel, he named the Son of God "the Word." As "the Word," the Son of God fully conveys and communicates God. The Greek term is *logos*; it was used in two ways by the Greeks. "The word" might be thought of as remaining within a person, when it denoted his or her "thought or reason." Or it might refer to "the word" going forth from a person, when it denoted "the expression of his or her thought"—such as speech. As a philosophical term, the *logos* denoted the "principle of the universe," even the creative energy that generated the universe. In both the Jewish conception and the Greek, the *logos* was associated with the idea of beginnings—the world began through the origination and instrumentality of "the Word." This is seen in Genesis 1:3 where the expression "God said" is used again and again.

John may have had these ideas about "the word" in mind, but most likely he originated a new term to identify the Son of God as the divine expression in human form (John 1:14). He is the image of the invisible God (Col. 1:15), the express image of God's substance (Heb. 1:3). In the Godhead, the Son not only reveals God, but also reveals the reality of God, which is a central theme throughout John's Gospel. John used a similar title in his first epistle: "the Word of life" (1 John 1:1–3). And in Revelation 19:11–16, Jesus is presented as the King of kings and Lord of lords, who has a name on Him: "the Word of God."

Before coming to earth, "the Word" lived in the beginning with God and was Himself God. This is a paradox beyond explanation: how can one be with God and yet also be God? What we gather from the first verse is that "the Word," who is both the Son of God and God, lived in face-to-face fellowship with God His Father. The last verse of the prologue (John 1:18) tells us that the Son was in the bosom of the Father. In Jesus' intercessory prayer (John 17) He revealed that the Father loved Him before the foundation of the world. We cannot imagine the extent of their union and communion.

"The Word's" first act was to work with God in creating the universe. His second great act was to come to men as the light of life. The essential nature of "the Word" is "life" (Greek, *zōē*), and this life gives light to people who live in darkness. The divine life resided in "the Word," and He made it available to all who believe in Him.

KEY VERSES

John 1:1;
1 John 1:1;
Revelation 19:13

Work

Greek expression: *ergon*
Pronunciation: *EHR gawn*
Strong's Number: *2041*

The Bible presents a positive perspective on "work," which begins with God. Unlike other ancient religious writings which regarded creation as something beneath the dignity of the Supreme Being, Scripture unashamedly describes God as a "worker" (Ps. 8:3; Isa. 45:9). This biblical description of a working God reaches its climax with the incarnation of Jesus. The "work" which Jesus was given to do (John 4:34) was the unique task of redemption. But He was also a worker in the ordinary sense. His contemporaries knew Him as "a carpenter" (Mark 6:3). In New Testament times carpentry and joinery were muscle-building trades. So Jesus was no pale weakling, but a working man whose hands had been hardened by years of toil with the ax, saw, and hammer. Hard, physical labor was not beneath the dignity of the Son of God.

If the Bible's teaching about God enhances work's dignity, the Bible's account of mankind's creation gives all human labor the mark of normality. God "took the man and put him in the garden of Eden to till it and keep it" (Gen. 2:15). And God's first command, to "fill the earth and subdue it" (Gen. 1:28), implied a great deal of work for both man and woman. In an important sense, people today are obeying that command of their Creator when they do their daily work, whether they acknowledge Him or not. Work did not, therefore, arrive in the world as a direct result of the fall into sin; though sin did spoil working conditions (Gen. 3:17–19). Work was planned by God from the dawn of history for mankind's good.

God is a working God who is pleased when His people work hard and conscientiously. That conviction lies at the heart of the Bible's teaching about Christian attitudes toward secular employment. And quite naturally, the New Testament extends the same positive emphasis to cover all Christian service, paid or unpaid. Jesus said that the world is God's harvest field, waiting for Christian reapers to move in and evangelize (Matt. 9:37–38). Paul used the same agricultural illustration and added another from the building trade to describe the Lord's work of evangelism and teaching (1 Cor. 3:6–15). Church leaders must work especially hard, he said (1 Thess. 5:12), to stimulate all God's people to be involved in the Lord's work (1 Cor. 15:58). All Christians should see themselves as "God's co-workers" (1 Cor. 3:9).

KEY VERSES

John 4:34;
1 Corinthians
3:13–15

W

World

Greek expression: *kosmos*
Pronunciation: *KAWSS mawss*
Strong's Number: *2889*

The Greek word behind "world," *kosmos*, is fascinating. It literally means "that which is ordered or arranged"; hence, we get our English word "cosmetics" from *kosmos*. *Kosmos*, however, has several uses in Greek literature and in the New Testament. *Kosmos* meant: (1) the universe created by God with design and order (Matt. 13:35; John 17:24; Acts 17:24); (2) the planet earth, which includes the idea of earth as the dwelling place of human beings (John 11:9; 16:21) and of earth as contrasted with heaven (John 6:14; 12:46); (3) all of humanity (Matt. 5:14; John 3:16; 1 Cor. 4:13); (4) all of human existence in this present life, with all of its experience and possessions (Matt. 16:26; 1 Cor. 7:33); and (5) the world order as alienated from God, in rebellion against Him, and condemned for its godlessness. The ruler of this world is the devil (John 12:31; 14:30; 16:11; 1 Cor. 5:10)—as John said, "... the whole world is under the control of the evil one" (1 John 5:19). Christians are not of this world (John 15:19; 17:16), even though they live in the world and participate in its activities (John 17:11). The believer is regarded as dead to the world (Gal. 6:14; Col. 3:2-3), and the Christian is to be separated from the world (Jas. 1:27).

The discourse of Jesus on the night before the crucifixion contains much teaching about "the world." According to John's account, the world cannot receive the Spirit of truth (John 14:17). Christ gives a peace which the world cannot give (John 14:27). He offers love, while the world gives hatred and persecution (John 15:19-20). The world's hatred of God is also directed against the followers of Christ (John 15:18-21). But, although the disciples of Jesus have tribulation "in this world," they are to be of good cheer, for Jesus has overcome the world (John 16:33).

Our relationship with the world is an indicator of our relationship with God. Those who love the world are void of love for God the Father (1 John 2:15). The Scripture points out that "all that is in the world, the lust of the flesh and the lust of the eyes and the pride of life, is not of the Father but is of the world" (1 John 2:16, RSV). The world and its desires or lusts are transient, passing away, but the follower of God's word abides forever (1 John 2:17; 2 Cor. 4:18).

KEY VERSES

John 3:16;
14:27; 15:19;
1 John 2:15-17

Worship

See also: *Worship, p. 214*
Greek expression: *proskuneō*
Pronunciation: *prawss koon EH oh*
Strong's Number: *4352*

The word *proskuneō*, "worship," means to encounter God and praise Him. The Jews had done this for centuries—some with reality and others just in form. Unfortunately, many Jews had become far too dependent on a physical place, the Temple, for their worship. When Jesus arrived on the scene, He proclaimed that He was the temple of God; in resurrection, He would provide the spiritual dwelling where God the Spirit and people, in spirit, could have spiritual communion (Matt. 12:6; John 2:19–22). In other words, worship would no longer be in a place but in a person—through Jesus Christ and His Spirit the worshipers could come directly to God (John 14:6; Heb. 10:19–20).

This shift in worship—from physical to spiritual—is the theme of John 4, a chapter that recounts Jesus' visit to the Samaritans. After Jesus' encounter with the Samaritan woman, she acknowledged that He must be a prophet, and then launched off into a discussion concerning the religious debate between the Jews and the Samaritans over which place of worship was the right one—Jerusalem or Mount Gerazim. The Samaritans had set up a place for worship on Mount Gerazim in accordance with Deuteronomy 11:26–29 and 27:1–8, while the Jews had followed David and Solomon in making Jerusalem the center of Jewish worship. The Scriptures affirmed Jerusalem as the true center for worship (2 Chr. 6:5–6; 7:12). But Jesus told her that a new age had come, in which the issue no longer concerned a physical site. God the Father would no longer be worshiped in either place. The true worshipers—Jew, Samaritan, or Gentile—must worship the Father in spirit and in truth.

Worshiping God "in spirit" corresponds to Jerusalem, and worshiping "in truth" is contrasted with the Samaritans' ignorant ideas of worship, God, etc. Formerly, God was worshiped in Jerusalem, but now the true Jerusalem would be in a person's spirit. Indeed, the church is called "the habitation of God in spirit" (Eph. 2:22). True worship requires a people to contact God, the Spirit, in their spirit, as well as have knowledge about the truth. New Testament worship must be in spirit and in truth; since "God is Spirit," He must be worshiped in spirit. Human beings possess a human spirit, the nature of which corresponds to God's nature, which is Spirit. Therefore, people can have fellowship with God and worship God in the same sphere in which God exists.

KEY VERSES

Mark 5:6;
John 4:20–23;
Revelation 4:10

W

Wrath

Greek expression: *orgē*
Pronunciation: *ohr GAY*
Strong's Number: *3709*

"Wrath" is a strong term, reserved in the English language almost exclusively for describing "God's anger" with human beings and their sinful actions. The Greek word *orgē* expresses the idea of "justifiable anger for unjust actions." It is used throughout the New Testament to describe God's anger toward the sins and unbelief of humanity.

The Old Testament and the New Testament both teach that God is storing up His anger for the great and final day of judgment. This day is frequently called the Day of the Lord. The concept of the Day of the Lord was developed by the prophets to warn Israel and the nations that no one can escape the righteous outpouring of God's wrath (Amos 5:18–20). This day was still spoken about by the New Testament prophets, John the Baptist and John the visionary (Matt. 3:7; Rev. 6:16–17).

Those who do not profess faith in the risen Christ remain in their sins and will be subject to God's wrath, whereas those who believe in Him are delivered (Eph. 2:3; 1 Thess. 1:10). The good news of the New Testament is that Jesus has come to deliver us from the wrath of God (Rom. 5:9). Those who have been delivered are reconciled with God because they are no longer under condemnation (Rom. 5:10; 8:1).

God's wrath will be poured out on the devil, his angels, and all who rebel against Him. This is graphically portrayed in the book of Revelation, as we see scene after scene of God executing judgment on the ungodly. God's stored-up wrath will be unleashed in awful ways, as He brings destruction on: the earth, those dwelling on the earth, the merchants of the earth, false religions, the antichrist, and all the enemies of the gospel. Ultimately, God's wrath will be satisfied when He has put the devil, his angels, and all unbelievers in the lake of fire, to be tormented for eternity in eternal separation from God (Rev. 14:10; 20:10–15).

KEY VERSES

John 3:36;
Romans 1:18;
Revelation 14:10

Index to Key Scriptures

Old Testament

New Testament